BLOOD OF THE PROVINCES

Blood of the Provinces

The Roman Auxilia and the Making of Provincial Society from Augustus to the Severans

IAN HAYNES

OXFORD
UNIVERSITY PRESS

OXFORD
UNIVERSITY PRESS

Great Clarendon Street, Oxford, OX2 6DP,
United Kingdom

Oxford University Press is a department of the University of Oxford.
It furthers the University's objective of excellence in research, scholarship,
and education by publishing worldwide. Oxford is a registered trade mark of
Oxford University Press in the UK and in certain other countries

First published 2013
First published in paperback 2016

Published in the United States of America by Oxford University Press
198 Madison Avenue, New York, NY 10016, United States of America

British Library Cataloguing in Publication Data
Data available

Library of Congress Cataloging in Publication Data
Data available

ISBN 978-0-19-965534-2 (Hbk.)
ISBN 978-0-19-879544-5 (Pbk.)

To my parents, my wife, and my children
with thanks

Preface and Acknowledgements

It is a tired but well-tried academic conceit to claim that one's particular interests are strangely overlooked while yet of far-ranging importance. To make such a claim about the *alae* and *cohortes* of the Roman army may seem especially ill-advised since many scholars, including some of the finest minds in Roman studies, have written about them. The men of these non-citizen regiments are often discussed as both products and instruments of Roman power, essential figures in the creation of provincial society. Yet it is perhaps a reflection of the wisdom of the scholars involved that for almost a hundred years no one has sought to write a single-volume study of their role across the Empire over three centuries. Indeed, Cheesman, author of the last such work, published in 1914, modestly described his monograph on these auxiliary soldiers as an 'essay' and, pending further work, focused overwhelmingly on the organization, recruitment and, briefly, equipment of these diverse bodies. The sheer amount of material that has surfaced since he wrote, the range of papers published, the awareness of changes in Rome's armies over space and time, and indeed the exponential upsurge in archaeological fieldwork all recall the risks in attempting a single-book treatment of the topic. At the same time, new ways of looking at cultural change, ethnicity, and gender mean that established readings of the Roman Empire are being continually revisited. Yet I believe that this growth in data and debate is precisely what makes it so important to attempt a new study of the *auxilia*.

The justification here is not simply that, representing as they did more than half of Rome's land forces, the men of the *alae* and *cohortes* warrant fresh study in their own right. To depend too heavily on this reason would obscure the ways in which, over time, they came to share ever more characteristics with their better-known legionary counterparts. My argument is rather that reviewing the rich body of evidence associated with auxiliary soldiers and their families offers new insight into how, at the humblest of levels, individuals were incorporated into the networks that defined the Roman Empire. Accordingly, this study focuses more on community than combat, and while hoping that students of military equipment and tactics will find much of interest, I trust that discussion of other topics such as cult, routine, and language will engage students with quite different interests in the archaeology of empire. A study of these military communities, examining all these themes and more against developments in provincial society, affords many opportunities for discussion across diverse areas of specialist expertise.

My interest in the *alae* and *cohortes* dates from before my doctorate on the *auxilia*, completed almost two decades ago. The fact that I have changed many of my views on the subject since then in no way lessens my gratitude to those who, as supervisors and mentors, the latter both formal and informal, enriched my graduate experience; indeed, if anything it only increases it. They helped me to think differently and more deeply about the experience of life in the Roman Empire and to continue to challenge my own assumptions. I am pleased to acknowledge my ongoing debt therefore to Sheppard Frere, Alan Bowman, Greg Woolf, and the late John Lloyd for many stimulating conversations. Colleagues at

Oxford, London, and Newcastle in archaeology, classics, and history often offered inspiration, whether or not they realized they were doing so at the time, and I thank them all. In the case of the Newcastle community, I note also a particular debt to leading authorities in the world of frontier studies whose expert knowledge has enriched my understanding of this field, notably Lindsay Allason-Jones, David Breeze, Paul Bidwell, Nick Hodgson, Rob Collins, and Alex Croom. My debt to my friends at Vindolanda should be no less evident within this book.

Field projects remain an essential and intensely fruitful environment in which to advance both knowledge and understanding of the archaeology of the Empire's provinces, and I would like to thank those I have had the privilege to work with in the field over the years: the archaeologists of the Museum of London, Oxford Archaeology, English Heritage, Landesdenkmalamt Baden-Württemberg at Ladenburg (Germany), the teams at Apulum/Alba Iulia, Vințu de Jos, Oarda and Salsovia/Mahmudia (all Romania), at Debelt (Bulgaria), the Lateran (Rome), and most recently at Birdoswald and Maryport. The generosity of fellow fieldworkers has never failed to impress me, but I wish to acknowledge particularly the kindness and expertise of Doru Bogdan, Alexandru Diaconescu, Kathleen Hawthorne, Gill Hey, Sophie Jackson, Paolo Liverani, Claudia Melisch, Alfred Schäfer, Jamie Sewell, Harvey Sheldon, Rob Somers, Sebastian Sommer, Giandomenico Spinola, Florin Topoleanu, Lyudmil Vagalinki, and Tony Wilmott. Fieldwork commitments often impose a heavy burden on those we hold dearest, and I would like to thank my wife, Mary, and our children, Isabelle, Claire, Emily, Laura, Luke, and Lucy for their understanding during my extended absences from home.

As the manuscript has emerged, I have taken ruthless advantage of the generosity of friends and colleagues (what a pleasure it is that these are one and the same). Adrian Goldsworthy, Lindsay Allason-Jones, Tony Birley, and Simon James all kindly read the entire manuscript in draft, and thus enriched the final product. Adrian Goldsworthy in particular has graciously endured more discussions of the book than anyone should have had to, and I am most particularly indebted to his generosity. OUP's anonymous referees provided very helpful observations and I would also like to thank them for their contribution. Carol van Driel-Murray, Jen Baird, Clive Bridger-Kraus, Elizabeth Greene, Tony Spawforth, and the late Denis Saddington kindly commented on sections of the draft to my considerable benefit. Readers with particular expertise in other areas than Roman studies have kindly reviewed the document too, notably Scott Ashley, Averil Goldsworthy, Paul Kielstra, and my father-in-law, Michael Meaney. Frances McIntosh and Emma Morris assisted with different aspects of related administration. Many others helped illuminate specific points, and I note my appreciation in the text. Any errors remaining or misleading hypotheses advanced remain, of course, mine.

Particular thanks should be given to Martin Millett and Greg Woolf, who have remained encouraging throughout this book's long gestation, and to the funding bodies who have supported my work over the years: the Arts and Humanities Research Council, the British Academy, the British School at Rome, and the Deutsche Akademische Austauschdienst. I owe a further debt to the tremendous librarians of the Ashmolean/Sackler library, Oxford, the joint library of the Roman and Hellenic Societies (ICS), London, and the British School of Rome.

It remains now to acknowledge with gratitude those who have given permission for the use of images for this volume. These contributors reserve copyright.

D. Baatz, fig. 3.4; J. Baird after original by van Knox, held at Yale University Art Gallery, fig. 11.2; J. Baird, Mission Franco-Syrienne d'Europos Doura, fig. 11.1; J. Alan Biggins and David Taylor, fig. 1.3; Mike Bishop, fig. 13.2; The Trustees of the British Museum, fig. 16.3; Sorin Cociş, fig. 16.5; Colchester and Ipswich Museums Service, fig. 22.1; Robert Collins, fig. 1.1; Carol van Driel Murray, fig. 17.5; Adrian Goldsworthy figs 3.3, 17.3, 17.4, and 18.3; W. Groenman-van Waateringe, fig. 3.2; Louise Hird, fig. 7.1b; Istanbul Archaeological Museums, fig. 6.1; photo: Alan Bülow-Jacobsen, fig. 20.1; Simon James, after la Mission Franco-Syrienne à Dura Europos, fig. 10.1; Sonja Jilek, fig. 11.5; fig. 13.3 redrawn from original by Tudor published in *Latomus* 1963; J. P. Laporte, fig. 21.2; fig. 10.3 relevé et mis au net par Corinne Licoppe dans le cadre des fouilles des Principia dirigées par Maurice Lenoir; GDKE Landesmuseum Mainz, Ursula Rudischer, figs 16.2, 17.1, 17.2, 18.1; Valerie Maxfield, fig. 10.2; Musée Calvet Avignon, fig. 15.1; Archivo Fotografico dei Musei Capitolini, figs 2.1, 22.2, and 22.3; Ioana Oltean, fig. 14.1; Museum of London, fig. 21.1; Römerhalle Bad Kreuznach, fig. 16.1; Römisch-Germanisches Museum/Rheinisches Bildarchiv Köln, fig. 15.2; fig. 16.4a reproduced by kind permission of the Society of Antiquaries of London and J. Bayley from original work by Judith Dobie first published in J. Bayley and S. Butcher, *Roman Brooches in Britain* J, 2004; fig. 11.6 reproduced by kind permission of the Society of Antiquaries of London from *Antiquaries Journal* 64, G. C.Boon, 1984; Society of Antiquaries of Newcastle upon Tyne, figs 3.1, 16.4b, 18.2, and 18.4; Tyne and Wear Archives and Museums, fig. 12.3; The Vindolanda Trust, figs 1.2, 12.1, 12.2 (taken by the author); Zolt Visy, fig. 9.1; Yale University Art Gallery, figs 11.3 and 13.1. Carlie Lindgren drew or redrew (with permission) figs 3.1, 3.2, 3.4, 7.1, 10.3, 11.4, 11.5, 11.6, 13.3, 16.4, 16.5, and 21.2.

Contents

**Part VI Pen and Sword: Communication and
Cultural Transformation**

**Part VII Auxiliary Veterans and the Making
of Provincial Society**

List of Figures

List of Tables

Abbreviations

AE	L'Année Épigraphique
AJA	American Journal of Archaeology
ANRW	Aufstieg und Niedergang der römischen Welt
BAR	British Archaeological Reports
BASP	Bulletin of the American Society of Papyrologists
BGU	Berliner griechische Urkunden (Ägyptische Urkunden aus dem königlichen Museen zu Berlin)
BJ	Bonner Jahrbücher des Rheinisches Landesmuseum
BMC	Coins of the Roman Empire in the British Museum
CBA	Council for British Archaeology
ChLA	Chartae Latinae Antiquiores
CIL	Corpus Inscriptionum Latinarum
CIS	Corpus Inscriptionum Semiticarum
CPL	Corpus Papyrorum Latinarum
CSIR	Corpus Signorum Imperii Romani
Doc. Masada	H. M. Cotton and J. Geiger, with J. D. Thomas, Masada II: The Yigael Yadin Excavations 1963–1965. Final Reports: The Latin and Greek Documents (Jerusalem, 1989)
FIRA	Fontes Iuris Romani Anteiustiniani
GRBS	Greek, Roman and Byzantine Studies
IDR	Inscriptiones Daciae Romanae
IEJ	Israel Exploration Journal
IG	Inscriptiones Graecae
IG Bulg	Inscriptions Graecae in Bulgaria repertae
IGLS	Inscriptions grècques et latines de la Syrie
IGRR	Inscriptiones Graecae ad Res Romanas Pertinentes
ILS	Inscriptiones Latinae Selectae
JBAA	Journal of the British Archaeological Association
JEA	Journal of Egyptian Archaeology
JRA	Journal of Roman Archaeology
JRMES	Journal of Roman Military Equipment Studies
JRS	Journal of Roman Studies
LIMC	Lexicon Iconographicum Mythologiae Classicae
O. Bu Njem	R. Marichal, Les ostraca de Bu Njem. Libya Antiqua, suppl. 9 (Tripoli, 1992)
O. Claud.	J. Bingen et al., Mons Claudianus, ostraca graeca et latina, I. IFAO, Documents et fouilles 29 (Cairo, 1992)

O. Flor.	R. S. Bagnall, *The Florida Ostraca: Documents from the Roman Army in Upper Egypt*. Greek, Roman and Byzantine Monographs 7 (Durham, NC, 1976)
OJA	*Oxford Journal of Archaeology*
O. Krok.	H. Cuvigny, *Ostraca de Krokodilô: la correspondence militaire et sa circulation. O. Krok. 1–151* (Cairo, 2005)
O.Wâdi Fawâkhir	O. Guéraud, 'Ostraca grecs et latins de l'Wâdi Fawâkhir', *Bulletin de l'Institut Français d'Archéologie Orientale 49* (1942), 141–96
PAT	D. R. Hillers and E. Cussini, *Palmyrene Aramaic Texts* (Baltimore, Md., and London, 1996)
P. Amh.	B. P. Grenfell and A. S. Hunt, *The Amherst Papyri* (2 vols, London, 1900–1901)
P. Berlin	R. Marichal, *L'occupation romaine de la basse Égypte: le statut des auxilia P. Berlin 6.866 et P. Lond. 1196* (Paris, 1945)
P. Dura	C. B. Welles, R. O. Fink, and J. F. Gilliam, *Excavations at Dura-Europos*, Final Report V, Part I: *The Parchments and Papyri* (New Haven, Conn., 1959)
P. Fayum	B. P. Grenfell, A. S. Hunt, and D. G. Hogarth, *Fayum Towns and their Papyri* (London, 1900)
P. Gen.	Nicole, J. (ed.), *Les Papyrus de Genève*, I (Geneva, 1896–1906); 2nd edn by P. Schubert and I. Jornot with contributions by C. Wick (Geneva 2002)
P. Grenf. II	B. P. Grenfell and A. S. Hunt, II, *New Classical Fragments and Other Greek and Latin Papyri* (Oxford, 1897)
P. Hamb.	P. M. Meyer (ed.), *Griechische Papyrusurkunden der Hamburger Staats und Universitäts-bibliothek* (Leipzig and Berlin, 1911–24)
P. Lond.	F. G. Kenyon and H. I. Bell (eds), *Greek Papyri in the British Museum* (London, 1893–1917)
P. Mich.	*Papyri in the University of Michigan Collection*
P. Oxy.	B. P. Grenfell, A. S. Hunt, et al. (eds), *The Oxyrhynchus Papyri* (London, 1898–)
P. Paris	J. A. Letronne, W. Brunet de Presle, and E. Egger (eds), *Notices et textes des papyrus du Musée du Louvre et de la Bibliothèque Impériale* (Paris, 1865)
PPS	*Proceedings of the Prehistoric Society*
P. Vindob.	H. Harrauer and R. Seider (eds), 'Ein neuer lateinischer Schuldschein: *P. Vindob. L 135*', ZPE 36 (1979), 109–20
REG	*Revue des études grecques*
RIB	*The Roman Inscriptions of Britain*
RIU	*Die römischen Inschriften Ungarns*
RMD	*Roman Military Diplomas*
RMR	R. O. Fink, *Roman Military Records on Papyrus* (Cleveland, Ohio, 1971)
SB	*Sammelbuch griechischer Urkunden aus Ägypten*
SCI	*Scripta Classica Israelitica*

SEG	*Supplementum Epigraphicum Graecum*
SHA	*Scriptores Historiae Augustae*
Tab. Vindol. II	A. K. Bowman and J. D. Thomas, *The Vindolanda Writing-Tablets (Tabulae Vindolandenses 2)* (London, 1994)
Tab. Vindol. III	A. K. Bowman and J. D. Thomas, *The Vindolanda Writing-Tablets (Tabulae Vindolandenses 3)* (London, 2003)
TAPhA	*Transactions and Proceedings of the American Philological Association*
TLL	*Thesaurus Linguae Latinae*
ZPE	*Zeitschrift für Papyrologie und Epigraphik*
ZRG	*Zeitschrift für Religions- und Geistesgeschichte.*

1

Introduction

Blood of the Provinces

Their dead are still remembered in the low rolling hills of Dobrudja. At Adamklissi, in southeast Romania, the remains of an elaborate ceremonial complex commemorate the *fortissimi viri*, 'the bravest of men', killed in the service of Rome.[1] Most eye-catching of the surviving monuments is a large tropaeum (see Fig. 1.1). Restored today to a height of almost 40 metres, it projects once more its uncompromising message. Topped by the sculpted arms and armour of the vanquished, it combines the time-honoured form of a victory memorial with a powerful representation in cartoon frieze of the bloody reality of war and Roman vengeance. Two almost identical inscriptions dedicate this grim trophy to Mars Ultor, Mars the Avenger, and offer a date: the Emperor Trajan's thirteenth period of tribunician power.[2]

To understand the full significance of this message, however, it is necessary to look beyond this great trophy, for it is but one of three monuments laid out together in an isosceles triangle. At the apex of this triangle, 864 Roman feet away, lies a great circular mausoleum. Excavations beneath it have revealed a pit containing the bones of oxen, representing perhaps traces of the funerary rites for the fallen. At the other corner of the base, directly north of the tropaeum, lies an altar; it too stands precisely 864 Roman feet from the tumulus.[3] Carved upon it in serried rows were the names of the dead. Fragments of these inscriptions reveal that the altar did not just commemorate the Roman citizens—the senior officers and legionary soldiers—who fell, but also members of the non-citizen auxiliary cohorts. Their place on the altar testifies to an evolution in Roman society; for auxiliaries were no longer conceived of as mere helping forces but had become an indispensable resource comprising over half of the Empire's land forces.[4] Listed by regiment, the names and origins of these men commemorate staggering diversity. Entries for a single auxiliary regiment, for example, show that it contained men

---

[1] For the the complex see Florescu (1960), Richmond (1982: 43–54), and Sâmpetru (1984).

[2] 10 Dec. AD 107 to 9 Dec. AD 108.

[3] Sâmpetru (1984: 18–19).

[4] As many auxiliary soldiers as legionaries and guardsmen combined under Tiberius (Tacitus *Ann.* 4.5). Cheesman (1914: 168): the *auxilia* probably amounted to 220,000 men, compared to 156,800 legionaries. Kraft (1951: 21–68): 220,000 men serving in the Empire's regular non-citizen regiments in the 2nd century AD, compared to 180,000 in the legions.

Fig. 1.1. The *tropaeum* at Adamklissi, Romania as it appears today following its reconstruction in 1977. The original monument was constructed in AD 107/8.

from two central European provinces, Noricum and Raetia, an African, two Britons, three Spaniards, and twelve Gauls.[5]

The presence of auxiliaries such as these on the altar reminds us of two very important things about the Roman Empire. The first is that it was capable of incorporating widely different peoples into its own network of power. The second was that it had to—it was dependent on this process to survive. Incorporation was the ongoing process that lay at the heart of the Empire's longevity. It was the key not just to conquest but also to the retention of conquests. And it was in its ability to keep hold of its conquests that Rome proved a uniquely successful master of empire.[6] The Adamklissi monuments attest in stone the mechanism that drove this achievement. A couple of years before the completion of the tropaeum, the great historian Tacitus had written 'It is by the blood of the provinces that the provinces are won.'[7] The complex at Adamklissi shows just how right he was.[8]

Yet while Tacitus's observation, placed in the mouth of an auxiliary commander, Iulius Civilis, also commemorates the role of non-citizen soldiers in Roman hegemony, it refers to a very different landscape. Tacitus' account refers not to the lands between the Black Sea and the Danube under Trajan, but to the Rhine during the tumultuous events of AD 69. Though the sentiment represents

[5] *CIL* 3.14214 = ILS 9107. Though this cosmopolitan array may reflect wartime recruitment patterns rather than those preferred during peacetime.

[6] Mann (1986: 251).

[7] *Provinciarum sanguine provincias vinci* (*Hist.* 4.17).

[8] Civilis here refers to auxiliary recruitment in the region, but in reality both auxiliaries and legionaries were recruited in the provinces at this date.

contemporary discourse on Roman power rather than a real speech, the choice of Civilis as a mouthpiece for the underlying argument is significant. The claim combines arrogant boast with profound insight. In fact it was largely the citizen soldiers of Italy who, aided by their allies, carved out the territories of the Empire under the Republic. Yet in the perpetual reassertion of the *pax Romana*, in the operation of Roman authority and in the wars of the Principate, it was indeed very often the provincial blood of auxiliaries to whom Tacitus/Civilis referred that sustained the imperial edifice. Civilis, commander of Batavian auxiliaries *and* a member of the Batavian tribal elite, chose to lead his men against the legionaries on the Rhine, and encouraged the commanders and men of other auxiliary units to join him. Led by a man who could operate both with and against Roman armies, the revolt thus exposed the Empire's one great weakness. It was intensely vulnerable to those provincials who, armed and trained to protect its interests, chose instead to pursue their own.

Rome's histories are full of dark tales of the enemy within. Over two centuries before Civilis, a former commander of native auxiliaries, Viriathus, had capitalized on experience of Roman fighting methods when leading a force in Spain against the Romans. Other notorious auxiliaries turned enemies were Jugurtha, Tacfarinas, and Arminius. Tacfarinas famously led a major uprising in Africa in the reign of Tiberius, while Arminius achieved notoriety as commander of the German forces who massacred Varus's legions in the bloodbath of the Teutoburg Forest in AD 9.[9] In subsequent revolts against imperial authority on the Danube and the Rhine, ancient writers repeatedly claim that Rome's most resilient and dangerous opponents were the men who had once served her.[10] Nor was it simply the leaders of these conflicts that she had to fear; in many instances some of the best troops available to the Empire's opponents were allegedly rank-and-file deserters from Rome's own armies.[11]

The cooption of potentially lethal adversaries was profoundly important to the Empire. An array of incentives was available to local leaders, but they are far from the whole story. Ordinary members of the rank and file could and did dissent from their leadership. Mutinies are well attested in the Roman army. Furthermore, it is evident that many men took the individual decision to desert, a constant concern to the authorities.[12] Desertion was endemic in many pre-industrial armies, and could—if unchecked—render them essentially ineffective. As with other imperial powers, the Romans found that both carrot and stick proved efficacious in keeping their auxiliaries on side. Money proved an obvious inducement; 'loyalty . . . made lucrative' has long been an elementary step towards securing allegiance amongst the guardians of empires.[13] And indeed, in Roman narratives, Civilis' followers do demand more pay.[14] Terror might well serve as the other, reinforced through the

---

[9] For Arminius's career: *Ann.* 2.10. For Tacfarinas see *Ann.* 2.52. Gannascus, a former auxiliary who turned pirate, appears in *Ann.* 11.18.

[10] Velleius Paterculus (II 110) for Roman experience with Pannonian rebels (AD 6–9).

[11] As with the armies of Jugurtha (Sallust *Bellum Iugurthinum* 103), Tacfarinas (Tacitus *Ann.* 2.52), and Decebalus (Dio 68.9.5).

[12] See Tacitus *Ann.* 2.52, 13.35; Sallust *Bellum Iugurthinum* 103; Dio 65.5.4, 68.9.5; Digest 49.16.4.1–9. See also Campbell (1984: 303–14).

[13] Omissi (1994: 235).   [14] Tacitus *Hist.* 4.19.

casual brutality of military discipline. Yet it is clear that even used together these were insufficient. Organized non-citizen soldiers, as Civilis' forces demonstrated, could still band together, subvert or crush legions, and force the imperial authorities to negotiate with them.[15] Something more was required. As this book demonstrates, a range of culturally specific dynamics enabled the Roman authorities to minimize this risk. Not all of these were initiated by the authorities themselves; many emerged from local initiatives and traditions. Together they incorporated into the network of imperial power individuals and communities that might otherwise have threatened the emperor's peace. Auxiliary units were not, of course, the only military forces caught up in this network; the legions, the fleets, and myriad irregular forces were bound up with it too, but the *auxilia* offer unique insights into the way it operated over space and time.

For a long time, discussion of the army's contribution to the Empire has focused on quantifying its role in maintaining the *pax Romana*, developing infrastructure and disseminating culturally charged information. Many of the arguments that have emerged from this discussion result from erroneous assumptions about the role of the army in the state. The approach here is different. Between the reign of Augustus and the end of the Severan dynasty over two million men would have enrolled in the *auxilia*; their experience and impact would have varied dramatically from place to place and from one date to another. Generalization in this regard is therefore problematic. When examining the *alae* and *cohortes*, an understanding of the diverse evolving provincial societies amongst whom they were raised and served is essential. Units of the *auxilia* are both instruments and products of Roman imperialism, but they are also much more; *alae* and cohorts were living, evolving communities in their own right.

Most familiar to students of the Empire is the notion that the recruitment of auxiliaries, together with the subsequent discharge of many of them as Roman citizens, contributed to the transformation of provincial society in a manner favourable to imperial interests. This argument will be examined in detail here, but unlike other studies, there will be closer attention to the soldier's own experience between enlistment and retirement. How we understand the significance of the beginning and end of a man's career depends fundamentally upon how we understand what takes place in its duration. Each stage and every aspect of the soldier's military service has something new to reveal about the way that individuals were incorporated into imperial society.

What is striking is that this process of incorporation was so often successful in Roman terms. Even Civilis' actions may be seen as legitimate intervention in the Civil War, rather than indigenous revolt against the Empire.[16] Certainly his 'revolt' did not ultimately prove fatal to imperial control; and the Batavians and their erstwhile allies were rapidly reincorporated into the Roman order. Their kin

---

[15] Tacitus *Hist.* 4.62.

[16] Urban (1985) and Wiedemann (1996) see the Batavian Revolt in these terms. Wiedemann (1996: 280) argues that Tacitus sought to conceal an awkward truth: that the Batavians and some Gauls were in fact those who supported the ultimately successful Flavian cause, while the citizen legions and some other Gauls provided the bedrock of Vitellian support. It is important to note that this view also exposes the discomfort Roman commentators felt in their dependency on non-citizen forces.

continued to serve and die in the armies of Empire for generations to come. Indeed, they are listed amongst the dead at Adamklissi.[17]

In focusing on soldiers of the *alae* and *cohortes* and their families and dependants, this study examines the crucial process of incorporation at the lowliest levels. Marginalized even in many studies of the Roman army, themselves marginal in so much of contemporary scholarship, auxiliary soldiers and the formations in which they served are both classic products and vital instruments of the Empire's ongoing capacity to incorporate the diverse into the whole.[18] They are, furthermore, the invisible made visible. Our knowledge of rural settlement has grown dramatically through major survey projects and innovative excavation in the last few decades, but all too often, students of the Empire find themselves at a loss when they seek to address the fate and experience of the mass of the provincial population. In many provinces, the lives and beliefs, homes and graves of the majority have received scant scholarly attention. Yet those who enrolled in even the humblest units of Rome's armies—the *auxilia*—have become much more accessible to modern researchers. Partly as a result of the very nature of material culture in the provinces and partly as a result of academic fashion, there are vastly more data currently available for these men than those they left behind in the Empire's villages. This may not entirely satisfy those who see in this study another discussion of cultural change through the prism of a relatively privileged group, but it does make the most of an archaeological reality. The experiences of the poorest of the poor are notoriously hard to access through historical analysis. It is often forgotten, however, that material poverty can render people archaeologically invisible too. Enlistment into the army, which drew recruits from a broad spectrum of backgrounds, changed that, but it also affected the way individuals accessed and used material culture.

AN IMPERIAL INSTITUTION

Such concerns were not, however, high on the agenda of the brilliant scholars who initiated systematic study of the *auxilia* well over a century ago. Nurtured by a wide-ranging classical education, these men lived and worked in a world of living empires amongst an intelligentsia that frequently turned to Rome's imperial past for inspiration. Theodor Mommsen, a towering figure whose celebrated *Römische Geschichte* continues to reward readers over 150 years after it was first written, wrote extensively of the *auxilia*.[19] His ambitious programme of excavation on

---

[17] *AE* 1963: 102.

[18] I claim a place for these men and their families alongside those other neglected groups now receiving scholarly attention with the growth of postcolonial scholarship and, particularly, the achievements of the subaltern studies group. They too engage in the 'third space' of colonial interactions (Bhabha 1989) that bridges the simple colonist/colonized dichotomy. Revolts and rebellions are only the most extreme examples of the enduring capacity of auxiliaries to assert agency in an unequal setting; postcolonial analysis has identified many other devices used by marginalized groups to assert a level of autonomy (Mitchell 1990). For the wider implications of postcolonial theory for archaeological thought, see especially van Dommelen (2006).

[19] Mommsen's *Römische Geschichte* was published between 1854 and 1856. His 'Die Conscriptionsordnung der römischen Kaiserzeit', published in 1884, was to prove profoundly influential.

Rome's Rhine frontier yielded vital archaeological insights into their camps and fortifications. His contemporaries Alfred von Domaszewski and Conrad Cichorius were also to have a formative impact on subsequent scholarship; von Domaszewski's papers continue to be cited extensively in new surveys of Roman military life,[20] while Cichorius' key articles on the auxilia have proved so valuable that over 110 years after their initial publication a fresh attempt has been made to update them comprehensively.[21] The research interests of these scholars encompassed many fields, but they all shared a desire to understand how the *auxilia* operated as imperial institutions. Significantly, it was an interest they could entice leading figures in their own imperial governments to share; Mommsen's high-level contacts, for example, assured for him the assistance of the German army in his fieldwork.[22]

The sense that military organization, rank structure, and recruitment were especially important areas reflected interest in the *auxilia* as an arm of imperial governance, and in turn defined the agenda of much subsequent research.[23] Cichorius, for example, itemized all known references to the auxiliary regiments of the Roman Empire in two encyclopedic articles of the 1890s. In both the original and re-edited version, units are catalogued wherever possible on the tribal or ethnic element of their title. It is a device that has much merit in compiling encyclopedia entries, but only limited value for attempts at understanding the cultural mix that the *auxilia* represented. Understanding the *auxilia* within provincial society requires that we go beyond these categories.

The first and most influential book to be wholly dedicated to Rome's auxiliaries acknowledged the intellectual legacy of these early pioneers. In his *The Auxilia of the Roman Imperial Army*, published in 1914, G. L. Cheesman expressed his particular debt to Mommsen and von Domaszewski's studies of army recruitment and organization. The debt was a very real one, for though over half of Cheesman's monograph was dedicated to analysis of these two themes, tactics, deployment, and equipment were included, but received relatively less attention. Not only was the study of recruitment and organization well served by the evidence of inscriptions, then one of the most intensely scrutinized sources of evidence in Roman studies, but these themes also resonated powerfully with the interests of leading scholars of Cheesman's generation.

Cheesman's interest in 'the extent to which a ruling race can safely use the military resources of its subjects and the effect on both parties of such a relation' recalls what has indeed been an enduring concern for emperors, kings, presidents, and prime ministers through the ages, but it must also be seen within the context of his own lifetime.[24] There are certainly echoes here of the early 20th-century belief that Roman studies were especially relevant to the challenges faced by

[20] von Domaszewski's *Die Rangordnung des römischen Heeres*, first published in 1908, was revised and reissued by Brian Dobson in 1967 (Domaszewski 1967).
[21] Cichorius, vols 1.1 (1893) and 4 (1900) of the *Realencyclopädie der classischen Altertumswissenschaft*. These have been revised by Spaul (1994) and (2000). Though full of admiration for Spaul's ambitious undertaking, I should note that there are several areas where I disagree with his reading of the evidence.
[22] See Marchand (1996: 173–4); James (2002: 10).
[23] As seen in M. P. Speidel (1989).   [24] Cheesman (1914: 7).

contemporary empires.[25] Only three years before Cheesman's monograph was published, his Oxford mentor Francis Haverfield noted in the first volume of the then new *Journal of Roman Studies*: 'The methods by which Rome incorporated and denationalized and assimilated more than half of its wide dominions . . . concern in many ways our own age and empire.'[26] If the tone seems anachronistic in our postcolonial milieu, it was nonetheless as grave a concern to Cheesman and his peers as it was to Tacitus and his audience. Enrolled into one of the British army's territorial divisions, Cheesman fought and died alongside soldiers drawn from Nepal, India, Australia, and New Zealand in a campaign that for many symbolizes the most obscene instance of colonial exploitation of imperial manpower—Gallipoli.[27]

Cheesman's perspective may make us uncomfortable, therefore, but that is no reason to dismiss it and arguably a good one to revisit its rationale. Indeed, the view underscores both the important role of incorporation in imperial government and the brute fact that it is not an equal relationship. Where problems arise, however, is in the perception of the participants. While Cheesman showed a willingness to look beyond imperial administration at one level, examining as he put it 'both parties', he followed an established tendency to categorize his subjects in what are misleading terms. Neither the simple labels of 'Roman' and 'Native' nor the seemingly more compelling ethnic and tribal names used in imperial administration constitute adequate tools for studying cultural transformation in the Roman world. Their ancient use illuminates state ideology, but as we will see their contemporary application to archaeological evidence is deeply problematic. The body of scholarly literature decrying the use of Roman/native oppositions is so vast that it cannot be summarized here, but it is necessary to stress that, more generally, there has been a seismic shift in academic understandings of ethnicity since Cheesman's day, even if this shift has not been noted by all students of Roman provincial archaeology.[28] While notions of shared 'culture' and origins continue to be seen as a vital element of ethnicity, it is now appreciated that the ethnicity 'only makes sense in a context of relativities, of processes of identification'.[29] Our understanding of past peoples and places has been distorted by our over-ready acceptance of the the names given to them by Rome and its predecessors. Treating exonyms, the names used by outsiders, as though they were the endonyms, or preferred names of the groups themselves, is inevitably misleading. With the recognition that ethnicity is not a biological or linguistic given, but is deeply sensitive to context, comes the understanding that individuals can switch ethnicities and even adopt multiple ones, using an almost infinite array of artefacts while doing so.

While he produced much of lasting value, Cheesman's work generated enduring misconceptions about the interplay of ethnicity and military identity. His belief, for example, that 'oriental regiments' continued to receive fresh drafts of recruits from

---

[25] For background see Hingley (2000).

[26] Haverfield (1911: xviii). See also Freeman (1996, 1997, 2007).

[27] I thank Major Peter Cottrell for the information about Cheesman's military service.

[28] See Jones (1997: 33) for a discussion of Roman/native oppositions within a wider-ranging assessment of the archaeology of ethnicity.

[29] Tonkin, McDonald, and Chapman (1996: 23); Gardner (2007: 198).

their homelands on the basis that 'good archers were born in Syria, and could not be made elsewhere' is demonstrably false, but it reflects the thinking underpinning recruitment practice in British colonial forces during his lifetime.[30] In early 20th-century India, particular castes and tribes were deemed suited to different types of military service. Furthermore, regiments in the British and Indian armies continued to receive recruits from the same area where they were first raised. Despite numerous claims to the contrary, we now know that Rome did not actually employ similar practices with its eastern units; but in fairness to Cheesman it must be acknowledged that we know this because we have considerably more evidence, from a far greater range of sources than was ever available to him.[31] It should also be acknowledged that the idea itself is not implausible; the Batavians were treated in this way, though Roman exploitation of this particular people was instrumental in creating their ethnic identity, rather than responding to it.[32]

Eric Birley, Cheesman's foremost intellectual heir and himself the founder of a distinguished dynasty of Roman scholars, was certainly influenced by his experience of contemporary armies in his work. Birley often stressed how his study of Rome's land forces benefited from his work as an intelligence officer, processing evidence for the German army's organization during the Second World War.[33] Orders of battle could be reconstructed from the fragmentary record of inscriptions, he argued, in much the same way as it could from the partial glimpses afforded through espionage and captured documents. The stress placed on this parallel reminds us, of course, that the emphasis here was especially on administrative structure—the social contexts of these armies were very different and would have afforded limited opportunities for comparative study.

Birley's immense contribution to Roman studies was not confined to military organization, but his influence on this field was particularly great, being felt not simply through his own valuable papers but also through the work of his students. Here and elsewhere, with the work of Kraft on the recruitment of the *auxilia* as with Cheesman's own essay, inscriptions were the main source of information, and the study of organizational structures a clear priority.[34]

Accordingly, when in the early 1980s Holder and Saddington produced their respective monographs on the *auxilia* the emphasis was firmly on ancient historical sources and their capacity to illuminate the evolution of structures.[35] Both approached with compelling thoroughness the evidence for the early *auxilia*, Holder examining it from Augustus to Trajan, Saddington from Caesar to Vespasian. Both displayed admirable awareness of the wider implications of their studies, but each also avoided being drawn into lengthy discussion of archaeological evidence other than inscriptions. Given the huge growth in data in recent years, the attractions of this strategy are readily appreciated.

[30] Cheesman (1914: 83–5). The British Indian Army maintained the practice of reinforcing existing units with drafts of men from their home areas.

[31] As Kennedy noted in his unpublished thesis, 'As the register of this evidence at the end of this work shows, most was unknown to Cheesman, almost half has only been published since 1940' (1980: 5).

[32] Roymans (2004); Driel-Murray (2003).

[33] E. Birley (1952: 226; 1988b: vii). The implications are considered by both Alston (1995: 4) and James (2002: 19–21).

[34] Kraft (1951).   [35] Holder (1980) and Saddington (1982).

A further consequence of the growth of data has been a tendency to study provincial armies rather than the army or the *auxilia* together. Von Domaszewski was the first scholar to stress that the Romans actually thought of their land forces as provincial armies rather than as a single monolithic institution.[36] This is evident both from the wording of discharge certificates, which list the units in a single province, and even from some epitaphs, in which the provincial army to which a soldier belonged is sometimes recorded.[37] Accordingly, this trend in provincial case studies has a useful basis in ancient practice. Beginning with Cagnat's 1913 study of the Roman army in Africa, there has been a steady growth in the number of monograph and long article studies on regional/provincial armies and regional/provincial *auxilia*.[38] Most recently the pattern has developed of examining aspects of military culture, such as religion, in distinct zones.[39]

It is not therefore hard to see why M. P. Speidel, himself the author of many key papers on the *auxilia* and Roman army studies, was able to conclude his agenda-setting paper with a very positive review of progress in the study of Roman military *organization* already made.[40] Much has indeed been achieved by scholars, and there are clear and established goals for students wishing to advance its study. Yet identifying the organizational machinery of the army is only part of the challenge. Institutional structures have real consequences for those who come into contact with them, but they can be applied and lived in a range of very different ways. The study of Roman military organization is but one part of the study of life in Rome's armies.

Here it is necessary to note an issue that has become problematic in the study of the *auxilia*. The vast majority of progress made in the study of organization reflects the advances made by epigraphers and, to an extent, papyrologists. Inscriptions including military diplomas have furnished us with a clear understanding of organizational structures and terms of service within the *auxilia*. It is also possible to argue with conviction that we now know of at least 95 per cent of the *alae* and *cohortes* which served between the death of Augustus and the Severan

---

[36] von Domaszewski (1895: 5, n. 12). Speidel (1989: 102–3) called for further study of provincial armies. See also James (1999: 14; 2001: 78; 2002: 38–9) and Haynes (1999: 7).

[37] e.g. the reference to the army of Moesia Inferior on an epitaph commemorating the wife of a decurion serving in the *Ala Atectorigiana* (*AE* 1890, 27 = *ILS* 2537).

[38] The main studies of regional/provincial armies are Cagnat (1913) and Lesquier (1918) for Egypt, Stein (1932) for Germany, Sherk (1955) and Speidel (1983) for Asia Minor, Sherk (1957) for Macedonia and Achaia, Le Roux (1982) for Spain, Holder (1982) for Britain. To these largely epigraphical studies we should add the archaeological guides prepared for the Limes conferences, notably that of Kennedy (2000), Visy (2003), Morillo and Aurrecoecha (2006), and Bidwell and Hodgson (2009). Studies of the *auxilia* of provincial armies are Wagner (1938) for Noricum, Pannonia, Moesia, and Dacia, Beneš (1978), and Țentea and Matei-Popescu (2004) for Dacia and Moesia; Alföldy (1962) for Dalmatia, Alföldy (1968a), for Germania Inferior, Roxan (1973) for Mauretania Tingitana, Benseddik (1977) for Mauretania Caesariensis, and Le Bohec (1989) for Numidia and Africa Proconsularis. To these categories we should add those which consider regions and provinces from the perspective of their role as sources of soldiers, notably Roldan Hervas (1974) for Spain, Jarrett (1969) for Thrace, and Kennedy (1980) for Syria.

[39] e.g. Stoll (2001a) for the Near East and Irby-Massie (1999) for Britain.

[40] M. P. Speidel (1989). The review focuses on military organization in particular, not Roman army studies generally, a point omitted from Alston's (1995: 3–5) criticism.

period.[41] It is notable that only a handful of units have been discovered since Cichorius first catalogued them in the late 19th century. Yet the riches of this information can give researchers false confidence, and a tendency has grown to attempt to use inscriptions and diplomas as a body of data that can be analysed statistically to reveal cultural changes within the *auxilia*, for example evolving recruitment patterns. It will be clear that I have tended to avoid such an approach throughout this work unless I believe that there are sufficient controls and sufficiently rich data sets to make the analysis statistically significant. We may know of most of the regiments that existed, but in many cases only a couple of inscriptions survive for institutions of several hundred men which endured for centuries. A close contextual reading of the surviving data is always necessary.

ARMIES AND COMMUNITIES

The growing trend to see Rome's armed forces as communities as well as imperial institutions reflects developments in both historical and archaeological studies. MacMullen's seminal 1984 paper 'The Legion as a Society', which actually also considered auxiliary units, opened up new avenues of research by stressing the social dynamics that ran alongside the institutional structures.[42] Already by this time, however, the dramatic growth of excavated data and the emergence of new thinking in archaeological theory were inspiring other scholars to explore this theme. Research into the social aspects of Roman military service has since been advanced not only within established scholarly networks concerned with such themes as frontier studies, military equipment and, most recently, the study of military diplomas, but also more generally among students of the Roman provinces.

Yet the study of Rome's armed forces as communities at once throws up a series of challenges. The first of these is: what does it actually mean to be a community? The term was already tired and overstretched in scholarly circles long before it was first introduced into Roman studies. Indeed, a 1955 survey found that over 94 different applications of the term were already in scholarly use.[43] It is necessary therefore to note that it is used in two interrelated ways in this volume: the broader 'occupational community' of soldiers and the local, co-located groups of soldiers, their families, and servants which formed distinct 'military communities'.

'Occupational communities', notably police and emergency services, have been extensively studied by sociologists since the 1960s, but it is clear that their defining characteristics are not limited to the modern world. Their key attributes were shared by Roman soldiers.[44] Three attributes of classic 'occupational communities' contribute to a shared sense of belonging. First, members share work that carries particular responsibilities and dangers. Second, they enjoy 'marginal status'—a product of the tension between their recruitment from lower-class social groups and their privileged status as the instruments of state power. Third, their work is both intentionally and incidentally exclusive. Members

---

[41] Spaul (2000: 5).   [42] MacMullen (1984).   [43] Hillery (1955).
[44] See here Gerstl (1961), Salaman (1974: 29), and Haynes (1999: 9).

enjoy particular privileges that others do not share, but the circumstances of their work affect their freedom to interact with other groups. I believe that we may see these factors at work in Rome's armies, where it was reinforced by a common oath and manifested in a tendency for people from widely differing locations to adorn themselves in remarkably similar ways. James has argued that it is more useful to write of 'the community of the soldiers' than of a single Roman army.[45] This community has, he adds, notable similarities to the notional 'imagined communities' conceived by Anderson to understand the rise of nationalism in the modern world.[46] Individuals widely separated by distance and time could nonetheless evoke a sense of shared belonging to a wider entity. While there were in fact many armies at the emperor's service, there are clear indications that military identity coalesced around certain themes under the Empire; significantly, this process was not simply imposed from above. This insight resonates strongly with what we know of occupational communities, for their members develop common bonds over and above those formally instituted by their employers. Indeed, such groups are characterized by exceptional degrees of empathy, despite the fact that they might be stationed at widely dispersed locations and never come into contact with more than a fraction of their fellow professionals.

There is clear evidence for distinct subcultures within this occupational community. Whenever it was faced with the competing ambitions of commanders, it proved quite capable of fragmenting. Regional and provincial armies were demonstrably willing to confront one another in the Empire's many civil wars. Much of the explanation for this must lie with leadership and self-interest, but the pattern of fragmentation raises questions about the degree to which the armies in these conflicts differed from one another. How different, we must ask, was the experience of serving in the army of one province from that of serving in that of another? The stock commentaries of ancient authors routinely contrast the lax conditions of the east with the brutal demands of military service in the west, but our evidence can take us beyond such simple oppositions.[47] So entrenched is the habit of writing of 'the Roman Army' that scholars often overlook the tendency to assume that much of the archaeological evidence for the intensely studied provincial armies of the northwestern provinces and, to a lesser extent, the Danubian lands is representative of all. It is a tendency reinforced by the fact that there were indeed multiple similarities between all these armies, both in their relationship to the emperor and in their organizational structure, but it is also potentially very misleading. Excavated data reveals that many aspects of soldiers' lives, from cult practice to diet, varied significantly across the Empire. As will become apparent, I believe that these variations are better understood as regional rather than provincial traits. Administrative divisions sometimes reflected, and sometimes helped sustain, genuine cultural variations within the Empire, but they did not and could not simply demarcate such potentially fluid phenomena. What applied in wider provincial society also applied in part to the military community: institutions might look similar, but the lives of the communities they governed could still be very different.

[45] James (1999; 2001: 79). [46] James (1999: 15, 18) citing Anderson (1991).
[47] Wheeler (1996).

Yet, as James has demonstrated, there is another level of complexity to embrace. For despite the absence of evidence for dress regulations and systematic imperial prescriptions on military equipment, there was a remarkable similarity in what soldiers wore from one end of the Empire to the other. He views this as evidence of a different pressure, a collective evolution rather than an imposed order that defined the image of a soldier in the Roman world. Such an argument offers a radically different way of understanding the relationship of imperial structure to material culture. I would suggest that it also helps us to reconsider the roots of our understanding of community in the Roman Empire, for the term ultimately derives from the Latin verb *communicare*—a term that signifies both communication between individuals and putting into common stock, or sharing. This link between exchange of information, belonging, and sharing offers a useful way of understanding our data. The patterns of behaviour reflect the pattern of information exchange amongst soldiers as opposed to that with and between other communities within the Empire. James supports his view by noting the evolution of the dynamics that lead people to emulate one another's dress, noting that opposing armies often copy the other side's equipment.[48] Within military communities the need for individuals to stress their membership as part of a common group is particularly strong— indeed, it is a survival mechanism—so there can be a strong social pressure to dress in similar ways even in the absence of regulatory instructions to do so.[49] The strength with which auxiliaries came to feel these ties is strongly suggested by the repeated reference to *contubernales* or tent mates in the correspondence at Vindolanda and elsewhere.[50]

The degree to which Roman soldiers came to resemble one another in turn raises a further question about institutional identity. Written sources continually stress the difference between auxiliaries and other soldiers, yet we know that the initial criterion behind the creation of the *auxilia*, non-citizen status, became increasingly irrelevant. How far did auxiliaries actually represent a discernibly different category of soldier in the Roman world? Recent studies have challenged long-held beliefs that auxiliaries received different pay and benefits from their legionary counterparts, and even that they were equipped differently, but they have not been widely accepted.[51] Maxfield, for example, has observed that artefacts commonly associated with the dress of legionaries have been found at sites or in provinces that would appear to have contained auxiliaries only.[52] In this volume I will argue that in fact auxiliaries remained a sufficiently well-defined body to warrant particular study, but that the increasing blurring of distinctions between their rights, deployment, and dress and those of the legions must be understood as part of a wider, quintessentially Roman pattern of incorporation. The same point applies to the relationship between the *alae* and *cohortes* with which this volume is concerned, and the altogether less well-understood formations collectively referred to by

---

[48] James (1999; 2004: 251–4).

[49] Banton (1964) and Cain (1971) note the particular force of this dynamic in military and police communities.

[50] The term is also used for 'comrade' and 'companion'. It is used extensively by the soldiers at Vindolanda; see e.g. *Tab. Vindol.* II.181.14; 310.2; 311.ii.2; 343.29; 346.ii.4; 349.ii.

[51] See Alston (1994) for an alternative view.   [52] Maxfield (1986a: 68); p. 275.

scholars as *numeri*.[53] These are omitted from most of the major works on the *auxilia* and treated as a distinct group primarily because, as Le Bohec argues, the *numeri* 'n'importe quelle sorte de troupe n'entrant pas dans les cadres tradition-nels, c'est-à-dire légions, ailes et cohortes auxiliaires'.[54] In this work, I shall discuss them only when their story relates directly to that of the *alae* and *cohortes*. The variations between *numeri* appear to have been great, with some being raised as temporary levies and preserving their own dress, while others appear to have evolved into altogether more permanent formations organized in a very similar manner to regular units.[55] Yet while the old divide between the citizens and non-citizen units collapsed over time, other status distinctions emerged within the armies that became ever stronger. The most important of these distinctions will prove to be that between the status and character of cavalry units and infantry regiments, discernible not only in their equipment and pay but also in the layout and space of their quarters and their traditions of funerary commemoration.

While distinctions may be observed at this level of analysis, it is altogether harder to trace individual regiments in the archaeological record. As we have seen, the study of regimental histories has a long pedigree; most of the formative studies of the *auxilia* stressed this aspect. It is easy to see why they did so: not only did soldiers and officers alike refer to the titles of their regiments, but many of the *alae* and *cohortes* endured for centuries—indeed, several existed as named entities for over 400 years. Such longevity and the occasional hints in the sources of regi-mental traditions make this an attractive avenue for text-based research, but also a problem for the archaeologist. The reappearance over time of a regimental name in our documentary sources may well reflect continuity of a kind of community, but in reality it often masks dramatic change. Sources of recruits, languages spoken, cult practice, deployment, and dress could and did change radically. The difficulty is that it is seldom if ever possible to trace the presence, movement, and history of individual auxiliary units through artefacts alone. Unless an object actually carries the name of a unit, there is no certain way of assigning it to a given formation; even then, in the absence of good contextual evidence, the possibility remains that the artefact was dropped at its findspot by a passing soldier, telling us little of the actual history of the unit involved.[56]

The radical change of circumstances and appearance that units could undergo during their existence is easily demonstrated with a single example: the *ala Atectorigiana*, a regiment that as part of the army of Lower Moesia may once have paraded before the Adamklissi memorial. In this case it is possible to combine the evidence of inscriptions with other data to paint a picture of the transformation. Our understanding of the regiment's early history is grounded entirely on the numismatic evidence; Celtic coins from southwestern France

---

[53] The term *numerus*, which simply means 'unit', is ambiguous. It was sometimes used by the Romans to refer to a regular force and in other cases to distinguish an irregular formation from a regular one. For example, in *AE* 1927: 95 the term appears to be used to refer to *cohors I Claudia Sugambrorum*.

[54] Le Bohec (1989: 145).

[55] As may have been the case with *cohors XX Palmyrenorum milliaria sagittariorum equitata*. See p. 81.

[56] Reece (1997). Bishop and Coulston (2006: 260–61) suggest that unit identity may be discernible from military equipment.

commemorate the Gallic leader Atectorix, a man widely believed to have been the unit's founder.[57] The Gallic flavour of the regiment in its early years is affirmed on the memorial of an early recruit found at Saintes,[58] but in later years the *ala* travelled widely. A late 2nd/early 3rd-century tombstone shows that some or all of the regiment was stationed in the Crimea in modern Ukraine at that time. The figure carved on this impressive monument, found by chance near the 19th-century battlefield of Balaklava, preserves no trace of the unit's Gallic past. Rather, it reflects the regiment's service in Lower Moesia, for it depicts not a Gaulish horseman, but a rider styled on the Thracian Hero, the ubiquitous messenger divinity of the Danubian provinces.[59]

Even where it is possible to tie a unit to a particular phase of occupation at an excavated site, it is ill-advised to assume that all of the artefacts discovered at the site are linked to the regiment based there. Documents such as 'Hunt's *Pridianum*', a papyrus report listing the deployment of one cohort, also in the army of Lower Moesia, show just how many detachments could be serving away from regimental headquarters at any given time.[60] At the time the document was compiled the unit, *cohors I Hispanorum veterana equitata*, was stationed outside the province at Stobi in Macedonia. On just one day in the early 2nd century the cohort had two detachments in Gaul, another outside the province at the mines of Dardinia, further patrols north of the Danube, and another contingent gathering cattle in Thrace. Furthermore, soldiers were deployed to at least three other military installations. The fact that the cohort was originally raised in Spain and that the document was discovered in Egypt only underscores the extraordinary picture of mobility conveyed by the *pridianum*.

The near-contemporary Vindolanda tablets tell a similar story, revealing not simply the degree to which units in the army of Britain could be fragmented[61] but also the extent to which military stations could house men from multiple contingents at any given time. In addition to the regiments known to have had their headquarters at Vindolanda, fragmentary writing tablets strongly suggest the presence of detachments from other units within the fort (see Fig. 1.2).[62] The pattern of accommodating more than one unit at a single site is strongly attested at bigger installations, notably the so-called 'legionary fortresses', where there is often epigraphic evidence for auxiliary cavalry units stationed alongside legions.[63] Given this complexity, it is useful to distinguish between those individuals who are members of a given regiment and those individuals who are, at any given time, co-located at a given place. This distinction is the more important because it underscores the fact that in archaeological terms we have to be aware that we cannot confidently distinguish between the latter and the former.

In contrast to the broader groupings that formed part of the community of soldiers, 'military communities' are primarily considered here as local entities. They consist of the individuals who generally encountered one another on a daily

---

[57] E. Birley (1978b: 265).   [58] *CIL* 13.1041.
[59] Carter and Mack (2003: 160, fig. 10.71).   [60] *P. Lond.* 2851 = *RMR* 63.
[61] *Tab. Vindol.* II.154.   [62] For example the *equites Vardulli* recorded in *Tab. Vindol.* II.181.
[63] Q. Herennius Silvius Maximus is recorded as *Legatus legionis II Italicae et alae Antoninianae* (*CIL* 9 2213 = *ILS* 1164). I note the controversies associated with this text, but I am convinced that the correct reading is indeed *et alae*.

Fig. 1.2. Strength report of *cohors I Tungrorum* from Vindolanda, England (*Tab. Vindol.* II.154). Late 1st century AD.

or at least weekly basis, the group that consists not only of fighting men but also of the military families, servants, and tradesmen dependent upon them.[64] Recent attempts to identify the non-soldiers within these communities have highlighted the problems inherent in trying to isolate them archaeologically, yet they have also opened up some important avenues for further research.

---

[64] James (2001: 80) uses the term 'Regimental Community II' for these groups.

Amongst the most recent developments has been the commitment to engender-ing military communities. Carol van Driel-Murray's groundbreaking analyses at Vindolanda used a study of footwear to demonstrate the presence of women and children within the confines of the 1st-century fort.[65] There has also been a wider debate, led by Lindsay Allason-Jones, about the challenges of 'sexing' artefacts in military assemblages, and a series of attempts by Pim Allison to engender Roman military space through high-resolution spatial analyses.[66] While the extent to which this project can be successfully pursued is debated, there can be absolutely no doubt that it has been triumphantly successful in two regards. First, it is now widely accepted that the occupancy of forts was not confined to military males. Second, and partly following from this point, is a growing interest in understand-ing military sites as a whole—in looking simultaneously at the activities that take place both within fort walls and in the settlements that lay immediately outside them. We are now much more aware of the fluidity of movement across sites.[67] The most advanced research programme to examine this now operates at Vindolanda, and comprises a sustained excavation strategy designed to explore intra- and extramural areas of the Severan and post-Severan period in an integrated manner (see Fig. 1.3). The project is already allowing for a more sophisticated analysis of spatial variation and temporal change than has hitherto been possible.[68]

Given such exciting developments in archaeological research, it is sometimes chastening when new textual evidence comes to light that shows an even greater complexity within the military community. Far from stopping at some notional soldier/non-soldier divide, archaeologists increasingly aspire to acknowledge that gender, age, status, occupation, and beliefs all impact on the way that individuals appear in the archaeological record.[69] Women and children, neither of which are monolithic identity groups anyway, are not the only individuals overlooked in many analyses. Slaves are often invisible too. When very occasionally we catch a glimpse of them in the written sources, they can radically challenge our precon-ceptions. The stir that followed Alan Bowman's translation of a letter from a *cornicularius*, a junior officer, to a slave is a fine example of this. Showing scant regard for our assumptions about the way two individuals of widely differing legal status should address one another, the Vindolanda *cornicularius* addressed the slave with the warm, informal, and remarkably egalitarian greeting of *frater*.[70] The contrast with other literary references to slaves and servants in military contexts is sharp, and reminds us that even amongst slaves, living conditions varied dramat-ically, making attempts to identify them archaeologically even more difficult.[71]

Both written and archaeological sources attest the complexities underpinning site formation. When dealing with the evidence of finds assemblages in and

---

[65] Driel-Murray (1995; 1997; 1998). Her work at Vindolanda has since been taken forward by Elizabeth Greene.

[66] Allason-Jones (1995; 2001: 21–4), who notes the problems inherent in trying to identify particu-lar groups and, indeed, identifying the gender of an artefact's user. For attempts to map gender in Roman forts see Allison et al. (2004), Allison (2005; 2006), and the response of James (2006).

[67] Allison (2005).   [68] A. Birley (2010).   [69] Hill (2001).

[70] *Tab. Vindol.* II.301, amended in Bowman and Thomas (2003: 159).

[71] Horace's observation that one of the fates awaiting an adulterer in hell was that *calones*, soldiers' servants, would urinate on him is an example of the low status such men held (*Sermones* 1.2.44). For a commitment to identifying slaves in the archaeological record, see Webster (2008a; 2008b).

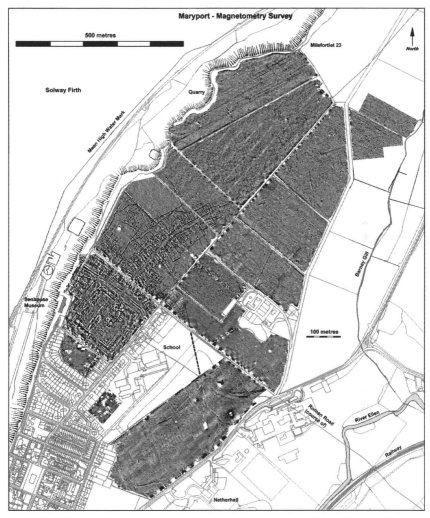

Fig. 1.3. This greyscale magnetometry plot from Maryport, Cumbria, gives some impression of the size extramural settlements could achieve, but even this impressive plan is incomplete. Parts of the Roman conurbation lie beneath modern housing, while even in the open land to the east, excavation has revealed traces of settlement that did not respond to geophysical survey.

around forts and fortresses, it is generally better for us to think in terms of military communities than specific regiments. Only exceptionally do artefacts preserve explicit record of the identity of their owners; even to suggest a simple link between arms and armour and professional soldier status is potentially misleading, and even where a link may be made reuse and adaptation must always be considered. To complicate matters further, finds assemblages in the Roman Empire do not divide neatly into military and civilian—a fact that makes it

difficult to identify military presence on the basis of artefacts alone.[72] In general
the archaeological identification is rightly made on a combination of finds and
structures; but while this appears to work well for military communities stationed
in the forts and fortresses of the west, it is altogether harder to identify with
conviction such groups in towns generally and in the settlements of the east more
particularly.

This in turn highlights the difficulties inherent in discussing military/civilian
interaction in the provinces, a theme of considerable importance. The degree to
which military communities are seen as culturally distinct, and the degree to
which they are seen as influencing local societies, are heavily influenced by the way
this interaction is understood. Back in 1983, Brent Shaw provocatively argued that
the bloody suppression of the Gordianus revolt of AD 238 by, amongst others, the
legion at the heart of the Numidian garrison indicated that that force operated as a
'total institution'.[73] Here was a body that could live alongside civilians for generations, yet turn on them with horrific violence in support of a distant emperor
none of its soldiers had ever seen in person. Drawing on Goffman's work on
asylums, Shaw argued that *Legio III Augusta* should therefore be understood as a
highly introspective entity, socially and culturally isolated from the surrounding
population.[74] The inward-looking character of the legion, he argued, came from
shared routine, common acts of worship, a particular relationship to the emperor,
and a tendency towards intermarriage.[75]

Other scholars subsequently attempted to apply Goffman's 'total institution'
model to the units of the Roman army, but ultimately found it to be unsatisfactory.
Pollard used it to analyse evidence for *cohors XX Palmyrenorum* in the Syrian town
of Dura-Europos, but concluded that even with the rich evidence from that site for
soldiers' quarters, language, and religious life, a more nuanced understanding was
required. At Dura, Pollard argued, the soldiers' particular religious practices and
the practice of institutional endogamy reinforced a separate identity, but nonetheless coexisted alongside documented instances of intermarriage and incorporation
of veterans into the pattern of civilian life. Significantly, he concluded his analysis
by noting that while the epigraphic and papyrological evidence that permitted this
analysis at Dura are exceptionally rich, other artefactual evidence from the site is
not as well recorded as elsewhere and could conceivably offer a different picture.[76]
More significantly still, while retaining these insights, Pollard's later monograph on
the Roman army in Syria avoids using the term 'total institution' altogether,
preferring instead to speak of 'institutional identity'[77]—a term which recalls in
some respects the notion of 'occupational community' discussed above.

The application of the total-institution model to the Roman army certainly has
an attraction to it. Indeed, it even offers through its discussion of 'disculturation'
insights into the process of transformation that enlistment induced.[78] As a whole,
however, the model proves too rigid to address the dynamic we find in the
archaeology of military bases across the Empire. Certainly Pollard is not the

---

[72] See Gardner (2007: 16, 262–3) for problems with the notion of a military assemblage.

[73] Shaw (1983: esp. 144).   [74] Goffman (1961).   [75] Shaw (1983: 144–8).

[76] Pollard (1996: 226).   [77] Pollard (2000: 7–8).

[78] Goffman considers the role of 'disculturation' and 'untraining' in integrating new members into
the asylum environment (1961: 12).

only researcher to have turned to it for inspiration but ultimately found it unsatisfactory. In a comprehensive study of the religion of the Roman army in the Near East, Oliver Stoll examined the concept thoroughly, before concluding that it failed to capture the particular character of the military community because it did not truly reflect the complex dynamic of soldier/civilian interaction in his region. This, Stoll argued, was best understood as 'Zwischen Integration und Abgrenzung.'[79] While then going on to offer some profoundly useful insights as to the internal dynamics of military units, including notably the force and role of 'mateship', he was less forthcoming about models for the hybrid relations he saw between these units and wider society.

Other scholars such as Alston have preferred to stress the ties between soldiers and civilians.[80] His analysis drew on the papyrological evidence from Egypt, a body of data that has a distinct advantage over other archaeological evidence, because while artefacts and structures may demonstrate contact between the two groups, they tell us relatively little about how this operated on a day-to-day level. An object alone cannot tell us if it was exchanged in fear or friendship. Alston instead used documents to illuminate the extensive networks that linked soldiers to non-soldiers, and advocated a model which saw the army much more closely associated with civil society. In short, he stresses integration.[81] When discharged as veterans into wider society, Alston rightly observes, former soldiers often blended back into the wider population. This analysis contains much of value, but it should be remembered that it does not in fact rule out soldiers' capacity to terrorize civilians; rather, it stresses that soldiers are human too and that they will have relations with their families, those from whom they need supplies, and those civil administrators with whom they have to deal. It has been rightly noted that the tales that emerge from Alston's Egyptian papyri are notably different from those that come from Palestine, from the New Testament and the Mishnah.[82] The latter convey a sense of brooding menace exceptionally punctuated by humane exchanges between individual soldiers and civilians.

Overall, it is surely necessary to consider the relationship of military communities with wider society on a sliding scale. Our knowledge of the Empire shows that there were, overlying the pattern of casual violence that enforced the *pax Romana*, episodes of both blood-soaked conquest and times of extended peace. We should not envisage a single model for soldier/civilian relations across the diverse cultural landscape of the provinces. Rather, the evidence indicates that, as members of classic occupational communities, auxiliary soldiers, their families, and their slaves could live alongside other provincials yet confine their interaction with them to certain types of exchange. Much of the contact that occurred was in the procurement of essential supplies and the discharge of duties. A clear sense of insiders and outsiders was maintained, as the use in the Vindolanda tablets as such characterizations as *transmarinus* and *brittunculi* suggest.[83] In times of heightened tension the proclivity of these occupational communities to become

---

[79] Stoll (2001a: 16–19 and 45).   [80] Alston (1995; 1999).

[81] Alston (1995: 101) argues that 'the level of integration demonstrated by the soldiery demand an absence of real hostility' between soldiers and civilians.

[82] Bagnall (1997: 507).

[83] 'Overseas man': *Tab. Vindol.* II.344. 'Little Britons': *Tab. Vindol.* II.164. 5.

inward-looking grew, but other circumstances might ameliorate, even if they could never wholly eradicate, such divisions. Members of the military community might be seen as 'others' because of their association with imperial power, but the degree to which they might appear different, alien, and accordingly perhaps threatening could vary dramatically. Was it what they rode, what they ate, how they spoke? The conspicuous differences could owe as much to an individual's origins as to his association with the greatest army of the ancient world. Did those soldiers born and bred in one's own community somehow mitigate the sense of distance between soldiers and civilians? I suspect that it did.

A final point here is the need to unpack the term 'civilians'. The relationship between local officials and the army was probably quite different from that between soldiers, the urban poor, and peasant farming populations, but there was most likely widespread variation across groups too. Surveys of provincial landscapes, comparing the richly documented urban centres with the diverse settlements of their rural hinterlands, reveal considerable variation in the degree to which farmsteads, hamlets, and villages in the provincial countryside attest the reach of Rome. Such variations have inspired some leading thinkers to stress the diversity of experience within the Empire as an alternative approach to its study.[84] There are regions where neither architecture nor artefact reflects the Empire's reach, yet many such places probably provided recruits for the *auxilia* at some time or another. Others known to have been associated with the *auxilia* certainly did. Indeed, in the tribal lands of the Batavi, traces of military equipment have been widely identified even in humble farmsteads and rural temples.[85] Here, in an area where Roman urbanism never really took root, we see a very particular manifestation of the impact of Rome and her auxiliary soldiers. Clearly the making of the Empire involved very different transformations from place to place.

THE *AUXILIA* AND THE MAKING OF EMPIRE

While Tacitus' Civilis may have had the peoples of the Rhine firmly in mind when he argued that 'it is by the blood of the provinces that the provinces are won', this book proposes that this pithy phrase has a more general relevance. While few areas were so intensely exploited for auxiliary recruitment as Civilis' homelands, the ongoing enlistment of provincials across the Empire into the auxilia, their military service, and life on subsequent discharge played a significant role in the creation of provincial society. If we are to characterize this role accurately, however, it is necessary to appreciate both its extent and its limitations.

The contributions of auxiliary soldiers to the republican conquests that won so much of the Empire are ill-documented, but their contribution under the Principate has seemed assured. In many thematic studies and provincial surveys, the auxiliary soldier appears in discussions of the cultural changes that made the Empire. Various academic studies have attributed demographic changes to his recruitment, the introduction of new fashions to his travels, and the bolstering of

---

[84] Mattingly (1997; 2002; 2004; 2006; 2011).   [85] Nicolay (2002; 2008).

local civil society to his engagement when at last he takes his well-earned retirement. To these services, we may add the attention paid to his role as an imperial enforcer and, from time to time, his active contribution to building projects in the civil sphere. There is an element of truth in all these notions, but the degree to which we choose to emphasize them and others depends to a large extent on how we understand the processes which formed both the *auxilia* and the Empire. In doing so, we must remember that the regiments of auxiliaries stationed across the provinces were themselves 'contact cultures', not mini-models of metropolitan Rome.[86]

No term has been more widely used to explain the evolution of provincial society and the cultural impact of service in the *auxilia* than 'Romanization'. It is now generally appreciated, however, that there are crippling limitations to the use of the term when discussing changes in material culture.[87] While it is wholly reasonable to acknowledge that societies and individuals adjusted their way of doing things when they encountered the Roman state, and that profoundly significant similarities occured, describing this as 'Romanization' is problematic. The term has been taken to cover too many widely differing and sometimes conflicting phenomena to advance detailed analysis. This point is most elegantly made by Woolf: 'Romanization has no explanatory potential, because it was not an active force, the course of which can be traced through a variety of indices, and the level of which can be measured.'[88] The term also carries with it intellectual baggage that debilitates debate. There was no one Rome provincials sought to emulate, and there was no agenda to make them do so. Rome was constantly changing. It represented widely different things to different people. For some it was a living, breathing city, to others an imperial abstraction, but it was never a static blueprint for life. The artefacts associated with imperial hegemony over the provinces often differed from place to place, and in many cases even from those to be found in Rome itself. The uses to which they were put must be assessed with reference to local context at least as much as by what we can surmise of the manufacturers' intentions.[89]

Some studies of the *auxilia* have nonetheless fought a rearguard action in the Romanization debate. Auxiliaries have been depicted as ideally placed to drive cultural transformation, as the perfect intermediaries between the core and the periphery of empire.[90] It is easy to see the attractions of this view, for not only did many auxiliary soldiers become Roman in the legal sense of receiving Roman citizenship on discharge, but the actual nature of military service brought auxiliaries into concentrated contact with many vital elements of imperial cultural

[86] Foster (1960) coined the term. Woolf (1998: 15) advances it in a Roman provincial context.
[87] For particularly thoughtful criticisms see Woolf (1998), Mattingly (2002; 2011), Hingley (2005). A fine response to this trend in Anglophone scholarship can be found in Alföldy (2005), and it is to be regretted that many critics of the term 'Romanization' have not engaged with his arguments. Overall, however, the term remains problematic.
[88] Woolf (1998: 7).
[89] Freeman (1993) offers the single best summary of the problems inherent in conflating the presence/absence of artefact types with assumptions about the ways in which they were used.
[90] R. W. Davies (1974: 338) claims that the ordinary soldier was 'more than anyone else' responsible for the development of Romanization. For an assessment of the claim that the army played a role in the 'Romanization' of the eastern provinces, see Gilliam (1965b).

style. In my early work I also framed my discussion of cult practice, the use of Latin, and written communication within the *auxilia* in terms of 'Romanization', though I have always resisted seeing this as part of a deliberate ancient strategy to turn the *alae* and *cohortes* into enclaves of Roman culture.[91] Other scholars disagree. As has already been observed, the loyalty of auxiliary soldiers had fundamental implications for the security of the emperor's interests; auxiliaries were no ordinary provincial subjects. Accordingly, it has been argued that there was an added pressure to ensure that auxiliaries 'bought into' Roman civilization; Rome's attitude elsewhere might be laissez-faire, but amongst the auxiliaries it has sometimes been argued that the circumstances of military life meshed with a more programmatic approach to win men's allegiance not just to an emperor but to a way of life.[92]

Yet there was always a strong body of opinion that was prepared to contest this perspective, and indeed which challenged its applicability to the army even before the concept of Romanization fell from favour in Anglophone studies of provincial archaeology. As far back as 1954 Mann argued: 'Twenty-five years in the army did not necessarily produce a civilized person fitted for the fostering of the urban civilization of the Empire.'[93] Certainly, the more comprehensively we examine Roman military communities in the archaeological record, the more inadequate the concept appears.[94] Though the image of the provincial enlisted into military service and intensely exposed to the language, concepts, and artefacts of empire would appear to represent an ideal example of the imagined process in action, the reality was more complex. In the service of the emperor the soldier was indeed exposed to a spectrum of practice found across large parts of the Empire, but often this was manifested in regional or provincial styles quite alien to those of contemporary Rome. And, as has been reiterated above, his role as a servant of Rome was not the auxiliary's only identity. In his relations with others, local customs or those of the lands of his birth may have proved of greater significance. These must also be considered in our analysis. Rather than offering a simple view of military service as an instrument of Romanization, therefore, this volume examines individually the diverse elements that characterized the lives of soldiers and their families within the looser conceptual notion of incorporation.

---

[91] Haynes (1993; 1999b: 173).

[92] e.g. Richmond (1962a: 197) argues: 'But much more was it evidently a matter not of pride but of specific imperial policy—one of the "arcana imperii", if we will see it so—to imbue the auxiliary regiments, Gauls, Spaniards, Dacians, Britons or Germans, with the traditions of the Roman world.' Hoey held a similar view of the role of the *feriale Duranum*, a religious calendar associated with auxiliary soldiers (Fink, Hoey, and Snyder 1940: 206–10 especially 209). See p. 202.

[93] Mann (1954: 506), referring here specifically to Egyptian legionaries; nevertheless the logic applies with equal force to the impact of military service on auxiliaries. Garnsey and Whittaker (1978: 242) offer similar reservations. Challenges to the Romanizing capacity of military service have been expressed with greater frequency in more recent years; thus 'It might be questioned whether military service really made natives into Romans' (Cherry 1998: 93).

[94] Saddington (1982: 187–92; 1991; 2009a). He poses the question 'How Roman did auxiliaries become?' and concludes 'Essentially the message remains mixed. . . . Thus in terms of legal status the imperial auxiliary became a full Roman. But as far as his life-style and cultural milieu are concerned the choice remained his as to how much, if anything at all, he might adopt from the civilization of Rome' (2009a: 1023). The distinction between legal identity and lifestyle is crucial, but I would qualify this conclusion slightly: the auxiliary was not a wholly free agent in what he selected to adopt—the full range of 'Roman civilization' was not open to him.

The advantage of the term 'incorporation' over other explanatory models is that it conveys the force with which Roman systems of classification ordered and integrated individuals into provincial society, but does not conflate this pull with debates about the notional 'Romanity' of different patterns of material culture.[95] A further advantage of the notion of incorporation is that it evokes the image of forming/joining a body. And indeed, the Empire is better understood as a body in which different parts served different functions and in which each element contributed to the particular shape of the whole. The multiple Latin senses of the etymological root of 'incorporation', the word *corpus*, are helpful here. To Roman writers this term did not just refer to a body, living or dead; it was also used to indicate the body politic, a corporate body, or a community. Rome's definition of distinct communities, such as *civitates*, or status groups, such as citizens, had profound significance for the rights and obligations contained within them.[96] Their relevance reached across imperial society and had a powerful resonance not only for civilians but also for soldiers, whose career opportunities were determined by them, and whose membership of them is frequently recorded on their funerary monuments.

Important as many of these classifications were in law, it is abundantly clear that their meaning and significance changed over time. The value and nature of Roman citizenship during this period is a fine example of this. And, as with Roman citizenship as other legal and communal identities, there were few neat correlates between the way these were lived and their legal force. The soldiers of the *alae* and *cohortes*, and to a degree their families and dependants, would have embodied the authority of Rome to many of the provincials they encountered. But in a still more subtle, anthropological, sense, their patterns of consumption, of dress, of routine could embody many different faces of the Empire over time and space.[97] What may appear to one viewer to be a Roman soldier might be someone whose behaviour at home, off duty, or even on patrol bore more relation to practices from far-flung imperial territories than to anything seen on the streets of Rome. In this sense, then, there is an important parallelism between the processes by which communities were incorporated into provincial society and the manner in which individuals embodied facets of that society.[98] For this reason, it is vital for any study of life in the *auxilia* to consider it alongside the broader trends that made provincial society.

[95] Important alternative models include those based on postcolonial studies of discrepant experience (Mattingly 1997, developed to the fullest extent in Mattingly 2006), creolization (Webster 2001), globalization (Hingley 2005), and crystallization (Greene 2008). James (2001b) explores the role of 'incorporation events' in transforming Roman Britain.

[96] For the extension of rights to communities according to their merits in Roman eyes, see Siculus Flaccus, *De condicionibus agrorum* 7–8, Th. 98–9. For Roman citizenship, see Gardner (1993).

[97] For the role of daily routine in replicating social structures see Giddens (1984: 60–64). Much important progress has been made in the study of 'embodiment' within archaeology in recent years, and I acknowledge particularly my debt to Meskell and Joyce (2003). I thank Ollie Harris for discussing embodiment theory with me.

[98] I adopt a structurationist approach to the *auxilia*; both the social system and the individual can be examined within a broad unified framework. For the writings at the heart of the structurationist project see Bourdieu (1977; 1990) and Giddens (1979; 1984). Structuration theory has been notably applied by Andrew Gardner in a series of works on the later Roman period (2004b; 2007).

At first glance such an explanation may seem no less susceptible to modernizing assumptions than Cheesman's concern with the martial relations of 'races' did 100 years ago. Certainly it echoes contemporary discussion of 21st-century globalization, but the structured differences that lay at the heart of Roman imperial incorporation were fundamentally different from those of our own era.[99]

With regards to law, three key distinctions had a particular relevance to everyone living in the Roman Empire during the first two centuries AD. These were whether an individual was a citizen or a non-citizen, whether free- or slave-born, and whether a civilian or a soldier. Crucially, these are culturally specific; Rome's particular understanding of citizenship is widely recognized as of profound importance to the development of empire. No less important is her creation of professional armies, which creates, as Carrié has observed, not only new military identities but the very notion of 'civilian'.[100] Furthermore, reinforcing the parallelism observed above between the communal and the individual is the way in which social mobility operated. Not only did individuals receive status from the communities of which they were a part, but communities as well as individuals could be promoted and demoted within imperial systems of classification. Thus a city may be promoted to the status of a *colonia*; an individual may be granted citizenship. As noted, this system served incorporation by placing every community and individual within an imperial scheme of rights and obligations.

Part of what makes the *auxilia*, itself conceived of as a non-citizen force, so interesting is that its very existence testifies to the enduring importance of these powerful categorizations. For much of this period the auxiliary soldier was more likely to be a non-citizen, yet his service was often a vehicle to citizenship. Though there were exceptions in practice, the auxiliary was supposed to be free-born, yet his life in the service of the state could be likened to servitude. Finally, he was a soldier, in a society where the distinction between civilian and soldier was being codified for the first time. The impact of this distinction on societies where men had once moved regularly between the roles of fighter and farmer was of profound significance. Though I will argue that each of these attributes is important to our understanding of the process of incorporation, it is vital to remember that what they meant in practice varied over time and place. Material possessions facilitated incorporation in a different way. The networks of communication that bound together the Empire enabled not only the efficient replication of elaborate structures and expensive goods but also mass production of a plethora of more mundane items. These are found in widely varying quantities in settlement archaeology, reminding us that some communities were much less affected than others. Nevertheless, in many areas the increasing number of goods in production and circulation transformed the lived environment, and these places lay overwhelmingly within the Empire. In such places the contrast between the sheer quantities of artefacts found in the Roman period as opposed to late Iron Age contexts is startling. Many people were now living in a material world of a wholly

---

[99] This echoes recent work on globalization; see Wilk (1995) and more particularly Hingley (2003: 118; 2005). Yet globalization is not a wholly satisfactory model for the wider dynamics involved, for there is a clear sense from both documentary and archaeological sources that these tools lose their potency at the edges of imperial territory.

[100] Carrié (1993).

different order to their forebears. As such goods permeated communities they created dependencies, tying the communities into a wider network of exchange and communication. Whether in a town's construction of a new theatre or a woman's purchase of a new brooch, newly disseminated styles became the currency of much social differentiation. The results of these patterns of negotiation have been likened to 'bricolage' where, especially at elite levels, individuals and groups picked and mixed diverse elements from a range of choices.[101] Extensive though this choice could be, it was not wholly liberating, for as some goods emerged, so too others fell out of circulation; as new crafts were developed, old ones died. Furthermore, the means of many were too limited to buy into new fashions and commodities. Only for some was the emulation of Rome an aspiration—for most, these objects were adopted because they were convenient—but consciously and subconsciously these artefacts helped define their owners' places in local society. Crucially, of course, most of these artefacts did not come from Rome or even emulate styles familiar in Rome. Many were still essentially local products, just produced in greater quantity and disseminated over larger areas. It was less their genesis that mattered than their ready availability. There was therefore no single imperial material culture, though crucially, several forms and types of artefact gained much greater currency. The evolving material landscapes of the Roman provinces attest to the degree to which such readily available artefacts tied people into regional and imperial networks, while also illuminating the remarkable rapidity with which fashions could change.

For change they certainly did; we are now aware of the far-reaching character of the 'cultural revolution' that transformed the Roman world under Augustus, the time that not coincidentally also sees the creation of permanent auxiliary forces in Roman service. Less extensively documented, however, are the other 'cultural pulses' which ran through the provinces in the decades the followed.[102] Again and again the networks of communication and exchange that tied the Empire together pumped new ideas across the provincial landscape, but not all came from the heart of the Empire and many manifested themselves very differently across it. The Danubian provinces are a case in point. Once on the margins of imperial culture and influence, they became a centre of military power. They produced their own emperor, sending their hero cults and soldier sons with their barbaric clothing and speech far across the provincial landscape and into the very heart of Italy itself. In this book, I have tried to show how these pulses operated, and how they demonstrate that the process of incorporation was very much ongoing and alive throughout the first two centuries AD.

---

[101] Terrenato (1998). Gosden's (2004: 110) observation that 'Roman expansion brought a new set of cultural resources to the natives' and that 'these resources could be used, refused or subverted depending on their resonance with local cultural ways' needs to be qualified by recognition that no single common set of resources was available, and that individuals did not have unlimited access to those that were, nor unfettered scope to apply them as they wished.

[102] Mattingly (2002: 539) acknowledges the importance of these 'pulses' while critiquing the Romanization paradigm: 'For a variety of reasons, there are phases in Roman history when profound redefinition of what it meant to be Roman (or what the empire was about) created cultural pulses that emanated from the capital.' Acknowledging the existence of these pulses is important but, as I seek to note here, they did not all emanate from Rome. Some began in the provinces.

This book begins by examining the *auxilia* as systems of structures, rights, and privileges within the wider network of imperial power (Part I), outlining the broad cultural trends linked to its evolution. The aim is not, therefore, to provide a history of the *alae* and *cohortes*, though those with limited knowledge of the *auxilia* will I hope find it also serves to provide a useful orientation. To facilitate this, Part I follows a traditional approach to the organization of the evidence, drawing extensively on written sources and ordering the analysis chronologically. Yet it also seeks to go beyond traditional narratives by outlining the ongoing impact of incorporation on provincial society, observing how different groups are brought into the imperial fold at different times, and noting how transformation in the *auxilia* is often linked to wider change, particularly the 'cultural pulses' noted above. The volume continues (Part II) by examining one of the most fundamental themes in the study of the *auxilia*, recruitment. Earlier studies have tended to focus on quantifying sources of recruits at different times and places, but this discussion seeks to do more. It lays a crucial foundation for the rest of the volume by scrutinizing recruitment not only in the imperial context of taxation, the levy, and the raising of new regiments but also in the context of notions of identity, provincial society, and the experience of individual recruits. This study of recruitment accordingly offers a vital insight into the incorporation of communities and individuals within provincial society. In the process it reveals how for almost 100 years scholars have misread several vital clues to its operation.

Once enrolled into the *auxilia*, the new recruit found himself living within a home from Rome, a place in the provincial landscape to which he was posted on the orders of Rome. Here he lived as part of a military community, a distinct population. Archaeological evidence lies at the heart of understanding life in this community. Rather than focus on fort buildings and camp layouts, this study (Part III) examines the minutiae of life within military outposts for soldiers and the civilians who lived alongside them. Here we see the material force of incorporation and the intersection between imperial, provincial, and local at the humblest of levels. From the use of razors to the regulation of life to the time of the regimental clock, the soldier's body was bound into wider imperial culture. Yet even in the military community there was real scope for variation. And so it is that in the evidence for such things as diet, preparation of food, and interaction with civilian followers, local variations are clearly discernible.

No less vital to our understanding of incorporation is cult practice (Part IV). The study of religion in the Roman army has a long pedigree; its power to bind military communities together has been much discussed since the discovery of the so-called *feriale Duranum*, a list of festivals celebrated at Dura-Europos in Syria. Yet new archaeological evidence demonstrates that the dynamics of cult in military communities were far more complex than these discussions suggest, and indicates that the process of incorporation worked at an altogether more subtle and potent level. This chapter goes beyond the papyrological and epigraphic evidence for cult and considers the direct residues of votive practice.

Equipment and tactics played crucial roles in defining auxiliary soldiers in provincial society and are discussed in Part V. Military dress defined men's status both within the emperor's armies and within wider society. How it developed is therefore of paramount interest. Archaeological evidence reveals how, in a classic example of incorporation at work, the process of absorbing communities into the

Empire actually led to the continual redefinition of soldierly appearance. This should be understood as an amalgam of provincial fashions. The same evidence also demonstrates the difficulty inherent in examining ethnicity archaeologically. 'Ethnic' identities were manipulated, created, promoted, and suppressed in the Empire. This becomes apparent through detailed discussion of the degree to which allegedly ethnic or tribal patterns of dress and practice actually survived within the *auxilia*.

Part VI examines the way in which one of the chief mechanisms of incorporation, language, operated amongst the *auxilia*. Evidence from military communities across the Empire illuminates not only the evolution of the spoken word in provincial society but also the degree to which ordinary lives came to depend on writing. Seen as part of Roman cultural style, the use of the written word is both of general interest and of particular military importance. Here indeed the pen proves as mighty as the sword.

For many scholars, the soldier's most important contribution to the making of empire comes at the end of his career when, having acquired skills and modest wealth, he was discharged back into provincial society. The veteran is frequently seen as an instrument of transformation in his own right. Yet when the diversity of veterans' experiences is considered (Part VII) it becomes clear that this was by no means always the case. As a relatively well-documented group within wider provincial society, however, these men still have much to tell us about how the Empire was made up.

The volume concludes with a discussion of the lives of four named auxiliaries, serving in separate parts of the Empire between the early 1st and mid-3rd centuries AD. Each of these men embodied distinct elements of what it meant to be a Roman soldier. Consideration of the similarities and differences in their lives underscores just how effective *auxiliary* units were as vehicles of incorporation. The discussion demonstrates how widely different individuals were drawn into it during its evolution over the centuries, contributing to its role in the making of empire.

Part I

The *Auxilia* and the Structures of Imperial Power

2

The Formative Years

From the Late Republic to the Death of Tiberius

The ideologies of Roman imperial power famously coopted a miscellany of origin myths. Collectively and individually these stressed the way in which diverse groups, be they the disparate band that first followed Romulus and Remus or the abducted Sabine women, became incorporated into the Roman people.[1] The crucial principle was that one could become a Roman—that it was not necessary to be born one. Were it not for her very particular notions of citizenship, community, and conflict, neither Rome's empire nor her *auxilia* could have evolved in the way they did. Yet despite their recurrent emphasis on cosmopolitan interaction and openness to foreign borrowings, ancient accounts of the Republic leave the auxiliaries and allies who helped Rome to power in the shadows. Incidental references to the granting of citizenship to exceptional individuals, to the employment of 'helping forces' under obligations of treaties, and to the absorption of defeated peoples in the aftermath of battle appear in Roman accounts from at least the 3rd century BC. Yet it is not really until the Social War (91–88 BC) that we see these converging in a manner that foreshadows the world the emperors knew.

It was in Ascoli Piceno (Asculum) in the Apennines that the Social War erupted, and it was here in 89 BC, after a year-long siege, that the Romans broke the back of the rebellion. In a practice familiar to soldiers through the ages, many of the missiles carried messages to their intended victims, so it is possible to see that some were directed at the besiegers, others against the defenders. All use the same language, Latin, a medium that underpinned the cultural ties between the opposing sides; indeed, the war ultimately strengthened those links. The very name of the war commemorated the bitter truth that it was a conflict between the Romans and their *socii* (allies). While the Senate had extended the rights of citizenship by stages to the people of Italy, there remained many communities within the Peninsula which endured the obligations of citizens but enjoyed few of the privileges. These were the people who provided the *alae*, a term not yet synonymous with cavalry, the wings of troops that fought alongside the legions of Rome's citizen forces. These were sizeable contributions; each *ala sociorum* had the same strength as a legion. Yet despite these commitments, Roman

---

[1] Livy 1.4–13; Ovid *Fasti* 2.381–422; Plutarch *Life of Romulus*.

entitlements were granted sparingly. Rome had no absolute objection to the idea of people becoming Roman citizens; it just was not quite ready for them yet.[2]

Velleius Paterculus, writing his history under Augustus, recalled this as a time when the 'whole of Italy' rose against Rome.[3] In 90 BC pragmatism led the Senate to extend citizenship first to those communities which had remained loyal and then to all but those deemed the most savage and implacable rebels. Thereafter it was only a matter of time until military force settled the remainder. Rome saw once again the value of shrewd diplomacy and the capital of citizenship, but it was haunted long after by the disaster. The dependency of Rome on allied manpower was rendered painfully obvious by the conflict. Even the reduction of Asculum required the efforts not just of her citizen forces and remaining Italian allies but also of auxiliaries from distant lands, men whose story must also be told.

In the end, however, the Roman settlement followed a significant course. The citizenship for which so many had died was extended even to the defeated, and as the pool of citizens changed, so Rome's armies had to change too. The number of legionaries grew dramatically; the ranks of the old *alae* could now join the *legio*, the force derived from the citizen levy. As the allies had hitherto provided light troops and cavalry in higher numbers,[4] Rome needed to seek new sources of such men. It already knew where to look. Spain was already a significant source of manpower; in the decades to follow it would become essential.

Significantly, the most famous archaeological relic of the Social War was not a sling shot—though quite a number from this period have been found around Ascoli Piceno—but a bronze plaque (see Fig. 2.1), not an artefact of war but a symbol of integration. The plaque commemorates the rewards granted by Pompeius Strabo, the Roman commander, to a troop of Spanish horsemen, the *turma Salluitana*.[5] The plaque records that in 89 BC, these men received citizenship and *torques*, *armilla*, and *phalerae*, military decorations, for their services at Asculum. So lavish were the awards, one commentator has argued, that it is quite possible it was the Spaniards who broke the deadlock of this terrible Italian siege.[6] Whether or not this was the case, the importance of their service to Rome was clearly recognized without embarrassment by the authorities. There was already a long tradition of honouring exceptional individuals with citizenship, but this particular award offers a portent of things to come. By the mid-2nd century AD almost a sixth of all auxiliary units had received a block grant of citizenship at some stage in their history.[7]

The relevance of all these events unfolding at the heart of the Republican Empire is clear enough. Rome's relationships with subject communities did not stop at assigning rights and obligations; they also opened the prospect of further promotion. In the Roman world both communities and individuals could be promoted to higher legal status. Rome was not wholly a free agent in this regard:

---

[2] Gaius Gracchus advanced the idea of awarding Roman citizenship to all Latins, and Latin rights to all *socii* as far back as 123 BC. Latins living in Rome received the citizenship in 94 BC.

[3] Velleius Paterculus 2.15.

[4] I follow the insightful analysis of Keppie (1984: 79) here.

[5] *CIL* 1 709 = *ILS* 8888.

[6] M. P. Speidel (1994b: 123) argues that they must have been amongst the first to cut their way into the town.

[7] Maxfield (1986b: 37).

Fig. 2.1. The famous 'Bronze of Ascoli' (*CIL* 1. 709) records the granting of citizenship to members of a *turma Salluitana* in recognition of their contribution to the Roman victory at the battle of Asculum. Musei Capitolini, Rome.

pragmatism sometimes forced her to extend rights, and it was also necessary to respond to local situations. Communities could become Roman, and their free-born members could benefit accordingly. It appears that this was the experience of the *turma Salluitana*. Notably, the contingent's title includes the term used for a cavalry troop under the empire, *turma*. Furthermore, thirty men, the number frequently assigned to such formations under the Empire, are listed on the plaque. Yet it also evident that the structure of auxiliary cavalry contingents had yet to take the form known under the Principate. Whatever their structure, however, it is interesting to see, through the case of this *turma*, the recognition of such contingents as entities through which soldiers could receive citizenship for service to Rome. Here, the unit is the vehicle through which they are rewarded *en masse*, for it is what originally brought them into wider participation in Roman affairs and what now sees them joining the ranks of the citizens. The development of block grants under the Empire will be examined below. At this time, however, the Roman grant comes through the agency and patronage of a powerful citizen, the commander Pompeius Strabo. It will be several decades before one man, the emperor, becomes the ultimate source of all such grants. It will take still longer for the grant of citizenship for long, but often less conspicuously heroic, service to become established. By the end of the emperor Claudius' reign, however, bronze plaques commemorating such awards would adorn Rome in their hundreds.

There is one further, profoundly important point to consider. As the story of the horsemen of the Bronze of Ascoli demonstrates, this is not just an Italian tale. Looking down the list of the troopers' names. it is possible to see how the events that unfolded in this Apennine town play into the wider history of provincial incorporation.[8] Twenty-seven of the thirty men who were to become Roman citizens had Iberian names, but some of these had already acquired Latinate endings. Three had adopted Latin *praenomina* and *gentilicia*,[9] but dutifully recorded themselves as sons of Iberian fathers. This may reflect shifts in linguistic identity, at a time when other parts of the Iberian peninsula are still generations away from Roman hegemony and there was hardly a native settlement to be seen that Rome would recognize as a city. The archaeological evidence from this time reveals few traces of material culture from Italy, and even in contemporary Roman camps in Spain, traditional Iberian weapons—instruments that were assuredly not simply trophies but rather models which inspired emulation amongst the legions themselves—have been recovered.[10] While the evidence shows individuals being brought into networks of Roman power, it is clear that there is no simple material counterpart to this process. In terms of the artefacts of war at least, Rome's armies were adopting and absorbing Spanish attributes at least as much as their Spanish allies and enemies were the intrusive ideas of Rome. This evolving amalgam, which changes the face of Rome in her territories, is a fine example of early incorporation.

FORGING PROFESSIONAL ARMIES: THE CIVIL WARS OF THE LATE REPUBLIC

The suffering of the Roman world did not, of course, end with the resolution of the Social War. In addition to confronting external threats, such as the expansion of Mithridates in Asia Minor, Roman armies were to confront one another repeatedly before Octavian's victory of 31 BC brought an end to civil war under the Republic.

Shortly after the Social Wars came to a close, a dispute over the command of Rome's force against Mithridates marked a return to chaos. On one side was the famous Marius, a man frequently credited with opening up military service to the less prosperous classes. On the other was Sulla, who marched on Rome to win back control of the command he had been pledged. Sulla's entry to Rome at the head of an army set a terrifying precedent: Roman armies were to return to terrorize the city on many later occasions. The clash between Sulla's men and those whose sympathies had lain with Marius had major repercussions, both for Rome's handling of Mithridates and for its Spanish territories. Networks of power, patronage, and influence were not confined to Rome after all, but extended far beyond Italy.

In Spain the conflict sparked the Sertorian War, a savage conflict that drew the son of Pompeius Strabo, the young Pompey, into its orbit. Here archaeology is beginning to shed light on the brutal nature of the contest and the Republican army in action. Excavations at Valentia have exposed the obscene cost of failure.

---

[8] For analysis of these soldiers' names see Untermann (1990: 195–7) and Adams (2003: 281).

[9] Forename and clan name respectively.

[10] For settlement patterns see Keay (1988: 52). For military equipment from Cáceres el Viejo, a near-contemporary Roman base in Spain, see Ulbert (1985, pls 25.195–9, 201) and the valuable observations of Bishop and Coulston (2006: 56).

The city had backed Marius and was stormed by Pompey. In the vestiges of the sacked town, archaeologists recovered the remains of several victims.[11] The partial skeleton recovered from one of them reveals that he had been manacled and a stake forced lengthwise through his body, before his legs were hacked off. It is a rare glimpse through the archaeological prism of intimacy, mitigated by distance in time, at what was at stake for commanders, communities, and soldiers at war.

At this time, when the old institutions buckled under the pressure of a growing Empire, society endured the curse of great men, private individuals, leading great armies. Pompey was undoubtedly one of these, but for the study of the *auxilia* the most important was certainly Julius Caesar. That this is the case is partially, it must be acknowledged, a reflection of our sources; Caesar wrote prolifically and highly favourably of his own achievements on and off the battle field. Yet with the benefit of hindsight it is possible to see that the military operations he conducted in Gaul had lasting consequences for the future of the *auxilia*, especially when they were succeeded by victories in the Civil Wars that followed. Nor is it hard to see why one of the premier studies of the *auxilia* takes the later years of Caesar as its starting point.[12]

The key to victory in the Civil Wars lay in the ability to raise manpower. In the build-up to open conflict, and throughout the battles that followed, ancient observers repeatedly stressed the strategic significance of recruiting grounds. The orator Cicero, for example, reacted with alarm to the news that Antony would control the fertile recruiting grounds of Gallia Comata, precisely because it was such an important source of auxiliary recruits.[13]

All informed observers clearly recognized the importance of Gallic auxiliary cavalry, but it is clear that it was not just Gauls who provided Rome's armies with trusted horsemen. The Civil Wars found Spanish cavalry once more on campaign in Italy. Speidel has astutely observed that the tombstone of one Marcus Valerius of the *ala Patrui*, found at Larinum in Apulia, could date only from between 44 and 31 BC.[14] Valerius' epitaph records that he came from Leonica, not far, therefore, from Valentia. His memorial is vitally important, not only because it gives us an early date for the formation of an *ala*, but also because it hints at a style of organization well established under the Principate, for Marcus Valerius was a decurion, a troop commander.

The men of the *ala Patrui* were not the only auxiliary horsemen to enter the fray. Another Italian memorial, this one recovered at Minturnae (Traetii), records an *ala Scaevae*.[15] As with the *ala Patrui*, the title seems somewhat informal compared to the great names of most regiments under the Principate; it simply states the name of the current commander, but this is in itself very telling. By far the most likely candidate for the commander is the war hero Caesius Scaeva, one of Caesar's centurions. In fighting against the forces of Pompey in Albania in 48 BC he managed to acquire 120 holes in his shield in a single day.[16] Other accounts recall his wounds and the loss of an eye.[17] Whether or not that warranted his promotion to *praefectus equitum*, or whether he simply commanded the *ala*

---

[11] Ribera i Lacomba with Calvo Galvez (1995: 28–9 and fig. 9).

[12] Saddington (1982). For the *auxilia* at this time see also Yoshimura (1961: 476).

[13] Cicero *Phil.* 5.2, 5–6.   [14] Speidel (1980). *CIL* 9.733 = *ILS* 2499.

[15] *CIL* 10.6011 = *ILS* 2490.   [16] Caesar *BC* 3.59.   [17] Valerius Maximus 3.2.23.

without any such formal title, is open to question. What is clear is that in Caesar's forces in particular, men could be on active service for decades, and there was ample scope for rapid career advancement. Furthermore, there is the clear sense of patronage at work. Scaeva is a protégé of Caesar; Scaeva is the man who leads the *ala* into battle. The troopers under his command are led into Roman service through a series of personal relationships that lead to the highest powers in the Republic.

The same essential role of patronage may be seen in the case of other forces under Caesar's command, though their structure probably varied considerably. Some of the Gallic units, for example, appear to have been little more than the *ritterliche Gefolgschaft*, the mounted followers of individual nobles.[18] The men who raised and commanded them were able to gain, maintain, and sometimes extend their influence through participation in the new order. Successful commanders enjoyed the patronage of important Romans, but they also achieved and/or retained the martial status that was clearly important within the social structures of many western European societies at this turbulent time.[19] This is most apparent in the story of a cavalry unit which was commanded by two Allobrogan brothers, Raucillus and Egus.[20] They were the second generation of their family to benefit from Caesar's patronage: their father had fought alongside him in Gaul. Their rise to greater power and influence was, however, interrupted when their own men reported them to Caesar for submitting fraudulent pay returns to their Roman paymaster. The two men subsequently switched allegiance to Pompey, searching, it would seem, for a way both to avoid punishment and to acquire a new patron. By offering pay and booty, through extending patronage, Roman commanders were able to bring these irregular formations into the body of their forces. Notably, in this case, the relationship is not simply between the Roman commander and the tribal elite; rather, members of the unit are depicted appealing to Caesar's authority, a fact that suggests a certain level of integration was already achieved.

Snapshots of the cavalry of the Civil Wars underscore two key points. First, though essentially non-citizen forces (for the legions had very few cavalry at this time), they are actually considered worth mentioning by ancient writers. Such units have identities and histories in Roman eyes. They are tacitly understood to enjoy a certain status. That they did so should not surprise us. A man had to have a significant income to learn to ride into battle and to maintain a horse; this much was as clear from Roman tradition as it was from contemporary native practice. Second, while mounted contingents take diverse forms, there are clear hints of the developments of later years. It is true that when we are told the size of cavalry forces, they are often somewhat irregular in size, but accounts use elements of technical vocabulary which become widely used in the *alae* and *cohortes* of later periods. Despite this, in sharp contrast to the legions, we must remember that there is no absolute proof that any auxiliary unit survived the Civil Wars to become part of the new armies of the Empire. Some units may have endured, renaming over time concealing their origins, and question marks hang over the

[18] Dobesch (1980: 419) and Roymans (1990: 40) discuss the importance of the *ritterliche Ger-folgschaft* in Celto-Germanic society.
[19] Cunliffe (1988: 127).   [20] Caesar *BC* 3.59–61.

antiquity of some of the *alae* named after their commanders, but the end of the conflict would have marked the end of many contingents.

Significantly, other units of non-citizens receive less attention both in Caesar's commentaries and in other contemporary accounts. Allied contingents such as those provided by the Numidians appear from time to time, as they will through-out Roman history, but less is said about those who accompanied Caesar through-out his campaigning career. War bands in which infantry ran alongside cavalry into battle receive a mention, but the suggestion that these are the ancestor formations of later part-mounted cohorts is surely wrong.[21] The Augustan part-mounted cohorts had the wrong proportion of infantry to cavalry to be used in this way. Rather, these curious contingents are included in the narrative more as a curiosity which illustrates Caesar's capacity to innovate and galvanize the exotic in order to achieve victory. Relationships with other auxiliary formations seem short-lived. Balearic slingers and Cretan archers served Caesar in Gaul, but do not appear in his commentaries after 57 BC, implying that they were sent home once they had completed what was required of them.[22] While they are often cited as examples of early auxiliaries, there are no examples of troops from these regions serving within specialized formations in the *auxilia* after this time.

Non-citizen infantry units are seldom acknowledged in the Civil War narra-tives, and even though there are earlier references for the grouping of such men into *cohortes*, the term is relatively seldom used for them. Caesar's contemporary Sallust, for example, wrote of *cohortes Ligurum* in his account of the Jugurthine War (112–105 BC).[23] The paucity of examples might be considered curious, for, despite its somewhat confusing etymology, the technical meaning of the term was much better established than that of *ala*. Legions had been divided into cohorts from at least the late 3rd century BC, albeit on an ad hoc basis, and the term was subsequently extended to infantry units in the auxiliary forces.[24] How far the internal organization of such contingents was arranged remains unclear, but it is by no means impossible that it was broadly similar to that found under the Principate. Our lack of information reflects limited interest amongst writers in the identities of these smaller, low-status units.

More is known of the legionary formations that accompanied the great com-manders. Here we see a range of practice that has significant implications for later military organization. Prior to his battles with Pompey, Caesar had responded to concern in Rome about his military conduct by getting his governorship in Gaul extended and enlarging his army at his own expense. The most striking addition to his force was a legion raised in Transalpine Gaul, which was to become in time a permanent part of the Empire's legionary force, *Legio V Alaudae*.[25] Significantly, this force was raised from non-citizens. Keppie has suggested that the fact that Caesar never referred to this legion by name in his commentaries, but refers to them rather as 'cohorts', indicates an unease with news of the device reaching his reading public.[26] Expediency was one thing, acceptable form another. Yet in fact 'legions' were to take far more irregular form than the Alaudae, 'the Larks', did in

[21] Keppie (1984: 100, 182–3) considers but rightly discards this possibility.
[22] Keppie (1984: 100).   [23] Sallust *Bellum Iugurthinum* 38; 77.
[24] Polybius *Hist.* 11.20 for legionary cohorts at Illipa in 206 BC.
[25] Suetonius *Caesar* 24.2.   [26] Keppie (1984: 140–41).

the years to come. Caesar often stresses this when he talks of his enemies' forces. Thus we learn from him that Pompey enrolled a *legio vernacula* from the native population of Spain.[27] The militia of the kingdom of Pontus became an impromptu *legio* in 47 BC.[28] A range of local rulers and allies from Asia Minor to Africa organized their forces on Roman lines to contribute 'legions' to the carnage of the Civil Wars. *Legio XXII Deiotariana*, for example, was raised from the forces of King Deiotarus of Galatia.[29]

What is one to make of this diversity? First of all, of course, it speaks of crisis, but second, it attests to Roman pragmatism. Ultimately, Roman dominion over both fellow Roman and barbarian depended on the capacity to mobilize and motivate bigger armies. Again, citizenship served as capital. The idea of using and employing non-Romans for sustained periods was regarded as natural. But only one thing really appears to have been regarded as wholly unacceptable: for slaves to fight as gladiators was unremarkable, but there was still a notion of honour that debarred soldier slaves from the ranks of Roman armies. All these principles and taboos were reinforced, rather than ripped apart, in the carnage of the Civil Wars.

TRANSFORMING A LEGACY: AUGUSTUS AND HIS SUCCESSORS

With his victory at Actium in 31 BC, Octavian inherited the moral legacy of Caesar, the armies of his enemies, and hegemony of the Roman world. Determining the fate of the professionals in the sixty legions now under his command was of paramount importance.[30] Part of his response was to settle older veterans in newly founded colonies. The other was to retain battle-hardened soldiers and units as part of a standing army. Many of Rome's legions, including those with unorthodox origins discussed above, made the transformation from Civil War armies to servants of the emperor. Much less is known of the fate of the *auxilia*; the *ala Atectorigiana*, which received its name from a Gallic leader, may have had its origins in Caesar's time, but it is first recorded under Augustus.[31] Amongst the infantry units, it has been argued that some of the earliest *cohortes Ituraeorum* could have originated from the Civil War levies of Caesar,[32] and the discovery of an early inscription referring to a Ituraean cohort at Philae (Assuan) suggests that these units had long histories.[33] Here again, though, it is impossible to prove a Civil War origin. Complicating matters is the fact that many very early infantry units, including perhaps the first Ituraean formations, were also named after their commanders. Indeed, the practice of referring to some cohorts by their current

---

[27] Caesar *BC* 2.20; *B. Hisp.* 7.4; 10. 3.   [28] Caesar *B. Alex.* 34.40.

[29] Here we might note the formations of the kings of Mauretania and Numidia (Caesar *B. Alex.* 62; *B. Afr.* 48). For the origins of *Legio XXII Deiotariana* see Caesar (*B. Alex.* 34. 39–40). See Keppie (1984: 141) on the creation of new legions.

[30] Keppie (1984: 132–44).   [31] p. 42.   [32] Kennedy (1989: 238).

[33] *REG* 89 (1976), n. 772. This inscription from the temple of Isis at Philae has been convincingly dated to 24–22 BC: Speidel (1988: 780).

commanders' names in the genitive survived until at least AD 27.[34] Sometime thereafter, a regularization of nomenclature ensured that this practice was abandoned in formal documentation, confounding modern scholars attempting to trace the earliest records of formations only known in later sources by the names of the communities from which they were raised. The implications of these changes for the study of recruitment will be discussed later in this volume, but for now it is worth noting how the new order celebrated the contribution of subject peoples to the Empire.

Much has rightly been made of the power of images in the age of Augustus.[35] For it is in the projection of images that we see how the new emperor transformed his legacy into a potent cultural revolution. The reach of this transformation is perhaps best seen in the Forum of Augustus, itself funded *ex manubiis* (from war booty),[36] which was a structure that inspired multiple Roman fora across the provinces. For the visitor to the forum, and most especially to the foreign dignitaries brought here to swear allegiance, the messages it communicated were explicit and imposing. As Ovid's vivid account stresses, the complex commemorates the military triumphs of Rome and Augustus, a sight fit to make Mars himself rejoice.[37] Its message was underscored by the way in which personifications of the peoples conquered by Augustus were complemented by later dedications of provincial communities. Spain, finally conquered under Augustus, sent 100 pounds of gold to decorate its own part of the panoply.[38]

The temple to Mars Ultor stood at the heart of the new forum. It was a dedication that was, as we saw at Adamklissi, to find echoes in later generations even in remote reaches of imperial territory. In the Augustan period, however, there is little in any of this monumentality to stress the dependence of the emperor on other peoples for his victory. That remarkable document, the *Res Gestae*, which can still be seen today carved into the temple of Augustus at Ankara, Turkey—a document that summed up for Augustus the scale of his achievement—makes no reference to the auxiliaries on whom so much had depended.

In Rome itself, the contingent closest to the *auxilia*, the paramilitary *corporis custodes*, a bodyguard of Germanic warriors, was discreetly housed across the Tiber to make it less conspicuous to the local population. Following the Varus disaster of AD 9 even this was disbanded briefly, probably to reassure those Romans terrified by the implications of the catastrophe.[39] Archaeological evidence, in the form of the Germans' funerary monuments, may suggest that even when they were present these soldiers mitigated their alien appearance. Coming from a tradition to which such monuments were alien, they adopted stelae virtually indistinguishable from those of the citizen soldiers of Rome, the Praetorian guardsmen, alongside whom they served. The sensitivity to public opinion suggested by the billeting of the *corporis custodes* across the Tiber should not be seen as primarily about fear of armed non-citizens. Augustus had good reasons to play down his dependency on military force more generally. He conspicuously refused to address the men who brought him to power as *commilitones*, or fellow

---

[34] Latest use of this formula: P. Vindob. L 135. 2–3 *cohors A* [. . .] *Habeti*. For the implications for this practice and a possible example of it in the case of the *cohortes Ituraeorum*, see Speidel (1982).
[35] Zanker (1988).   [36] *Res Gestae* 21.   [37] Ovid *Fasti* 5.533.
[38] Claridge (2010: 178).   [39] Suetonius *Aug.* 49.

soldiers, in the aftermath of the Civil Wars, believing such intimacy poor for discipline, unsuited to peace, and insufficiently respectful of the new imperial family.[40] Later emperors were as keen to embrace this term as Augustus was to avoid it, for it stressed the special relationship between emperor and soldiers upon which imperial power depended. Even the Praetorians, who as Roman troops might appear more acceptable to citizens than the members of the *corporis custodes*, were carefully dispersed within the city. It was not until the reign of Tiberius that the vast and conspicuous *Castra Praetoria* was built at Rome, and even then it was built outside the city limits.

In addition to the *Res Gestae*, three key memoranda known to have been written in his own hand survived his death: his will, his instructions for his funeral, and his record of the Empire's resources.[41] His will notably did not include gifts for non-citizen soldiers, though it included household troops, legionaries, and men serving in the citizen cohorts.[42] But ultimately there was no denying the importance of the non-citizens to the Empire's might, and at the head of the list of imperial resources he had meticulously documented the numbers of both citizens and non-citizens in arms.[43] The items that followed listed taxation liabilities, territories, and the holdings of empire.

In many ways the list of the Empire's resources was the most extraordinary document of the three, for it did not just detail the dramatic expansion of imperial territories, it quantified their contribution to the treasury. Those implications were enormous. From the parts of northwest Spain that now released vast quantities of precious metals for the imperial coffers, to the Danubian territories of Pannonia and Moesia, Augustus' reign witnessed the remarkable advance of Roman control. Egypt became part of the Empire. New territories in Asia Minor (Galatia) and in the Near East (Judea) were absorbed along with their institutions and armies. Still more ambitious expeditions were envisioned, though they were not all realized, and goods produced in the Empire travelled well beyond the furthest imperial outposts. Red slipped wares, classic features of Roman imperial mass culture, could be found from the Bay of Bengal to Britain.

Of clear importance to Augustus as he wrote his memorandum was the census. One of the most radical devices of the Augustan revolution was the census of provincial populations, first recorded in Gaul in 27 BC. While the census of citizens was an ancient Roman practice, rooted in the need to track the pool of military manpower for the legions and to assess the taxation liabilities of the citizen body, its extension to all provincial subjects marked a profound transformation. Documentation and classification of the local population aroused suspicion and resistance from west to east. In Gaul, resistance which necessitated the presence of members of the imperial family is well attested.[44] When the census

[40] Suetonius *Aug.* 25.1.   [41] Suetonius *Aug.* 101.

[42] Tacitus *Ann.* 1.8 states *legionariis aut cohortibus civium Romanorum trecenos nummos viritim dedit*. Suetonius *Aug.* 101 mentions only legionaries.

[43] In Tacitus *Ann.* 1.11 the formulation is *quantum civium sociorumque in armis*. The *auxilia* are not therefore explicitly alluded to, but it is clear that Tacitus' intention is to emphasize the comprehensive nature of the record and to contrast citizens with non-citizens; surely in this instance the *socii* are both auxiliaries and allies.

[44] Livy *Epit.* 134 and Dio 53. 23. 5 refer to 27 BC. In fact the subsequent censuses in Gaul of 12 BC (Livy *Epit.* 139) and AD 14 (Tacitus *Ann.* 1.32.2) were also times of high tension.

was imposed in Judea in AD 6, messianic leaders saw it as an instrument of slavery and launched a devastating revolt. Their wrath fell heavily on those who collaborated with the innovation.[45] Yet from a Roman perspective, all this instability was the price to pay to unlock the resources of the provinces. It is clear that, as with the original Roman census, assessing the human resource was an integral part of this process. Treaties with newly incorporated communities took into account their potential manpower contribution as well as their tax base.[46] Whereas before, perhaps, recruitment of the *auxilia* was sporadic, there was now, at least in theory, a comprehensive body of data upon which recruiting officers could draw.

What was Augustus to do with the military legacy he had inherited? In a well-known but fictitious episode in Dio, Augustus' advisers Maecenas and Agrippa present him with two contrasting visions of the future of the army.[47] Maecenas' vision of a new full-time army triumphs over that of Agrippa, who argues for a continuation of traditional practice, fearing the risks a professional army might bring to both state and emperor. The account was written with a much later debate in mind, and addressed the alleged and real causes of the crisis that had mushroomed by the early 3rd century AD, yet it touches on a matter of profound significance—the formal creation of a professional army. Formal creation because, although there were men in the armies of Caesar who had known little other than military service for pay, the decision to establish a permanent Empire-wide institution which made its oaths to one man was a dramatic step with profound consequences. Hitherto, of course, oaths had been made to individual commanders; the switch marked a vital shift towards an imperial system.

One of the most pressing consequences of the new professional army was the need to generate money to pay full-time soldiers. Conservative estimates suggest that up to 40 per cent of the state's disposable income went into paying for the emperor's guards, the army, and the newly formed navy.[48] The vast bulk of this, of course, came from poll taxes and land taxes levied on the provinces. Italians enjoyed exemption from direct taxation until the Augustan reforms of AD 6/7, and even then their contribution to the army budget, through death duties and taxes on auctions, represented a small outlay for most citizens and a fraction of the total sum the army devoured. In a book that focuses on the 'blood of the provinces', it is well to remember that the army, legions and *auxilia* alike, were essentially funded by the sweat of provincial labour.

A consequence less often noted is that the creation of professional soldiers essentially creates another category, that of the civilian.[49] At the senior levels of the army, it continued to be possible to move between what we would think of as civil and military duties, but for most people in the Roman world, the new arrangement meant that they were one or the other. This distinction was to grow in significance and in signification as time progressed.

---

[45] Josephus *Ant. Iud.* 18.I.1 (1–10) and *Bell. Iud.* 2.8.1 (117).

[46] The best-attested case of a treaty arrangement where recruitment was agreed as an alternative to taxation was the *antiqua societas* with the Batavi (Tacitus *Germania* 29; *Hist.* 4. 12), p. 112.

[47] Dio 52.27.1–5.

[48] Campbell (2002: 85), following Hopkins (1980) for these figures, which assume an annual revenue of between 800 and 1,000 million sesterces.

[49] Carrié (1993: 103).

Once the idea for a permanent force had been agreed, there was a need to establish the basic structure of the army. It was accepted that auxiliaries, who had played a crucial if often understated role in the wars that brought Octavian to power, were an essential part of this. Yet for a number of reasons the sort of sleight of hand that Caesar had used, and downplayed, to build his *Alaudae* from non-citizens, was not adopted. Rather, non-citizens were not allowed to join the legions: the *auxilia* would remain separate. Part of the transformation and indeed, it would seem, part of Augustus' instinct was to preserve the status of citizen. This much is clear from Suetonius, who stresses the emperor's unwillingness to 'taint' native Roman stock by creating too many new citizens or manumitting too many slaves.[50] Indeed, such was the cultural climate that even honourably discharged auxiliaries did not normally receive citizenship; changes to this policy under Claudius were to have major legal implications in provincial society.

While the Augustan scheme did distinguish auxiliary units from the legions, and as the state itself distinguished non-citizens from citizens, we may already detect processes that accelerated the incorporation of these units into the imperial system. There are hints of standardization, for example, and their command becomes a useful step for young men seeking to advance themselves within Roman society. The evidence that we have for this time is frustratingly incomplete, but it is clear that many of the processes identified below were still at an early stage of development under Tiberius. Accordingly, the evidence for changes under Augustus and Tiberius will be considered together, though where a later evolution can be discerned it will be highlighted.

The system of command appointments in the *auxilia* does not appear to have been formalized early. In the early Julio-Claudian period there was no clear hierarchy of ranked commands but rather a series of appointments.[51] Many of these were held by members of the equestrian order, as in the later Empire, but senators and centurions also served in this capacity. The experiments with senatorial appointments did not outlive Augustus' Principate. Suetonius notes that he had allowed *alae* to be commanded jointly by two young men of senatorial class. This initiative was first and foremost aimed at qualifying more men for entrance to the Senate; but while it also briefly extended the opportunities for military command to more young aristocrats, it was ultimately found to be an unsatisfactory system.[52] To such arrangements we should add the role of local elites, men who commanded regiments such as the *ala Atectorigiana*, *cohors Trumplinorum*, and the *ala Indiana*. The precise formation date of the first is uncertain; it may have been formed under either Caesar or Augustus, and was presumably named after its founder/most famous commander, Atectorix.[53] While the short life story of the *cohors Trumplinorum* can only be reconstructed from a single inscription, this is enough to suggest that this north Italian infantry unit was operating under one of its own chieftains.[54] By contrast, the formative moments of the *ala Indiana* are relatively well attested. It was formed and led by a Gallic noble, Iulius Indus, to respond to the Treveran revolt under Tiberius. Local factors were thus as great a

---

[50] Suetonius *Aug.* 40.   [51] Holder (1980: 141).   [52] Suetonius *Aug.* 38.2.
[53] E. Birley (1978b: 265–6), following Mommsen (1905: 145).
[54] *ILS* 847, Saddington (1982: 57–8).

force as ever in the construction and shape of new auxiliary regiments. Men like Indus were already part of the provincial establishment; his daughter was to marry the procurator of Britain, Iulius Classicianus. To see him simply as the leader of a local war band in the service of Rome would be to miss the way in which his role was similarly plugged into Roman networks of power. At the same time it is necessary to remember that these networks were under constant development; accordingly it is not surprising to see variation in command appointments continuing into the reign of Claudius, with a few exceptions even surviving the Flavians.

Changes in unit nomenclature, noted above, represent a related process that similarly testifies to the increasing standardization of the auxiliary units. While the *ala Indiana* and the *ala Atectorigiana* were to preserve the names of early commanders in their titles for generations, the practice of identifying regiments by their current commanders, often also associated with irregular formations in more modern armies, had clearly been abandoned well before the Flavian period.[55] The abandonment of the practice reflects the advent of a more ordered system.[56] But in the Roman world it may have additional force, as the emperor's monopoly on the legitimate command of armies is asserted.

In fact, this very shift towards provincial, ethnic, and tribal titles clearly reflects the wider pattern of provincial incorporation. As Augustan administration took effect it rather artificially preserved some of these titles, and indeed created others to facilitate the classification of subjects. It was natural that the Augustan auxiliary system should follow the same course, and that in doing so it would also reflect the emperor's own legacy and achievement. A very high proportion of the Augustan *auxilia* came from provinces where Caesar had campaigned extensively (for example Gaul) or where Augustus had extended Roman hegemony (for example northwestern Spain).[57]

Given the broad pattern of standardization and incorporation that these features attest, it is important to ask how far the regiments that were raised— each on average no more than 500 men strong—actually had any independent identity. This question will emerge again and again throughout the book, and the survival of distinctive attributes will be noted; but for the moment it is worth simply addressing this question in terms of operational command and deployment. Of particular importance is the degree to which these formations were merely seen as appendages to designated legions. While legionary commanders were powerful figures who often took overall command of mixed forces, there is little to suggest that they had permanent control of these contingents. Cheesman, for example, reviewed the arguments for and against the dependency of individual regiments on larger legionary formations. His overall conclusion was that, while auxiliaries might be brigaded with such forces for protracted periods, no auxiliary regiment was permanently subordinated to a particular legion. No evidence has since come to light to challenge this verdict.[58]

Archaeological and textual evidence raises the question of the frequency with which such regiments were stationed together. It has been argued that '[i]t was not

---

[55] P. 110.

[56] It is possible to find many examples of irregular units named after their commanders, from the American Civil War to the British Indian Army and beyond.

[57] P. 106.   [58] Cheesman (1914: 49–52).

Augustan strategy to waste troops by splitting them up into penny packets'.[59] Auxiliary regiments were brigaded with legions prior to offensive operations, sometimes in vast quantities. In a contemporary eyewitness account, Velleius Paterculus describes how 10 legions, over 70 cohorts, 14 *alae*, 10,000 or so veterans, further volunteers, and the cavalry of one friendly king were gathered in a single camp.[60] The description, which recounts events in the Pannonian War, records exceptional circumstances, but the accommodation of large campaigning forces was obviously widely practised at this time. In Germany, large fortresses, such as that at Neuss, were sometimes enlarged to accommodate as many as four legions, and lay on key invasion routes. Others like that at Cologne, had an additional summer camp in the vicinity, capable of holding over 20,000 men. It would have been at these bases, as Velleius explains, that the *auxilia* would have gathered prior to the campaigning season. The presence of auxiliaries within legionary fortresses on a more permanent basis is also documented, and recent analysis of buildings and artefacts at the Augustan fortress at Nijmegen has claimed that distinct but contemporary zones of auxiliary and legionary occupation can be observed.[61] It is, however, too often overlooked that even now, at this formative time in their history, auxiliary units were operating independently. Saddington makes this point very well, noting not just the establishment of smaller forts on the Rhine but also the fact that auxiliaries were the only troops that operated within the so-called 'unarmed' provinces of the time.[62]

Accounts such as those of Velleius Paterculus indicate that regular auxiliaries were already grouped into *alae* and *cohortes* under Augustus. The earliest specific reference to the hybrid part-mounted units appears in an inscription of approximately the same date which attests a *cohors Ubiorum peditum et equitum*.[63] We should note here in passing that the later form *equitata* has yet to be adopted, an indication that the evolution of military terminology still had some way to go. The existence of several early memorials to decurions and centurions, commanders of *turmae* and *centuriae* respectively, further suggests that the sub-unit structures familiar to students of the 2nd century AD were already present. But detailed reconstruction of unit size is something that must be approached carefully at all times, and hesitantly now. Not only do military units of similar types vary dramatically in manpower even in the most regular of modern armies today, but strength reports from late 1st-, 2nd-, and 3rd-century Roman units reveal notable differences in dispositions.

A fragmentary inscription from Coptos in Egypt has been cited as evidence for the size of sub-units at this time.[64] It originally recorded the number of men and officers detached from each of the two legions, three *alae*, and seven cohorts that provided manpower for a programme of fort rebuilding. A sum of 788 *milites/* infantrymen drawn from 10 centuries and 61 cavalrymen are recorded under the auxiliaries' contributions. As Holder notes, these figures would fit fairly closely with the figures advanced from later sources, of *c*.80 men per century and 30 men per *turma*, though we should note that the number of *turmae* is not actually

---

[59] Wells (1972: 247).   [60] Velleius Paterculus 2.113.1.   [61] Franzen (2009).
[62] Saddington (1982: 194).   [63] *CIL* 10.4862 = *ILS* 2690.
[64] *CIL* 3.6627 = *ILS* 2483. Holder (1980: 6) argues for an Augustan date; Saddington (1982: 61) argues for a date under Augustus or Tiberius.

specified.[65] Yet difficulty remains with the dating of the inscription. While most commentators, believing that all the units of the army of Egypt must have been involved, observe that the number of legions in the province was reduced to two only after AD 23, there is uncertainty as to how long after that the project could have taken place. The original suggestion that the inscription must be relatively early because one of the legions it lists, *Legio XXII Deiotariana*, still had large numbers of men in its ranks from the area where it originated, Galatia, requires qualification. Asia Minor remained a significant source of manpower for Egypt into the 2nd century AD;[66] doubts remain therefore as to the actual date of this important text, and accordingly it will be best to discuss unit strengths and structures below, under Claudius, where our evidence allows us to speak with more conviction.

The armament of these early auxiliaries will be discussed in later chapters; but without wishing to simplify a complex issue, we may observe that even under Augustus most units were using broadly similar equipment to that carried by their successors over a century later. In material terms, the Augustan era was formative in defining the image of the Roman soldier. Two examples will suffice to illustrate the challenge and potential of exploring the material culture of the *auxilia* during this transitional period.

Archaeologists have demonstrated that the first phase of Roman occupation at the Basler Münsterhügel in Switzerland began shortly before 15 BC.[67] In this occupation level, excavators discovered a single Roman coin, a possible Sequanian coin, and six Gallic coins bearing the lettering TVRONOS CANTORIX. They also discovered fragments of cooking pot of a central Gallic type and a typical Gallic brooch. As no CANTORIX coins were present in the lower Late Iron Age strata on site, it was assumed that their presence represents the arrival of a new group who originated from central France. Their military identity seemed to be confirmed by the graffiti, T(VRMA) TOR(I), found on site. The excavator, Furger-Gunti, observes that these artefacts were found alongside Roman weapons and ceramics of types indistinguishable from those found at the Roman forts of Oberaden and Dangstetten.[68] The impression of immersion in military mass culture is strong, but the finds assemblage clearly preserves traces of other artefacts redolent with different and equally intrusive cultural affinities.

A second example would be the research at Kalkriese, site of the defeat of Varus and his command in AD 9.[69] Battlefields are not mausoleums, preserving the dead and their artefacts, but complex sites subject to multiple disturbances.[70] What has survived is, however, illuminating: a cavalry facemask of the type still in use in the *auxilia* right up to the end of our period and fragments of the segmented armour commonly associated with legionaries.[71] Significantly, the latter had often been seen as a later development; the Kalkriese excavations show that it was already a

---

[65] Holder (1980: 6–7).

[66] For further discussion: Kennedy (1985: 156–60) and Alston (1995: 30–31).

[67] For this analysis see Furger-Gunti (1981).   [68] Furger-Gunti (1981: 234).

[69] Harnecker (2008); Harnecker and Tolksdorf-Lienemann (2004); Wilbers-Rost (2009); Wilbers-Rost et al. (2007).

[70] Rost and Wilbers-Rost (2010).

[71] See also Franzius (1995: 78 for the helmet and 76, 79 for the segmented armour).

feature of Augustan armament. No less meaningfully, the first hints to the identity of the site took the form of coin finds, including a notably large number of countermarked *Lugdunum* series I *asses* recovered from the area over the years.[72] These coins, which provide an interesting counterpoint to the Gallic coins of the Basler Münsterhügel, illustrate an essential and unifying draw on the allegiances of auxiliaries and legionaries alike: pay from the imperial coffers.

The story of Varus is in many ways a profoundly important one for our understanding of incorporation of territory and soldiers in the late Augustan period. It reveals both the strengths and limitations of the new system.

The year AD 6 was not a good one for Rome. On the Danube, a mass levy of the Pannonian tribes, called with a view to enlisting more auxiliaries, showed the tribes at once the potential of their combined strength and the inequities of imperial demands. A Roman enterprise therefore brought together the agents of regional revolt, individuals whose own experience in Rome's armies made them especially deadly enemies. Suppressing the uprising was an exhausting undertaking, involving, as we have seen, not just Roman troops but also the forces of friendly kings. In the east the Empire also faced fierce resistance, and Varus, then governor of Syria, had to confront a major uprising in Judea. To suppress this uprising required not only all the legions in Syria, but also four *alae* and as much support as he could muster from local kings. Without auxiliaries and native allies, it would have been impossible for Rome to triumph, since the deployment of legions was actually very finely balanced. Later that year, on the death of its king, Herod the Great, Judea was absorbed into Roman control; all the Herodian apparatus of power was simply coopted by the Romans. Even Herod's forces, it appears, were simply translated into regiments of the *auxilia*.[73]

To Roman eyes, however, Germany now appeared to offer a more promising area of expansion. Archaeological evidence from Waldgirmes makes it clear that the process of reducing the lands beyond the Rhine to provincial status was under way.[74] A new city was built, a focus for the new province. Varus, now in Germany following his operations in Judea, felt at ease marching his vast army through German territories in AD 9. After all, he was assured by a trusted auxiliary commander, Arminius, that the peoples beyond the Rhine were just waiting to embrace the new Roman order. Yet once the army was on the march, Arminius' forces melted away to join forces with the local tribesmen lying in wait to butcher the disoriented soldiers under Varus' command. This was another disaster, still more traumatic than the first, which showed the limitations of incorporation of peoples and soldiers. Rome was still frighteningly dependent on those whom her writers dismissed as mere auxiliaries and allies.

Rome's response to this catalogue of horrors is intensely interesting. With the exception of the German bodyguard in Rome, there is little evidence for the disbanding of auxiliary regiments; rather, many more were created. Yet such was the crisis that these new formations were recruited first, in the aftermath of

---

[72] The presence of these coins, minted between 8 and 3 BC, points to a strong military connection. The absence of *Lugdunum* series II which were produced from AD 10–14 suggests a *terminus ante quem* that fits the historic date of the Varus disaster. For this and for the rest of the coin series see Berger (1996), Chantraine (2002), and Schlüter (1999: 150–52).

[73] P. 117.   [74] Becker and Rasbach (2003).

the Pannonian revolt, of citizen volunteers and later, following the Varus mas-
sacre, of slaves freed and pressed into service. It has been suggested that as many
as 44 units of *cohortes Voluntariorum* and *Ingenuorum* were raised at this time,
though only 18 such cohorts are known in the epigraphic record.[75] Whatever the
precise quantity, the number of men required was considerable. The device of
using citizens in detached cohorts was already familiar to Augustus, but the
pattern of freeing slaves and impressing them into military service was of much
greater antiquity. This form of conscription had been adopted in the aftermath of
Cannae in 216 BC, when 50,000 citizens and allies perished in a single bloody day.
So even in this crisis, pragmatic response followed Roman precedent: slaves did
not fight for Rome. Furthermore, another crucial precedent was maintained.
These may have been auxiliary formations, but they were distinguished from
other auxiliaries: their officers held the status of tribunes, rather than the more
common post of prefect, and their soldiers were bequeathed the same amount as
legionary soldiers were in Augustus' will.[76] Even here the distinction between
citizen and non-citizen soldier was very publicly protected.

What is less clear is how far these distinctions were sustained in the years
that followed. There is no unambiguous direct evidence that non-citizen soldiers
received donatives after this, nor is there any proof that they were eligible for
individual military decorations, *dona*. This has convinced some leading authorities that the distinctions found under Augustus remained enforced well beyond
his death.[77] Indeed, Gaius Caligula's donative of AD 37 specifically records *citizen*
troops in the provinces as beneficiaries—a wording that strongly implies that non-
citizen troops did not receive the award.[78] After this date, though, as Campbell
notes, it must have become increasingly difficult for members of the imperial
house to exclude, and thus alienate, such a large part of the armies on which they
depended.[79]

While these questions of rights and privileges reveal something of how the
different units of the *auxilia* were integrated into Roman structures, they also raise
questions about the impact of this process on individuals. How did the pay and
service conditions that accompanied them affect the lives of the auxiliaries, their
families, and their dependants?

The hardships of military service at this date are well documented, and we shall
return to their implications later, but it is clear that auxiliary soldiers reaped real
benefits from military service over and above the prestige that arms bearing
carried in some societies. Suetonius claimed that Augustus standardized promotion awards, length of service, and pay for all soldiers, and we know that men
received their pay three times a year.[80] Their pay was not increased again until the
reign of Domitian (AD 81–96), a fact that underscores both the lasting impact of

---

[75] Speidel (1976). The high numbers come partly from the fact that a *cohors XXXII Voluntariorum*,
the highest numbered auxiliary unit, is known. Yet it would be a mistake to assume that there were
therefore at least 31 other *cohortes* in that series. The most comprehensive listing of known citizen units
may be found in Spaul (2000: 20). For further discussion see p. 119.

[76] Tacitus *Ann.* 1.8. There is no reference at all to other auxiliary soldiers in this passage, strongly
implying that they were not so fortunate.

[77] This view is advanced particularly strongly by Maxfield (1981; 1986b).

[78] Dio 59.2.3.   [79] Campbell (1984: 168).   [80] Suetonius *Aug.* 49.

Table 2.1. Estimated pay in sesterces of Roman soldiers from Augustus to Maximinus (after M. A. Speidel 1992 and Campbell 1994)

Reign	Legionary infantryman	Auxiliary infantryman	Auxiliary cavalryman of a *cohort*	Auxiliary cavalryman of an *ala*
Augustus	900	750	900	1,050
Domitian	1,200	1,000	1,200	1,400
Severus	2,400	2,000	2,400	2,800
Caracalla	3,600	3,000	3,600	4,200
Maximinus?[81]	7,200	6,000	7,200	8,400

Augustan policy and the burden it placed on the state. Precisely how much auxiliary infantry soldiers received at this time is unclear; most authorities believe that they received less than legionaries,[82] but almost all now concur that cavalry received more than infantry.[83] Indeed, if Speidel's widely accepted calculations are correct, the men of the *alae* received more than those of the legions. Even allowing for the costs involved in maintaining a mount, this is a telling distinction: the auxiliary cavalry would have been, in material terms at least, better off than their citizen soldier comrades (see Table 2.1).

Assessing the relative wealth of an auxiliary infantryman in relation to, say, the work of a farm labourer is difficult. In later periods it may be argued that the *per diem* earnings of both were equivalent, but the fact that the soldier was guaranteed his pay was itself a big difference.[84] Furthermore, the soldier was guaranteed something to eat, whatever the harvest, while the peasantry could often be at the mercy of localized but devastating famine. As in the police forces of many modern developing nations, being a government employee offered ample opportunities to enhance one's earnings. It is highly likely that extortion was so routine as to become an accepted part of a soldier's income. Being a soldier of the emperor allowed scope to augment one's pay by demanding bribes—less exotic no doubt, than occasional war booty, but a steady and sure source nonetheless. John the Baptist's guidance to the soldiers not to extort money and to be content with their pay may have been a harder lesson than most western moderns realize.[85]

[81] Herodian's (6.8.8) claim that Maximinus doubled the soldiers' pay should be treated with caution, and may have been invented to show the ruler in a bad light.

[82] Alston (1994), however, disagrees, and argues that the belief that there were different pay rates for legionary infantry and auxiliary infantry owes much to 'Roman imperial military historiography' (p. 113). While his detailed commentary and judicious caution are essential reading, I find that the view that 'it is very difficult to see any major difference in the treatment of soldiers from the different units in this period' problematic. First, we know that the Roman army was quite capable of paying soldiers performing similar duties different pay on account of their particular unit's status—Hadrian makes this quite clear when distinguishing *equites* from cohorts from those serving in *alae*. Second, I believe that there are differences in the discharge benefits granted to men from different units, as indicated by *FIRA* 3.171 discussed below.

[83] Breeze and Dobson (2000: 183–4) cite both Watson's (1969) calculations and those of M. P. Speidel (1973) and M. A. Speidel (1992), allowing for both possibilities in the 2nd century. They argue that if the auxiliary cavalry were paid more than legionaries, this difference could have been offset by the cost of maintaining a horse.

[84] Campbell (1984: 177).   [85] Luke 3:14.

Though the successive Augustan reforms of service conditions are quite well known,[86] the detail is perhaps less important than the general situation as it pertained to the *auxilia*. We see auxiliary soldiers serving very long periods in the ranks without receiving citizenship. Indeed, although we find some citizens serving in the *auxilia* in units that were raised amongst the *peregrini*, free-born non-citizens, they are few indeed.[87] Where they appear they are often decurions or centurions and are quite probably direct entrants. However much military service in the Augustan *auxilia* may have increased the number of provincials with close links to the imperial system, it did little overall to increase the number joining the civilian body. It is only under Tiberius that we see direct evidence for auxiliaries receiving grants of citizenship, but even here the practice seems irregular and sporadic, as indeed does the length of time soldiers served. The latter was to prove a significant cause of discontent in the Rhine legions as men awaited discharge. Holder has argued that problems with the army and, indeed, the rebellions in Thrace and North Africa may have inspired the emperor to extend citizenship to some auxiliary soldiers.[88]

The implications of changing conditions at this time for soldiers' immediate families are harder to discern, for they are sadly still less well attested. This is partly because we do not have the information provided by diplomas for later periods, and partly because the inscriptional evidence for the army as a whole is scantier for the early Julio-Claudian period than for the late 1st to early 3rd-centuries AD, when the 'epigraphic habit' generated more surviving monuments. It may indeed be the case that soldiers were more likely to raise families in later years, when units were less frequently on campaign,[89] but we know for a fact that soldiers' families were part of military life even at this stage. The army that followed Varus in the disaster of AD 9 was, for example, accompanied to its doom by numerous military families and servants.[90] Much has been made of an official ban, believed to date from the time of Augustus, on soldiers marrying.[91] The point reflects changes in Roman law, but it should not be assumed that it led to a radical transformation of human behaviour. Various explanations have been put forward for the ruling, including discipline and the problems for both soldiers and the authorities of soldiers trying to maintain families on their own salaries. It might also be considered, as it seldom is, in the context of Augustan rulings on marriage.[92] For most of the population, even in Rome, marriage conventions had grown increasingly informal, Augustan legislation, geared partly to tackle a falling Italian birth rate, stressed particular rites of marriage. It intended to force marriage upon many, to build up once again the 'native stock' with which Augustus was concerned. The hearts and bodies of campaigning soldiers were less likely to be in harmony with the emperor's ideals. Furthermore, as any well-informed military historian would observe, many a campaign army in more recent times has been accompanied by families under utterly extraordinary conditions,

---

[86] Keppie (1984: 147–8).

[87] Holder (1980: 46–7).

[88] Holder (1980: 47 and table 4.1) notes that of 17 soldiers known to have served 26 years or over under Tiberius, at least 6 had not received citizenship after 30 or more years in the ranks.

[89] Roxan (1991) and discussion below, p. 131.   [90] Dio 56.20.2–5.

[91] Phang (2001: 345–81).   [92] P. 348.

unsupported by officialdom and casually discarded as strategy demanded. Dependants sought not citizenship or privilege but rather, in an often cruel and difficult world, the security of a wage earner, protector, and loved one. Much confusion has resulted in scholarly circles from the implausible assumption that in the absence of a right to *matrimonium iustum* soldiers did not form more permanent unions.

Beyond the family there came also the servants. Their presence in both earlier and later periods is well attested, and they are depicted with increasing frequency on the tombstones of cavalry troopers. There is, however, little direct evidence for them in the Julio-Claudian period. Yet one monument from around this time does indeed appear on balance to refer to a *lixa* of *cohors III Thracum Syriaca*.[93] *Lixae* were low-status free-born and freedmen who sold goods and services to the army.[94] They could, and did on occasion, don armour for combat, but they were not counted as part of a unit's regular fighting strength. Marcus Titius, who died in Syria at the age of 40, seems to be a rare early example of this underrepresented part of the military community. His memorial must stand for thousands of such men whose very being was dependent upon service to the army, rather than in the army. In Marcus Titius' case, the degree to which this role defined his own identity is even carved into his tombstone, where beneath a fine carved imperial eagle there is even a reference to the auxiliary regiment to which he was attached.

The Augustan system, then, witnessed a transformation that reached deep down through society, moulding the lives even of itinerant servants. Yet it was not without its problems. The crises of the Pannonian Revolt and the Varus disaster marked the dangers inherent in both incorporating new territories and depending on auxiliary forces. Mutinies on the Rhine revealed the dangers inherent in building a professional army. Nor did such challenges cease with the death of Augustus, for in the reign of Tiberius we see imperial lamentations at the paucity of good recruiting material and a further revolt, notably by Thracian warriors terrified of conscription into the *auxilia*.[95] Although Rome continued to raise fresh legions from Italy down to the reign of Severus Alexander, it chose not to conscript there for the frontier armies.[96] The result was that Italians became increasingly rare in the legions, almost disappearing from their ranks in the eastern provinces by the end of Tiberius' reign and from those in the west by the time of Hadrian.[97] Given its unwillingness to impose the *dilectus* on Italy, what could the state do to ensure the supply of men it so desperately needed?

---

[93] M. P. Speidel (1980; 1981b). The ambiguity here is over whether *lixa* is the deceased's cognomen or his job. I follow Speidel in believing that the latter is more likely.

[94] Thorburn (2003).

[95] Tiberius' concerns about the shortage of volunteers and the quality of available manpower seem plausible enough given conditions in the army at the time (Tacitus *Ann*. 4. 4). The outbreak of the Thracian revolt (Tacitus *Ann*. 4. 46) and its consequences are discussed below, p. ***.

[96] Mann (1963).   [97] Mann (1983: 192–3).

3

'Together under the Name of Romans'

The *Auxilia* from Claudius to Trajan

The interdependence of military performance and imperial power was rendered especially explicit under Claudius. In reviving and realizing dreams of conquering Britain, Claudius simultaneously grasped the opportunity to display martial prowess to his people and triggered a chain of events of considerable importance for the army. In time, Britain was to become home to a tenth of the Empire's land forces.

Yet while the invasion of Britain was perhaps the most treasured of his military acclamations, it was actually only one of twenty-seven during his reign. His fourteen years on the throne were to witness the expansion of Roman influence in the east, notably around Palmyra and the Black Sea, the impressive achievements of Suetonius Paulinus' army in the Mauretanian War, and the formal incorporation of client kingdoms in Lycia (AD 43), Judea (AD 44), and Thrace (AD 46). In the East, this pattern of incorporation was to follow a pattern that began in the reign of his predecessor Gaius Caligula and which intensified under Vespasian.

Under such circumstances it is not surprising to see growing textual and archaeological evidence for the incorporation of both military communities and soldiers into a more standardized system of titles, obligations, and rights. Some of these developments, such as granting the privileges of married men to soldiers, were a response to earlier developments.[1] Married men had previously enjoyed legal privileges and exemptions that soldiers, who were not allowed to marry, could not share. Claudius here introduced a more humane ruling.

Alongside a growing consistency in the practice of naming units, we see a clear tendency to group regiments within provincial structures. The notion of provincial armies is not merely established but is made explicit at several levels. Not only do several career inscriptions of equestrians record the province in which their regimental commands took place, but the military diplomas issued to soldiers on receipt of citizenship are arranged on a provincial basis too. We will discuss these documents more below, but for the moment it is sufficient to observe that they are issued on a province-by-province basis and list only the regiments granting citizenship to soldiers within a given province's boundaries. Such a development follows naturally from the evolution of the concept of *provincia* from the responsibility granted to a governor through to a demarcated region with clearly defined territory and army.

---

[1] Dio 60.24.3.

Though by no means typical of all provinces, the experience of Judea is illuminating. Claudius had in fact returned the provincial territory of Judea to a local ruler,
Herod Agrippa I, at the beginning of his reign—an interesting example of the
flexibility with which territories could actually move from Roman to local authority with imperial blessing. Yet with the death of Herod Agrippa in AD 44, it was
decided to bring the territory firmly into the system of Roman provincial administration. What is fascinating about this is the way that the Romans essentially take
over local command and control mechanisms and use them as their own. The most
obvious example of this is the king's army, which may well have formed part of the
auxilia.[2] Josephus tells us that some of the regiments within this force behaved so
badly after the king's death that Claudius considered sending them away to Pontus.
Determined lobbying by the community—whether by the soldiers themselves or
the towns where they were stationed—stayed the imperial hand.[3] The soldiers were
therefore allowed to remain. In addition to demonstrating the local character
retained by some units of the *auxilia*, this episode also illustrates some of the
cultural ties that formed within provincial armies.

It would be a mistake, however, to assume that such ties were a universal feature
of the army in provincial society. In another lobbying episode, this time in the west,
soldiers from several provinces expressed shared grievances to Claudius.[4] Their
objection was that their commanders were overworking them on building and
mining projects in order to impress the emperor. The fact that this complaint, led
by soldiers from Germany, could involve men from so many different regions
without involving higher command reminds us that the Empire's communications
network allowed extensive unofficial exchange too. It also further supports the
argument that we need to see the army as a community of soldiers, whose character
was as much defined by grass-roots movements as it was by imperial edicts.

As far as the organizational development of regiments goes, we may observe
several interesting developments. Suetonius tells us quite specifically that Claudius
confirmed the hierarchy of equestrian officers' command appointments within
the *auxilia*.[5] The very existence of the *auxilia* was thus further formalized as an
integral element in the advancement of these privileged citizens. Many of these
men came from the provincial elite, and some, such as the mystified tribune who
interrogated the Apostle Paul in Jerusalem, were first-generation citizens.[6] On
discovering that Paul was a citizen from birth, the tribune, a cohort commander,
confessed that he had had to pay a great deal of money for his own grant. Again
we see how the ever more profound incorporation of individuals into the structures of imperial power works at multiple levels.

Assessing the degree to which internal regimental organization was standardized by this time remains frustratingly difficult. We do have a fragment of a
Claudian *pridianum* which detailed the strength of the *ala Commagenorum*.[7] The
very existence of this formation is of some interest in its own right, as the client

---

[2] This is based on the belief that Herod the Great's own soldiers were subsumed into the *auxilia*
stationed in the region, as argued by Holder (1980: 14).

[3] Josephus *Ant. Iud.* 19.364–6.

[4] Tacitus *Ann.* 11.20. In this case legionaries are the main agents, but they write on behalf of
members of the provincial armies.

[5] Suetonius *Claud.* 25.   [6] Acts 22: 26–9.   [7] *ChLA* 11.501.

Table 3.1. Theoretical strength of auxiliary units under the Principate (M = *milliaria*) (after Breeze and Dobson 2000: 161, but with adjusted figures for *turma* strengths)[8]

Unit type	*Centuriae*	Men per centuria	Infantry total	*Turmae*	Men per turma	Cavalry total	Total
Cohors peditata	6	80/100	480/600				480/600
Cohors peditata M	10	80/100	800/1000				800/1,000
Cohors equitata	6	80/60	480/600	4	30	120	600/720
Cohors equitata M	10	80	800	8	30	240	1,040
Ala				16	30	480	480
Ala M				24	30/36	720/864	720/864

kingdom of Commagene was actually a nominally independent client kingdom at this time. Yet like Judea, it had been Roman-governed territory before and would become so again. It is likely that the *ala* had been raised for Roman service during the kingdom's earlier absorption under Roman rule. Sadly, given the enigmatic character of the last two surviving lines of the papyrus it is difficult to say anything about the unit's internal organization, but it is clear that at one stage the *ala* had twelve *decuriones* and 434 men.[9] If this was its total complement (and this must be questioned), then the unit would have had fewer *turmae* (twelve) than the norm of sixteen *turmae* attested at later periods. Again, however, it is vital to counsel caution before assuming that absolute standardization of unit organization was deemed desirable at any date (see Table 3.1).

It is also at about this time that we have our first really solid archaeological evidence for purpose-built structures designed to house a single auxiliary unit.[10] This comes in the form of the much-cited Valkenburg I fort in Holland which was built *c.* AD 40 to house *cohors III Gallorum equitata*, a part-mounted cohort.[11] To appreciate why this site is so important in Roman studies, it is necessary to note that not only is it one of the earliest excavated forts believed to have been occupied by a single auxiliary unit, it is also rare amongst the early turf and timber forts in that wooden elements have survived. The excavators were not, therefore, wholly reliant on the interpretation of features cut into the subsoil to recover the plan. So not only does the fort embody the principle that auxiliary forces could be stationed away from the legions, but it also reveals such down-to-earth details as latrine locations and room partitions.

---

[8] Breeze and Dobson (2000: 161) for 32 men per *turma*, following Arrian *Tactica* 18, while I follow Hodgson's (2003: 86–90; Hodgson and Bidwell 2004: 134) calculation of 30 men. The arguments for larger *turmae* in an *ala milliaria* are more complex, but I find little compelling evidence to support the notion of *turmae* with 42 men.

[9] Holder (1980: 9).

[10] In a wide-ranging paper Richmond (1955) sought type sites where fort and building plans could be linked to unit types. The dangers of assuming a simple fort-to-unit correlation are now widely recognized, as has been noted in the introduction.

[11] Glasbergen and Groenman-van Waateringe (1974).

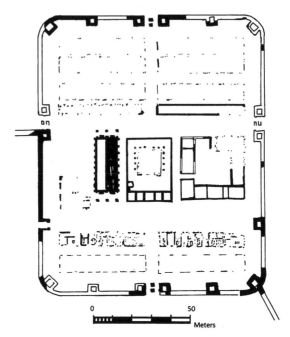

Fig. 3.1. Plan of the Wallsend fort, England, *c.* AD 125.

Extensive examination of another, much later stone fort, Wallsend in Britain, home of a different *cohors equitata* under Hadrian, provides a telling comparison with Valkenburg (see Fig. 3.1).[12] On the one hand, the extensive excavation of barrack blocks at the British site illuminates the style of infantry accommodation used in both and still found in 3rd- and 4th-century sites. The essential element is a *contubernium* block, regarded as the likely accommodation of a *contubernium*, the eight-man sub-unit of an infantry century. It is divided into two rooms, which scholars describe as *arma*, for the front room and the storage of military equipment, and *papilio*, the rear room designated as living quarters. This terminology and arrangement is based on the tented lines of Roman army camps and seems to be of some considerable antiquity. Excavations at Wallsend show that a passageway ran alongside the front *arma* to provide unencumbered access to the rear room. The same arrangement can be seen at Valkenburg. At this level it is clear that the organization of soldiers' living space in the forts of the West remained constant for most, perhaps all of this period. Our knowledge of the situation in the east is so partial that although some thoughts on it are offered later in this volume, any attempts to generalize are precarious.[13]

Wallsend also furnished excellent examples of the organization of cavalry stables, soldiers living on one side of the building in rooms allocated to groups

---

[12] Hodgson (2003).

[13] Hodgson and Bidwell (2004). The classic study of Roman barracks remains Davison (1989).

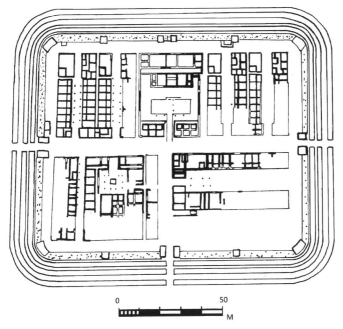

Fig. 3.2. Plan of the Valkenburg fort, Holland, *c.* AD 40.

of three men, while on the other side horses were stabled, again in groups of three. This pattern follows one identified at diverse forts across the Empire: while most of the examples identified are post-Flavian, there is clear evidence for the use of this type of stabling by the time of Claudius.[14]

Yet while these essential elements reveal remarkable continuity, their organization shows significant variety, and in the case of Valkenburg I (see Fig. 3.2) offers a good example of the difficulty of drawing unambiguous conclusions about unit organization even when the unit in residence is known and the fort plan almost fully exposed. The site is known to have housed a *cohors equitata*. In the site report, Glasbergen and Groenman-van Waateringe proposed that the unit consisted of four centuries of approximately 78 men each and two *turmae* of 32 soldiers each. Drawing on the same site data, and focusing primarily on the number of available rooms, Hassall posited six centuries of 64 men and four *turmae* each of 32 men.[15] Hassall's reconstruction fits better with the theoretical strength of units derived from later figures, but as he notes, 'the precise way in which these troops and their officers would have been housed in the barrack accommodation at Valkenburg remains not at all clear'.[16] While at one level this probably reflects the general state of evolution under Claudius, we must remember that neat matches between fort layout and theoretical strength or units are

---

[14] Hodgson and Bidwell (2004: 131–6). The identification of combined barrack/stable buildings was made by Sommer (1995).

[15] Glasbergen and Groenman-van Waateringe (1974); Hassall (1983: 109).

[16] Hassall (1983: 109).

relatively hard to find. While the Hadrianic layout of Wallsend obligingly matches the arrangement of barracks we would expect for the unit stationed there, many forts of the 1st–3rd centuries conspicuously fail to do so.

While equestrian career inscriptions, papyrus strength reports, and excavated forts all point towards the growing incorporation of the *auxilia* into the imperial system, evidence for the intensified absorption of soldiers and their families into Roman provincial society comes in a very different form, that of the bronze diploma. The earliest auxiliary diploma so far discovered dates from AD 54.[17]

Diplomas have an exceptionally important role to play in our understanding of the *auxilia*, for they document not only the granting of citizenship to individual auxiliaries but also the rights extended to their families. Furthermore, as noted above, they are a vital source of information about provincial armies, recording as they do the names of the *alae* and *cohortes* in the province where the beneficiary was stationed. Though diplomas with similar wording, extending similar rights, were issued to sailors, legionaries did not normally receive them. Other types of diploma were issued to the emperor's household troops and, very exceptionally, to discharged soldiers belonging to the so-called *numeri*, or irregular units, an amorphous category discussed below.

What diplomas commemorate is a shift in thinking. Whereas it had long been possible for distinguished individuals to receive an award of citizenship on account of exceptional service to Rome, we now see the systematic extension of citizen rights to an entire category of individuals, auxiliaries who have served a minimum of twenty-five years.[18] It should be noted that this practice was not yet synonymous with discharge; only later does granting citizenship generally coincide with the award of veteran status.

Scholars have repeatedly linked this important development to Claudius. In a famous speech partially preserved on bronze tablets discovered in Lyons in 1524 and recorded in a subtly altered version by Tacitus, the emperor argued that the aristocrats of Gallia Comata should be allowed to stand for senatorial office.[19] Ultimately his decision to grant them this right was not especially revolutionary, and very few Gallic senators are known after this date, but the arguments given are intensely illuminating. Though Tacitus wrote his account of the debate that proceeded this ruling much later and with an eye to his contemporary audience, his version is convincing. One side lamented the fact that those peoples who had so recently fought against Rome might supplant Rome's ancient families. One sentence, particularly difficult to read, even has them recalling the Roman bugbear of the *terror Gallicus*, referring to the Gallic assault on the Capitol in the fourth century BC.[20] This is ironic given that when auxiliary diplomas are later granted, copies of them were displayed on the Capitoline. Roman imagination may have continued to have been haunted by centuries-old defeats at the hands of the Gauls, but Roman pragmatism ultimately triumphed: incorporation rather than exclusion prevailed.

Claudius' response, by contrast, stresses the degree to which the Romans had, from their founding under Romulus, absorbed other peoples. His argument

---

[17] *CIL* 16.2. For the Claudian evidence see Beutler (2007).   [18] Holder (1980: 47–8).
[19] *ILS* 212. Tacitus *Ann.* 11.24.   [20] Tacitus *Ann.* 11.23.

emerges beautifully from Jackson's splendid translation, 'I find encouragement to employ the same policy in my administration, by transferring hither all true excellence, let it be found where it will ... in order that not individuals merely but countries and nationalities should form one body under the name of Romans.'[21] To hold the conquered apart as alien was, he argued, the fatal mistake of Lacedaemon and Athens. This then is a classic statement of one of the most profound differences between Roman and Greek identity, and a notion of considerable importance for the evolution of the *auxilia*.[22]

It is not difficult to see how such an approach could have translated itself into the systematic extension of citizenship to auxiliaries, especially as the experiences of living memory had shown the emperor both the challenges involved in recruitment and the vital importance of auxiliary regiments on campaign or in internal policing. Nonetheless, it is striking how conspicuous the transformation would have been. It would not have been quite so simple to extend the new rights as might at first appear: significant legal manipulation was required to accelerate the incorporation of the conquered into the body of citizens.

The vast majority of free-born imperial subjects in the provinces were either *dediticii* or *peregrini*. *Dediticii* had lower status, they belonged to communities that had surrendered unconditionally to Rome, and they could not in theory become Roman citizens.[23] This was an avenue open only to *peregrini*. Of course the Roman system allowed for the promotion of a community's status, and accordingly the conquered *dediticii* could become members of a newly formed *civitas peregrina*.

The surviving diplomas indicate that Claudius instituted the practice of awarding citizenship to auxiliaries who had served twenty-five years and to their children. Citizenship was not, however, granted to the soldier's wife, but recognition of the marriage, via a grant of *conubium*, was assured. The wording explicitly notes that this grant can only be extended to one wife. This somewhat complex application of *conubium* is a product of Roman law. It begins with the assumption that the auxiliary came from a *civitas peregrina* despite the fact that many probably did not. Then, in order to legitimately give citizenship to the children, it delves deeper into legal fiction. Because there is a real risk to the state that some of the wives of soldiers might actually be from *dediticii*, all are treated as such, and the assumption is made that the soldier had made the union in ignorance of his wife's actual status.[24] A grant of *conubium* allowed what would otherwise be a socially disabling situation to be avoided. A mother from the *dediticii* could have citizen children.[25]

That such an elaborate fiction needed to be constructed at all tells us several important things about family formation in the army. First, it assumed that many serving auxiliaries already had a 'wife' even if their unions were not recognized in Roman law prior to the grant. Second, it assumed that she might well be from amongst the *dediticii*. This is important because, while some site-specific evidence and many generalizing hypotheses point towards units becoming 'inbred' as soldiers marry the daughters of other soldiers, the extension of *conubium*, at least

<hr>

[21] Jackson (1936: 287–9).
[22] Tacitus *Ann.* 11.24.   [23] Jones (1960: 130–32).
[24] As Simon James has kindly reminded me, many wives would probably have been slave-concubines of their spouses first.
[25] Mann (1986).

retrospectively, authorizes marriage with members of the wider community—even, indeed, from recently conquered peoples.[26] Finally, it is important to note that the diploma essentially demanded a choice from the soldier: he has to name the one wife with whom he was to have *conubium*. How far this in practice restricted polygamous relationships is of course impossible to assess. What the whole issue does do is demonstrate not only how soldiers were pulled closer into the body of imperial society, enjoying a privileged position, but how their families were drawn into new networks too. That the wife was the least favoured in this arrangement is in itself a reflection of the spread of Roman influence, part of a pattern which may well have seen a diminution of women's status in many provincial societies. Yet status is a complex notion, and while such arrangements contributed to female subordination within the Empire, marriage to a soldier may well have enhanced a non-citizen woman's standing in her local community too, through assuring better access to goods and foodstuffs. The range of possible scenarios is huge and our knowledge of them ridiculously limited.

A MATURE SYSTEM? DEVELOPMENTS UNDER THE FLAVIANS

For many scholars the Flavian period marks the end of a transition that began under the Republic.[27] Indeed, by the death of Vespasian most elements of the military system had already reached the form they were to retain well into the 3rd century. The evolution of the *alae* and *cohortes* reflects this trend, and accordingly, the overall impression is of a professional force with broadly standardized command structures and service conditions. Yet this growth towards maturity was not without its pains. Rebellion and Civil War preceded the rise of the Flavians and played a vital role in the whole process. Were it not for the horrors of both, it is perhaps unlikely that we would know as much as we do about the 1st century army. Tacitus is particularly moving when recounting the tumultuous events of AD 69 in his celebrated *Histories*; he probably knew the territories set ablaze during the Batavian revolt from personal experience. Fortunately for students of the Empire, it was also a tale that could only be told well by reflecting on the more humble participants and victims; auxiliaries were numerous in both categories. His *Annals*, covering AD 14 to AD 68, are more problematic for students of military history because they often detail events more distant from the author's life and experience. The insights into events and peoples in northwest Europe offered in his *Agricola*, a somewhat unreliable biography of his father-in-law, the fighting and reforming governor of Britain, and the important commentary on the tribes and peoples of Germany recorded in the *Germania* also prove useful.

---

[26] Shaw (1983: 144; 148) of *Legio III Augusta* at Lambaesis in Numidia. He is, however, careful to note that his analysis refers to the '*discernible* patterns'. Given that we do not have diplomas for the legions, there is no source of other information on marriage to women from outside the military community to balance that provided by the inevitably slanted sample drawn from those people who erected or were commemorated on tombstones—the primary source for families in *Legio III Augusta*.

[27] Saddington's (1982) seminal study of the development of auxiliary forces ends in AD 79.

In the Near East, the Jewish Revolt (AD 66–AD 74) claimed the attention of historians. We are fortunate that Josephus, a minor protagonist, recorded the events in his extraordinary work of Roman propaganda, the *Jewish War*. His writings, including the *Antiquities* and his autobiography, illuminate the complexities of provincial incorporation and the operations of the Roman army. Furthermore, for the first time in the Near East, there is substantial archaeological evidence for military operations to place alongside parts of the narrative. The remarkable works of Masada, scene of the final siege of AD 74, preserve details of the minutiae of military life. From the outstations with their billets divided into *contubernia*, through the associated settlements for civilian followers, to the rudimentary jottings of Roman soldiers on papyrus, the complex proves a remarkable source of information.[28]

Yet it is not just conflict that generates a greater range of evidence for this period, it is also culture. While military campaigns across the Empire resulted in the deposition of more equipment, and the construction, destruction, and abandonment of more forts and fortresses, so also did broader fashions in provincial society. The growth in the 'epigraphic habit', the cultural practice of using inscriptions, and the increased use of carved funerary reliefs dramatically enrich our knowledge of the *auxilia* in war and peace. The lessons that emerge from this rich database will be examined later; the current focus must remain with the place of the *auxilia* in the administration of Roman power.

Perhaps the most obvious lesson to emerge from the accounts of both Josephus and Tacitus is that by the AD 60s auxiliaries emerge as significant agents of change within provincial society. They are no longer (if indeed they ever really were) helping forces ancillary to the legions; rather, they are a significant source of power in their own right.

The episode discussed above under Claudius, when the *ala* and *cohortes* recruited from Sebaste and Caesarea managed to lobby their way out of reassignment after particularly scandalous behaviour, illustrates that this was not a wholly new development.[29] What is clear, however, is that it marks an increasingly important trend. In Josephus' account of the tense months preceding the Jewish Revolt, the role of the Sebasteni in retaining control is consistently stressed.[30] In one noteworthy case, the *ala* is employed to suppress lethal rioting sparked by the killing of a Galilean in Samaria.[31] While this particular intervention was militarily successful, surely the fact that Samaritans were thus employed to confront Jews bent on revenging one of their own people could only have exacerbated simmering tensions.

When the Civil War erupted, each side recognized the legions as the key strategic assets, the big players, but auxiliaries were inevitably embroiled in the fighting from the outset. A Tacitean aside indicates that many auxiliaries were already in Rome in AD 69,[32] but it is elsewhere that we see them playing politics. Notably it was an auxiliary cavalry regiment, the *ala Siliana*, which won over four major north Italian *municipia* to the cause of the imperial pretender Vitellius. What is especially

---

[28] Schulten (1933), Richmond (1962b), and, for documentary evidence recovered, Cotton, Geiger, and Thomas (1989: 17–32).

[29] P. 52.   [30] Josephus *Bell. Iud.* 2.58; 63; 74 and 236.   [31] Josephus *Bell. Iud.* 2.236.

[32] Tacitus *Hist.* 1.38 refers to helmets and shields meant for auxiliaries being held in the *armamentarium*.

significant here is that it was the decurions, the troop commanders, who were behind the move. They were bound to Vitellius, but the regimental commander's allegiances do not even get a mention. Such was their success in bringing over such major centres that they were reinforced by other auxiliary units of Gallic, Lusitanian, and British origin.[33] We should note that the *ala* was originally in Italy because it was in the process of being redeployed. A march through Italy was an integral part of many military journeys from Europe to Africa.

As different governors and armies declared their allegiances to successive contenders, so too did the auxiliary forces under their command. In Africa, peculiar rumours circulated about Lucceius Albinus, the procurator of both Mauretania Caesariensis and Mauretania Tingitana. He was believed to have styled himself Juba, following the former African leader, and adopted the trappings of kingship. He certainly drew extensively on Moorish irregulars, as well as his extensive auxiliary force. It would be fascinating to know more, but what we can discern in this episode is both the perpetuation of regional traditions in the conflict and their ultimate subordination to wider imperial allegiances. The Moors were ultimately won over by an emissary from the army of Germany, which enjoyed an impressive reputation across the provinces, and not by affectations of traditional kingship. Of some note, though, are the consequences of Albinus' downfall, for the three named associates whose deaths Tacitus records were all auxiliary officers.[34]

In the army of Britain the role of the auxiliaries is even more striking. When tensions flared up between the governor, Trebellius Maximus, and the Twentieth Legion violence followed, but the *auxilia* did not immediately participate. Tacitus discusses their deteriorating relations with the governor separately, and when, after some delay, they do decide to desert him, Trebellius has no choice but to flee the province.[35] As Denis Saddington observes, while Tacitus uses the episode as a device of opinionated auxiliaries to argue for a disgraceful collapse of discipline, one in which mere auxiliary troops openly insult a consular governor, the incident actually demonstrates how influential such troops had become.[36]

Yet it was the contemporary uprising on the Rhine that more than anything exemplified the dynamics of local allegiance, the dependency of the authorities on the *auxilia*, and the military maturity of the *alae* and *cohortes*. The Batavian revolt led by Iulius Civilis, himself a commander of auxiliaries, is often regarded as a defining event in the history of the *auxilia*.[37] Not only did the revolt bring in Batavian units which, being supplied with an ongoing stream of Batavian recruits, might be expected to preserve tribal allegiances, it also attracted other local auxiliary formations and even witnessed the defection of legionary forces. Roman accounts identify a range of incitements and incentives in the motives of the rebels. While these include reaction to a mishandled levy and demands for improved service conditions, there are also clearly more complex motives amongst the elite. These factors are discussed further elsewhere, in the discussion of recruitment, but in the context of this discussion it is useful to emphasize that this was ultimately to be seen as a regional rebellion within the framework of the

[33] Tacitus *Hist.* 1.70.   [34] Tacitus *Hist.* 2.58–9.   [35] Tacitus *Hist.* 1.60.
[36] Saddington (1982: 128).   [37] Tacitus *Hist.* 4. See also pp. 113 and 122.

Roman system, not a tribal revolt against it.[38] Furthermore, as Tacitus grudgingly acknowledges, auxiliary units abandoned the rebellion and returned to the Roman fold before some of the legionary mutineers. This may explain why there is no clear evidence for a systematic strategy after the rebellion to break the ethnic identity of auxiliary units and to separate them from their place of origin. Rather, the imperial response follows a familiar pattern. It recognizes what students of the *auxilia* often underestimate, that many other loyalties can trump ethnic allegiance: Batavians, for example, were to be found fighting on both sides. New units were certainly drafted in to replace those destroyed or cashiered, but even a devastating revolt on this scale did not lead to a policy of foreswearing the use of locally raised soldiers to guard frontiers; rather, the local elite probably witnessed some significant realignment. The Gallic Iulii, for example, faded from view at around this time.[39] In many units, evolving recruitment patterns were sufficient to ensure that local loyalties were diluted. Native commanders disappear. Yet this dynamic did not greatly impact upon Civilis' own people. Indeed, the special practice of enlisting Batavian soldiers into Batavian units under Batavian leaders clearly continued after the revolt.[40]

Part of the explanation for this no doubt lies in Roman pragmatism. The Batavians had convinced the Romans of their military effectiveness, both as allies and as enemies, but part of it may also reflect the need for a swift settlement at the end of the Civil War. The victor, Vespasian, now had a huge task before him.

The strategies employed to restore imperial order and win the loyalties of the provinces varied from region to region and from one community to another. In the Near East a huge military effort was required to win the Jewish War. Here the primary aim was the capture of Jerusalem. Rome's armies were at their most lethally effective when they could target a major urban centre, when they could take and hold strategically important ground, rather than when they were engaging dispersed opponents. Yet Jerusalem was a major challenge. Three legions (about 16,000 men), six *alae*, and 23 cohorts (a further 14,500 soldiers), together representing over a seventh of the Empire's regular forces, and contingents sent by four kingly allies (approximately 18,000 men combined) were committed to the war.[41] As Millar has argued, this episode exposes three important truths about Roman power.[42] First, there was no sustained regional nationalism yet to challenge Rome. Exhausting as the combat with the Jews proved to be, it was almost exclusively with Jewish forces; had gentiles joined the uprising, Rome could hardly have contained it. The second point follows from the first. Rome's armies may be the biggest permanent force in antiquity, but there was a limit even to their capacity to engage in warfare on multiple fronts. Without at least 'passive acquiescence' from the majority of the population and generally peaceful borders, Rome could not hope to govern. Finally, there was a pronounced dependency upon allies who, as we have seen, provided a third of Vespasian's force.

In the years that followed the siege of Jerusalem this dependency was to undergo a marked shift—one that had some significance for the *auxilia*, for we do not see

[38] P. 115. For revolts in the Roman world see Dyson (1975).
[39] Drinkwater (1978).   [40] P. 116.
[41] Josephus *Bell. Iud.* 3.4.2 (64–5); Millar (1993: 76).   [42] Millar (1993: 76).

such large contingents of *royal* forces on campaign again. When *c.* AD 72/73 Roman troops invaded Commagene, one of the kingdoms that actually supported them during the Jewish War, they were helped by forces of other kingdoms, amongst them that of Sohaemus of Emesa. Sohaemus had also furnished troops for the reduction of Jerusalem, but Josephus' reference to his support in this instance is the last reference to the dynasty to appear in our sources.[43] One consequence of this was that new recruits and units entered the Roman army from Commagene; another was that in time Emesene units would appear too; but perhaps the most significant development was a fundamental shift in Rome's depositions in the Near East. What was once a 'bridgehead' now resembled an 'integrated provincial and military system': what was once peripheral to the power games of the west was now an arena in which emperors could be acclaimed, sustained, and deposed.[44]

In those provinces where the initial conquest was but a distant memory, the emperor employed quite different strategies of incorporation. At about the time his forces invaded Commagene in the east, Vespasian extended Latin status to the communities of Spain. This was a shrewd device, for it brought prosperous and strategically important territories into ever closer association with Rome. Epigraphic evidence indicates that at least eighty towns successfully applied to take advantage of this offer, while archaeological evidence indicates a growth in urbanism.[45] As is widely recognized, the incorporation of provincial societies does not just stop with their absorption into provincial structures, but continues through ongoing competition for rights and status, a process which can often, as here, manifest itself materially.

The incorporation of civil communities was one challenge, of course, but at the heart of the Civil War crisis there lay another, still more pressing concern. How might the allegiance of armies be won and sustained? It was a question that had profound consequences for the Flavian handling of the army. It is thus rather disappointing that the literary sources have little to say on the matter. Suetonius tells us that Vespasian was something of a disciplinarian, but illustrates his observations with vignettes of little value. He describes how a young man had his commission rescinded when he approached the emperor reeking of perfume, and how a contingent of *vigiles* had its shoe allowance refused.[46] Yet there is some evidence for development and innovation in his reign and again under Domitian.

One of the most important developments has already been noted. We see that auxiliary units are now sufficiently embedded within the imperial system to be common, albeit still minor-league power players. Josephus and Tacitus offer two rather different perspectives on the impression this created. Josephus, writing with a Jewish background and for an audience that consisted largely of the literate non-Greek speakers of the Interior, neighbours of Rome needing to be discouraged from challenging her power, tends to subsume the *auxilia* under the broader label 'Romans'. Soldiers are distinguished by the type of unit in which they served, rather than by whether or not they are from non-citizen units. Interestingly, some of his accounts indicate that soldiers from auxiliary units cooperated informally with their legionary

[43] Josephus *Bell. Iud.* 7.7.1–3 (219–45).   [44] Millar (1993: 80).
[45] Mackie (1983: 215–7) and Keay (1988: 57).   [46] Suetonius *Vesp.* 8.3.

counterparts, as with an improvised scaling party during the siege of Jerusalem, which contained a score of legionaries and a couple of troopers from *alae*.[47]

For Tacitus, as we have seen, the difference between the legions and the *auxilia* is still something to be stressed. Alongside his distaste at the disorder in Britain in AD 69 when *even* auxiliaries insulted the governor, we should note his celebrated comment on a later episode.[48] In an account of the battle of Mons Graupius in the early AD 80s, Tacitus describes how his father-in-law, Agricola, chose to use the auxiliaries to do most of the fighting to save Roman blood.[49] In reality, the writer probably knew that the citizen/non-citizen distinction between the troop categories was less than absolute, but the very fact that he can make such a point, as late as the reign of Trajan, is telling. Clearly his audience would have felt that a clear difference existed between the statuses of these different parts of the campaigning army.

Despite the methodological problems inherent in calculating the proportions of citizens to non-citizens in the *auxilia*, the balance of evidence indicates that a growing number of individual citizens enrolled in the *alae* and *cohortes*. In some cases, the evidence is distorted by the growing habit amongst non-citizens of adopting the *tria nomina*, the names normally associated with citizens, on enlistment.[50] Of course, the very practice of coopting such names suggests that auxiliaries had closer links to the citizen body. The process of enrolling citizens into the *auxilia* may have started very early, and Holder argues for the presence of citizens in the ranks of non-citizen units as early as the reign of Augustus.[51] Kraft claimed that as many as half of his sample of Flavio-Trajanic auxiliaries from the Rhine and Danube were citizens.[52] While the precise details of his analysis can be debated, and the ratio of citizens to non-citizens might have varied significantly from region to region and unit to unit, the general trend he identifies is unmistakable.

To the growing number of individual citizens found within the ranks we can now add those who received citizenship on the basis of block grants to entire regiments. Block grants are not without precedent, as the award to the Spanish horseman of Ascoli demonstrates, but the systematic scale of the new awards indicates something innovative. In a time of bloodshed and strained imperial coffers, block grants of citizenship were an attractive, economical, and effective way of rewarding reliable soldiers. We might also argue that they offer evidence of the extension of that principle that saw Vespasianic grants of Latin status to the *municipia* of Spain. Although it has been argued that the earliest block grant to a unit, commemorated with the title *civium Romanorum*, took place under Claudius or Nero,[53] the earliest datable use of this title by an auxiliary unit is actually from the AD 70s.[54]

---

[47] Josephus *Bell. Iud.* 6.7.1 (68).

[48] Tacitus *Hist.* 1.60.   [49] Tacitus *Agric.* 35.2.

[50] The methodological problems and the hazy relationship of the *tria nomina* with citizenship are discussed on p. 101.

[51] Holder (1980: 49).   [52] Kraft (1951: 80–81).

[53] For a Claudian introduction: Maxfield (1981: 231–2), also Birley (1952: 10–12) on the basis of *RIB* 159, which records *Ala Hispanorum Vettonum* with the title *civium Romanorum*. As Holder (1980: 31) notes, however, the inscription is more likely to be Vespasianic in date.

[54] Kraft (1951: 100–101); Holder (1980: 30–32). The earliest reference to a unit carrying the title that can be reasonably confidently dated is to *cohors I Breucorum c.R.* (*AE* 1972: 721 = *ILS* 1374). Details of the equestrian commander's career indicate that the inscription must date from the AD 70s.

If this was indeed a Flavian development, it certainly fits with other economical devices for bolstering military morale, inspiring competition for honour—that classic instrument of transformation under the Empire—and winning allegiance.[55] For example, the first attested use of the title *torquata*, which indicates the award of the elaborate neck collar of Celtic origin, dates from *c.* AD 74.[56]

In examining the motives behind such imperial largesse it is important to acknowledge that another has been advanced: this is the belief that, at a time when the ethnic or tribal origins of many auxiliary units were no more than distant memories, something more needed to be done to preserve a sense of regimental unity or *esprit de corps*. This is possible, but I strongly suspect that granting of such awards was, like the occasional award of imperial titles, as much a way of cementing the relationship of emperor and soldier as it was of sharpening military efficiency. The first consideration always held precedence over the second in the Roman Empire.

Finally, a further testimony to the growing importance of auxiliary units within the military system comes in the creation of milliary units: double-sized regiments of a notional 1,000 men. It is not too much to see in this initiative an indication of the degree to which the value of the *auxilia* had become recognized. A milliary regiment was a force to be reckoned with; its deployment required special consideration. Only in utterly exceptional circumstances, for example, were two or more *alae milliariae* ever stationed together in the same province. Normally, only one was ever under a single governor at a single time. Just as the disposition of legions required careful planning to ensure that no potentially seditious consular governor had too much manpower at his disposal, so now the larger milliary units had to be weighed in the balance of power.

What did this mean for the ordinary soldier? First, as seen above, there was a higher chance that he would either be a citizen or be serving alongside citizens, even if *cives Romani* were still in the minority. Second, heightened imperial interest in his welfare was in evidence. While it must be acknowledged that this interest was probably somewhat uneven in practice, there is a clear tendency towards regularizing soldiers' end-of-service conditions. From the AD 80s military diplomas commonly show soldiers receiving citizenship at the same time as honourable discharge.[57] Yet in the end the awkward subject of money could not be overlooked: Domitian was ultimately obliged to raise the salaries of soldiers.[58] The raise marked a substantial increase in military expenditure, the first increase in basic pay since Augustus, and Domitian's critics did not hesitate to argue that even he regretted the decision.[59]

So by the end of the Flavian period, it is possible to see a significant maturity in structures of empire, army, and *auxilia*. Though much of his contribution has been hidden by the hostile writers and the formal condemnation of his memory,

---

[55] For the currency of honour in imperial government under the Empire, see Lendon (1997).

[56] Awarded to *ala Tauriana Torquata*, a unit of Gallic origins. The title is first recorded on the career inscription of one of its former commanders, who can be shown to have commanded the *ala c.* AD 74 (*AE* 1939: 60; Holder 1980: 35).

[57] Holder (1980: 48), following Mann (1972: 236–7).   [58] Suetonius *Dom.* 7.3.

[59] According to Dio, Domitian regretted his decision but decided to reduce the number of soldiers rather than attempt to reduce pay to the previous level (67.3.5).

Domitian probably consolidated many of the military achievements of his predecessors. In particular, wounded by the attempted revolt in AD 89 of Antonius Saturninus, the legate of Upper Germany, the emperor extended the tendency towards dispersing units rather than concentrating them where they could be readily manipulated by imperial pretenders. Accordingly he reduced, but did not quite ban, the number of double-legionary fortresses.[60] How this affected the *auxilia* is difficult to judge, but it probably reinforced the established pattern of dispersing units. In theory at least, such an arrangement might have allowed military communities to develop in a degree of isolation from one another, but in practice there remained a high level of communication and exchange between them. Furthermore, the growing crisis in the Danubian provinces was about to pull the army in a different direction. Under Trajan, the Empire was to witness once more the concentration of vast campaigning armies, large elements of which were drawn from the *auxilia*.

CONQUEST BY PEN AND SWORD: THE EMPIRE UNDER TRAJAN

As the process of incorporation steadily saw new peoples added to the Empire, and others bound still further into the structures of imperial power, so the very fabric of Rome changed. Monuments financed *ex manubiis* expressed both martial prowess and the ideals of the Roman order. This practice, which we saw in the Forum of Augustus, was repeated in the construction of the Colosseum and the Temple of Peace under Vespasian, and again in the remarkable Forum of Trajan. This complex reminds us that while there is much about the reign of Trajan that recalls that of his august predecessor, there were significant developments too. The point was picked up in the ritual acclamation by the Senate too, when they wished that emperors might be 'luckier than Augustus and better than Trajan'; they recognized the two as great imperial leaders whose rule was nevertheless marked by different strengths.[61]

In Trajan's Forum, as in that of Augustus, the visitor would see images of great Romans and cowering foes, but Trajan's Forum took this quite literally to new heights; it contained an extraordinary monument of enduring influence, Trajan's Column. As a commemoration of the conquest of Dacia, the Column was an epic monument to an epic conflict, one that ultimately transformed Rome's strategic situation on the Danube and brought the rich lands of Transylvania into the empire. It was not until the late 3rd century that the Empire had to relinquish this territory, but up until that time it contributed lavishly to the imperial coffers. Indeed, Dacian gold funded much of this extraordinary building effort. Yet despite

---

[60] Suetonius *Dom.* 7.3 claimed that he banned double-legion fortresses, but he clearly did not. The double-legion fortress of Nicopolis, Egypt, continued in full use for several decades (Keppie 1984: 194). It also appears that the fortress at Apulum in Dacia was occupied by two legions simultaneously in the early 2nd century AD (Alexandru Diaconescu, pers. comm.).

[61] Eutropius 8.5.3.

the attention lavished on this triumph, it was only one of several wars of conquest launched at this time.

Towards the end of his reign Trajan was to launch his armies into battle with another ancient Roman enemy, Parthia. The move contrasted both his own operations in Dacia and conflicted with his successor's policy. At least two, and quite possibly three, of the new provinces the emperor formed across the Euphrates were almost immediately abandoned. Yet while the newly won territories were swiftly discarded, the campaign that briefly secured them had enduring consequences. Millar has noted that it actually launched a new phase of relations with the Near East which had repercussions well into the 3rd century. This phase was marked by determined attempts, realized in the 190s, to reduce northern Mesopotamia to the status of a province, and by the fact that it was now increasingly the emperor who led these campaigns in the field.[62]

To these developments should be added the incorporation of the Nabataean kingdom. The acquisition of this allied territory seems to have been achieved with comparative ease. Tried and tested mechanisms of incorporation, such as the development of a Roman road network, the introduction of the census, and the absorption of the royal army into the *auxilia*, are all well documented here.[63] The swiftness of the Nabataean transformation underscores Trajan's reputation for competence. He enjoyed, amongst historians at least, a superlative reputation as a diligent administrator. It is a reputation that owes much to the surviving letters of Pliny the Younger, a remarkable source of information for provincial administration, but one which must, of course, be read with circumspection.[64] While Pliny was in fact writing of his experience of administration in an 'unarmed province' in Asia Minor, he raises important issues relating to the recruitment and deployment of the auxiliaries who provided the military personnel under his jurisdiction.[65]

What then did all this activity, this juxtaposition of conflict and good governance, mean for the development of Rome's armies? How did it impact upon the *auxilia*? Part of the answer may be found in the carved figures of Trajan's Column itself (see Fig. 3.3).

Too close a focus on the images on the Column can easily mislead. Scholars who have read these stone scrolls literally have given rise to elaborate fiction,[66] yet there are conventions in the artwork that clearly reveal a deeper pattern of meaning. For our purposes, one of the most important is the way in which four broad types of figure are used to represent the vast majority of the Roman fighting force. The first is the soldier clad in plate armour carrying a curved rectangular shield: he appears in combat frequently, but if there is any building to be done, he and he alone appears to do it. The second type wears chain mail and carries an oval shield: he may appear either mounted or on foot. The third type represents archers from the east clad in long, flowing oriental garments. The fourth type is quite distinct; he often brandishes a club and fights bare-chested, and is at once a barbarous and a heroic figure. While arguments as to precisely what soldiers really

[62] Millar (1993: 99–100, 104).   [63] Graf (1997) offers a comprehensive overview.
[64] For a critique of this reading see Woolf (2006).
[65] Recruitment: Pliny *Ep.* 10.29–30; deployment: *Ep.* 10.19–20.   [66] e.g. Rossi (1971).

Fig. 3.3. This scene from Trajan's Column shows several distinct types of Roman soldier. To the left of the main group of standard-bearers shown in the upper register, it is possible to identify a legionary-type soldier in segmented armour; in the lower register march auxiliary figures in mail with oval shields, archers, and bare-chested irregulars.

wore may continue, the division is almost universally acknowledged to show the legionaries, regular auxiliaries, auxiliary archers from the Orient, and irregular forces respectively which served Trajan in the conflict. Interestingly, the auxiliary figures participate in nineteen of the twenty major battles depicted on the Column. Furthermore, they fight alone or alongside irregulars in twelve such scenes.[67] Thus while it is still regarded as essential to distinguish them from legionary formations, it is nonetheless accepted that they play much more than an ancillary role in combat.

So the Column suggests, at last, public imperial acknowledgement that the *auxilia* have truly come of age. This impression is reinforced by other sources. It is not coincidental that one of the most important studies of the *auxilia* pursued their development up to the reign of Trajan, but no further.[68] But the Column may also illuminate aspects of the story too. For however important it clearly was to the scheme that the different types of soldier were differentiated, there is abundant evidence that the artists who depicted them had not really seen the army of conquest in action. Where did they get their models from?

The answer may well lie quite close by, for, as noted above, auxiliaries had been embroiled in Italian warfare for generations, visiting Rome on several occasions, and Trajan's reign saw a regular auxiliary formation permanently stationed in the capital. The old paramilitary formation of *custodes* was replaced by the *equites singulares Augusti*, and while this mounted unit was not simply just another

---

[67] Rossi (1971: 118–19).   [68] Holder (1980, esp. 2).

provincial *ala*, it owed its appearance and recruits to just such regiments. Surviving tombstones of the *equites* from this date show them in similar poses and dress to their comrades in the Rhine armies.[69] Under Trajan the particular reputation of the German armies was maintained and the tradition of German bodyguards sustained. Yet, ironically, it was Trajan's own campaigns that were ultimately to lead to a change in this association.

Whether type figures on the Column were modelled on different types of household troops, rather than on campaigning armies, the broad message is clear. There can be no doubt that the vital combat role of auxiliaries was being publicly acknowledged. The men of the *alae* and *cohortes* were now accorded a place in the triumphal art of Rome.[70] It was a natural development of the Augustan system, but it probably would have appalled Rome's first emperor nonetheless.

Before departing Rome for the provinces, it is worth glancing at the depictions of Rome's enemies on the Column. While these are often ludicrously stylized, it is clear that a couple of real observations imprinted themselves firmly on the memories of the campaigners. The Dacians' distinctive curved swords are almost ubiquitous, and the heavily armoured cavalry of the Sarmatians is especially distinctive. The peoples of the Danube were to make a major impression on Rome's armies, and it is clear that the armament of the Sarmatians in particular was to influence the *auxilia*. It is no surprise therefore to find that a regiment raised under Trajan, the *ala I Ulpia contariorum*, was equipped with the distinctive two-handed Sarmatian lance, the *contus*.[71] It was a pattern of fighting quite alien to Roman tradition, but one soon to be employed across the Empire.

Even under the warrior emperor Trajan, however, the Roman Empire could not expand on all fronts. In those areas where there was little expansion, the period was marked instead by a consolidation and rationalization of troop deployment. Watchtowers, which had previously only been used to control movement across rivers, were now increasingly used to police the artificial 'stop lines' in Germany and Britain. Small fortlets were incorporated into such schemes, further dispersing the manpower of auxiliary units. In Germany, the development of the frontier as a means of demarcation and regulation, in a form that had begun to emerge under Domitian, was accompanied by economic development. Trajan was not merely a military man; he also recognized the importance of civilian development behind the frontier.[72] In Britain, a consequence of Domitian's decision to arrest operations in Scotland had led to a concentration of forces on the Tyne–Solway line. The existent Corbridge–Carlisle road evolved into a frontier line, controlled by a series of forts spaced half a day's march apart. To Trajan too, it now appears, we must credit a rationalization of military deployments on the fringe of Roman territory in Africa.

---

[69] Busch (2003).

[70] P. 282.

[71] Roman sources certainly regarded the *contus* as a Sarmatian weapon, though in reality the link between weaponry and ethnicity was far from exact, it is stressed by Tacitus (*Hist.* 1.79). See also Coulston (2003).

[72] *Colonia Ulpia Traiana* and *Civitas Ulpia Sueborum Nicrensium* were both founded during this period.

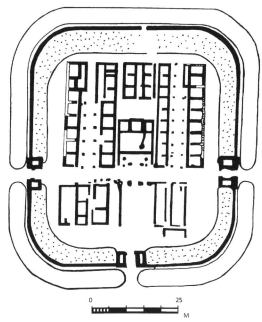

Fig. 3.4. Plan of the *Numeruskastell* at Hesselbach, Germany. Early 2nd century AD.

It has been suggested that the emergence of infant frontier systems may have fostered the introduction of new types of units, commonly termed *numeri*, to the army.[73]

Excavations at Hesselbach (Germany), the *Numeruskastell*-type site, indicate that the fort there was designed for one such unit (see Fig. 3.4). Ceramic evidence suggests that the site was established *c.* AD 100.[74] The fort contains many of the elements of buildings and layout familiar to other Roman military establishments in the west and has its own headquarters building, but the complex would not have been capable of housing a full *ala* or cohort. Both the appearance of such sites and the increasing use of the term *numerus* in Roman military contexts have led colleagues to suggest innovation around the late 1st century AD.[75]

Developing this theme, several scholars have argued that the emergence of *numeri* is itself a symptom of the degree to which the *alae* and *cohortes* had become absorbed into the Roman system. They were, so the view goes, too 'Roman' and had lost much of their original fighting efficiency as ferocious barbarians.[76] Yet such an

---

[73] The key surveys of the *numeri* are Callies (1964), Southern (1989), and Reuter (1999).

[74] Baatz (1973).

[75] A further factor in the debate is the reference to *nationes* and the *De Munitionibus Castrorum*, but there are clear problems in basing any arguments on the origins of the *numeri* on this document. Scholars remain divided on the relationship between *nationes* and *numeri*, as well as the actual date of the *De Munitionibus Castrorum*. For the latter debate see p. 81.

[76] Cheesman (1914: 89); Watson (1969: 16).

argument not only conflicts with auxiliaries' active participation in battle scenes on the Column but also fails to explain the ongoing creation of regular units.

At the heart of the problem here is the failure to recognize the sheer diversity of soldiers under Roman command. Roman armies used irregulars at most periods of Rome's history. While it is true to say that there was a movement towards grouping some of these under Roman commanders and in regular forts, the fact is that these 'units' (for that is all the term *numerus* actually means) were highly diverse in form and character. By the mid-3rd century there were some that strongly resembled established *cohortes*, but it is clear that there were many that did not. The contingents not only varied in size and were designated by very different titles; they were also recruited on a very different array of criteria. Special diplomas, significantly different in form from those of the *alae* and *cohortes*, were issued in a few cases, but for the most part their soldiers stood little chance of receiving Roman citizenship.[77] This diversity does not accord therefore with the idea of a single type of force created with a single goal in mind, but rather of a (perhaps more economical) fashion that brought irregulars into the system. It drew from a range of traditions with origins in the local militias, allied armies, and occasional alliances of the Julio-Claudian period. It was as good a way to bring the *dediticii*, who could not normally acquire Roman citizenship, into the Roman fold, as it was, for example, to translate *civitas* militias into more permanent formations. It was a flexible approach—one that could as easily be employed by armies of conquest as by armies of occupation.

Nor was this the limit of Roman pragmatism. While Trajan's Parthian War made little use of the allied kings of old—most of whom had, after all, been absorbed into the imperial system by the early 2nd century—other campaigns clearly used allied troops under their own commanders. The famous Moors of Lusius Quietus are depicted on the Column, wearing traditional dress and fighting led by tribal leaders.[78] Even a century after the reforms of Augustus, service with Rome could still take many forms.

Given that such diversity still existed within the army, it is important to ask how far the standardization many scholars expect to see within the *alae* and *cohortes* had advanced. Various sources illuminate this question, but in doing so they only raise further questions. At one level there does seem to be a growing precision in the use of regimental titles. The reign of Trajan reveals a general tendency to write the full titles,[79] a practice which may reflect the growth and further codification of the army list.[80]

At another level it is important to consider evidence for the internal organization of units. Thus we know that around the time of Trajan's Dacian campaigns *cohors I Hispanorum Veterana quingenaria equitata*, stationed in Moesia Inferior,

---

[77] See Mann (1954) *contra* Rowell (1939) and Vittinghoff (1950).

[78] For a survey of Moorish irregulars fighting for Rome, see Southern (1989: 92–4).

[79] Wagner (1963: 327); Saddington (1982: 177).

[80] The notion of 'an army list' may itself be anachronistic. It is clear that rigid rules were not applied to regimental titles across the entire Empire. Some units in different provinces may have shared the same title. Nevertheless, there must have been some attempt to document auxiliary regiments, similar to that known to have been employed for legions.

consisted of 546 men, including 119 cavalry.[81] Additions to the rolls thereafter raised the total number of soldiers to 596, but sadly the detail of these additions is unclear. While this makes the debate about sub-unit size difficult, we may observe that the regiment had six centurions for its infantry and four decurions for its cavalry; in structural terms, therefore, it conforms to the modern expectations of this category of regiment. A slightly later document (AD 117) recording recruits enrolled in another *cohors equitata*, this time from the army of Egypt, indicates that that regiment also had six centuries; it provides no information for the cavalry contingent, presumably because its recruits came through different channels.[82] Neither of these units was double-strength. While these fragments broadly support the view of a common organizational structure, other near-contemporary evidence is confusing. A strength report recovered from the period 1 ditch at Vindolanda, dated *c.* AD 85 to *c.* AD 92, records the strength of *cohors I Tungrorum* on the 18 May in an unspecified year.[83] This infantry cohort had 752 men under arms, placing it at around the conjectured strength of peditate milliary units, but only six centuries, in contrast with the ten for ten centuries that we might expect from ancient sources. While various explanations have been advanced to explain this apparent anomaly, the possibility that standardization was rarely achieved must be acknowledged. Later documents, discussed below, also reveal significant variation from the supposed norm.

Maintaining regiments at their desired strength remained a concern for provincial administrators. Pliny, who had only auxiliary soldiers to reckon with in his duties in Bithynia, corresponded with Trajan on this matter on at least two occasions. The correspondence reveals that the army drew not only on volunteers but also on conscripts and men paid by those called up in the levy to replace them. While military pay had increased significantly under Domitian, it is clear as ever that money was not a sufficient incentive in and of itself. Other attempts were made to improve service conditions. The practice of issuing diplomas to serving soldiers dies out under Trajan.[84] From this point on we rarely see men serving beyond twenty-six years, and where we do, it is almost always because warfare delayed the granting of discharge.[85]

At about the time this practice becomes formalized, a final rationalization of legionary rights and privileges takes place. Trajan's reign was to see the last of the great colonial foundations. The *coloniae* of Sarmizegetusa in Dacia, Oescus in Moesia Inferior, Ratiaria in Moesia Superior, Poetovio in Pannonia Inferior, and Timgad in Numidia, established to house discharged legionaries, are the last monuments to a tradition that could be traced back to Rome's conquest of Italy. Even these grand cities accommodated only a small percentage of the discharged citizen soldiers, but hereafter there are no examples of mass settlement of veterans. Dacia, for example, had provided a ready source of land for *colonia Ulpia Traiana Sarmizegetusa* and its huge territory, but future colonial foundations would have

---

[81] *P. Lond.* 2851 = *RMR* 63. The document records unit strength on the 1st January of an unknown year in the late 1st or early 2nd century AD. See p. 14.

[82] *ChLA* 11.497.

[83] *Tab. Vindol.* II.154. Though initially published as associated with period 2, it is now accepted that the tablet was recovered from an earlier context: A. R. Birley (2009).

[84] Last known: AD 110 (*CIL* 16.164).   [85] Alföldy (1968b: 226–7); Holder (1980: 49).

required significantly greater outlay on the part of the government, for expansion was slackening and territory within the Empire was already under established owners. This, and perhaps, the preference amongst some soldiers to settle close to their military stations, was to lead to important changes in the impact of veterans upon provincial settlement patterns.

Given the dramatic differences between the experiences of Roman armies at this time, between the campaign forces operating in Dacia and the east and those which were largely responsible for maintaining the imperial writ in pacified provinces, we may be sure that military families had very different experiences of service life. In legal terms, though, some general observations may be offered. First, the ruling that a serving soldier could not marry remained in force. The hardship that this could cause soldiers' families is made explicit in a ruling made by the prefect of Egypt in AD 117.[86] In turning down a request from one Lucia Macrina, a widow, to recover a deposit from the estate of her deceased husband, the Prefect shows mastery of both local practice and Roman law. Such deposits, he observes, were actually dowries. If he authorized the return of this dowry to her, he would have to acknowledge that she was legally married, and that he could not do. This is a classic example of the twin tracks of incorporation colliding. Lucia had married into the military community through the rights established in local tradition, but the imperial authorities could not legally honour such an arrangement, and she ended up much the poorer as a result.

Other Egyptian rulings reflect the implications of the marriage ban on children. Accordingly, the local marriage of Chrotis to her fellow Alexandrian citizen Isidorus of *cohors I Thebaeorum* inevitably raised the question of their son's inheritance rights.[87] Here, more happily, the prefect concluded that while Isidorus' son could not have been considered legitimate, as Isidorus was a serving soldier, the will could be honoured as he had made his son an heir legally. What a relief this ruling must have been to the family, but what a chore it must have been too, to take this all the way to the attention of the Prefect. It is worth noting in passing that the opposition between local and imperial is made especially explicit in this document, for it reveals that Isidorus actually used a Roman name, Iulius Martialis, when in the army.

Under Trajan, who repeatedly stressed his special concern for the welfare of soldiers, we see some emphasis on a flexible, beneficent application of the law.[88] This emerges in individual cases, as when Pliny asks the emperor to grant citizenship to the daughter of an auxiliary centurion,[89] but it also appears more generally in the *Digest*. Trajan is explicitly credited with instructing governors to treat poorly or incorrectly written military wills sympathetically.[90] In noting this, the *Digest* links his generosity to that of Titus and Domitian. Significantly, in writing to governors, Trajan refers to the soldiers as *commilitones*.[91] In addressing them in this manner, in employing the very term Augustus had famously refused to use, Trajan reaffirms the increasingly explicit mutual dependency of emperor and soldier.[92]

---

[86] Mitteis and Wilcken (1912: II.2 no. 372).   [87] *FIRA* 3.19.
[88] Campbell (1984: 284–5).   [89] Pliny *Epistulae* 10.106–7.
[90] Dig. 29.1.1–2; 1.24.   [91] Campbell (1984: 284).
[92] For Augustus' refusal to address the soldiers in this manner, see Suetonius *Aug.* 25.1 and above.

This was just one of the many ways in which Trajan's reign set the agenda for his successors. While many, but by no means all, of his conquests were abandoned, he changed the shape of the Empire and directed imperial attentions afresh to the Danube and the East. The deployment and redeployment of military units literally paved the way for later frontier lines. Organizational structures within the army were now firmly established. Soldiers' families now had to be reckoned with in a different way. All of these developments proved to be profoundly important for his successor.

4

A New Provincialism

Hadrian and the Antonine Revolutions

Under Hadrian two especially conspicuous phenomena marked the incorporation of provincial society: a surge of investment in urban centres and the development of demarcated frontiers. Both reveal the interests and commitments of this well-travelled emperor, while each manifestation reflects the importance of local culture and geography. Complementing these phenomena was a further change: Italy was now regarded as provincial territory, not a land apart from the provinces. Hadrian's journeys through the Empire helped drive a building boom, while his visits to provincial armies led directly to the construction of new linear barriers in Britain, along the Rhine and Danube, and in Africa, while the Near East witnessed judicious disposition of major legionary fortresses. Underpinning these broad developments was direct knowledge of the needs of different provincial territories and a decision to abandon the expansionist strategies of his predecessor.

This did not, however, mean that the soldiers of Hadrian's armies were spared combat. In addition to the low-intensity conflicts that never quite made it into our historical sources, there were major wars in Britain, Dacia and, most memorably, in Judea. Overwhelmingly, however, military archaeology tends to reflect a growing stability as new lines of defence are established which physically demarcate provincial communities, though such systems were not universally introduced and even in those territories where they did exist there was real variation in form. Nevertheless, the Hadrianic impulse had a lasting effect on the study of the army and Empire, giving the appearance of coherence to an important body of frontier research, widely known even amongst its Anglophone exponents as *Limesforschung*. The substantial advances in our knowledge that have resulted are the subject of an elegant recent synthesis by Breeze, who manages to convey both the geographical and chronological diversity of Roman 'frontier systems' within a single volume.[1] Much of our view of the Roman army, both during the 2nd century and, perhaps less advisably, during earlier periods, has emerged from the field of frontier studies. It is worth noting, therefore, just how strongly German and British scholars and frontiers dominated the formative early years of *Limesforschung*. It has been an enriching movement, but to appreciate its achievements it is necessary to view them in a wider context, lest the study of Rome's armies be cut off from the societies that produced them.[2]

---

[1] Breeze (2011).
[2] For a constructively ambivalent view of this special relationship see James (2002: 12–13).

For Holder, the Hadrianic period marks the finale to the development of the *auxilia*, one which placed them 'on an equal footing' with the legions'.[3] It is nonetheless clear that real differences between the legions and the *auxilia*, and indeed between different branches of the *auxilia*, remained. This is certainly the impression left by the surviving evidence for the building of Hadrian's Wall, where legionary working parties are recorded completing much of the work on forts and curtain walls, while auxiliaries are only explicitly credited with digging a section of the *vallum*.[4] Furthermore, while such sources as the Vindolanda tablets should warn against making simplistic distinctions between regimental bases and units in garrison, it remains the case that the *limes* forts were generally constructed with a particular auxiliary cohort or *ala* in mind, while the large fortresses were principally occupied by legions, albeit sometimes in association with an *ala*.

As Hadrian travelled his Empire, anxious regimental commanders looked on as their soldiers paraded and performed their manoeuvres for imperial approval. A remarkable inscription from Lambaesis in Africa records a series of just such operations undertaken under the eyes of the emperor in AD 128.[5] Significantly, not only does each force, *Legio III Augusta*, the *ala I Pannoniorum*, and *cohors VI Commagenorum*, perform separately, but where both cavalry and infantry contingents are represented within a regiment they perform separately too. The emperor is generous in his compliments; he makes clear that he has lower expectations of the cavalry of mixed cohorts than he does of the cavalrymen of the *alae*. The differences in status and ability of the cohorts and *alae*, so clear in the history of the two types of formation, were clearly still marked at this date.

Hadrian's interest in military matters is also widely attested in our ancient sources.[6] Of these, one of the most interesting was Arrian of Nicomedia, one-time governor of Cappadocia and a historian of Alexander the Great. The increased respect for and interest in provincials and provincial culture that characterizes the Hadrianic period is echoed in Arrian's comments about the emperor.[7] In his military writings he praises Hadrian for encouraging troops to use traditional war cries.[8] What that meant in practice will be discussed later, but it is interesting to see that such an argument could be both believed and regarded as complimentary at this time. It is a further reminder that incorporation did not require homogenization.

Yet it was not just in military manoeuvres that Hadrian took an interest. Indeed, the historical sources stress his involvement in every aspect of military life, right down to the appearance of soldiers' quarters.[9] Here Hadrian clearly objected to the trappings of civil life in a military environment, frowning on gardens and excessive architectural decoration.[10] The extent of Hadrian's inspections and innovations

---

[3] Holder (1980: 2).

[4] *RIB* 1365 records the work of *cohors I Dacorum*. Hadrian's comments in his address to auxiliary troops at Lambaesis, however (see below), suggest that they were expected to undertake more involved building work elsewhere in the Empire at this time.

[5] *ILS* 2487: 9133–5. For further work on Hadrian's speeches to the army in Africa see Le Bohec et al. (2003) and M. P. Speidel (2006).

[6] Davies (1968a). In addition to the writings of Dio and Arrian, note Fronto *Principia Historiae* 8–9 and *SHA Hadrian* 10.

[7] Saddington (1975: 116).   [8] Arrian *Tactica* 44.1.

[9] Dio 69.9.   [10] *SHA Hadrian* 10.4.

was clearly regarded as exceptional; most emperors had much less contact with the frontier armies. So we may accept the view of Dio, writing several decades later, that Hadrian's reforms had lasting impact, even if it would be unwise to attribute all changes to his intervention.[11] Modern claims, for example, that he instituted the cult of *Disciplina* to aid in this transformation now appear exaggerated.[12]

Finally, amidst all this talk of manoeuvres, discipline, and military reform, it is important to recognize that the period also saw further developments of importance to military families. These reinforce a general trend, discernible from at least the reign of Claudius, towards improved conditions for service families while nonetheless retaining the official ban on military marriage. In AD 119, the text of a letter from the emperor himself was displayed at the headquarters of the double legionary fortress of *Legio III Cyrenaica* and *Legio XXII Deioteriana* in Egypt.[13] It recorded that Hadrian wanted to interpret more leniently the rules of inheritance, so that children of serving soldiers who died intestate might nonetheless inherit from their fathers. As such children were technically illegitimate, the ruling essentially marks a move towards the recognition of military marriages; its tone further suggests that it applied to all soldiers, citizen and non-citizen alike.[14]

Important as such rulings clearly were, they surely reflect a more general trend, a trend that the wider policies of the emperor had in turn reinforced. For with the new frontier policy and the abandonment of territories briefly won by Trajan, there was a greater sense of stability. The civilian communities of the border areas, some in towns only a few miles from the frontier, quickly began to flourish. Occupants of the forts' extramural settlements, many of them civilian dependants, clearly benefited too. They enjoyed a growing level of security in the knowledge that the regiments on whom their livelihoods depended were less likely to move than before. Though there are grave dangers in generalizing from the small number of surviving diplomas, it is notable that the proportion naming the wives and children of diploma holders is very markedly higher (75.8% as opposed to 37.3%) under Hadrian than under his predecessors.[15] This supports the impression that the growing permanence of military stations not only aided family formation but also mitigated pressures on families formerly occasioned by conflict, relocation, and instability. The archaeological record shows therefore that in many areas the extended military community enjoyed a more settled existence than they had done for decades. The implications of this for regimental communities, recruitment, and relations with the local population were considerable.

ANTONINE REVOLUTIONS

The regime that followed was not supposed to be revolutionary. Hadrian had done his best to ensure that. In leaving the reins of imperial power in the steady and

---

[11] Dio 69.9.

[12] von Domaszewski (1895: 44) but now requiring severe qualification. See p. 205.

[13] *BGU* 140.   [14] Campbell (1994: 158).

[15] Roxan (1986: 269–70). The sample consists of 51 pre-Hadrianic diplomas and 29 dated between 117 and 140.

competent hands of Antoninus Pius, Hadrian had every reason to assume that continuity rather than change would mark the imperial order. Yet even his diligent interventions in provincial society and his shrewd choice of an heir were unequal to the forces with which Roman emperors now had to contend.[16] Our sources show that this was a time of powerful transformation. Not only were Hadrianic wall systems abandoned in some areas, but there was even a serious attempt to reduce large tracts beyond the frontier to the status of provinces.

Initially Pius began conservatively enough. In the towns of the Empire, Pius proved himself a worthy successor to Hadrian; his reign frequently saw the completion of building projects launched by the travelling emperor. Italy especially benefited from his largesse. On the frontiers, even departures from his predecessor's strategic dispositions suggest that Pius was serious about realizing Hadrian's vision. While we should never forget the potential propaganda value to an emperor of successful military operations, both the abandonment of Hadrian's Wall for a newly established line between the Forth and the Clyde, the Antonine Wall, and the extension of the Rhine frontier in Germany can be understood as part of a wish to consolidate rather than expand.[17] The moves allowed for shorter frontier lines, and incorporated excellent farmland. In theory at least, they were more sustainable and more able to meet the increased need for food production that their huge garrisons brought. Reorganizations on the border with Parthia and on the Danube *limes* also suggest an emphasis on consolidation. Yet it was not enough to prevent crises breaking out towards the end of Pius' reign. The emperor's last years were marked by conflict in the northwest provinces, on the Danube, to the east and, with the Moorish War, in Africa. While ancient commentators insist on Pius' preference for peace, fighting played a significant role in his reign.[18]

The same was true, only more so, under the emperor Marcus Aurelius. In the east, Parthian attacks led to a major Roman campaign under Aurelius' co-emperor, Lucius Verus. Though accounts of the events were viciously satirized by Lucian of Samosata in in his work on the writing of history, *Quomodo historia conscribenda sit*, Rome's military response was both highly competent and successful. A friendly king was installed in Armenia and Roman control beyond the Euphrates extended. In AD 171 rich Spanish settlements in Baetica were targeted by North African raiders. A year later Egypt was rocked by the rebellion of the mysterious Boukoloi. But worst, by far, was the situation in the Danubian provinces. Destruction deposits, coin hoards, and wall building all reflect the catastrophic effect of raids from across the Danube, raids that even penetrated Italy and Greece.

It is no coincidence that the greatest monument in Rome to Marcus Aurelius, a column probably completed under Commodus, his son and heir, testifies powerfully to the savagery of war. The population of Rome are not here spared the horrors of the frontiers. Often unfavourably compared to Trajan's Column, on which it is clearly modelled, this monument in fact has a different role. It too commemorates fighting on the Danube, this time recording combat with the Marcomanni and the Quadi (AD 167–180), but its focus is even less concerned

---

[16] A. R. Birley (1974: 17).

[17] Breeze and Dobson (2000: 89) note that the political benefits of a short sharp campaign and the merit of moving the frontier lines closer to 'main centres of resistance' could have informed the move.

[18] Pausanias, *Description of Greece* 8.43.

with the detail of the campaigns than was its better-known predecessor. Rather, the image here, in stylized cartoons, commemorates the suffering of both Romans and their combatants in especially graphic style. This is no second-rate imitation, no crude propaganda; rather, it is a meditation on the dangerous forces which an emperor might hope to contain, but could seldom really master.[19] In a world beset by plague and battlefield carnage, Aurelius had to confront both.

For all that the erection of the Column by Commodus might suggest of filial loyalty, the new emperor decided not to follow his father's counsel. He abandoned combat north of the Danube and with it his father's vision of two new provinces, Marcomannia and Sarmatia. There were also miltary setbacks in Britain when raiders from the north crossed a wall, presumably Hadrian's Wall, and destroyed many Roman units in the process.[20] Though there is little direct archaeological evidence for a disaster in Britain at this time,[21] it is not unreasonable to accept that the security of the province was compromised.

Amidst this tumult, the Antonine emperors showed a proper awareness of the importance of the army. Pius appears in full armour at the head of his troops on some coins, while Commodus appears alongside his father on others, possibly ones minted for a donative.[22] So a close association with the army was perceived as necessary both for an emperor who never left Italy and for a father seeking to win acceptance for his son and successor-in-waiting. This should not occasion surprise, but the claim that Marcus actually addressed his own son as 'fellow soldier' is striking.[23] So too is the amount that Marcus offered in donatives to his soldiery.[24] Despite the crippling financial burdens the state faced, this wise and restrained ruler nonetheless paid a huge donative on his accession; the troops in Rome alone received 240 million sesterces. If, as seems likely, the legions also received the donative the additional sum offered to provincial armies would have amounted to at least 1,000 million sesterces more. No wonder Marcus refused to grant a further donative at the end of his German campaigns.[25]

The archaeology of the middle and late Antonine period is revealing. While evidence from many cities attests to flourishing populations within the interior, rapid change is notable on the frontiers. Most conspicuous is what Bishop and Coulston identify as a revolution in military dress.[26] A significant number of excavated military sites were occupied briefly during this period, offering an un-diluted glimpse of the arms and armour of the time. Notable shifts in equipment types can be seen in assemblages dating from between the reign of Hadrian and that of Severus, at sites as far apart as the Antonine Wall and the Danubian frontier. The extent of change, in a relatively short period, reflects the degree to which provincial armies remained in active contact with one another. Innovations in one zone were swiftly adopted in another, but we should not assume that this resulted from some form of central direction. There is also evidence for a wider cultural evolution within Rome's armies at this time. But the cultural changes also reveal other patterns,

---

[19] Brilliant (2002: 506) emphasizes that the Aurelian monument, rather than being a poor copy of Trajan's Column, is 'one of the most dynamic and demanding of Roman imperial works of art'.
[20] Dio 73.8. [21] Frere (1987: 147).
[22] *RIC* 3. 1046 shows Marcus Aurelius presenting Commodus to a group of soldiers.
[23] Herodian 1.5.3. [24] *SHA. Marc.* 7.9.
[25] *SHA. Marc.* 7.9. [26] Bishop and Coulston (1993: 109–21).

amongst them the increasing importance of the Danube in forming Roman military identities. This is evidenced not only in the figural tombstones discussed below but also in the spread of new weapon types of Danubian origin. A notable example of this is the two-handed lance, the *contos*, used by auxiliary soldiers.[27] Its use spreads, it would appear, with the redeployment of campaigning armies. The *ala I Cannanefatium*, redeployed from the army of Pannonia to Numidia, is a case in point. This regiment served in Pius's wars with the Moors. Men from its ranks who died in Numidia are depicted on gravestones armed with the *contos*. The fact that a unit of *Cannanefates*, originally raised in what is now Holland, could be rearmed with a weapon associated with lands far to the east indicates the extent to which units had evolved. Ethnic origins did not bind the appearance and character of established auxiliary regiments at this date. By no means all changes in military appearance were limited to arms and armour. Changes in footwear and garments may also be seen at this time, and unlike the *contos*, they appear to have been adopted not just by a number of units but across entire provincial armies.[28]

Given the growing number of citizens attested in the *auxilia*—auxiliary diplomas after AD 140 even use the phrase 'Roman citizenship to those who do not have it' is a clear acknowledgement of their presence—it is important to ask how great a distinction really remained between the legions and the *auxilia*. Three arguments have been advanced to suggest that the status distinction had been substantially eroded by this date. The first is that there was a clear tendency in many parts of the Empire to recruit legionaries and auxiliaries from the same communities.[29] It has even been conjectured that auxiliaries may have received incentives to enlist which were similar to those offered to prospective legionaries, namely the granting of citizenship on enrolment.[30] Neither of these claims is convincing. The first claim may work for some parts of the western Empire, but it certainly does not hold true when examined in the light of richer documentary evidence in the Near East.[31] Furthermore, even when the same communities were being mined for recruits, it must be remembered that each would contain individuals of varying status, health, and physique. It does not therefore follow that the sources of recruits were necessarily indistinguishable. As for the claim that citizenship was extended to some of those enlisting into the *auxilia*, not only is there no evidence for this, but there is considerable evidence for non-citizens in the *auxilia* throughout the Antonine period and beyond. The fact that a papyrus strength report of the *cohors I Augusta praetoria Lusitanorum* from Egypt reveals that the regiment received transferees from *Legio II Traiana* in 156 is sometimes advanced to suggest the diminution of difference.[32] It has been argued that the fact that there is nothing in this document to suggest that the men were being punished or demoted is significant.[33] Now it may be that they were not, and that such a transfer was now routine and unexceptional, but in reality the evidence

---

[27] Bishop and Coulston (1993: 109–11) for the new sword type and the role of the *contos*.
[28] P. 269.   [29] Dobson and Mann (1973: 195).
[30] Roxan (1986: 278–9) offered this as a thought exercise, but did not believe it herself and offered compelling arguments against it.
[31] A point Gilliam (1965a) made strongly with reference to the men of *ala veterana Gallica* in AD 179 (*P. Hamb.* 39) and *cohors XX Palmyrenorum*. See also Roxan (1986: 279).
[32] *RMR* 64.   [33] Holder (1980: 49).

does not allow a firm conclusion. This is a brief entry: other fuller documents would once have existed detailing the circumstances of each soldier's history, while contemporaries would not have had to document the status implications of the transfer to one another.

What is clear is that distinct *alae* and *cohortes* continued to be formed during this period—a move that is in itself an indication of the resilience of this troop type. Some of these new units have acquired a special place in the study of the Roman army because their organization, membership, and activities are especially well documented. It is therefore useful to consider them briefly here, prior to a fuller consideration in later chapters.

Altogether some fifty-six soldiers from *cohors I Hemesenorum milliaria sagittariorum equitata* are known to us, some of whom came from the unit's home town, Hemesa. At the Pannonian site of Intercisa in Hungary, archaeologists have unearthed some of the regimental base and the cemetery associated with it. A combination of the false belief that the regiment was an early foundation and the striking evidence for the presence of many Syrian soldiers at the site has contributed to the widespread misconception that eastern archer units continued to receive recruits from the community from which they were raised long after they had gone overseas.[34] It is now believed that this formation was raised in Syria under Marcus Aurelius and redeployed to the Danube as late as AD 180, and therefore no special recruitment practices are required to explain the presence of the Syrians.[35] The argument that the emperor and his officers laid a special emphasis on perpetuating eastern ethnic enclaves within the *auxilia* no longer appears necessary.

Still better attested is *cohors XX Palmyrenorum milliaria sagittariorum equitata*, sometime garrison of Dura-Europos on the Euphrates. This site, too, has played an influential role in forming our understanding of the army. Extensive excavations unearthed papyri relating to the unit's structure and routine. The relevance of these documents to the rites and rituals of auxiliary units will be discussed in much further detail elsewhere in this book, but here it is useful to note the evidence for the creation and organization of the unit. It seems most probable that it was created in the AD 160s out of an irregular formation of Palmyrene archers, providing an example of a staggered incorporation into the Roman military system.[36] If so, it is a reminder that Rome was still conscious of the difference between regular *alae* and *cohortes* and the so-called *numeri*. If such differences had ceased to matter, conversion would have been unnecessary.[37] Of further interest is the structure of the unit. The most frequently cited source for the organization of auxiliary regiments is *De munitionibus castrorum*, a text on the proper layout of a camp that was either a theoretical treatise or record drawn from actual practice on an unknown campaign. There is good reason to believe that this document dates to the time of Marcus Aurelius, for it attests to the brigading together of four milliary *alae* in one force, a concentration unattested at any other date.[38] In this document, the strength of a *cohors equitata milliaria* is given as ten

---

[34] P. 136.   [35] Mann (1974: 259); Kennedy (1980: 121–2).

[36] Kennedy (1980: 213–27).   [37] Kennedy (1980: 220).

[38] E. Birley (1966; 1982a). It is important, however, to acknowledge Frere's (1980) view that the document dates to the reign of Domitian, and to note other translators of the text who, regarding it more as a theoretical treatise, also see it as late 1st or early 2nd century in origin (Lenoir 1979: 111;

centuries plus 240 cavalry.[39] The latter, it is generally assumed would be most naturally divided into eight *turmae* of thirty men each. Yet *cohors XX Palmyrenorum* actually has only six centuries and five *turmae*. While this might be explained by the contingent's irregular origins, it is probably best to take it as just another indication of the degree to which 'exceptional' patterns of organization were more usual than contemporary scholars tend to accept. One final point is of interest here: close reading of the Dura rosters reveals that soldiers generally joined the cohort as infantrymen, and appointment to *eques* only usually came after ten years' service.[40] The evidence that the movement from foot soldier to horseman was regarded as a promotion after such a relatively long period further underscores the prized status of cavalrymen.

The last of the units to be discussed here is the *ala Sarmatarum*, a formation which also appears to have been created under the Antonines. Dio records that 5,500 Sarmatians were sent to Britain by Marcus Aurelius in AD 175.[41] Marcus' decision was probably primarily determined by a need to secure the Danubian frontier rather than an especial wish to reinforce Britain. Once on the island, surrounded by sea and by a substantial number of soldiers with whom they had little if any cultural links, the Sarmatians posed no risk to that embattled war zone. Many of these forced migrants were settled in the area around Ribchester in Lancashire. Significantly, material from Ribchester attests to the presence of both a *numerus*, later termed *cuneus*, recruited from amongst these men, and also a regular *ala Sarmatarum*.[42] There is no need to see in this any ambiguity in the naming of regiments; rather, it is clear that an *ala* was also raised from amongst the men brought over. A 17th-century sketch recording the tombstone of a decurion in the *ala* shows him brandishing his long lance in two hands, commemorating incidentally the arrival of trans-Danubian fighting styles in this distant province.[43] The influence of this great region, of both its Roman armies and their powerful enemies, was strong indeed. Another tombstone, this one erected by a *singularis consularis*, or governor's guardsman, from the *ala*, records a family group.[44] Here the soldier commemorates his son, wife, and *socaere tenacissimae*, his 'most steadfast' mother-in-law, all of whom have quite conventional Roman names. The transplanted community had clearly settled into its new home.

Such commemorations bring us back to the question of soldiers' status and the legal position of military families. The Antonine period saw two changes take effect; the first was relatively minor, but the second had far-reaching implications.

From the time of Julius Caesar onwards, soldiers' rights to make wills had been enlarged, extended, and codified in various ways. Yet the change believed to have taken place under Pius marks a new departure, for this closely guarded right is extended to the *tiro* or recruit.[45] The emperor is crossing a line here, because the recruit is technically a civilian. Thus extension of this right marks the slight

---

Gilliver 1993: 33; Miller and DeVoto 1994: 61–2). None of this essentially changes my basic point here, however, that *cohors XX Palmyrenorum* does not fit the only known ancient source for the 'general' organization of milliary equitate cohorts.

[39] *De mun. castr.* 27.   [40] Gilliam (1965a: 74–81).   [41] Dio 71.46/16.

[42] For the *numerus*: *RIB* 583; for the *cuneus*: *Notitia Dignitatum Oc.* 40.54; for the *ala*: *RIB* 594 and 595.

[43] *RIB* 595.   [44] *RIB* 594.   [45] *Digest* 29.1.9.1.

shifting of a fundamental distinction in the Roman world: the division between soldier and civilian. On balance, however, it is difficult to see how radical the impact of this change could have been. In contrast, the change to discharge rights must have been very radical indeed.

Some time in November/December 140 the Empire ceased to award citizenship to the children of honourably discharged soldiers who had been born while their fathers were serving.[46] An exception was, however, made for the children of decurions and centurions, who continued to receive citizenship. This change, which would have seen a small but nonetheless significant drop in the number of people receiving citizenship annually, is clearly attested. It appears not only in the wording of the diploma certificates but also in that rare and important category of provincial records, the *epikrisis* documents. These documents detail the provincial prefect's hearings and the challenge of interpreting Roman law as it applied in the particular setting of Egypt.[47] The realization that other provinces would have had their own hearings, traditions, and records, now all lost to us, underscores the multiple complexities of incorporation. What is significant, though, is that both diploma and *epikrisis* records are in harmony with one another, giving us a sense of the reach and power of this transformation.

There is no scholarly consensus as to why this change came about. One early idea was that Pius was concerned that more citizen children meant fewer recruits for the *auxilia*,[48] yet it is clear that large numbers of citizens were still joining the *alae* and *cohortes* at this time. Another, that the motive was to encourage celibacy and thus foster good discipline, overlooks the fact that other arms of service were not treated in this way and that, furthermore, there is no hint of this attitude in official policy towards ordinary soldiers.[49] A further suggestion is that the authorities were alarmed at the number of soldiers' children receiving citizenship. While the notion that this was somehow seen as barbarizing the community of citizens should be treated with caution, it is nevertheless possible that the number of peregrine children so honoured shocked the authorities.[50] We have already seen that the proportion of auxiliaries declaring their families on diplomas reached a peak under Hadrian. Close reading of the diploma formulae at the end of his reign also suggests an attempt to clarify the situation, prevent abuses, and reduce the number of grants.[51] Awards are specifically made in the present tense, to ensure that earlier wives (and perhaps families) of soldiers cannot claim these precious rights alongside others. As with the Antonine extension of the frontiers, therefore, what may at first be deemed innovative is essentially driven by the desire to implement more fully an older idea. For those soldiers and families directly affected by it, however, the ruling of AD 140 was no less revolutionary for all that.[52]

---

[46] A diploma of AD 148 shows that the change has been implemented (Roxan 1986: 268).

[47] Mann and Roxan (1988).

[48] Lesquier (1918: 320).

[49] Mommsen advanced this idea in his discussion of *CIL* 3.2015. Fleet diplomas remain unchanged, suggesting that the issue was not in fact linked to general ideas of military discipline.

[50] For concern over the spread of citizenship to 'barbarian' folk, see Kraft (1951: 117–21). Phang (2001: 78) argues against this notion. For a commitment to reform abuses, see Wolff (1974: 492–6).

[51] Various rewordings are found from 138 onwards (Roxan 1986: 273–4).

[52] Eck (2007).

While citizen auxiliaries unofficially married to citizen women may have suffered less from this arrangement, and their sons would have had the option of gaining citizenship on enlistment,[53] even their families were now at a disadvantage. The sons were essentially obliged to enlist if they wanted to claim citizenship, the daughters remained non-citizens. For other groups the situation was much worse. The exceptional power the existing legal position gave to soldiers, allowing them essentially to abandon their 'wives' and children when choosing who, if anyone, to name on their diploma, only grew.[54] Roxan has noted that by depriving children born during military service of citizenship, the position of the wife was potentially further weakened. By the time her husband received citizenship she was likely to be beyond childbearing age. If he wanted citizen children, he could remarry and disown his existing family with full legal impunity. Even the families of devoted fathers clearly also suffered from the ruling.[55]

The drama of it all emerges once again through hearings of the prefect of Egypt. In AD 142, two years after the ruling, Octavius Valens, an Alexandrian citizen serving in an auxiliary cohort, petitioned that his three sons receive the same citizenship. The prefect swiftly established, however, that all three were born while Valens was in the army, and accordingly ruled them illegitimate. He notes in passing that this would be the case whether the father served in a legion, cohort, or *ala*—a comment that strongly suggests, incidentally, that soldiers of these units were still believed to have different entitlements in other respects at this date. Valens' parting plea, 'What wrong have the children committed?' is swiftly waved aside by the prefect, despite the difference holding the citizenship could have made to their lives.[56]

It is very tempting to link these changes to a gap in the archaeological record: no auxiliary diplomas are known between May 167 and early 177.[57] While it is possible that this striking gap may be reflect a halt in production or indeed the issuing of only wooden rather than both bronze and wooden variants, the explanation may also lie in the behaviour of veterans. The rights diplomas had once ensured soldiers' children had clearly been coveted, but now, without those rights, the diplomas were of less value and perhaps therefore fewer veterans bothered to acquire them. In the fleet and in the urban cohorts the rate of issues remains broadly constant, but not so in the *auxilia*. One wonders if the sheer size of Aurelius' accession donative was at least partly an attempt to compensate for the unpopularity of Pius' ruling.[58]

---

[53] Roxan (1986: 271).   [54] Gilliam (1978: 118–19).

[55] Roxan (1986: 276) examines four diplomas that actually name spouses after this date in support of this sad hypothesis.

[56] Mitteis and Wilcken (1912 II.2, no. 372, col 5.I).

[57] Roxan (1986: 275) and Greenberg (2003: 415, fig. 1). Eck (2003) notes this date range and suggests that it may be linked to an economy measure during the Marcommanic Wars, but this hypothesis is itself linked to his belief that all veterans ordinarily received diploma. If, as I believe, veterans purchased their own diploma, suspending provision would not have saved the state money.

[58] *SHA Marc.* 7.9. thank Simon James for raising this possiblity with me.

5

Shifting Fortunes

The *Auxilia* under the Severans

If the Antonine Period was marked especially by external pressures, the reign of the Severan dynasty was moulded by the experience of civil war. The struggle for hegemony taught its founder, Severus, several brutal lessons, lessons he paid for in full. The era witnessed dramatic shifts in fortunes: the rise and fall of cities, a rapid rise in the influence of the east, and a noteworthy enrichment of the soldiery. So pronounced was the dynasty's emphasis on its armies that it stretched beyond the emperors themeselves to their immediate circle, Severus' wife, the empress Julia Domna, received the title of *Mater Castrorum*, mother of the camp.[1] Tensions between the declining power of the Senate and the growing influence of the army became acute. But the most important shift under the Severans came not under Severus but under his son Caracalla, with the extension of citizenship to all the empire's free-born subjects.

The fears and hopes of this age were played out across the Roman world, but they were especially visible at the heart of the Empire. An appreciation of how the very fabric and population of Rome changed during this period is invaluable to understanding why contemporary historians wrote of the dynasty with fear and loathing. For while Severus spent much of his reign in the midst of campaigning armies on the fringes of empire, he also brought those armies to Rome itself. The city became an armed camp, and the ratio of soldiers to civilians reached an all-time high.

Gone now was the sensitivity of Augustus to the deployment of his Rhenish bodyguard: instead, the *equites singulares* who succeeded them were now doubled in number. A second fort was added close to the first to accommodate this growth, ensuring that a thousand auxiliary cavalrymen could now reach the historic centre of Rome in mere minutes. The establishment of the *Palatium Sessorianum* nearby demonstrates how, by the 3rd century, emperors were happy to reside amidst their soldiers. But the *equites singulares*, filled with men sent from the *alae* of the frontiers, were not the only soldiers whose presence attested the growing hold of provincial armies on the heart of empire. Where once exotic auxiliaries in Italy were drawn from Spain and Germany, the new arrivals came overwhelmingly from the Danube provinces.[2] They came to bolster not only the ranks of the horseguard, as they had done since Trajan, but also those of the legions and the

---

[1] Levick (2007).   [2] Coulston (2000: 82–6, 99) for the changing military complexion of Rome.

Praetorian Guard. Contemporaries famously stressed how savage and alien these men appeared to them.[3] Even allowing for a certain amount of literary licence, the alleged provincialism of Rome's own 'armed and belted men', and the presence of so many auxiliaries amongst them, underscores how close the *auxilia* could now stand to the centre of imperial power.

Something of the assertiveness of this new group may be found in the funerary monuments of the city. Whereas the paramilitary guardsmen of the Julio-Claudian *corporis custodes* had preferred discreet, nondescript memorials, the new guardsmen and their peers erected substantial monuments. This practice must be understood as part of what Bishop and Coulston have termed a 'renaissance' in the use of figural gravestones in *some* of the military communities of the Empire.[4] This renaissance testifies both to the wealth and status of soldiers and to distinctive changes in their appearance at this time. The use of Danubian iconography—especially that linked to the Thracian Hero—is especially marked, and indeed many such monuments have been found on the Upper and Middle Danube.[5] It is notable, however, that areas that produced large numbers of figural tombstones in the 1st and early 2nd century, notably Britain and the Rhineland, produce far fewer such monuments at this time. Often this is because the soldiers actually came from that region themselves, but increasingly the evidence points to changes in fashion that transcended the soldiers' origins.

While the civil war that had led to Severan victory had been proved especially long and brutal because the main contenders had each commanded substantial provincial armies, it would be wrong to see the conflict and its aftermath in terms of simple provincial or regional loyalties. Severus himself drew upon supporters from widely dispersed parts of the Empire. Archaeological evidence attests to his largesse to those who supported him. The famous African city of Lepcis Magna offers a vivid example of the impact of imperial patronage, but so too do many of the Danubian settlements. Research at many of these sites is now revealing an expansion of building under his reign.[6] In several cases this appears to coincide with promotion in city status. *Canabae* become *muncipia* and *municipia* become *coloniae*. A similar pattern may be found in the Near East, where Severus' actions reveal the raising up of some cities and the humiliation of others, such as as Berytus, which lost much of its territory as a punishment for supporting another contender, Niger. Conversely, the promotion of Laodicea first to metropolis or mother city status was followed with further promotion to the stature of *colonia* four years later in 198, all on account of its support for Severus.[7]

Millar observes that the 'malleability' of communal identities reflected in these promotions attests the importance of the local over the regional.[8] Ultimately, the competition for status which ultimately made such awards and punishments meaningful essentially undermined any growth of a wider regional identity. But there were broader patterns at work here, under both Severus and his successors.

---

[3] Dio 75.2.6.   [4] Bishop and Coulston (1993: 26).   [5] P. 376.

[6] Nicopolis ad Istrum in Bulgaria, which received Severus' gratitude for its generous donation to his campaigns (*IG Bulg* 2.659), seems to have thrived after his accession. Archaeological evidence comes in the form of a marked peak in official inscriptions from both buildings and statue bases during his reign (Poulter and Blagg 1995: 12).

[7] Millar (1993: 123).   [8] Millar (1993: 124).

Both Caracalla and Severus Alexander continued to promote cities in the manner of Severus, and in doing so made increasing use of the Roman title *colonia*. It is a device that reflects how the east was being drawn more closely than ever into the Roman fold. Yet, as was ever the way with incorporation, intensifying the ties to any one region had ramifications far beyond it. Rome's burgeoning interest in the east was reflected by Syria's growing hold over Rome. The force of that hold was to be seen in the fall not only of Macrinus, successor of Caracalla, but also of the exotic figure who replaced him, Elagabalus, chief priest of the sun god of Emesa.[9]

Wider concern with the east was also marked in Rome by the dedication of an Arch to Severus and his sons Caracalla and Geta in AD 203.[10] In celebrating both the restoration of the state and the extension of imperial territory, the wording of the dedicatory inscription records the ancient ambitions of many emperors. In this context, however, it refers to two hitherto elusive achievements: victory over Parthia and the foundation of a province of Mesopotamia. These conquests were to fundamentally change the balance of the power in the Near East, and were accompanied by a major redeployment of soldiers.

Part of the need for extra manpower was met by the recruitment of new legions. Just as Marcus had raised two legions in Italy in AD 165, so Severus raised another three *c.* AD 196.[11] This is a fascinating example of conservatism in Roman military administration. Even in the late 2nd century emperors persisted, as they had done with all new legions from the time of Augustus, in raising fresh formations from Italy itself. In this respect, it would appear, the legions remained distinctive. By contrast, there was not a problem with raising fresh auxiliary units outside Italy; indeed, it remained standard procedure.

The creation of new legions was one thing, supplying them with recruits quite another. Evidence from one of the regiments based in the east, the *Legio III Cyrenaica* stationed at Bostra in Arabia, reveals that in the 3rd century it was drawing recruits from rural communities with scant exposure to Greco-Roman urban culture.[12] Even in the early days of the Principate, when many legions in the west still contained Italians, the east had drawn in non-citizens, preferably from Hellenized cities. But by the 3rd century they were looking still further afield, beyond the areas with long-established Greek pedigrees and into Semitic-speaking communities. There was now little to distinguish the recruits joining some of them from those enrolling in the *auxilia*.

With the *Constitutio Antoniniana* of AD 212 the legal distinctions between legionary and auxiliary recruits were swept away. All free-born subjects were now citizens. The transformation is reflected in the rolls of *cohors XX Palmyrenorum*, where large numbers of first-generation citizens make an appearance.[13] The *alae* and *cohortes* were no longer non-citizen formations. Though part of a wider process of incorporation that drew the *auxilia* into the core of the army and the soldiers into the body of citizens, this was undoubtedly an important milestone. It also underpinned the distinction between both legions and *auxilia* and the other

---

[9] Millar (1993: 145).   [10] *CIL* 6.1033.

[11] Mann (1963: 485–6). Mann also reads Herodian (6.3.1) to suggest that Severus Alexander raised the *Legio IV Italica* in Italy in preparation for his Parthian campaign. The passage does not, however, specify a legion (A. R. Birley, pers. comm).

[12] Mann (1983: 42).   [13] Gilliam (1965a).

forces at Rome's disposal which remained an essential part of Rome's armies. Employment of irregular forces continued on a large scale, but so too did experiments with special formations. Caracalla had, for example, a much-resented force of *Leones*, who allegedly contained Goths and slaves in their ranks.[14] While some of the evidence of their irregular aspect may be no more than literary propaganda, there is nothing inherently improbable about claims that such men joined the army at this time.[15] In many respects they were, therefore, just one of the latest exemplars of incorporation, combining soldiers travelling from the peripheries of provincial society to a place at the heart of empire with others of more conventional stock.

Though reflecting a gradual rather than a dramatic shift, the archaeological evidence also suggests that the old distinction in dress and equipment between the legions and *auxilia* had disappeared by the end of the Severan period.[16] All troop types now used long swords, weapons that had once been the preserve of auxiliary cavalry.[17] Excavated evidence leaves little doubt that the basic troop-type division employed on Trajan's Column, and perpetuated in highly stylized form on the Arch of Severus, owed little to the appearance of contemporary soldiers.[18] The principal distinction now was between infantry and the different forms of cavalry.

As noted above, some of our key evidence for changes in dress comes from funerary monuments, and the many fine 3rd-century examples speak evocatively of a wealthy and confident soldiery. Indeed, in Rome itself, Coulston's suggestion that we might be able to see in this assertive soldiers defining themselves against a hostile civilian population is a compelling one.[19] As noted, hostility towards the increasingly prosperous armies of the time is a marked feature of contemporary commentators.

Describing Severus' campaigns in Britain in wholly misleading terms Dio addresses the notorious advice of the dying emperor to his sons.[20] While Caracalla rapidly disregarded his father's wish that the two work together, murdering his brother in short order thereafter, he clearly took his famous dictum on the army to heart. 'Enrich the soldiers, scorn the rest' became Caracalla's maxim in an even more profound sense than his father had intended. Severus was generous towards his soldiers, and under him their position as *honestiores*, distinguished from the bulk of the provincial population, the *humiliores*, was confirmed.[21] It was a distinction that counted for much, particularly as the old division between citizens and non-citizens fell away. The emergence of this new distinction, discernible by the mid-2nd century AD, ensured that the *honestiores*, initially those of the Senatorial and Equestrian orders and of curial classes, enjoyed important legal privileges, and indeed a different scale of punishments for crimes in comparison with the *humiliores*.[22] That soldiers now shared privileges with the *honestiores* was

---

[14] Dio 77.14.3.   [15] M. P. Speidel (1994b: 67).
[16] Bishop and Coulston (1993: 209): 'by the early third century, differentiation between legionaries and auxiliaries had practically disappeared.'
[17] Bishop and Coulston (1993: 126). Longer swords over time: James (2011: 32, fig 8 and 185).
[18] Coulston (2000: 93).   [19] Coulston (2000: 96).   [20] Dio 76.15.2.
[21] *Digest* 49.18.3; Mann (1983: 66).   [22] Garnsey (1970); Rilinger (1988).

very significant.[23] Such treatment was now combined with acts of calculated generosity. Severus had also allowed soldiers to wear gold rings, once an exclusive right of the Roman elite.[24] But for many soldiers, the single biggest change concerned money.

Severus had been the first emperor to raise the soldiers' pay since Domitian, but Caracalla increased it yet again within a few years of his father's death. According to Herodian, he was able to do this partly because he squandered all the resources his father had gained confiscating the fortunes of his opponents' supporters, but it is also clear that Caracalla significantly increased taxation. Indeed, this emerges as the primary motive in extending citizenship through the *Constitutio Antoniniana*, for the taxes on citizens were simultaneously doubled and they went to fund the *aerarium militare*, the military treasury.[25] The claim that, on the murder of his brother, he announced to his *commilitones* that he only wished to live to enrich them sounds at once tyrannically infantile and disturbingly plausible.[26] Caracalla certainly went to great lengths, discussed below, to build a special relationship with the troops and to appear as a fellow soldier, one who would guard their interests. It appears, however, that some provincial armies, notably those who had been loyal to his murdered brother, Geta, required more convincing of this special relationship than others.

The precedents of Severus and Caracalla's reigns were clearly dangerous. The failure of two of Caracalla's successors, Macrinus and Severus Alexander, to live up to the army's inflated expectations clearly contributed to their undoing.[27] Alexander enjoyed, after all, some real military successes in his reign. The Persian invasion of Mesopotamia in AD 230 was countered and the province recovered. There is no reason to believe that the especially large numbers of loyalty declarations from this time are wholly formulaic. Yet at the same time the stress on loyalty also reflected the stress under which loyalty might be placed. While better fiscal management reduced Alexander's scope to buy the men's allegiance, it was warfare on the Rhine and Danubian frontiers that brought the young emperor down. The soldiers were no longer convinced that Alexander was really their type of emperor. He was too readily dismissed as a weak, unmilitary figure dominated by his mother.[28] The soldiers sought a real fellow soldier as their emperor, one who would see to their interests. With the death of Alexander at the hands of his own soldiers, the Severan dynasty came to an end.

What did the growing influence of the soldiers mean for their families? While it is difficult to gauge how much the increase in salaries would have made a difference, because inflation may actually have outstripped it, there are other signs of improved conditions. It appears that in general, military families enjoyed greater stability than ever before. The itinerant lifestyle of earlier generations was

---

[23] James (2011: 199). In most respects soldiers, and most certainly veterans, enjoyed the legal privileges of the *honestiores*. See *Digest* 49.18.1.3 and the discussion by Alston (1999: 62). Note, however, Le Bohec's (1994: 88) reservations.

[24] Reinhold (1971: 287); Herodian 3.8.5.

[25] Dio 77.9.4–5; A. R. Birley (1988: 190).

[26] The remark was addressed to the Praetorians, but took on a wider resonance (Dio 77.3.2).

[27] Macrinus specifically blamed Caracalla's pay rise for his impossible predicament (Dio 78.36.2).

[28] Herodian 6.8.3 and 6.9.5.

possibly less common, for when armies went on campaign many of their families stayed behind. This at least is the implication of an important passage in Herodian.[29] In what was an increasingly common pattern, soldiers from the Danube were sent to reinforce armies in the east, while eastern units often made the journey in reverse. When Severus Alexander set out to recapture Mesopotamia he followed this practice, but the successful operations of his army were soon soured by news from their Danubian homes. News that German tribes had breached the *limes* meant that many in his army were desperate to return home and protect their families. The temporary encampments that were once found alongside forts had long since become permanent settlements with stone houses, and it was understandable that soldiers' families should have felt more secure in such quarters than enduring the rigours of campaign.

That the imperial authorities encouraged such developments is perhaps suggested in the ancient sources. A brief comment in the *Digest*, datable to the 220s, notes the issuing of land along the frontiers to veterans.[30] The *Historia Augusta*, a notoriously unreliable source, goes a stage further. It says that Severus Alexander granted such lands to veterans on the condition that their sons followed them into the ranks.[31]

It is frequently argued that the Severan period saw the overturning of the Augustan marriage ban.[32] Herodian refers somewhat ambiguously to this right in a passage in which he charges Severus with corrupting the army and militarizing the state.[33] The historical date for the alleged reform is AD 197, after Severus' victory over Clodius Albinus in the battle of Lyon.[34] The difficulty hinges on the translation of *gunaixi . . . sunoikein*. This could be translated as either 'the right to live with women' or the 'right to marry women'; up until recently most commentators have taken it to mean the latter. The discovery of a diploma of AD 206 issued to a soldier in the *ala Herculana* in Egypt makes it clear, however, that soldiers' 'marriages' did not enjoy full legal recognition under Severus.[35] If they did, it would have made no sense to grant *conubium* at this date. And indeed, there is evidence that grants of *conubium* were still being made to discharged veterans at a much later date, under the reign of Maximinus. Such a grant is also recorded on a diploma issued to a member of the *equites singulares* in AD 237.[36]

If there is any substance to Herodian's claim at all, therefore, it must be that Severus relaxed discipline to allow soldiers to cohabit routinely with their female partners. That some such cohabitation must have been arranged periodically, at the very least, is evidenced by the number of soldiers who had families; but the implication of Herodian's observation might be better understood as larger numbers of soldiers living outside the fort walls, and perhaps even more civilians living inside them than was already the case. The camp becomes less the soldier's home and more simply his place of work.

Whatever the precise arrangements and their impact, it is clear that the Severan period saw a significant improvement in the status and conditions of soldiers' families. In the ongoing pattern of empire, we see again the power of incorporation

---

[29] Herodian 6.7.3.   [30] *Digest* 21.2.11.   [31] *SHA Sev. Alex.* 58. 4.
[32] Phang (2001: 17, 18–19, 381–2).   [33] Herodian 3.8.5.
[34] Hasebroek (1921: 99–100); Phang (2001: 18).   [35] Eck (2011).
[36] Garnsey (1970: 50–51). The diploma concerned is *CIL* 16.146.

drawing auxiliaries and their families ever deeper into evolving networks of rights and privileges.

THE LIMITS OF INCORPORATION

The limits of incorporation are perhaps best exemplified in the short reign of Maximinus Thrax. The received story of his life, the tale of an auxiliary cavalry-man who becomes emperor, would appear a fitting finale for our analysis. Yet even if we chose to dismiss this tale as a creation of Herodian, embelished in the *Historia Augusta*, it is clear that Maximinus' reign witnessed key developments in *Integrationspolitik*. His three years in power coincide with the discharge of the last of the auxiliaries enrolled before the *Constitutio Antoniniana*. They also saw the Empire change in a fundamental way. Maximinus' life represents the culmination of the ideal of the emperor as fellow soldier; he was the first to wear the purple and to fight in the thick of the battle line.[37] Yet as the first of the so-called soldier emperors he was also herald of a new and more dangerous age. His reign marked the last great clash between emperor and Senate, exposed gaping fault-lines within the dynamics of incorporation, and marked the beginning of the drama known to historians as the Third Century Crisis.

While the origins of Maximinus are disputed, what is unequivocally the case is that his rise to power must be seen in the context of the Danubian armies. Later nicknamed Thrax because of his Thracian/Lower Moesian origins, he had commanded Panno-nian troops under his predecessor, Severus Alexander.[38] In a world where the powers of the armies had grown, he fulfilled what appeared to be the single most important qualification: he could lead them to victory. And indeed, his operations on the Rhine were proclaimed a triumph in AD 235, mere months after his succession.

Yet victory on the frontier was still not enough in the Roman order, and in Rome trouble was brewing. Maxminus gave little thought to securing support there, leaving dignitaries waiting for the moment when they might commemorate his succession in traditional style. For this fighting emperor, however, there were too many other priorities. He swiftly moved from the Rhine to confront new enemies on the Danube. Prioritizing provincial action over senatorial courtesies was to prove a dangerous, if understandable, mistake, for when Gordian I led a revolt in Africa the Senate condemned Maximinus, formally depriving him of his powers.[39]

The events that followed reveal much of the character of the army and its relationship to provincial society. Maximinus turned towards Rome. Once again there were many auxiliaries in his force, but they were very different in origins and appearance from the Spanish horsemen with whom we began our story. The irregulars were notably conspicuous amongst them. Moors, extensively used by the Roman army over the years, were there in force. They had served Rome well in

---

[37] Herodian 7.2.6.
[38] Syme (1971: 179–93). Maximinus is not in fact recorded as Thrax before the *Epitome de Caesaribus* (written *c.* AD 395). As Syme observes, however, it is quite likely that he did come from one of the Thracian provinces, if not *Thracia* itself then *Moesia Inferior*.
[39] Herodian 7.7.2; *AE* 1935.164.

the Rhine campaigns and their leader in the 2nd century AD, Lusius Quietus, whose career is noted above, had gone on to become a consul. Now they were an integral part of Maximinus' new invasion of Italy.

Alongside these irregulars were other units, regiments whose appearance spoke of distant cultures and frontiers. There were oriental archers with reflex bows. Cataphract cavalry, of the type Roman soldiers jokingly termed *clibanarii* or 'oven-men' on account of their extensive armour, were seen in flesh and metal for the first time on Italian soil.[40] If the armies of the Severans had seemed alien, that of Maximinus must have seemed still more so. Yet within these forces even more revolutionary changes were taking place. These changes again testify to the Roman tendency to incorporate men and ideas from elsewhere.

An inscription from Intercisa in Hungary that records the career of a decurion in one of these remarkable *alae* tells us much about the army around this time.[41] His name was Barsemis Abbei, and he came from Osrhoena, an area reduced to a province as recently as the reign of Septimius Severus. The peoples of this region became an increasingly important source of recruits at this time, and several irregular units were formed from them. Yet rather than being seen as second-tier troops, it is evident that the Osrhoene soldiers were especially respected, appearing at the heart of many campaign armies. Furthermore, as the career of Barsemis indicates, they were sometimes detached to other units to train them. For Barsemis began in a *numerus Hosroruorum/Osrhoenorum*, became a decurion in the *ala Firma Catafractaria*, and ended up a training officer for *cohors Hemesenorum sagittariorum*. The very fact that a man who may well have been a non-citizen could transfer through such posts reveals much about how the army had changed. The growing role of ethnic units was soon to reduce the regular *auxilia*, and indeed their legionary counterparts, a second-class role.

As Maximinus began his invasion of Italy, events in Africa were reaching a horrific climax. The legionary legate in Numidia remained loyal to the Danubian emperor. His forces slaughtered the Senate-backed contender, Gordian, and his son at Carthage. Then they vented their fury on the civilian population, slaughtering not only the landowners who had backed Gordian but many more besides.[42] A couple of key points emerge from this gory tale. The first is that in the richly networked world of the Roman Empire the original uprising, with its resentments against high taxes and its strong local leadership, could never simply be a regional revolt. The disturbance had profound implications, both in terms of the reason for the taxes, the financing of distant wars, and in terms of senatorial politics. The second lesson comes from the bloodletting itself. Shaw sees it as notable that an army that had been stationed in Africa for so long could turn on the civilian population in this way.[43] Even after generations of service in the provinces, the military community was still first and foremost at the service of the emperor. It might bring, through its recruitment and through its families, many provincials ever closer into the orbit of Roman power, but its relationship with local populations was always ultimately secondary to its interdependence on imperial power.

---

[40] Herodian 8.1.10.   [41] *ILS* 2540; p. 138.   [42] Kolb (1977) for the revolt.
[43] Shaw (1983: 148). Sadly, of course, there are all too many examples of armies doing just that even in our own time.

Part II

The Human Resource

The Recruitment of the Auxilia *and
its Consequences*

6

The Captive Body

Individual Recruitment

Rome's harvesting of provincial manpower was an unprecedented achievement with extraordinary consequences. It was almost as important as her capacity to harvest natural resources, for it sustained for generations the ranks of guardsmen, legionaries, sailors, and auxiliaries essential for the preservation of the emperor's writ. In the case of the *auxilia* alone, recruitment has been repeatedly cited as one of the most important instruments of cultural transformation within the Empire.[1] As a mechanism of incorporation, one of its most tangible products was the steady growth of the citizen body as enrolled auxiliaries went on to honourable discharge and citizen status. Yet the way in which this capacity was exploited varied significantly across time and place. Rome did not harvest its human resource evenly. Furthermore, a moment's reflection on the size of the *auxilia*, which required no more than 10,500 recruits annually and quite possibly significantly less, reminds us that many communities in an Empire of 50 million or more souls were seldom directly affected.[2] Recruitment was, after all, closely linked to other forms of taxation—imperial expectations and local capabilities varied significantly.[3] Both must be studied if recruitment is to be fully understood. Processes of incorporation, as men were absorbed first into the military corps and subsequently into the citizen body, were themselves dependent upon other changes within provincial society. The incorporation of local elites is an essential element of the same story. These diverse strands did not advance in isolation, but neither did they take the same form across provincial society.

This chapter presents two glimpses of the way in which individuals were pulled into service within the auxilia. The first examines elite participation in early 1st-century Thrace; the second details the experience of recruits to an auxiliary unit in Egypt almost a century later.

---

[1] Millar (1981: 5): 'the recruitment of non-citizens into the auxiliaries and their discharge as citizens was one factor in the Romanization of the provinces.'

[2] The highest estimate: Haynes (2001: 63). Cherry (1998: 95–6) argues that at any one time the estimated 150,000 auxiliaries formed at the most 0.3% of the population. For the population of the provinces at between 44–54 million with a further 6 million for Italy, see Hopkins (1978: i.68). Scheidel (2010: 432) would accept a lower figure, believing that 15,000 recruits were required annually for the legions, *auxilia*, and navy combined.

[3] As Enloe (1980: 50) has observed, levies are best understood as a form of taxation in most empires.

Fig. 6.1. Masked helmet from the tumulus at Vize in Turkey. Early 1st century AD. Istanbul Archaeological Museums.

In 1938 Arif Müfid Mansel excavating at Vize (ancient Bizye) in Turkey opened a magnificent tumulus.[4] Silver cups adorned with scenes of Bacchic revelry, gold rings set with delicately carved intaglios, fine candlesticks and bronze lamps discovered in the tumulus attest to the wealth and classical connections of the deceased. Complementing these are the symbols of military power: an iron sword, a suit of scale armour recalling the martial traditions of the east, and a spectacular silvered helmet complete with face mask (see Fig. 6.1). It is the helmet that has perhaps attracted the most attention, for it carries all the classic symbols of Roman dominion. Save for its moulded face mask, the form of the helmet is instantly familiar to any student of 1st-century auxiliary cavalry tombstones—its Attic form with brow plate and skull covered with a representation of human hair.[5] Yet this is no ordinary trooper's helmet, for the hair is topped with an oak leaf crown, while trophy-bearing victories disport themselves on the cheek pieces. Clearly the deceased was prepared to associate himself with the triumphant iconography of the Empire.

Though many rulers on the fringes of Roman power who would have delighted in such treasures, the setting and dating of this particular assemblage would have

[4] Mansel (1941: 151–89); my thanks to Oğuz Yarligaş for discussing the excavation.
[5] Robinson (1975: 118).

suited one particular individual very well.[6] The tumulus almost certainly commemorates Rhoemetalkes III, the last Sapeian king, and the man who with Roman backing was nominated king of all Thrace in AD 38.[7]

When in AD 26 the tribes of Thrace feared that the demands of Rome would grow beyond the familiar requirements of foreign powers, namely mercenaries and short-term alliances, they rebelled. The imposition of a regular levy was quite a different matter. Tacitus himself likens it to a form of enslavement.[8] The tribes' fears, that their clans would be broken up and mixed with outsiders and then sent to foreign lands, were to be amply borne out.[9] Exploiting local politics to suit imperial ambitions, a well-established strategy, the Romans brought in other Thracians to suppress revolt. King Rhoemetalkes I had already led his countrymen in support of Roman operations to suppress mutinous auxiliaries and their kin in the Pannonian War of AD 6–9.[10] Now his namesake, Rhoemetalkes II, commanded Thracians still loyal to Rome, and in doing so, essentially led the way for Rome to tap what was to prove one of her most important sources of manpower for the *auxilia*.[11] Reward from Rome came to the family in various forms, including in the nomination of Rhoemetalkes' successor, Rhoemetalkes III as king of all Thrace in AD 38. With the chaos that threatened to follow his death in AD 45, Rome found it suited her interests better to incorporate Rhoemetalkes III's dominions as a province. With the creation of this province of Thracia recruitment of soldiers intensified.

The Vize tumulus offers a striking snapshot of a Thracian noble in the formative politics of provincial society. We see here a dynamic enacted in different local settings across much of the Roman world at this time. The symbols and capital of Roman power are manipulated by local leaders, often as instruments against their neighbours, but these leaders thus become ever more dependent on Roman capital—wealthy, powerful, but captive bodies nonetheless.[12] Their military power grows as it is linked to their capacity to oblige Roman interests. This is particularly evidenced in Thrace, a region destined to become one of the most important reservoirs of military manpower tapped by Rome.[13] Though particularly spectacular, the assemblage of Vize is not unique in the potent juxtaposition of wealth, indigenous tradition, and Roman military equipment—the well-known villa site of Chatalka recalls a similar blend.[14] In time, as members of the Thracian elite become obliged to seek power and influence within a new Roman order, civil symbols become more potent or at least more accessible than those of the old martial order. Within a few decades of the death of Rhoemetalkes, the responsibility for the levy passed to members of the new Roman Thracian administration—indeed, we even find a *phylarch* (local magistrate) involved in its execution.[15]

---

[6] The dating is partly based on the helmet style, though Mansel saw a link between the tomb decoration and the early Augustan 'Second Style' wall paintings in the House of Livia.

[7] Hoddinott (1981: 45, 130).   [8] e.g. Tacitus *Ann.* 4.46 and *Hist.* 4.17.

[9] Tacitus *Ann.* 4.46.

[10] Velleius Paterculus 2.112; my thanks to Matthew Schueller for discussion.

[11] Tacitus *Ann.* 4.47.

[12] Roman military equipment emerges in an impressive array of archaeological contexts prior to and during the early phases of provincial incorporation, from the rich tomb of Es Soumâa in Algeria (Waurick 1979) to the Folly Lane harness fittings of England (Niblett 1999: 143–5). For an excellent discussion of the possible social context of such material, see Creighton (2001, 5–6).

[13] Zahariade (2009: 59–112).   [14] Bujukliev (1986: 71–4).   [15] *IG Bulg* II.517.

A very different glimpse of enlistment emerges in a papyrus of 24 February, AD 103, a letter received from the prefect (governor) by the commander of a cohort of Ituraeans stationed in Egypt.[16] The letter instructed him to enter six young men into the ranks of his regiment. A copy of the document was duly filed in the regimental records office; the men's military career had now begun. The record is brief, but richly informative. The names, ages, and distinguishing marks of the men are given. It was a reminder that their bodies now belonged to the army. Should they try to run away, their distinguishing marks—on one a scar on the eyebrow, on another a scar on the side of the forehead—will help ensure that they are identified and returned. Their literal incorporation into Rome's armed forces had now begun.

So important was this process that it had begun with an examination by the prefect himself or his immediate representatives. Tight control of the army, in both imperial and senatorial provinces, ensured that this process was carried out at the highest levels of provincial administration, even when such a small number of men were involved. The Oxyrhynchus papyrus on which this text is recorded explicitly states that the prefect had approved the men concerned. The parallelism between the human resource and the natural one is clear here. In Egypt, as quite probably in most other provinces, it was the prefect's office that coordinated supply of food and equipment to army units. Records of the complex process of supply show how some villages were instructed to provide commodities for auxiliary regiments over 300 km away.[17] The prefect was central, therefore, to supplying all that was needed for the provincial army to operate.

The prefect's approval was no mere formality. To reach this stage, a recruit had to be able to prove that he was of appropriate status. 'Appropriate', of course, was a Roman definition and though it followed some Empire-wide rules, there were further province-specific criteria. To join the *auxilia* in Egypt, for example, we know that it was not sufficient simply to be free-born; native Egyptians were not permitted to enlist. Free-born status was considered everywhere essential, except in the exceptional case of the rushed creation of the *cohortes ingenuorum* detailed above. Less than eight years after the prefect's letter, the governor of Bithynia discovered that two slaves had attempted to enter an auxiliary unit. The matter was serious enough to be directed to the emperor immediately. His response was that if they had volunteered they should be executed; otherwise whoever was responsible for presenting them should be punished.[18]

The army respected the Empire-wide distinction between citizen and non-citizen, just as it did that between free-born and slave. Auxiliaries were not required to have citizenship, though as we will see a growing number did so by the early 2nd century; but for legionaries to enrol without citizenship was a grave offence. The distinct enlistment criteria for the two parts of the army were clearly enforced.[19] Another papyrus from Egypt records that in AD 92 an *optio* of the *Legio III Cyrenaica* had to swear an oath that he was a freeborn Roman citizen.[20]

---

[16] *P. Oxy.* VII.1022 = *CPL* III.

[17] *P. Amh.* II.107 of AD 185: villagers from the Hermopolite *nome* supplied barley for the *ala Heracliana* at Coptos.

[18] Pliny *Letters* 10.29–30.

[19] There is evidence for non-citizens serving in the legions from the end of the 1st century AD, but it nonetheless appears clear that citizens were the vast majority of the legionary body (Forni 1953: 103–5).

[20] *CPL* 102.

What would have happened if he had proved to be free-born but not a Roman citizen is unclear, but it was clearly still a serious matter. As noted in the previous chapter, imperial interest in these matters is further demonstrated by a change in the rights given to discharged auxiliaries from late AD 140. Their children were no longer automatically entitled to citizenship. The most plausible suggestion is that this was intended to help with auxiliary recruitment. Male children may then only have received citizenship on enlistment.[21]

Even in its earliest stages, then, the recruitment process reinforced the categories of legal status that defined the Roman world and one's place within it. But it quickly becomes clear that recruitment had still more complex relations within the social order. While the Roman soldier would have been appalled at the notion that he was in any sense a slave, there can be no doubt that particularly in the 1st century, his condition bore some resemblance to that condition.[22] In this we see again the paradoxes that are central to the Roman definition of the soldier: the privileged man with fewer rights than other free men, the richly armoured warrior who might yet be called to back-breaking labour. Different recruits, volunteers and conscripts alike, no doubt viewed this paradox differently. In some provincial societies, military service was probably linked to higher status, in others to drudgery. For some men, the discipline of the army liberated them from the constraints of tribal society and allowed a level of social mobility that was otherwise impossible. We cannot know how each community viewed enlistment, but it is worth remembering that in more recent armies curious divisions have emerged. Bengali soldiers of the East India Company were, for example, of markedly higher status and frequently better educated than their British-born equivalents;[23] the imbalance in status between those perceived as auxiliaries and those understood to be of greater military standing generated situations ripe for discontent and, in some cases, violence. Certainly tensions between auxiliaries and legionaries did arise, and competing claims of status cannot have helped alleviate them. On one occasion the crowing by a Gallic auxiliary about his victory in a wrestling match with a soldier of the Fifth Legion goaded the legionaries to wipe out two entire auxiliary cohorts.[24] It is quite possible that some of the pressure emerging from diverse attitudes to military status were alleviated by divisions within the *auxilia*. In general the cavalry units, a number of which appear to have arisen from the entourage of indigenous nobles, enjoyed higher status, kept more servants, and undertook fewer labour-intensive building projects. Furthermore, the well-connected were able to employ the Empire-wide currency of patronage to ensure better postings.[25] Letters of recommendation made all the difference to life in the Roman army.

What is clear is that for those with the means and the inclination it was possible to avoid conscription. This is evident from Trajan's letter to Pliny in which he describes three categories of recruit: the *voluntarii*, *lecti*, and *vicarii*. The *lecti* were conscripts, while the *vicarii* were men substituted by others in their place. Such a system must, in practice, have reduced the pool of quality recruits at the army's

---

[21] Roxan (1986: 265–6). See also pp. 83–4, 'The Auxilia and the Structures of Imperial Power'.

[22] Josephus *Bell. Iud.* 2.70 sees soldiers as of servant class.

[23] It is also worth noting that particularly humiliating punishments, such as flogging, were outlawed in the British Bengal Army before they were outlawed in the British Army itself (Mason 1974: 202–3).

[24] Tacitus *Hist.* 2. 68.   [25] See pp. 328–9, 'Tongue, Pen and Sword'.

disposal, but it was just too Roman a practice, with its ready response to privilege, to be dropped. Idealized images of the Roman army frequently understate the degree to which conscription was a regular feature of provincial life. In part this is because of a peculiar scholarly belief that inevitably the average man would find nothing more appealing than a secure career in one of history's most famous armies. The reality was probably rather different. Though assured meals and a regular income were probably very genuine incentives to many, twenty-five years tied to military service and the real likelihood of being separated from friends and family permanently were surely far from universally appealing. In fact much of the confusion appears to stem from ancient sources on the end of the *dilectus*— sources which in fact are referring to Italy, rather than to the Empire as a whole. In reality, even at the apogee of the volunteer army men were still hunting down draft dodgers in the Empire's villages. Recruitment's power as an instrument of incorporation owes much to the fact that it was not in any sense restricted to willing candidates.

Discussion of conscription and exemption inevitably raises questions as to the kind of men who actually found their way into the ranks of the *auxilia*. Many commentators have drawn heavily on the recommendations of Vegetius, which while of a later date are widely believed to recall practice under the Principate. While a certain amount of scepticism is required when dealing with this material, it offers some interesting insights into Roman ideals. Vegetius advises that soldiers should be recruited from the 'more temperate', northern lands, rather than the south, for he sees the men of such regions as more virile.[26] This preference is certainly evident in the actual pattern of recruitment. He then goes on to argue that the recruits should be sought from the country rather than the town.[27] While this preference recalls a literary *topos*—the generally unimpressive attributes of the urban male—it nonetheless would also fit with what we know of the army and the wider population.[28] Simply put, the vast majority of the population lived in the countryside anyway. What is more interesting from the point of view of this study, however, was that military life was ultimately a species of urban life. Soldiers themselves were either billeted in towns or stationed in fortlets, forts, and fortresses with pronounced town-like features. Much of the incorporative experience of military service involved taking those from rural communities less exposed to the Empire's towns and introducing them to this lifestyle.[29] Finally, Vegetius emphasizes the moral calibre of the ideal recruit. They were not to be drawn from inappropriate professions, such as pastry cooks and textile workers, but from hearty physical professions, such as smiths and huntsmen.[30]

A defining feature of much recent research into recruitment is the study of the soldiers' names. The prefect's letter suggests some of the difficulties inherent in this nonetheless valuable approach. The first point of interest is that each of the six men enrolled has three names, the *tria nomina* normally associated with the Roman citizen. Are we to assume that every one of these auxiliary recruits was a citizen? It is certainly possible, but it is far from certain. By the end of the 1st

---

[26] Vegetius 1.2.   [27] Vegetius 1.3.

[28] e.g. Cato *Res Rustica*, pr. For military service in towns corrupting: Tacitus *Ann.* 13.35; Vegetius 1.3.

[29] See pp. 145–64.   [30] Vegetius 1.7.

century some *peregrini* were adopting this fashion.[31] This makes it very difficult to assess the growing number of citizens in the *auxilia*, itself a reflection of the ongoing incorporation of provincial society. Attempts to calculate the changing ratio of *peregrini* to *cives* on the basis of surviving epitaphs and documents must be regarded with considerable caution, but reinforce the impression that more and more citizens were making themselves at home in the ranks of these non-citizen formations.[32] Several soldiers give explicit information about their citizen status. Growing numbers of citizens in the *alae* and *cohortes* would, over time, narrow the gap between the *auxilia* and the legions. Nevertheless, in the day-to-day reality of provincial society, citizenship came to mean less, until in the edict of Caracalla in AD 212 it was formally extended across the free-born of the Empire.

Leaving aside the fact that Roman servicemen are known to have changed their names on enlistment to facilitate their integration,[33] the names of individuals have often been seen as a key to ascertaining their origins. While this form of analysis may be useful under the early Empire, it becomes less convincing when applied to 2nd- and 3rd-century nomenclature. Evolutions in naming are themselves a feature of imperial incorporation. Naming practices outgrew the associations they once held, and in time provinces developed stocks of names.[34] A single family could include members with traditional Latin names and others with names of decidedly local origins. Given such practices, it seems entirely unlikely that their owner perceived them as either Roman or non-Roman names; they were simply interchangeable. No greater tribute to the impact of incorporation upon provincial society need be sought.

If we do, however, review the name origins of our six recruits, one point stands out. None of them has a name that would associate them with the regiment's homeland. One, a Saturninus, carries a name most strongly associated with the African provinces, miles from the Lebanon Mountains of the Ituraeans. This is a crucial point, as not only did the ethnic unity of auxiliary units break down with subsequent drafts of recruits, it breaks down also in the Syrian units—long regarded as an exception. We will return to this point later, but for the moment it is worth noting one other challenge that faces the student of auxiliary recruitment. In the vast majority of cases, our knowledge of the rank and file within a regiment at any given time consists of a couple of inscriptions at most. When, exceptionally, a longer list of soldiers survives, it quite frequently defies our expectations. One such exceptional document is a papyrus of AD 117.[35] It records that when *cohors I Lusitanorum*, another unit in the Egyptian army, received a draft of 123 new recruits, the men came not from the unit's original base in Spain, nor from Egypt, nor from the neighbouring African provinces, but from Asia. Though this draft may have arrived to replace severe casualties incurred during

---

[31] Lesquier (1918: 219–23) notes that the *tria nomina* are not a reliable indication of Roman citizenship.

[32] Kraft (1951: 80–81) attempted to tabulate this change on the basis of data from the Rhine and the Danube, suggesting that while only 7 of 92 known auxiliaries of the Julio-Claudian period were citizens, 38 of 97 Flavio-Trajanic auxiliaries had this status, as did 27 of 53 who died between the ascension of Hadrian and c. AD 170. Le Bohec (1994: 98) has reproduced these figures as part of a generalized argument about the increasing numbers of citizens.

[33] *BGU* 423.22–3: a sailor tells his father of his new name.

[34] As Tomlin (1988: 97) suggests of the people of Roman Bath.   [35] *RMR* 74.

the Jewish Revolt of AD 115–116, the particular circumstances preceding its arrival are irrelevant to the material point. Rome's armies were prepared to reach as far as was required to keep them up to strength, and had little interest in the problems that this might present later generations of epigraphers. Understood in this light, the cosmopolitan mix of men on the Adamklissi memorial becomes more readily comprehensible.[36] Yet such a mix is inherently frustrating to those who seek more from the rich array of inscriptions that testifies to the diverse make-up of the army. Might some clues as to the existence of ordered imperial practice be recovered amidst this complexity?

[36] *CIL* 3.14214 lists 21 soldiers from a single unit. See p. 2.

7

Geopolitics

How Rome Selectively Exploited the Manpower of the Provinces

The way in which the raising of auxiliaries was conducted across the Empire has much to tell us about the diverse impact of incorporation. From the perspective of the authorities, it can be considered in two forms. Most accessible to enquiry is the issue of where regiments were raised. Here, unit titles often indicate the place of formation. More complex is the question of how to maintain units at full strength after they had been created. Analysis of the evidence suggests that while there were regions such as Thrace which made a major contribution to both the creation of entire units and the ongoing supply of manpower, there were also regions such as the Iberian Peninsula which went from being key providers prior to the Flavian period to becoming a minor source thereafter. It is important to try to get behind the dry statistics that suggest varied exploitation of manpower resources, and to appreciate some of their social implications.

It is appropriate to begin this discussion with a review of the creation of auxiliary regiments; taken together, the roll of these units—over 80 *alae* and over 300 *cohortes*—offer a fascinating snapshot of Rome's perception of her world.[1] We do not know for certain at what level the decision to establish permanent regiments was taken, but it seems impossible that it was at anything less than the highest levels of government. The association with high-level decision-making and the fact that a high proportion of these units were established in the formative years of the Julio-Claudians, the time when so many long-lasting treaty arrangements with the peoples of empire were established, makes it all the more interesting to see how the manpower demands of the new foundations first manifested themselves.

Even the so-called 'ethnic' and 'national' titles of these new formations reflect a sea change in the geopolitics of the ancient world. Though scholars often treat them as if they reflect a more ancient reality, it quickly becomes apparent that they reflect Roman notions of provincial society. As always, there is some truth in these perceptions, but there is also a clear element of selectivity to them. This is most

---

[1] Spaul's study of *alae* (1994) and cohorts (2000) identifies 86 *alae* and 302 cohorts. Le Bohec (1994: 96) finds 383 auxiliary units. I follow these figures in preference to the far larger one of MacMullen (1984: 571) of 486 regiments.

evident in the titles of units that carry the names of provinces—entities which few if any provincials could have identified with before imperial incorporation. It is also, however, a feature of many other contingents carrying tribal names which were ostensibly raised, as Cheesman argued, because 'clan spirit' amongst them remained so strong.[2] This argument about 'clan spirit' will require further investigation.

Many of the tribal or regional names adopted during the Roman period were either distorted,[3] created,[4] or perpetuated by imperial authorities when they might otherwise have died out. We can not always see the link between regimental origins and provincial administrative units, but in most cases some such connection may be made. Thus the units of northwestern Tarraconensis discussed below were raised on the *conventus* system introduced by Augustus to help govern an area with few major settlements;[5] the units of Gallia Belgica are frequently associated with the Roman *civitas* system, ostensibly based on existing tribal units; and the regiments drawn from Syria carry the titles of ancient city states—necessarily the basis of Roman administration in the Near East.[6]

Over three-quarters (78.5%) of the auxiliary regiments that sustained the Empire came from Europe; indeed, rather over half (56%) came from western Europe alone. Asia provided about 15% of the units formed and Africa the remaining 6.5 per cent.[7] At first glance, these figures would appear to support conventional Roman rhetoric of martial races, the war-like peoples of the Celtic west contrasted with the faintly effeminate but prosperous peoples of the east.[8] Such distinctions are the common currency of more recent imperial discourse.[9] But Roman need for military manpower had frequently demanded that she looked beyond mere stereotypes to supply her armies. Furthermore, when we look beyond these broad trends, we find a far more nuanced handling of the human resource, one that shows subtle principles of social engineering applied with equal vigour to west and east alike.

A greater challenge lies in determining the relative contributions of regions to the ongoing provision of manpower required to sustain units once they had been created. While we can be confident that we know the origins of the vast majority of auxiliary regiments,[10] the same cannot be said of the individuals who served in their ranks. What is known comes in the first instance from *origines* specified on epitaphs and diplomas, and these survive intact for only a minute fraction of the

---

[2] Cheesman (1914: 57–8).

[3] Strabo, for example, notes the Roman distortion of geopolitical terms in the case of Gaul (*Geog.* 177, 4.1.1) and Asia Minor (626, 13.4.12).

[4] e.g. the Batavi (Tacitus *Germania* 29).

[5] Mommsen (1884: 47).

[6] Cheesman argues, 'The distinction was not necessarily connected with the position of *civitas foederata* in the technical sense' (1914: 58 n.1). This is partially correct, but does not detract from the fact that units were clearly raised on the basis of Roman perceptions of territory.

[7] See Le Bohec (1994: 96) and Haynes (2001: 63–4) for figures.

[8] See Strabo *Geog.* 4.1.14 and Caesar *De Bello Gallico* 6.15. As Webster (1996) reminds us, we must treat these observations with caution.

[9] For parallels between notions of martial races in Roman and modern empires, See Driel-Murray (2003).

[10] After over a century of intense research, the number of auxiliary units known to scholarship has only increased by about 7 units.

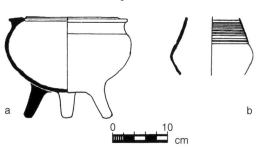

Fig. 7.1. Two examples cited by Swan (2009: 30 and 72) in support of her view that cooking pots and drinking vessel types may reveal the ethnic origins of recruits. (**a**) A Gallic tripod bowl from Claudian Hoffheim (after Ritterling 1913). The fact that this form is not found in indigenous settlements on the Lower Rhine at this date may suggest that it came with auxiliary recruits from elsewhere. (**b**) A *vase tronconique* in North Gaulish Grey Ware from late 1st/early 2nd century Vindolanda (after Hird 1977). This is also an intrusive form, and may reflect the attested presence of northern Gaulish units at the fort.

men who once served in the *auxilia*. Attempts to supplement these with onomastic analyses of soldiers' names enlarge this number but, as noted above, this approach can be intensely problematic.

Other, more archaeological attempts to trace the origins of recruits have been advanced on the basis of transplanted artefact types. The work of Swan, which links the presence of different ethnic groups to the distribution of distinctive cooking and drinking vessels, has been the most warmly received and comprehensive attempt (See Fig. 7.1).[11] Yet it must be acknowledged that our knowledge of the drivers of culinary fashion remains partial, and explanations unrelated to recruitment practice may explain the presence of such items. Inscriptions, by contrast, offer very direct evidence for recruitment.

An exhaustive study of the epigraphic evidence for the recruitment of individuals is beyond the scope of this chapter, but it is important to note that the surviving documentation reveals different patterns to that attested by the titles of those units raised during the 1st century. Though the surviving evidence must be understood to reflect several cultural phenomena, such as variations in epigraphic consciousness, and differing research histories, there are some interesting points that emerge. The difference between the known sources of units and the main sources of individual recruits across three centuries lies not simply in the fact that the Empire had conquered new territories in the 2nd century AD and had therefore opened up new sources of manpower, such as Dacia. There are also differences in the way in which long-provincialized territories behaved. Spain, Gaul (here including lower and upper Germany), Pannonia, and Thracia emerge as the four most important sources of known individual recruits prior to Hadrian. Unsurprisingly, northern Gaul with the Germanies and Pannonia, areas with a frontier territory and large numbers of military units, continue to provide large numbers of recruits well into the 3rd century. Spain, which was to prove so important in the early 1st century, ceases, however, to be a significant supplier of auxiliaries after the Flavian period.

[11] Swan (1992; 1997; 2009).

Conversely, Thracia, which had a tiny military garrison (one cohort), continued to be a major source of recruits well into the 3rd century. It appears on balance not only that some areas were more intensively exploited for their human potential than others, but also—and this is important—that this did not only apply to frontier provinces proper. In addition to these major sources of recruits there were areas which, while they did not produce recruits in quite the same numbers, seem to have been exploited for the benefit of other zones. The most obvious example of this phenomenon is Asia Minor, which was to prove an important source of manpower for Egypt, but which like Thracia had a very limited military presence.

Sadly, the state of our evidence seldom allows for a detailed reconstruction of the social and political context of recruitment. What evidence we do have suggests that local conditions were a very significant factor in the creation of the imperial *auxilia*. Recruitment of auxiliaries did not just serve to provide a force to maintain Roman rule: the very process of recruitment itself advanced the incorporation of provincial society. It is illuminating to look at the different circumstances in which Rome raised auxiliaries. In what follows, Rome's relations with mountain peoples (often dismissed as bandits), Rome's use of existing social structures, the creation of special treaty arrangements, the conversion of royal armies, and the raising of units of citizens in crisis situations will be examined. It will be clear that these categories are not exhaustive, and that individuals continued to be enrolled from across the provincial landscape and most notably in the frontier zones, a phenomenon discussed further below, but I would nevertheless suggest that the patterns they reflect were intensely significant.

MOUNTAIN PEOPLES

The province of Hispania Tarraconensis made a major contribution to the *auxilia*. In the early 1st century AD it provided the army with more than one *ala* in eight, and more than one auxiliary cohort in seven. As the largest of Rome's three Iberian provinces, it was well known for its extraordinary mineral wealth, its thriving industry, and its influential elite. In the first half of the 1st century, the colonies within the provinces of Baetica and Lusitania provided the requisite legionary recruits. Why then was this prosperous land raising large numbers of rough and ready manpower for the *auxilia*? A closer examination of the provinces' geography provides the answer—exploitation of natural resources also required exportation of human resources. A very high proportion of the units raised in Tarraconensis come from the northwest of the province.[12]

Spanish scholars have examined the circumstances behind this pattern in some detail.[13] They emphasize the importance of gold in northwest Tarraconensis and the large number of troops sent to secure it.[14] Field survey has identified 231 gold

---

[12] At least 20 infantry units (Spaul (2000: 70) lists 18, but the two units of Cantabri he identifies should be added) out of about 44 from Tarraconensis as a whole. At least 4 *alae* were also raised, all from amongst the Astures.

[13] I thank Esther Perez for discussing this with me.

[14] Roldán Hervas (1983: 129–31); Pastor Muqoz (1977: 162–3).

mines in the region, demonstrating just how important this area was to the imperial purse.[15] The focused combination of imperial interest and military might at a time when army reforms were generating the new permanent *auxilia* meant that the populous tribes of the northwest were an attractive source of manpower.[16] As García y Bellido observes, however, there was a further consideration: recruitment into the Roman army may have served as a way of weakening local communities which might have resisted the transformation.[17] Certainly the Romans had difficulties controlling this area and its mountainous terrain. The northwest was the last part of the Iberian Peninsula to be incorporated into the Empire, but fighting there was difficult. The Cantabrian War, planned to bring the region under imperial control, ran from 27 to 22 BC, but three years after a peace treaty, the Cantabri revolted again. The large military presence was clearly insufficient to pacify the area. Thereafter, the Cantabrians' near neighbours, the Astures, rose against imperial authority under Nero. Though scholars have rightly challenged the accuracy of Strabo's descriptions of the peoples of Spain, his claim that the Cantabri, Astures, and their neighbours were particularly challenging reflected the protracted difficulties Rome encountered in attempting to control the region.[18] Writing just before intensive Roman recruitment in the region began, he significantly emphasizes also the character of these groups as mountain people. Archaeological fieldwork in the wider region shows that there was much that might have appeared primitive and threatening to Roman ideas. While there was fairly extensive lowland settlement, there was no significant development of villas before the beginning of the 2nd century, and *castros*, villages of round houses surrounded by defensive walls, survived in the region well into the imperial period.[19]

Accordingly, Roman administrators negotiated with *castella* and *gentes*, pre-existing political and social structures, rather than the more urbanized and centralized groupings with which they were most comfortable.[20] All the while, however, the imperial infrastructure designed to facilitate mining operations advanced. Asturica Augusta (modern Astorga), chief town of the Astures, functioned as the centre of Augustan operations in the Cantabrian War. It became a *municipium* and was a district (*conventus*) capital by AD 1. Excavations have revealed public buildings of exceptional size dating from the Julio-Claudian period, notably a basilica 90m long. Yet rather than offer employment to large numbers of young men, the development of town life, road networks, and mining operations led to their de facto expulsion from the area. With over 50 gold mines within 50km of their new tribal capital, the Astures still provided men for seven cohorts and four *alae* stationed elsewhere. Their neighbours were also intensely 'farmed' for recruits: the people of Bracara Augusta (Braga) and Lucus Augusti (Lugo) provided seven and five cohorts respectively.[21] As Millett has observed, the

---

[15] Concentrated in the modern Asturias and León (Bird 1984).

[16] Pastor Muqoz (1977: 162–3); Pliny *Nat. Hist.* 3.28.

[17] García y Bellido (1963).   [18] Strabo *Geog.* 3.3.7.   [19] Keay (1988: 69).

[20] Millett (2002: 168) speculates that the *princeps* of the *populi*, the small rural communities referred to by Pliny, oversaw the levies of recruits in northwest Iberia.

[21] Two of the cohorts raised from Lucus Augusti and two from Asturica Augusta were mixed with men raised from the Callaecians, a neighbouring group.

withdrawal of a substantial portion of the communities' young men, never to return, may have stunted development locally and perpetuated the 'fragmented and relatively conservative' character of rural society in the region.[22] I believe that García y Bellido is correct, and that we must see in this measure the determination to reduce the threat of banditry and unrest in an area of profound importance to the imperial coffers.[23] The fact that Augustus is known to have taken a direct interest in the suppression of banditry in Spain adds weight to this theory, for the formation of so many regiments clearly required imperial sanction.[24]

Elsewhere we certainly see evidence for the recruitment of groups identified as bandits into the army, but it is hard to tell whether it was systematic or whether indeed it was used to support regular forces.[25] Under the Principate, for example, Marcus Aurelius allegedly recruited bandits in Dardania and Dalmatia.[26] There were also clearly people who saw a link between *not* recruiting men and the potential for banditry. Dio argues, for example, that a consequence of Severus' decision to stop recruiting praetorian guardsmen from within Italy was that the number of brigands haunting the roads grew.[27] More importantly he regards as one of the advantages of a professional army the fact that it enrols those who might otherwise feel obliged to earn a living through brigandage.[28] So we need to ask if on occasion the choice of recruiting grounds was forced on the authorities. Remarks on the martial qualities of mountain peoples may also mask a pragmatic response rather than an imperial initiative. In the 6th century, for example, Procopius mentioned that it was finally found best to recruit the Tzani of the Antitaurus mountains (eastern Turkey) into the army rather than to pay them subsidies or to fight them.[29]

Looking at the peoples harvested for service in the *auxilia*, there may be evidence for earlier initiatives of the kind Procopius recorded. This is striking in the more mountainous regions. Mountains and mountain people proved a grave problem for the Roman authorities. In a significant way they represented a sort of 'internal frontier'.[30] For incorporation to advance, the interest was more in containing these areas than transforming them. They were amongst the most difficult of all territories to control. There were few major settlements to capture or destroy and few individuals powerful enough to agree treaties with. These elements, which were integral to incorporation elsewhere, were notable by their absence. Victories might be won, but they were temporary affairs. Enemies might disperse and regroup.

---

[22] Millett (2002: 167–8).

[23] García y Bellido (1963). I have avoided discussing directly the famous bronze inscription (*CIL* 2.2633), now joined by new discoveries that appear to discuss the new administrative arrangements introduced under the Julio-Claudians. This is primarily because none of these texts touches directly on military matters, but some scholars have challenged the authenticity of the documents. This is noted by Collins (1998: 63) in the case of the inscription and by Richardson (2002) in the instance of the tablets discovered during 'unofficial excavations' in 1999. If a forger is at work, may I request that he/she focus with some urgency on the circumstances behind the raising of these units?

[24] Cassius Dio 56.43 tells the story of Augustus' highly pragmatic response to the remarkably successful bandit Caracotta.

[25] Shaw (1993: 339). See Grünewald (2004) for the malleability of the terms *latrones* and *leistai*.

[26] *SHA Marcus Aurelius* 21.2.7.   [27] Dio 75.2.5.

[28] Dio 52.27.5. This from a fictional debate between Augustus' advisers, Agrippa and Maecenas.

[29] *Hist.* 1.15.19–25.   [30] See Isaac (1990: 54–67).

Much of the population lived below subsistence level. Low-level banditry remained intensely difficult to suppress. Sometimes interest in mineral resources sucked Rome into these regions, but the perceived poverty of many mountain peoples meant that the authorities rarely launched a sustained effort to master them. In ordinary circumstances, tackling banditry was not a pressing imperial concern, the state's energies being focused instead on exploiting resources and raising taxes.

It is interesting, therefore, to see links between mountains, 'brigands', and recruitment running right the way through our period. Such links are strong in those areas that provided large numbers of recruits. Thrace is one such area.[31] Not only did it produce at least twenty-two of Rome's infantry cohorts and at least eight *alae*, it continued to provide large numbers of men for the army right the way through to the late Empire.[32] Indeed, military recruitment must be understood as an important theme in understanding Roman Thrace. The mountainous regions set afire in the Thracian Revolt have generated in more recent centuries a rich folklore centred on tragic bandit heroes.[33] If we look closer at Roman literature we find further telling evidence for such associations. In Apuleius' *Metamorphoses*, a dashing hero masquerades as a bandit leader. He dupes the bandits holding his beloved by launching into a speech that is a clear parody of an army recruiting pitch. But what is especially interesting here is the name he adopts. He calls himself Haemus, after the Thracian mountain range famous for banditry—the very area of the revolt of AD 26.[34] It is impressive that Apuleius, living in Africa but setting his tale in Thessaly, could be confident that his listeners would make the connection. The region's reputation had clearly travelled far. Furthermore, it is evident that the association was not just a literary set piece. That this episode really reflects the vicissitudes of life in this Balkan province is admirably demonstrated by evidence recovered from the sanctuary of Asklepios Zymydrenos (Batkun, Bulgaria). Some time in the late 2nd or early 3rd century AD, one Aurelius Dionysodorus dedicated a fine marble column in fulfilment of a vow to the god. Upon the inscription he records the challenging activity for which he had invoked divine aid: the recruitment of brigands as soldiers.[35]

INCORPORATING WARRIOR BANDS

While it was recognized early, therefore, that mass conscription could contribute to imperial security, there was also growing awareness that its implementation could have a dangerously destabilizing affect. Terrifying rebellions could result from a mishandled *dilectus*. The Thracian revolt of AD 26 was by no means the

---

[31] By no means all Thracian units came from mountainous regions, however; some came from Lower Moesia, north of the main mountain ranges (Saddington 1982: 161–2).

[32] Jarrett (1969) counted 28. I believe, however, that there were 20 *cohortes Thracum*, 2 *cohortes Bessorum*, 8 *alae Thracum*, and 3 *alae Thracum et Gallorum*. For further discussion See Spaul (1994; 2000).

[33] For ancient and modern banditry in the region, see Wolff (2003: 69–94) and Stavrianos (1957) respectively. I thank Kathleen Hawthorne for discussion of this theme.

[34] Apuleius *Metamorphoses* 7.4–6.

[35] *IG Bulg* 3, 1. n. 1126; Nicolay Sharankov, pers. comm.

first or last such uprising. The Pannonian revolt twenty years earlier had been triggered by Dalmatian auxiliaries who rebelled while being assembled for operations in Bohemia.[36] Even men from tribes with a long history of loyalty to Rome could rebel on being confronted by the rigours of enlistment. Tacitus' famous account of the luckless *cohors* of *Usipi* recalls the men who, sent from Germany to active service in Britain, elected to kill their commanders and the soldiers placed in their ranks for instruction, and sailed for home, encountering numerous hardships en route.[37] By far the best way for Rome to operate was to raise the men it wanted from within existing systems, exploiting local power structures in order to minimize resistance and disruption. The approaches adopted again reflect the synthesis of imperial and local, crucial for the incorporation of provincial society.

In many parts of the Celtic west, Rome confronted societies for whom raiding was the precise antithesis of antisocial behaviour. The practice must be seen in the context of one of the most profound social changes in Late Iron Age society in the West: the emergence of warrior bands consisting of mounted fighters.[38] Raiding reinforced social cohesion, binding the leaders of war bands to the men under their command, providing an arena in which the martial rites of passage, so essential to status and identity, could be enacted. It has been suggested, by analogy with studies of the Yamomami of the Amazon rainforest, that this image may have been exaggerated: that martiality took on a new force as a result of the threat and opportunities introduced by imperial Rome.[39] There can be no doubt that Roman influence must have generated new tensions in much of western Europe. But it is clear from the archaeological evidence that raiding behaviours were not solely a result of such transitions. Pre-Roman artefacts from these regions emphasize martial splendour that ran beyond the merely symbolic. Whatever the case, Rome was itself confronted with both a challenge and an opportunity: in her territories, raiding behaviours were often disruptive and counter to imperial interests, but elsewhere, where she required military action, they could be extremely useful.

Some of the earliest cavalry units emerged out of such situations. The best-known case dates from AD 21, when a Treveran noble led a picked force on Rome's behalf to help suppress a local revolt.[40] Tribal feuds provided Iulius Indus with the incentive to take the Empire's side against his fellow Treveran, Iulius Florus. The force he led almost certainly became the *ala Indiana*—a regiment that went on to serve the Empire in Britain and Germany. The unit's origin should be understood against the background of local politics, and the struggle for supremacy between native noble families, both of which enjoyed Roman citizenship. Such contests moved to other arenas in time, however, and there is no evidence of Treveran aristrocrats behaving in the same way after the AD 60s.[41] Indeed, the Gallic Julii, the elite families granted citizenship under the Julio-Claudians, virtually disappear from our sources at this time.[42] Their disappearance may well be attributed to a decline resulting from their loss of military status.[43]

[36] Cassius Dio 55.29.   [37] Tacitus *Agric.* 28.   [38] Creighton (2000: 14).
[39] Webster (1996: 111–23).   [40] Tacitus *Ann.* 3. 42.
[41] Alpinius Montanus, a Treveran auxiliary prefect who defected to Civilis in AD 69, is not in quite the same situation (Tacitus *Hist.* 3.35).
[42] Drinkwater (1978).   [43] Wightman (1985: 73).

How the internal dynamics of these early formations operated is difficult to assess, but a passing reference to a Gallic unit in Julius Caesar's service offers us some idea. Some of Caesar's units, the forerunners of the earliest *alae*, appear to have been little more than the mounted following of individual nobles. Successful commanders enjoyed the patronage of important Romans, as Indus had, for example, but they also achieved and/or retained the martial status that was so important within the social structure of their society. The tale, recounted above, of the two Allobrogan brothers who jointly commanded a cavalry unit in Caesar's service is a case in point. In or around 49 BC, the brothers were reported to Caesar by their own men for submitting falsified claims to the paymaster. Though the men in the unit were operating under tribal leadership, they knew where their pay was coming from. The traditional clientship network had been incorporated within a Roman one[44]—though we may note that in the eyes of these Gauls, Caesar's Roman identity may have been secondary to his role as a warlord.

Again, though this model of recruitment is best attested in the west, the model could clearly be applied in an eastern context too. Sociopolitical factors were no less important in the creation of Parthian regiments within the *auxilia*.[45] Parthia lacked a standing army. To those Parthians who sought wealth and prestige on the battlefield, the opportunities in their own territories were sometimes limited. For such men, Kennedy notes,[46] there were two options: they could seek employment as professional soldiers elsewhere, or they could become retainers to Parthian noble families. Either option could lead to subsequent service in the Roman *auxilia*. Parthian aristocrats, much like their Gallic counterparts under the Republic, often appear in Roman service and/or as Roman hostages.[47] These men were accompanied, following the Parthian feudal tradition, by large numbers of retainers.[48] An Augustan funerary inscription discovered at Clissa, near Salona in Roman Dalmatia, records one T. IVL. MAXIM. C. IVL. THIRIDATIS F. DEC. ALA PHARTHO.[49] The epitaph's findspot recalls Tacitus' account of the Parthian contingent, led by Ornospades, which served Rome in the Dalmatian revolt.[50] A number of details recorded on the inscription indicate that Maximus was no ordinary auxiliary recruit: he offers his place of birth (*origo*) as Rome, and was born to a citizen father, something rare among auxiliaries at this early date. The possession of citizenship and the father's name could even suggest that this decurion was the son of the Tiridates who sought to recover the Parthian throne in 26/5 BC.[51] Even if Maximus were not the son of that Tiridates, his *origo* and citizenship suggest that he was born into a prominent Parthian family living in Rome as exiles or hostages. A second early epitaph, this time from Mainz in Germany, attests a Parthian serving in the *ala Parthorum et Araborum*. Here too it is possible that the deceased had an aristocratic connection. The offering of the

---

[44] Caesar *De Bello Civile* 3.60. See also Slofstra (1983) and Wightman (1985: 129).

[45] Petersen (1966).   [46] Kennedy (1977: 530).

[47] For Parthians serving with Rome, see Kennedy (1977). For Parthian hostages, see *Res Gestae* (32.2) and Strabo (*Geog.* 16.1.28). For the service of Gallic hostages, see Braund (1984: 16) and Roymans (1990: 35).

[48] Kennedy (1977: 529).   [49] *CIL* 3.8746 = *ILS* 2532.   [50] *Ann.* 6.37.

[51] Kennedy (1977: 523), however, argues that were this the case Maximus would have been commanding the regiment, not merely a *turma*.

soldier's *origo* as Anzarbus in Cilicia may suggest a link to the pretender Vonones, who was resettled in Cilicia by Rome at the request of King Artabanus.[52] It is likely that his journey into the *auxilia*, and that of many others, was a mere side-effect of Arsacid dynastic factionalism. It was the losers in these conflicts who, exiled from their homelands, sought advancement in Rome's ranks.[53]

The debate about Maximus' background and rank underscore another point sometimes overlooked in the general discussion of recruitment. Suitable individuals were sometimes directly appointed to the centurionate and the decurionate.[54] Gilliam argued that the state sometimes made direct appointments 'to obtain literate and educated men to help deal with the paper-work and administrative functions of the army'.[55] He supports his thesis with a number of cases in which officers held the rank very shortly after, or even from the date of, their enlistment. A man named Hierax, for example, held the rank of centurion from the year of his enlistment,[56] while at Cherchel the gravestone of a *decurio alae* records his death after a mere four years of military service, far less than we would normally expect him to serve before achieving such a post.[57] Again, the implication is that he was directly appointed to the rank. While Gilliam is surely correct to note the administrative benefits of direct appointments, the approach had an added advantage when Rome sought to incorporate fighting men of a range of different statuses. This must have made it easier to transfer some warrior bands directly into Roman service.

TREATY ARRANGEMENTS WITH SPECIAL GROUPS

Yet the most pronounced example of auxiliary recruitment through local mechanisms must undoubtedly be the case of the Batavi. Well known from the accounts of Tacitus, whose comments are worth recording verbatim, the peculiarities of the Batavian experience are also admirably attested through a growing number of other sources. In his account of the German peoples, written *c.* AD 98, Tacitus wrote:

> Of all these peoples the most manly are the Batavi . . . they are not insulted by having tribute demanded of them, and there is no-tax farmer to oppress them, they are exempt from such burdens . . . they are reserved for war, to be, as it were, as arms and armour.[58]

Besides the important statement that the Batavi enjoyed a special status, Tacitus's comments here highlight two important points.[59] The first is that the provision of military support is linked in the Roman administrative mind to taxation. Exemption from taxation and tribute is here permissible because of the martial potential of these people. Given that the Batavi may have had to provide 5,500

[52] Kennedy (1997: 528). *AE* 1976, 495.　　[53] Simon James, pers. comm.
[54] For discussion of the background of centurions, decurions, and *principales*, see Holder (1980: 86–99).
[55] Gilliam (1957: 168).　　[56] *P. Mich.* 164.18–20.　　[57] *CIL* 8.9389.
[58] *Germania* 29, translation by Hutton (1970).
[59] Tacitus argues that the Mattiaci also enjoyed this arrangement. There is, however, no epigraphic evidence for this claim.

men from a possible 6,000 households, this was not necessarily a lighter burden.[60] Assessment of the human resource, this passage reminds us, runs alongside assessments of the natural resources throughout the Roman period. The census is as concerned with people as it is with their property.

The second point, closely linked to how the Batavi are assessed, is how they are viewed. To Tacitus there was something special about them; indeed, his description is perhaps the fullest expression of an imperial ideal, the martial race honourably harnessed to Roman service. The notion of martial races has been a familiar feature of colonial discourse right up to modern times.[61] In reality it emerges from a blend of grass-roots knowledge and wishful thinking. Just as the 'martial races' that served the British Empire were described in great detail by the officers who recruited them, men whose work bordered on real ethnology, so the comments of Tacitus, a man who would have had some familiarity with the region to which the Batavi belonged, appear to reflect real experience.[62] Yet, as more recent studies of 'martial races' have observed, they are more often those who can be reconciled to imperial hegemony, not those who constantly oppose it.[63] Both sides can see in the arrangement a kind of honourable collaboration—events that expose this façade are likely to be very dangerous indeed. Quite probably Rome's perception of the Batavi grew out of the events of 12 BC, when Drusus found them useful allies in his operations in Germany. Certainly it was aided by Rome's willingness to distinguish them from the Chatti to whom they once belonged. Whatever its source and development, the view of the Batavi as a martial race had an enduring impact on the development of Batavian tribal society. Essentially, imperial power thus helped mould Batavian identity.[64] Significantly though, this did not mean that Batavian culture simply came to resemble that of metropolitan Rome; indeed, in some ways it acted as a brake on such a transition.

Rome's manpower demands upon the Batavi appear to have had far-reaching implications. Pollen evidence from Kops Plateau at the heart of their territory suggests that cattle grazing rather than settled cultivation remained the norm throughout the Julio-Claudian period.[65] Pastoral farming would not have required a large labour force, relative to arable farming, during the periods when many men were away on campaign.[66] Yet analysis of the wider region of the Dutch River area also suggests that even the grazing potential of Batavian lands was limited by winter and spring flooding.[67] How long a growing population could have employed this particular subsistence strategy is questionable.[68] Driel-Murray argues that the population must have increasingly depended upon horticultural cultivation of smaller plots for food, noting that this would have

---

[60] Willems (1984: 234–7).

[61] Driel-Murray (2003). Roymans (2004: 221–34) also offers a detailed consideration of 'ethnic soldiering' amongst the Batavi.

[62] See Mason (1974: 345–61) for notions of the 'martial classes' and 'warlike races' in British India.

[63] Killingray (1999: 15).   [64] Roymans (2004).   [65] Willems (1984: 233–4).

[66] For the 'warrior economy', see Nash (1984: 100–101).   [67] Kooistra (1996: 71–3).

[68] Lindsay Allason-Jones (pers. comm.) has suggested to me that the regular inundations of sea water and their consequent implications for settlement and farmland may have forced a certain amount of migration out of the tribal area. This may also have made military service with Rome more attractive.

helped conserve scarce resources such as fodder.[69] She further suggests that evidence for the introduction of *potstal* regimes, whereby cattle are kept for longer because they are valued principally as sources of manure for fertilizer, reflects growing agricultural stress at the end of the 2nd century.[70] Such a scenario would fit well with the concept of 'ethnic soldiers' who are frequently drawn from relatively impoverished groups.[71] It would also readdress the lop-sided way we have tended to view Batavian transformation, perceiving it as dominated by elite males. In fact, as Driel-Murray observes, these farming practices almost certainly depended principally on women and children.[72] There are strong reasons to believe that the combination of agricultural marginality and military service actually had disastrous implications for the Batavi. In the late 2nd century, when I believe the traditional recruiting arrangement probably came to an end, the economic situation appears bleak.[73] This is in no sense a traditional model of Romanization; rather, it is a case of incorporation where the state ultimately drains a community of life to serve its own needs.

Several attempts have been made to assess the impact of this process by establishing the proportion of the male population that was enlisted. Willems concluded that the total population in the 1st century AD stood at between 30,000 and 40,000 people in 4,000–6,000 households.[74] Keeping all the Batavian units serving Rome at their total establishment strength of about 5,500 men would, he observes, place considerable pressure on a population of this size.[75] With one *ala*, eight cohorts, the imperial guard, and the fleet to serve, this figure would have been large to begin with, but over time more and more would also have joined the legions. The sheer scale of demand may account for the number of instances in the ancient sources where brothers are shown serving together.[76] If, as these figures would suggest, almost every household had a soldier in the Roman army, most of them in the *auxilia*, the impact on local society would have been enormous.

These conclusions alone support the claim that martiality was not only a defining element of Batavian life, but also one underpinned by service with

---

[69] Driel-Murray (2003: 205).

[70] Driel-Murray (2003) cites Lauwerier (1988: 134) for analysis of cattle at age of slaughter. The fact that cattle are being slaughtered at a later age strongly suggests that they are valued for traction and manure rather than simply for meat.

[71] It is interesting here to compare the image of the noble, wild warrior depicted in early Dutch work on the Batavi (Hessing 2001) with that of a vulnerable and marginal group, as understood by Driel-Murray (2003: 206).

[72] Driel-Murray (2003: 205–6).

[73] Based on the lack of evidence for special recruitment in the late 2nd century and the impression that some forms of weapon deposition are becoming less frequent. Driel-Murray (2003: 214) reaches similar conclusions by a different means, noting the extraordinary implications that the collapse of ethnic soldiering had in parts of India.

[74] Willems (1984: 234–7).

[75] Despite my admiration for Willems' reconstruction, I cannot agree with his assumption that the figures should be based on allowing 'socio-economic life to go on more or less undisturbed' (1984: 235); rather, it seems to me that the very demands of military service could have redefined the terms of socioeconomic relations within the community.

[76] Roymans (1993: 40 n. 27). This certainly appears to be the case in Tacitus' accounts. Epigraphic evidence for the phenomenon is less clear, however. The term 'frater' used on tombstones of the guards at Rome need not mean biological brother.

Rome. Evidence for weapon offerings at cult sites in the Batavian tribal area long after such practices had been abandoned elsewhere in Gaul appear to be an archaeologically visible consequence of this situation.[77]

Scholars debate the extent to which *alae* and *cohortes* raised from the peoples of the lower Rhine had their origins in local militias.[78] Though the titles of regiments from other regions may suggest that such a process was employed, hardly any proof remains to show how these units were first constituted. The literary evidence is generally confusing, while interpretations of the archaeological data are fraught with difficulty. Many attempts to explain the region's weapon graves through such frameworks are based, I believe, on a misunderstanding of the way that Roman law applied in early provincial society.[79] Tacitus' reference to 'auxiliaries *and* the Batavians', and to the latter's operation under the leadership of Chariovalda *dux Batavorum* in campaigns of the early 1st century, do imply irregular non-Roman units.[80] By the time of the Revolt of AD 69, however, Batavian auxiliaries were clearly ordered into regular formations that can be distinguished from mere tribal bands.[81] Whenever this transition took place and indeed however far advanced it was, it is clear that Batavian nobles were integral to its completion. Significantly, the trigger for the Batavian Revolt was a *dilectus*— this is doubly interesting as the Batavians were already active in providing large numbers of auxiliaries, sailors, and guardsmen for the Empire through their own leaders. Tacitus mentions the grievances of these leaders and laments the inept way in which the levy was conducted, but he does not identify what may have been the main motive for disaffection among the indigenous elite.[82] The arrival of outsiders to conduct the levy essentially undermined the native aristocracy: it rode roughshod over the detailed knowledge that locals would have applied to the process and disrupted the networks of patronage integral to traditional levies.[83] In essence it made explicit to the entire community the erosion of their power—the impression of honourable cooperation in a shared undertaking was impossible to sustain in such circumstances.

It is notable, however, that the Batavian Revolt ultimately accelerated incorporation rather than provoked brutal suppression. Though the leaders of the Revolt may have had very different motives, it is clear that many of the rebels' demands recall a synthesis of imperial and local military thinking. There was a request, for example, for more mounted men to be employed.[84] Mounted men had higher

---

[77] Roymans (1993) on the transformation of a martial elite. It is important to remember, however, that very few areas have been as intensely studied as the landscapes of the Batavi, so it is difficult to assess how atypical they really were.

[78] Kraft (1951: 37–40) saw a process whereby militias and local units were later integrated into the *auxilia*. Alföldy (1968a: 86–93) was sceptical about the degree to which militias, local levies, and regular auxiliary forces could be genuinely distinguished from one another in the first decades following incorporation.

[79] P. 253.

[80] Auxiliaries and Batavians, *Ann.* 2.8; Chariovalda's actions and companions in *Ann.* 2.11 recall those of a tribal warleader, not a regular officer.

[81] See particularly the distinction between regular units and levies in *Hist.* 4.22.

[82] Ibid. 4.14.

[83] Kraft (1951: 40) also regards the use of Roman recruiting officers amongst the Batavi as an innovation.

[84] Tacitus *Hist.* 4.19.

status in both societies and commanded higher pay, a reflection of a distinction that was to remain of lasting importance in the cultures of the *auxilia*. At a higher level, it is clear that Batavian units continued to be manned by Batavians wherever they were and even to be commanded by them. This was no doubt aided by the fact that few such units left western Europe. For all the carnage that the Revolt witnessed, imperial authorities and Batavian elite were ultimately able to continue their special relationship for several generations.

Correspondence associated with the best-known member of this group, Flavius Cerialis, prefect of the Batavian cohort at Vindolanda *c.* AD 100, has attracted considerable scholarly attention. It has even been suggested that a letter written to him by a decurion beginning with the address *Masculus Ceriali regi suo* recalls the survival of Batavian terms of address alongside Roman ones, though I find this explanation unnecessary.[85]

Further evidence suggests that Batavian units continued to be commanded by Batavians well after Cerialis' command. A 2nd-century tombstone records the commander of *cohors III Batavorum*.[86] The tombstone does not give the prefect's origin, but it does state that his wife came from the *civitas* capital of the Batavi, Ulpia Noviomagus.

At a less elevated level it is clear that Batavians continued to serve in Batavian units well after the revolt. M. Ulpius Fronto, for example, was discharged from *cohors I Batavorum milliaria c.R.* in Upper Pannonia in AD 113. His diploma makes it clear that both he and his wife were Batavians.[87] A further diploma, found at Elst, a *vicus* within Batavian territory, was issued in AD 98 to a man who had served in a Batavian *ala*. This individual, who is recorded alongside his Batavian wife and children, must have been recruited *c.* AD 73, four years after the Revolt.[88] The findspot of the diploma may, incidentally, suggest that Batavian units continued to be stationed on Batavian territory even then.

CONVERSION OF ROYAL ARMIES AND REGULAR FORCES

At the height of the Batavian Revolt its instigator, Iulius Civilis, allegedly snarled, 'Let Syria, Asia and the East, which are used to kings, act the slave.'[89] The phrase is a cocktail of truth and irony. As a Batavian nobleman and the commander of an auxiliary unit, Civilis had himself facilitated the military exploitation, here again likened to enslavement, of his own people. What he and his forebears had done was not in fact so different, despite the hyperbole, from that which had happened in the East. In the east, however, it was royal armies rather than just militias and war bands that were absorbed into the *auxilia*. Once again, we see how the imperial appetite for manpower deftly exploited local circumstances.

---

[85] *Tab. Vindol.* III.628. A. R. Birley (2002: 80) nonetheless regards it as more likely that the term *rex* is here used as 'a form of extreme flattery' of the type applied to patrons. Cuff reviews the use of the term, revisiting a parallel in a letter to an auxiliary officer from a *cohors Ituraeorum*, and concludes that it 'provides insight into the Batavians' enduring cultural identity' (2011: 155). I am less convinced.
[86] *AE* 1944, 97.   [87] *RMD* 86.   [88] Roxan (2000: 309).   [89] Tacitus *Hist.* 4.17.

Perhaps the best-known example of this process actually concerns the creation of a citizen unit established following Nero's incorporation of Pontus into the Empire.[90] In AD 64 part of the royal army was converted into a cohort, organized and equipped following a Roman model and dispatched to guard Trapezus on the Black Sea. Meanwhile the former royal fleet became the *Classis Pontica*. It is a striking example of the mechanics by which client kingdoms were absorbed, but it was certainly neither the first nor the last time such strategies were adopted.

It is fascinating, for example, to consider the fate of the army that once served Herod the Great. Herod's funeral entourage was a remarkable ensemble. Just as the Romans had exploited the potential of several regions for their *auxilia*, so too had King Herod. Accompanying his cortege in 4 BC were Gallic, German, and Thracian troops.[91] Herod understood, better perhaps even than his Roman masters, how valuable it was to have an army that could not easily side with the people against the powerful. Though little is known of how these exotic units were raised, maintained, and equipped, it has been suggested that they were subsequently subsumed into the Roman *auxilia*.[92] In several respects, however, they are the least interesting part of Herod's force, for the savvy ruler had also raised a large contingent of soldiers from amongst his own subjects, the Sebasteni. In the disturbances that followed the king's death, these troops, 3,000 in all, were the ones who stood by the Romans as other elements of the royal army deserted.[93] Reading accounts of their loyalty and ability, it is hard not to recall the exploits of the Batavi. They too are led by remarkable leaders with Latin names, they stand by the Romans against the rest, and they even rescue some legionary troops from imminent destruction.[94] In the religious and cultural mix of the time though, such loyalty was almost inevitable, for as Herod knew well when he raised the force, the Sebasteni could never have made common cause with the majority Jewish population.

Sebaste was Samaria: Herod had renamed the city and its surrounding region to honour Augustus; he had built a palace there and lavishly decorated the city itself.[95] Contemporary accounts emphasize the distance between the region's Samaritan occupants and the wider Jewish population.[96] The two communities were rival claimants to the inheritance of the Pentateuch.[97] Both appear to have been parallel societies that shunned contact with one another. In both cases these tensions could and did flare up into communal violence.[98] When it did, the Romans sometimes used the Sebasteni to bring it under control. Rome knew how to exploit the divisions in local society. Accordingly, Sebasteni of Herod's old guard ultimately found their way into the *auxilia*.[99] Their importance as an

---

[90] Ibid. 3.47.   [91] Josephus *Ant. Iud.* 17.198.

[92] Holder (1980: 14) attractively suggests that Herod's Thracian units may have been incorporated into the Roman army. There is admittedly no direct documentary evidence to support this claim.

[93] Josephus *Bell. Iud.* 2.53.

[94] Rufus and Gratus (Josephus *Bell. Iud.* 2.53). *Bell. Iud.* 2.63 records a legionary contingent rescued by Gratus and his Sebastenians.

[95] Saddington (1982: 50, 99).

[96] e.g. the parable of the Good Samaritan (Luke 10: 25) and the story of the Samaritan Woman (John 4: 9).

[97] For the background, see Millar (1993: 341).   [98] e.g. Josephus *Bell. Iud.* 2.263.

[99] e.g. the *ala Sebastena* (Benseddik 1977; Spaul 1994: 196). We only have certain evidence for one *ala* and one *cohors* of Sebasteni. This would be far fewer than the 3,000 Sebasteni under arms on the

effective local force remained for several generations. When, after an extraordinary episode in which these soldiers insulted the daughters of the local friendly king Agrippa I, the emperor Claudius threatened to deport them, they sent him an embassy that persuaded him to let them remain in Judea.[100] They appear to have remained there until after the Jewish War. Both the known *ala* and *cohors* were in Syria by AD 88.[101]

The relationship between auxiliary recruitment and the incorporation of client kingdoms is strongly suggested in the titles of many regiments. Royal armies most probably provided much of the manpower for these contingents. Strong hints of this strategy are evident from the reign of Augustus well into the 2nd century, and from territories spanning the lands of modern Turkey, Syria, and Jordan. The complexities of Rome's relationship with the kingdom of Commagene, for example, are reflected in the raising of successive sequences of *cohortes Commagenorum*. At least one *ala* and one *cohors* may have been raised following the first annexation of the kingdom in AD 17, but a number could not have been recruited until the final annexation of the kingdom in AD 72.[102] With the annexation of Nabatea under Trajan, a similar process is suggested. Six *cohortes Ulpia Petraeorum* appear in the line of battle.[103] These most probably contained the remnants of the formidable Nabatean army.[104] How their conversion into Roman units was undertaken is lost to us; perhaps a minimum of change was required. Yet we do know that, unlike some client armies, they were not organized on a Roman model before incorporation. The terminology of the Nabatean army, as recorded on surviving inscriptions, overwhelmingly though not exclusively followed Hellenistic traditions.[105] An interesting exception is suggested by a tomb inscription from Medain Saleh in Saudi Arabia, in which the deceased is recorded as a QNTRYN, a transliteration, it would appear, of *kenturion*.[106] More significant perhaps is the transition from a small permanent force, supplemented as required by local levies, to a collection of long-service units of the Roman army amounting to six thousand men.[107] Was it possible to simply convert the similar-size contingents the Nabateans had formerly loaned Rome, or did a more complex process of conversion take place? Future research may yet provide the answer.

What emerges from this review is that local circumstances were carefully considered in the raising of new units and large bodies of recruits more generally. There are good reasons to emphasize the incorporation of existing bodies of troops, albeit with some adaptation in the process, rather than consistently raising

death of Herod the Great (Josephus *Bell. Iud.* 2.53). It is possible therefore that only part of the force was converted to regular Roman service: Speidel (1982/3: 234).

[100] Josephus *Ant. Iud.* 19.364–6.
[101] As seen on *RMD* 3 = *CIL* 16. 35. Evidence for the cohort comes from Syria (Spaul 2000: 453), but the *ala* was subsequently transferred to North Africa. Benseddik (1977) believes the tombstone (*AE* 1980, 972) of an *eques* from this regiment found at Cherchel dates from the late 1st century, though he allows for a 2nd-century date. Spaul suggests that the move coincided with the Hadrianic reorganization of the province (Spaul 1994: 196).
[102] Kennedy (1980: 44, 91–4, 97–101).   [103] Kennedy (2000: 40–43).
[104] For the Nabatean army See Graf (1994).   [105] Ibid. 274–90.
[106] Kennedy (2000: 41).
[107] For the Nabatean contribution to the Roman army in Judea in AD 67 (Josephus *Bell. Iud.* 3.4.2 (68)), see Kennedy (2000: 43).

contingents from scratch. Not the least of these, I would suggest, consists of the fact that many of these units had an embedded social role. Converting such military communities into Roman entities allowed the imperial system to pene-trate more deeply into local networks of power. This was as true whether it concerned the channelling of a war band's energies or a royal army's policing responsibilities. In lands where military duties stretched far beyond territorial defence, incorporating an army essentially assured rapid control of a myriad of other administrative apparatus.

Furthermore—and this is a lesson that has been too readily forgotten in recent times—*not* converting existing formations can itself be a recipe for disaster. To exclude a large group of young men trained in arms and sometimes indoctrinated with ideals of martial prowess from the new military system would have been to invite failure. In this sense imperial authorities may have been aware that they dared not fail to take advantage of the opportunities existing units offered. The modern reader only has to look at recent experience in Iraq to see the conse-quences of failing to preserve and redirect large military formations. A large number of those opposing the new government were men who found themselves without livelihoods when Republican Guard units were disbanded. Conversely, initial progress with intransigent militias came when the state offered them cash, uniforms, and other equipment.[108] Their initial wish was to be allowed to fight together under their own commanders.

CRISIS RECRUITMENT OF CITIZEN UNITS

Incorporating existing forces was not always and everywhere applicable, of course, and on occasion military imperatives might require more dramatic recruiting initiatives. A final example of the Roman capacity to exploit the human resource imaginatively to sustain the *auxilia* comes with the raising of the *cohortes Volun-tariorum*. These units were composed of citizens and freedmen, men not normally found in the Augustan *auxilia*. Though much about these units remains ill-understood, including indeed quite how many there were, it is clear that they were numerous, and that the very first were raised in the earliest days of the *auxilia* in response to the crisis conditions of the Pannonian War and the Varus disaster.[109] To ensure that some sense of Roman propriety was maintained, these cohorts were commanded by a tribune rather than a prefect, as would normally be appropriate for their size.[110] Furthermore, in the will of Augustus men of the first generation of recruits were specifically awarded a donative of equivalent value to

[108] e.g. the early strategy in Fallujah in April/May 2004. It appeared to be taking effect and was for a while seen as inspiration for further emulation elsewhere. Interestingly the initiative was deeply distrusted by the Iraqi defence ministry, which saw the support for diverse militias as a recipe for further splits along ethnic and religious lines. See *The Economist* (2004: 42–3). Since then the Awakening movement has had a mixed history in the Iraqi government's attempts to harness the manpower of different factions.

[109] Macrobius (*Sat.* 1.11.32).

[110] M. P. Speidel (1976), Holder (1980: 64–72), and Saddington (1982: 142–4). Le Glay (1972) examines the distinctive arrangements for the command of these units.

that of their legionary counterparts.[111] Though termed *voluntarii*, it is clear that this was a euphemism.[112] Compulsion was used to raise the regiments of freedmen.[113] The title obscured the fact that Rome was using slave-born soldiers, something that was strictly prohibited at other times.[114] Velleius Paterculus recalls how, as the emperor made the direst of predictions, the authorities used quintessentially Roman social networks to get their men.[115] Men and women were forced to hand over suitable slaves in their possession. The slaves were rapidly freed, receiving citizenship in the process, and then conscripted immediately. Though surviving units continued to draw citizen recruits for several decades, they ultimately adhered to the Roman form of incorporation outlined here.[116] Peregrine recruits went on to join their ranks, receiving citizenship only on their discharge.[117]

The raising of auxiliary recruits thus demonstrates several features of Roman administration. We see the way in which imperial administrators view the peoples under their jurisdiction. In some cases, the view that an ethnic group is particularly predisposed towards martial behaviour is deliberately exploited by the authorities, often with lasting effects. Such policies have a real impact on ethnic identity, as the case of the Batavi, where units retained links to their homeland, clearly demonstrates. It was also clearly significant in other provincial territories, such as Thracia, where links to specific units were dropped but the area became widely known as a source of military manpower. In some cases recruitment emerges as part of a more holistic process, aiding pacification of a territory and thus facilitating imperial control. The ability to incorporate potentially threatening peoples must have brought with it an added security in frontier areas. Martial energies could be engaged in the service of the Empire, rather than in opposition to imperial interests. The whole procedure of recruitment and of redeployment was designed to be as smooth and simple as possible. Rome had the capacity to suppress revolts arising from these actions, but she did not, indeed could not, rely on military force alone. Ultimately, Rome's monopolization of pay and rewards allows her to tap the human resource, but transforming local social structures proved no less important. It is only at the end of the Flavian period, when her redirection of elite energies into civil competition is largely achieved, that the danger of local uprisings linked to native auxiliaries appears to subside. Even then, however, the processes of incorporation continue apace. In the next section we will see how the ongoing supply of recruits necessary to maintain these units contributed to the transformation of provincial culture.

---

[111] Tacitus *Ann.* 1.8.   [112] Saddington (1982: 144).

[113] Saddington (1982: 143–4) successfully refutes Kraft's (1951: 93) argument that these were not the units referred to by Macrobius.

[114] For prohibitions on slave-born recruits, see p. 279.   [115] Velleius Paterculus 2.111.

[116] Holder (1980: 65, table 5.1). Drawing on the evidence for these units up until the reign of Trajan, he argues that of 21 soldiers known, 20 were citizens.

[117] A non-citizen from Cappadocia is found in *cohors XXXII Voluntariorum* in the second half of the 1st century (*CIL* 13.7382). *CIL* 16.38, a Dalmatian diploma of AD 94, lists *peregrini* enlisted into *cohors VIII Voluntariorum*. Holder (1980: 65) tentatively suggests that these two exceptions might indicate wartime needs.

8

Recruitment and the Limits of Localism

So far the discussion has focused on the impact of recruitment on the individual and on the community from which he came, but another major consideration is the impact of recruitment practice on the changing character of the *auxilia* themselves. Here there are two major issues that require consideration. The first concerns the circumstances under which units were moved away from their place of origin. Such movements potentially had devastating consequences for a unit's relationship with its home community. The second concerns the degree to which army units in general and auxiliary regiments in particular became increasingly 'local' in character as a result of the continued influx of new recruits.

To begin, it is important to consider the rationale affecting the deployment of the *alae* and *cohortes*. Just as the raising of large numbers of men reveals much about the way that imperial power operated across the provinces, so too does the deployment of units. Major modern armies concerned with internal security have often found it expedient to station soldiers raised in one area of their dominion a long way from their homelands. This essentially binds the unit still more tightly to central authority. Furthermore, it ensures that the unit is less likely to form allegiances amongst the local population.[1] Interestingly, as Cheesman observed a long time ago, this was not Roman policy.[2] Imperial policy instead reacted to local circumstances. So long as a region was relatively quiet and the troops did not participate in disturbances contrary to the emperor's interests, there was a good chance that they would be left where they were.

Rome did not make a regular practice of moving auxiliary units after their formation. Movement of large military formations involved considerable organization and effort, and though this was clearly not beyond the capabilities of imperial administrators, it was equally clearly kept to a minimum. Sometimes, the unrest it caused simply was not worth the effort, even when the move was actively under consideration for punitive reasons. Thus as we saw above, when the Sebasteni were threatened with deportation to Pontus following their lamentable behaviour in AD 44, the emperor was won over by their embassy and desisted. A couple of decades later the Sebasteni still provided the 'Roman' military presence in their home towns.[3]

---

[1] See Killingray (1999: 15) for this phenomenon in recent police forces and armies.
[2] Cheesman (1914: 67–73).
[3] Josephus' claim, *Ant. Iud.* 19.176, that in AD 59 the garrison of Caesarea was composed mainly of Sebasteni and Caesareans may be a reference to men rather than to units (M. P. Speidel 1982/3: 235).

Units were moved therefore, only if they posed a security threat where they were stationed, or if other areas urgently required reinforcement and no other troops were available. In an empire as large as that of Rome, even this was enough to ensure that many regiments ended up far from their area of origin, but this was not part of any specific policy to break up the ethnic composition of units. Had such a policy existed we might expect that regiments would have been continually on the move as each started to fill with recruits from its new station. In fact there is every reason to believe that many units spent their early years close to home. That the process of redeployment was essentially reactive is apparent from the aftermath of two famous early rebellions.

The first of these, the Pannonian War, took place in the Danubian provinces in AD 6. Descriptions in the literary sources indicate that rebels came both from regular auxiliary units capable of operating in large formations[4] and from Dalmatian and Pannonian irregulars.[5] Between them these groups had been largely responsible for Roman security in the region. It took three years to reimpose Roman control, and after this time it is clear that Rome was in no mood to trust her interests to the same guardians. Julio-Claudian inscriptions show the appearance of Pannonian and Dalmatian *alae* and *cohortes* along the Rhine and even on the other side of the Mediterranean, in the African province of Mauretania Caesariensis.[6] Not a single such regiment ever appeared in its area of origin again. The responsibility for defending this crucial stretch of the Danubian frontier fell instead to regiments from all over the Empire.

However great an impact the Pannonian war had on Roman thinking, it did not result in Empire-wide changes in the levying and deployment of non-citizen soldiers. Right up until the late AD 60s the security of the Rhine depended heavily on locally raised militia, *alae* and *cohortes*. As we have seen, the leaders of the Batavian Revolt exploited this to the full in AD 69 when they appealed for unified opposition to the imperial authorities. In the aftermath, the Batavians preserved some of their ancient rights,[7] but even so there was a significant reorganization. With the exception of the *ala Batavorum*, which may itself have been reformed, all pre-existing units were either destroyed or reorganized and sent outside the province.[8] Many Batavians were sent to Britain.[9] Otherwise, of the units raised on the Rhine only *ala I Cannanefatium* and *cohors I Germanorum c.R.* are found there at a later date, but neither was stationed anywhere near the epicentre of the revolt. They served instead in the army of Upper Germany, a force largely unaffected by the rebellion. To ensure stability, the provincial army at the heart of the disaster was reconstituted with new regiments brought in from outside the region. Evidence for the new arrivals comes from two military diplomas issued to soldiers serving in the army of Lower Germany a few years after the uprising. Between them these diplomas, dating to AD 78 and AD 80 respectively, list six *alae* and eleven cohorts; not one of these regiments originally came from the province.[10]

---

[4] Velleius Paterculus 2.110.   [5] Dio 55.29.

[6] Units redeployed to Germany, for example, are recorded on *CIL* 13.11962; *CIL* 13.7508; *CIL* 13 8316; and *RMD* II. 79. For redeployments to Africa see *CIL* 8.6308; *AE* 1921, 31; *CIL* 8.7508; *CIL* 8.21040; *CIL* 8.21041.

[7] P. 116.   [8] Roxan (2000: 309).   [9] Tacitus *Agric.* 36.   [10] *CIL* 16.23 and 16.158.

Rome's response to the Pannonian, Thracian, and Batavian revolts—and it is worth emphasizing that it was always a response, not a pre-emptive strategy—was to replace compromised forces with *alae* and *cohortes* drawn from other areas. A logical extension of this essentially reactive policy may be seen in the later acquisition of provinces. In both Britain and Dacia, where the incorporation of territory was accompanied by much hard fighting, locally raised units are virtually absent.[11]

So much for the movement of units; what about the movement of the men upon whom their existence depended? For over a century now scholars have worked diligently to understand the mechanisms by which Rome maintained the strength of her armies. A consensus has emerged that by the end of the 1st century at least most auxiliary units maintained their strength through a process often termed 'local recruitment'.[12] Certain exceptions are allowed: some provinces, such as Egypt, are deemed exceptional, while some unit types—there is no absolute consensus—are believed to have continued to recruit from their area of origin instead. These alleged exceptions will be discussed further below, but it is necessary first to examine the problems inherent in the concept of 'local recruitment'.

'Local recruitment' is a problematic concept because it conflates several distinct understandings of local which have widely differing implications. At the micro-level, there can be no doubt that military communities themselves became a source of many recruits; the children of soldiers' families were in turn enrolled. Thus the *canabae* of the legions and the extramural settlements around auxiliary forts may be envisaged as an increasingly important source of manpower. Assessing how important a source they were is, however, essential. To what extent could an 'army caste' have emerged in provincial society? How far could units have become closed communities, unleavened by the influx of outsiders? Third-century legislation may have attempted to enforce the enlistment of soldiers' sons, but could units themselves have ever become self-replicating?

Problematically, local is also understood to indicate recruitment in the broad area within which a unit was stationed. This is generally left vague in discussion, but it may perhaps be understood as within the same 'frontier zone' or within a few days' travel of the regimental headquarters. More frequently, however, it is used simply to indicate from the same province. Given the cultural diversity that existed within provinces, it needs to be asked whether the term 'local' is really a useful one. It would be possible for a recruit to arrive from a location within the same province as the garrison yet to speak a different language and worship different gods from those of the people living both inside and outside the fort walls. Finally, and in the most elastic use of the term 'local', we see it used to include recruitment from neighbouring provinces.[13] Here the term essentially refers to the relative distance between the recruits' homes to their units. Yet the

---

[11] Only one auxiliary unit from Britain ever served within the province; this was the *cohors I Cornoviorum*, and even it was moved to quite another region—from the Welsh Marches to Northumberland.

[12] Cheesman (1914: 79); Kraft (1951: 62–3).

[13] Holder (1980: 123) concludes that 'local recruitment' becomes 'pervasive' after the Civil Wars of AD 69–70, but he argues for certain exceptions. He defines 'local recruitment' as including recruitment from neighbouring provinces.

documented distances between these show that a journey from one to the other could still represent several weeks on the road, and passage through very different provincial communities.

It is more meaningful to understand what takes place Empire-wide as recruitment from the nearest convenient source. Though scholars often speak as if recruits could be found with relative ease in quantity across the Empire, the evidence suggests that this is not quite how contemporaries saw the situation. There were, as the writings of Vegetius demonstrate, elite ideas about what made good recruit material. The degree to which this affected actual practice is debated. More importantly, however, there were times when reserves of manpower were more readily available—notably in the aftermath of imperial expansion—and others when it was at a premium.[14] It will be argued that in this sense the human resource was like many of Rome's natural resources: there were times of relative plenty and times of shortage; this sort of oscillation must be considered when trying to seek simple patterns of the evidence. In practice, there would have been times when it was more convenient and less disruptive and therefore unpopular to draw recruits from a relatively distant source than to gather them locally. Roman administration was wholly capable of adapting flexibility to changing sources of commodities and people.

It will be helpful to begin with a summary of the traditional position before examining those situations it fails to explain. The section will then conclude with an examination of the degree to which the military communities could themselves generate 'local' recruits.

When in 1884 the extraordinarily influential Theodor Mommsen discussed the ongoing requirements of regiments for recruits, he was strongly influenced by the evidence for North Africa. Then as now, this was in raw statistical terms the finest data available. For example, the extensive series of epitaphs recovered at Lambaesis, Numidia, recording soldiers in *Legio III Augusta* provide an unparalleled opportunity to examine chronological change in recruitment patterns. Altogether we know the origins of some 809 men who served in the legion between AD 14 and AD 235.[15] Of the known recruits, 81 per cent of those enrolled in the legion before the reign of Hadrian were non-African, yet by AD 225 the situation had changed dramatically: every one of the known recruits was African-born. A further transition was evidenced: whereas up until the reign of Hadrian fewer than 5 per cent of recruits gave *castris*, i.e. the civilian settlement attached to the legionary base, as their place of birth, by the reign of Antoninus Pius that had climbed to 34 per cent. The legionaries' dependants were still producing recruits for the *III Augusta* at this rate several decades later, in AD 225.[16] To early commentators it all appeared a splendid example of Roman progress: the agents of the centre were succeeded in their mission by the children of the provinces. And certainly there was a real transition in the province: rapid urban growth, with its burgeoning communities of citizens, generated a larger pool of recruits. In fact this is not strictly local recruiting. The majority of African recruits did not actually

---

[14] For Tiberius' concerns see Tacitus *Ann.* 4.4.

[15] Le Bohec (1989). The legion features extensively in the work of Forni (1953).

[16] Cherry (1998: 94, table 3.1); Le Bohec (1989: 70).

come from the area around the regimental base; rather, they came from the growing towns of the eastern part of the province.[17] Other commentators subsequently introduced the legion's experience into their discussion of auxiliary recruitment, suggesting that it offered parallels.[18]

Yet in fact, even in extensively documented Africa it is impossible to prove that local recruitment predominated in the *auxilia*. Indeed, it cannot even be demonstrated on the available evidence that the majority of auxiliaries came from within the provinces in which they were stationed. This is not simply because there are far fewer records of individual auxiliaries. The evidence that does exist underscores the importance of external sources of recruits.[19] Only three of the twenty-six individually attested auxiliary soldiers whose *origo* is known came from North Africa.[20] Furthermore, there is explicit evidence for large drafts entering the region from elsewhere. While an analysis of soldiers' names from the Tripolitanian garrison of Vezereos may suggest that many of the men there were of African origin in the Severan period,[21] another inscription of about the same date records the arrival of 1,000 Bessi from Thrace.[22] The men that formed the Bessian contingent were most probably auxiliaries of some kind, as they were placed under the control of a tribune of the *numerus Syrorum Malvensium*. When their collective origins are added to those discussed above, we are obliged to acknowledge that rather more than half of all the known soldiers, legionary and auxiliary, stationed in Africa came from Thrace. I am not suggesting here that this evidence is wholly representative of the overall situation, but rather emphasizing the limitations in the data. In raw statistical terms it is not possible to argue that even regional recruitment became the norm for the army of Africa. Again, it might be argued that the draft's arrival was in response to some exceptional circumstance, in preparation for a campaign perhaps, but we should be hesitant in assuming that this was the case.[23] The problem with counting individual epitaphs is that a single discovery can too easily destroy a fine hypothesis.

For M. P. Speidel, the tombstone of the tribune in charge of the Bessian contingent offers an insight into the processes by which drafts were selected and dispatched. He suggests that there was some sort of central agency in Rome that planned recruitment Empire-wide.[24] Certainly the text admirably illustrates the remarkable complexity underpinning an operation that must have been reasonably common in imperial times,[25] the movement of large bodies of recruits across the provincial landscape. Here we see the commander of a Syrian auxiliary unit named after its Dacian headquarters, a man who was himself born in Upper Germany, bringing a contingent from Thrace to Africa overland. Given what we saw earlier of the level of attention to detail shown in the support of the Egyptian army, some sort of Empire-wide coordination is a real possibility.[26] Yet it might be worth recalling that regimental formations in very large armies have even recently

---

[17] Shaw (1983: 144). [18] e.g. Cheesman (1914: 78–9).

[19] Critiqued in Cherry (1998: 95). [20] Ibid. [21] Lassère (1980).

[22] *CIL* 8.9381 = *ILS* 2763. M. P. Speidel (1977a) dates this inscription to the Severan period.

[23] Ibid. 342 suggests that these men were brought into Africa in connection with operations in the early 3rd century.

[24] Ibid. 169. [25] See ibid. nn. 6 and 9.

[26] As M. A. Speidel (2007) suggests in his study of *ChLA* X 422.

sent recruiting officers great distances on their own initiative to areas known to be fertile recruiting grounds.

The *surviving* evidence from Britain also raises questions about the degree to which the principle of local recruitment operated.[27] Holder argues that British recruits offer a notable exception to it.[28] Indeed, there are only two references to British recruits serving in auxiliary regiments in Britain. One is a tombstone which records a Brigantian in a *cohors II Thracum* on the Antonine Wall, the second a diploma recording a soldier from Gloucester who served in *cohors I fida Vardullorum*.[29] Mann attributed this absence of evidence to a lack of 'epigraphic consciousness' amongst Britons, and this may indeed be a partial explanation, but it does not seem to me to be the whole explanation.[30] Even if it is accepted that Britons were generally less inclined than other provincial peoples to record their lives in inscriptions, a life lived in military service exposed every man to the power of words in stone.[31]

What makes the paucity of evidence for Britons in the British armies striking is the large number of Britons attested in the Danubian armies during this time. Of the two *alae* and 15 *cohortes* styled *Britannica*, *Brittonum*, or *Brittanorum*, all but two serve on the Danubian frontier; seven are found in the new provinces of Dacia. There are also multiple attestations of individual British soldiers there. Of these, the most noteworthy are five 2nd-century diplomas, one of which records a man enrolled in *cohors I Brittonum c.* AD 129, almost half a century after it had been posted overseas.[32]

The belief that the presence of Britons in such numbers overseas and their relative absence at home is explained by the wild and intractable nature of a people who were fundamentally too dangerous to serve in their own homelands is— however pleasing it may be to certain national sentiments—probably misplaced. A more convincing argument is that the phenomenon is linked to defending the Danubian frontier from a new wave of Dacian assaults. It is clear that this was deemed a higher priority than continuing operations in Britain, even if Tacitus dismisses the redeployment as an inept waste.[33] It is no coincidence that almost all the diplomas that survive from British auxiliaries in British units in Dacia indicate that the men would have enrolled in the early to mid-AD 80s. Their units probably accompanied established regiments, such as *Legio II Adiutrix*, known to have deployed from the British army to the Danube at this time. While some Britons were deployed in British units, it is likely that others were drafted wherever required. A Briton is certainly recorded on the Adamklissi memorial in the very mixed ranks of an unknown auxiliary unit.[34]

---

[27] Dobson and Mann (1973) offer a useful review of the evidence, though more data is now available.

[28] Holder (1980: 123).   [29] Tombstone: *RIB* 2142. Diploma: *CIL* 16.130.

[30] Mann (1985).   [31] P. 322.

[32] Ivonercus received a diploma (*RMD* 47) in AD 154, suggesting that he enlisted *c.* AD 129. Other Britons in British units in the Danubian armies include Lucco (*CIL* 16.49), Novantico (*CIL* 16.160), and Longinus (*CIL* 16.163). All of these men were enrolled in the AD 80s, most probably prior to, or contemporaneously with, the redeployment of *Legio II Adiutrix* and other units of the British army to the Danube.

[33] Tacitus *Agric.* 41.   [34] *CIL* 3.14214 v.18.

Nor is there anything especially surprising about finding a Briton, Ivonercus, entering *cohors I Brittonum* so long after the unit left Britain.[35] Several explanations are possible. The generic 'British' *origo* given on the diploma may suggest that he received his nationality from his father.[36] Had he been born in Britain he might have been more likely to give a tribal or urban origin. Alternatively, he may have been amongst those men conscripted in the aftermath of Hadrian's wars in Britain—though if this is the case his likely enrolment date would seem to be late. Ultimately, we will never know, but what we can say categorically is that there was no attempt to treat British recruits or British units specially; the latter had a range of diverse peoples within their ranks too.[37]

However many recruits Britain actually provided for its own garrison, it remains clear that a very large number of men continued to enter the provincial army from outside, most notably from northern Gaul and the Germanies. A high proportion of units in the British garrison were originally raised there and indeed, much of the army that originally invaded Britain had come from this region. Crucially, northern Gaul and the Germanies had a long-standing role as a source of army recruits. In fact this region remained a convenient source of manpower for Britain well into the 3rd century. Colleagues habituated to believe that 'local recruitment' was the norm at this time, therefore, risk attaching undue importance to the presence of Gauls and Germans in units of Gallic and German origin in the late 2nd and 3rd century. Thus the attested presence of such men in *cohors I Tungrorum* at Housesteads at this time need not indicate a special connection between the unit and its Belgian homelands akin to the treaties that sustained the Batavi.[38] Men from these regions were reinforcing auxiliary units of all origins at this time. Furthermore, if the evidence for another Tungrian unit in the same provincial garrison is considered, we can see that the evidence rather reinforces the notion that recruiting from the source that is most convenient at a given time is a more likely explanation than recruiting to maintain ethnic stock. In the mid-2nd century, different groups within *cohors II Tungrorum equitata* at Birrens (Scotland) dedicated altars on which they commemorated their origins. One group came from the vicinity of the unit's homelands,[39] another from elsewhere in Germania,[40] while the third, a group from Raetia, came from another province altogether.[41] The latter contingent may well have been recruited while a detachment from the cohort was in the region.[42]

Before leaving Britain, we should consider an interesting hypothesis advanced by Anthony Birley that touches on the most mundane workings of recruitment in the province.[43] Birley suggests that an inscription recording a census of the Anavionenses of northern Britain was linked to the raising of *numeri*. We know that British *numeri* were sent to Germany at about this time, a fact that underscores the impression of strong ties between the two provincial armies. He argues that the *censores*' role was to assess not foremost taxes in money, but how many

---

[35] See above, p. 126.   [36] Spaul (2000: 197).

[37] *RMD* 35: a Pannonian in *cohors I Britannica*. *RMD* 63: a Thracian in *cohors I Brittonum*.

[38] *Contra* the impression in Crow (1995: 56–63).   [39] *RIB* 2108.

[40] *RIB* 2107.   [41] *RIB* 2100.

[42] See Holder (1982: 122) and Jarrett (1994: 49–50) for a vexillation recruiting soldiers in Raetia.

[43] A. R. Birley (2007: 306–18).

men the community could contribute. A fragmentary text from Vindolanda, perhaps a rations roll, may in turn indicate that Anavion[enses?] were attached to the cohort in residence, the *cohors VIIII Batavorum, c.* AD 98–104/5.[44] Furthermore, he argues, the well-known tablet that refers dismissively to the fighting methods of the *Britunculi*, or little Britons, may relate to their training.[45] Whether or not Birley's erudite speculations are correct, they certainly offer a very plausible picture. Moreover, it is attractive to imagine the scenario advanced: that auxiliary soldiers—in this case Batavians—contributed to the incorporation of Britons within the Roman army.

While neither the African nor the British armies offer compelling evidence for the primacy of local recruitment, it is clear that there were areas where units did draw recruits from the immediate vicinity of their bases. Ironically, the strongest case for truly local recruitment actually comes from Pannonia, the province that hosted one of the biggest revolts of local troops ever experienced by the Empire.

Epitaphs and diplomas recording soldiers in the Pannonian garrison indicate that local recruitment was well under way by the early 1st century AD. They show that men were enlisting from the Pannonian *civitates* of the Drave and Save, the Breuci, Colapiani, Coranacates, and Sisciani.[46] Mócsy suggests that the number of men recruited from amongst the Colapiani reflects the strategic importance of this tribe during Tiberian operations in the province.[47] A similar explanation may, perhaps, account for the drawing of recruits from the other tribes. Recruitment of Pannonians for the Pannonian garrison is also recorded in Tacitus's account of AD 50.[48] By this time Rome was recruiting more widely in the province, needing to draw on a bigger pool of candidates. Thus we find Iasi and north Pannonians in the ranks of regiments stationed there.[49] The consolidation of the Danube frontier in the late 1st and early 2nd century witnessed the adoption of new recruiting areas, however, this time among the Azali and Eravisci. This clearly resulted from the deployment of the vast majority of the provincial garrison in the *civitates* of the two tribes; for example, at least nine auxiliary forts lay within the territory of the Eravisci. Just how important the contribution of these tribes to the garrison was is illustrated by the origins of soldiers given on the thirty-one diplomas from the Pannonias issued between AD 96 and AD 167.[50] The other *civitates* that are named are those of the Azali and Eravisci. In this region, it is clear that recruits were drawn extensively from wherever units were based.

Culturally, this pattern produces some very striking results. Ethnographic evidence from the two *civitates* indicates that forms of native dress, non-Latin names, burial practices, and religious symbolism survived amongst these peoples until well into the 2nd century AD.[51] Roman citizenship spread relatively slowly; the earliest known grant of citizenship to an Eraviscian noble was under Nerva.[52]

[44] *Tab. Vindol* III 594. As Birley notes, there is no parallel for Anavion as a personal name.
[45] *Tab. Vindol.* II. 164 is also a period III text. It is therefore also provisionally dated to AD 98–104/5, the time the Batavian cohort was in residence.
[46] See e.g. *CIL* 3.4372, 4373, 4376, 4377 and *CIL* 16.2 and 4.   [47] Mócsy (1974: 51).
[48] Tacitus *Ann.* 12.29.   [49] Mócsy (1974: 51–2) cites *CIL* 16.20 and 31 for this trend.
[50] These are *CIL* 16.47; 49; 61; 69; 71; 73; 89; 97; 99; 109; 113; 116; 119; 123; 132; 164; 175; and *RMD* 62, all incidentally discovered near fort sites, and *CIL* 16.42; 64; 84; 92; 96; 100; 103; 104; 12; 178; 179; 180.
[51] Mócsy (1974: 61–3, 158).   [52] Mócsy (1962: 35).

Furthermore, the Hadrianic municipalization of the Danube area left the *civitas peregrina* of the Azali virtually untouched.[53] Accordingly, the character of the area and the recruits who sprung from it would have been 'decidedly rustic and plebeian', just the sort of material that would have delighted Vegetius.[54] Local recruitment in these territories had implications not only for the Azali and Eravisci within Pannonia but also for the forms of provincial culture that evolved beyond their borders. We may see this in the forts and their dependent extramural settlements within the new Dacian territories. The distinctive brooches that appear in the forts and extramural settlements, and the depictions of soldiers' wives in Eraviscan costume, all indicate that cultural trappings of these tribes were exported, both with Pannonian recruits to the units sent to Dacia and with the families of serving soldiers who had lived south of the Danube before Trajan's conquest took them north.[55]

Thus far, analysis of recruitment patterns has necessarily dwelt on the identities and movement of individual servicemen. These individuals were, after all, the focus of the provincial administrators' efforts to classify, quantify, and supply men for military service. But, as has been demonstrated, the impact of recruitment on provincial society did not stop with the men themselves. It had wider implications. Amongst those for whom its implications were profound were soldiers' families. These lie at the heart of any debate as to how far army units became self-reproducing, both biologically and culturally. If military families came to be the primary producers of future recruits, then the chance of individual units perpetuating distinct—one might even say incestuous—attributes grows. This was certainly an important prop in Shaw's argument that the legion at Lambaesis was a 'total institution'.[56]

Though very occasionally auxiliary soldiers cite their origins as *castris*, 'born in camp', the phrase is much less frequently used amongst them than amongst legionaries.[57] There are probably several reasons for this. Some of those born in the *canabae* settlements attached to the legionary fortress would end up in the *auxilia*, but the children of legionaries, being citizens themselves, might well enter the neighbouring legion if they sought a military career. It is often argued that the extramural settlements attached to the forts where most auxiliary regiments were stationed would also have operated in this manner.[58] Certainly these could house quite large communities including many military families. Yet because they had a different legal status from that of the legionary camps and their *canabae*, they could not be cited as a place of origin. An entry in the *Digest* clearly states that *vicani* (inhabitants of *vici*) should be registered in their *civitas*.[59] While it is not certain that all extramural settlements attached to auxiliary forts were termed *vici* by their occupants, it is clear that some of them were. It is also quite possible that some soldiers preferred to cite as their origin what was more properly their cultural affiliation. In some cases, the children, say, of Batavian parents born overseas may well have chosen to identify themselves as Batavians, despite never having set foot in the tribal territory itself. Driel-Murray has asked whether, in the case of a soldier of *cohors I Batavorum*, M. Ulpius Fronto, and his wife, Mattua,

[53] Mócsy (1974: 145).   [54] Ibid. 158.   [55] Cociş (2004).
[56] Shaw (1984).   [57] e.g. *CIL* 8.3101.
[58] Mann (1963: 145); Webster (1998: 230); Sommer (1989: 28).   [59] *Digest* (50.1.30).

both Batavians, their three daughters, Vagatra, Sureia, and Sata, would actually have considered themselves Batavian too, and if in turn they would have passed these identities onto their (soldier?) children.[60] These too might have been born in the camp's extramural settlement, but we would not be able to tell that from surviving documentation. Any attempt to quantify, however loosely, the proportion of soldiers who may themselves have grown up within military families must fall back on two rather problematic approaches. The first analyses the epigraphic evidence in an attempt to determine what proportion of soldiers actually had families. The second seeks to estimate the number of military followers by looking at the size of the settlements attached to forts and other military outposts.

Evidence for civilian settlements linked to military establishments has been found across the Empire, from the short-lived siege camps of Masada in Israel to the far more established settlements of the Rhine frontier. In the northwest European provinces, where they have been most intensively studied, it has been possible to demonstrate the presence of so-called 'military *vici*' adjacent to at least 64 per cent of known British forts, 84 per cent of those in Raetia, and 87 per cent of those in Upper Germany.[61] Furthermore, in these regions as in the Masada example, there is strong evidence that many settlements were founded at the same time as their associated forts.[62] Close reading of the archaeological evidence from *inside* the Empire's forts and fortresses suggests furthermore that many of these civilians even spent time within the bases themselves.

Merchants, vendors, and servants will receive attention in due course, but our principal interest here is in the families, most especially soldiers' families, amongst this throng. Women and children clearly constituted a large part of any army's following. In the literary sources, they are often mentioned only incidentally, such as when they are caught up in the horrors of the Varus disaster in AD 9.[63] To ancient writers, after all, these people were marginal to the great narratives of Roman history. Yet to the soldiers they were surely anything but irrelevant. Many readings of the evidence have argued that relatively few soldiers formed families in the early Principate. They hold that it was not until later that soldiers' rights to live with women were regularized, and argue further that the mobility of early armies would have made any sort of stable relationship difficult.[64] Yet a glance at the history of recent armies where similar conditions prevailed indicates that whatever difficulties existed, people would strive to overcome them. In the 19th century, in the Peninsular War, large numbers of unofficial wives and children followed their soldier 'husbands'/fathers throughout a terribly demanding campaign. When the campaign was over, they were abandoned at the dockside. Only the handful of women whose marriages were officially recognized were allowed to

---

[60] Driel-Murray (2003: 210) on *RMD* 86. This fascinating question has major implications for the study of recruitment. Might other groups have simply preferred to identify themselves by a tribal or ethnic link despite being second- or even third-generation expats?

[61] Sommer (1989: 25).

[62] Sommer (ibid.) notes that it is possible to *prove* archaeologically that an extramural settlement was founded at the same time as a fort in 44% of cases. The actual proportion of contemporaneous foundations could be much higher.

[63] Dio 56.20.2–5.

[64] See Roxan (1989: 463) for the difficulties in maintaining family life under the early Empire.

accompany their spouses back to Britain.[65] Had the sea not intervened, many more would surely have followed. We must, I think, envisage a similar situation in the Roman army. The legal situation demonstrated that the authorities took no responsibility for these people; it did not mean that they did not exist.

What evidence we do have indicates that such relationships were widely understood to exist. Diploma formulae from the post-Claudian period clearly demonstrate that soldiers did form unions with women—otherwise it would not have been necessary to establish the status of those unions after a soldier had been discharged and awarded citizenship. The use of the term *uxor* or 'wife' in the formula indicates that men were understood to be married, but it was only with the grant of *conubium*, conveyed at honourable discharge, that the soldier's marriage was recognized under Roman law.[66] In Egypt, special tolls specifically for 'soldiers' women/wives' were levied on travellers from Coptos to the Red Sea.[67]

The toll rates from Egypt remind us that soldiers travelled long distances with their families. We know of the rigorous travelling some families undertook precisely because they never completed their journeys. Ulpia Dana, the Mauretanian wife of a decurion serving in the much-travelled *ala Atectorigiana*, was buried in Rome.[68] It appears that she died on the journey from Africa when accompanying her husband on his way back to his unit in Lower Moesia.[69] The lot of many itinerant families was made relatively easier by the fact that the Roman army preferred to move large formations by land and to avoid long sea crossings.[70] As this case demonstrates, however, sea crossings did not act as a barrier to civilian followers. Evidence for this comes also from Britain, where a German family group, apparently with military associations, is attested at Old Penrith. A tombstone commemorating the family records two brothers and a girl of 4.[71]

The nature of the evidence makes it difficult to identify chronological or regional patterns in the creation of military families. A survey of 787 tombstones recording serving auxiliaries argued for some patterns.[72] Such inscriptions, our primary source, are, however, unevenly distributed through time and space. As the author of the survey observes, in some places the data they offer us are wholly misleading.[73] In Egypt, for example, only eight auxiliary tombstones are known, and the families

---

[65] Weller (1992: 361 n.1); Adrian Goldsworthy, pers. comm.

[66] The most common version of the formula is *conubium, cum uxoribus quas tunc habuissent.*

[67] *IGRR* I 1183.

[68] *CIL* 6.33032 = *AE* 1890, 27.

[69] A view also held by M. P. Speidel (1977a: 169, n. 10).

[70] In the 1st century AD, for example, *Legio IX Hispana* went from the Danube down through Italy before taking the shortest possible sea route over to Africa (Tacitus *Ann.* 3.9; M. P. Speidel 1977a: 169).

[71] *RIB* 934.

[72] Roxan (1991).

[73] Of these epitaphs, 250 refer to wives or *libertae*, freedwomen partners. This is insufficient to identify regional patterns. When the figures are broken down into regional groupings they appear to confirm Saller and Shaw's (1984: 142) analysis that there 'was a low level of family formation and family ties' in the British garrison. Yet it is surely difficult to argue for such patterns when only 7 auxiliary tombstones from the province refer to family ties. The paucity of references could also reflect other local trends, such as the alleged lack of 'epigraphic consciousness' in British families (Mann 1985). If the models of Roxan, Saller, and Shaw are correct, however, it may explain why the British garrison drew so many recruits from elsewhere. Military families would have furnished the provincial army with an even smaller pool of recruits than elsewhere.

of auxiliaries scarcely appear on the epigraphic record, yet such families are referred to regularly on surviving papyri.[74] Nonetheless, the survey did support the generally accepted hypothesis that there was a higher instance of family formation at later periods.[75] The same study then used diplomas to argue for a similar conclusion, noting that only 38 per cent of diplomas issued before AD 117 named soldiers' families as compared to over 69 per cent of those issued afterwards.[76] Importantly, an increase in military families would coincide in broad terms with growing stability on the frontiers and the increasing permanence of postings.[77]

Determining what proportion of any given unit would have been composed of soldiers' children is virtually impossible; in every case it rests upon a series of uncertainties. Furthermore, multiple local patterns ensure that what might be appropriate to one station would prove wholly inappropriate to others. Calculations also depend on how we reconstruct ancient populations. The most compelling study to come out of the exciting recent debates on Roman demography was sceptical about any attempts to reconstruct the age profiles of ancient populations. It observed, however, that in the absence of hard data, model life tables would be 'good to think with'.[78] Yet even the roughest calculations demonstrate that units could only have received a small proportion of the recruits needed from military families in the extramural settlements associated with each fort. A military family population several times the size of the unit would be required, and most extramural settlements simply are not that big, even if they were exclusively occupied by military families, and we know that they were not.

While it is clear, therefore, that there would have been a steady flow of outsiders coming into every regimental community to top up its numbers, it is less clear how much of an opportunity there was for those wanting to leave it. Soldiers were, of course, confined by their professional obligations and could be released only by desertion, death, sickness, or discharge. What of their sons? How much of an alternative to service in their fathers' regiments young men growing up in a *vicus/* fort setting would have had must have depended a great deal on the station. In some places, isolated postings must have ensured that the boundaries of the military community defined the limits of opportunity. Young men in such situations were often indeed captured bodies, trapped by expectation and convention. Tendencies towards hereditary soldiering were no doubt strong in some areas, and in the 3rd century it allegedly became enforceable.[79] As Simon Jones has noted, however, any attempt to enshrine such a practice in law would likely indicate that a significant proportion of sons were choosing not to follow their fathers into the profession.[80]

The cultural implications of all this may well have been amplified by a further trend, argued by a number of scholars principally from the epigraphic evidence. This is the view that for the most part soldiers married into the families of other soldiers. This was certainly a significant phenomenon, though attempts to quantify it are marred both by the sheer paucity of evidence and by the misleading character of that which we do have.[81] Attempts to calculate its frequency draw

---

[74] Roxan (1991: 465).   [75] Ibid. 462.   [76] Ibid. 464.
[77] Cheesman (1914: 116); Mann (1963: 149); Maxfield (1995: 7).
[78] Scheidel (2001: 26), in this case quoting Golden (2000: 32).
[79] *HA Sev. Alex.* 58.4; *Probus* 16.5.   [80] Simon James, pers. comm.
[81] For the importance of 'daughters of the regiment' as the mothers of the next generation, see Wells (1997).

largely on data from legionary families in North Africa.[82] It is important to recognize that such figures may not apply with equal force to auxiliaries, and also to recall that members of indigenous populations in many regions are less likely to leave inscriptions than individuals who have grown up in military families.

Quantifying the importance of this institutional endogamy relative to formation of partnerships with local civilians is impossible. There were clearly cases, such as in the army of Syria, where as early as AD 69, soldiers had become tied to the local civilian population through ties of friendship and marriage.[83] It may not be a coincidence that the famous speech in which Mucianus appals his local audience with the prospect that their army might leave them took place in the great city of Antioch.[84] There could have been far greater scope for soldier–civilian relations where soldiers were stationed in cities than when they were in more sparsely populated frontier zones. Almost certainly in this, as in so much else, there was real regional variation. For a host of reasons, including local tensions and cultural practices, the degree of intermarriage would have varied. Conceivably, intermarriage may have been less likely the further removed the men of the garrison were from the wider population in terms of language and culture, but it is clear that such obstacles were frequently crossed.

Where units remained in one place for an extended period, provided a significant percentage of their own recruits, and intermarried, there was a greater chance that cultural relics from the unit's place of origin or previous station would be maintained. The wider regimental community was thus not simply Roman or Roman military, but also a particular evolving synthesis of provincial cultures. Such a dynamic is certainly best able to explain otherwise extraordinary survivals. Thus a 3rd-century tombstone found at Birdoswald in Cumbria records a child called Deciba[lus],[85] the name of the Dacian king defeated by Trajan. The name seems curiously apposite given that the unit in residence was *cohors I Aelia Dacorum*, but that regiment appears to have arrived in the region many decades before. Decibalus can hardly be understood to have been a drafted recruit—he was far too young. The most reasonable conclusion we may draw from the evidence is that the name remained popular among men in the regiment and their families for several generations.[86] Significantly, the same regiment retains the Dacian falx sword on its dedications for just as long—further evidence perhaps for some sort of cultural memory or regimental tradition.[87] Confusingly for scholars, it has recently been suggested that ethnic identity might have remained so strong in some of these places that soldiers and their families gave not their actual place of birth on their documents and tombstones, but the ethnicity with which they most strongly identified. If this idea is correct—and it is currently impossible to prove—it could have major implications for our analysis.[88] The possibility that a man who describes himself as Batavian and another who regards himself as Syrian might both have been born on, say, the Lower Danube would be a great setback for historians. While it seems less likely to me that such a practice occurred on diplomas, which were after all legal documents, it is a possibility that we should not ignore when looking at private dedications such as inscriptions.

[82] Shaw (1983: 148) and Cherry (1998: 99–140, esp. 133).   [83] Tacitus *Hist.* 2.80.
[84] Ibid.   [85] *RIB* 1920.   [86] Birley (1988b: 96).
[87] P. 289.   [88] Driel-Murray (2003: 210–11).

Reviewing the evidence, we must accept that auxiliary regiments were kept at strength by a range of means. Each of these processes had significant cultural implications, for the man, the regimental community, and for provincial societies more generally. Volunteers, conscripts, and substitutes were in varying proportions present in the ranks throughout the period. Sources of recruits varied from province to province, both in terms of the peoples enrolled and in terms of the degree to which local, provincial, and regional recruitment were employed. A further complication came in the response to local crises—a sudden shortage of men might lead to emergency reinforcements.

To reiterate, it is clear that as units became established they increasingly drew on recruits from their immediate vicinity, but overall it is wrong to assume that this became the primary source of manpower. In most areas truly local recruits are seldom found within the evidence. This is not necessarily because, as some claim, outsiders are more likely to record their origins while locals find it superfluous. In the cosmopolitan community that was any provincial army, origins were still worth recalling. We have enough evidence to indicate that in many settings, amongst them the armies of Pannonia, locals gave their origins too. Rather, recruits were drawn, throughout the period, from the nearest convenient source. Even where this was within the same province, it could still ensure a cosmopolitan mix. Just as the tensions behind the origins of several early regiments demonstrated, differences between neighbouring communities could still be real. In fact, though, our evidence frequently shows drafts of recruits moving from one province to another. Often pragmatism ensured that these were provinces that were reasonably close to one another. This must have helped ensure that the British army continued to have a strongly Gallic/Germanic aspect. But at other times, the arrival of drafts in a territory depended on where the largest number of men was available. Thus the presence of so many British units and recruits in Dacia owed much to the pacification of the island at the time Rome was expanding north of the Danube.

There are some significant patterns in all this complexity. The key to appreciating them lies in recognizing that recruitment operated in a way that related closely to other processes of supply and taxation within the Empire. With these too, of course, ad hoc arrangements and imperial whims created temporary and localized peculiarities. There is a parallelism between the human resource and the natural one. Just as a glut in wine production might affect the patterns of wine consumption in some regions, so might a surge in available manpower following fresh conquest affect the supply of recruits. Men from such regions would be disproportionately represented in areas with particular shortages. It is clear that the pattern of recruitment did not therefore fall evenly. In general, peoples who could, through agriculture or industry, contribute less to the imperial coffers were more likely to be exploited as a human resource. Such groups were often perceived as a threat to imperial interests too, so recruitment served the further role of reducing the pool of potentially hostile manpower. Peoples on the fringes of the Roman world or on the relatively 'under-urbanized' zones within it were accordingly absorbed into the imperial system. The result at regimental level was on occasion bewildering, but at imperial level it led in a similar direction. As I noted in the discussion of the Adamklissi memorial with its cosmopolitan war dead, the exotic mix found within units was also a powerful testimony to the incorporation of provincial society.

9

Ethnic Exceptionalism?

Examining 'Special' Recruitment Practices

Had emperors wished to preserve the ethnic qualities of their fighting units, there is every reason to believe that they could have done so. The imperial system was entirely capable of moving men and materials across the Empire when it so desired. Given that a special recruiting arrangement existed for the Batavi, one might wonder why similar agreements should not exist with other groups.

The claim that there was something special about the recruiting practices of British units has already been discussed and dismissed. But other claims have been made for special recruiting practices. This section will assess these claims and will argue that, contrary to what has been suggested by other scholars, the evidence does not support the existence of special recruiting practices sustaining ethnically distinctive enclaves of soldiers. The ranks of regiments were open to men of widely differing origins. It is often the mixture of men alongside, of course, the official function of these units that leads them to develop as distinctive communities—discrete not only from the provincials around them but often also from other elements of the army.

Of the various claims made for special recruiting practices designed to ensure a notional ethnic homogeneity, the most enduring is that certain eastern units, in particular regiments of archers, continued to receive recruits from their place of origin. This was the opinion of Domaszewski over a century ago and continues to be believed even today.[1] Cheesman was a firm believer in the notion, Kraft spoke of the practice applying to 'oriental' units in general, while Mann was rather more specific, citing 'exceptions in the case of specialized troops like mounted archers'.[2] Speaking of the *auxilia* before Trajan, Holder makes a more general claim that 'the regiments from the East . . . generally retained their ethnic composition whatever the distance' from their area of origin.[3] So widespread is this belief in exceptional recruiting practice that it has been used to explain an extraordinary range of phenomena in provincial society. Hitherto only one scholar, David Kennedy, has challenged this claim.[4] This section examines the arguments that there were

---

[1] von Domaszewski (1895: 52).

[2] Cheesman (1914: 82–4). Kraft (1951: 63) explains how he reads the evidence from the Rhine and the Danube. See Mann (1963: 147) for mounted archers.

[3] Holder (1980: 121).

[4] I owe a particular debt to Kennedy's (1980) rigorous analysis of the evidence for auxiliary units raised in Syria.

special eastern exceptions to the general policy, and considers what they tell us of both ancient and modern views of Rome's subject peoples. It argues that the current consensus reflects a misapplication of colonial conceptions of martial races to Roman practice. What emerges from closer analysis is the altogether more interesting evidence for the evolution of distinctive hybrid communities as a by-product of imperial policy.

The notion that Rome had a special policy towards some eastern peoples largely originates from a cemetery in Hungary. To date, more than 2,500 graves have been excavated around the Roman fort of Intercisa in Dunaújváros, Fejér County (See Fig. 9.1). Over 800 of these were uncovered before Cheesman published his classic work on the *auxilia*.[5] Some of these, at least, dated from after AD 180, when the fort was remodelled to receive its new garrison, *cohors I Hemesenorum milliaria Antonina Aurelia sagittariorum equitata civium Romanorum*, a regiment of archers raised from the territory of Emesa in Syria. Information from the epitaphs and religious dedications recovered played a crucial role in convincing scholars that this unit, and others like it, preserved a distinctive ethnic character through special recruiting methods. The sheer volume of data recovered added credibility to this attractive theory. *Cohors I Hemesenorum* was for a long time the best-known auxiliary regiments in the Roman army. It was also, as we shall see, one of the least well understood.

At the heart of the theory were two mistaken beliefs. The first was that the regiment was raised in the early 2nd century, shortly after the annexation of Emesa. Many scholars were happy to attribute a Trajanic date to the foundation.[6] Rossi somewhat imaginatively even claimed to have identified the cohort on Trajan's Column in the form of bowmen with long flowing gowns.[7] Such an early foundation date would indeed have raised questions as to how the unit could still have had so many easterners in it by the time it reached the Danube in the late 2nd century. The only explanation would then have seemed to be special recruitment practices. The second mistaken claim was that the majority of soldiers serving in the regiment at Intercisa came from the lands of the former Syrian kingdom.

In fact there is actually no evidence at all for an early 2nd-century foundation date. Rather, all of the available evidence favours the creation of the regiment in the AD 160s.[8] If we accept that the unit was founded in the AD 160s and stayed in the east for a few years after it was raised, it comes as no surprise at all to find Syrians serving in its ranks on its arrival in Pannonia less than twenty years later. The rebuilding of the fort at Intercisa c. AD 180 may have coincided with this move, although it has been suggested that the unit arrived in AD 176.[9] The first datable reference to the regiment being at Intercisa comes from a building

---

[5] Between 1906 and 1913, 846 cremation and inhumation graves were excavated.

[6] Baur and Rostovtzeff (1929: 56 n. 1); Wagner (1938: 142).

[7] Rossi (1971: 189).

[8] See Mann (1974: 259) for formation of the unit between AD 161 and AD 169. Kennedy (1980: 121–2) argued that the regiment was founded c. AD 162. I owe the following assessment of the origins of recruits to the regiment to him.

[9] For 180, see Fitz (1972: 47). Visy (2003: 118) argues that the unit replaced the *ala I civium Romanorum* when it left in AD 176.

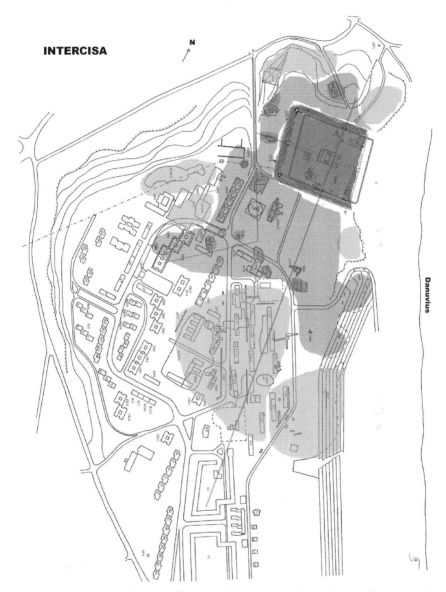

Fig. 9.1. The Roman settlement of Intercisa, Hungary, superimposed on modern Dunaúj-város. The parallelogram-shaped stone fort, which lies to the northeast, measures 176 × *c.*200m. It nevertheless represents only a fraction of the overall site, and is surrounded to the north, west, and south by extramural settlement. The cemetery areas that lie beyond are almost as extensive as the settlement itself.

inscription *c.* AD 180–183.[10] The earliest precisely datable reference to a soldier from the regiment records one Aurelius Bazas.[11] The text records his honourable discharge under Valerius Pudens, governor of Pannonia Inferior *c.* AD 192–4. If we work on the generally accepted principle that honourable discharge followed twenty-five years' service, Bazas would have been enlisted *c.* AD 167–9.[12] The non-Emesene origo of Bazas is itself interesting, indicating that non-Emesenes were already being recruited before the unit reached Intercisa.

A further problem with the claim that the unit continued to receive drafts from Emesa is the fact that only six of the fifty-six known soldiers of the regiment actually cite Emesa as their *origo*.[13] Four of these are named M. Aurelii, one does not give a full name, and that of the sixth has been lost. The name M. Aurelius could suggest that the soldiers concerned acquired citizenship either on retirement or in the block citizenship grant recorded in the regimental title, under Aurelius. There is therefore nothing to prevent them from having been recruited at the time the regiment was created. Similarly, *praenomen* and *nomen* indicate that most of the soldiers with Semitic names and/or from Syria received citizenship under Aurelius.[14] The presence of at least five Semites who give a city other than Emesa as their *origo* only reinforces, rather than undermines, the argument that *cohors I Hemesenorum* would have recruited in much the same way as other auxiliary units.[15] What has been missed by some scholars is simply that some of this local recruiting was conducted in Syria before it moved to Pannonia *c.* AD 180. Only one of the dateable inscriptions which refer to unit personnel serving in the regiment over twenty-five years after this move—by which time the last men enlisted in Syria had been discharged—mentions an easterner.[16] The soldier Barsemis was, however, an Osrhöenian who came from Carrhae, a city over 160 miles from Emesa. Such a distance may seem local to a contemporary scholar, but 2,000 years ago it could have meant a quite different cultural milieu. Furthermore, Barsemis had not enlisted into the unit, but rather joined it after holding two postings, one in an *ala* and the other in a *numerus*. His isolated case may hardly be argued as an example of special recruitment practices.

There is nothing to suggest that the remaining men in the regiment were even from the east. While Cheesman and others were confused as to the foundation date of the regiment, other scholars exacerbated the problem by offering wholly misleading readings of soldiers' name origins. Repeatedly, soldiers with names unknown or rare within Syria yet widely found elsewhere were attributed to the east. In fact the names of all the other men in the cohort would fit perfectly well in western contexts. As a result of the work of Mann and Kennedy, we can now see that accepted readings of the men's names are at best unsubstantiated, at worst

---

[10] *AE* 1964, 104.   [11] Barkóczi et al. (1954: no. 311).   [12] Fitz (1972: 47).

[13] Barkóczi et al. (1954: nos 129, 130, 132, 133) and *Albia Regia* 11 (1970), no. 452. The sixth text (*CIL* 16.131) may be restored to read *Hemes]a ex Syr(ia.*

[14] For M. Aurelii with Semitic names, See Barkóczi et al. (1954, nos. 16, 39, 340) and *Alba Regia* 11 (1970), no. 464. Although the name could have been given under Caracalla, the important point to note here is that it need not have been.

[15] M. Aurelii who offer Syrian origins but who do not come from Emesa record their origins as Apamaea (Barkóczi et al. 1954, no. 134), Arethusa (ibid. no. 23), and Edessa (*Alba Regia* 11 (1970), no. 446).

[16] *ILS* 2540. Barsemis' career most probably dates to the mid-3rd century AD, when many Osrhöenians appear in Roman service (Fitz 1972: 149; Speidel 1975: 229; Kennedy 1980: 133).

wishful thinking. The sum of this evidence suggests that *cohors I Hemesenorum* employed an entirely conventional recruiting pattern. When in Syria, it drew its recruits from there; when it moved to Pannonia it received recruits from the region around Intercisa.

What applies to the Hemeseni clearly applies to other eastern archer units. Cheesman supported his influential claims for special recruitment practices with reference to the history of two other regiments, the *ala I Augusta Ituraeorum sagittariorum* and the *cohors I Augusta Ituraeorum sagittariorum*. Again Cheesman based his hypothesis on foundation and overseas posting dates that are now contested. Contrary to his belief, there is no secure evidence for the existence of the *ala I Augusta Ituraeorum* before AD 98, when it appears on a Pannonian diploma. Rebuilding in the late AD 80s at the unit's station of Arrabona in the same province may be associated with the regiment's arrival. Whether or not the regiment was an early foundation (and there are reasons to argue that it was not), it was quite probably in the east until at least the late AD 80s. The often-cited Ituraean recipient of a diploma of AD 110, who would have enrolled in the regiment *c.* AD 85, is not therefore evidence for special recruiting. He may just have joined the *ala* on its foundation or at least immediately prior to its departure from Syria. Non-easterners, including a Batavian, a probable Spaniard, and a scattering of other provincials, are also found in the regiment's ranks. This further argues against a practice of recruitment geared towards sustaining ethnic unity. The argument from Cheesman's third alleged example, the *cohors I Augusta Ituraeorum*, is even less convincing. The one Syrian known from within its ranks was in fact from Cyrrhus, not Ituraea. Though little archaeological fieldwork has been undertaken in the area, we know enough about Cyrrhus from literary sources to say that it supported a very different society to that of the Ituraeans. In addition to being over 160 miles from the northern borders of the Ituraean principality, it was a well-established Greek city dominating a rich and fertile landscape far removed from the rugged terrain of the Lebanese mountains and Bekaa Valley. Rather than indicating special recruiting practices, therefore, the presence of this Syrian demonstrates that the regiment did not retain an Ituraean character. Further evidence that eastern archer units did not rely upon replacement recruits from their place of origin may come in the form of a recently discovered diploma which was probably discovered in Bulgaria.[17] The diploma was issued to a soldier in *cohors I Hamiorum*, a regiment of archers later stationed in Britain, who would have enlisted *c.* AD 107. His *origo* is given as MOMS, which Birley has convincingly argued is an engraver's error for MONT (ana), Mihailovgrad in northwest Bulgaria.[18]

Preservation of strong ethnic links was very much a feature of the British army of Cheesman's time. Emergency recruiting could dilute these links, but especially in the British Indian Army, real attempts were made to preserve the alleged or real ethnic character of regiments. In part this was because of a strong belief in 'clan spirit', a term widely used by Cheesman himself,[19] but it also allowed the army to capitalize on special fighting skills within particular units. Cheesman was too good a scholar simply to assume that the same practice was followed across the Roman

---

[17] Eck, Holder, and Pangerl (2010).   [18] A. R. Birley, pers. comm.

[19] e.g. Cheesman (1914: 57 and 58).

army, and indeed demonstrated that for the most part it was not, but confronted by a partial understanding of the eastern units he argued for an exception. Perhaps the contemporary background convinced him that certain types of fighting men could only be born in certain places, not made elsewhere. This is all despite the fact that no such requirement really pertains to archers.[20] Constant training can ensure exceptional proficiency in archery, and service in the Roman army offered plenty of scope for that.

It was not just the origins of the recruits in *cohors I Hemesenorum* at Intercisa, however, that wrongly convinced Cheesman and others that the regiment was receiving fresh drafts of men from the east. It was also the evidence for the culture of the regiment. Two religious dedications, discussed in detail below, show an ongoing association between the regiment and its place of origin. In around AD 201, over thirty years after the cohort was founded in Emesa, the regiment constructed a temple to Elagabalus, the patron god of that city.[21] Most, probably all, of the initial recruits would have gone by this time. Thirteen years later, soldiers of the same regiment dedicated an altar to the same deity. How could such a link be maintained without a steady flow of recruits from Emesa?

As noted, even when the cohort arrived at Intercisa it was far from a purely Emesene entity. There is little value, therefore, in imagining the regiment as a simple ethnic enclave. Not only were there recruits in its ranks from other Syrian communities, but the regiment would have contained officers and experienced hands seconded from elsewhere on its formation. Such secondments were essential if a mass levy of recruits was to be converted into a credible military unit.[22] Yet language and culture must have helped distinguish the new arrivals from the provincials who surrounded them. Transformed through military service, the Hemeseni thus formed a distinct nucleus around which a regimental community grew up. We know that this was distinctive enough and attractive enough for veterans to stay close and for former legionaries of Emesene extraction to settle nearby. Alföldy has described this sort of community as a classic *Militärgesellschaft.*[23] This is a useful formulation, but it does not adequately encompass the dynamics that have less to do with those cultural aspects which, preserved and/or transformed through association with the army, were not in fact military in origin. When the initial recruits were discharged, therefore, the cultural link to the east did not evaporate; it remained very much a part of the local area. Those veterans' children who enlisted in the ranks may have perpetuated the association. Even new recruits drawn from elsewhere would have absorbed and sustained the distinctive culture generated by the mixture of Emesene expats and military circumstances. Such a process explains how an eastern temple could be constructed, dedicated in Roman fashion, and could flourish four decades after the regiment arrived in Pannonia. Once the building was consecrated it became as much a part of the regimental community's religious landscape as other shrines, and soldiers from the cohort were naturally quite happy to worship there. At the same time the worship of Elagabalus at Intercisa illustrates one way in which the

---

[20] Ibid. 84.

[21] *ILS* 9155. Fitz (1972) argues for a date of AD 201.

[22] For stiffening newly raised units with seconded personnel (Tacitus *Agric.* 28).

[23] Alföldy (2000: 49).

regimental community operated as a parallel society. The men of the cohort and, one suspects, their families related to a deity largely unknown elsewhere in Pannonia, and indeed most of provincial society at this time. It was not until the accession of the emperor Varius, commonly known as Elagabalus, in AD 218 that the cult became more familiar.

If soldiers from the unit, whether native-born Emesenes or successive generations steeped in regimental culture, continued to worship Elegabalus, it might be asked whether or not there were other indicators of eastern culture at the site. Did other eastern practices survive amongst them? Excavations at the site actually reveal few indications of such survivals despite claims to the contrary. What is known of the fort, with its fine *principia*, indicates a fort type well within the range of military bases from the western Roman Empire. The civilian settlement which concentrated at the southern end of the fort prior to the Marcommanic Wars (AD 167–AD 180) spread during the time of the Hemeseni to surround much of the installation. To the south of the extramural settlement lay the cemeteries, and evidence for ethnic survivals has been sought in this area. Might it be possible to identify distinctive funerary rituals? Did traces of eastern dress continue to be worn? In fact it is not possible to offer a distinctive case for either proposition.

The excavators noted that deceased soldiers from the unit were cremated in accordance with widespread military practice, not inhumed as one might expect in eastern communities of this time.[24] That soldiers from the cohort were cremated is clear from the predominance of cremation burials from the late 2nd and early 3rd century and from some of the finds recovered from these cremations. A fine military-style belt was, for example, found within a cremation grave dated to this period.[25] Although a face pot deposited in another such burial was identified as eastern, the type fits entirely into the repertoire of face pots found in the western provinces.[26] Identifying soldiers with any certainty is notoriously difficult in Roman military contexts and identifying their families is no less so, but the finds from two contexts have been linked to the military. A child, believed by excavators to be the offspring of a soldier of the Hemeseni on account of an eastern coin found within the grave, contains little else to suggest an exotic eastern style of life or death.[27] It must be acknowledged, however, that this is a weak premiss. More strikingly, a family tombstone shows a soldier's wife who clearly followed Empire-wide fashions. The hairstyle of Aurelia Baracha, wife of Germanius Valens, a soldier of *cohors I Hemesenorum*, recalls that depicted in 3rd-century portraits of the imperial family.[28] It is interesting to note in passing that Aurelia may have been identifiable as a soldier's wife here by her adherence to Roman fashion, while in neighbouring provinces, such as Dacia, many soldiers'

---

[24] Sági's (1954: 116) sees the Hemeseni conforming to what he imagines to be an alien rite to them. He argues: 'Es muß daher die Rolle der Armee bei der Romanisierung des Landes beachtet warden, das sie auch bei anderen Einzelheiten der Bestattungssitten nachweisbar ist.'

[25] Ibid. 82–5.

[26] Visy (1977, cover and caption).

[27] Sági (1954: 71, Grave 17). The coin is 'eastern' in that it was minted at Byzantion, a long way, of course, from Emesa, but it was on this basis that the excavators advanced an association of the inhumed child with the unit. Clearly this argument is weak, but the very fact it is made at all indicates how few discernibly 'eastern' artefacts were found within the cemetery.

[28] Sági (1954: 190–91, pl. 38.4).

wives were conversely distinguished from their neighbours by their retention of Pannonian tribal dress.

Much of this discussion simply underscores the well-attested difficulty inherent in discussing ethnic identity on the basis of funerary rites. Yet it also suggests that, for all its eastern associations, the regimental community at Intercisa was also marked by its adherence to wider cultural patterns. This is both a reflection of its mixed composition and an expression of its military character. The social dynamics that characterized regimental communities could vary significantly, and their material manifestation can accordingly be very difficult to read. What they share, however, is their capacity to generate wholly separate social networks.

Part III

A Home from Rome

Daily Life in the Auxilia

10

Military Service and the Urban Experience

Amongst the most important lessons we can learn from the extensive fieldwork that has taken place at military bases across the Empire is that these installations varied significantly in form. Even without the diverse watchtowers and fortlets and the temporary camps, which themselves housed troops, there was real diversity in structures and settings. While the playing card shaped forts and fortress commonly found in the west displayed many shared features, the differences between them, in both construction and development, were often substantial.[1] In some cases, too, army units were stationed in towns, though our understanding of the detail of how this worked is limited. In the east, as is widely recognized, the range of settlement types employed was wider still: soldiers were often stationed in cities or fortified places first constructed prior to the arrival of Rome.[2] Even the purpose-built fortifications constructed there under the Empire show marked differences from the forts of the west and, indeed, from one another. The diversity in east and west is still more marked when the organic growth associated with extramural settlement is considered. Yet it is possible to offer useful generalizations about military life in all these very different bases. Of these, the most important observation is that military life was a form of urban life.[3] The soldier's daily activities may differ from his fellow town-dwellers, his life might be ruled by the military clock rather than by other imperatives,[4] but he was still essentially an urban creature. The Romans themselves recognized this, and ancient writers use the analogy of town life to describe life in both temporary camps and more permanent fortifications.[5]

To characterize more precisely the relationship of military life to city life it is useful to scrutinize the evidence for the army *in* towns. The best known source of information for this remains Dura-Europos in Syria. This city on the Euphrates not only preserves important insights into life in a Roman base; it also remains the only case where both the 'civilian' and 'military' parts of a city have been

---

[1] Chorus (2008) has recently suggested that the construction methods used on the fortifications of early Roman forts on the lower Rhine reflect diverse building traditions used by their auxiliary occupants.

[2] For the reuse of pre-existing forts in Arabia Nabatea, see Kennedy (2000: 24).

[3] For fort life as urban life, see also M. A. Speidel (1999); Lendon (1997: 247).

[4] For military clocks, see *CIL* 13.7800 for a clock of *cohors I Flavia* at Remagen, Lower Germany. von Petrikovits (1975: 75; 174 fn. 79) discusses *CIL* 3.1070 = *ILS* 5625, and suggests that there may have been a regular position within army units designated to maintain the unit clock (1975: 174, fn. 79).

[5] Livy (44.39.5). Josephus *Bell. Iud.* 3.87 and Tacitus *Hist.* 2.80 both draw parallels between aspects of life in cities and forts.

extensively excavated.[6] Importantly, changes to the city during its occupation by Roman army units reflect both pragmatic cooption and localized adaptation. This combination helps us identify what the authorities deemed the essential elements of a military settlement. As this chapter will demonstrate, for all the variation found in military bases, certain key attributes were deemed desirable across the Empire. Significantly, while Dura-Europos would have looked very different from many of the forts and fortresses in the west, had say a 1st-century auxiliary from the Rhine been able to see this Euphrates stronghold in the 3rd century, he would have nonetheless found many elements within it that he would recognize.

When the first triumphant Sassanian troops retook Dura-Europos from its Roman garrison in or around AD 256, they beheld a rather different city from the one their Parthian predecessors would have known 150 years before (see Fig. 10.1).[7] Many of the most dramatic changes resulted from the garrison's determined but doomed attempts to protect this outpost on the Euphrates from its sophisticated besiegers. Properties adjacent to the western walls had been covered in a huge earthen rampart constructed to reinforce the defences—a measure that simultaneously disturbed and preserved an impressive array of perishable artefacts. Buildings too were pressed into service. A sanctuary near the Palmyrene (western) Gate was, for example, turned into an arms depot containing hundreds of stone shot, arrow heads, and a store of spears.[8] Elsewhere the transformation was of a different order and scale.[9] In the north and northeast, there were buildings of a quite alien form constructed to accommodate the needs of Roman soldiers and administrators. There was an elaborate palace occupied by the Dux Ripae (in block X3/5), a complex with courtyard and basilica (in E7), even a house with a partial peristyle (J1). Yet as the Persian victors ransacked properties, inconsiderately disrupting traces of the Roman occupation in the process, they must have noticed that the garrison was never confined to these new buildings. A significant number of Roman soldiers were clearly housed in townhouses first built in the city's Partho-Palmyrene heyday, some of which had been substantially altered for the purpose decades before the siege began.[10]

Dura's suitability as a Roman outpost in the 2nd and 3rd centuries AD owed much to its history; from its Seleucid foundation in the late 4th century BC onwards it promoted an urban style that the Romans came to share.[11] The regular street grid and substantial walls, both probably constructed in the second half of

[6] Altogether the 10 seasons of excavation led by Rostovtzeff and Cumont opened up about 20% of the city. Subsequent Franco-Syrian research at the site has not been on the same scale, but it has played a vital role in building our understanding of structures and stratigraphy at the site. The results of these campaigns are reported in Leriche and Gelin (1997). The author would like to thank Simon James and Jennifer Baird for their insights into the archaeology of Dura.

[7] James (1985: 120–22). There is reason to believe that the Sassanians had actually held it briefly only a few years before the final siege in AD 252–3. The arguments for this are best summarized in James (2004: 23–4).

[8] For the discovery see Leriche and Mahmoud (1994: 416–17).

[9] Downey (2000).

[10] For the origins of the houses, see esp. Rostovtzeff et al. (1936: 24). Evidence for the housing of soldiers at Dura is well summarized by Pollard (2000: 54–6).

[11] For the foundation, see Grainger (1990: 43–4). For Seleucid policy on veteran settlement and urbanism, see Cohen (1978). For the wider background, see Pollard (2000: 37–48).

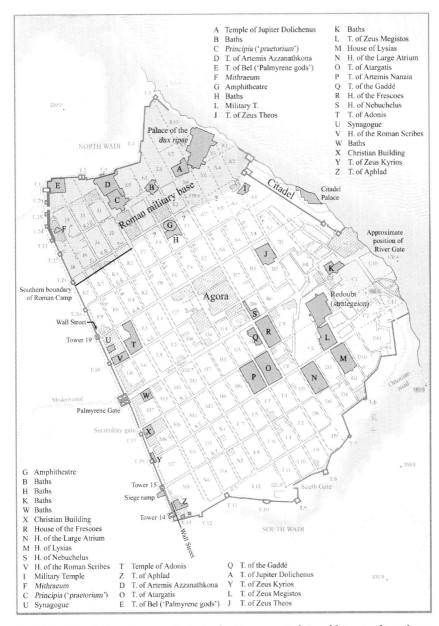

The map legend reads:

A   Temple of Jupiter Dolichenus
B   Baths
C   *Principia* ('*praetorium*')
D   T. of Artemis Azzanathkona
E   T. of Bel ('Palmyrene gods')
F   *Mithraeum*
G   Amphitheatre
H   Baths
I   Military T.
J   T. of Zeus Theos
K   Baths
L   T. of Zeus Megistos
M   House of Lysias
N   H. of the Large Atrium
O   T. of Atargatis
P   T. of Artemis Nanaia
Q   T. of the Gaddé
R   H. of the Frescoes
S   H. of Nebuchelus
T   T. of Adonis
U   Synagogue
V   H. of the Roman Scribes
W   Baths
X   Christian Building
Y   T. of Zeus Kyrios
Z   T. of Aphlad

Map labels: 220.2; Palace of the *dux ripae*; NORTH WADI; Roman military base; Citadel; Citadel Palace; Approximate position of River Gate; Southern boundary of Roman Camp; Wall Street; Tower 19; Agora; Redoubt (*strategeion*); Ottoman road; Modern road; Palmyrene Gate; Secondary gate; Tower 15; Siege ramp; Tower 14; Wall Street; South Gate; SOUTH WADI; 213.6; 220.9

G   Amphitheatre
B   Baths
H   Baths
K   Baths
W   Baths
X   Christian Building
R   House of the Frescoes
N   H. of the Large Atrium
M   H. of Lysias
S   H. of Nebuchelus
V   H. of the Roman Scribes
I   Military Temple
F   *Mithraeum*
C   *Principia* ('*praetorium*')
U   Synagogue
T   Temple of Adonis
Z   T. of Aphlad
D   T. of Artemis Azzanathkona
O   T. of Atargatis
E   T. of Bel ('Palmyrene gods')
Q   T. of the Gaddé
Y   T. of Zeus Kyrios
L   T. of Zeus Megistos
J   T. of Zeus Theos

Fig. 10.1. Plan of Dura-Europos, Syria, in the Roman period. In addition to the military base in the northern part of the city, Roman soldiers controlled the gates and walls around the perimeter. Block E4 lies immediately north of the city's amphitheatre.

the 2nd century BC, were exploited by successive occupants.[12] When the Parthians took over the city in c.113 BC they too laid stress on the importance of the fortifications.[13] A brief Roman takeover under Trajan was followed by more permanent annexation in the AD 160s. Thereafter the city received several contingents of Roman soldiers. Initially these seem to have consisted only of auxiliaries, but from c. AD 208 more men were added, some of them legionaries.[14] In addition to legionary detachments, Dura-Europos housed men from several auxiliary regiments including *cohors II Ulpia equitata sagittariorum* and *cohors XX Palmyrenorum*. The latter cohort specifically identified Dura as its *hiberna* or headquarters/winter camp.[15]

While enduring uncertainties about the identification and phasing of many buildings pose difficulties for those trying to assess the impact of Rome on the city, some points are clear. The most conspicuous adjustments to the city following the army's arrival are found in the north and northeastern part of the city, though some military handwork can be seen to the west near the so-called Palmyrene gate. It is very important to acknowledge that by no means all military activity was confined to the city itself, and that there were developments to meet the army's needs outside the old walls, but enough evidence survives from within the city boundaries to reveal much about the relationship between militarized space and urban space.[16]

Initial restructuring involved the conversion of at least one town house into a barrack block and, significantly, the introduction of bath-houses in blocks E3, M7, and C3.[17] New and growing demands on water were clearly a feature of the arrival of a permanent military presence.[18] Magnetometry survey also suggests a heightened density of ovens and hearths in those parts of the city associated with the presence of military personnel.[19] Special provision must have been made for the soldiers' food supplies too. Their growing importance is certainly underscored in a later guard roster of *cohors XX Palmyrenorum*; the granaries are one of a handful of locations which the garrison is detailed to guard.[20] Overall, though, relatively little major structural alteration seems to have been required within the city walls initially. Soldiers could be billeted in existing buildings, while senior officers could take over and use, with little significant alteration, existing houses for their own dwellings.

By the second decade of the 3rd century more changes had taken place; archaeology reveals the remains of a substantial headquarters building and the presence of a wall seemingly built with the intention of separating off the northwest of the city.[21] An amphitheatre—a feature relatively rare in the cities of the east but familiar enough in the west—was built by detachments from two

---

[12] For dating, see Leriche (1997a; 1997b) discussed by Downey (2000: 155, 157–8).

[13] For the Parthian takeover, see Bellinger (1947: 66). For the walls, see Leriche (1986: 61–82; 1987).

[14] Dabrowa's (1981: 63–4) analysis of the strengthening of the garrison has gained widespread acceptance.

[15] *P. Dura* 89 i.5.

[16] I owe a great deal to Simon James for drawing my attention to the complexities of the archaeology beyond the city walls.

[17] I follow Pollard (2000: 52–3) here, but note (Jennifer Baird, pers. comm.) that the upper storey of the E4—the converted house/barrack—was a Roman addition.

[18] Jennifer Baird, pers. comm.   [19] James, Baird, and Strutt (2011: 6).

[20] *P. Dura* 106 = *RMR* 13 dating to AD 235–40. Soldiers guard the granaries and main gates.

[21] Recent excavations by Simon James (pers. comm.) have demonstrated that this wall did continue to the east.

MONS CLAUDIANUS

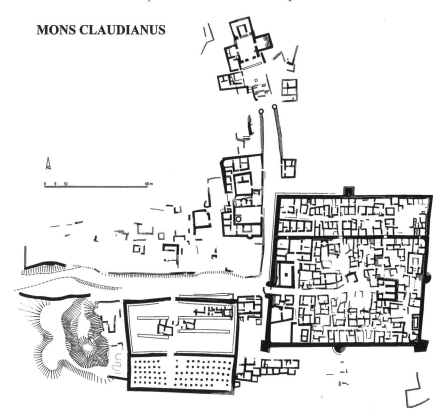

Fig. 10.2. Plan of the quarry base at Mons Claudianus, Egypt. The densely packed interior of the main base differs markedly in appearance from forts known in the west; it was home to both soldiers and civilians. To the north, overlooking the settlement, lies the Temple of Serapis built by *cohors I Flavia Cilicum*. The animal lines lie to the west.

legions.[22] That auxiliary soldiers were also actively engaged in the building programme is demonstrated by the discovery of an inscription recording the completion of a temple by a working party from *cohors II Ulpia equitata sagittar-iorum*.[23] These men were supervised by a centurion from *Legio IIII Scythica* responsible for the working parties enlarging the parade ground. Though the name of the deity to whom the temple was dedicated does not survive, enough remains of the structure to show that it was distinctly classical in form and quite alien to the other shrines and temples of the city.

Despite the particularities of Dura, the essential features here are those found at permanent camps across the Empire. Not only that, but they are elements that are established early in the development of forts and fortresses. The rectilinear street grid, here a legacy of late Seleucid planning, plays as much of a role here as it does in the forts and fortresses of the west from the Augustan period onwards. There were, it is true, military installations in the east that parted from this model—the cluttered interior of Mons Claudianus in Egypt's Eastern Desert, for example (see Fig. 10.2), or a plethora of smaller installations where the buildings were

---

[22] Rostovtzeff et al. (1936: 77–80, no. 630).   [23] *AE* 1931, 113.

constructed directly against the enclosure wall—but this layout was the single most familiar way of ordering large military centres.[24] That essentially the same ideals of street grid and *insula* blocks were fundamental to urban planning in Roman cities across the Empire hardly requires mentioning. In some towns, of course, they remained but an aspiration, but for many new foundations they essentially provided the framework for urban life.

Public space in civil Dura, however, evolved along a different trajectory. By the time the Romans took over the city the ancient agora had long since ceased to function as an open space. This must have made the introduction of major Roman administrative buildings all the more conspicuous. Foremost of these was the *principia* (headquarters building) established in the north of the city (see Fig. 10.3).[25] Despite misleadingly terming it a *praetorium* in their reports and plans, the excavators rightly recognized the parallels between this complex and headquarters buildings then known from Lambaesis in Africa, Saalburg in Germany, and Newstead in Scotland.[26] The construction of the building took place in what appears to have been a 'little developed' area and involved enlarging an east–west street to the front of the complex and adorning that street with a colonnade.[27] We now know that the same essential building form, built around a courtyard and accompanied by a basilican hall, is a hallmark feature not only of forts from Britain to the Danube and the Sahara but also of new towns. In Roman eyes, after all, the *principia* required much the same built space as did a forum. Meeting space, both open and covered, was required for information to be exchanged and justice enacted. The only conspicuous difference between many of the fora and *principia* of the west, it has been argued, was in the absence of a temple from the latter. Yet even here, the difference is not perhaps so great, for a chapel lay against the rear wall in the centre of the *principia*'s basilican hall in forts both great and small.[28] It is possible that the holes in the floor of this room in the Dura actually mark the stands for the standards.[29] Whether or not this was so, the trappings of cult were certainly represented in the complex; archaeologists found the remains of a substantial altar in the centre of the courtyard.[30] Cult activity was clearly as much a part of life in the *principia* here as it was in any of the more elaborate civil fora known from elsewhere in the Empire.

There has been some discussion as to whether or not this complex served both the legionary and auxiliary contingents in the garrison or just the former; the building, unusually, had two tribunals.[31] It is certainly commonly asserted that the *cohors XX Palmyrenorum* used the neighbouring temple of Azzanathkona as its headquarters. While this may indeed be the case—and urban-based auxiliary units

[24] Peacock and Maxfield (1997).   [25] Rostovtzeff (1934: 201–18).

[26] Ibid. 206.   [27] 'Tenth Street' (ibid. 207).

[28] For this now widely recognized phenomenon, the authors of the report were obliged to cite the evidence assembled by von Domaszewski (1895: 9).

[29] Rostovtzeff 1934: 214).

[30] The altar was 2.10 × 1.83m with steps leading to the top (ibid. 211).

[31] The vast majority of scholars follow Rostovtzeff (ibid. 216, 227) in linking the absence of references to the auxilia within this building to the idea that they did not use it. This situation is contrasted with the number of references in the neighbouring temple, where two inscriptions and many papyri refer to auxiliary regiments (ibid. 226–9).

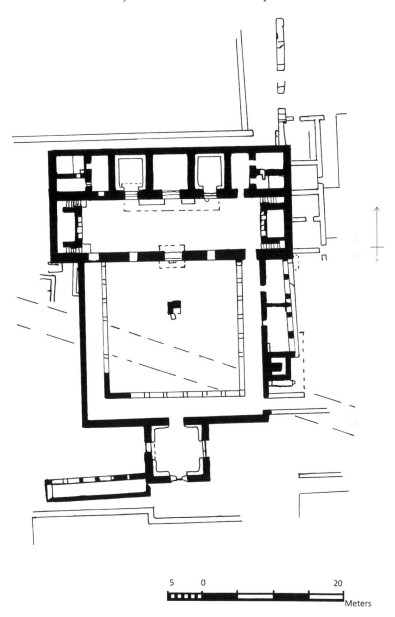

5   0   20
                                      Meters

Fig. 10.3. Plan of the *principia* at Dura-Europos.

probably often did make use of such structures—there remains some ambiguity in the evidence, and Reeves has rightly noted that the argument rests partly on anachronistic views of the inferiority of auxiliary units.[32] What is clear, however, is that the *principia* was a conspicuous part of the urban environment in the area where many auxiliary soldiers were stationed. Few can have failed to recognize its importance. In essence the headquarters was just as much a focus as the forum of a Roman town. Indeed, it seems quite likely that such courtyards were themselves designated fora by their military users.[33]

Less than 20m to the west of the *principia* and the Temple of Azzanathkona lay a house with a partial peristyle (J1).[34] This may well have served as the commanding officer's house. There is excellent access from the house to an alley running along the rear of the *principia*, making the whole arrangement immensely convenient for such an officer. Though the building might have looked somewhat out of place in the mixture of Mesopotamian architecture found at Dura, it would again have been familiar in military settings across the Empire. Such buildings were essentially traditional Mediterranean town houses, hence the peristyle aspect. What a commander needed, as a place for both work and leisure, was basically just a large house. Following partly from the assumptions made about the *principia* at Dura, there has been the tendency to associate this house specifically with the resident legionary detachments, but this too is open to question. What is clear is that it was again part of the military landscape within which soldiers worked. It seems quite possible that, given that a town house was all that was really required, several senior officers at Dura simply occupied other appropriate commandeered properties where a commander could have received petitioners and visiting dignitaries, conduct much of his paperwork, and keep his family. Whatever the precise details of officers' housing, the synthesis of Roman urban style and military function remains pronounced.

To this transformed cityscape must be added two other elements, both essential components on the military environment, albeit components most commonly outside fortifications. The military bath-houses of Dura (C3, E3, F3, M7, and X3), considered further below, are clearly a distinct innovation in that city, and contrast with the facilities used by the civilian inhabitants.[35] Though bath-houses have become a vital element at military centres across the Empire, it is important to note that they do not observe a single style of architecture. In several regions, indeed, military bath-houses are actually little different from their civilian equivalents. In the northwestern provinces, for example, bath-houses found near forts are commonly of the simple Reihentyp plan, a form of bath developed not in Italy but in Roman Gaul.

---

[32] Reeves (2004: 39–40) challenges these assumptions, noting that in fact there is no *epigraphic* evidence for the twentieth cohort in the building, though *cohors II Ulpia* and two legionary contingents are attested.

[33] For ancient references to this part of a camp as forum, see M. A. Speidel (1999: 81), to which add Hyginus Gromaticus, writing *c.* AD 100, who uses the term for the centre of a camp (*De limitibus constituendis* 12).

[34] Rostovtzeff (1934: 235–7).

[35] Rostovtzeff et al. (1936: 84–105), but see Pollard's (2000: 52–3) comments for F3 and his discussion of the history of the baths in the city.

The other element, discussed in detail in Chapter 7, is the provision of temples and shrines. It is clear that several of the temples built prior to the Roman takeover drew soldier devotees from the new garrison. Indeed, the temple of Mithras (J7) was even rebuilt by Roman soldiers. Yet there was also change. The construction of a classical-style temple in the vicinity of the barracks by the cohort of archers added a feature that would have looked familiar in almost any major city in the Empire. It is a project that recalls building projects at many military stations. Whether in the rugged terrain of Egypt's eastern desert, overlooking the remote camp of Mons Claudianus, in the territory of the Hemeseni's Danubian camp at Intercisa (Hungary), or by the British outpost fort at High Rochester, auxiliary troops actively contributed to building a sacred landscape.[36]

At this stage it is important to examine how it was that a major Roman force could fit so relatively easily, spatially at least, into a long-established city. To understand this we have to appreciate not simply that Roman camps were traditionally structured around ideals of the proper organization of Roman society but also that cities of all sorts were fundamental to the making of the Empire.

Important as Rome itself was as an ideal city for many, it was actually the notion of city life that was vital. Politically the Empire was nothing if not an empire of cities. Greco-Roman thinkers concurred that ordered life, indeed *civilized* life, was urban life. Cities, surrounded by their territories, were thus the cells that made up the imperial organism.[37] Like cells, they varied in form, history, and function, but united they constituted something much bigger. In the Roman world these diverse entities interacted to build an Empire, mediating between their diverse populations and the demands of imperial governance. Just as each city, or city-state, was incorporated into the body politic, so it in turn incorporated. Hamlets, villages, and people fell under its sway, sustaining it, perpetuating it, and depending upon it for their very identity and meaning in provincial society.

In such a world, the Roman soldier was inevitably an urban creature too. This was not just because power and influence in the Roman world radiated outwards from urban centres, but because where such centres did not exist to accommodate him they had to be constructed. Ancient writers saw this clearly, likening the camp to a 'walled city' and recognizing that routines found within it could be seen on the streets of Rome itself.[38] Modern scholars have stressed the point too, looking both at the social dynamics involved and at the transition of settlements from one category to another.[39] In a world in thrall to *urbanitas*, the construction of new forts and fortresses inevitably involved the partial perpetuation of ideals of town life. Yet there was a tension in this process, for while the same core principles of ordered living were imposed on soldiers, towns were regarded as subversive of military virtues.[40] Here we encounter again that conflict at the heart of the auxiliary's Roman identity: the trade-off between a vision of civilization and the

---

[36] The temple of Serapis at Mons Claudianus was built by *cohors I Flavia Cilicum* (*CIG* 4713f = *IGRR* 3.1255). For the Hemeseni at Intercisa, see *ILS* 9155. The dedication slab at High Rochester is *RIB* 1272.

[37] Woolf (2003: 73).

[38] Vegetius 1.21. For the parallel between urban and military routines Josephus *Bell. Iud.* 3. 87 and Tacitus *Hist.* 280.

[39] M. A. Speidel (1999).　　[40] Tacitus *Ann.* 13.35; Vegetius 1. 3.

daily realities of life in the emperor's service. For Rome it was essential that a broad balance be maintained. Soldiers needed to be kept under close control, at once indulged and restrained in a manner alien to the daily lot of the civilian population. Yet the ideas that underpinned this balance were themselves well established in the history of Rome's citizenry. The mundane routines of the soldier illuminate this, reflecting not just his military occupation, nor simply his existence as an instrument of Roman power, but rather the degree to which incorporation into the Empire's network of power could intrude into daily life.

This is all the more important when it is remembered that the vast majority of recruits to the *auxilia* did not grow up in towns. This is known not so much from the set-piece literary descriptions of the urban recruit as a pampered creature, undesirable for military service, but from our knowledge of the provincial land-scape.[41] Many of the Empire's most fertile recruiting grounds prove to have been areas that were determinedly rural. How the routines of life in military instal-lations affected these predominantly rural recruits, and how their impact played out across the wider community found at every major military centre, is an issue of abiding interest. Understanding the dynamics involved tells us as much about the influence of military service on individuals as it does about the diverse species of urban life that allowed the Empire to incorporate, accommodate, and endure.

The need to look beyond buildings and to focus on communities and routines stems from two particular concerns. The first is that archaeology constantly demonstrates that the built environment is only a part of any story. To understand the differences and similarities between lives, times, and places, it is necessary to look beyond the resemblance in buildings and plans; it is vital to evoke a sense of how that space was lived.

The second concern lies with the diversity of Roman military installations. Con-trary to the received image of the Roman soldier, there were many diverse ways of garrisoning troops. This diversity owes much to the disparate forms of settlement that fell under the Empire's hegemony. In the provinces of the east, long-established towns such as Dura could be used to accommodate soldiers, reinforcing their dominion over surrounding territories. Roman soldiers are attested stationed in the towns of the east long before the first permanent forts of the west were constructed. Yet as (with the exception of Dura) their bases there remain poorly understood, the dominant image of the fort or fortress remains that of the great playing-card-shaped installations, dominating the landscape. The stark resemblance of such forts found from the Clyde to the Euphrates, and from the fringes of the Sahara to the banks of the Danube, inevitably tempts scholars to see these forts as quintessential homes from Rome. This is an impression strongly reinforced when we see how installations built miles apart, yet within years of one another, show a remarkable likeness to one another. Clearly this resemblance is of more than merely superficial interest. It reflects real similarities of purpose and organization, but it is not the whole story.

Even in the more familiar type of site there is clear change over time. From the emphasis in the early Julio-Claudian period on vast centres capable of accommo-dating campaigning armies, we see a movement towards altogether smaller forts

---

[41] Tacitus *Ann.* 1.31. The single largest sources of recruits to the *auxilia*, northern Gaul, northern Spain, and Thrace, remained some of the least urbanized provinces of the Empire.

and fortresses. As part of this trend permanent fort sites were established, very often though by no means universally around the core of a single *ala* or *cohors*, from the mid 1st century AD onwards. Geopolitical imperatives converged to generate new, much smaller entities based on the same Roman principles of ordered living.[42] In time, a new permanence evolved which was at least as much a response to local geography and provincial circumstances as it was to imperial desire. This was determined at least as much by the need to deploy soldiers where they could be sustained and supplied as it was by any strategic imperatives. Accordingly there is real variation across the Empire. As a result of the work of Gregory, much more is now known about Roman military architecture on the eastern frontier, but despite the rapid development of research in the eastern Empire many scholars' perceptions are heavily framed by evidence from the west.[43] Forts such as Tell el Hajj on the Euphrates, which resemble the playing-card-shaped forts of the west, are in a clear minority in the east. For in Syria, as in many of the urbanized eastern provinces, there was little need to build an urban home for the soldiers when well-placed towns and sometimes even pre-existing forts were already available.

Even in provinces with substantial number of forts and fortresses, there are good reasons to believe that soldiers were stationed in towns.[44] In the west, even where the distribution of forts and towns appears to be mutually exclusive, military equipment is often found in similar quantities at both categories of site.[45] The implication is clear: soldiers were to be found in towns across the western Empire too. Forts and towns are not opposed phenomena—they are different aspects of a broad cultural movement. The recent call emanating from one 'under-urbanized' province to include forts in future discussions of urbanism needs to be considered for all.[46] For those prepared to heed it, it offers at once a broader understanding of settlement history and a greater sensitivity to local peculiarities.

Yet such aspirations only underscore the scale of our ignorance. Despite thousands of excavations at military sites, there remain entire categories of installation and substantial areas where no real investigation has taken place. Even in intensely surveyed and excavated provinces, the inner workings of key fort types remain unclear. Temporary encampments, for example, were being used by Rome long before Augustus, and continued to serve campaigning armies in the centuries following Maximinus. They are known from across the Empire, from the Near East, the Danubian lands, the Rhine, and Britain. The numbers of these camps discovered in Britain alone, 478 to date, is at once a testimony to the role of aerial photography and an alarming indication of how many such camps must still linger unknown across the provinces.[47] Yet even in these British examples, little is known of their interior layout.[48] Another category, still more mysterious, is that of the praesidium. This name is found used in many different provinces, but it appears frequently in ostraca from Egypt. The term may be taken to mean any garrisoned area, and for that reason can include forts and towns,[49] but it is clear

---

[42] The dispersal of units made sense not just to facilitate control over communications routes but also to alleviate problems of supply and the risk that a large concentration of troops might be used against the imperial house.

[43] Gregory (1995–1997).   [44] Bishop (1999: 113).   [45] Bishop (1991) for Britain.

[46] Millett (2001: 64).   [47] Jones (2006: 15).   [48] Ibid. 115–18.   [49] Vegetius 3.8.

that it could also include smaller purpose built structures.[50] Our knowledge of the workings and layout of the Egyptian praesidia still comes principally from documentary evidence. We know that they often had civilians around them, that they had buildings, and that some even had a *tyche* (protective spirit), but we know very little more.[51] Quite probably they took a range of forms even in that one province. To these two examples, we could add many others. Diverse watchtowers, signal stations, fortlets, and turrets that ornamented frontiers and communication networks across the Empire; analysis of finds from such sites indicates a different pattern of life again from that found within the permanent forts.[52]

Appreciating the degree of variation should therefore make us approach the apparently familiar topic of daily life in the Roman army with humility. For many reasons the vast majority of archaeological evidence of soldiers' quarters comes from inside the more permanent playing-card forts of the west. The sheer quantity of data from these sites makes them some of the best known in all provincial archaeology. Yet while this allows for the identification of certain common trends, there was also variation; military communities, just as their urban civilian counterparts, could respond very differently to local circumstances.

The civilians alongside whom the soldier lived played an important role in both defining and mediating these circumstances. While, by definition, military installations would have had a higher proportion of fighting men within their walls, it is nonetheless clear that there were many others living alongside them, people whose very presence made these centres more like other towns. Not only were there women and children, craftsmen and merchants, but there were enough slaves and servants to ensure that even in a base containing a few hundred soldiers, a range of statuses and specializations characteristic of urban life were represented. Reconstructing the dynamic that took place must remain a major challenge, however.

Dura is one of the relatively few places where it has been possible to explore this dynamic in detail. The rich combination of sources from the city has ensured that there has been much discussion of the civilian presence as well as the military one. Civilians linked to the garrison are clearly attested. A papyrus found within the city records a divorce between a soldier serving in *legio IIII Scythica* and a woman by the name of Aurelia Ammima, who describes herself as a Durene.[53] It seems most likely that she met her ex-husband when he was stationed at Dura. No doubt many other soldiers met their wives in similar circumstances. Theatrical entertainers and prostitutes are attested as part of the extended military community too. Writing found on a building in block G5 less than 150m from housing known to have been used by soldiers indicates not only that the building accommodated both (overlapping?) groups but that their presence at the site was actively facilitated by the military.[54] Indeed, Pollard thinks it likely that they were army

---

[50] For the versatility of the term, see *TLL* X.2, fasc. VI, cols 883–92.

[51] For *tyche*: *O. Claud.* 225; Maxfield (2003: 159).

[52] Compare e.g. the archaeological evidence gleaned from watchtower WP 5/4 on the Wetterau-limes (Schallmayer 2007) with that recovered from the turrets of Hadrian's Wall (Allason-Jones 2001). In the former case, the analysis is further enlivened by illuminating archaeobotanical analysis (Kreuz 2007).

[53] *P. Dura* 32. Pollard (2000: 157) rightly notes the importance of this testimony.

[54] Rostovtzeff et al. (1944: 166–7).

slaves.[55] Whether or not this is the case, it is clear that slaves also formed an integral part of the soldiers' immediate society. Finally, we should note that there is clear evidence for ongoing links between serving soldiers and veterans. A telling example of this is found in a Dura papyrus recording the case of a veteran of *cohors III Augusta Thracum* who bought a vineyard in AD 227. The contract of sale was signed in camp and its signatories clearly included men still serving in the unit.[56]

Yet despite the uniquely rich combination of evidence that Dura offers, determining the nature of exchange between the military community and others living at Dura remains difficult. Differences in setting, context, status, time, even personality would all have played a role. It is no particular surprise to find evidence for exchanges with merchants and with local councillors, both figures who loomed large in the life of the Empire's cities. Yet it remains very hard to say with certainty from the evidence how relations functioned with city-dwellers who were neither within the *familia* of the soldier nor officials or merchants. Pollard, who has addressed this issue in detail, recognizes some exchange, but sees the military force and its immediate dependants as a group apart.[57] He sees what he terms 'institutional identity' as a key divide, not ethnicity or even language. This resonates with the sense of the soldiers and their followers as a parallel society; coexistence with the wider urban community was possible, sometimes even it would seem amicable, but there remained the risk of dramatic confrontation too. It is easy to see here how the archaeological difficulties are twofold: the dating of phases of use of buildings and their identification is crucial to the argument, but so too is evidence we cannot really hope to obtain with the spade—namely the degree to which the soldiers and wider civilian population of the town actually identified with one another.

Ancient accounts of Antioch on the Orontes might suggest that quite a high level of intermingling was possible. Luxurious Antioch, provincial capital of Syria, has some things in common with its humbler neighbour on the Euphrates. It too was a Seleucid foundation, having been established by Seleucus I Nicator in 301 BC. As such it had strong military connections and powerful walls to protect it. The Romans frequently imposed troops upon these Seleucid cities, so well suited were they to their particular needs. While there is doubt as to whether Antioch ever really housed a legion, as has been suggested, there is no question that it accommodated many Roman solders over the years before it too finally fell to the Sassanians in the AD 250s.

Perhaps it was the prosperous notoriety of Antioch that inspired it, but the city acquired a reputation as a place that welcomed the soldiery to its heart and corrupted them in body. In AD 69, Tacitus tells us, the relationship between soldiers and citizens in Antioch was so close that it virtually provoked a riot. The thought of their legions being sent from their comfortable billets to the brutal conditions of the Rhine was allegedly met with resistance on all sides. Tacitus ingeniously uses the term *contubernio*, a term that recalls the close camaraderie of the military *contubernium* to describe the soldier/civilian relationship. He observes

> For the provincials were accustomed to live with the soldiers, and enjoyed association with them; in fact, many civilians were bound to the soldiers by ties of friendship and

---

[55] Pollard (2000: 188).   [56] *P. Dura* 26.   [57] Pollard (2000: 111–67).

of marriage, and the soldiers from their long service had come to love their old familiar camps as their very hearths and homes.[58]

Tacitus is by no means the last writer to lament the lure of Antioch; a similar tale emerges in the notoriously unreliable *Historia Augusta*. As he geared up to campaign against the Persians in AD 231–2, Severus Alexander allegedly felt the damaging impact of the city on his forces. After lambasting the indiscipline of his soldiers, he saw them disperse not to the camp, but to diverse inns and homes elsewhere. Of course these two episodes, even if we accept them at face value—and they do smack suspiciously of literary *topoi*—refer to different circumstances. In the first we see units that have allegedly lived near the city for long enough to build a lasting rapport with the townspeople. In the second we see a campaigning army that goes to seed through too much exposure to the good life of *urbanitas*. Yet it is possible to accept that there was a struggle for balance here—from an official point of view, co-location of troops had real benefits. Substantial cities were by defin- ition close to good communications routes and had developed systems of supply. Rome was in many ways perpetuating the agenda they were established to advance. On the other hand, the human factor in high strategy carried its own momentum, drawing the soldier closer to an experience of town life. For soldiers, the proximity of a major civilian settlement was a place where they could 'make love, drink, and wash', and in any civilian society there were those who saw an opportunity in this and those whose lives were blighted by it.[59] For in addition to the misery that the mere billeting of soldiers could cause, there was ever a risk that armed men might run amok amongst their civilian hosts, underscoring through fire and sword the profound divisions between those who served the emperor and those who were merely his subjects.

Even where soldiers were based in purpose-built forts and fortresses, the extended military community actively contributed to the creation of an urban environment. The military *vici* and *canabae* outside these great centres lent a greater density and variety to these substantial settlements. In recent years, a dramatic growth of interest in the archaeology of these areas has expanded our knowledge of them considerably, yet the amount of attention lavished upon them remains small in comparison with the work undertaken on the forts and fortresses themselves.[60]

As emphasized in the introduction to this volume, there has also been a dramatic growth of interest in the civilian element of the military community in recent years. The possibility that surviving evidence reflects changes in patterns of family formation in the army has been discussed above, along with the acknow- ledgement that this is not a late development: even from the Augustan period large numbers of civilians lived in the vicinity of soldiers. Tablets from the Swiss legionary fortress at Vindonissa, sometime home to a number of auxiliary units, support this picture.[61] The tablets allude not simply to military activities and

---

[58] Tacitus *Hist.* 2.80.3. The translation given is Moore (1980).

[59] *Historia Augusta: Severus Alexander* 53.

[60] The pioneering work of Sommer (1984; 1988; 1989; 1991) has been followed by a major growth in geophysical survey and aerial photographic analysis of extramural settlements.

[61] M. A. Speidel (1996).

structures, but to dice games and bars. They also refer to a diverse array of civilian residents including women.[62] Crucially, the latter are not the widely attested wives of officers, but women who lived with ordinary soldiers. Some of the civilians at Vindonissa clearly lived in numbered quarters within the camp, but how such individuals lived in smaller bases is unclear.

As discussed in the introduction to this book, the degree to which artefactual evidence can illuminate not just the presence of civilians, but also different types of civilians, within Roman forts has been much debated in recent years. There is no doubt that the study of artefact distribution, when considered alongside discard strategies, can identify distinct activity zones in a way that is not wholly dependent on assumptions about how buildings of particular types were used. While it is reasonable, for example, to see barrack blocks as the places where soldiers were quartered, it is not necessary to assume that all parts of every barrack block were in fact used in this manner throughout the occupation of a fort. It is also important to ensure that any such analysis includes not only substantial areas of fort interiors but substantial areas of the fort/*vicus* complex as a whole.

At present, the archaeological investigation of military communities is constrained by the way in which these sites have been excavated. It is surprisingly rare to have high-quality data from large areas of both the fort interior and its extramural area recovered by the same method and dating from contemporary phases. There are, however, some cases, and of these it is particularly appropriate to mention work at Vindolanda.[63] Here, consistency in recording techniques and a structured programme designed to comprehensively sample both the interior and the exterior of the 3rd- and 4th century fort and extramural settlement assess the notion of the fort wall as the 'great divide' between activities. While a contraction of activity into the fort itself is archaeologically visible in the 4th century, analysis of the 3rd-century evidence indicates that artefacts of similar types are often found both within and without the walls. The clear implication, of course, is that there were significant overlaps between the types of activity which took place within the fort and beyond it at this time. It is hoped that in the future, such research will be developed further to examine the relationships between forts and their extra mural settlements during the 1st and 2nd centuries AD.

Identifying activity zones is one important area in which our knowledge of fort/*vicus* sites needs to develop. There are others. We still need to know much more about the way the buildings within these complexes were used, and to acknowledge that even when buildings of similar form are found at different sites, there may have been significant differences in the way they were used.

It is often forgotten, for example, that reconstructions of the use of internal space within barrack rooms remain overwhelmingly hypothetical. This is despite the fact that our knowledge of these very familiar structures has advanced

---

[62] Ibid. nos. 35, 38, 45, 47.

[63] Of other possible examples, I note the comprehensive excavations of the 1st-century AD fort at Elginhaugh, Scotland, and its annexe (Hanson et al. 2007). What makes the Vindolanda excavations particularly relevant to this discussion, however, is the particular emphasis built into their 5-year research design and the recent Ph.D analysis conducted by Andrew Birley (2010), the director of excavations at Vindolanda.

markedly in recent years.[64] Not only might non-soldiers have shared space within these rooms—more recent fighting forces certainly accommodated families in this manner—but there was also considerable room under the eaves which may also have been used by servants and others that is seldom considered.[65] The truth is that we simply do not know how the space immediately beneath the roof was used; relatively sophisticated arrangements would have been possible beneath the eaves.

It is, however, increasingly apparent that within the walls of the camp there was space for a complex social hierarchy, many elements of which would have been familiar to city-dwellers. Clues to the ways that military hierarchies related to civilian ones may also be found in the soldiers' own accommodation. Centurions and decurions occupied spacious quarters at the end of each block. Evidence from the German fort at Echzell demonstrates that at least sometimes these were lavishly decorated with fine plaster just as elaborate as that found in the towns.[66] These quarters would have provided ample space for families and servants. Cavalry troopers were allocated rooms to every three men.[67] Little is known of the way in which the interior of these rooms were organized, and there was probably considerable variety in their layout. As noted above, a factor that is not always considered is the roof space, which would have provided significant supplementary space for storage and extra sleeping areas. Markedly less space was allocated to the infantryman than to the cavalryman in barracks, a feature that comes through clearly in both the literary and archaeological sources.[68] Here, it would seem, accommodation was designated to groups of up to eight men. Each *contubernium* had its own sleeping room (*papilio*) and store room (*arma*). It is harder to see where additional servants could have stayed, though roof space was surely also an option here, but it is notable that our sources suggest that the infantry had fewer attendants in general. This difference in the allocation of space, accompanied by the difference in terms of slaves and attendants in the cavalry lines, and indeed by distinct smells—that of horses and the lime used to neutralize horse waste—meant that the cavalry barracks would have been experienced in a manner discernibly different to the blocks occupied by the infantry.

In theory at least the walls, the gates—guarded by day and closed by night—and the system of passwords served to distinguish those within the camp from those outside. It is, however, far from clear how these barriers actually inhibited day-to-day movement in peacetime. Much must have depended on the local circumstances, still more on the regime of a particular commanding officer and his centurions or decurions. Certainly the areas around the forts and fortresses of the army rapidly acquired substantial civil settlements, whose very existence

---

[64] Davison (1989); Hodgson and Bidwell (2004).

[65] Hodgson and Bidwell (2004: 136) consider the possibility that servants lived in the roof space of barrack blocks, but there is no proof that they could not also have shared ground-floor living space, however cramped their presence might seem to make it.

[66] Baatz (1968).

[67] Research by Sommer (1995) and Hodgson (2003) has demonstrated that horses were stabled on one side of each cavalry barracks and men on the other. Now that this has been appreciated, it is possible to state with confidence that three men occupied each accommodation compartment in cavalry barracks. The pattern has been identified in Britain, the Germanies, Raetia, and the Danubian provinces.

[68] *De mun. castr.* 25.

suggests some interaction between those within the walls and those beyond. These settlements made a particular contribution to the sense of the camp as an urban centre. Some element of official planning is evident, but there is also often a sense of freer development reminiscent of the organic growth of urban centres. Their buildings, even in the frontier communities of the northwest, reflect first and foremost guiding principles of Roman architecture. In both the *vici* outside the forts and the larger *canabae* of the fortresses, forms of urban governance evolved. Yet it remains clear that these centres were essentially under the dominion of the army commanders. Even where, as often happened on the Rhine and the Danube, they grew up close to civil settlements, they preserved a distinct legal identity. In time, many went on to become cities in their own right—a promotion that was a particular feature of Septimius Severus' transforming reign.

It is not just in the layout and occupancy of military installations that archaeology reveals a close association between urban life and the experience of auxiliaries and their legionary counterparts; a similar theme emerges from the study of artefact assemblages. The degree to which the range and type of artefacts found within auxiliary forts can resemble those found in small towns within the same region can be quite striking.[69] No doubt future studies will enlarge our understanding of this association, which remains marked despite some differences between the 'discard strategies' or patterns of artefact abandonment and disposal practised by military communities and townspeople.[70] For the moment, however, it may prove still more fruitful to examine the particular pattern of associations linked to one artefact type, the coin.

Coin finds touch on so many fundamental issues in the archaeology of the Roman provinces that it is difficult to do more than to recall some elements of their role and diverse character here. Yet some reference to them is vital, for in the Roman world the relationship of coin to both the urban fabric of the Empire and the very existence of the army is of intense importance. Coins illuminate the making of empire in a very particular way. Just as systems of coinage, with all their connotations of identity and authority, illustrate the interplay of power that creates provincial society, so the routine use of coin reflects the incorporation of individuals into networks of imperial power. Payment of soldiers in coin was a key factor in the dissemination of coin.[71]

In general terms, coins reflect broad patterns within this Empire of cities. Many of the long-established Greek urban communities of the east produced their own bronze coinages right up to the second half of the 3rd century. In the west, by contrast, where the city was generally a recent development, there was no real parallel for this; local coinages seldom survived the Flavian period. Many were the fluctuations in the production and provision of coinage over time and space, but the army has been seen as both the most important consumer and a major agent of distribution. Though there is no neat parallel between the still ill-understood local 'mints' of the east, the handful of minting centres in the west, and the forts and fortresses of empire, it is clear that military installations were sometimes

---

[69] As discussed by Allason-Jones (2001: 23 and references).
[70] Bishop (1989) discusses discard of military equipment at fort sites.
[71] Duncan-Jones (1990: 38, 44); Pollard (2000: 179–211).

active in producing coinage themselves.[72] As quasi-urban centres, they were natural places for such operations. Evidence of the minting of so-called *limesfalsa*, attributed to the need to ensure small change for the soldiery, is well known from major legionary centres, but it has also been found at the site of a number of auxiliary forts in later contexts. Both Ilişua and Hoghiz in Romania, for example, have produced spoilt bronze casts.[73] While at Housesteads, a coin mould was recovered from the extramural settlement. The discovery has been seen as evidence for illicit activity, but may reflect more widespread semi-official practice.[74]

The very history of the *auxilia* is linked to the cread of coinage in the west. Coins, after all, replaced the lure of booty in the service of Rome.[75] Rome here continued an earlier practice for the paying of mercenaries. In the early 1st century AD, many military stations in the northwest provinces show a rapid and dramatic turnover in the supply of bronze coinage—a process which clearly indicates that the expenditure of soldiers' money resulted in it being dispersed more widely in the cash-strapped civil settlements further afield. Here, then, the army may be seen as playing a key role in facilitating the growth of coin-based exchange in the civil sphere, a process which accelerated the incorporation into wider provincial society. By the late 1st century this turnover had slowed significantly; it appears that towns were able to rely upon an existing pool of coinage, the regional mint at Lugdunum is closed, and Rome is able to supply demand directly. This stage represents both local sustainability and centralized supply of the army.[76]

The patterns of the east are more complex, but a number of significant themes are apparent. One is the need for money-changers to change local coins into coins that could pay Roman taxes. In addition to the notorious scope for corruption, this process again asserted the power imbalance that drove incorporation. Local use patterns have to be incorporated within imperial systems. Complicating matters, of course, was the fact that many local coinages also carried the head of the emperor on one side while carrying the symbols of their community on the other. Because of the existing habit of coin use, well established even amongst the urban poor by the early 1st century, the army's impact on coin circulation was probably less than it was in the provinces of the northwest.[77] Yet the army's relationship with coins is still well attested.

That the crucial relationship between emperor and soldiers was routinely underscored by the payment of men in coins that bore the emperor's head is everywhere clear. Sometimes the message of the authorities was reinforced by countermarking. The way in which soldiers used coin—the quantities received, the denominations used, the transactions involved—is less clear in some parts of the Empire than in others, though in both east and west it appears that soldiers used locally produced low-value coinage before other sources became available. Where evidence for patterns of daily coin use in the army survives, it is important. Though there are dangers in assuming that soldiers used cash widely in transactions within forts, I believe that we can and should see both the camps with their

---

[72] e.g. RIC 66. See Reece (1987: 16).   [73] Cristian Gazdac, pers. comm.
[74] Crow (1995: 70).   [75] Maxfield (1981: 57).   [76] Wigg (1997).
[77] Also, of course, because of the smaller size of the military population.

dependent settlements and the major towns as characterized by the extensive use of coin.[78] This represents a marked contrast with the situation in the multiplicity of rural settlements that make up the Empire, but it does not automatically indicate the same patterns of use. Pay scales, themselves much debated by scholars, did not always translate into the supply of ready cash to the soldiery. Some sums were no doubt held on credit, others were exchanged in kind, with national coin values helping to determine the worth of the transaction. Yet there is clear evidence for routine use of hard cash by soldiers—a practice which could have both positive and negative implications for the civilians with whom they came into contact. It is thus interesting to find, in a fragmentary document that records the purchase of a camel by men of an *ala*. that the transaction involved silver drachmae, local rather than imperial currency, albeit easily convertible.[79] But it is downright alarming to read in a merchant's accounts from about the same date entries showing sums as high as 400 drachmae being paid to a soldier 'on demand'.[80] Seldom do we see military extortion so crudely attested. Clearly soldiers had every bit as much interest in acquiring hard cash as they had in receiving it from their paymasters. Indeed, much of the discussion of how military pay was delivered has ignored the likelihood that many soldiers probably received a lot of cash this way.

Some of the most evocative evidence for the actual coinage used by soldiers again comes from Dura. Three hoards were discovered in the barracks. While we should remain ever mindful of the danger in constructing elaborate tales around hoard finds, it is likely that these were buried by Roman soldiers prior to their final catastrophic battle with the besieging Sassanid Persians. Here, squirrelled away, are their savings—largely bronze coins from Pontic and Mesopotamian mints.[81] It is a salutary reminder of the multiple local elements in every military station that the emperor's men would also place their hopes in a regional coinage. Yet this is also appropriate: as the next chapter demonstrates, it is in the evidence for daily routine recovered in and around military barracks that the local and regional dimensions of what becoming Roman meant in the *auxilia* are most readily observed.

---

[78] Fort sites in Britain have an exceptionally high coin loss pattern for the 1st and 2nd centuries AD. Large towns are the only other settlements in the province with significant quantities of early coinage (Lockyear 2000: 413, 415 fig. 12, 416 fig. 13).

[79] *P. Gen.* 35.

[80] *SB* 9207.

[81] Rostovtzeff, Bellinger, Hopkins and Welles (1936, 179–81, hoards 14–16); Pollard (2000, 196).

11

Incorporation through Routine

The Power of Everyday Life

For a student of archaeology, close attention to the context of artefacts is absolutely essential for distinguishing what de Certeau calls the 'strategies' from the 'tactics' of daily life.[1] Authority, imperial or other, might establish a built framework strategically to foster and reward certain behaviours, but even walls of stone can be differently interpreted by those they enclose. It is said that during his tour of military installations in AD 121, Hadrian was appalled to see a range of civil decorative schemes and gardens in the camps and set about banning them.[2] Apparently, the humanizing transformation of the fort into an urban living space conflicted with an imperial ideal of military discipline. To appreciate better the impact of life in camp on individuals, and the degree to which individuals were themselves able to transform their environment, we must go beyond looking at the plan of buildings and examine mundane routine and the tactics of daily life.

Discussion of daily life in the Roman army almost invariably focuses on the duties performed by soldiers, on the changing of the guard, the detailing of patrols, and the ongoing cycle of training. Recently, certainly, there has been some attempt to consider life off-duty, but still the minutiae of everyday life are overlooked. Yet ancient writers recognized the way that consumption associated soldiers with Rome in the eyes of outsiders, and defined their particular niche within provincial society to insiders. Thus Dio, himself a former army officer, could make Boudicca claim that Roman soldiers 'need (kneaded) bread and wine and (olive) oil, and if any of these things are not available to them, they succumb'.[3] The remark underscores the importance of routine in defining identity. Indeed it is here, in the realm termed *habitus* by sociologists, that we see most clearly the extent and the limits of cultural transformation.[4] Daily routine played a fundamental role in incorporating auxiliaries into the structures of empire. At the most basic, subliminal level the soldier himself incorporated the products of that society into his own body, literally internalizing the diverse cultures of consumption that

---

[1] De Certeau (1984).

[2] *SHA Hadrian* 10.4.

[3] Dio 62.5.5.

[4] Giddens (1984: esp. 60–64) discusses the role of routine in recreating social structures, noting the character and role of routine at different levels of consciousness (1984: 5–8).

Fig. 11.1. E4 House, Dura-Europos: southwest corner of courtyard.

collectively defined the Roman world. This form of incorporation through consumption attests the extraordinary power of mundane routine.

Finds from the barracks of Dura-Europos underscore this point. A fine example
of the soldiers' quarters uncovered there is House E4 (see Fig. 11.1). Having
undergone 'ruthless conversion' *c.* AD 165, the 'house' embodies the contrasts
and commonalities between domestic civilian and military life (see Fig. 11.2).[5]
Analysis of graffiti from its walls suggested to the excavators that the adapted
block housed men of *cohors II Ulpia equitata*.[6] Whether or not this was the case, it
seems almost certain that auxiliaries were amongst the occupants.[7] Significantly,
the remodelling did not simply replicate the purpose-built barrack blocks familiar
elsewhere in the Empire, for this would have required the total demolition of the
existing house, but the substantial reordering of the building's interior does show
that it was organized around the same basic assumptions. Though the team
responsible for the examination of the building were no doubt influenced in
their interpretation by what was then known of barrack blocks in the Empire's
purpose-built forts and fortresses, the similarities that they were able to observe do
appear significant. Once E4 had been converted, the excavators estimated, it was
able to accommodate between sixty to ninety soldiers; this gave it much the same
capacity as envisaged for other barrack buildings across the Empire, allowing it to
accommodate a century of soldiers.[8] Furthermore, essentially the same principles
of command and control seem to be applied. One part of the block (room 23),
distinguished by the presence of a Latin calendar on the wall (see Fig. 11.3),[9]

---

[5] Rostovtzeff et al. (1936: 28 and 31).   [6] Ibid. 29.

[7] Simon James (pers. comm.) notes the uncertainties surrounding *cohors II Ulpia*'s location at this
time, and has suggested that the building might equally well have housed either a mixed group of
legionaries and auxiliaries or a contingent of *cohors XX Palmyrenorum*.

[8] Rostovtzeff et al. (1936: 29).   [9] Ibid. 40–42, no. 622.

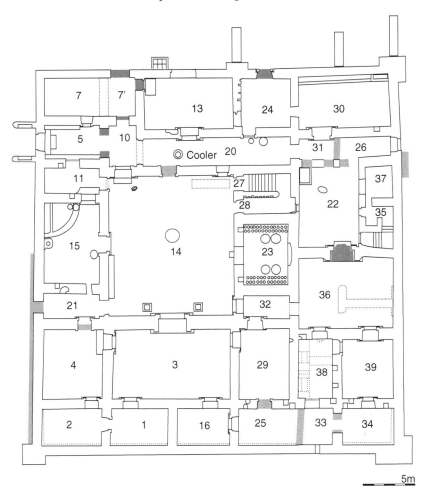

Fig. 11.2. Plan showing the layout of E4, Doura-Europos, following its conversion into a military barracks. Rooms 4, 2, 1, 16, 25, 20, 39, 38, 7 and perhaps 34 are interpreted as barrack rooms. Room 23 appears to be an officer's room. Room 30 was a stables and room 33 a bath.

appears to have served as accommodation for an officer. While the calendar provides a useful reminder of the importance of measuring time for the smooth running of military operations, the proximity of the officer's accommodation recalls practice elsewhere. The presence of centurions' or decurions' quarters within each barrack block seems to have been standard across the Empire, ensuring a higher level of supervision and rapid communication between officers and men. It is also clear that here, as elsewhere, food preparation took place within the soldiers' quarters; indeed, a cheerful graffito in Room 21 appears to boast of a duty cook's culinary excellence.[10] In this case, conversion for military use had

---

[10] Ibid. 40, graffiti no. 621.

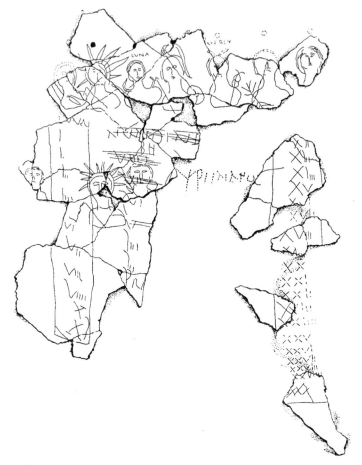

Fig. 11.3. Latin Calendar from House E4, Dura-Europos. The seven divine heads appear to indicate a seven day week. This is particularly noteworthy in a city where papyrological evidence indicates that other calendar systems were in use. Yale University Art Gallery.

generated a single major kitchen range—an interesting discovery, as it is often assumed that most of the food preparation took place in the rooms of individual *contubernia* at this date. In addition, a large pithos and five amphorae capable of holding wine and olive oil—commodities central to Roman drinking, food preparation, and personal grooming—were discovered within the block (room 36).[11]

Roman notions of hygiene were also represented in the conversion process; a preexisting room was partitioned to accommodate the installation of a new bath complete with conventional Roman hypocaust (Fig. 11.2, room 33).[12] Importantly, such innovations were not restricted to house E4. As noted above, other Roman

[11] For the find, see ibid. 27. Unfortunately it is not possible to establish exactly how these amphorae were used. See also Pollard (2000: 187, 202).

[12] Rostovtzeff et al. (1936: 24).

baths, closely related to one another in plan and form and radically different in form from traditional Durene buildings, appear elsewhere in the city at about this time. One lies only a block away from E4. Though initially attributed by the excavators to 'the intensive Romanization of municipal life',[13] Pollard is surely correct to link the construction of these baths to the army.[14] Finally, we may note that what appears as a significant trend in the built environment of the city also emerges in the small finds evidence. Archaeologists working at Dura-Europos recovered a range of small bronze objects identical to finds from Roman military sites in the west. Amongst these discoveries were artefacts that may be clearly identified as razors.

Razors are but one example of how the most humble artefacts play an active role in defining cultural affiliations. The 3rd-century framed razors from Dura, directly comparable in form and decoration to examples from Italy, the Balkans, and the western provinces, clearly evolved from the basic triangular razor popular amongst ordinary soldiers in the 1st century. Together they attest to an Empire-wide practice. Neither form was the particular monopoly of the military community, any more than shaving itself, but such razors notably emerge as familiar finds at sites associated with the army.

The Romans had a long-established suspicion of beards and the bearded up until at least the reign of Hadrian. Beards were associated with Greeks, philosophers, and the poor. Not only were they regarded as undesirable, therefore, but they ran into direct conflict with early Roman notions of manhood.[15] In the imperial armies, as in a great many later ones, the relationship of hair to masculinity was no less important than in civil society. Tacitus links the slide into barbaric treachery of the auxiliary commander Civilis to his refusal to cut his hair.[16] Control and order were abandoned when he reaffirmed his native roots. Maintaining the self-mastery required of the *vir* initially involved distinguishing oneself from the bearded through the arduous routine of shaving. When beards become more acceptable, it required that they nevertheless remained firmly under control. Maintaining the delicate beards shown on soldiers in Dura's famous Terentius fresco must have required at least as much effort as keeping the chin resolutely stubble-free, requiring both shears and razors.

What lends significance to this distinction is the fact that in the Roman world shaving was not the quick battery- and/or shaving cream-aided chore of today, but a lengthy process dependent on a regular supply of hot water. The provision of communal baths with regular supplies of hot water no doubt helped, but it is clear that shaving took place elsewhere too. One of the reasons, no doubt, why Dio's Maecenas identified soldiers as the carriers of wood and charcoal was that they had to invest a significant amount of time in gathering it for fires.[17] In addition to heating, cooking, and supplying the furnaces of the unit baths, they needed wood to be able to heat water for washing in their accommodation.[18]

---

[13] Ibid. 104.   [14] Pollard (1996: 52–3).

[15] Balsdon (1979: 215) wonders if the townsman in Olbia who drew the contempt of the local community for keeping his hair short and shaving regularly (Dio Chrysostom *Or.* 36.17) was a former auxiliary.

[16] *Hist.* 4.61. Though the incident recalls a vow made by Caesar (Suetonius *Caesar* 67.2).

[17] Dio 52.25.7.

[18] For soldiers and the gathering of fuel, see *RMR* 47.ii.9 and Croom (2011: 36–8).

Nor was wood gathering the only time-consuming routine to punctuate the soldier's day. Experiments with a reconstructed razor similar to those found at Dura suggested that a full clean shave might take anything up to three-quarters of an hour. The wealthiest Romans had slave barbers, and even the less wealthy were often prepared to pay somebody else to do the work for them. All this indicates that regular shaving was not an easy option. Yet in all the 1st century AD tombstones of auxiliary soldiers where the chin is visible, it is cleanshaven. In this sense, and in others, the auxiliary soldier adopted fashions associated with the more affluent and urbane members of Roman provincial society.

In a world where a multiplicity of hairstyles existed, not least amongst the peoples from whom the *auxilia* were enlisted, the adoption of traditional Roman coiffures by so many auxiliaries need not have been a foregone conclusion.[19] This becomes clearer still when one considers the remarkable and often preposterous range of haircuts imposed on and adopted by soldiers in modern armies. It would be possible to write a history of military hair, with its wigs, powders, short cuts, and extraordinary regulations. So it is worth considering how styles emerged in the Roman army and how they were sustained. Claudian's comment that 'Sygambria' should have its locks shorn to serve under Roman standards may be viciously sarcastic, but the very observation may suggest that certain minimum standards were enforced in the later Roman army,[20] and this may well have applied to the Principate too.

Minimum standards are one thing, but fashion may be another. There are certain moments in the history of Roman military hair when the soldiers' preferences appear to resemble those of the reigning emperor. For example, much has been made of Hadrian's beard and the increasing depiction of bearded soldiers from about the same date; a contrast with an earlier Roman preference for cleanshaven chins is often stressed. Trajan's Column, which was actually completed under Hadrian, shows officers, legionaries, and both regular and irregular auxiliary soldiers with beards, though many of the military figures remain beardless. While scholars have long since lost confidence in the Column as an accurate portrayal of the army, and later representations of soldiers in monumental art seem still less realistic, there is no reason to doubt that the fashion was adopted by lower-ranking soldiers at about this time. More humble provincial depictions, such as the Croy Hill relief,[21] also reflect the change; but what drove it? The established view that Hadrian's beard is an expression of his philhellenism has come under increasing scrutiny lately.[22] Is it possible that other factors might be at work? Most recently Simon James has suggested that some imperial hairstyles might represent a deliberate adoption of military hairstyles by emperors rather than the adoption of imperial fashion by soldiers. And indeed, it is tempting to see in the 'shaggy-haired' locks of later 2nd-century portraits or the close cut of Maximinus Thrax in the 3rd rough styles that recall those most convenient on campaign.[23] Perhaps the answer is a bit of both: as emperors became more dependent on stressing their relationship with the army, it was useful to project

---

[19] For long hair amongst Rome's enemies and allies, see M. P. Speidel (2004: 175–80).
[20] Claudian *Eutrop.* 1.383.   [21] Coulston (1988b).
[22] Opper (2008: 69–71).   [23] James (2011: 189–90, 216).

closeness to the soldiery through their appearance. At the same time, imperial likenesses would have been conspicuously displayed throughout military bases across the Empire on statues, frescoes, and coins offering a model that soldiers could readily adopt. Whatever the explanation, the increasingly strong relationship between imperial and military hair reflects the impressive degree to which soldiers were incorporated into the network of ideas that helped define the face of the Empire.

Hair care was linked to another important Roman routine, bathing. Regular bathing would help to reduce infestation with lice, as well as fleas and ticks, and the ailments they carried.[24] In Rome itself and at many major metropolitan centres, the ritual of the bath was also linked, among other forms of grooming, to the removal of body hair. Indeed, there appear to have been at least two types of specialist for the latter, the *depilator* and the *alipilus*.[25] It is far from clear, however, whether soldiers would have availed themselves of these services. What is certain, though, is that in bathing, the bodies of soldiers were themselves immersed in Roman debates on cleanliness. As many recent studies have shown, notions of cleanliness are about much more than the presence or absence of dirt: they are also linked to complex ideas about health and status.[26]

As the introduction of Roman bath houses at Dura attests, bathing became a routine part of military life. By the 2nd century virtually all military installations, from the deserts of Egypt to the lowlands of Scotland, had a bath complex associated with them. It is less easy, however, to establish when bathing became commonplace in military circles. The earliest known example of a bath-house attached to a military station is the celebrated, and distinctive, timber model constructed at Vindonissa *c*. AD 25–30, but it was not until somewhat later that baths became commonly associated even with the larger fortresses. The association of bath-houses with forts in several provinces comes later still. Baths are not found in auxiliary forts in Britain until the late 1st century—for example, they first make an appearance at Elginhaugh, a site abandoned *c*. AD 86.[27] From this time onwards, however, baths do appear to play an important role in the lives of auxiliary soldiers. A near-contemporary writing tablet from Vindolanda emphasizes the official dimension of auxiliary soldiers' participation in Roman bathing culture, recording their work in building a bath-house.[28]

An interesting argument for why baths appeared so much later at auxiliary sites comes from Paul Bidwell.[29] He argues that this development reflects the impact upon official policy of the changing cultural backgrounds of auxiliaries. He suggests that, by the end of the 1st century, in contrast to earlier generations, bathing was no longer alien to either the upbringing or the expectations of these men. Interestingly, however, this alleged change in expectations does not involve a wholesale adoption of the bathing habits of legionaries as represented at fortresses. Legionary bath suites in the western provinces tend to incorporate a *palaestra* or exercise courtyard, a feature originating in the public spaces of the Mediterranean

---

[24] Jackson (1988: 49).   [25] Wissemann (1984: 80–9).

[26] Elias (1992); Douglas (1995); Lindenlauf (2004).   [27] Bidwell (1997: 78).

[28] *Tab. Vindol.* II.155.3. The tablet does not specify the source of the men, but I follow the editors in believing that it must indicate soldiers.

[29] Bidwell (1997: 79).

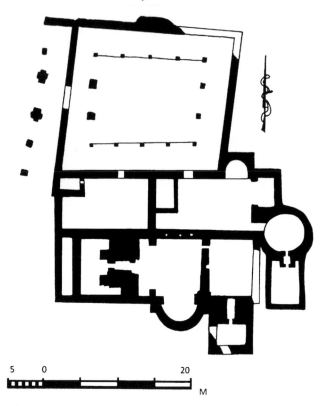

Fig. 11.4. Red House baths, Corbridge, England. The substantial *palaestra* lies to the north.

world, yet those found outside forts do not. This distinction is all the more interesting when considered in the context of the Red House site at Corbridge in Britain (see Fig. 11.4). Here the baths that appear to serve the fort do contain a *palaestra*, but the fort contained the *ala Petriana*, the regiment destined to become the highest-status auxiliary formation in the provincial garrison.[30]

Soldiers were probably some of the most active bathers in provincial society even before military bath-houses were established. Sauer has, for example, demonstrated military involvement in the development of spas on the Upper Rhine.[31] Here, of course, the bathing was often linked to hopes for health and healing, but particular notions of hygiene and relaxation would have been on display too. Much of this activity dates from the decades immediately following the death of Augustus, but there are still earlier examples of the phenomenon. Analysis of coin offerings at the Augustan spa at Bourbonne-les-Bains, for example, convinced Sauer that the site was already drawing a large number of soldiers to take the waters in the late 1st century BC.[32] In Britain, too, it has been suggested that several military tombstones found at Bath, such as that of Lucius Vitellius Tancinus, a trooper in the *ala Vettonum*, commemorate soldiers drawn to the baths of Sulis Minerva in the (in this case unfulfilled) hope of reinvigoration.[33]

---

[30] Daniels (1959: 85–176).   [31] Sauer (1999: 53).   [32] Ibid. 62.   [33] *RIB* 159.

The picture of the soldier as a regular bather and spa visitor is confirmed by other epigraphic evidence. An inscription from Aljustrel in southern Portugal indicates that soldiers there were privileged by being allowed free access to the baths linked to the mines.[34] Though the surviving regulations from this site date to the 2nd century, it is quite possible that similar arrangements existed before. The absence of a fort bath was not therefore a barrier to Roman hygiene, but it suggests that for many auxiliaries before the Flavian period it could not have been a common feature. Once access to baths became more available, possibly even on a daily basis, soldiers were able to enjoy a routine seldom experienced by those who inhabited neither towns nor villas.

The strong association between soldiers and bathing makes particular sense in a Roman context, for the Roman soldier was understood to be a particularly sweaty being.[35] Various widely read military treatises argue that soldiers should be 'trained by sweating'.[36] This is in marked contrast with Celsus' advice to a largely civilian audience that exercise should stop as soon as a light sweat has been achieved.[37] Sweating is, in fact, so strongly linked to the image of soldiers from the 2nd century BC to the 4th century AD that it eventually becomes a legal term for active service.[38] Allusions to the sweat of warrior emperors must be understood as flattery, not impertinence. Pliny's poetic assurance to Trajan that he won his soldiers' admiration when on field manoeuvres, his sweat and dust mingled with their own, underscores the potent—even pungent—notion of the emperor as co-soldier.[39] Emperors on campaign therefore naturally sweated more than others. Claims that Maximinus Thrax collected enough of his sweat in cups 'to exhibit two or three pints of it' a day, may be mere fiction, but they underscore the link between soldiering and sweating in the Roman mind.[40]

At the end of the working day, particularly when their commanders had chosen to take literally the advice of Vegetius and his predecessors to exercise the men until the sweat ran off them, there might reasonably have been quite a queue for the baths.[41] Indeed, it is possible that bathing was even prescribed as part of military routine alongside the exercise which preceeded it.[42] While in the military sphere sweat contributed to a particular kind of masculinity—a glowing testimony to hard work—it was not seen as necessary to be permanently caked in dust and perspiration. The fact that many auxiliary installations did not generally have bath-houses prior to the Flavian period may have meant that in the early years they emanated a more pungent and consequently 'barbaric' odour than their legionary counterparts.

Bathing was more, of course, than simply a device for removing sweat and dust. As Yegül observed, 'not to bathe would be un-Roman'.[43] Experimental bathing in the newly reconstructed Roman bath house at Wallsend demonstrates that an individual could progress rapidly through a reinvigorating and cleansing bathing sequence. This, and the fact that bath-houses would have been kept operating 24

---

[34] *CIL* 2.5181 = *ILS* 6891.

[35] For sweat as a Roman military quality, see Carrié (1993: 115–17).

[36] The phrase appears in Onasander's *Strategikos* 10.4, a treatise of the 1st century AD.

[37] Celsus *De Medicina* 1.2.6–7.   [38] Carrié (1993: 116).   [39] Pliny *Panegyricus* 13.1.

[40] *SHA The Two Maximini* 4.3.   [41] Vegetius 3.4.   [42] Simon James, pers. comm.

[43] Yegül (1992: 4).

hours a day to avoid structural damage due to constant cooling and reheating,[44] might suggest that most members of the garrison could have enjoyed a daily bath if inclined and permitted to do so.[45] To do so would, however, have required a significant departure from the ideal routine of the Roman metropolis as advocated by Martial and lived by Augustus.[46] It would also have reduced time for cleaning and maintenance of the baths. Ensuring that everyone had access to the hot room would have been impossible unless access to the baths was staggered over much longer than the allegedly optimal three to four hours of the afternoon. The Wallsend reconstruction, based on the remains of Chester's bath that once served the *ala II Asturum*, allows only eight seats in the hot room of a complex originally designed to serve a cavalry regiment of almost 500 men and an unknown number of civilian users. Even if each trooper only spent five minutes seated in the hot room, it would have taken over five hours for the entire regiment to progress through the sequence of chambers.[47] Accordingly it is clear that for most soldiers the military bathing routine probably varied significantly from that of the elite. Military duties may have also have made emulating such routines unfeasible.

What is notable, however, is that the changing room is huge—easily sufficient to allow forty to fifty people to stroll, exercise, and chat without the slightest risk of claustrophobia. So big is the room, indeed, that today it can be used to house special functions and business receptions. The size of the original room certainly suggests that the authorities expected soldiers not simply to pass through it but to use it as a place for socializing.

Judging by evidence from other sites, other members of the wider military community, such as the families of soldiers and other occupants of military *vici* and *canabae*, clearly also availed themselves of these facilities. Excavations at the legionary baths at Caerleon have, for example, uncovered an admission token, female jewellery, and a milk tooth, finds that suggest that the baths were also being used by non-soldiers, women, and children. Earlier work at the baths of Vindolanda yielded women's hairpins.[48] So it is perhaps possible to envisage the presence/absence of the bathing habit as something that distinguished the community living in and around Roman forts from the occupants of their wider hinterland. Recent historical assessments of the living conditions of modern colonial armies emphasize contrasts between the notions of health and hygiene that characterized the lines of colonial troops, local auxiliaries, and indigenous settlements.[49] Perceptions of appropriate or ideal conditions could diverge widely and in accordance with very disparate views of 'science', tradition, society, and

---

[44] The damage to fabric from reheating and cooling has been observed in the reconstruction baths at Xanten (Clive Bridger-Kraus, pers. comm.).

[45] Night bathing does not appear to have been usual behaviour in Roman metropolitan circles (Yegül 1992: 33).

[46] Martial identifies the 8th hour (2 p.m.) as the best time for bathing (Martial 4.8). Augustus clearly considered 6 p.m. to be uncomfortably late (Suetonius *Aug.* 76.2).

[47] This is of course only a theoretical figure. We do not know how many individuals actually bathed daily, or indeed how many of them used the full range of baths and rooms in the complex.

[48] Davies (1976: 124).

[49] e.g. Arnold (1985: 168) and Peers (1999: 30–31).

religion. Just as diet could mark identity, so too did the treatment of the body.[50] Routines linked to health and hygiene marked boundaries between communities.

Amidst the jumble of military graffiti found in the military quarters within House E4 at Dura-Europos, the excavators identified an incomplete text on a door jamb, referring to olive oil (Fig. 11.2, room 21).[51] Olive oil was clearly as much in use here as it was in the force that confronted Boudicca a couple of centuries before. It was used in bathing as a cleaning agent, moisturizer, and massage oil,[52] but it was also employed elsewhere in medicine, lighting, food preparation, and the maintenance of military equipment. As its use spread beyond the Mediterranean under the Empire, olive oil was often introduced, and probably initially perceived, as an aspect of Roman cultural style. From an archaeological point of view, the very versatility of the product raises problems. For while its movement and bulk consumption is greatly aided in the western provinces at least by analysis of amphorae distribution, its use by individuals could have taken a range of forms.

Significantly, Roman writers disapproved of some of the recorded patterns of use. Pliny the Elder, for example, expresses disgust at the practice of oiling skin at the gymnasium. Yet how different was this in reality to the practices attested in many Roman baths? One wonders what Pliny might have thought of an incident recorded in the Talmud. Fearing a patrol of soldiers who arrived in their town, the townspeople fed them and rubbed them with oil, offering hospitality so that they would not themselves be harmed.[53] What Roman traditionalists might have regarded as effeminate affectation actually symbolized imperial hegemony in this particular episode.

Whatever the use, the centrality of olive oil to the Roman soldier's daily routine is made explicit not simply by the discovery of oil amphorae at military sites but by their presence at military sites in regions with no history of olive oil consumption or production. Detailed studies of sites in both Britain and Germany demonstrate the particular concentration of Dressel 20 olive oil-carrying amphorae at military sites.[54] In Britain, indeed, Dressel 20 amphorae are the single most common form of amphora on military sites, and appear there with greater frequency than they do at any other category of site until *c*. AD 250.[55] Underscoring the prominent role of the military consumer in Romano-British oil consumption, Funari notes that provision was ensured by a complex distribution system. A free market, political distribution, and individual unit-level contracting made sure that soldiers at all installations received this 'somewhat imposed product'.[56]

Reviewing the British evidence, Funari asserts

> the active role that the material world plays in discourses of power and identity is clear in the case of olive oil in Britain. People's identity and position in the world were linked to olive oil in different ways. Olive oil was a potent symbol of a dominant

---

[50] An interesting recent study of nail cleaners in Roman Britain underscores this point. Nail cleaners are mainly found in the southern part of Roman Britain, and seldom in those areas associated with the military. They are also rare in Gaul, Germany, and the Danube provinces (Crummy and Eckardt 2003: 44–69).

[51] Rostovtzeff et al. (1936: 36 no. 615).   [52] Mattingly (1996: 224).

[53] tos. Betzah ii.6 cited in Isaac (1990: 116).

[54] For Britain: Funari (2002: 238). For Germany: Remesal Rodriguez (2002: 300–301).

[55] Sealey (1985: 145).   [56] Funari (2002: 240).

power, particularly as it was part of a military supply network. . . . In Britain, it probably first meant a symbol of voluntary adherence to the Roman Empire. The Roman army played a pivotal role in this respect, as its supply network helped to expand Roman values and mores. For soldiers from northern lands and for native Britons, the use of olive oil was first a statement of allegiance.[57]

While this last comment is perhaps a bit strong, there is no doubt that oil use was culturally charged. The potency of this symbol in the northwestern and Danubian provinces was of course enhanced by the fact that the very scent of olive oil distinguished its users from non-users.[58] While similar claims are less compelling for the garrisons of the Mediterranean provinces and the Roman Near East, olive oil production may have had a special connection to military consumers there too. There is an ongoing debate amongst archaeologists working in Syria as to whether the region saw a switch to a monoculture of olive oil in this period in order to capitalize on the army's needs, and furthermore whether or not this was partly a result of investment by veterans in this resource.[59] However the question is ultimately resolved—and to a certain extent resolution awaits further archaeological survey—it is clear that there was a general increase in olive oil production in Syria during the Roman period.

In a profound sense, therefore, the soldier's use of olive oil reflects his incorporation into the networks of power that characterized the evolving Empire. Back in the 2nd century BC, it was already possible for Cato to list olive farming as one of the most profitable agricultural products.[60] In time, the Empire's needs for these products led to intensification in key parts of the provinces. And ultimately, those areas themselves went on to generate the elites who would one day rule the Empire. Thus the Guadalquivir valley in Spain, a key source of olive oil for the army, was the *patria* of both Trajan and Hadrian, while Lepcis Magna in Libya was the homeland of Septimius Severus.[61]

What applies to olive oil also applies more generally to the way soldiers ate and prepared food. Here, patterns of consumption reveal still more of the particular blend of cultural ideas that informed what the soldier ate, how he prepared it, and what he ate it off. Dio's claim that kneaded bread ranked along with wine and oil as the soldier's vital needs underscores the symbolic importance of bread in Roman society.

To a Roman, to 'know the colour of one's bread' was to know one's place in society;[62] it is not then surprising that there was a particular type of bread for

---

[57] Funari (2002: 263). Soldiers may also have used olive oil in other ways. See Frontinus *Strategemata* 1.4.7; 2.5.23) for other uses of olive oil. Sealey (1985: 145) cites P. M. Barford's suggestion that olive oil would also have been particularly useful for maintaining leather.

[58] In a similar way to how in Athenian society the scent of olive oil identified those who had access to the gymnasium as distinct from the wider population (Lindenlauf 2004: 91, discussing Xenophon *Sym.* 2.4).

[59] Pollard (2000: 201–4, 247–9). The debate follows claims by Tchalenko (1953–1958), based on survey work several hundred km west of Dura-Europos at the limestone massif east of Antioch. Tate (1992) offers further evidence for the development (either foundation or expansion) of olive farming in northern Syria from the 2nd century AD.

[60] Cato, *De agricultura* 1.7.   [61] Mattingly (1996: 245).   [62] Juvenal *Sat.* 5.74–5.

soldiers, the *militaris panis*.[63] In many parts of provincial society, bread baked from wheat was actually quite unusual. In northwest Europe, for example, it was not until at least the early 2nd century that wheat overtook barley in popularity at many major settlements.[64] Furthermore, comparison of pollen plots with macro-faunal evidence from a number of smaller rural settlements indicates that those communities that harvested wheat did not necessarily do so for their own consumption, but rather for the benefit of the army.[65]

By contrast, ancient writers argue that barley was eaten by soldiers only when there was a desperate shortage of food or when they were undergoing punishment.[66] This attitude to barley is in part a reflection of Mediterranean tradition. Barley was much less important in Italy than wheat,[67] and it appears that barley bread was regarded as only fit for slaves in some societies.[68]

That these conventions did have a real day-to-day significance for the auxiliary soldier is clear from the environmental evidence. Even in those provinces where there was no strong tradition of bread wheat production, forts were well supplied, and there is clear evidence that the army was careful to ensure that this supply was well maintained.[69] Examination of the remains of a 2nd-century ship that sank by the *limes* fort at Woerden (Holland) indicates that it was used to transport wheat, presumably to the auxiliary garrison there.[70] Similarly at the auxiliary fort of Loughor (South Wales), abandoned *c.* AD 110–120, it is clear that real efforts were made to supply the soldiers with bread wheat. The high proportion of bread wheat in the site sample clearly came from outside the vicinity of the fort, for none of the farms of south Wales was producing it at this time.[71] As part of the ongoing process of incorporation into provincial society, many local agricultural regimes moved into wheat production in the 2nd and 3rd centuries, ensuring that the need for long-distance shipment of such products became less necessary. Yet while wheat continued to be important, it should not be overlooked that some units came to consume more barley than the historical sources would allow.[72] There was, therefore, a degree of adaptation to local conditions.

The very supply of grain to the soldiers was itself famously bound up with the Roman networks of power that pulled the Empire together. Trips to collect grain were themselves a part of the routine activity of the auxiliaries stationed at Dura-Europos.[73] Reinforcing the emperor's bond to his soldiers was the fact that the growing number of imperial estates played an important role in meeting the army's needs. This much is clear from a Dura papyrus recording the issue of barley *ex praedis fiscalibus*.[74] Even this impressive resource was, however, unable to meet more than a fraction of the army's needs. Failure to ensure corn supplies

---

[63] Pliny *NH* 18.67. Cato offers a recipe for military bread (*Res Rustica* 70). Junkelmann's (1997) book of the same name in fact ranges across a much wider range of themes, but contains useful comments on bread and bread making (1997: 128–36).

[64] Groenman-van Waateringe (1989: 99).

[65] Finds at sites such as Assendelver Polders and Wijster indicate that wheat was not playing an important role in local diet, even though it was being grown nearby (Groenman-van Waateringe 1989: 100–101). See now also Kooistra (1996).

[66] Suetonius *Aug.* 24; Polybius *Hist.* 6.38.3.   [67] Pliny *NH* 18.74

[68] *Athenaeus* 7.304b.   [69] Groenman- van Waateringe (1989: 99).

[70] Haalebos (1986).   [71] Davies (1997).   [72] Davies (2002: 182).

[73] Perkins (1959: 41).   [74] Fink (1971: no. 91).

to the city of Rome or to the army of Empire was a crisis of imperial proportions, a disaster to be avoided at all costs. As such it fell to senior officials and local worthies across the Empire, not just in those areas with large garrisons, to prioritize it.[75] Thus, for example, Pliny had to allocate soldiers to assist in the buying of corn in Paphlagonia.[76] Similarly, local elites in Asia were made responsible for the supply of substantial quantities.[77] Though the authorities paid for corn, it should not be assumed that they relied on the market to supply this vital resource; rather, they instructed individuals to sell at a price that the imperial authorities, not necessarily the vendors, considered appropriate.

The way in which the burden of supply was spread throughout the population is best illustrated in the case of a single *ala* in Egypt. In AD 185 the prefect of Egypt ordered that a single *nome* supply 20,000 *artabae* of barley for the *ala Heracliana* stationed at Koptos. Those responsible for organizing the tax at a local level then divided this amount amongst the villages of the *nome*, the elders of each village supplied the amount for which they had been assessed, and they were in turn paid from government funds.[78] In a sense, it is less important to establish how the mechanisms of supply worked than to recognize that to a certain extent supplying the army with grain absorbed the energies of provincials and administrators miles away from the soldiers themselves.

In peacetime, then, soldiers could rely on a regular issue of grain from the *horrea* (granaries) that were an essential feature of military establishments. As papyri from Dura attest, the granaries were one of the key points within the camp/city that were guarded by members of *cohors XX Palmyrenorum*.[79] It is easy to see why all military commanders would have emphasized the security of these buildings. The guarantee of a regular corn supply must have been a significant change for soldiers recruited from communities accustomed to the perils of subsistence farming. It reminds us that the very notion of a routine of eating, not just the manner in which it was undertaken, was distinctive. In a world where fluctuations in local conditions could quickly bring villagers to starvation, certainty that one's next meal was assured placed one in a privileged position indeed. In this sense the granary was itself an enduring symbol of Roman power. Through the granary, soldiers were not only able to take resources from the local population; they were also able to sustain themselves when that population could not. Granaries assured the army's staying power, the key to its long-term dominance. The very issue of a wheat ration served to differentiate members of the military community from outsiders; but it is interesting to note that not all beneficiaries were necessarily soldiers themselves. Evidence from Dura-Europos, Mons Claudianus, and Vindolanda shows that the army issued resources to civilians associated with the army.[80] On one of the Vindolanda tablets, for

[75] Erdkamp (2002).   [76] *Ep.* 10.27.

[77] e.g. Flavius Damianus of Ephesus, who supplied 200,000 *medimni* of corn for the army in AD 166–167 (*AE* 1913, 170).

[78] *P. Amh.* 107 and 108.

[79] Perkins (1959: 376–83, nos 106–10); *P. Dura* 106 (*RMR* 13) and *P. Dura* 108 (*RMR* 14).

[80] Whittaker (2002: 209). For Dura, see the supply of muleteers (*P. Dura* 64). For civilians on the ration roll at Mons Claudianus, see Gilliam (1986: 115–17).

example, an individual named Primus, a non-soldier who may have been a slave, appears as a recipient of rations.[81]

On campaign, similar networks of supply were mobilized, but soldiers carried sickles and were frequently tasked with harvesting key crops.[82] This was a laborious chore, and early auxiliaries drawn from those societies where it was performed by the infirm, elderly, and women might well have considered it demeaning.[83] This is another example of the peculiar combination of chores that characterized the professional Roman soldier in contrast to the elite warriors of many provincial societies.

Still more indicative of this peculiar blend is the actual practice of preparing bread. Soldiers milled their own grain, and shared quern-stones for the purpose within their centuries and occasionally within their *contubernia*.[84] Like sweating, making bread was so fundamental to Roman military life that emperors made great show of doing it themselves. On campaign Caracalla, for example, ground his own corn and made it into a loaf that he then baked in order to identify with the soldiers under his command.[85] Most often, however, it appears that bread was baked in batches by each century with, as the excavators of the auxiliary fort of Fendoch (Scotland) suggested, *contubernia* taking turns to perform the duty.[86] One wonders how those auxiliaries, drawn to the profession of arms because they perceived it as being a 'manly' thing to do, responded to performing a task that was in many provincial societies a female responsibility.[87] This is all the more interesting as elsewhere in Roman society baking was itself considered a demeaning task. Though there is ample evidence for ovens in Roman military installations, most often in the ramparts themselves, bakers themselves were frowned upon. Vegetius, for example, even argued that bakers, along with brothel owners, were inappropriate candidates for military service on account of the disreputable nature of their occupations.[88] So the eating and preparation of bread among the *auxilia* may, therefore, be considered a culturally distinct aspect of military service with which many soldiers would have been unfamiliar before enlistment. Tasks considered menial elsewhere in provincial society were redeemed by their association with military service and thus with the ruling power. Through this peculiar combination of mundane tasks, the soldier's particular place within the body of provincial society was routinely reaffirmed.

---

[81] *Tab. Vindol.* II.180.

[82] Josephus *Bell. Iud.* 3.5.5 and Trajan's Column.

[83] e.g.Tacitus *Germania* 23.

[84] Excavations have recovered many handmills bearing centurial marks but only one that refers specifically to a *contubernium* (*CIL* 13.11954a).

[85] Herodian 4.7.5. Bread ovens have recently been discovered in the marching camp at Kintore, Scotland: see Dunbar (2002: 4).

[86] Johnson (1983: 198–9) supported by a bread stamp from Mainz (*CIL* 13.6935). The excavators of Fendoch noted that the number of rampart ovens corresponded to the number of centuries (Richmond and McIntyre 1939: 138).

[87] Consider, e.g. the biblical references that suggest that in the Roman Near East grinding corn was a chore often performed by women (Matt. 24: 41; Luke 17: 35).

[88] Vegetius 1.7. Bakery work was so undesirable that it was occasionally allocated to convicts; see the Theodosian Code (*c.* AD 364) (9.40.3, 5–7, 9, and 14.3.7, 17).

Alcohol consumption is frequently associated with military communities. At Dura-Europos, Baird has suggested that the arrival of the army may be associated with an increase in the number of inns and food shops in the area of the Agora.[89] Wine is also the third element of Dio's list of a soldier's vital supplies. Again, it is a product of Mediterranean origins that comes to be associated with the expansion of Roman hegemony in some regions. Again, there is extensive evidence for its use amongst auxiliaries across the Empire. The wine of the Greek East served by a soldier to Christ on the Cross appears to be synonymous with the *acetum* of the Vindolanda tablets.[90] This is the sour vinegary wine that men received as a daily allowance and was served as a safe alternative to water. Yet set against the evidence for wine's ubiquity, there is also clear evidence for social and cultural variations in consumption. Discoveries at forts with auxiliary garrisons of *tituli picti* on amphorae show that finer wines were available. This is also clear from the Vindolanda tablets. In one interesting example, only better-quality wines and large quantities of beer are noted; there is no reference at all to *acetum*.[91] The tablet makes three references *ad sacrum*, allowing for the interpretation that the special issues might be related to the celebrations of festivals.

The reference to beer is also significant. Documentary evidence, and discoveries of beakers, make it evident that, despite the widespread availability of wine across the Empire, the provinces may be divided into beer-drinking and wine-drinking regions. Though wine was widely available at Vindolanda, for example, it is quite clear that the fort fell into the former group. Official interest in beer provision comes across in the tablets; a decurion wrote to Cerialis, commanding officer of *cohors VIIII Batavorum*, to express concern over shortages.[92] In another tablet brewers actually appear amongst unit personnel.[93] Beer consumption may be a reflection both of regional supply networks and of the particular wishes of the soldiers within the fort. At the time these documents were composed, the Vindolanda unit mostly contained men from Lower Germany, itself a beer-drinking area. It would be interesting to compare patterns of beer consumption with a unit stationed nearby but drawn from the Mediterranean. Unfortunately such information is not yet available.

The wine/beer divide is important because it emphasizes that, of course, a significant amount of a soldier's eating routine would have been influenced by local factors. Yet, in what might be a metaphor for the creation of provincial cultures across the Empire, even mundane local patterns of consumption converge with imperial ones on a soldier's plate. At the top end of the unit hierarchy, evidence for such blends comes from the kitchen of the aforementioned Cerialis. This room, Room VIII of the period 3 commanding officer's house, was found to contain several fragments of tablets related to food and food preparation.[94] A tantalizing reference in one of these fragments contains the word *batavico[..,*

---

[89] Baird (pers. comm. and 2007: 423).
[90] The 'common wine' of Luke 23: 37. *Tab. Vindol.* II.190.c.25; 202.a.2n.
[91] Ibid. II.190.   [92] Ibid. III.628; Whittaker (2002: 217–18).
[93] *Tab. Vindol.* II.182.
[94] Period 3 is dated *c.* AD 97–102/3. It is during this time that Cerialis commanded *cohors VIIII Batavorum* at Vindolanda.

apparently as part of the recipe for a dish served with garlic paste.[95] The term
suggests that the cooks prepared something 'in the Batavian fashion', indicating a
culinary survival in the Batavian regiment.[96] We might note in passing the way in
which information about a native eating style is preserved for ongoing use in a
Latin document. The recipe should be viewed alongside another contemporary
document from the same kitchen that lists vessels including *paropsides* and
acetabula.[97] There is some scholarly debate as to what these dishes actually looked
like, itself an indicator of the need for a certain amount of culturally specific
knowledge required even to name them. *Paropsides* may have been used as serving
dishes for fine foods or as side-plates.[98] An *acetabulum* probably served as a
vinegar bowl. The use of separate vinegar bowls is alone a reflection of the
sophisticated degree to which Roman ideas about eating penetrated the household
of Cerialis, even if he sometimes ate dishes prepared in the traditions of his
homeland. The likelihood that the two vessel types were actually of the same
form and simply of different sizes, further underscores the degree of cultural
knowledge involved in their routine use.[99]

Cerialis was, of course, in the senior ranks of the *auxilia*. Like his notorious
fellow countryman, Civilis, he was a man at home in two worlds. Yet as those two
worlds, Roman and Batavian, continued to converge it is highly likely that many
further down the ranks behaved in similar ways. The problem for the archaeologist is that the mere presence of raw material does not directly illuminate how it
was used. Nevertheless, it is possible to gain some significant insights. First, it is
possible to look at patterns of meat supply and note what these tell us of cultural
change in the Roman army set against society at large. Second, seasonings give
clues to the evolving nature of provincial cuisine and the army. Finally, as the list
from Cerialis' kitchen suggests, the study of the vessels themselves can offer vital
insights into eating practices.

The choice of what meat to eat and what not to eat is itself a choice of some
significance. It is conditioned by the availability of local resources, but these
resources are often themselves a reflection not just of natural conditions but
also of conscious decisions about supply and subsistence. Extensive survey of
faunal assemblages from sites across the Roman world reveals much about these
choices. Perhaps the most significant point is that it is possible to recognize
archaeologically a pronounced 'Roman' meat diet which is notably rich in pork.
This is, however, the diet favoured by middling to prosperous occupants of the
city of Rome itself and its immediate surrounds.[100] It is not emulated by the mass
of the provincial population, and indeed is far from universal throughout Italy.
Surveys of military meat diet, once considered insignificant but now recognized as

---

[95] *Tab. Vindol.* II.208.2.

[96] For this translation see A. R. Birley (2002: 151). Bowman and Thomas (1994: 180–81) note that
the occurrence of the word could indicate that the Batavians brought some of their culinary traditions
with them. See here also Trow (1990: 107).

[97] *Tab. Vindol.* II.194.

[98] Juvenal *Sat.* 3.141. Hilgers (1969: 238) for serving dishes. Bowman and Thomas (1994: 164) for
side plates.

[99] Gwladys Monteil, pers. comm.   [100] King (1999b: 189).

a real feature of daily eating patterns, reveals different preferences.[101] While the total number of samples available for meta-analysis in the most recent survey is strongly skewed towards the western provinces, a reflection of different patterns in fieldwork and on-site sampling, it is nonetheless possible to note real regional variation.[102] Furthermore, it is possible to see that hunting provided a significant source of meat, thus reinforcing the local element within faunal assemblages.[103]

Within the western provinces King has identified a 'military' pattern of meat consumption under the Principate.[104] This is characterized, not by the high pork ratio of Rome, but rather by a high cattle ratio. He sees this pattern originating north of the Alps in the 1st century and drawing in part on indigenous dietary practices there. It is surely no coincidence that a high proportion of the army in the western provinces came from this region. Over time, this pattern becomes common at military sites too, a transition seen in the British data.[105] Thus the incorporation of local patterns of consumption and supply appear within a regional setting. King suggests that this transition, so closely associated with the Roman army, is better understood as dietary 'Gallicization' or 'Germanization' than Romanization.[106] Yet, as has been noted, those who prefer to work with the concept of Romanization argue that its primary affect was to spread and expand regional patterns, not necessarily to generate Empire-wide ones.[107] One may therefore select from a smorgasbord of 'izations' if one's tastes fall that way, but the essential point remains that evolving regional meat preferences can be observed in faunal assemblages associated with military units.

Indeed, elsewhere in the Empire different patterns are discernible. First- and 2nd-century sites associated with the army in Egypt have virtually insignificant quantities of cattle bone in their assemblages.[108] Even allowing for the greater meat weight contribution of these animals, their contribution is very small. This may in part be a reflection of difficulties supplying and maintaining such animals in desert outposts, but it is nonetheless a very pronounced pattern.[109] Pig bones, by contrast, dominate the faunal assemblages—a fact that distinguishes military sites from most contemporary civil ones in the region.[110] At present there is too

---

[101] Groenman-van Waateringe (1997) estimates that the meat consumption at the auxiliary fort of Valkenburg (Holland) approximated to 1lb of meat a day. This contrasts with environmental evidence taken from latrine deposits at Bearsden (Scotland) that did not appear to suggest a significant level of meat consumption (Breeze 1996: 77–8), but it appears to be consistent with faunal evidence from other auxiliary forts.

[102] King (1999b) marshals evidence from 79 British military sites (16 'legionary sites' and 63 'auxiliary sites') and 65 German ones (9 'legionary' and 56 'auxiliary'), as against 4 from Romania and Bulgaria combined, and a total of 11 military sites from the Roman Near East.

[103] Davies (1971: 127) and King (1999a: 147, table 3).

[104] King (1984: 190–92, 198: 1999b: 189).   [105] King (1984: 192).

[106] King (1984: 190–92, 198; 1999b: 189).   [107] James (2001).

[108] The bone assemblage from Al Zarqa contained no trace (Leguilloux 1997), while only 0.2% of the assemblage from Mons Claudianus was from cattle (Veen with Hamilton-Dyer 1998). Three separate assemblages from the military/urban site of Berenike also contain low proportions of ox bone, at 4.6, 6.5 (both in van Neer and Lentacker 1996) and 14.7 (van Neer and Ervynck 1998) respectively (King 1999b: 196, table K).

[109] King (ibid. 189–90) notes the role of the command economy is supplying these particularly remote locations.

[110] Ibid. 183 and van Neer (1997).

little evidence from Egypt and the Near East to enable us to determine whether military and civil dietary patterns subsequently converged.

Within these wider patterns there are some indications of a division between legionary fortresses and sites associated with the *auxilia*. While allowing for the fact that auxiliaries could be found at the former and some legionaries spent time at the latter, and that the terminology is potentially misleading, there is no doubt a distinction in bone finds between the two. This is most evident within the largest data set, that from Britain. Here the 1st century witnesses a generally higher ratio of pork at legionary sites as opposed to a higher proportion of sheep/goat at those of the *auxilia*.[111] Perhaps the importance of pork at legionary fortresses is a reflection of higher-status units with closer cultural ties to Rome.[112] High pork assemblages certainly tend to be most pronounced at earlier legionary sites, where more men with ties to Italy would have been stationed.[113] These sites also generally show a *lower* percentage of sheep/goat bones than do auxiliary forts in Britain.[114] It is interesting to note, however, that in time, patterns of meat use at auxiliary sites come to emulate those of fortresses. This could reflect the consolidation of supply lines, a process that had its own cultural implications. That this was the case is suggested by study of culling age at different sites. Evidence from the fort of Eining in Southern Germany, for example, shows that a high proportion of the animals consumed were older animals. This contrasts with the slaughter pattern at the legionary fortress of Caerleon in Wales, where there is a preference for younger ones.[115] King has suggested that the explanation for this is that legionary sites were wealthier, more prestigious, and perhaps better able to exercise selectivity in the supply of meat than their auxiliary counterparts.[116]

One further distinction between site categories may be distinguishable in the faunal evidence. Though, sadly, there remain few cases where comparable data from both the military installation and its associated settlement (*vicus* or *canabae*) are available, when these are present there is a clear phenomenon. In each case that this author has seen, there is a higher proportion of cattle bone in the extramural settlement than in assemblages from the installation itself. Part of the explanation for this may lie in the fact that tanneries were most likely located beyond the camp walls. Yet where tanneries have been excavated, it is clear that the carcasses were sent elsewhere, for it is mainly heads and hooves that appear in their bone reports. Another explanation is that the butchery of larger animals would have been most sensibly conducted outside rather than within forts. The distinction may owe less to meat-eating preferences than to different activities in the two areas.

Finally, as with patterns of beer and wine consumption, it would be very interesting to see whether or not preference for particular meats reflects the ethnic composition of the garrison. Yet thus far the only data available that allows such comparisons to be made suggests that this was not a significant factor. Soldiers therefore appear to have made do with the meat resources the army could provide for them. At Eining, for example, it is not possible to see any difference in patterns of meat supply to successive auxiliary garrisons of Gauls, Tungri, and Britons.[117]

---

[111] King (1984: 189).   [112] King (1999b: 183).   [113] Ibid.
[114] King (1999a: 139).   [115] Eining: Lipper (1982); Caerleon: O'Connor (1986).
[116] King (1999a: 146).   [117] Lipper (1982), observed by King (1999a: 144).

The dependency on local supply systems for meat was not necessarily, of course, an absolute obstacle to the survival of distinct culinary traditions. In her study of the dietary acculturation of the modern Marathi population in Madras, Katona-Apte has observed that the community prepared foodstuffs that were alien to their own cultural tradition in a manner that was distinctly their own.[118] To do this simply required access to different spices and cooking equipment. There is no reason why auxiliary soldiers and their families should not have done the same thing. Might study of spices and ceramic assemblages from forts reveal ethnic currents in daily routine?

Travelling merchants were an integral part of the wider military community. Merchants and soldiers advanced Roman expansion on and beyond the frontiers of empire. Military markets presented multiple opportunities to these men who, hardy and cosmopolitan as their soldier clients, traversed vast distances in their professional careers. It is not at all surprising to see traders from the Near East travelling amongst soldiers of the northwest. Such men probably played a key role in ensuring the presence of exotic spices at military sites across the Empire. Birley, for example, tentatively suggested that the Salmanes who buried his 15-year-old son at Auchendavy on the Antonine Wall was there to sell eastern foodstuffs.[119]

Certainly spices travelled the length and breadth of the Roman world. Traces of pepper were recovered at Oberaden in Germany—a testimonial to the fact that from at least the Augustan age the military community could access food resources from distant Asia.[120] Such access was clearly not limited to officers or legionaries. A double leaf from Vindolanda preserves accounts of cash transactions between ordinary soldiers and someone who is quite probably a merchant.[121] Alongside items of clothing and footwear, these soldiers were able to buy pepper. The widespread availability of pepper and other spices had, of course, a greater significance than simply allowing individuals to preserve certain culinary habits. It also helped ensure that in military circles people from widely different provincial backgrounds could enjoy equal access to flavours less accessible in the civilian world. Again, the flavours are not Roman in the sense of coming from central Italy; they are Roman in that they are available across the Empire as a result of the networks of that empire. Pepper and spices therefore helped to incorporate raw local materials into a range of culinary experiences that itself enlarged as a direct result of the growth of Roman hegemony.

That a defining feature of that growth was the emergence of new regions of cultural exchange is most evident, however, in pottery assemblages associated with both military and civil communities. In the heady days of the Augustan cultural revolution, fine tablewares and wine amphorae from Italy could be found across the Empire and beyond. Yet it is ultimately regional patterns of pottery production that are important, as these reflect the development of Roman provincial society. These regions are distinguished from the networks of cultural exchange that preceded them in two ways. First, they are defined by the increase in

---

[118] Katona-Apte (1975: 326).   [119] *RIB* 2182 and A. R. Birley (1988: 128).

[120] Whittaker (2002: 204–34) cites De Romanis (1997: 141) for a discussion of the wider implications of the pepper finds.

[121] *Tab. Vindol.* II.184. The 27 fragments of this tablet were recovered from a building that may have been either a barrack block or a workshop (Bowman and Thomas 1994: 135–6).

the proportion of the population that can access similar materials. Second, they are generally larger than the exchange networks of earlier periods. Though there is clearly no universal ceramic assemblage discovered throughout the Empire, the defining characteristics shared by these regions result from a Roman cultural emphasis on intensified production and improved communications. Does the diversity that results allow us to offer anything more than broad generalizations about the unifying force of dietary routines in the army and the wider Empire?

At a very basic level, we must recognize that the soldiers of the *auxilia*, unlike some of the communities from whence they came, lived in a pottery-using environment. Across the Empire it was assumed that soldiers needed pottery. If, as in Dura-Europos, a sufficient range of existing pottery was already available, then the soldiers would simply use it.[122] If, however, this was not the case, as in much of the highland zone of Britain after the conquest, provision had to be made. This essentially pragmatic strategy reinforced regional patterns in pottery use. Amongst the pots used by soldiers in northern Britain, for example, were two distinctive forms whose origins lay far outside the northwestern provinces, the flagon and the *mortarium*. The latter, though not itself of Roman origin, became in time one of the most familiar forms of Roman pottery in the west. Long-distance supply from both within and beyond the province was used to ensure supply of the requisite vessels. Closer to the bases, auxiliaries sometimes produced their own pottery, but more often it appears that the civilians associated with them were responsible for production. Ultimately, in some areas, the basic assumption that soldiers needed pottery led to the growth of separate regional/provincial pottery traditions.[123]

A fascinating example of this phenomenon may be seen in the spread of Norico-Pannonian products into Dacia after the Roman wars of conquest there in the early 2nd century AD. Distinctive and intrusive forms of tripod vessel accompanied units for the new garrison that had originally been stationed in Noricum and Pannonia. Soldiers in these provinces had long been accustomed to using versions of local wares, as the tripod vessels produced in the auxiliary fort kilns at Carnuntum (Austria) in the second half of the 1st century AD demonstrate (see Fig. 11.5).[124]

The close relationship between eating and pottery use has led some scholars to consider linking the distribution of certain pottery types to the movement of particular contingents of soldiers.[125] Interestingly, though, in most of the cases that have been advanced the suggestion has been that either irregular levies or

---

[122] The arrival of the Roman army in Dura in the 2nd century AD was not accompanied by any dramatic shift in the pottery assemblage. Dyson (1968: 26, 66) notes that the earliest discernible shift comes with the importation of large quantities of vessels in the second quarter of the 3rd century.

[123] A fine example of this is the development of Romano-British pottery production in Wales, a region hitherto overwhelmingly aceramic (Davies 2002: 172–5).

[124] Gassner, Jilek, and Sauer (1997); Swan (2009: 14, 18–20).

[125] Swan (1992; 1997; 1999; 2009); Swan and McBride (2002). In what follows it is necessary to remain mindful of Cooper's (1996) observation that too much 'cultural baggage' is sometimes associated with the presence or absence of pottery types. People will adopt, with relative rapidity, pottery forms which are most convenient.

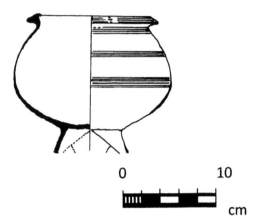

Fig. 11.5. Tripod vessel with Norico-Pannonian-style feet from the Carnuntum Auxiliary Kilns, Austria (after Gassner, Jilek, and Sauer 1997).

legionary soldiers were responsible.[126] Yet there are cases where a tantalizingly close link between the presence of certain members of the *auxilia* and the appearance of a particular form of ceramics demands further investigation. For example, the appearance of 'Raetian-type' *mortaria* in the area around Birrens (Scotland) in the 2nd century is striking.[127] The distribution of this pottery generally falls within Raetia, Noricum, and Germania Superior (Switzerland, Austria and Germany), yet here it is at a fort in southern Scotland. It is tempting to make an association between the epigraphically attested fact that a detachment from the unit at Birrens, *cohors II Tungrorum*, went to Raetia and brought back recruits from the province on its return to Scotland.[128] Yet the process might have been still more complicated, for we know that potters at Wilderspool near Manchester actually started to produce this pottery, and in this case there is no need to assume a connection with a unit recruiting in Raetia. A different explanation is possible, therefore, but it too depends on viewing the army as the vehicle for the new style.[129]

If ideas about pottery forms could travel with the army, it is equally likely that ideas about how they should be used travelled too. The difficulty lies in determining how this worked. It is possible that the refined knowledge of tableware use displayed by Cerialis, and discussed above, was not evenly spread amongst the rank and file. We know by contrast that some of his soldiers in the Vindolanda garrison were using traditional north Gaulish vessel types at this time (see Fig. 7.1 (b)). It is probable that even within the army, different status groups used pottery

---

[126] Uslar (1934) argues for irregulars on this basis at Zugmantel and Saalburg, but note also later work (Uslar 1980) on material from Heddernheim in which the phenomenon is placed within a broader context. On Hadrian's Wall the relationship of 'Frisian' or 'Housesteads' ware to the presence of Frisian irregulars is suggested by Jobey (1979: 127–43), though see now Wilmott (2000: 1–3). For legionary forces see Swan (1992; 1999) and Swan and McBride (2002).

[127] Swan (1997: 289–90).

[128] *RIB* 2100. The possible connection is noted by Swan (1997: 291).

[129] Wilderspool is associated with the *Legio XX Valeria Victrix* (Swan 1997: 288).

differently. Within the fort at Bearsden, for example, the distribution of Samian ware was found to congregate around the *praetorium* and the centurion's quarters at the end of each barrack block.[130] When we come to food preparation, our knowledge is more limited. The distinctive *mortarium*, for example, would have been put to a range of uses. Furthermore, it is evident that in some regions this vessel was used differently. For example, a markedly higher proportion of the *mortaria* found in Britain compared to those discovered elsewhere display traces of use with boiling water.[131]

A major priority for pottery studies, then, is to discover what vessels can tell us about food preparation, but there are already some interesting results emerging. Vivien Swan has drawn attention to the spread of certain forms, and argued that they link new culinary routines to the arrival of recruits from particular regions.[132] The spread of distinctive casseroles, platters, and braziers along the British frontier in the 2nd and early 3rd century AD is, she argues, a case in point. These clearly descend from North African vessel forms and are linked to certain eating practices. Their appearance and production at York suggested to Swan a link to the growing number of troops from North Africa at this time, though she recognizes that non-African potters and users probably adopted the form too. Indeed, the vessels are produced at a large number of sites conventionally associated with auxiliary troops.[133] Swan's wide-ranging research raises important questions about the cultural legacy of eating habits within the provincial armies, revealing quite diverse practices.

For the most part, however, the picture that emerges of military eating and food preparation is that of collective acts by small groups of ordinary soldiers. No separate eating halls have been identified in military installations; soldiers prepared food and ate it in their own barracks. This is suggested both by evidence from House E4 at Dura-Europos, where both activities clearly took place in the living quarters, and by the artefacts found at barrack blocks across the Roman world. There are differences, certainly, but the overall picture remains the same. While E4 seems to contain a central cooking area, evidence from barracks excavated elsewhere suggests that cooking in the lines took place in still smaller compartments within the barracks. Not only have most of the *contubernium* compartments properly excavated in western forts contained a hearth, many have also been found to contain hand mills.[134] Furthermore, while pans appear to have been held by individual soldiers in some units, it is clear there were shared items (see Fig. 11.6).[135] Larger cooking vessels and pots seem to have been shared within *contubernia*, perhaps in much the same way as other common items such as tents. A large bronze pot found at Nijmegen, for example, bears inscriptions giving the regimental (*cohors II Thracum*) and centurial and *contubernium* names

---

[130] Breeze (1977: 135).   [131] Hilary Cool, pers. comm.

[132] Swan (1992; 1997: 290–93). Though Swan's arguments focus on the legionary communities, particularly here the potters associated with *Legio VI*, it is clear that the general trends she illuminates also have relevance for the *auxilia*.

[133] Swan (1997: 291).

[134] For hearths in barracks, see Davison (1989: 231), with additional comment by Hodgson and Bidwell (2004: 140–41), who focus on the auxiliary barracks on Hadrian's Wall.

[135] e.g. pots found at Newstead in Scotland have century or *turma* titles scratched alongside personal names: *RIB* 2415.65–8.

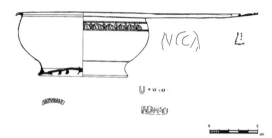

Fig. 11.6. This 1st-century AD pan (*trulleus*) found at Caerleon was stamped ALA I TH (for the *ala I Thracum*), the numeral LI was punched on the inside of the handle, while a graffito records a personal name (*RIB* 2415.39). This combination of marks indicates unit-level participation in the provision of individuals' cooking equipment.

and numbers. Such an arrangement would no doubt have reinforced the bond of the *contubernales* to one another and facilitated logistical arrangements. Furthermore, in the cosmopolitan mix that was the *auxilia*, it must have accelerated familiarity with diverse eating habits and culinary taboos. The mix that emerged from the soldiers' cooking pots must often have echoed the diverse mélange that constituted provincial society.

In matters of daily routine, from bathing to baking, the auxiliary soldier absorbed and embodied key assumptions about the Roman order. His place in that order was defined quite literally in his sweat and in his bread. Yet total homogeneity of routine was unattainable and anyway unnecessary in Rome's armies. The conditions of and resources for everyday living inevitably varied from place to place. Thus the soldier's routine also placed him, in his privileged position, in a situation where he could feed off the evolving regional patterns that characterized provincial society. This, then, was incorporation at two levels, enforced and expedited by the needs of the army. It was more than anything else, however, a reflection of the way the soldier's body was controlled and incorporated into the military body, and that body was in turn a product of the structures of empire.

Part IV

Through the Eyes of Believers

Religion, Ritual Activity, and Cult Practice

12

Sacred Space and Sacred Time in the *Auxilia*

Even after more than a century of intense study, our understanding of the cults and beliefs of Rome's armies remains partial. Excavations continue to yield data that confounds earlier analyses, introducing new layers of confusion and ambiguity to a field that has long prided itself on order and categorization. The long-standing tendency to frame debate around a notional religion of the Roman army is proving increasingly inadequate. The difficulties are profound. First, work in the study of cult practice in military contexts has often neglected the widespread criticism of the term 'religion' as an analytical concept, artificially grouping together quite disparate phenomena. Defining what was understood as religion under the Empire remains far from straightforward.[1] It is better, I believe, to refer to cult practice, the external form of worship.

Thereafter there remains a tendency to underplay the degree to which all practices varied across Rome's armies.[2] Some scholars have, it is true, attempted to identify differences between the cult practices of legionaries and auxiliaries in monumental art and in cult dedications, but this approach only takes us so far.[3] In fact, as the dynamics of incorporation would require, there are multiple commonalities between cult practice in legionary and auxiliary formations. But while in some cases these practices are virtually indistinguishable from one another, in others significantly different traditions are either homogenized or given the superficial appearance of similarity by shared rituals.

Underlying this complexity is a further problem: attempts to disaggregate elements of a perceived religious system end up producing distinctions which would probably have been thoroughly alien to the soldiers themselves. Frequently the interconnections between different areas of cult practice, both within military communities and between the military and civil populations, were more important than the distinctions scholars make between them.

As long ago as 1895 von Domaszewski, author of the first major study of religion and cult in Rome's armies, argued that such research should be wide-ranging, incorporating the study of structures, sculptures, coins, and site plans as

---

[1] Beard, North, and Price (1998: 211–44).

[2] Though Stoll (2001a; 2010) has been consistently careful to emphasize the importance of this point.

[3] Goldsworthy (1996: 271–6) discusses the association of auxiliary-type figures and head-taking in monumental art—an echo of Celtic ritual practice. Stoll (2001a) divides many of his tables of dedications by the armies of the Roman Near East between auxiliaries and legionaries.

well as inscriptions.[4] Since then an impressive body of research has grown up, but important archaeological evidence has still often been overlooked. The study of structured deposits, which are frequently amongst our more revealing sources for cult practice, has only recently received serious scholarly attention.[5]

SACRED SPACE AND RELIGIO CASTRENSIS

Scholars have often stressed the apparently solid Romanity of the camps in and around which cult practice was performed. Fishwick, following Helgeland, has argued, 'a Roman camp on the frontier was regarded as a religious microcosm of Rome, the archetype for all military camps'.[6] Rüpke, whose own work has done so much to illuminate the character of cult in the camps, similarly points to the profound religious aspect of such centres.[7] The topography of forts and fortresses reveals much the same ancient Roman religious vision as the early towns on which they were modelled.

Emphasizing this dimension was the combined affect of a large amount of visual imagery, each piece affirming through repeated viewing the cosmology of the evolving imperial state. Images of the emperor, statues and plaques, would have been familiar features. Their presence of course was not merely decorative; it was an extension of the principle articulated by Severian.[8] This was that the emperor's image should stand in courts, markets, meeting houses, and theatres, indeed wherever the governor might have to act, in order to lend his acts appropriate authority. The 'religious art' that decorated military installations ranged from small intaglios, shrines, and figurines, privately owned to more substantial statuary. Among the latter we see, unsurprisingly enough, images and dedications to Fortuna in military baths, just as we do in their civilian counterparts. But other deities, such as Mars and Victory, are used significantly more frequently than in civilian settings. Sculptural fragments from Housesteads and Risingham, for example, indicate that gates were sometimes adorned with images of these gods.[9] Vegetius shows that their names served as passwords to enter forts.[10] Even on the dress of the occupants in many military installations, these gods were a common sight. They were popular on military equipment, featuring, along with images of the standards, on swords and belts.

As time progressed, art and public text in the forts reflected a growing trend in Roman religious expression. Deities came to be given the features of emperors, a process known as identification. In many cases the association presented in this art would have been immediately apparent to anyone with small change to hand, for coins not only carried the image of the ruler, they too underwent this transformation.[11]

---

[4] von Domaszewski (1895: 1).

[5] Bradley and Thomas (1984). Though in many ways an awkward phrase—for, as Hill (1995: 94–7) emphasizes, all 'human activities are symbolically structured'—the term should serve as a powerful inducement to further reflection on key contexts.

[6] Fishwick (1988: 352); Helgeland (1978: 1490).   [7] Rüpke (1990: 165–83).

[8] *de Mund. Creat. Or.* 6.5.   [9] Crow (1995: 33 fig. 17).

[10] Vegetius *De re militari* 3.5.   [11] Fishwick (1987: 29; 1992b: 71).

Yet despite the evident power of the fort or fortress as a conduit for Roman ideas, it is possible to misrepresent its impact. Some commentators have gone so far as to see military installations as offering a pure form of Roman religion, excluding, for example, oriental cults as a matter of official policy. This view is, however, demonstrably incorrect.

Another error is to think of the worship practices of soldiers as wholly distinct from that of wider society; the cult of the standards was certainly a particular feature of military life, but in general much of the cult activity that we see in camps echoed that found in provincial towns. It must be recognized that the term *religio castrensis* has misled many a scholar.[12] It derives exclusively from the writings of Tertullian, whose Montanist leanings led him to a particularly unbending understanding of Christianity. His aim was to stress that the camps, which by his day must actually have contained many Christians, were places which posed great peril to his co-religionists' souls. He therefore sought to stress the distinct and cultic, rather than to acknowledge the broader resemblance between camps and the wider community.

To understand the context—the built environment within which the rituals of the religious year were played out—we need to look again at the archaeology of military bases.[13] This is necessary if we are to see how far, if at all, camps represented distinct islands of religious culture. We need to be alert to both the diversity of sites and the depth of information they contain. As we will see again and again, the stations of Roman soldiers varied to a greater extent than usually acknowledged. Variation applies not just to their diverse geographical settings, but also to their associated civil settlements, where present, and their internal organ-ization. Many soldiers did not spend their days inside the signature playing-card installations that we take as representative of military bases Empire-wide. Some lived in outposts of varied form, others in native settlements, designated as *praesidia* yet often archaeologically indistinguishable from towns and villages without garrisons. All this must be considered when we think of such places as landscapes in which ceremonies were performed and ritual enacted. Yet even among those who lived in major military installations, the experience was far from uniform. Indeed, some of the diversity was linked very explicitly to cult activity. At Dura-Europos the army took over parts of temples for official use. When, in the early 3rd century AD, the military transformed the city, a pre-existing *mithraeum* was rebuilt and at least one temple was built by soldiers for soldiers. Even in the west, that part of the Empire where the army conformed far more widely to the ideal notion of the Roman fort, there is clear evidence that sacred space in the installation could be remodelled to honour and accommodate exotic deities. Even in Rome itself, the *castra peregrina* hosted the rites of eastern gods.[14] At Porolissum (Romania), on the frontier with free Dacia, the auxiliary fort is known to have housed a *mithraeum* within its walls, while a *dolichenum* has been discovered within the defences of the fort at Vindolanda (see Figs 12.1 and 12.2).[15] In the east, where much less is known of military installations generally, clear evidence nonetheless survives for the basing of units in and around temple

---

[12] *Ad Nationes* 1.12.   [13] P. 145.
[14] Lissi-Caronna (1986).   [15] Birley and Birley (2010).

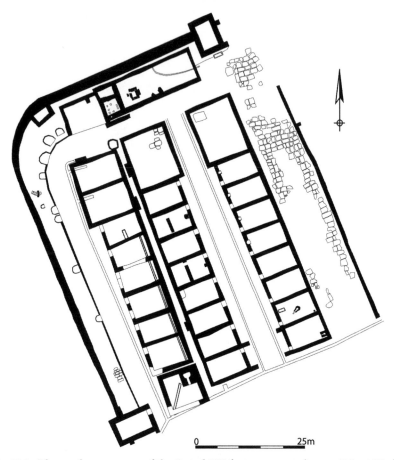

Fig. 12.1. The northwest corner of the Period VII fort, constructed *c.* AD 213, at Vindo-landa. The plan shows the *dolichenum*, the long building just inside the north wall, in its final phase of development (early 4th century AD), by which time the original structure (17.73 × 4.52m) had been expanded to the west. The temple was approached along an alleyway between two barrack blocks, and it appears that the southern entrance to this alleyway was elaborated with a gate or arch, possibly to make the approach appear more monumental.

sites. This is notably the case in Egypt, where for example a Trajanic fort was built around a temple to Thoth.[16]

Yet it is really in the detail of individual sites, in the walls and floors of buildings, in the makeup of ramparts and the fills of pits and wells, that we see how complex and how diverse the ritual dimension of military installations really was. Often it is only through the most diligent excavation that the extent of such activity becomes apparent, for much of it is easily overlooked.

---

[16] Maxfield (2009: 76).

Fig. 12.2. Altar from the Vindolanda *dolichenum* (1.05m high, 0.49m wide, and 0.48m deep), photographed during excavations on site.

At South Shields on Hadrian's Wall, for example, the painstaking examination of an early 3rd-century auxiliary barrack block revealed a series of stones marked with phallic symbols built into the wall (see Fig. 12.3). Significantly, these were placed so that they were in the front wall of the centurion's quarters and individual *contubernium* compartments. Being built face in to the wall, they were clearly *not* supposed to be visible to the human eye. The symbols were not therefore, casual decoration or grafitti, but a systematic pattern of placed deposits.[17] The excavators wonder if the particular placing of these stones was to ensure good fortune for the occupiers.[18] Certainly the association of the phallus with good fortune was a familiar one in the provinces, but to my knowledge there is no precise parallel for this practice in wall construction.

Elsewhere, the excavation of Roman forts and their associated settlements reveals a still greater level of complexity. This reminds us that clues to soldiers' dealings with the divine are to be found in the distribution of materials, not just in the fabric and layout of buildings.

Excavations at Kops Plateau, near Nijmegen in Holland, revealed three successive Roman forts and over 1,000 fragments of horse trappings, identifying the site as a home to cavalry contingents.[19] They also unearthed a number of enigmatic

---

[17] Croom (2001: 68); Nick Hodgson, pers. comm.
[18] Hodgson and Bidwell (2004: 143).   [19] van Enckevort and Willems (1996).

Fig. 12.3. One of a series of carved stones adorned with phallic symbols and built facing into the wall of Barrack IX at South Shields, England.

pits dug at different times around the middle decades of the 1st century AD. Six pits were found to have individual helmets in them, accompanied by purposely broken pots and in one case the remains of a chicken.[20] In another pit, the excavators found two helmets placed together. In no case was there any evidence that the helmets had been deposited with a view to subsequent recovery; certainly, no trace was discovered that suggested an attempt to protect the items from corrosion. These circumstances and the similarity to well-attested Iron Age special deposits support the excavators' interpretation that these were ritual offerings. Yet all but one of the helmets is of a type conventionally linked to the auxiliary cavalry, while the other, a modified imperial-Gallic helmet, may also have seen service in the *auxilia*. That this form of deposition was not restricted to helmets is suggested by the contents of other pits, most notably one of a Claudian date that contained a folded shield placed alongside several broken pots, and two of 1st-century date which appear to have contained saddles.[21]

The excavators rightly note that the pits they describe may be understood in the context of an indigenous tradition of votive hoards.[22] Yet aspects of the ritual attested here also appear in a still wider array of settings. The deliberate smashing or 'killing' of pottery vessels in votive contexts, for example, is part of the widespread phenomenon of fragmentation, a feature of prehistoric ritual behaviours across a vast array of societies back to the Mesolithic.[23] It is thus no surprise to find it archaeologically attested in very different settings in the imperial period. The widespread occurrence of this practice, then, suggests that peoples of diverse origins,

---

[20] Ibid. 126–8.   [21] Ibid. 133 for the shield; van Enckevort (1999) for the saddles.
[22] van Enckevort and Willems (1996: 128–34) draw on Levy's (1982: 17–44) criteria for defining ritual hoards. Though these criteria have been criticized (Bradley 1990: 10; Hill 1995: 97), they nevertheless offer useful insights into the character of the Kops Plateau hoards.
[23] Chapman (2000).

both indigenous and intrusive, could have recognized the breaking of the vessels as a significant ritual act and even shared a similar understanding of its meaning. As such, it may be dangerous simply to label it as either Roman or native.

Underscoring the problems of simple labelling is the character of the garrison at Kops Plateau and the individuals who interred the objects. The excavators suggest that the *ala Batavorum* might have been responsible.[24] This is certainly plausible, as the unit was stationed in the area. Yet, even if it were possible to ascertain that this contingent, as opposed to any other group, was responsible, ambiguities would remain, for though the *ala* was a Roman auxiliary regiment, it was also recruited and commanded in accordance with tribal tradition. To describe the men in this regiment or in any other contingent within the *auxilia* at this time as either native or Roman would be to promote a false dichotomy.

A further example, from 2nd-century activity at the fort of Newstead (Scotland), underscores the problem and potentials inherent in defining and interpreting 'structured deposition'. One hundred and seven 'pits'—a number of them were actually wells—were recovered in the fort and its annexes.[25] Though many of these were simply used to dispose of waste, some were clearly singled out for particular treatment.[26] This treatment included the deliberate deposition of 'significant' objects such as human bone, altars, arms and armour, seemingly selected for the purpose.[27] Such objects were found in only 37 of the pits, generally the deepest of those on site, and were notably often found alongside other rare 'significant' items.[28] A 6.1m-deep pit from the headquarters building of the fort, for example, contained human bone, horse bone, fragments of an altar, iron tools, and *militaria*. What is clear is that some of the other pits are backfilled wells, others are deliberately linked to boundaries—indeed they are dug under the fort and annexe walls.[29] Given the importance of boundaries, ditches, and walls in the Roman world, this fits quite well with Roman tradition, but it also fits naturally with rampart building practices in the Celtic west.[30] It is, of course, far from clear whether a conscious desire to follow a Roman or indigenous model was on the minds of the agents involved; both were arguably part of a broader and more ancient tradition. All that we may say is that there is ample evidence for both the incorporation of special items in walls and the presence of placed deposits in ditch terminals at Roman auxiliary forts,[31] while well closure rituals are attested across civilian sites in Britain and beyond and have clear prehistoric precedents.[32] The most recent commentators on the site are careful to note the way in which such cult practice blended into the ordinary routines of the site; there was no simple division between the sacred and the profane here.[33] This is evident right down to the level of the individual feature. Archaeologists can be too

---

[24] van Enckevort and Willems (1996: 135).

[25] Curle (1911); Clarke and Jones (1996: 109–13).

[26] It is important to note here that many scholars have seen the contents of these pits as common-place rubbish (Curle 1911; Frere 1987: 107; Manning 1972: 234). By contrast, as Clarke and Jones (1996: 109) note, other specialists have seen the whole combination as ritually charged, considering Newstead in effect one of the largest cult sites of the Celtic west (Ross 1967; Ross and Feachem 1976).

[27] Clarke and Jones (1996: 118).   [28] Ibid. 119.   [29] Ibid. 120–22.

[30] Clarke and Jones (ibid. 120), following (Owen 1992: 27, 31–2, 50–51), observe Bronze/Early Iron Age parallels for the practice in the immediate vicinity of Newstead, at Eildon Hillfort.

[31] Hooppell (1878: 41); Clarke and Jones (1996: 120); Bidwell and Speak (1994: 136).

[32] For the pits as part of regional tradition, see Ross and Feachem (1976).

[33] Clarke (2001: 81–2).

easily confused by the fact that many pits and wells which contained ritual deposits were subsequently backfilled with what else was then available. This apparent lack of purity confounds many modern expectations of ritual practice, but in fact it is entirely in keeping with the mundane realities of such practice in living societies.

The pits of Kops Plateau and Newstead are important for another reason. They underscore the ongoing rhythms of activity that harmonize the cosmos for a military community. The key moments of harmonization, whether in the entering or the leaving of a place, or in the opening or closing of the earth, are thus marked. In any community of this scale, such activities are being enacted somewhere almost all the time—a point we must remember if we wish to address the temporal dimension of cult activity in the army. Being a member of such a community inevitably involved routine familiarity with such patterns, however exotic they may seem to the modern viewer.

SACRED TIME AND PARTY TIME: THE RHYTHM
OF THE SOLDIER'S RELIGIOUS YEAR

Alongside these harmonization routines, so easily overlooked, there were more formally designated moments of sacred time. These were linked to notions of auspicious time and festival time, both of which could in turn be connected to one another. There is ample evidence for the importance Roman leaders placed on auspicious times for military undertakings, moments determined by the reading of signs and the examination of entrails. With festivals, calendars enabled soldier and commander alike to anticipate the sacred moments with rather greater certainty. It is evident that from at least the late Republic onwards public holidays entailed lighter duties for soldiers. Suetonius, writing in the reign of Hadrian, stresses the rigour of Julius Caesar's command by noting that he often made the soldiers turn out on duty at short notice, especially on public holidays.[34] That Suetonius can believe that this will resonate with his readership suggests that it would have been considered noteworthy during the imperial period too. While these days were clearly seen as an opportunity for merrymaking, we should not assume from this that they were days devoid of religious sentiment. Indeed, such celebrations were an integral part of cult activity during the religious year.

This section focuses on the rhythm of the soldier's religious year, but it is important to remember that the feast days and holy days celebrated in the Empire's forts and fortresses could have involved non-soldiers too. A tantalizing reference to what is almost certainly the *Matronalia* appears in a list of accounts produced for Flavius Cerialis from Vindolanda.[35] As Elizabeth Greene has noted, this festival honoured not only Juno Lucina but also mortal wives and mothers.[36] Women played the lead role in *Matronalia* rituals. Were these rituals confined to the occupants of the *praetorium*, or might other military families too have joined in the celebrations?

---

[34] Suetonius *Caesar* 65.   [35] *Tab. Vindol.* III.581.72.   [36] Elizabeth Greene, pers. comm.

The *feriale Duranum* has long dominated our understanding of the religious year of the Roman army. It is widely cited as the single most important source for the 'official' dimension of the soldier's religious experience. This festival calendar was discovered during excavations within the temple of Azzanathkona at Dura-Europos, Syria.[37] Other documents found with the *feriale* in Room W13 of the complex may suggest that it formed part of the regimental records of the *cohors XX Palmyrenorum*, an interpretation this author has also accepted. Yet a recent rereading of the *feriale* by Reeves has challenged this understanding, arguing that it is based on uncertain evidence and suggesting that this Latin festival document could instead be a civil calendar used by the *colonia* at Dura.[38] As Reeves observes, this raises the question of whether some of the festivals recorded, such as the *Rosaliae Signorum*, are city cult events rather than military events. The importance of this alternative reading to our understanding of the religious life of auxiliaries and indeed of the Roman state cannot be overemphasized. In this section I will therefore review the evidence for the calendar's interpretation before using it to provide an alternative structure against which other evidence can be examined.

To begin with, it is crucial to reconsider the archaeological context of our source. From the outset we must recognize that the site formation processes at Dura remain poorly understood. It is intensely perilous in particular to assume that the documents recovered were unearthed where they were originally used or stored.[39] The state in which the documents were found need not suggest that they had been archived in Room W13. They might simply have been dumped there. While Hopkins, the field director, conjectured that shelves supporting the documents may once have been present on the walls, no traces of such shelves were discovered, while the papyri were actually scattered across the room's north-western corner. Neither, he noted, 'were there any other remains of wood or leather to suggest covering for the documents'.[40] Furthermore, while many of the papyri found in this confused state were military, a number clearly were not, and documents that might have been expected in a military archive were absent.

None of this proves the precise purpose of the *feriale*, but it does alert us to much of the circular reasoning surrounding some of its interpretation. Under the circumstances, the excavators would have been extraordinarily fortunate to have found an archive entirely intact. In the garrison's need for materials to build improvised defences elsewhere during the final stages of the siege, shelving units may have been broken up and removed. The composition of the surviving group need not be so problematic; given that we do not really know exactly what an archive would have consisted of, the presence of older and non-military documents is not ultimately fatal to the interpretation. Furthermore, the possibility remains that illegible papyrus bundles found nearby, in Room W18, may actually have contained those records whose absence seems to pose a problem for scholars

[37] Fink, Hoey, and Snyder (1940: 1–222), repr. in Welles, Fink, and Gilliam (1959: 191–212, no. 54).
[38] Reeves (2004).
[39] Welles, Fink, and Gilliam (1959: 4); Reeves (2004: 79).
[40] Hopkins in Rostovtzeff (1934: 166). Reeves (2004: 78) draws attention to the absence of the shelves.

trying to interpret the area as an archive store.[41] The traditional understanding may yet stand, therefore, but it is evident that some of its foundations are shaky. Reeves's considered call for caution is well advised, and leads us, as she demonstrates, to look more closely at the wording of the document.

A closer reading is essential anyway, as we have no explicitly military religious calendar with which to compare this celebrated papyrus. Under the circumstances the best way to use the evidence of the *feriale Duranum* is to think of it as a document that framed time in an environment with a substantial military community. One way or another, the timing and character of the festivals would clearly have affected the soldiers' lives.

Scholars usually divide the contents of the calendar into three categories. By far the biggest category—27 out of the surviving 41 entries—were those devoted to emperor worship.[42] The bulk of the remaining entries consist of traditional festivals of Rome and Italy. Some honour the great gods of the Olympian pantheon. One, a surprise for many scholars, was dedicated to Vesta, a deity seldom attested in provincial contexts. Included within the traditional festivals are the *Quinquatrus*, *Neptunalia*, and the *Saturnalia*. Festivals with military associations, such as those dedicated to the standards and the *honesta missio*, are understood to constitute the third group. By no means all scholars agree, however, on which if any of the festivals properly belong to this category.[43] Furthermore, there are possible problems with the interpretation of both the entries linked to the standards and those linked to the *honesta missio*.

Over time, and in part as a result of the translation of the *feriale Duranum*, scholars have come to associate the ceremonies of *honesta missio*, the granting of honourable discharge to soldiers, with the date of the 7th January. This certainly is how Fink read the text, but as several scholars have observed, he based this on the surviving fragments of two words, the first the *ianu* of *Ianuarias* and the second, the letters *legio*. Neither the date of the 7th nor the term *honesta missio* appear anywhere. In several respects the 7th January would be a great date for such an event; it was, after all, the anniversary of Augustus' acceptance of the *imperium*, the highest military and judicial power Rome could bestow.[44] The date does appear to have been a 'highly significant' one for soldiers from the early 1st century AD onwards.[45] Furthermore, it appears to have been significant for the discharge ceremonies of the emperor's guard units.[46] Yet it is clear that this date was by no means always associated with the *honesta missio* in provincial armies,[47] and there remains a real debate as to whether legionaries and auxiliaries were actually discharged on this day.[48] At the very least, a careful reading of the papyrus

---

[41] Rostovtzeff (1934: 170). Reeves (2004: 79) notes this possibility, though the excavating team clearly thought that W18 was from a distinct part of the building.

[42] Fink, Hoey, and Snyder (1940: 6).

[43] Welles, Fink, and Gilliam (1959: 192) suggest that the category contains the *honesta missio* and the first stipendium, the anniversary of Septimius Severus' victory over the Parthians, the *Rosaliae Signorum*, and the *natalis* of Germanicus. Hoey (Fink, Hoey, and Snyder 1940: 203) omits the *natalis* of Germanicus, while Nock (1952: 188) omits both Germanicus and the Severan victories.

[44] Derks (1998: 54); Herz (1978: 1148); Scheid (1990: 459–60).

[45] Welles, Fink, and Gilliam (1959: 203).   [46] Ibid.

[47] Gilliam (1954: 190) and Welles, Fink, and Gilliam (1959: 203–4).

[48] See Gilliam (1954: 190) and Welles, Fink, and Gilliam (1959: 203).

demonstrates that the surviving evidence allows for a diversity of practice in terms even of the timing of this important ceremony. It could also undermine one of the arguments for the calendar's military identification, however.[49]

While considering the place of this ritual in the military year, it is worth considering what we know of the environment in which it took place. Our evidence for the practices of the emperor's horse guard indicates that the ritual took place in a military setting and involved the offering of vows to gods linked to the army and to the *numen* or *genius* of the emperor.[50] That so many themes interconnected within this one day illustrates that in many respects these three categories were not mutually exclusive; the image of the emperor and the presence of the standards would no doubt have been a common feature. Interestingly, Roymans and Derks have taken this interpretation further, and suggested that at least amongst the peoples of the lower Rhine, honourable discharge could have been accompanied by the dedication of military equipment at shrines to local deities. This is an attractive possibility, and one that reminds us that Empire-wide rituals could vary in form from place to place; but it is not necessary to assume that such dedications only occurred at such times.[51]

To return to the papyrus; though the document dates to *c*. AD 225–7,[52] it has been argued that it had a far wider significance in time and space than its immediate context might suggest.[53] No obviously local cults appear amongst the festivals, a fact that strongly suggests that the *feriale* was a universal calendar. It is widely understood to represent an evolved Severan version of a document that had its origins in the time of Augustus.[54] Certainly the hypothesis that the calendar started life as an Augustan conception for the army as a whole has an appeal. Not only does it accord well with the range of festivals included in the document, it also fits well with what is known of Augustus. Honouring the old gods formed an integral part of his strategy to 'restore' the Republic.[55] His vision of a new state and new army required a religious focus. Yet it would be wrong to rule out the possibility that later rulers attempted to do the same thing. It is certainly possible, for example, that Severus Alexander used such a strategy. An exceptionally large number of inscriptions dating to his reign stress the loyalty of his soldiers, a worrying sign for any emperor. A common calendar which stressed his divinized predecessors might have seemed a good strategy.[56]

Whoever was behind this initiative, it is clear that the strategy incorporated what modern historians term 'invented tradition'.[57] In addition to inculcating certain values and attitudes, invented traditions often serve to 'foster the corporate

---

[49] Reeves (2004: 82) notes the circularity of the argument; Fink's restoration fits because the calendar is understood to be military.

[50] Derks (1998: 54).   [51] Roymans and Derks (1994); Derks (1998: 52).

[52] Fink, Hoey, and Snyder (1940: 23).   [53] Ibid. 28–9; Gilliam (1954: 184–5).

[54] Nock (1952: 195–7, 203, 241) and Gilliam (1954: 183–6), challenged by MacMullen (1981: 110), but supported by Fishwick (1988).

[55] Suetonius *Aug.* 35.3; Nock (1952: 195).   [56] Also Reeves (2004: 76).

[57] Hobsbawm and Ranger (1983: 1) define 'invented tradition' as 'a set of practices, normally governed by overtly or tacitly accepted rules and of a ritual or symbolic nature, which seek to inculcate certain values and norms of behaviour by repetition, which automatically implies continuity with the past. In fact, where possible, they normally attempt to establish continuity with a suitable historic past'. For the link to nation-building, see ibid. 13.

sense of superiority of elites—particularly when these had to be recruited from those who did not already possess it by birth or ascription'.[58] Building such a corporate sense was crucial if Rome's cities and armies were to identify with their imperial masters. Ensuring participation in common devotions at common times not only facilitated this goal, but also engendered and perpetuated a collective memory, fostering a sense of community membership at the same time.[59]

It is easy to see how an element of myth-making in the ceremonies of the *feriale* could resonate with soldiers. Germanicus, a member of the imperial house lightly dismissed by Charlesworth as 'a versatile and amiable mediocrity', could have been celebrated for his importance in the east, but might also have been celebrated for his military significance.[60] There were other victorious generals, but aside from his local popularity in the Near East, Germanicus' most celebrated moments came after he avenged the most infamous disaster to befall Roman arms: he defeated those who slaughtered Varus' legions.[61] Revenge mattered to Roman soldiers. References to Mars Ultor—Mars the Avenger—within this document and elsewhere on military monuments, such as the Adamklissi altar, make this quite explicit.[62] A feature of the soldiers' collective memory was the importance it placed on avenging reverses to Roman arms.[63] In theory at least, a blow to one provincial army was a blow to all.

The centralizing aspect of the *feriale* and the mixture of feasts led some scholars to argue that the document was created as part of a policy designed to inculcate 'Roman' mores, a policy indeed of Romanization.[64] That a community in Dura, most of the members of which had grown up on the easternmost fringes of the Empire, should commemorate the same events as the people of Rome had two or three centuries before is certainly notable.[65] Equally noteworthy is the exclusion of all non-Roman deities: even the venerable Cybele, an alien deity long accepted in Rome itself, has no place within the document. Far from the evolving bricolage that defines other aspects of military culture and, indeed, the reality of religious practice in the provinces, this document appears to constitute a remarkably homogeneous expression of Romanity.

Richmond's sympathies clearly lay with this view. In a classic paper on 'The Roman Army and Roman Religion', he argued strongly that the *feriale* showed that the soldier's religious year was constructed not simply to win the soldier's allegiance during his military service but to transform him into a fine outstanding citizen when the time came to discharge him into provincial society. The argument, characterized by a strong sense of the division between legionary and auxiliary troops, is vintage Richmond, and thus worth quoting in full. The adoption and articulation of Roman thoughts and beliefs, he argues,

[58] Hobsbawm and Ranger (1983: 10).   [59] James (1999).   [60] Charlesworth (1934: 622).
[61] Webster (1998: 276). Tacitus *Ann.* 2.21–2F for Germanicus' role as avenger and his own memorial to Mars.
[62] See p. 1.
[63] The *feriale Duranum* records the celebration of the Circenses Martiales (Col. II.9) on 12 May. This date marked the anniversary of the dedication by Augustus of an *aedicule* to Mars Ultor (Hoey in Fink, Hoey, and Snyder 1940: 165, 204).
[64] Ibid. 206–10.   [65] MacMullen (1981: 110).

must have been a matter of pride to the legionary, however thinly or however crudely the lesson was inculcated. But much more was it evidently a matter not of pride but of specific imperial policy—one of the 'arcana imperii', if we will see it so—to imbue the auxiliary regiments, Gauls, Spaniards, Dacians, Britons or Germans, with the traditions of the Roman world. For these men, if discharged with good-conduct sheets unblemished, (honesta missione), were then to become Roman citizens, having earned by services rendered what they could never otherwise have attained. The military religious calendar can thus be seen not merely as an ordination of worship, but as having its effect upon not merely Roman citizens in esse, but Roman citizens in posse; as charging with loyal belief not only the existing but the potential citizen body. If its function is thus conceived it becomes a broader and bolder instrument of Imperial policy than might at first appear. Not a Test Act but an act of faith, a broadening of the political body coupled with a liberal diffusion of ancient and well-tried religious beliefs.[66]

Finely articulated as this claim is, however, it rests on shaky foundations and is weakly buttressed by an assumption that there was some kind of drive to Romanize soldiers. Even if we accept that the *feriale* is a military document, its role may be understood differently. As another early reader of the document observed, 'Between Akhanaton and the Sassanian monarchy it would be hard to find outside Judea any clear attempt by a state to direct the religious lives of its own members or subjects.'[67] The calendar's festivals would have had a very different impact on the spiritual life of different members of the Durene community.[68] Certainly, whatever the hopes of its initiators, there could be no guarantee that the programme of festivals would do more than create the impression of unity and loyalty. A more nuanced understanding of the document is therefore required. Gilliam, emphasizing the festival aspect of the calendar, argues: 'that is not to say that [these *feriae*] had no meaning and no effect at all. Such holidays, like the rest of the soldiers' routine, his use of Latin however limited, and his dress, helped serve to distinguish him from civilians and to remind him that he was a Roman soldier.'[69] Perhaps, however, the real distinction is between those who follow the calendar and those who do not. Certainly there are instances of individuals who were not serving soldiers participating in rituals that were primarily focused on the regiments that celebrated them. In an outpost city such as Dura in the mid-3rd century it is likely that many of the civilians within the walls would have been aware of, and quite possibly involved in, the cult practices of the soldiers whom they lived alongside.

How we understand the *feriale Duranum* thus clearly has significance for an altogether wider field than the study of the Roman army. The notion that some sort of Empire-wide religion or *Reichsreligion* existed that spanned provincial societies has been much discussed. Cancik and Rüpke see such a phenomenon as the agglomeration of multiple local syncretistic acts, which evolve in the particular circumstances of Roman provincial society.[70] Rives suggests that the emperor

---

[66] Richmond (1962a: 197).

[67] Nock (1952: 208). There are, however, dangers in assuming that a soldier in the Roman world would be treated in the same ways as 'members or subjects' of other ancient states.

[68] Nock (1952: 189, 223–9).   [69] Gilliam (1954: 186).

[70] Cancik and Rüpke (1997: III and 3–21). Woolf (2000: 619, fn. 26) notes the contrast between this and other top-down positions.

Decius may have attempted to establish a 'religion of empire' in his decree of AD 249, but that this was a new initiative.[71] If ever, under the Principate, an emperor had intended to create and impose a religion of empire, then surely we would find it here, actively imposed upon the one body on which the Empire depended—the army.

In fact it is possible to accept the notion that the *feriale Duranum* is one copy of a standard calendar issued to all units in the Roman army, yet still to recognize the considerable scope for diversity in actual practice. The guidelines provided by the calendar are a model of brevity, noting simply the date, the occasion, and the animal(s) for sacrifice. Liturgy, location, dress, and attendees are left unspecified. No details are given as to what form, if any, the post-offering banquet and accompanying speeches should take. Doubtless ideas of appropriate form circulated. We would, for example, expect the senior official present to make the offering. Other guidelines might even, of course, have been codified in another document, but to date no example of such a document has surfaced in a military context. Rather, the evidence that does survive allows for quite considerable diversity. The implications of this for our understanding of emperor worship will be considered below.

Certainly there were commonalities in the official religious practice of soldiers across space and time. The power and reach of Rome are nicely conveyed in the commemoration of the *natalis urbis Romae aeternae* on 21st April. How striking it is that this festival, recorded on a copy of the *feriale* found on the easternmost fringes of the Empire, finds echoes on an altar dedicated to Dea Roma on the same day by *duplicarii* at High Rochester, an outpost fort in northern Britain.[72]

Similarly, there is clear evidence for the widespread celebration of the *Saturnalia* throughout the military community.[73] An Egyptian document of AD 81, for example, records deductions from soldiers' pay for the *Saturnalia* held in their camp.[74] The tablets from Vindolanda, from a context a Roman world away, but only a couple of decades later, similarly attest the celebration of the festival. One letter requests that Candidus, slave of the commanding officer of *cohors VIIII Batavorum*, settles an outstanding bill resulting from the feast.[75]

There is also clear evidence that the will existed within the imperial house to coordinate at least some religious behaviours within the army. The link between soldier and emperor reaches its apogee in the oaths and official ceremonies that mark the soldier's career from its very beginning to its very end—with many points in between.[76] Loyalty mattered, and mattered desperately; it had to be reaffirmed, and reaffirmed publicly. Without the loyalty of Roman soldiers there would be no Roman Empire. But oath swearing was no mere act of secular pragmatism—it was understood by all parties to have a profoundly religious dimension.[77]

Assessing the extent to which imperial initiatives played a role in defining religion in military circles, however, remains difficult. We have already seen the

---

[71] Rives (1999).   [72] *RIB* 1270; *ILS* 2631.
[73] Hence the chant of soldiers addressed by Claudius' freedman Narcissus (Dio 60.19).
[74] Fink (1971: no. 68).
[75] *Tab. Vindol.* II.301. The Saturnalia is also mentioned in ibid. III.622.
[76] Campbell (1984).   [77] See below p. 216.

problems of interpretation linked to the *feriale Duranum*. It is often suggested that imperial initiatives sought to foster the promotion of certain deified virtues. The role of Hadrian in promoting Disciplina within the army is the most frequently cited example of this phenomenon.[78] There is, however, a curious pattern to the evidence for the cult's adoption. Though most commentators believe that it was probably followed across the army, the vast majority of known altars associated with the cult come from Britain and North Africa.[79] More recently, Gammon has noted that Disciplina was manifested in different ways even in these two provinces, and has argued that again it was local military culture that determined the form of an ostensibly imperial cult.[80] Certainly, given the number of finds involved, it is unlikely that this distribution is entirely a chance phenomenon. Rather, this is another example of different behaviours in provincial armies.

In an attempt to assess whether or not the *feriale Duranum* truly represented patterns of religious practice throughout the Roman army, Fishwick also looked at the distribution of dated inscriptions.[81] He noted that there was a sufficiently strong correlation between the dates given on many altars erected by military personnel and those given in the festival list to suggest that the army Empire-wide celebrated the same liturgical year. This may indeed indicate that, as he avers, there was a 'canonical festival list issued to . . . Roman troops everywhere',[82] but the examples he presents raise another point that his fascinating study does not address. While there is clear evidence that these dates were important, hardly any inscriptions explicitly refer to the festivals or divinities recorded in the calendar by name.

On the 23rd July, the festival of *Neptunalia* in the *feriale*, for example, we do indeed find soldiers making dedications. Yet when we look at the dedications themselves we see that they have little demonstrable association with the *Neptunalia* itself. Soldiers at Talmis in Egypt made offerings to the god Mandulis in AD 81, a legate at Mogontiacum in Germania Superior honoured Juno Regina and the *genius loci* in AD 218, and *cohors I Septimia Belgarum Alexandriana* at Vicus Aurelius in the same province sacrificed in honour of the divine house in AD 231.[83]

It is difficult to be clear what is going on here, and the possibility remains that the correlation of dates is coincidental.[84] Furthermore, very little is known about how the festival of *Neptunalia* was celebrated in the imperial period generally, and nothing at all about its military manifestation. It is entirely plausible that it had lost many of its original religious connotations by this time. What we can say, however, is that these dated dedications reflect local patterns and traditions just as much as broader ones. Mandulis was a nomadic Nubian deity in origin, though his cult centre south of the first cataract of the Nile drew pilgrims from a considerable distance during the Roman period. Indeed, his temple was constructed with the help of the Roman garrison, part of a regional policy to establish shared cult sites for the army and the nomadic peoples they were responsible for

---

[78] von Domaszewski (1895: 44).   [79] Stoll (1992: 123; 2001a: 205).
[80] Gammon (2004).   [81] Fishwick (1988).   [82] Ibid. 361.
[83] Mandulis: *IGGR* 1.1332; Juno Regina and the *genius loci*: *CIL* 13.6696; h.d.d. of the *aqua Alexandriana*: *CIL* 13.11758. Fishwick (1988: 357).
[84] Ibid. 361.

overseeing.[85] Meanwhile, a wholly different combination of imperial and local elements is found in the legate's dedication to Juno Regina and the *genius loci*.

There is nothing especially surprising about the mixture of dedications. The eminently, if not uniquely, Roman notion that some days were auspicious and others inauspicious may account for the selection of the same times for different acts of worship. But overall, the pattern of correlations attested by dated inscriptions reminds us of the danger of assuming that there was a clear demarcation between the feast days of the official calendar and the other elements of the soldier's religious life. It probably also reflects the fact that even 'official' events had a fair amount of local colour in them—a classic example of incorporation. Certainly there are a number of other indicators that suggest regional variation in the way that gods and emperors commemorated in the *feriale* were honoured. Even the popularity of the Olympian deities appears to vary, though this may be partly a reflection of the vagaries of the archaeological record. Mars, for example, scarcely makes an appearance in the epigraphy of the armies of Raetia and Germania Superior, yet he is widely honoured on regimental dedications in the British and Danubian provinces. Similarly, the divine couple Jupiter and Juno Regina seldom appear on altars from the Lower Rhine frontier, yet there is clear evidence for their worship by soldiers on Hadrian's Wall.[86]

Examining all this variety, is it possible to make any generalizations about sacred time in the lives of men in the *alae* and *cohortes*? Even if we accept the *feriale* as a military document or, failing that, accept that there were broad shared emphases on certain dates, we see that forms of celebration varied in impact and form across the *auxilia* and across the Empire. Certain key emphases, such as emperor worship, do (as will be shown) come through, and reinforce the sense of shared enterprise, but there is still scope for real diversity of practice. This variation underpins rather than undermines a broader cohesion; it lends force to the process of incorporation by allowing real local engagement with virtual imperial endeavour.

---

[85] Griffith (1929: 72–4); Frankfurter (1998: 108).   [86] Stoll (2001a: 205).

13

Centralizing Cult

The need for a more nuanced understanding of the centralizing role of cult in the auxilia has been brought home to me while excavating at Maryport on the Cumbrian Coast. The famous Maryport altars, the largest cache of altars ever to be discovered in Britain, were unearthed in 1870 and are frequently cited as evidence for a form of cult practice assumed to be common across the Empire.[1] In a powerfully influential paper written in 1939, Wenham argued that the discovery within a series of pits of the altars, which were clearly dedicated within a few years of one another during the 2nd century AD, reflected a military practice of ritualized burial.[2] He argued that the altars had stood beside the fort parade ground and that when, annually, oaths of allegiance to the Emperor were made, the previous year's altar was buried and a new one erected to replace it. This interpretation was rapidly adopted and disseminated by scholars, and influenced the interpretation of altar finds further afield.[3] Part of its appeal lay in the way it appeared to bring together evidence not only for sacred time and sacred space (here cult at the edge of the parade ground); part of the explanation for its widespread application lay in the idea that units could be expected to behave in similar ways across the Empire. Detailed analysis of the altars themselves accompanied by our re-excavation of the site make clear, however, that Wenham's argument is fundamentally flawed.[4] We can now see that the altars were in fact buried at the same time, centuries after their dedication, being used with a range of other stone sources as ballast for the construction of a substantial timber building. There is also no evidence at all that the area in question was ever a parade ground, and indeed its topography makes it highly unsuitable for such a role. It is also notable that only a couple of the altars mention the emperor in any capacity, and that while the majority are dedicated to Jupiter, other deities are represented too. Looking closely at the evidence from other sites, such as the Mainhardt group of altars from Upper Germany, which it has been suggested reflected similar practice,

---

[1] Most, but not all, of the altars discovered in 1870 were dedicated to Jupiter (*RIB* 815–17, 819, 822, 824–8, 831), and we now know from Wilmott's insightful work at Maryport that *RIB* 823, also to Jupiter, was buried in the pits too. A further dedication to Jupiter was discovered in one of the pits in the 2012 season. Other altars found in the pits were dedicated to Mars Militaris (*RIB* 838) and Victoria Augusta (*RIB* 842, 843).

[2] Wenham (1939: 21–2).

[3] See, e.g. E. Birley (1978a: 401–2). I was also initially seduced by this hypothesis.

[4] For the altars, see Hill (1997); for the evidence of the 2011 excavations, see Haynes and Wilmott (2012).

it becomes clear that other processes are at work there too.[5] Thus falls one of the most enduring factoids in the study of centralizing cult in the auxilia—the idea that we can currently show *archaeologically* that the making of vows took place in the same types of spaces at the same times across the Empire. This is not to claim that there were no areas of shared cult practice, but to recall that our actual evidence for it is much less strong than is frequently averred; conversely, evidence for regional variation is more common than is often suggested. With this in mind, we can better review the evidence for centralizing cult within the auxilia.

EMPEROR WORSHIP

Despite the common tendency to speak of the existence of an 'imperial cult' as if there were a single unified group of practices that bound together all devotions to the imperial house, patterns of emperor veneration varied significantly through-out provincial society.[6] The absence of a demonstrably cohesive system of Empire-wide common cult practice makes it more appropriate to speak of the phenomenon of emperor worship.[7] Regional analyses demonstrate how a broad array of rituals and symbols associated with such worship were used in different ways across the Empire.[8] Thus far, however, the extent to which such variation may have existed within the provincial armies has been little considered. This is partly because of the enduring tendency to think in terms of '*the* Roman army' as a monolithic entity, and partly because the very idea of diverse practice in such an important matter might seem to compromise imperial security. Divergent under-standings of the emperor amongst the soldiers could indeed be dangerous. Yet there was room for a range of devotions. As noted above, even if it is accepted that the *feriale Duranum* was a military calendar, it makes only two stipulations with regards to ritual for a particular festival: the date and the animal to be sacrificed. These constituted minimum expectations. Other sources of evidence actually suggest that beyond this, considerable variation was possible. Emperor worship's capacity to attract individuals into a Roman network of perceptions and hierarch-ies was not lessened by this variation, but rather strengthened by it. Incorporation worked through eliding imperial dynamics with local manifestations of religiosity.

Archaeological evidence for emperor worship certainly suggests variety. While some provincial armies produced an extensive array of dedications to the deified emperors so conspicuous in the *feriale*, other much bigger ones leave no traces of having done so. British dedications, for example, relate to the imperial *genius*, the *numen Augusti* or the *numina Augustorum*, not to the *divi* or *divae*.[9] These dedications are private ones, and need not reflect the public rites celebrated in

---

[5] Thus see, e.g. Baatz's (1993: 240) interpretation of the Mainhardt altar finds, which recalls the Maryport 'model' and contrasts with the initial analysis of the excavator (Goessler 1943: 173–4).

[6] Summarized in Beard, North, and Price (1998: 348–63).

[7] Gradel (2002).   [8] Woolf (2000: 619–20).

[9] Fishwick (1969; 1988: 350–51). The term *numen/numina* can refer to both living and dead emperors, the terms *divi* and *divae* only refer to deified ones. The only surviving dedication to the imperial *genius* is *RIB* 915.

Fig. 13.1. The Tribune Fresco from Dura-Europos, Syria, *c.* AD 239 (1.5 × 0.88m). Two figures are named on the fresco itself. The first, Iulius Terentius, tribune of *cohors XX Palmyrenorum,* appears in the centre sacrificing before the statues. The second, Themes Mocimi, a sacristan, stands by a *vexillum.* Yale University Art Gallery.

the calendar, but it is notable that the overall pattern is so different.[10] More diversity, rather than less, may lie behind the variations in the wording of dedications too. It is possible, even probable, that such variation indicates different practices in discharging cultic obligation. Thus, surviving inscriptions on imperial statue bases from auxiliary bases in Germania Superior tend to omit details of the commanding officer, while those from the Danube not only name them but also frequently include the name of the governor too.[11] There may even be significant variation in the representation of the emperor himself from army to army. Thus the fragments of imperial statues that survive from Germany, Raetia, the Danubian provinces, and North Africa all attest a preference for life-size or larger-than-life images of an armoured figure. Thus far, despite extensive excavation, British military sites offer much less evidence for a similar practice.[12] Though again it is certainly possible that some of these patterns are as much a reflection of the archaeological record as they are of ancient behaviour, the overall impression remains of a genuine variation in practice. The complexities involved in identifying and characterizing imperial cult practice may be examined with reference to two glimpses of the actual act of worship by members of the *auxilia.* The first is the Terentius fresco from Dura-Europos on the Euphrates (see Fig. 13.1), the second a record of ceremonies performed at Elephantine in Egypt.

---

[10] Fishwick (1988: 351).   [11] Stoll (1998: 159).   [12] Stoll (1992: 123, 197).

Inscriptions on the Dura-Europos Tribune Fresco make it clear that the scene depicts the commander of *cohors XX Palmyrenorum* attended by other soldiers.[13] He is pictured making an offering before three statues. The fresco invites interesting comparison with the *feriale Duranum*, dating as it does from the same time and coming from the same place. Some features of the scene would have been familiar to contemporaries across the Empire. Thus we see the commander sacrificing before his soldiers in a manner reminiscent of the Bridgeness Slab from Britain or cult scenes on Trajan's Column at Rome, as a priestly intermediary for those over whom he has authority.[14] The performance of such duties by community leaders was a hallmark of Roman religious tradition. Yet this image also contains many regional and local characteristics. In terms of artistic composition, its appearance echoes that of a civilian sacrifice scene from the same building, showing the eunuch Otes and a councillor—a much earlier painting that clearly relates to Palmyrene worship.[15] It is annotated in both Greek and Latin, and local *tyche* or spiritual guardians of Palmyra and Dura are depicted.[16] Stoll claims that the regimental sacristan/priest depicted in the scene clasps a *basom*, a bundle of twigs, in his left hand much as Syrian/Palmyrene priests did; I cannot, however, reconcile this with what I can see in the fresco.[17]

The combination of elements has led scholars to conflicting interpretations ever since the fresco was first published in 1922.[18] Most commentators hold that the three statues before which the tribune sacrifices represent a triad of Palmyrene deities.[19] Such an interpretation would suggest that the scene depicts an 'approved cult', a cult whereby units venerated the gods of the regimental homeland.[20] Others have argued that the image represents a scene of emperor worship.[21] Pekáry identified the three statues in the fresco as images not of gods, but of members of the imperial house, namely Pupienus, Balbinus, and Gordian III.[22] I must confess to having held both views. In mitigation, it is important to note that the mixture of elements that has generated conflicting interpretations was probably characteristic of the rituals of both emperor worship and local deities in the 3rd century.[23] Indeed, we might note that the flag, or *vexillum*, depicted at the scene, while clearly military in this context, also became part of the ritual panoply

---

[13] Cumont (1926: 94) argues that these are the *principales* of Terentius' cohort, but Devijver (1989a: 444) believes they are the equestrian commanders of other contingents.

[14] *CSIR* I.4 no. 68. In all of these the senior officer is the sacrifiant, even if the nature of the sacrifice/offering varies.

[15] Cumont (1926: 122–34, pls LV–LVII; 364–5) and Perkins (1973: 47).

[16] Stoll (2001a: 314) for a commentary on the accompanying figures.

[17] Krumeich (1998: 180 fn. 31) cited by Stoll (2001a: 373). This part of the fresco has suffered some damage, so the comment of Cumont (1926: 94) is particularly relevant here.

[18] Breasted (1922: 202) believed that the three statues represented emperors, Clermont-Ganneau (1922, 271) suggested that they depicted Palmyrene deities.

[19] Amongst advocates of this view: Cumont (1926: 89); Drijvers (1980: 106); Dirven (1999: 187: 302–7); Gawlikowski (1990: 2618); Kaizer (2006).

[20] Dirven (1999: 187, 302–7); Stoll (2001a: 368, 377–8).

[21] Pekáry (1986), whose arguments were accepted by Fishwick (1990: 595).

[22] Pekáry (1986). He had argued previously for the identification of the statues with Severus Alexander, Septimius Severus, and Caracalla (1985: 127).

[23] See Dirven (1999: 187) for the argument that while this was a Palmyrene cult, it had assimilated Roman practices, and Dirven (2007) for the issue of the fresco and the imperial cult.

of many cults. Another relief from Dura, for example, depicts a cult banner that looks remarkably like a Roman standard, between the figures of Atargatis of Hierapolis, the so-called Syrian Goddess, with Hadad, her consort. Scholarly confusion therefore reflects not only our ignorance but also genuine ancient ambiguities. The most successful religious symbols in a polytheistic world were those that could sustain the greatest number of readings. Despite determined reappraisals of the archaeological evidence from the site and its broader cultural context, I think it unlikely that a full consensus will ever emerge.[24]

A glimpse of military emperor worship in provincial society is preserved in the papyrus day-book of a *strategos*, a regional governor, from Egypt.[25] Interestingly, the entry is closely contemporary with the *feriale Duranum*, recording as it does the celebrations of the emperor Severus Alexander's birthday at Elephantine on 1 October, AD 232.[26] The ceremonies involved both civic officials and officers from the nearby garrison at Syene, a force that included *cohors I Flavia Cilicum equitata* centurions, *beneficiarii* and *principales*, joined the *strategos*, the civilian head of administration, in rites at the *caesareum*, the municipal temple dedicated to emperor worship. Several readers have suggested that both civil and military officials were represented in the ceremonies in the military shrine, though the papyrus is unfortunately fragmentary at this point.[27] Wreath placing, a eulogy, and a procession followed, and the whole celebration concluded with a banquet back at the *caesareum*. Here too it is possible to see the local aspect of imperial cult, and in this case, the local aspect is Egyptian. What is especially interesting about the reference is that we can compare it to another dedication for the emperors by the Syene garrison. These were matching obelisks erected to the welfare and victory of Antoninus and Verus by *cohors I Flavia Cilicum equitata* in AD 166.[28] The choice of obelisks as a medium is telling: the emperors' soldiers are happy to use an Egyptian form of great antiquity to assure the welfare of their imperial ruler.

Four important points with a general significance for the study of universality and diversity in the army's 'official' religious practice emerge from the account. First, key elements within the celebration resemble those attested in less complete sources from across the Empire—there is a broadly similar expectation across the provinces as to what such ritual should contain. Thus whatever variations do exist, the most important points remain intact, and throughout provincial society people are making offerings for the same reasons at the same time. This is a crucial point, undiminished by the discussion of diversity in practice, for it still engenders a wider sense of community and common purpose. This is not entirely *Reichsreligion* or 'religion of empire' in the way that Cancik and Rüpke understand it. It is not a product that arises from multiple local acts of syncretism, which evolve towards a form of coalescence through the particular channels of communication and exchange that characterize the Empire. There is an element of direction, but that element is never expected to dictate all elements of practice.

---

[24] Pekáry (1986) and Heyn (2011). The problems inherent in analysing the building in which the temple was found, long mislabelled as the 'Temple of the Palmyrene Gods', are set out in Downey (1988: 105–10).

[25] *P. Paris* 69.   [26] Entries for October are missing from the *feriale Duranum*.

[27] See Col. III, 1.10. Fishwick (1992b: 589).   [28] *AE* 1974, 664.

This brings us to the second point within the framework of 'military religion': there is real scope for regional variation. Officers down to the rank of *beneficiarius* are attested participating in ceremonies that reflect the particular situation and traditions of the region in which they serve. In the case of these accounts, the ceremonies reflect the circumstances in Elephantine.[29] Third, by no means all soldiers or local civilians are active participants in the rites that take place. This is in keeping with the main principles of Roman cult, but it does raise the important question of the extent to which ordinary soldiers were both affected by and distinguished through formal celebrations of the type often grouped under the term *religio castrensis*. The final point that emerges is that the rites of military duty did not stop at the camp wall or the parade ground. Contrary to early mistranslations of the Elephantine document, it is clear that the account does not refer to events in a fort, but rather to events at an urban temple.[30] It will no doubt be objected that this is simply a civil festival which attracts a level of senior military involvement, but at some stage we need to confront the fact that where we have evidence for participants in ritual, military, and civilian elites are often seen offering cult alongside one another at the same events.

Having examined the variation in forms of emperor worship, it is now necessary to consider the depth of their impact. That cults of emperors could involve serious religious devotion was seldom actively considered until the important work of Price.[31] Scholarly emphasis on the use of emperor veneration as a political tool obscured the fact that these cults were not received simply as the instruments of pragmatic government.

That some of those soldiers who participated in these rituals were affected is suggested by the text of three inscriptions analysed by Fishwick.[32] In the first, an officer responsible for the camp hospital and armoury at the legionary camp of Lambaesis, in North Africa, made a dedication to the 'divine house' of the Severi in the dative.[33] This formulation, surely not a carver's error, indicates that the dedicator attributed to the living imperial family 'divinity', something which the emperor Augustus had understood to be achievable only after death.[34] Fishwick's second example, a mid-3rd-century metrical text from the *principia* of the legionary fortress at Bonn erected by the governor of Germania Inferior, bluntly incorporates Caesar into a list of gods.[35] Though such a practice has some ready parallels in the Greek world at an earlier date, for example in the Julio-Claudian Sebasteion at Aphrodisias,[36] in the Latin west the direct identification of the imperial house with the gods reflects a pattern that emerges most strongly in the mid-3rd century.[37] Fishwick notes that in this particular case the articulation of this equation 'at the religious centre of legionary headquarters, surely tells

[29] Fishwick (1992b: 590).

[30] von Domaszewski (1899: 159–62) originally understood this document as a military one, and his reconstruction of the text was based on this assumption. Yet the restorations of Wilcken and Blumenthal are ultimately more convincing.

[31] Price (1984).   [32] Fishwick (1992a).

[33] *CIL* 8.2563. The inscription dates to the triple reign of Septimius Severus, Caracalla, and Geta. Fishwick (1992a: 65–6).

[34] Ibid. 66, and for the Augustan perception, Fishwick (1992b: 472).

[35] *CIL* 13.8007 = *ILS* 1195. Fishwick (1992a: 66–9).

[36] Smith (1987: 135) and Fishwick (1992a: 68).   [37] Ibid. 69.

something of the psychological impact of a liturgy that focused on the emperor and his family in festival after festival throughout the year'.[38] A third example, which Fishwick would like to see as 'a purely private dedication', appears to have been erected *c*. AD 213–217 by an officer of the *Legio XXII Antoniniana Primigenia Pia Fidelis* quartered at Mogontiacum.[39] In this text the empress Julia Domna is conceived as endowed with the qualities of Dea Caelestis. The association is all the more interesting given that there is now no reason to believe that such a conception was officially encouraged, contrary to the claims of earlier scholars.[40] Again Fishwick observes that 'the liturgy and ceremonial of the Roman army, as revealed by the *feriale Duranum* in particular, will have played a major role in creating the psychological framework of the texts'.[41] This seems to me to be a compelling analysis, though it is ultimately impossible to distinguish whether dedicants' statements are driven by real belief or 'political' expediency.

Illuminating as these examples are, all are from legionary contexts, and all are associated with officers and/or officials. These are precisely the individuals who would in a military context act as cult functionaries. What of soldiers lower down the social spectrum? How far did this psychological framework affect them? Were they passive observers at the rituals, eagerly awaiting only the festivities that accompanied them, or was their involvement more substantial and far-reaching? It is, of course, entirely possible that a sizeable chunk of the soldiery celebrated these days on light duties, drinking excess alcohol and harassing the locals, but there is good reason to believe that for many, the rituals of the day had a real significance beyond these activities.

Assessing the character of an individual's religious belief is difficult at the best of times. One is dependent on the way in which that individual behaves, speaks, or writes for some kind of indication. Even then, the impression gleaned may be entirely misleading. Grasping the quality of religious belief among ordinary soldiers a couple of thousand years ago is more difficult still, yet archaeological evidence gives some clues.

As noted above, our information for religious experience of individuals in the 1st century AD is markedly poorer than that for the 2nd and 3rd centuries. It is not until then that we start to get larger numbers of inscriptions and historical accounts of soldier's responses to the practice of emperor worship. Nevertheless, evidence from military dress does suggest some interesting patterns. Though there is clear evidence for the mass production of swords and belts, it is clear that soldiers actively selected and embellished these items according to their own tastes.[42] The very rarity of plain sheaths further indicates that we should not assume that such items necessarily represent special awards or the possessions of high-ranking soldiers.[43] These conclusions raise questions as to what the decorative motifs on soldiers' swords and belts actually meant to them. Certainly, religious themes are present, and one common motif on sword sheaths is a *sacellum* or shrine. Though no simple answer may be offered, as some designs may simply have

---

[38] Ibid. [39] *CIL* 13.6671. Fishwick (1992a: 69–72).

[40] Mundle (1961: 228). [41] Fishwick (1992a: 72).

[42] e.g. Pliny *NH* 33.152. A papyrus of AD 27 records an *eques* of *ala Paullini* using a silver sheath with ivory inlay as security for a loan (*P. Vindob.* L135).

[43] See Bishop and Coulston (1993: 76) for the rarity of plain sheaths.

proved more visually appealing and fashionable than others, it would be wrong to dismiss the broad trends as irrelevant to the beliefs of soldiers. A recent study of the iconography of decorated *gladii* and belts of types worn by both legionaries and auxiliaries in the northwestern provinces suggests the existence of some significant patterns.[44] Künzl observes that *gladii* of the Mainz type, a form that evolved in the Republic and survived in use until the mid-1st century AD, attest to the use of about forty different themed decorative motifs.[45] In contrast, *gladii* of the Pompeii type, a style in use from the second half of the 1st century, reflect choices made from a repertoire of fourteen themes.[46]

Of particular interest are the variations in decorative themes over time. Members of the imperial house—in these cases Augustus, Tiberius, Germanicus, Iulia, Gaius Caesar, and Lucius Caesar—feature nine times in the sample of thirty-four Mainz-type *gladii*, yet members the Emperor and his family are entirely absent from the later sample of fourteen swords of Pompeian form. That the practice of representing emperors in this medium had not, however, stopped by this time is demonstrated by the presence of portraits of Trajan and Hadrian on a sheath from Leiderdorp in the Netherlands, but it does appear to have become less common. Similarly, the classic iconography of Rome and Roman power—Roma, the wolf, the globe—appear on the decoration of Mainz-type swords, but not on Pompeian ones. What emerges most strongly in later weapon decoration are the deities Mars and Victoria, and the representation of the standard.

The symbolic unity of belt and sword, combined tokens of the soldier's special status, was apparently reflected in similar iconographic decoration of both.[47] It is thus hardly surprising to find trends in the decorative motifs used on belt plates. Examples embossed with images of the *lupercal* (the wolf with Romulus and Remus) and others with a bust of Tiberius are known from southern Britain, Upper Germany, Raetia, and Noricum.[48] The archaeological context of these examples indicates that they are Julio-Claudian in date. Thereafter such images become less common, until during the Antonine period a complete change in belt fittings occurs.[49] The new fittings with their openwork designs allow less scope for such figural decoration. Yet the link between belt decoration and religious belief is not ultimately abandoned; rather, it receives spectacular affirmation in a new manifestation. Not only is the eagle, a clear reference to Jupiter, retained on many of the new-style *balteus* from the 2nd century on, but individual belt plates in the form of letters spell out hopes and prayers (see Fig. 13.2). Baldrics are decorated with *phalerae*, requesting that Jupiter the Greatest and the Best protect the wearer's unit, and are known from the finds of belt fragments from western Europe, the Danube, and African provinces.[50]

How might we best understand these trends? The early presence of imperial images and symbols of Rome may reflect the dynamic of the Augustan cultural revolution. It was at this time that the link between the imperial house and the army, always important, was established. Quite probably a number of those specially decorated swords presented to officers and men by the emperors to

---

[44] Künzl (1994).   [45] Ibid. 39.   [46] Ibid.   [47] Ibid. 40–49.
[48] Bishop and Coulston (1993: 98).   [49] Ibid. 119.
[50] See below, p. 262. Also Bishop and Coulston (1993: 130–35).

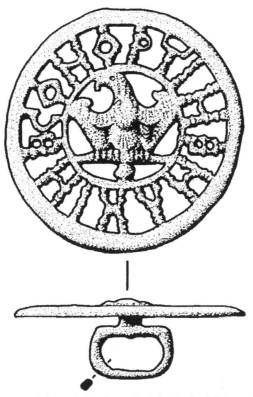

Fig. 13.2. Third-century baldric fitting from Carlisle, England (70mm in diameter). The baldric carries the prayer OPTIME MAXIME CON(SERVA) *RIB* II.3, 2429.2. Tullie House Museum, Carlisle.

help consolidate this relationship were themselves copied. Then and thereafter, many soldiers also expressed a genuine commitment to the gods of Rome such as Jupiter and Mars, whose feasts are conspicuous amongst the events recorded on the *feriale Duranum*. The decoration of equipment fittings also reflects the very real identification of soldiers with the cults of the standards, a phenomenon famously observed by Tertullian: *signa adorat, signa deierat, signa ipsi Iovi praefert.*[51] Though we might note that contrary to Tertullian's claims Jupiter appears even more popular, in terms of sheer quantity of iconographic and other references on equipment, than do the standards. The popularity of Victory, though hardly surprising in military contexts, is not notably stressed in the *feriale*. Indeed, the only surviving reference to her within it is in the particular context of Victoria Parthica. Her image was, however, a familiar sight in military camps, and it is highly likely that it was prominent at cult events.[52] More striking perhaps is

---

[51] *Ad Nationes* 1.12.

[52] A relief of Victory standing on a globe, now in the Clayton Collection Museum, Chester, came from Housesteads, where it probably adorned the south gate. In North Africa, a Victory makes an appearance in a fresco at Castellum Dimmidi in the so-called *bâtiment des fresques* (Picard 1944).

the relative absence of imperial images on the personal equipment of soldiers after the mid-1st century AD. This would appear to run counter to other trends, including the growing importance of the cults of emperors. It seems highly unlikely that this is because of an official restriction, but equally implausible to suggest that soldiers of all people were untouched by the pretensions and propaganda of the imperial house. Further discussion of this phenomenon will have to await new research.

It is interesting to note, however, that when a soldier in Apuleius' 2nd-century *Metamorphoses* lost his sword, his main fear was of the spirit that tied him to his oath to the emperor—the *sacramenti genium*.[53] An inscription from Syria suggests that such a scenario need not have been literary exaggeration. The text reads simply *genio sacramenti veterani*.[54] For a group of veterans to make such a dedication suggests that the oath meant more than simply a formal procedure. Oath-taking was an important part of the Roman soldier's religious year, and this soldier at least grasped the profound supernatural aspect of it all. He understood that this had a personal relevance for him.[55]

However emperor worship was commemorated on the soldier's military equipment, it is nonetheless clear that it continued to grow as a force in provincial society. Three episodes from the late 2nd/early 3rd century convey the diversity of responses to this trend that most likely existed amongst auxiliary soldiers.

One rare glimpse comes from a graffito discovered at Al-Muwayh in Egypt. Composed by a trooper serving in the *ala Vocontiorum*,[56] it reads *pro salutem imperatore feliciter* (sic).[57] Its translation by the editors of *Année Épigraphique* as *Vive l'Empereur! Bonne chance!* neatly captures the sentiment behind its composition. The notion is simple enough, lacking any of the complex nuances intertwined with the inscriptions cited by Fishwick. It also differs markedly in composition from a contemporary surviving formal dedication left by the same *ala* in the fort at Admedera, suggesting that the soldier's graffito is not simply copied from familiar examples of official documentation.[58] For this soldier—Dida, son of Damanaus, a Dacian—the emperor's wellbeing was a matter of personal interest, and this may owe much to the psychological framework engendered through the cult routines of the *feriale*. This framework did not stand alone; the special relationship between soldier and emperor was reiterated at multiple levels, from the oath he swore, to the head on the coins with which he was paid, to the repetition of the imperial image throughout the camp. In a world where provincial subjects in remote areas could remain in ignorance of the name of their ruler, the soldier had no such chance.[59] He was in a profound sense closer to the person of the emperor than most in provincial society. Not infrequently it was the emperor himself who choose to assert the tie—identifying himself rhetorically as one of the

---

[53] Apuleius *Metamorphoses* 9.41.   [54] *AE* 1924, 135.

[55] For oath-breaking as contrary to divine law, see Seneca *Ep*. 95. 35, and as an act of impiety, see Philostratus *Vit. Ap*. 5.35.5.

[56] The graffito most probably dates to before AD 183, when the regiment is believed to have moved to Syria.

[57] *AE* 1996, 1647; Stoll (2001a: 220).   [58] Ibid. 221 and 443, no. 4; *CIL* 3.1.130 = 14160(2).

[59] One recalls the observation of Synesius of Cyrene that some North African peasants believed they were ruled by Agamemnon (Syn. *Ep*. 148).

commilitones or fellow soldiers.[60] Dida's graffito captures the sense of a link to the emperor, offering best wishes for his ruler's welfare at the same time as providing a little humdrum detail about his own military career, but perhaps unsurprisingly, more sophisticated notions of the emperor's relationship to other gods are absent.

Altogether more remarkable is an incident recorded in the *Historia Augusta*.[61] While few scholars would trust the *Historia Augusta* as a reliable record of events, the incidental detail supplied in this tale combines to make it seem entirely plausible. After visiting *Luguvallum* (most probably Carlisle) in Britain, the emperor Septimius Severus was confronted by a macabre practical joke. A black soldier, a noted joker from a *numerus*, approached him with a wreath announcing: 'You have routed the world, you have conquered the world. Now, conqueror, become a god.' Both the soldier's joke and the emperor's mortified reaction rely on shared understanding of a *double entendre*, for what might be a simple reference to emperor worship is also a reference to death—an appeal for the emperor to 'meet his Maker'. The soldier uses his colour and the wreath to underscore this second meaning, for blacks appeared on stage as people of the underworld, and at Roman funerals holding wreaths.[62] That a soldier in a provincial auxiliary unit was able to construct such a joke indicates the extent to which Roman beliefs were disseminated. That he had the courage to do it is even more impressive. Apparently the emperor's god-like aura did not dazzle all his soldiers.

A final, important insight comes from early Christian writers. Though great care is essential when approaching Christian accounts of soldier martyrdoms as sources of information, such accounts do reflect the fact that many *milites* or prospective recruits recognized in the cult ceremonies linked to the emperors profoundly religious elements *that demanded personal involvement*. Tertullian begins his famous *De corona* with a contemporary account of a soldier who refused to wear a wreath-crown at a ceremony that incorporated the distribution of a donative from the Severan imperial house.[63] His description of the event, which took place in the autumn of AD 211, records the initial amused reaction, followed by the growing anger of the hero's fellow soldiers as well as his officers— a reminder that the pressure to conform to such practices was not simply imposed from the top.[64] Peer pressure was most probably a very real force in generating outward conformity to cult behaviour in the army.

It would seem, then, that the forms of religion commemorated in the military calendar were not merely superficially relevant to ordinary soldiers. To varying but significant degrees, soldiers accepted and adopted the importance of deities, divinities, and basic concepts affirmed in the Roman religious year. Ton Derks has argued that the particular forms of ceremony and liturgy to which the soldier was exposed helped to transform the behaviour of auxiliary troops. This exposure complemented the declining opportunity to participate in traditional rites of manhood among the indigenous population; raiding was no longer an option, opportunities for martial display were constrained, and the soldier was anyway

---

[60] Campbell (1984: 32–59), and p. 72. [61] *Historia Augusta: Severus* 22.4–5.
[62] See also Thompson (1989: 121). [63] Tertullian *De corona* 1.1–3.
[64] Tertullian's account should also be read in the context of his own evolving Montanist beliefs. As Nock (1952: 223–6) notes, many Christians do not appear to have seen a religious conflict within their participation in the ceremonies of the *feriale*.

obliged to spend his time in a parallel society, separated from whatever 'old ways' survived. The transition was from warrior to soldier, from barbarity to Roman *virtus*.[65] The idea is certainly an attractive one, and there is good reason to believe that soldiers did absorb aspects of Roman devotional practice, as we will see below. It would also have been (one suspects) an attractive idea to those commanders of the imperial house who honoured the personified Roman virtues on behalf of their troops.

The cults experienced by soldiers were not of course restricted to such features of religious expression. The definitive features of military religion were in fact the veneration of the standards and the military *genii*.

STANDARDS, *GENII*, AND *COLLEGIA*: CULT IDENTITIES WITHIN THE REGIMENTAL COMMUNITY

The standards are, of course, the symbols *par excellence* of the Roman military community. In times of peace, they lie at the heart of the camp; in times of war, at the heart of the battle force. They represented much, much more than mere banners. As Oliver Stoll has shrewdly observed, 'Die signa stehen für das loyale Regiment, das Regiment oder die jeweillige Garnisonstruppe steht für Rom, und Rom ist der Kaiser.'[66] The standard thus serves as a symbol of the unit's allegiance to the emperor and the soldier's allegiance to his unit. So important were they, indeed, that the highest representatives of Rome might swear binding oaths in front of them.[67] The standards are therefore a classic example of the capacity of material culture to embody symbolic links and facilitate incorporation.

Such lofty notions would not have been lost on the common soldiers themselves, for the standards occupied a central place within their own daily routine. The actions of the standard-bearers marked the pitching or striking of camp; so much so, in fact, that the term *signa tollere* came to represent striking camp in Latin speech.[68] Located in the *aedes principiorum*, their shrine often literally stood over the chests in which the soldiers' own pay was stored. Standards and, with them, the strongbox were guarded night and day with a sacristan in attendance.[69] The horror of losing a standard are alluded to many a time in the classical sources, while the punishments inflicted on those who allowed it to happen are recorded in the undated 'Laws of Rufus'.[70]

The *signa* were thus central to the regimental psyche.[71] On special occasions they were also anointed with oils in the way that favoured statues were.[72] They were thus in many respects treated as *kleine Götter*, as Jorg Rüpke observes.[73]

---

[65] Derks (1998: 54). For the complex meaning of this term, see Alston (1998).

[66] Stoll (2001a: 294). 'The *signa* stand for the loyal regiment, the regiment or garrison stands for Rome, and Rome is the emperor.'

[67] Tacitus *Ann.* 16.46 notes Paetus' sworn guarantee that not a Roman would enter Armenia until imperial orders reached him as to Nero's intentions.

[68] Webster (1998: 133).   [69] Stoll (1995). See also below, p. 150.

[70] 'Laws of Rufus' 27; Brand (1968: 156).   [71] Helgeland (1978).

[72] Pliny (*NH* 8.3.23); Suetonius *Claud.* 13.   [73] (1990: 187).

Their special treatment has led many scholars to see in the reference to the *Rosaliae signorum* or crowning of the standards, within the *feriale Duranum*, further evidence for military ceremony, though this point has been debated.[74] In turn, the floral decoration on a carved stone from Corbridge convinced Richmond that the standards there were bedecked with flower garlands at special festivals.[75]

Festooned with images of beasts and/or emperors, the intensely religious dimension of the standards could arouse strong reactions among contemporaries. Josephus recalls the notorious 'affair of the standards'. Pontius Pilate, procurator in Judea, attempted subterfuge to get the standards of an auxiliary regiment into Jerusalem during the night.[76] In Roman terms he behaved, initially at least, with subtlety—the images of the emperors were kept under cover.[77] But on learning of the ruse and the religious taboos it had broken, the local population responded with horror.[78] Pilate then sought to insist at the point of a sword that the imperial images on the *signa* be allowed; but faced with the prospect of mass martyrdom on the part of the outraged Jews he backtracked and ordered the standards removed.[79]

Altogether different motives surfaced in another violent reaction to the standards: the removal of imperial images from the standards of those units that sided with Civilis in the Batavian revolt of AD 69.[80] Tacitus, describing this episode, recounts the sense of shame, real or imagined, that accompanied the mutinous troops. But here the objection to images is political, not religious. It is notable that the units nevertheless retained their *signa*, and that the Gauls alongside whom they fought carried standards too.[81] No inherent hostility to such totems existed amongst the people of northwestern Europe. Indeed, the Roman standards and those of their indigenous counterparts surely recall a common origin.[82] This made the standard an extremely effective device for rallying many auxiliaries to the Roman fold.

When thus considered, the three-horned bull depicted on the *vexillum* of the *ala Longiniana* has a special significance.[83] The *vexillum* is shown on a tombstone, which can be dated to the reign of Claudius, and is being carried by Vellaunus, an *eques* in this Gallic *ala*. The three-horned bull was a popular motif in Celtic religious art, the triple horns ritually symbolizing a multiplication of the animal's strength. Green notes that over fifty such depictions are known from Gaul.[84] It is an interesting testimony to the manipulation of symbols in the Roman world that this regiment adopted a Celtic religious icon as a sign of its unit identity under Rome.

---

[74] Reeves (2004: 82–7) offers an alternative reading of the evidence, noting that *signa* could refer to non-military standards.

[75] Richmond (1943: pls V.2 and XB.2).   [76] Josephus *Bell. Iud.* 2.169.

[77] Jospehus *Ant. Iud.* 18.55.

[78] Josephus *Bell. Iud.* 2.170–71. Here, of course, the religious taboos were linked to the Roman's use of graven images.

[79] Josephus *Bell. Iud.* 2.172–4.   [80] Tacitus *Hist.* 4.62.   [81] See also Webster (1998: 134).

[82] For the totemic aspect of the earliest Roman military standards, see Keppie (1984: 67).

[83] *CIL* 13 8094. Webster (1998: 148) argues that the feature depicted as projecting from the centre of the bull's head has more the appearance of a feather than a horn. I follow Lehner (1908: 283–6), however, in interpreting it as a third horn.

[84] Green (1976: 13).

A similar pattern may well be echoed in *cohors I Gallica*. Between AD 165 and AD 191 members of the regiment made at least three dedications on the occasion of 'the birthday of the little boars', *ob natale aprunculorum*, at Villalis in Spain.[85] The name of the ceremony echoes that of the *natalis aquilae*, the birthday of the eagle, which indicates the day particular to each legion when it celebrated its foundation. Indeed, there is a connection, even in this local context, for we find members of the cohort participating in the *natalis aquilae* of the nearby legion at Luyego in AD 181.[86] Centurions are the senior officers of the unit represented in these dedications, though it is notable that in the contemporary anniversary commemorations of another unit, *cohors I Celtiberorum*, imperial freedmen play a conspicuous role.[87] Though the *natalis* celebrations are therefore clearly part of a broad Roman military tradition, it is tempting to see the particular association of the cohort with little boars as a reference to its Gallic roots. The boar, a popular totem amongst the Gauls, was certainly a popular animal symbol within the Roman army as a whole, but the little boar may indicate something more particular.

Even the animal-skin headdress of the standard bearer, with all its totemic overtones, resembled the indigenous traditions of some provinces. Webster suggests, for example, a parallel with the masks worn by some of the Germanic tribes.[88] Where the totem animal is not conspicuous, and the standard is decorated with an array of discs and crescents, the *signifer* still retains this distinct garment as a surviving fine tombstone of the standard bearer of *cohors V Asturum* demonstrates.[89]

Reinforcing the Roman dimension of the cult of the standards was the cult of the *genii*. Two inscriptions from High Rochester link the *signa* of *cohors I Vardullorum* with the *genius cohortis*.[90] Both appear to be 3rd-century and both were dedicated by the regiment's commanding officer.[91] The *genii* were at once the most Roman and the most ubiquitous of deities.[92] Their Romanity is reflected in both their antiquity and their adaptability. Their beginnings are truly ancient, so much so that their precise origins are unrecoverable to even the most dedicated of philologists,[93] but they were already a familiar part of the Roman religious scene when in the late 3rd century BC sacrifices were being offered to the *genius populi Romani*.[94] The *genii* remained a defining feature of Roman religion well into the late 4th century AD.[95]

Adaptability, itself a defining aspect of Roman civilization, is reflected in the mutability of the *genii* themselves. Understood as the sum of an individual or community's life force, they could be readily recognized in settings ranging from the domestic to the state. By at least the end of the 1st century AD, they had established a following in Rome's armies, and indeed more evidence for the *genii* comes to us from the Roman military than any other element of Roman society.[96]

---

[85] *AE* 1910, 6 = *CIL* 2.2556; *AE* 1910, 1 and *AE* 1966, 188.   [86] *AE* 1967, 230.

[87] *CIL* 2.2552 = *ILS* 9125 (AD 163) and *CIL* 2.2553 = *ILS* 9127 = *AE* 1910, 4 (AD 167), both from Villalis.

[88] Tacitus *Germania* 45; Webster (1998: 139).   [89] *CIL* 13.8098.

[90] *RIB* 1262 and 1263.   [91] *RIB* 1262 dates from AD 238–41.

[92] M. P. Speidel (1978a: 1542).   [93] Otto (1910).   [94] M. P. Speidel (1978a: 1543).

[95] *Cod. Theod.* 16.10.12 for AD 392.   [96] Cesano (1922: 475).

Furthermore, when over time the concept of *genius* evolved into the notion of a deity of place, it did so in both the army and wider provincial society.[97] Once again, the capacity for the study of the army to illuminate broader trends in the Empire is affirmed.

A bronze tablet from Vindonissa (Switzerland) constitutes the earliest reference to a *genius* of a military unit known thus far. The tablet commemorated the discharge of a vow by a member of *Legio XI Claudia pia fidelis*; the regiment stationed at Vindonissa from AD 70 to AD 101. Establishing the earliest known dedication by an auxiliary regiment is less straightforward, but a good candidate would be the dedication to *genius praesidis et monti[s]*, by the prefect of *cohors VII Breucorum equitata*, discovered at Knodara, Cyprus.[98] The regiment's stay on Cyprus may have been linked to disturbances among the Jewish community in AD 116/17.[99]

It is highly likely that senior officers such as tribunes and prefects played an important role in introducing the notion of the *genii* to auxiliary units. Certainly they are highly represented amongst those dedications that can be demonstrably linked to the *auxilia*. With their exposure to religious ideas in both the civil and the military sphere, they were well placed to introduce these beliefs. But the important point to note about the *genii* is that they were not simply promoted and celebrated at unit level; they were also widely celebrated by sub-units of varying type and size. In such cases there is no reason whatsoever to see regimental commanders as the instigators. Sometimes groups of no more than fourteen individuals would cooperate in the financing and fronting of such dedications.[100] A range of specialists made dedications, and this partly served to distinguish them from the common soldiery amongst whom many, quite possibly all, of them would have begun their careers.

In this respect the *genii* offer an interesting perspective on the organization of army units, one that might allow us to map the way in which relationships operated across institutional boundaries. This is noteworthy in the way that different specializations come together to dedicate to a particular *genius*, but also in the way in which some sub-units are not represented. We find *genii* for most units—legions, *alae*, and cohorts—but not for legionary cohorts or for any *contubernia*. In the former case this may be, as Speidel suggests, because the legionary cohorts had no officers of their own and there was little strong feeling for the cohort identity within the legions.[101] In the latter case, though, the men who shared meals, barrack rooms, and tents together must have had very strong social bonds, so it would appear that contingents that consisted exclusively of ordinary soldiers were not considered appropriate bodies for the patronage of *genii*. Such men came, however, to find that almost all aspects of their working lives brought them into contact with these divine figures. They drew protection from the *genius* of the unit, they honoured the *genius* of the standard, and their very camp and its buildings had their own *genii* too. The notion of the *genii* thus became almost ubiquitous within the auxiliary units, leaving few if any soldiers

---

[97] M. P. Speidel (1978a: 1550).   [98] *AE* 1953, 171.
[99] Mitford (1950: 55); Spaul (2000: 326).
[100] See the case of *collegium victoriensium signiferorum* below.
[101] M. P. Speidel (1978a: 1544).

oblivious to its force. It was an aspect of Roman life that touched the life of even the most ordinary soldier.

The sort of evolution possible can be seen at the 'German Dura-Europos',[102] the 5.2ha fort of Niederbieber. At this important site, excavations from the 18th century onwards have brought to light one of the most important collections of inscriptions and sculptures to survive in any military context.[103] Those that may be dated with confidence were erected between AD 221 and AD 246, but it is likely that most if not all were still in use at the time of the fort's violent destruction in AD 259/60. To glance at the texts and figures is to see how ubiquitous the *genii* could truly be. Within this one fort we find *genii* presiding over the records office and the granaries, over entire units, and over diverse specialist groups. Thus we see not only the collective dedications of the *vexillarii* and *imagniferi*, but also later the *baioli*, or couriers, with the *vexillari*. In the latter case, a total of fourteen members of a *collegium victoriensium signiferorum* are named as co-dedicants. Even the combat medics have their own *genius*. The visitor to the fort would have confronted, almost at every turn it seems, in bronze and stone, crowned and uncrowned, the familiar figure of a protective spirit, hand reaching out in offering, arm wrapped around a cornucopia.

The collection is all the more interesting when we note that there is no evidence for the presence of regular *alae* and *cohortes* at the fort at this time. Rather, our information indicates that two *numeri* were responsible for most, perhaps all, of the dedications. By this date, it would appear that religious practice in the irregular units had come to give every appearance of regularity.

As the role of the *collegium victoriensium signiferorum* at Niederbieber demonstrates, soldiers of certain ranks could also be bound together in their activities through more formal associations. *Collegia* were an important feature of Roman civil life, but their very importance meant that they were sometimes feared as a threat to the public order. Introducing such clubs, each with their own constitutions and treasuries, many with their own buildings, was therefore potentially risky in a military setting. Nevertheless, it is clear that they came to thrive in this environment, promoting once again a particularly Roman synthesis of religion and community identity.

Excavations in of the *principia* of the cavalry fort of Slăveni in Romania yielded some evidence of how the *collegia* achieved this feat. The *principia* appears to have been constructed in the early 3rd century, when the fort was extensively rebuilt.[104] From this time onwards the site was associated with the *ala I Hispanorum*, until it was abandoned by the authorities. Thereafter the *principia* was subjected to 'squatter occupation'. It is in the remains of this squatter occupation that Romanian archaeologists discovered multiple fragments of inscriptions and reliefs. These included dedications to Fortune and to the emperor Philip the Arab and his house, conventional dedications in a headquarters, but also to Bacchus and the Thracian Rider. Though none of these were found *in situ*, Tudor has plausibly

---

[102] As Stoll (2001a: 133) describes the site.   [103] Stoll (2001b).

[104] See Tudor (1963: 242). I thank Andrew Pegler for introducing me to this paper. Tudor uses the term *praetorium*, but the range of material and structures uncovered indicates that this building was in fact a headquarters building. For the extensive rebuilding of the site in AD 205, see *CIL* 3.14216, 16 = 13801.

0   5
cm

Fig. 13.3. *Collegium Duplariorum* relief from Slăveni, Romania (0.34 × 0.32m).

suggested that they all came from the shrine in the headquarters.[105] Of particular importance for the study of *collegia* in the *auxilia* was a marble plaque discovered alongside this material (see Fig. 13.3). Burnt fragments from this piece were found in association with hearths in three separate rooms, but it was nevertheless possible to recover most of its parts.[106]

The plaque shows a mounted figure riding from left to right, approaching a tree. The composition immediately recalls the influential image of the Thracian Rider, a form emulated to a quite extraordinary extent in art forms across the region in the 2nd and 3rd centuries AD. It is probable that the Rider is indeed depicted for, as noted above, the excavators recovered another relief explicitly linked to him in the same building, though in one case the characteristic attributes of the dog and serpent are absent. On the right side of the plaque stands a bare-headed male figure in the act of sacrifice. Tudor believes that this represents the dedicant himself, sacrificing in the Greek manner with head uncovered,[107] but it may represent a *genius*. Though the sacrificing figure does not carry a cornucopia, he closely resembles many such figures in all other respects. The accompanying inscription advises us that the plaque was dedicated for the *collegium duplariorum*

---

[105] Tudor (1963: 242).   [106] Ibid. 242–3.   [107] Ibid. 243.

and set up by one Iulius Marinus.[108] That a local divinity may be honoured in this way within an official setting is notable. It is a clear indication of the extent to which the regimental shrine had come to resemble other holy places across the provinces. It was no longer—if indeed it ever was—the exclusive domain of the standards, as the shrine could become a home of many gods. Marinus gives no information about himself, but we may reasonably assume that he was himself one of the members of this association of soldiers on double pay.[109] In such a relatively small association, consisting perhaps of no more than twenty members, no further information was required; other members would immediately have known the identity of the dedicant.

Though all the evidence suggests that this *collegium* was part of an auxiliary regiment, the plaque itself recalls evidence from a legionary fortress in North Africa. The rich crop of inscriptions from Lambaesis in Algeria famously provides one of the best sources for the *collegia* of any Roman army unit. The inscriptions are broadly contemporary; they also postdate the accession of Septimius Severus, the emperor widely believed to have permitted these guild-like associations in the military.[110] There is also a strong connection with the *principia*; indeed, the rooms occupied by the *collegia* may be located within it. Finally, at Lambaesis too we see the collective power of the *duplicarii*. A hundred and nine *duplicarii* are named on a dedication to Elagabalus. Here though, interestingly, they form part of a larger group, a *schola* of *principales*. The term *schola* incorporates again the sense of a recognizable community of individuals, and is sometimes used in a sense akin to *collegium*; but it can also refer to the meeting place of a group, an ambiguity that sometimes confuses archaeologists.

Travelling across the Empire again and returning to the evidence from High Rochester on the northernmost frontier, we find that similar associations existed there. The tribune of *cohors I Fida Vardullorum* made a dedication to Minerva and the *genius* of what is sadly an unknown *collegium* in AD 213.[111] As commander of the garrison, he may well have acted in his capacity as patron of the association. Another commander of the same regiment, this time acting also as commander of the *numerus Exploratorum Bremeniensium*, appears on a dedication by the *duplicarii* of that unit to Dea Roma.[112] The dedication brings us in a full circle, for it demonstrates how the ties that could pull a group of men together within the regimental community could also be harnessed to Rome.

THE CAMPESTRES: DEITIES FOR CAVALRYMEN

The last metaphor seems apposite for the study of the Campestres, for they were venerated by a very distinct group of worshippers, the auxiliary cavalry. Nearly forty inscriptions are known attesting these deities, and they follow a distinct

---

[108] IDR 2.505: *[Optim?]um collegium dupl/[ari]orum Iulius Marinus posuit.*
[109] There are, of course, varying spellings for this rank including *duplares, duplarii, duplicarii,* and *dupliciarii.*
[110] Le Bohec (1994: 192).   [111] *RIB* 1268.   [112] *RIB* 1270.

pattern.[113] Infantrymen do not make dedications to the Campestres, but horse-men do. The study of the Campestres thus underscores an important theme within the *auxilia*: that the cavalry formed a distinct subculture within the larger body. The particular status of horsemen within armies has been a common feature of military life over the centuries, but its distinct religious manifestation within the Roman army is especially interesting. What makes it all the more so is the way in which it varies from province to province.

Seventy-five metres from the Roman fort at Gemellae, on the edge of the Sahara, lie the remains of one of the best-preserved temples to the Campestres.[114] The rectangular structure, with an apse in its northern wall, stands next to what was most probably a parade ground. The walls were constructed of unbaked bricks covered with baked calcite. Inside, the building was decorated with a fresco depicting among other motifs a woman, a horse, and a *vexillum*. Most probably the woman is one of the Campestres, for the same structure retained two 3rd-century altars to the goddesses.[115] Of particular interest are the remains of sacrificed animals found at the foot of the altars. It is clear from the surviving horns that gazelles were the animals of choice. While this makes perfectly good sense for a cavalry unit, whose troopers might well have sought to emulate the gazelle's grace and speed,[116] the Campestres must have had to accept other animal sacrifices elsewhere in the Empire, where gazelles were less readily available.

Nor was it just in terms of sacrificial animals that the cult of the Campestres varied. The goddesses were known, and thus to a certain extent conceptualized, differently by cavalry units across the Empire. Thus, for example, the Campestres are associated with the Matres in Britain, but not in Rome, where the emperor's horseguard worshipped them.[117] What is clear, however, is that the Campestres originated as Celtic deities who came to have significance for horsemen of many ethnicities serving in the army. The deities' Celtic origins, albeit veiled by their Roman name, emerges from their frequent association with the horse goddess Epona.[118] Their worship is another classic example of how in its incorporation of subjects into the Empire, provincial society reappropriated local symbols and concepts.

The Celtic origins of the Campestres again demonstrate that even within the armies of Empire, soldiers might express ties to places and peoples far from Rome. In this instance, however, the link still serves to perpetuate an imperial rather than a local identity, the persona of the Roman cavalryman. The next section will examine another distinct element of religion in the Roman *auxilia*, the practice of so-called Approved Cults. Here, it appears, the sense of regimental community was fostered through identification not simply with Rome, but with the patron

---

[113] E. Birley (1977: 108–10).

[114] Baradez (1949a: 17–18; 1949b: 104); Davies (1968c) ; M. P. Speidel (1977c).

[115] AE 1976, 735 and *Libyca* III, 156 to *Dii Campestres*.

[116] As Davies (1968c) observes.

[117] M. P. Speidel (1994b: 142). I am less convinced, however, by his other claims for regional variation in the cult or of his understanding of the relationship of Mars Campester to the Campestres. For a discussion of the alleged link between them, see E. Birley (1978a: 1513).

[118] von Domaszewski (1895: 50).

gods of the peoples among whom the regiments were raised. It is interesting to note that this practice is not seen as being in conflict with the incorporation of diverse peoples into the Empire; rather, it is used as a vehicle to facilitate it. Analysis of the practice illuminates our understanding both of the evolution of identity in Roman provincial society and of the way diverse religious sentiment could be directed towards imperial interests.

14

Distinct Cult Communities within the *Auxilia*

COMMUNAL DEDICATIONS TO THE GODS OF REGIMENTAL HOMELANDS

The ascendancy of Varius to the imperial throne in AD 218 caused something of a sensation on the Roman religious scene, for the new emperor made a most determined attempt to promote the alien forms of worship of the sun god Elaga-balus.[1] In at least one community in the west, however, Elagabalus, the patron deity of Emesa, was already well known. The community was at Intercisa, in Pannonia Inferior, and centred on the soldiers of *cohors I milliaria Hemesenorum sagittariorum*. Sometime around AD 201 this regiment constructed a temple to the god of their homeland.[2] Thirteen years later, soldiers of the same cohort followed this with a further sign of their commitment, an altar *Deo patrio Soli Elagabolo*.[3] At this time Varius and his evangelistic zeal were still four years away from the imperial throne.

The cohort's sustained connection with this deity, coupled with the mistaken belief that the regiment continued to recruit from Emesa long after its arrival in Pannonia, have convinced some scholars that it should be seen as an 'approved cult'.[4] While the cult is unknown at this early date from other military contexts, it appears to have official support at Intercisa. Certainly the building dedication indicates official sanction, naming not only the regimental commander but also the governor.[5] Yet I must confess that I find that the notion of specific 'approved cults' rather unnecessary. Outside those beliefs which invited official *disapproval,* such as Judaism, Christianity, and forms of worship involving human sacrifice, there was widespread tolerance for religious practice in the Roman Empire. There are so many examples of imperial officials making dedications to 'non-Roman' deities that the practice hardly requires explaining in the civil sphere. What seems

---

[1] Varius better known as Elagabalus reigned from June 218 to March 222.

[2] *ILS* 9155. The dating of the inscription is based on the period of the governor's office. Fitz (1972) argues for a date of AD 201.

[3] *AE* 1910, 133.

[4] Identified as a category by von Domaszewski (1895: 52), enlarged upon by E. Birley (1978a: 1516–23), critiqued by Haynes (1993: 144). Stoll (2001a: 136) accepts the idea of 'approved cults' and terms them *halboffiziell*, though he acknowledges this formulation is only a *Hilfskonstrukt* (2001a: 155).

[5] *ILS* 9155.

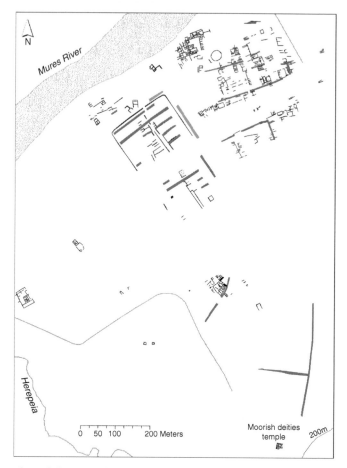

Fig. 14.1. Plan of the site of Micia on the banks of the river Mureş, Romania. This important fort appears to have housed at least two auxiliary units at a time. The extensive conurbation has been revealed partly through excavation and partly through aerial photographic survey. The temple to the Moorish deities lies to the south.

to have caused confusion here is rather the mistaken belief that the Hemeseni continued to receive recruits from Emesa when we now know that they did not.[6] I propose that what actually happened was that the Elagabalus cult was transplanted to Pannonia when the cohort arrived, still containing many first-generation Eme-senes in its ranks. The erection of the temple on behalf of the unit was a shared endeavour, and the cult continued to thrive as part of the local religious landscape, contributing to the particular character of the regimental communities at Intercisa. It is interesting to note that when in AD 214 a further dedication is made to the deities, it is made simply on behalf of the soldiers of the regiment, and that no

---

[6] See p. 136. E. Birley (1978a: 1516) makes a mistaken association of the worship of eastern deities to special recruitment practices.

senior officers or officials are named. These dedications, which we might also note are in Latin and using very familiar formulae, thus testify to an interesting cultural synthesis that offers an important insight into local and imperial notions of ethnicity, not to a distinction between 'authorized' cults and other practices.

It is important to emphasize that the archers at Intercisa were not exclusively bound up with their Emesene deity. Regimental personnel were responsible for the construction of temples to other deities too, including one to the Capuan goddess Diana Tifata.[7] Isis and Liber Pater also received cult,[8] while an easterner attached to the unit is depicted on an altar making a conventional offering to Jupiter.[9]

None of this should, however, be taken to indicate that the veneration of deities associated with regimental homelands was unimportant. Indeed, as the strikingly ethnic character of some regimental standards indicates, some units drew strength from commemorating their roots.

Striking examples of this phenomenon come from Micia, in Romania (see Fig. 14.1). This substantial fort complex on the banks of the River Mureş has recently been the focus of new archaeological research both on the ground and from the air.[10] Importantly, progress on the ground has been matched by that in the air. Aerial photographic survey of the site has revealed surrounding settlement stretching up to 1km east west along the river bank.[11] Micia emerges from this as a classic argument for why fort sites always need to be assessed with reference to the wider debate on urbanism in provincial society.[12]

In the Roman period Micia housed several major military formations and boasted several substantial monuments including a small amphitheatre. One of the longest-standing elements of its garrison was *cohors II Flavia Commagenorum equitata sagittariorum*, stationed at Micia from at least the reign of Hadrian to the first half of the 3rd century A D. During this long period of service, the regiment left ample testimony of its religious life. Many of the cult inscriptions that actually give the regiment's name are to regular Roman deities—Jupiter, Mercury, Minerva, and Fortuna—but a couple appear to reflect the regiment's particular Commagenian connections. The first, to Dolichenus, is not necessarily compelling evidence of such links, as this deity attracted widespread devotion across the Roman world. His strong showing in the region around Micia may be attributable to the regiment's own activities, for not only was Dolichenus widely popular in military circles, Roman Dacia was a land of many peoples. The second altar, that dedicated to Jupiter Turmasgades, is however altogether more distinctive.[13] To date only six dedications to this deity are known from outside the Roman Near East. What is most striking about this one is that it is quite clear that the prefect made the dedication on behalf of the regiment. Again, the regiment had long since lost any of its original recruits, and had been stationed in the west for ten years at the very least when it made this offering. How far the cult of Turmasgades would

---

[7] *AE* 1910, 140, reread in *RIU* 1059.   [8] Isis: *AE* 1965, 10. Liber Pater: *AE* 1971, 329.

[9] *CIL* 3.10307. The easterner here was Barsemis Abbei, a transferee from the *ala Firma Catafractaria*.

[10] Excavations have recently been conducted by Deva Museum and by Prof. Petculescu of the Institute of Archaeology at Bucharest.

[11] Oltean, Radeanu, and Hanson (2005).   [12] Millett (2001: 64).

[13] See also Sanie (1981: 99–103).

have retained a form recognizable to the inhabitants of Commagene at this time is uncertain, but it is clear that distinctive features of cult iconography, such as the outsized eagle swooping down on a deer or goat attested at Dura and Rome, reached Dacia.[14]

What makes Micia especially interesting is that it is home to more than one unit that honours the deities of its homelands. Moorish soldiers were also active in this regard.[15] An inscription of AD 204 refers to the restoration of the *templum deorum patriorum*,[16] and Birley suggests, not unreasonably, that the original structure was constructed when *numeri Maurorum* first arrived in Dacia under Marcus Aurelius.[17] The temple was identified and investigated during the 1930s. Its buildings, which covered 19.05 × 16.95m, encompassed a triple *cella* of a type familiar from Roman Africa.[18] Archaeological evidence from the site, therefore, suggests that this cult did not simply travel in name only; there was a real link to North African practice. But it also reminds us that, at least in terms of both epigraphy and architecture, this practice manifested itself in terms of Roman provincial culture.

Given the relative paucity of unit dedications to the deities of their homelands—I believe that no more than five can be convincingly argued Empire-wide—it is interesting to note two instances from the same site.[19] Is this just a coincidence? One possible explanation concerns the particular circumstances at Micia. The site was home to several units in garrison at any given time. Is it possible that in such a setting we may also see these practices as a further way in which regiments might distinguish themselves from one another?

Temples clearly helped to provide an element of cult continuity over time; initially built perhaps when a high proportion of soldiers came from the place where the regiment was raised, the cults were subsequently sustained by the descendants of those families and veterans of the early drafts settled nearby, but ultimately they became just another feature of the local religious landscape. Certainly their existence contributed to something approaching regimental tradition in some units, but it must also be understood as part of a larger phenomenon in provincial society. This was the expression of distinct religious and ethnic identity, quite often anachronistically, within the norms of expression that spread with the incorporation of empire.

PRIVATE DEDICATIONS TO ANCESTRAL GODS

It is poor scholarship to be cynically functionalist when considering religious practice. The fact that participation in a common cult contributed to incorporation need not necessarily mean that religious devotions were anything less than genuine. In addition to the formal regimental dedications, we do find private offerings in a similar vein. Thus Claudius Victorianus, for example, a trooper in a

---

[14] The group stands above an inscription dedicated to Turmasgades (*CIL* 3.8027): Gilliam (1974).
[15] See also Benseddik (1977: 137).   [16] *AE* 1944, 74.   [17] E. Birley (1978a: 1518).
[18] Bărbulescu (41992: 1319–38); Rusu-Pescaru and Alicu (2000: 92).
[19] These are Intercisa, Micia (2), Porolissum, and Castellum Dimmidi.

cohors Maurorum, venerated *Dis patriis Manalpho et Theandrio* while he was stationed in distant Pannonia Inferior.[20]

There is no doubt that many individual soldiers remained tied to the cults they knew from before they enlisted. The evidence that survives thus raises some interesting questions about the extent and character of religious knowledge among the peasantry and urban poor in provincial societies. In many cases soldiers might also practise their beliefs in a way that distinguished them within the larger regimental community. This is not simply a continuation of the way that *collegia* work, but rather is a statement of tribal or national identity and a reflection of distinctive worship. One of the most striking examples of this phenomenon comes from Birrens, Scotland. Here, distinct groups of men within the ranks of *cohors II Tungrorum equitata* set up a remarkable series of inscriptions in the middle decades of the 2nd century. Soldiers from the Vellavian district of Germany erected an altar to the goddess Ricagambeda,[21] while men recruited in Raetia set up an altar to Mars and Victoria Augusta.[22] Other soldiers, drawn from the Condrustian district, made a dedication to Viradecthis.[23] Such a distinctive group, which has few parallels within the Empire, may suggest that certain very particular circumstances lay behind this series.[24] Were some elements within the regiment inspired to assert their identity in this way after witnessing the group dedication of another contingent? Was there an element of competition here? Though the reassertion of such distinct identities within a single regiment could have been divisive, it is noteworthy that even these acts of distinction are undertaken in a similar way. Each is in Latin and each on a Roman altar constructed in the distinctive style that characterizes the regiment's epigraphy.[25]

That the Birrens series does not, however, simply reflect an isolated occurrence is suggested by evidence from the very heart of the Empire, from Rome itself. Excavations in the 19th century revealed an ancient 'hall' complete with marble floor on the Caelian Hill, which preserved dedications made by the emperor's horseguard. These men, with their close links to the provincial *auxilia,* have a fascinating story to tell. The hall, vividly described by Lanciani in 1885, still contained many of its forty-four marble pedestals *in situ.*[26] Some carried dedications to Olympian dieties, others to gods with determinedly provincial origins. Thus, even in this proximity to the emperor, Beellefarus, an eastern deity, could, for example, be worshipped alongside Toutates Meduris from Gaul.[27] There was clearly no bar on soldiers presenting dedications to their native gods within the confines of military camps. Evidence from elsewhere in Rome shows that guardsmen honoured the diverse religious traditions of the provinces. Special priests trained in the cults of their homelands served some;[28] funerary stelae rich in particular religious iconography distinguished others.[29] Close analysis of one of

---

[20] *CIL* 3.3668.   [21] *RIB* 2107.   [22] *RIB* 2100.

[23] *RIB* 2108. According to Caesar, the lands of the Condrusi lay between those of the Eburones and the Treveri (*BG* 6.32.1).

[24] *RIB* 2101 may also have belonged to this series, but only the left-hand upper corner survives.

[25] For the distinctive style, see Tomlin (1995: 795).

[26] M. P. Speidel (1994b: 139).   [27] Ibid. 38 and 36.

[28] e.g. Praetorians from the city of Philippopolis serving in different cohorts of the guard made a shared dedication to their native god Aesclepius Zimidrenus (*ILS* 2094).

[29] See p. 376.

the cults honoured by guardsmen and provincial auxiliaries alike further illuminates the way in which religious practice underwent transformation in provincial society. This is the cult of Hercules Magusanus.[30]

FROM LOCAL GOD TO REGIONAL DEITY: THE CASE
OF HERCULES MAGUSANUS

Historically, many of the guardsmen came from the Batavi of the Lower Rhine—so many, indeed, that the guards were frequently referred to as 'the Batavians'.[31] It is thus no particular surprise to find members of the horseguard drawing on this link in their religious devotions. They dutifully erected an altar to Hercules Magusanus for the safe return of the emperor.[32] Magusanus, who originated in the Lower Rhine area, attracted many military devotees. His following among the garrison of Lower Germany is not only attested epigraphically, it is also vividly evoked by the number of items of military equipment found at his sanctuary at Empel (Holland), along, perhaps, with those found at other sanctuaries in the region.[33]

What is notable, however, is the way his worship spread. In addition to the evidence from Rome, there are several dedications by soldiers beyond the Lower Rhine. A *duplicarius* of the *ala I Tungrorum* dedicated an altar to the god at Polmont, near Edinburgh, for example; while a *stator* of the *ala II Pannoniorum veterana* did the same at Gherla in Dacia Porolissensis (Romania).[34] The Polmont inscription appears to be a fairly straightforward example of cult transfer; both the god and the regiment originate from the lower Rhine. The same may apply in the second case. Schäfer believes that Aurelius Tato, the Gherla dedicant, also had a Rhine connection, though he acknowledges that the man's cognomen is too common to prove any such link.[35] A further dedication to Hercules Magusanus comes from Razbionei (Romania), a fort perhaps not coincidentally once occupied by a Batavian unit, *ala I Batavorum*.[36]

Plenty of documented examples illustrate the phenomenon of cult transfer by soldiers, whereby worship of essentially regional or local deities is transported to another region and established there, but there is relatively little discussion of what it actually involved. The presence of inscriptions attesting a deity's name in widely dispersed parts of the Empire is but part of the story; in the process of his or her travels, the god could come to acquire new attributes and associations, be depicted differently and even worshipped differently. The cult of Hercules Magusanus gives us some insight into the role played by soldiers in these transformations.

---

[30] See also Genevrier (1986: 371–8).   [31] See p. 378.   [32] *CIL* 6.31162.

[33] Roymans and Derks (1994) for Empel; Nicolay (2003; 2008).

[34] *RIB* 2140 and *AE* 1977, 704.

[35] Schäfer (2001: 260). In fact, though Schäfer may well be correct, it is clear that the god's journey to Dacia need not have relied on the movement of soldiers. A powerful civilian, Publius Aelius Maximus, also honoured Hercules Magusanus in Dacia (Husar 1995: 140).

[36] Moga (1996: 185); Haalebos (1999: 202) considers the likelihood of a link between the dedicant and the *ala*.

On an early, possibly Flavian, altar from Ruimel on the lower Rhine, the god is commemorated as Magusanus Hercules by a *sumus magistrates civitatis Batavor*.[37] The dedicant's title appears to reflect the continuation of non-Roman tradition amongst the local tribe, the Batavi.[38] In this capacity, too, he appears to mediate between Roman and native notions of the god. Derks believes that the mediation that led to name-dualling was in fact an initiative of the local elite.[39] Already, however, difficulties of terminology arise, for in an important sense the local elite clearly do not remain 'non-Romans' for long. Furthermore, the frequency with which the phenomenon occurs across the Empire, including areas where there was no native elite to mediate, suggests that Roman soldiers and officials played a pivotal role in the process.[40] Certainly the use of epithets was well established in Roman religious tradition. Jupiter, for example, might variously be styled Conservator, Custos, Depulsor, Stator, or Victor, to name but five of the many epithets associated with him. Some of the soldier devotees would have been native in origin, others outsiders, but significantly all soon came to see the god not as Magusanus, nor Magusanus Hercules, but rather as Hercules or Hercules Magusanus.

The extent to which soldiers understood Hercules Magusanus as the Hercules of classical myth becomes apparent when we look at two further dedications, both offered by legionaries.[41] A statue from Xanten shows him with the apples of Hesperides, while a depiction on an altar from Bonn shows him reining in Cerberus.[42] Both images show the god naked, with a lion-skin over his shoulders and a club. Their Mediterranean antecedents are obvious. The same applies to a sculpture found in Laurieston, Scotland, no great distance from the Tungrian *duplicarius*' dedication to Hercules Magusanus. Both sculpture and inscription may have come from a nearby shrine, suggesting perhaps that a similar image of Hercules Magusanus lay in the mind of soldiers in the British garrison.[43]

Similarly, Derks has drawn on the evidence from Empel to show how soldiers promoted new ways of worshipping the god. Offerings from the temple site appear to range in date from *c.* 100 BC to AD 500.[44] The practice of dedicating weapons to the gods, a feature of the site from the Late Iron Age, continued well into the Principate. Fragments of late La Tène swords, albeit vastly outnumbered by coins and brooches, complement fragments of Roman weaponry including sword sheaths and a helmet.[45] Even if we focus on the military equipment discovered, only a small part of the total finds assemblage, we should not assume that simple continuity is at work. We know that the Batavi only arrived in the area some time between 51 and 13 BC, but it is not yet possible to tell what impact their arrival had upon the way the already established cult site was understood.[46]

---

[37] *CIL* 13. 8771 and *AE* 1994, 1281.

[38] The precedence of the native name in this example of name-dualling and the reference to this particular 'monocratic' system are both significant in this discussion (Derks 1998: 89).

[39] Derks (1991: 236–7; 1998: 100–101).   [40] Webster (1995); Zoll (1995).

[41] Derks (1998: 113).   [42] Xanten: *CIL* 13.8610, Bonn: *AE* 1971, 282.

[43] The statue is obviously Hercules, but lacks the animal skin. The possibility that the two come from the same shrine is advanced by Bailey (1992: 1–4). I am most grateful to David Breeze for pointing out this reference to me.

[44] Roymans and Derks (1990: 447).   [45] Ibid. 447–9.   [46] Carroll (2001: 111).

Magusanus may well have been an immigrant god who took over the sacred spot and adopted some of its rituals in the process.

The Roman period subsequently brought with it changes to the right to carry and dispose of arms. Roman equipment of the type found at the site was unlikely to be deposited as booty. This has led Roymans and Derks to suggest that offerings of Roman military equipment were linked to the private rituals of discharged soldiers at the time of their *honesta missio*.[47] They may be right, but there is as yet nothing to prove their hypothesis, and plenty of evidence to indicate that soldiers did dispose of their weaponry while in service.[48] The question is further complicated by the special conditions that applied to the Batavi;[49] was Roman military law really enforced amongst them anyway?[50]

Whatever the explanation, it appears that some indigenous votive traditions survived into the Roman period. Analysis of continuity and change in ritual must, however, consider more than just what is offered. It must also consider the way in which it is offered. Derks has shown that Roman rituals of the vow were introduced to the Magusanus cult site at Empel.[51] He has also suggested that this introduction owed much to soldiers.[52]

One splendid find from the sanctuary, a plaque (60 × 50 × 70mm), records that a veteran of *Legio X Gemina Pia Fidelis*, Lucius Genialis, *v(otum) s(olvit) l(ibens) l (aetus) m(erito)*.[53] Sadly, the plaque has long since become separated from whatever it was originally attached to, but the presence of this familiar formula is sufficient to suggest that aspects of the Roman votive tradition were enacted at the shrine. Derks notes that there is in fact plenty of evidence from the region for the *solutio*, or payment, of vows. The term appears both on commemorative altars and on objects offered by way of payment in many provincial settings. But there was much more to the Roman ritual of the vow than the *solutio*, as traditionally vows began with a ceremonial opening—the *voti nuncupatio*.

If, as seems highly probable, the complex rituals of the Roman vow were practised at Empel, who actually introduced them to the site? All the evidence suggests that soldiers were responsible.[54] Soldiers were one group within provincial society who we know were repeatedly exposed to the practice of *voti nuncupatio*; the ritual is referred to explicitly in the *feriale Duranum*.[55] Legionaries may have played an early role in the dissemination of this practice, but it is clear that they were not alone. Auxiliary soldiers emerge as an important category of dedicants and vow makers from the Flavian period onwards.[56]

All this rather creates the impression, not simply of continuity or change, but of what we might call a 'cuckoo cult'. Roman ideas of proper cult gradually transformed Empel, pushing those who did not subscribe to their understanding to the peripheries. Military and civic notions of worship came to dominate. Sacred space

---

[47] Roymans and Derks (1994: 10–38); Derks (1998: 52).   [48] See p. 196.

[49] Tacitus *Germania* 29. See p. 112.

[50] The laws do include punishments for soldiers who lose (*alienasse*) arms (*Digest* 49.16.14.1), but this is not quite the same thing. Men could always replace weapons that they intended to dedicate. Furthermore, one of the Carlisle tablets makes it quite clear that lost weaponry in the late 1st century was considered a routine matter, not a criminal offence (Tomlin 1999: 137).

[51] Derks (1995; 1998: 215–39).   [52] Derks (1998: 88, 238).   [53] *AE* 1990, 740.

[54] Derks (1998: 238).   [55] Col. 1.2–6.   [56] Derks (1998: 90).

was now monopolized by cult buildings and demarcated by altars. Those who preserved the old ways could be dismissed as victims of *superstitio*, unable to communicate properly with the gods. The transformation was pronounced. In such circumstances it is difficult to argue that the soldiers of Polmont, Gherla, and Rome were still worshipping the Magusanus of their forebears.

One further aspect of this transformation needs to be noted. The role of auxiliaries and others in spreading the cult had a significant implication for provincial identity. While the god was first understood to be a local manifestation of Hercules, in time he came to be identified as a figure of regional importance. Under the Gallic Empire, Postumus issued three series of coins with the legend HERCVLI MAGUSANO on the reverse.[57] In each of them, however, Hercules appeared with club and lion-skin. No finer example need be sought of the relationship of cult to the evolution of provincial identity under the Roman Empire.

THE MYSTERY CULTS AND THE *AUXILIA*

Yet there are other examples of religious groups that reflect significant changes within provincial society. No discussion of cult communities would be complete without reference to the mystery cults. These groups had, by definition, to have a clearly defined membership. One had to be an initiate to learn the mysteries of each faith. At the same time, however, it is very important to stress that these groups have been awarded too great a prominence in the study of religion in the Roman army more generally. Their distinctive shrines and exotic practices have drawn a level of scholarly interest disproportionate to their actual impact on the military communities.

Best known and most intensely studied of the mystery cults is undoubtedly Mithraism. The association of Mithras with army units has been strongly emphasized in a few provinces. This is most notably the case in Britain, where the vast majority of known *mithraea* were located in the vicinity of auxiliary forts.[58] Yet analysis of the evidence for the cult from across the Empire shows that any claim that it was a military cult is fundamentally misleading.[59] In fact the vast majority of adherents came from civil society. Claims that the army was a major force in propagating the cult must therefore be disregarded.

What is clear, however, is that despite its contrived appearance of exotic eastern exclusivity the cult was exposed to several broad currents that affected religious practice across the provinces. There was, for example, an adherence to the importance of vows, attested in the classic formula V.S.L.M on altars at many *mithraea*. There was also a high level of conformity to Roman epigraphic and iconographic convention. Though some elements of the rituals, such as the grades of initiates, were highly specific to Mithras, other elements, such as the bull

---

[57] See *RIC* V.2, esp. p. 342, no. 68, and p. 349, no. 139. Cristian Gazdac, pers. comm.

[58] An apparent exception, the Walbrook *mithraeum*, was close to the Cripplegate fort in London.

[59] Gordon (2009).

sacrifice and the use of snake vessels, resemble those of other mystery cults.[60] The similarities suggest that common expectations as to what an 'eastern' cult should look like arose in the Empire, most probably in Italy itself, and influenced the forms these cults took within provincial society. Similarly, it is evident that even the Mithraic communities strongly associated with military installations were not immune to the impact of trends in local religious ideas. Thus, we find a rough-hewn mother goddess figure in the Carrawburgh *mithraeum* and a Mithraic initiate depicted as the 'Lion Companion', a local term of Aramaic derivation, of Mithras dressed as a Palmyrene archer in the late *mithraeum* at Dura.

As with all cults, we have better evidence for the participation of officers than ordinary soldiers. This is quite probably as much a reflection of relative wealth and influence as any other factor. Officers and wealthy veterans were better placed to donate the altars and reliefs *mithraea* required; they were probably also most likely to have reached the senior cult ranks of *Pater,* or Father. Yet the evidence from the Dura *mithraeum* leaves no doubt that ordinary auxiliary soldiers partici-pated in the cult. Mithraic graffiti scribbled on the site's walls offer a source of information about devotees that is lacking from the inscribed monuments. Many of the names recorded in this fashion are the same as those in the records of the *cohors XX Palmyrenorum*, and indeed some of those named do refer to themselves explicitly as members of that unit.[61] Regrettably it is not possible to determine whether the humblest soldiers were ever allowed to surpass their superior officers within the grades of initiates. What we may say with confidence, however, was that even within the confines of this exclusive cult, the essential vehicles for proper form in Roman provincial society were reaffirmed to the participants. Inscrip-tions, altars, vows, and sculptures all formed an essential part of Mithraism.

---

[60] The discovery of snake pots at Liber Pater sanctuaries in Cosa (Collins-Clinton 1977: 32) and Apulum (Bolindeţ 1993: 123–41) indicates that this vessel type was not, as previously thought, unique to Mithraism.

[61] Francis (1975, 433).

Part V

Arms and the Men
Equipment, Tactics, and Identity

15

Armoury of the *Bricoleur*?

The Disparate Origins of Auxiliary Equipment

Arrian's descriptions of the pageantry of the *Hippika Gymnasia* are probably the most frequently cited passages of his *Ars Tactica*, written in the reign of Hadrian.[1] These cavalry sports must have been a remarkable sight. Even from a distance some of the mounted men would have stood out, their metal-clad faces shining god-like with reflected light. They were men of status—the finest riders in the regiment—and their heads were encased in elaborate masked helmets. Long yellow horse-hair plumes, painted shields, and fine tunics competed in a blaze of colour, while above the ranks bright Scythian standards wove, fanged mouths gaping open, tails flapping as the breeze coursed through their slender bodies. Riders and mounts glided from one complex manoeuvre to the next. After masterly displays of the *Petrinus* and the *Toloutegon*, equestrian feats of the Celts, teams performed the famed Spanish manoeuvre named *Cantabrika*, discharging missiles at the gallop.[2]

Rich in symbolism, the *Hippika Gymnasia* were the most dramatic manifestation of the processes of incorporation at work in the *auxilia*. In this parade ground spectacular, auxiliary soldiers presented in both myth and reality the faces of Rome to her provincial subjects.[3] The imagery employed on artefacts associated with these performances recalls the Troy Game (*lusus Troiae*), a pageant celebrated by mounted patricians every spring in Rome.[4] Troy, mythical mother city of the Romans, was to prove a potent icon in the incorporation of imperial society.

---

[1] Probably as an encomium composed for Hadrian's *vicennalia*: Wheeler (1978).

[2] Drawn from Arrian's *Tactica*. For the appearance of the riders: 34.2; the *draco* standard: 35.3–5; Cantabrian Gallop: 40.1–7; *Toloutegon*: 43.2. Arrian stresses the importance of Celtic and Spanish terminology in 32.3.

[3] The vast majority of Roman cavalry, the group under discussion in this part of the treatise, were auxiliaries, and there is no absolute proof that other units had masked helmets and sports equipment (Webster 1998: 155; Bishop and Coulston 1993: 196). Nevertheless, we should not imagine that the creation and use of this armour was exclusively tied to *Hippika Gymnasia* (Bishop and Coulston 1993: 148; Garbsch 2000: 53).

[4] von Petrikovits (1952); Webster (1998: 156). Revived under Caesar in association with the dedication in 46 BC of the temple of Venus, the Troy Game was especially strongly promoted under Augustus, who ensured that members of the imperial family participated in the spectacle (Weeber 1974; Erskine 2001: 19–20). The Caesarian association of Troy with Venus and the Vergilian emphasis on its association with Aeneas celebrated a vision of Rome's origins favoured in Julio-Claudian ideology. For Vergil's account, see the *Aeneid* (5.503–603).

Tales of the Trojan War were increasingly presented under the Republic as a way of linking Rome's past to that of Greece, and allowed in turn a way for Greeks to 'approach' Rome.[5] What might have underscored an opposition between civilized Greeks and barbarian Trojans/Romans became a bridge between the mythical ancestries of both. The acclamation of Augustus as a descendant of Troy's Aeneas offered a new impetus to the celebration of this association. Such was the potency of Troy in Rome's rise to power that multiple provincial communities across the Empire seem to have found ways to link their own origin myths to it, binding themselves not merely to Roman power but to Roman pedigree.[6] With trained horses for combat and elaborate equipment at their disposal, the *auxilia* were able to provide the most lavish re-enactments of this incorporative ritual in the provinces. Concealing their own true faces behind masks, the riders' identities are transformed and re-presented through the material culture of Rome's armies.[7]

Arrian's famous description of the *Hippika Gymnasia* follows closely upon a less frequently quoted passage. Bridging the gap within the *Tactica* between a relatively straightforward account of Hellenistic tactics, which he draws from an ancient tradition of Greek military manuals, and his own, apparently innovative account of Roman and contemporary practice, Arrian indicates that for him the appearance and performance of Rome's cavalry, enriched by so many exotic borrowings, characterizes the spirit that made the Empire great. He argues that it bears comparison with the Roman assimilation of Etruscan clothing, Phrygia's Great Mother goddess, and Athenian laws, all matters of great moment in the Republic's history.[8] This can hardly be dismissed as hyperbole. There is nothing strange about finding here, in what might at first seem an obscure technical treatise, a statement that so readily articulates the reformulations of culture under the Empire. This is particularly true when we consider the author's background and interests. One of the first Greeks to serve as a provincial governor, he is also our key source for an impressive array of topics: the life of Alexander the Great, the thoughts of the Stoic philosopher Epictetus, the ancient lands of the Black Sea, Rome's relations with Parthia, not to mention the cavalry tactics of Rome's armies.[9] The special importance of Arrian's claim is that it reminds us that this process of cooption and absorption was not limited to the civil sphere. This empire and its armies are inextricably interlinked. Recent studies of both have usefully applied Lévi-Strauss's *bricolage* metaphor to examine the way in which new forms of 'Roman' identity emerge through the incorporation of pre-existing elements.[10] Is it appropriate to suggest that the same process was at work in defining the armament of the *auxilia*?

---

[5] Erskine (2001).

[6] For Gaul and Britain, see Roymans (2004: 236–8). His remarks on Britain follow from those of Creighton (2000: 141). The celebration of Aeneas, which Erskine sees as ultimately becoming the most important 'Trojan' element of Rome's heritage, is attested across the Empire from Asia to Spain (Erskine 2001: 255).

[7] Richmond (1982: 19) and Webster (1998: 156) both make this point, though the opposition with 'swarthy barbarian faces' is unfortunate; both 'barbarians' and 'Romans' came in many forms.

[8] *Tactica* (33.3–33.6). This link is partly to ease the reader from the section on ancient Greek tactics into those of the contemporary Roman world.

[9] Stadter (1980) for Arrian's life.

[10] Lévi-Strauss (1966: 16–36). Terrenato (1998) introduced the term into Roman archaeology when he applied it to the social and political transformations that took place in Italy under the Roman

A *bricolage* is made up of materials that are secondhand, not materials that are conceived and created afresh for a particular project. In the writings of Lévi-Strauss there is an explicit contrast between the figure of the *bricoleur* and the engineer. The engineer creates materials and tools for whichever new task he or she confronts; the *bricoleur* works from the residue of that which has gone before. While it is evident that there was no single *bricoleur* determining the form of dress worn by soldiers across the Empire for over two centuries, it is possible to discuss the factors that influenced the adoption of styles of military dress. This chapter seeks to advance that discussion, arguing that it is both an essential preliminary for the study of Roman military material culture and a vital complement to the study of the incorporation of provincial society.

With its cosmopolitan rituals and routines, the *Hippika Gymnasia* recorded by Arrian exemplifies the sort of pattern of appropriation manifested in *bricolage*.[11] The equipment he describes further suggests that a parallel process manifested itself in the material culture associated with the performance. This also attests the vital role of other regions in the creation of the *auxilia*, and indeed the army as a whole. As we will see, the masks and the standards appear to be adopted from other traditions again—this time from Danubian peoples. Emerging in Roman use amongst the auxiliary *alae*, some of these elements go on to wider use in the army; the serpent standards, for example, appear in the hands of legionary and other infantry troops by the later 3rd century AD.[12]

As the evolution of these standards in Roman hands demonstrates, the borrowing and adaption of military equipment was not confined to the spectacle of cavalry sports, but was instead widespread across the armies of Rome. Furthermore, such was the attraction of *bricolage* that it ultimately broke down some of the differences in appearance between different troop types in Roman service. While the legionary and auxiliary might have appeared distinct into the 2nd century, by the 3rd century it would have been increasingly difficult to distinguish them by dress on the battlefield. Different troop types were quite capable of borrowing from one another.

This point reminds us that the transformation of military dress in the Roman world involves two different but related processes. The first is the adoption by some of Rome's soldiers of equipment worn by allies or enemies. The second is the dissemination within the military community of the styles of these adoptions. It is possible for the first to occur without the second taking place. While the adoption of new forms of material culture in contact situations is a widely documented phenomenon, it is especially common in military situations. This is because, as van Creveld has explained, 'war represents the most imitative activity known to man'.[13] There is an intensely strong incentive to imitate the best weaponry and tactics encountered *irrespective* of its cultural associations, because matching it or bettering it will be the only way one side can hope to defeat another. But even in a

---

Republic. James (2004: 245) subsequently applied it to his rich discussion of the military equipment found at Dura-Europos.

[11] Whether or not the manoeuvres Arrian describes really hail from the regions to which he attributes them, it is significant that the Roman authorities were happy to accept the idea that their very armies, the bodies upon which they relied, had a distinctly cosmopolitan legacy.

[12] Coulston (1991: 106).   [13] van Creveld (1991: 174). I owe this reference to Simon James.

Fig. 15.1. 'The Warrior of Vachères' as displayed in the Musée Calvet, Avignon, France. Late 1st century BC.

relatively small army battlefield adoption of military equipment will only go so far; that dissemination of new adoptions occurs so widely across the Empire tells us something important about the patterns of communication and exchange that bound Rome's armies together.

Of the subject peoples that provided the models for military dress, few, it would appear, were more important than those of Gaul. Indeed, at one level Gaul may lay a credible claim to have created the military equipment of the Roman *auxilia*.[14] For during those crucial decades when the concept of a more permanent auxiliary force was taking shape, it was the Gauls, later accompanied by Spaniards and Germans, who appeared in the greatest numbers in Rome's non-citizen forces.

An impressive statue displayed in the Musée Calvet in Avignon testifies to the importance of this legacy. From the time of its discovery near the southern French village of Vachères over 130 years ago, scholars have debated the identity of the larger than life-size figure of a heavily armoured man (see Fig. 15.1). To some it has represented the quintessential Gallic warrior, to others a Roman soldier, and to others again a member of the imperial house.[15] Though most scholars believe the statue originally came from a funerary monument, its archaeological context is

---

[14] I am struck by the similarity between this claim and that by Vertet (1998: 130–31) that samian, so often regarded as an exemplar of 'Romanization', was in fact a Gallic rather than a Roman creation.

[15] For diverse early interpretations, see Espérandieu (1907: 35).

in fact unknown. Nevertheless, evidence accrued from the study of military equipment strongly supports the growing consensus that the figure represents a Gallic auxiliary who served in the armies of the Empire in the second half of the 1st century BC.[16] There is, in fact, no absolute need to oppose the identity of Gaulish warrior with Roman soldier at this period.[17] A man could be both at the same time.

What makes the Warrior of Vachères so interesting is that in terms of both general accoutrements and specific detail he closely resembles the appearance of the vast majority of Rome's auxiliary troops right through to the end of the 2nd century AD. I speak here not simply of arms and armour; even the very sleeves and cuffs of his tunic are directly paralleled on the tombstone of T. Flavius Bassus, a Roman cavalryman from the end of the 1st century AD, over 100 years later (see Fig. 15.2).[18]

Nor was his dress so distinctively different from that of the legions for much of the same period. Such similarities lead us to ask where these common traditions come from? The Romans themselves certainly believed that many of the items depicted on the Warrior were of Gallic, or more generic 'Celtic' origin. Varro, writing *c*.45 BC, held that the mail coat, the standard though not universal body armour of the *auxilia*, was a Gallic legacy.[19] This may or may not have been true; certainly mail has been discovered in a rich variety of non-Gallic contexts, some dating to as early as the 4th century BC. But even if a majority of Varro's contemporaries shared his opinion, it is noteworthy that mail was not understood to hold exclusively Gallic connotations. Indeed, mail was regarded as entirely appropriate armour for the *wealthiest* Roman citizen soldiers as early as the 2nd century BC.[20] That this form of armour became widespread in the auxilia is all the more noteworthy when one considers the amount of time it took to make a single shirt; experimental work suggests that the production of rings for a single mail shirt could take 200 days of work, while its assembly might take a further 30.[21]

The torque, worn here on the Warrior's neck, was to become an award for valour in the Roman army, and is depicted in later military contexts not only around soldiers' necks but also on armour and shield designs. 'Celtic' influence is also evident in the long sword or *spatha* depicted on the sculpture. Generations of Roman soldiers were to be armed with this weapon, which was to become the most common form of army sword in the 3rd century AD.[22] The warrior's shield, too, readily accommodates both indigenous and Roman conventions. The combination of oval shield and circular boss is echoed both by shields borne by Gallic warriors on the Tiberian Arch of Orange and by one carried by an auxiliary soldier on a column base from Mainz (see below, Fig. 17.1). If the Warrior had been

---

[16] Espérandieu (1907: 35) suggests the warrior was a Vocontian who had commanded auxiliary troops under Julius Caesar. Beck and Chew (1991: 46) also see him as a Roman auxiliary of Gallic origin. Robinson (1975: 165) argues for a late 1st-century BC date.

[17] For the equipment of Gallic auxiliaries during this period, see Pernet (2010).

[18] The parallel with the stele of Bassus is noted by Bishop and Coulston (1993: 100 and fig. 4.1).

[19] *De lingua latina* 5.24.116.   [20] Polybius *Hist.* 6.23.

[21] Sim and Kaminski (2012: 132).

[22] Beck and Chew (1991: 46). For the origins of the *spatha*, see Curle (1911: 184), Connolly (1981: 236), and Bishop and Coulston (1993: 71–4). James (2011: 29–30) notes that the term *spatha* could be very loosely used in the ancient world, and cautions against treating it as a strict technical term.

Fig. 15.2. Stele of T. Flavius Bassus, *eques* of the *ala Noricum* (*CIL* 13.8308). Late 1st century AD. Römisch-Germanisches Museum, Cologne.

depicted entirely as he went into battle, Rome's debt to the Gauls would perhaps appear even more pronounced. His head is left uncovered to enable the passer-by to gaze on his face (and Roman hairstyle?),[23] but in battle he most probably wore a helmet. If so, it would also have been familiar to a Roman contemporary, for most of the styles adopted by the Empire under the Republic and the early Principate had clear Celtic predecessors.[24] Finally, on his memorial our Warrior appears standing, but in life he most probably went into combat mounted. The decision

[23] See p. 169.
[24] This is as true for the Montefortino and Coolus-type helmets as for the Imperial-Gallic and Imperial-Italic forms (Bishop and Coulston 1993: 204).

not to represent him on horseback has deprived us of a glimpse of another innovation of Celtic origin that was to have vital importance for Roman mounted warfare, the Romano-Celtic saddle.[25] This stable platform was to enable cavalry to play just as important a role on the battlefield as their stirrup-riding counterparts would later do. It was to become an integral part of every trooper's equipment, be he an *eques* in an *ala*, *cohors equitata*, or legion.

The Warrior of Vachères affords a snapshot of one moment in the process whereby the Roman army, and in particular the Roman *auxilia*, adopted a general style of dress. It was not uniform, but it did involve certain expectations of what a soldier could reasonably be expected to wear on campaign.[26] As with such forms of representation, the statue has the advantage of depicting these accoutrements together in a single image and providing them with a broad cultural context. Unlike many forms of representation it appears, through analogy with known finds, to be largely free from stylistic and artistic conventions that would diminish its value as evidence. Yet the statue remains that of a single figure at a single moment in time. The apparent ubiquity of the arms and equipment it depicts should not disguise the fact that there was considerable variation in the dress of Roman soldiers over time and space.

In his survey of the equipment of auxiliaries, Cheesman argued that Tacitus' comments on the armament of Bosporan allies and a cohort from Pontus indicated that 'uniformity had always been the ideal of the Roman War Office'.[27] Yet there was no Roman War Office. Even if there had been, the machinery did not exist to allow central control over what soldiers wore.[28] No pattern books are known.[29] Occasionally, a great commander is credited with an important innovation, as Caesar often is with the practice of leaving untempered part of the iron shaft of the javelin or *pilum*, so that the weapon would bend on impact, rendering it unusable by the enemy.[30] There is, however, no proof that this move away from an earlier approach, whereby a wooden peg was used to help secure the javelin shaft, was a Caesarian innovation. Indeed, the change, which may be seen archaeologically, could have taken place significantly before Caesar's time.[31] Under the Empire, there is literary evidence for the involvement of the emperor and his governors, but this always seems to be directed at regional armies, not at Rome's forces as a whole. Even here, the evidence is somewhat ambiguous. The *Historia Augusta* credits Hadrian with improving the military equipment of the Rhine armies, but it is far from clear to what extent he actually did this in practice.[32] Furthermore, the comment implies that he was exceptional in the

---

[25] Connolly and Driel-Murray (1991).

[26] Robinson (1975: 9) on the dangers of assuming modern notions of 'uniformity'.

[27] Cheesman (1914: 132), commenting on Tacitus (*Ann.* 12.16 and *Hist.* 3.47).

[28] The restored reading of *Tab. Luguval.* 16.i.8 as *gladia instituta* by Tomlin (1999: 129) leaves open the possibility both that local commanders attempted to achieve some coherence (the term is otherwise unparalleled in association with weaponry) and that soldiers routinely used a range of swords.

[29] See Bishop and Coulston (1993: 202) for a rejection of notions of central control and for comment on the absence of pattern books.

[30] Caesar *De Bello Gallico* (1.25), but it is notable that Caesar makes no claim to originality in this regard.

[31] Keppie (1984: 102).

[32] *SHA Hadrian* 10.7; questioned by Bishop and Coulston (1993: 43).

interest that he took; emperors did not normally interest themselves in such matters. Lucullus, governor of Britain, was allegedly executed by Domitian because he had the temerity to name a new lance, the *lancea Lucullanea*, after himself.[33] This suggests some local initiative; but Frere plausibly suggests that the tale reflects imperial suspicions that Lucullus sought to win the loyalties of the provincial army.[34] Whether or not this theory is correct—and it must be allowed that it appears in a passage where Suetonius wishes to stress Domitian's bizarrely cruel and suspicious mind—it is likely that such actions could be interpreted as subversive. Had Lucullus also rearmed large numbers of soldiers with the weapons, his actions might have appeared in a similar light to the granting of donatives. It would have been a centralizing gesture. Most if not all governors would surely have hesitated to act in such a way. Certainly there is no direct evidence of any of them doing so.

To reiterate, then, there was no single individual or body to serve as a *bricoleur*, to orchestrate the adoptions of arms and armour worn by Rome's soldiers.[35] The *bricolage* that emerged grew up around consensus views as to the appropriate combination of equipment each troop type in Rome's armies should carry—there always remained scope for diversity. Military equipment was produced even at very small military installations; it was not until markedly later that arms factories emerged to support centralized production and dissemination of a unit's needs. This is clear, for example, from the discovery of moulds to produce belt buckles and plates at turrets and forts on Hadrian's Wall.[36] What is remarkable about these products is the degree to which they resemble those found on other 2nd- and 3rd-century frontiers.

Yet within this similarity, there was scope for diversity. In the first two centuries AD at least four distinct types of body armour, multiple different-shaped shields, and an almost unclassifiable array of spears were in use by regular infantry and cavalry units.[37] Even the most familiar weapon forms, such as the *spatha* or long sword, vary considerably in size from find to find.[38]

As Obmann observes, academic attempts to identify systematic reform of military equipment are often predicated on the notion that some form of uniformity existed.[39] This assumption is itself problematic. At present it is impossible to detect any sweeping Empire-wide change that may be linked to systematic reform. Part of the problem may lie in our ignorance of the dress of many provincial armies. But in all likelihood the real reason is that no such reforms ever took place. In the archaeological evidence, the most rapid change discernible is the so-called 'Antonine Revolution' in military equipment—an event, or series of events that actually appear to stretch from the end of Hadrian's reign to the beginning of that of Severus.[40] There is, however, no reason to link this

---

[33] Suetonius *Dom.* 10.   [34] Frere (1987: 105).

[35] James (2004: 251–4) reaches the same conclusion.

[36] Allason-Jones and Dungworth (1997).

[37] Marchant (1990: 1–6) illustrates the difficulty in classifying such missile weapons.

[38] The *spatha* varied in blade length from about 622mm (24in.) to 915mm (36in.).

[39] Obmann (1999: 191).

[40] Bishop and Coulston (1993: 109–21) tentatively identify this period as one of significant change. Elton (1994: 492) questions whether it is really correct to see this as a 'revolution'.

transformation to imperial reform. The dissemination of innovations during the Marcommanic Wars may be a partial explanation, but other factors most probably played a role too. In many parts of the Empire, this was a period of growing prosperity which witnessed significant changes across Roman provincial society. Though there are fundamental problems with importing 'class' terminology into a discussion of such societies, it is striking that this is the time to which many scholars attribute the emergence of newly assertive social groups in the provinces. Some scholars have spoken of the role of a new bourgeoisie, and while this term may be inappropriate, its application nonetheless reflects something of the changing social situation.[41] It is with these groups, a kind of *nouveaux riches*, that the soldiery, no longer peasants yet in no sense aristocrats, compared themselves. The time was ripe for an intensification of the search for new status symbols and the re-presentation and re-assertion of old ones. The form these searches took is considered below.

In all this variation, Coulston and others have seen hints of a 'hierarchy of design' that encompassed individual compositions for particular soldiers, fashions within units, and traits specific to provincial and/or regional armies.[42] That soldiers owned their own equipment is well attested. On the 25th August, AD 27, for example, an *eques* of the *ala Paullini* used his silver-plated helmet and a silver dagger sheath as security for a loan.[43] If ordinary troopers could own such richly decorated objects, there is no reason why they could not also commission them, ordering motifs to meet their particular tastes. Equally clear is the fact that units produced and repaired much of their own arms and armour. One of the Vindolanda tablets records that in the course of a single day 343 men were undertaking work in *officinis* (workshops). The document is incomplete, and it is not possible to ascertain all of the tasks that they undertook. Yet while some of their activities concerned construction, others were clearly concerned with dress.[44] Certainly another tablet from the fort refers to both shield and sword makers (*scutarii* and *gladiarii*).[45] There is no reason to doubt that these men were themselves auxiliaries. Production at unit level not only allowed for variation between regiments, it could also facilitate the perpetuation of regimental traditions if so desired.

Finally, regional variations in what the soldiers carried and wore are suggested by historical and archaeological sources. Ancient writers record that several of the great Mediterranean cities continued their traditions of providing arms for local armies into the Principate.[46] Artefact studies also reflect the diversity of equipment types, though our appreciation of its extent suffers as a result of the geographical imbalance in published material. Provinces such as Britain and Germany are well served, while other areas are poorly understood. This makes it difficult to determine the extent to which provincial armies may have differed in appearance from one another. The sheer diversity of forces to which these armies

---

[41] Whittaker (1995: 28–9) on social change in mid-2nd-century provincial societies.

[42] Coulston (1998: 175); Deschler-Erb (1991); Bishop and Coulston (1993: 196–8); Stary (1994).

[43] *P. Vindob.* L135.   [44] *Tab. Vindol.* II.155 notes cobblers (*sutores*).   [45] Ibid. I.3.

[46] Tacitus (*Hist.* 2.82) suggests that towns were selected by Vespasian to perform this role, but a tradition of expertise determined this choice. Dio (69.12. 2) recalls the production of arms by cities under Hadrian.

were opposed would itself suggest that a variety of forms of 'Roman' equipment was employed. Britons, Germans, Sarmatians, Parthians, Nubians, and Numidians, to name but a handful of examples, all fought in very different ways. Armies on both sides of Rome's frontier were capable of adapting to one another, thus creating an ongoing dynamic. Different responses were necessary and different cooptions were possible. By no means all adaptations necessarily followed from battlefield innovations, however, and authorities on military equipment have been quick to emphasize the equally important role of cultural change. Much of this change may itself reflect the recruitment practices of armies at particular moments in time.[47]

In fact a range of weapons—from swords with 'cocked hat' hilt guards found in Britain[48] to the javelins with bronze pyramidal heads known mainly from the Danube region[49]—suggest distinctive local adoptions by army units, some of which may be connected to the enlistment of men from different areas. Their spread may also reflect troop movements; Magness has, for example, suggested that the discovery of these javelins beyond the Danube reflects troop movements. More specifically, she proposes they attest to the presence of a detachment from the Raetian-based *cohors IV Tungrorum* known to have been in Mauretania Tingitana at this time.[50]

Javelin heads are, however, far from the only type of military equipment found in this North African province to exhibit clear parallels with arms and armour in use elsewhere in the Empire. The publication in 1994 of almost 500 bronze and other items of military equipment from Morocco extended the geographical coverage of military equipment studies.[51] But a close investigation of the material within the catalogue demonstrates how such diverse objects as mask helmets, sword scabbard runners, and belt plates in use by the provincial army were essentially identical to those found in other provinces. The movement of units only explains part of this phenomenon.

The single most important site for our knowledge of the military equipment of Rome's eastern armies—indeed, for any of her armies—is the caravan city of Dura-Europos in Syria.[52] Many pieces of arms and armour were lost with the fall of the city to the Persians *c.* AD 254–7. The dramatic circumstances of the city's end contributed to their extraordinary preservation. In the evocative remnants of a collapsed siege mine, the equipment of trapped fighters survived. Arms stored in towers were similarly preserved when the towers fell. There is so much outstanding information from the site that it seems almost churlish to lament the fact that we do not know for certain the full character of the Roman garrison during the siege. *Cohors XX Palmyrenorum* appears to have been present, but Dura had accommodated a range of troops from the 2nd century onwards, including a *cohors II Ulpia equitata*, an irregular unit of archers and detachments of legionaries. Nevertheless, the range of armament does permit some useful observations. In addition to attesting to the adoption of heavy cavalry equipment from peoples outside the Empire, material from this site on Rome's easternmost frontier shows

---

[47] Bishop and Coulston (1993: 203).   [48] (Bishop 1994: 16–18).
[49] Petculescu (1991).   [50] Magness (1995: 492).   [51] Boube-Piccot (1994).
[52] James (2004).

the extent of standardization across the Empire at this time. In his report of the military equipment from the site, Simon James notes:

> One of the most striking characteristics of the Dura assemblage is the degree to which so much of it matches finds from other Roman frontiers, not only in general form, but often in the finest details of manufacture and decoration. Finding so many martial artefacts on the Middle Euphrates which are near-identical to, and often indistinguishable from, discoveries made at other Roman military sites as far away as Scotland and Mauretania demonstrates a remarkable empire-wide tendency towards uniformity and homogeneity, albeit with limited variation, in much military equipment in the third century AD.[53]

The examples from Morocco and Syria remind us that variation in arms and equipment in Rome's armies was not infinite—aspects remained the same over vast areas. This reinforces the point made when discussing the Warrior of Vachères. Somehow, assumptions as to the most appropriate forms of weaponry and clothing were disseminated across the Empire. In the absence of evidence to the contrary, we must see this as less of a top-down strategy than a result of the constant movement of men and ideas from unit to unit, fort to fort, and province to province.[54] Such a form of information exchange resulted for the most part in the copying, rather than the dissemination, of identical pieces of equipment. The next chapter looks away from the battlefield and towards the competition for status that drove so much change in provincial society in order to understand what drove this dynamic.

---

[53] James (2004: 251).   [54] Bishop and Coulston (1993: 202) and James (2001: 86).

16

Status, Competition, and Military Adornment

The Augustan Revolution that gave birth to the *alae* and *cohortes* generated profound changes in Roman society. Unprecedented social stratification coexisted alongside unparalleled social mobility.[1] Into such an environment, where status symbols were constantly being redefined and usurped, came new types of professional soldiers with money to spend and power to wield.[2] Analysis of the ways in which military identities were defined is only fruitful when we view their evolution against this wider background. Such identities also reflect the role of individual competition stimulating and responding to the rise and fall of fashions. As noted above, sweeping *empire-wide* reforms of military equipment are nowhere described in the ancient literature and nowhere apparent in the archaeological evidence.[3] The study of dress, arms, and other military equipment shows how soldiers and their dependants articulated their status in the changing societies of the provinces.

Inspiration for the socially mobile auxiliary soldier came from a variety of sources, not all of which lay in classical Roman tradition. Disposable income allowed the soldier to invest in trappings previously limited to the indigenous elite. This was not just a question of money, though that was important; it also reflected the redefinition of symbols of power that accompanied Roman hegemony over the provinces. Despite multiple laws aimed at preserving status symbols in Rome, up to, and including, the imperial purple, preventing the usurpation of these symbols proved impossible.[4] Status symbols traditional to the indigenous rulers of the Empire were still less protected. Not only had Rome little interest in their active preservation, but the very individuals who had depended upon them were themselves adopting new motifs to articulate their place in the new order. Much misguided emphasis has linked the introduction of Roman political power to the emulation of Roman material culture. In practice, upwardly mobile groups in many parts of the Empire would have been most influenced by the status markers that had greatest significance in their region, whatever the pedigree. Both the face-helmets of the masked riders and the armour of the Warrior of Vachères may serve to illustrate this point in the military sphere.

---

[1] Reinhold (1971).

[2] Alston (1998) notes the importance of linking discussions of shifting power relations at this time to the way in which masculinity is defined in the context of the Roman army.

[3] See p. 245.   [4] Reinhold (1971: 282).

Masked helmets known from across and beyond the Roman world reflect a range of uses for the form across time and space.[5] As noted, however, there appears a strong link with early masked helmets and lavish, high-status burials. In addition to the examples from the rich Thracian tumuli graves, a further piece is linked to a robbed tomb associated with the Sampsigerami dynasty at Homs in Syria.[6] Several generations after these artefacts were deposited in graves, similar ones were used to define status in rather different ways. Within Thracia and Moesia the masks continue to serve in funerary contexts, suggesting a link to local beliefs in ancestor worship and hero cults.[7] The masks may still confer status, perhaps aristocratic connections, but they do not necessarily reflect military power. At Varna in Bulgaria, for example, the 2nd-century AD grave of a young girl contained a face-mask of this type.[8] In the same century Arrian notes the role of these helmets as status symbols. Yet the status is different: no longer aristocratic, it denotes the finest riders within auxiliary cavalry regiments,[9] not necessarily the senior officers. Indeed, inscriptions on items in the Straubing hoard, deposited in the 3rd century AD, indicate that the men who were wearing such distinctive dress included junior officers, such as a *duplicarius* (a sub-officer within a *turma*) and a *capsarius* (a bandager/combat medic). Ownership inscriptions from other elaborate helmets similarly indicate that their use was restricted only to those that could afford them, not necessarily to those of any particular rank.

The dress of the Warrior of Vachères, like the helmets of the masked riders, illustrates how equipment once confined by custom and/or by law to a few—markers of distinction—is adopted across the *auxilia*, and comes to mark the status of soldiers. His monument is a testimony as much to the conspicuous consumption of resources as to anything else. Whoever decided to commission the erection of a two-metre tall statue was clearly of considerable means and quite prepared to advertise that fact. The point was powerfully emphasized in the painstaking depiction of the Warrior's own accoutrements of war. These were not cheap. Only a minority of fighters in the indigenous armies of Gaul could have afforded such objects. Assembling the links to make a mail tunic, such as the one depicted, probably represented at least 200 hours of work.[10] Access to the required quantities of metal, from the iron of the links to the bronze of the sword fittings, could hardly have been universal. Yet in the armies of Rome, it would appear that every regular soldier enjoyed access to these resources and could dress this way. Regular pay, sophisticated organizational structures, and networks of supply helped to make it possible.[11] The visual impact of this on contemporary witnesses, particularly upon those who were used to seeing such armour restricted to a minority of users, must have been strong. At first glance every man appeared as a chieftain, every soldier resembled a war leader.[12] For those early auxiliary recruits

---

[5] Over 80 such masks are known. Since the publication of Garbsch's (1978) catalogue there have been notable new discoveries from Morocco (Boube-Piccot 1994), Holland (van Enckevort and Willems 1996), Germany (Franzius 1995), and Britain (Worrell et al. 2011).

[6] Seyrig, (1952: pl. 26). Robinson (1975: 122).

[7] Kohlert (1980: 230–31). For 6th–3rd centuries BC examples, see Theodossiev (1998).

[8] Kohlert (1980: 228).   [9] Arrian *Tactica* 34.2.   [10] Junkelmann (1986: 166).

[11] Coulston (1998: 173) notes that in this respect the Roman army was 'historically unusual'.

[12] The visual impression may have been misleading, though. As much Roman military equipment was mass-produced, less care, effort, and expense may have gone into the fabrication of some items than into the individual possessions of high-status warriors in indigenous armies.

from societies that laid particular emphasis on the association of weapons with status, this may have been a strong inducement to enlist. They could emulate the status symbols and stature of their leaders simply by enrolling as humble soldiers in an alien army. Interestingly, this process had already taken place in the legions of the Roman army; mail's exclusive association with the wealthiest citizen soldiers in the 2nd century BC had long since become an anachronism by the time of Augustus.[13]

Conscious emulation probably also played a role in the acquisition and use of weaponry, though evolving fighting practices were surely significant too.[14] It is in the use of weapons that the soldier's status is most obviously asserted, but the relationship between bearing weapons and soldierly identity in Roman provincial society was almost certainly not straightforward.[15] Archaeologists have often misunderstood the literary sources when approaching this theme. Despite Brunt's sensitive consideration of the evidence for and against an imperial policy aimed at disarming provincial subjects,[16] the impression lingers in some works that possession of weapons under the Principate became the exclusive preserve of Roman soldiers. The existence of the *Lex Iulia de Vi Publica* is commonly assumed to have restricted the carrying of weapons to travelling and hunting. Yet it must be asked how any such legislation could be routinely enforceable across the provinces.[17] Its intention was not necessarily to deprive individuals of weapons so much as to restrict the bearing of arms in public settings by unauthorized individuals, render illicit the maintenance of private armies, and undermine disruptive martial ideologies.[18]

Singled out for particular attention in the discussion of weapon carrying is the sword. This weapon is sometimes seen as the particular mark of the soldier, a denominator of his particular status. This is, however, more a reflection of the situation in Rome itself than in the provinces.[19] We know that there were provincials who were not soldiers who carried swords as part of their duties. In Egypt 'sword-bearers' and even a 'chief sword-bearer' are found assisting the *archephodoi*, the rural police, who were surely also armed.[20] There are many other references to guards of various sorts. Though it would be folly to make casual generalizations from Egyptian papyri, it would equally be unwise to ignore the one area for which we have comprehensive information on policing in the

---

[13] Polybius *Hist.* 6.23. It is generally believed that mail was the standard armour of legionaries at least by the time of Caesar.

[14] See below, p. 257.

[15] Obmann (1999) discusses the relationship of weapons to military status.

[16] Brunt (1975).

[17] Jones's (1964: i.viii) astute observation of a later period applies as readily here. 'Many modern historians . . . have too readily assumed that Roman citizens obeyed the law, and that everything was done as the imperial government directed.' It is in fact clear that many non-soldiers continued to enjoy access to weapons. See also *Digest* 48.6.

[18] For the role of the *lex Iulia* with regards to public events and armed retainers, note James (2001: 83). For the law's significance for Gallic warrior ideology, see also Brunaux (1986: 18–21, 147), Wightman (1986: 585), and Whittaker (1995: 30).

[19] Coulston (2000: 91 and fn. 106).

[20] Alston (1995: 92 and 224–5, fn. 126). Alston notes that *archephodoi* appear in the papyrological evidence about 70 times in the 1st–3rd centuries AD, while 'sword bearers' appear about 15 times in the same period.

provinces. My strong suspicion is that such 'sword-bearers' were common figures in towns, villages, and estates across the Roman world. It is interesting that it is a title carried by non-soldiers that most strongly links weaponry to office and identity.

Misunderstandings as to the extent to which the provinces themselves were disarmed have real consequences for the interpretation of the archaeological record, for it is often assumed that if a Roman-period grave contains weapons, particularly weapons and native goods, it must belong to an auxiliary. Such figures are often seen as the only individuals likely both to have weapons and to act in such an 'un-Roman' manner. These blanket assumptions will not do. Mortuary contexts do not permit such simple readings of identity. There is a real danger that, in focusing on weapons in funerary assemblages, archaeologists give them greater significance than the deceased may have done.

'Weapons burials' are widely attested across the Roman Empire, but they do not represent a single cultural phenomenon. Local factors are clearly of crucial importance. Two such burials from Camelon in Scotland in the late 1st century AD,[21] for example, are entirely different in form, content, and ritual from one known from Chatalka in Bulgaria, though the examples are separated from one another by only a few decades at most.[22] At both sites it is easy to suggest associations with Roman authority, and entirely plausible to suggest links to the *auxilia*, but these are not the only or even the most important aspects of identity stressed. Nevertheless, there is one region where scholars have repeatedly emphasized links between weapons burials and Roman auxiliaries of various types. This is the Rhineland, and it is worth exploring the evidence from there in further detail.[23]

Grave assemblages including weapons first appear in the region during the late 1st century BC, about the time that Rome began to raise large numbers of auxiliaries from German tribes. Though he acknowledges other possible explanations for the weapon graves,[24] Wells suggests that these deposits reflect a dynamic process, in which local men create 'new identities around Roman categories', in this case the category of the auxiliary soldier.[25] Furthermore, he argues that this process also manifests itself in the cemeteries of the early Roman period in Free Germany, noting in particular sites such as Putensen and Ehestorf-Vahrendorf in the region of the lower Elbe.[26] If he is correct, his argument has interesting implications, both for Roman recruitment practice and for the reception of Roman culture beyond imperial territory. The attractiveness of the idea does not, however, necessarily make it correct.[27] In these turbulent years, when societies on both sides of the notional 'frontier' were under great stress, it is highly likely that weapons would have had greater importance for those who might be

[21] Breeze, Close-Brooks, and Ritchie (1976). Two burials are discussed, one of which contains two individuals.

[22] Bujukliev (1986: 71–4).

[23] The first survey of weapon graves in Roman provincial contexts was by Schönberger (1953).

[24] Wells (1999: 239).   [25] Ibid. 119.   [26] Ibid. 120.

[27] Here it is important to note the absence of literary evidence for recruitment beyond the frontiers at this time (James 2005: 274–6) while at the same time acknowledging that individual recruits from outside the Empire might have been deemed beneath the interest of ancient writers. Against Wells's attractive hypothesis, it is important to remember the ample evidence from modern colonial culture contact situations that weapons can travel even when their owners do not.

called upon to fight—such individuals were not necessarily auxiliaries in Roman service.

Archaeological material from the Moselle River region allows us to examine competing explanations of the phenomenon in one area at least. Furthermore, the fact that the community of the Treveri, a *civitas* for which we have considerable information, appears to have occupied much of this area makes it an interesting region to study.[28] Altogether, at least twenty-six so-called *Gladiusähnliche Kurzschwerter* or '*gladius*-like short swords' are known from Roman-period grave assemblages in the middle Rhine region.[29] These swords are understood to reflect some type of Roman influence—an association reflected in their similarity to a stamped Roman sword from Bell, Mayen-Koblenz.[30] None of them appear to post-date the Flavian period. The concentration of these and other items of apparently military equipment within grave contexts in the Moselle region is striking, and it is understandable that colleagues have sought to understand it as part of a unified cultural phenomenon.

Difficulties with this approach, however, become apparent quite quickly. Though they appear to offer a convenient common denominator, the swords prove to be associated with quite different assemblages. The contents of two graves from the important Treveran cemetery at Wederath-Belginum have, for example, attracted much comment. Graves 1344 and 2215 both contain short swords, both may be dated to before the mid-1st century AD, and both have been linked to men serving in the *ala Treverorum* or another Roman cavalry regiment.[31] This is an attractive hypothesis. It is useful to remember, however, that if we do not focus on the swords, but on other objects from the graves, or indeed on the *combination* of objects in the graves, other identities and other parallels might emerge. In addition to the sword and lance head discovered in 2215, for example, were fine ware vessels, a pitcher, a glass *balsamarium*, shears, coins, and a mattock (*dolabra*). The vessels of fine pottery and glass, the shears and coins might fit just as easily in, say, grave 1026 at the same cemetery, a grave profiled in the 'Körper- und Schönheitspflege' section of the site report.[32] Equally, a *dolabra* of a form familiar from Roman military contexts appears in another grave at Wederath (no. 697), accompanied by a number of weapons, but no sword.[33] Of course, the fact that other links are possible does not mean that the association of the sword graves with troopers of an *ala* is necessarily wrong; it merely suggests that there were other ways of expressing similar identities, and demands that we look at the whole assemblage of any grave under discussion.

Comparison of the assemblages associated with short swords at Wederath and elsewhere with other graves in the region is important, particularly if we are to understand them in the context of indigenous tradition. Similarities between these

---

[28] For surveys, see Wightman (1970) and Heinen (1985).

[29] For the term, see Schumacher (1989: 270).   [30] Ibid. 271.

[31] Krier and Reinert (1993: 67–8); Schumacher (1989: 274). Wells (1999: 120) does not argue the association with the *ala* specifically, but does believe that the deceased in Grave 1344 was 'a Treveri soldier who served in an auxiliary unit'.

[32] Goethert (1989: 275). The presence of a mirror, comb, and bronze spoon in 1065 underpin this characterization of the grave's contents.

[33] Schumacher (1989: 271).

graves and those from Goeblingen-Nospelt in Luxembourg are noted in the academic literature, yet it is the differences that may prove most significant. In 1966, archaeologists uncovered four burials at the Goeblingen-Nospelt site, each of which lay within a wooden chamber and was covered by an earth mound.[34] The remains of the dead had been cremated, but the goods that accompanied them had not. All these practices offer ready parallels with local Iron Age mortuary traditions. Each of the graves contains pottery, each contains lance points, and indeed three contain swords. The two latest graves, grave A (30–20 BC) and grave B (25–15 BC), also include Roman fine wares. If this were the sum total of their assemblages, all that might appear to distinguish them from a grave such as 2215 at Wederath would be the quantity rather than range of goods. There are, however, other distinguishing factors; most notably, the dead represented in A and B take wine serving sets with them into eternity. Furthermore, they take so many vessels with them that, along with the cauldron and pails accompanying B, they appear well equipped to host many a feast. This capacity clearly underscores their elite status in local society. But importantly, part of their status is also expressed through the inclusion of symbols first introduced into local graves in the mid-1st century BC. These make explicit reference to mounted warfare. Long, rather than short, swords accompany three of the deceased.[35] Furthermore, each of the four burials from the site contains either one or two spurs. Spur burials are also known from the late 1st century BC within the region at Konz and Thür.[36] If the sword burials discovered across the area and associated with troopers in *alae* actually commemorate men who served in the Roman cavalry, why do they not do the same? Is it because there are so many ways of celebrating the same type of status? Is it because there are changes in burial custom?

Answers to these questions may emerge through the examination of other assemblages in the region that are contemporary with the short sword burials. Most striking here are the graves discovered to contain cavalry helmets. A grave from Weyler in Belgium (*c.* AD 40/45), excavated in the 1980s, included a fine cavalry helmet of conventional unmasked type. The Hellingen (Luxembourg) grave, with its masked helmet, also dates from the second quarter of the 1st century AD, while another local burial, dating to the first half of the 1st century AD, this time from at Conflans (France), also contained a masked helmet. Yet none of these graves contains any weapons.[37]

Understandably, scholars have sought to link the masked-helmet burials from here with the better-known, but contemporary, Thracian examples. Though it is seldom suggested that in this case the deceased are themselves of Thracian origin, it has been argued that they were Gauls who encountered the tradition while campaigning in Thrace in the AD 20s and who brought it back with them,

---

[34] Haffner (1984), Metzler (1984), and Böhme-Schönberger (1993).

[35] The sword in Goeblingen-Nospelt Grave A was, e.g. 790mm in length (including tang).

[36] For the wider phenomenon of spur burials, see Völling (1992; 1993).

[37] Weyler-Schlamfeld: Fairon and Moreau (1983: 551–64); Hellingen: Krier and Reinert (1993); Conflans: Perdrizet (1911). For a convenient survey of the evidence, see Krier and Reinert (1993). On typological/chronological grounds I omit two helmet burials from the region: those of Trier-Olewig in Germany and Couvreaux/Villers-la-Loue in France.

choosing to be buried this way the best part of two decades later.[38] This is an interesting suggestion, but hardly a necessary one, particularly as its authors feel no such explanation is necessary for another western masked-helmet burial, that at Chassenard.[39] The fact that the Weyler helmet is of conventional type, and that the burial rites were so different, also suggests that no Thracian precedent is required.

While allowing for the fact that each grave assemblage was selected by different groups of individuals, who were themselves burying different individuals, and that simple categorization of grave groups may be impossible, it is conceivable that the evidence shows the evolution of certain conventions here. The Goeblingen-Nospelt series clearly reflects the representation of identity by a prosperous and influential group within Treveran society. In the years following Roman conquest these individuals made more explicit use of martial symbolism, underscoring the fact that they had successfully negotiated the retention or development of their influence in the new order. When smaller, less elaborate swords became more widely available across Treveran society, those who had access to them emulated the mortuary patterns of the elites as best they could. This is despite the fact that the swords themselves could only be associated with infantry combat, a form of fighting not previously associated with the native aristocracy. The short-sword holders may have seen service in the *cohortes*, in the militia, or as 'sword-bearers' of the type mentioned in Egyptian papyri. It is not necessary to claim that they served in the new *alae*. Rather, the men associated with these prestigious mounted units adopted new symbols, in life and in death, to distinguish them from the foot soldiers. In Roman service, they were paid better and they wore different equipment; in their burials they made this clear through the active inclusion of some items and the active exclusion of others. Thus we see an evolving pattern, in which the symbols of the mounted warriors of old are emulated and thus devalued by their native subjects—so that their successors, the new elite, proclaim afresh their status through the use of Roman trappings. I shall return to the importance of the distinction between foot and mounted troops below.

The historical sources certainly suggest a complex interplay between Treveran identity and Roman military service from at least the Julio-Claudian period. They also demonstrate the dangers of associating access to military equipment with acceptance of Roman authority. Iulius Florus, one of the leaders of the revolt of AD 21, was descended from Treveran ancestors who had received citizenship on account of their services to Rome.[40] He held, or believed he held, sufficient influence in Treveran society to attempt to induce an *ala* raised from his people to mutiny.[41] In Tacitus' account he has a counterpart, another Treveran with a similar lineage, Iulius Indus. This man, founder of the *ala Indiana*, appears in the narrative as the leader of a body of picked men fighting in the Roman cause.[42] In such an environment it seems highly likely that, for several generations, men

---

[38] See Krier and Reinert (1993: 63) and Reddé (1994: 668, fn. 34) for such a link. The further association of such a practice with men of an *ala Gallorum et Thracum* seems to me to be unnecessary.

[39] Krier and Reinert (1993: 63) follow Beck and Chew (1991: 105–6) in suggesting another identity for the occupant of the Chassenard burial in Gallia Lugdunensis, though Bishop and Coulston (1993: 96) wonder if a Thracian connection might not still be possible.

[40] Tacitus *Ann.* 3.40.   [41] Ibid. 3.42.   [42] Ibid.

related their status to the power of Rome. With the raising of regular *alae*, such as those described by Tacitus, it also seems possible that more men had greater access to better military equipment—and were thus able to display this status through it. It must always be remembered, however, that the contingents described by Tacitus appear almost incidentally in an account focused on elite ambition and revolt. There would have been other military organizations, militias and cohorts, serving in the region which do not appear in the tale. We should not try to squeeze the archaeological evidence for them into the literary framework we have inherited from Tacitus. The men in these organizations probably also expressed their status through weaponry, but their way of doing so need not simply echo the activities of their leaders.

Weapons cease to appear in the grave assemblages of the Treveri in the second half of the 1st century. During the same period, new patterns of elite expression appear in the archaeological record. Of these, the most notable is the development of elaborate rural houses of the type that are frequently termed *villae* in the academic literature.[43] These developments are not necessarily linked, and though it is tempting to envisage a scenario whereby the power-holders in Treveran society opt for the trappings of a settled lifestyle as more appropriate status symbols than those of war, many other explanations are possible. Precisely why weapon burials stop is unclear, but there are two strong possibilities. The first is simply that mortuary fashions changed as a result of currents in the religious life of the community that we ill understand. The second, a possibility that could also be linked to the first, places a strong emphasis on the events of AD 69. This was the year in which the Roman authorities lost control over large parts of the Rhine. In Tacitus' account, Classicus, a man of royal blood and the prefect of an *ala Treverorum*, and Iulius Tutor, another Treveran and prefect of the Rhine bank, were pivotal figures in a rebellion against Roman authority.[44] If Tacitus' account is accepted,[45] it becomes tempting to link the absence of weapons in grave assemblages from the late 1st century onwards to the imposition of new rules across and beyond the Treveran area designed to minimize the possibility of revolt. Armed assemblies and rituals involving weapons may have been restricted. Also possible, indeed probable, is that large numbers of indigenous armed men were removed from the territory, through death, deportation, and redeployment during the suppression of the revolt. Many of those Treverans who then found themselves in other lands may have abandoned the weapon burial tradition on arrival in areas where the local population did not attribute the same social significance to their rituals. Certainly some authorities have placed the end of the weapon grave phenomenon here at around AD 70, which would fit remarkably (suspiciously?) neatly with the end date of the Civilis 'revolt'.[46]

The Treveran example illustrates that equipment of the type used by auxiliaries could be incorporated into status display at different times and in different ways in

---

[43] Woolf (1998: 152).

[44] Tacitus *Hist.* 4.55. Woolf (1998: 21, fn. 70) is cautious about such claims, noting that it is more certain that those who claimed long pedigrees were rich citizens with military commands.

[45] Urban (1985) has reinterpreted this account, arguing that the actions of Classicus must be interpreted within the context of the Civil War and not seen as part of a tribal or native revolt.

[46] Krier and Reinert (1993: 65).

association with different identities. However, it is important to note that the practice of including arms in funerary assemblages was not a widespread one. Weapon burials, a familiar though certainly not common feature of provincial burials in the 1st century AD, become much rarer. Indeed, it is rare to find any examples within imperial territory in the 2nd and early 3rd centuries AD. With less exclusive status attributed to weapon-carrying by the soldiers themselves and with relative peace on the frontiers, the ritualized use of weaponry became less pronounced. An exception to this may be the lands of the Batavi, where the continued emphasis on armaments may be linked to the community's militarization by Rome.[47]

One of the problems with using grave assemblages as a source of information about identity is, of course, the fact that the assemblage reflects ritual practice rather than necessarily day-to-day routine. Other data may suggest different patterns. Funerary reliefs are an obvious source of information, though we should note that they only commemorate those soldiers who (or whose heirs) subscribed to such forms of representation. Such individuals and their associates may have embraced more readily the status markers depicted on the monuments than those of whom we have no trace. Funerary reliefs follow their own distinct fashions and stem from a tradition alien to most provinces, but while these attributes raise fresh interpretive problems, they also offer valuable potential insights. They certainly offer a different perspective from that recoverable from the study of burial goods. Grave stelae from the territory of the Treveri that commemorate soldiers follow the same general patterns as those elsewhere: infantry soldiers are depicted un-armoured at full or half-length, cavalry are depicted mounted and in the act of trampling barbarians.[48] The existence of a further category of monuments, however, of large mausolea decorated with battle scenes and weapon scenes is noteworthy. Fragments of these monuments are known from Wasserbillig (Luxembourg), Nennig (Germany), and Arlon (Belgium) and its environs. Neither the form nor decoration of these mausoleums is unique to the lands of the Treveri.[49] Yet they appear to be represented in greater numbers in the region than outside it—a reflection perhaps of their particular value to an elite seeking to express the military aspect of their status in a distinct way from the new classes of warriors and weapon-carriers created by Roman power.[50] The power struggles evidenced in Tacitus' accounts of the AD 21 and AD 69 revolts may suggest that such concerns were pressing for Treveran leaders. Interestingly, the fighting scenes all appear to depict troops dressed as regular auxiliary cavalry. On stylistic grounds, it appears that the monuments do not post-date the 1st century AD.

Across the Empire, auxiliary infantrymen are predominantly depicted on funerary reliefs without armour or enemies. Heads are uncovered. In exceptional cases,

---

[47] See Nicolay (2008) for the presence of armaments within Batavian territory.

[48] For the evidence from the territory of the Treveri, see Kreir and Reinert (1993: 71–81).

[49] When complete they most probably resembled the famous tomb of the Julii at Glanum (Saint-Rémy-de-Provence, France). For this tomb, see Rolland (1969), Picard (1963; 1964), and Gros (1986). For the comparison, see Krier and Reinert (1993: 73).

[50] The largest example of this monument type known from the Germanies is the tomb of a legionary veteran from Cologne (Precht 1975), so such monuments do not have to commemorate native elites. Nevertheless, the decoration of the mausolea in the Treveran area is distinctive in its depiction of regular auxiliary cavalry in action.

Fig. 16.1. Stele of Annaius Daverzus, *miles* of *cohors IIII Delmatarum* (*CIL* 13.7507). Early 1st century AD. Römerhalle Bad Kreuznach.

such as the Egyptian mummy cases, this allows for the painting of realistic portraits, but in most instances it appears there was little attempt to achieve an accurate likeness. Yet the depiction of a soldier's hairstyle—short and, in the 1st century, beardless—was a further indication of his particular identity. This may just reflect military fashion, though at least in later periods it appears to be obligatory. Where auxiliary soldiers are depicted bare-headed on funerary monuments, their hairstyles appear the same as those of their legionary colleagues, and quite unlike those of the barbaric natives carved on contemporary monuments. As discussed above, in uniform or out, hairstyle can readily indicate cultural allegiance.[51]

In terms of armament, the infantry soldier's sword, sword-belt and, under the early Principate, his apron is usually clearly shown, often indeed very carefully carved. In this respect there is little to distinguish auxiliaries from their legionary counterparts, as comparison of the representations of Annaius Daverzus (see Fig. 16.1) and P. Flavoleius Cordus (see Fig. 16.2) illustrate—though, as noted

---

[51] See p. 171.

Fig. 16.2. Stele of P. Flavoleius Cordus, *miles* of *Legio XIIII Gemina* (*CIL* 13.7255), Germany. First half 1st century AD. Landesmuseum Mainz.

their shields and missile weapons are of distinct types. Whether colours originally made it easier for a viewer to discern the difference between these categories of soldiers is unclear; too few painted reliefs have survived. On the stelae then, the identifying features of an infantryman's dress are clearly his sword-belt and apron.

Seen in terms of gender studies, a soldier's apron occupies a crucial place, quite literally protecting his masculinity. Recent work suggests, however, that the apron was of little protection against the risk of castration, and that it was inconvenient for the running soldier.[52] One marvels at the commitment of the researcher whose painstaking experiments led to these conclusions! Rather, it appears that the apron jingled, making a noise that signalled the presence of a soldier. Cordus is actually depicted on his memorial with his hand on his apron, twisting the straps. Sound, then, as well as sight, conveyed soldierly identity. The noise of the apron complemented the distinctive cacophony of hobnailed sandals, belts, and clanking swords.[53]

As with the apron, the weapons-belt or belts offered ample scope for decorative experiment.[54] The metal fittings which also served to prevent the leather curling and stretching could be styled in a range of shapes, and offered ample scope for embellishment. It now seems very likely that some of the decoration used conveyed information to the informed contemporary viewer. Certainly the range of types reflects regional production patterns, and in some cases may even have been distinct to particular units. As noted above (Fig. 13.2), by the end of the 2nd century both legionary and auxiliary soldiers were wearing belts with individual letters attached to them, spelling out mottoes or maxims such as VTERE FELIX and OPTIME MAXIME CON(SERVA).[55] These belt types became fashionable over large areas and have been found in the northwest provinces, Danubian provinces, and the Dura assemblage.[56] While some belt fittings used in military circles owe a debt to indigenous art, it is worth noting that this form with its Latin mottoes is one of a range of military artefacts created *de novo* in the Roman military community.

That belts should attract elaborate decoration is hardly surprising. Not only do they offer the individual wearer more ready scope for elaboration—the shield, body armour, and helmet offer less—but they also draw significance from the fact that they are connected very directly to the weapons themselves. Yet the very early date at which the belt took on an important military status reflects the fact that belts had special significance in Roman society. At least in Roman metropolitan settings, not to wear a belt with one's tunic was discreditable—it was to be *discinctus*.[57] Unbelted tunics were variously associated with low status, moral laxity, and effeminacy.[58] This view was still more pronounced in military settings. In a list of the punishments that could be inflicted on Roman soldiers, Suetonius advises us that they could also be forced to stand in front of their headquarters without their belts on.[59] The explicit claim that this punishment was deliberately designed to degrade the victim is illuminating. It shows how loss of his sword belt deprives the soldier of his military identity, by stripping him of the most potent

[52] Bishop and Coulston (1993: 99) quote Peter Connolly, pers. comm. Though the sound of the apron may also have helped to terrify enemies on the battle field, I wonder if, under the circumstances, many soldiers actually chose not to wear it in that setting.

[53] Ibid. 196.   [54] James (1999: 21).   [55] Petculescu (1991a).

[56] See James (2004: 79) for a Durene example and references. A new example has recently been identified in the finds from the Liber Pater sanctuary at Apulum (Haynes, forthcoming).

[57] Balsdon (1979: 220–21).

[58] For the association of unbelted tunics with low status, see Croom (2002: 33). Olsen (2010: 23) has brought together references for the negative connotations of such dress. See in this respect Cic. *Verr.* 2.5.31; Dio 46.18.1–3; Horace *Sat.* 1.2.26; Seneca *Ep.* 114.4.

[59] Suetonius *Aug.* 24.2.

symbol of that status.[60] By at least the end of the 3rd century AD, discarding the belt had also come to symbolize the rejection of military service.[61]

It is illuminating to note here the occurrence of military belts in funerary assemblages. The role of richly decorated 'military belts' as indicators of ethnicity, status, and rank is much discussed in the study of the later Empire. Belt sets in grave assemblages from the early Empire are seldom discovered in the western provinces, but they are known elsewhere. In Dacia, for example, graves containing what may be military belt fittings represent a small but significant phenomenon from the early 2nd century onwards.[62]

How might the apparently localized aspect of this phenomenon be explained? Petculescu, who has studied the data from the Danubian provinces, is careful to avoid suggesting that all the belts are deposited for the same reason, or indeed solely with soldiers. Literary exaggeration notwithstanding, there is good reason to believe that Roman Dacia contained an extraordinarily diverse array of peoples.[63] The pattern of settlement, with entire communities migrating into the region, allowed and perhaps encouraged groups from different traditions to emphasize their distinctiveness. Archaeologically, this diversity is reflected in the very distinct mortuary rituals discovered across the region.

A possibility must be that the strategies of distinction practised by these very different peoples had an impact on the practices of ritual deposition employed by soldiers. Some items of military equipment deposited in Dacian graves may well reflect the practices of those Norican or Pannonian peoples from south of the Danube who provided recruits for the garrison,[64] but it is also possible that in such a richly cosmopolitan area, soldiers and those associated with them found it important to stress their institutional links.[65] Perhaps not coincidentally, notable examples of these finds have come to light in graves within 10–20km of military installations, possibly therefore from those living within the boundaries of camp *territoria*. Many such settlers were probably veterans. More discoveries in the region may yet allow us to test the hypothesis that, for settlers connected to, but living some distance from, garrison posts, outward displays of military association were especially important.

That sword-belts hung from the shoulder were also treated as status identifiers in the provinces is also suggested in the representational evidence. Egyptian mummy portraits show men who are clearly identified as soldiers in this way, despite the fact that no weapons are depicted (see Fig. 16.3). The figures are dated stylistically to AD 160–170 on the basis of their hairstyles. Each wears a *balteus* over his left shoulder, and a cloak (*sagum*) pinned with a brooch. Unfortunately, there is some uncertainty as to the precise provenance of some of the finest examples, which are attributed, somewhat uncertainly, to er-Rubayat in the Fayum.[66] Commentaries on the pieces have tended to suggest that the men are

---

[60] For the association of soldiers with belts, see Pliny *Natural History* 33.152; Juvenal *Sat.* 16.48; Petronius *Satyricon* 83; Tacitus *Hist.* 2.88; Herodian 2.13.10.

[61] Woods (1993: 55–60).   [62] Petculescu (1995) and Ciugudean and Ciugudean (2000).

[63] Eutropius (8.6.2) speaks of settlers coming to Dacia from across the Roman world.

[64] Petculescu (1995: 110, 112, and 114–15).   [65] Ibid. 121–2.

[66] Walker and Bierbrier (1997: 86) observe that these are not typical of other portraits known to have come from er-Rubayat, and may come from elsewhere in the Fayum.

Fig. 16.3. Mummy portrait of a soldier in encaustic and tempera *c.* AD 160–170. From the Fayum in Egypt. British Museum.

officers, seemingly on account of the quality of the portrait, the gold cloak fastenings, and the fashion-conscious hairstyles. Such an attribution may be correct, but the amount that some ordinary soldiers in the west were clearly prepared to spend on both their memorials and their equipment suggests that we should not altogether rule out junior officers and *milites*. Similarly, uncertainty must remain as to the units with which these men served. Legionary troops were not stationed in the Fayum, and auxiliary units are therefore more likely.[67] It is to be hoped that more information will yet shed light on these splendid portraits.

---

[67] The precise nature of military deployments in the area is uncertain, but it is likely that auxiliaries served at Philadelphia, a settlement 12km from er-Rubayat.

This brief review suggests that, off the battlefield, infantry soldiers, both legionary and auxiliary, presented their status in similar ways. Though the types of equipment used to do this changed, the belt remained a crucial identifier and was one with which the men themselves strongly identified. This emphasis may owe something to the artistic conventions that governed the production of military funerary portraiture, but the presence of belt-plates to represent military equipment in graves, and the basic longevity of the convention in the face of changing traditions in tomb art, suggest that it reflected an enduring feature of soldierly behaviour. As noted, this in turn suggests the internalization, perpetuation, and evolution of an emphasis that had its origins in Roman republican tradition.

Cavalry tombstones differ dramatically and very deliberately from those of infantry soldiers. This very fact suggests that there was more than one kind of military identity. In the 1st century and much of the 2nd, the deceased is depicted armoured and in action (fig. 15.2).[68] Frequently a hapless naked man cowers beneath the rider's horse, underscoring a blunt opposition between Roman conqueror and barbarian victim. It is sometimes suggested that this composition developed from the iconographic tradition of the Thracian Rider/Hero, and that troopers in the Thracian *alae* were responsible for its dissemination.[69] This is wrong; the earliest examples are not linked with Thracian auxiliaries at all. The model was, in fact, already familiar in Italy long before Thracian auxiliaries were enrolled.[70] In the 2nd and 3rd centuries AD, however, the iconography of the Thracian Rider strongly influenced artistic conventions in the Danubian provinces. Multiple artistic syntheses attest the influence of this classic composition, and Thracians in the *equites singulares* even brought it to Rome. The funerary stela of Bithus in the Capitoline Museum (fig. 22.3), for example, depicts not only the rider accompanied by a running dog, but also a wild boar. The artistic composition is virtually indistinguishable from that used by contemporary civilians in Thrace; unlike the early *Reitergrabsteine*, the rider wears no body armour and carries no shield.[71]

Significantly, cavalry tombstones do adopt different forms in some provinces from the late 1st century AD onwards. The deceased appears at his *silcernium* or funerary banquet. Monuments depicting this banquet, commonly referred to in archaeological literature as *Totenmahlszene*, are a familiar feature of contemporary civilian practice. This move from the dust of the battlefield to the ashes of the funeral dinner may reflect a new willingness by troopers to convey their status in civil terms. It may even suggest that cavalrymen felt themselves sufficiently integrated within the wider provincial community to compete effectively for mutually prized status symbols. In many examples, the feast is but part of the overall decoration and the horse remains a significant element. This clearly

---

[68] Schleiermacher (1984).   [69] Anderson (1985: 18–19).

[70] Mackintosh (1986); e.g. the Loredan I stele displayed at the Archaeological Museum of Padova: Zampieri (1994: 111, fig. 152).

[71] The same combination of rider, dog, and boar can be found in civilian modes, e.g. a 3rd-century family tombstone discovered at Vranya, Bulgaria, and now in the Archaeological Institute and Museum, Sofia. The main military concession may be in the figure standing behind the rider in the Bithus monument, who is probably a groom or servant, but the identity of this figure is open to question. In his commentary on the tombstone, M. P. Speidel (1994a: 330) argues that the figure's helmet is adorned with a bird's head, a helmet style associated with the imperial guard. I regret to say that, despite repeated visits to the monument, I still cannot see this detail on it.

demonstrates that the deceased's identity as a cavalryman remains important. In some regions, such as Pannonia and Noricum, the tendency towards more peaceful imagery becomes increasingly pronounced. It is tempting to link this pattern to the high proportion of soldiers who are recorded on family tombstones from these provinces.[72]

Two features of cavalry tombstones are particularly noteworthy. The first is that they frequently depict grooms/slaves or other dependants. Of course, this is not accidental; the depiction is telling us something of the individual's wealth and status. Both are expressed through and within the wider community that formed around the deceased's regiment. While we know that some foot soldiers also had slaves, it is interesting that they seldom if ever appear. I believe that the distinction speaks not simply of the mounted soldiers' greater wealth but also of the social traditions that underpinned many of the earliest *alae*. In the Julio-Claudian period many of these regiments were formed from the more prosperous elements of indigenous society. A higher income, provided at an early date by Roman paymasters, was of course necessary to maintain a horse. This fact was recognized even in Roman tradition, lying as it did behind the origins of the knightly class, so it is unsurprising to find it presented so explicitly in the cavalry's own monuments. The fashion for representing grooms originates in the *alae* of the lower Rhine during the 1st century and subsequently spreads, becoming a familiar form even in Rome.[73] In its earliest manifestations the fashion may represent an additional device for underscoring the status of cavalry troops in a heavily garrisoned region, with vibrant indigenous traditions of martial display.

This is also why the horse is present on grave markers: the animal is not just an instrument of mounted warfare, it is a symbol of prestige. Affirming this link is the attention lavished on horse trappings in many monuments. These form the cavalryman's counterpart to the belt and apron of the infantry soldier. The horse trappings allowed for display, for dash, and for colour—they too reflect different traditions and patterns of production. As with all other aspects of material culture, they are also open to a range of users, but their form seems to have made them attractive to non-soldiers. James notes, for example, the 'military' horse trappings discovered with the late AD 50s burial at Folly Lane, Verulamium, in England. Found in another context, they might be attributed to cavalry troops, yet here as part of an indigenous burial they appear as items appropriated by a fashionable aristocrat.[74] The picture here is all the more complex because at this relatively early date, auxiliary cavalry themselves expressed a preference for the fine metalwork that seems to have once been an aristocratic preserve.

Appropriation of items of military dress by civilians is common even today,[75] but in Roman times it must have been all the more so. The civilian/soldier divide was itself a creation of Rome and in its infancy;[76] until the advent of the professional warrior there was no such thing as a civilian, so there was still plenty of scope for the negotiation of status identifiers. Furthermore, there was always

---

[72] Saller and Shaw (1984: 141).   [73] Coulston (2000: 96, fn. 130).

[74] James (2001: 83). For the finds, see Niblett (1999: 143–5, nos 8 and 9).

[75] James (2001: 83). The most alarming example of this phenomenon the author has witnessed to date was the fashion of wearing of NBC (nuclear, biological, and chemical warfare) suits at Newcastle discos in the late 1980s.

[76] Carrié (1993: 103).

Fig. 16.4. Examples of two Roman provincial brooch types researchers commonly associated with the military: (a) 'knee' brooch from Richborough (after Dobie in Bayley and Butcher 2004: 101): (b) P-shaped brooch from the fort at South Shields (after Allason-Jones and Miket 1984: 108).

potential for individuals to disguise themselves through the misappropriation of agreed symbols. Presenting oneself as a soldier, even if not in state pay, clearly appealed to enough individuals for late Roman legislators to attempt to do something about it. The legislation was particularly aimed at those individuals who used military dress as a guise in which to cajole their fellow citizens.[77] Significantly, this legislation specified not just weapons but also belts and cloaks as items of a soldier's dress.

The relationship of brooches to the soldier's self-image has been much debated (see Fig. 16.4). Studies of the distribution of 'knee' brooches in the northwest provinces have noted a correlation between their presence and military activity, leading to their interpretation as *soldaten-Fibeln*.[78] Their presence at military sites on the Danube is also notable, but if these were indeed soldiers' brooches, how were they worn? As Allason-Jones has noted, they were too small to fasten a cloak, and there were few other places on an armoured soldier where a brooch could actually be worn.[79] Their use to hold together a cravat is about the only other possibility.[80] Furthermore, another complication has often been overlooked. Recent analysis by Frances McIntosh of Britain's Portable Antiquities Scheme data suggests that in Britain at least, the type may have been widely copied and adapted for wear by civilians living far from the frontiers.[81] Certainly, more richly ornamented versions of the knee brooch can be found in late 1st- and 2nd-century contexts in southern England. Any association with military usage was thus far from exclusive, even if it may have initiated the style.

Knee brooches are not the only type to have been associated with the military. P-shaped brooches, which foreshadow the crossbow brooches of the later Roman Empire—brooches known to have had an official and/or military significance—are also particularly well represented at military sites. While it would be misleading to suggest that they are universally found in quantity at such sites, McIntosh's analysis of the Portable Antiquities Scheme data does show that they are notably markedly less common in rural areas than in military and urban centres[82]—a finding that suggests that they too had a particular link to state functionaries.[83]

---

[77] Amory (1997: 341); note also Halsall (2000: 174).
[78] For this type in Britain, see Bayley and Butcher (2004: 179) and Snape (1993: 20).
[79] Lindsay Allason-Jones, pers. comm.   [80] Ibid.   [81] McIntosh (2012).   [82] Ibid.
[83] It appears unlikely that this pattern simply reflects differences in the availability of such brooches, as they were quite common finds and were easily reproduced.

Fig. 16.5. Norico-Pannonian brooch from the fort of Buciumi, Romania (after Cociş 2004: 411).

At later periods, the brooch is one of the artefacts singled out for particular embellishment in order to convey the wearer's rank. Though this was almost certainly not the case in the first two centuries AD, the brooch may have conveyed other important visual information, such as the origin of the brooch wearer. While there may be some truth in this, it remains vital to remember, here as elsewhere, that an attractive, unusual, or convenient object may be adopted by a wearer regardless of its origins. Anyone on a long-distance journey in the Roman Empire would have been exposed to a range of different material cultures, and would have had considerable opportunity to adopt and abandon items of adornment as they travelled. Yet there are cases where it seems churlish to wholly rule out the notion that objects illuminate patterns of movement. One notable example concerns the use of Norico-Pannonian brooches in Dacia.[84]

A range of ceramic and representational evidence from Roman Dacia attests to the arrival of migrants from Noricum and Pannonia here during the 2nd century.[85] It is also clear that many units in the army of conquest were stationed in those provinces prior to the invasion. The forty-four Norico-Pannonian brooches recovered from Roman Dacia display a distinctive distribution which reflects these connections (see Fig. 16.5).[86] They come overwhelmingly from Dacia Superior, the area with the highest concentration of soldiers. While their depiction on funerary monuments from civil sites warns against arguing for a simple correlation with military users, the distribution of the objects themselves shows a very strong association with military sites. Eleven of the forty-four are known from the frontier site of Porolissum, several examples are believed to have come from the extra-mural settlements attached to forts, and ten are known to have been excavated within forts.[87] In his valuable analysis of the type, Cociş notes this pattern, but then tellingly suggests that it may contradict the evidence of funerary reliefs that these brooches were predominantly worn by women.[88] Given that it is now widely accepted that women were to be found in Roman forts,[89] it is no longer necessary to see a contradiction.

The dangers inherent in assuming links between jewellery use, military/civilian identity, and gender in the neighbourhood of forts have been clearly laid out by Allason-Jones. In a paper first delivered at the Theoretical Roman Archaeology

---

[84] For another example see Ivleva (2012) on British brooch types and the Roman army.
[85] See p. 185.   [86] Cociş (2004: 407), of 2,214 examples.
[87] Ibid. 408.   [88] Ibid.   [89] A reassessment led by Driel-Murray (1997). See also p. 16.

Conference in 1995, she noted that archaeologists were too often happy to assume that earrings, for example, were objects associated with females despite the fact that many of the men in attendance at the conference were obviously wearing them too; the assumption is thus unsafe.[90] Perhaps, she suggests, auxiliaries drawn from some peoples may have favoured this practice, however alien it may have been to the male occupants of Rome.[91] The same point may equally apply to brooch use.

So assuming that any example necessarily came either from a soldier, camp follower, or other civilian is fundamentally problematic. While students of the *auxilia* have long followed the Vergilian focus on 'arms and the man' in attempting to illuminate the presence of tribal and ethnic traits amongst soldiers, it is highly likely that much of the best evidence for these traits in fact comes not from *militaria*, but from other items of adornment, worn either by off-duty soldiers, male civilians, children or, in the case of the Norico-Pannonian examples, women.

One final item strongly linked to the identity of Roman soldiers remains to be discussed. This is the celebrated *caliga*, the hobnailed military boot. Distinctive in both appearance and in the sound it must have made, this boot appears in very diverse settings in ancient literature. Most famously, of course, it gives the emperor Gaius his nickname 'Caligula'.[92] Suetonius' comments on the dress and military associations of the future emperor's childhood suggest that, while he did indeed spend much of his time in military camps, the imperial house rather played up the association.[93] Juvenal is much taken by hobnailed boots and their link to the violent and threatening behaviour of soldiers in Rome,[94] but it is in the works of Josephus that one of the most vivid incidents linked to *caligae* appears. In AD 70, during fighting near the Temple of Herod in Jerusalem, a Roman centurion's nailed boots slipped from underneath him on the paving. He was promptly surrounded and killed.[95] Perhaps it was because of the military connotations of hobnailed footware that the Jews banned them for use amongst their own people.[96] Certainly *caligae* were known across the Empire and at its very heart. Their military association is preserved anachronistically in 3rd-century documents through the use of the phrase *milites caligati* to indicate soldiers below the rank of centurion/decurion. The term was still employed in the 'morning reports' of Dura's *cohors XX Palmyrenorum* for example.[97] Yet recent archaeological re-search raises interesting questions about the role *caligae* had in proclaiming military identity. Finds of shoe series from a number of military sites indicate that the style had fallen out of fashion in the AD 80s, to be replaced by a closed boot.[98] The reasons for the change are not clear, but as van Driel-Murray notes, consumer preference can clearly play a role in the rapid acceptance and equally sudden abandonment of footwear fashion.[99] Research also indicates, as in fact the tale of the young Caligula illustrates, that 'military' shoes were not just worn by adult males. In fact, a careful analysis of the sizes of shoes indicates that there were no particular gender distinctions in footwear use until late in the 2nd century.[100] Soldiers' wives, children, and dependants all appear to have chosen from a similar array of shoes to those worn by the soldiers themselves. Certainly a form of closed

---

[90] Allason-Jones (1995: 25–6).   [91] Ibid. 26.   [92] Suetonius *Caligula* 9.
[93] Ibid. 8.   [94] Juvenal *Sat.* 3.248, 16.25.   [95] Josephus *Bell. Iud.* 6.85.
[96] James (1999: 21), citing Roussin (1994: 188).
[97] See e.g. *P. Dura* 82.ii.1. This papyrus is dated to AD 223–235 by Fink (*RMR* 47).
[98] van Driel-Murray (2001: 190).   [99] Ibid. 195.   [100] Ibid. 194.

boot resembling that believed to be worn by the Vindolanda soldiers was worn by women living in the fort *praetorium* prior to the reign of Hadrian.[101]

The soldier and, it would seem, his dependants enjoyed a wide range of choice in what they wore. Influencing and influenced by fashion, it is clear that individuals emphasized different aspects of their dress and equipment in different times and in different places. Members of the *auxilia* must be seen as active agents in this exchange. An evaluation of the evidence suggests that many of those who formed the wider communities dependent upon army regiments in turn appropriated military symbols. But the process was constantly evolving. The identity of an auxiliary soldier in the 1st-century Rhineland, for example, was not expressed in quite the same way as it was by another in 2nd-century Egypt. Furthermore, even members of contemporary auxiliary contingents within a region used differing strategies to assert their status. Thus the infantry echoed their legionary counterparts, while the cavalry stressed their particular status as mounted troops. Yet for all this diversity, it is also possible to see how notions of a common soldierly identity encompassing both legionary and auxiliary soldiers evolved. When soldiers tried to distinguish themselves from one another, they used the same sorts of items to do so, such as side arms, belts, and brooches, because these things were seen as important. The new common identity, which evolved through competition for status symbols, also reflected the soldier's position in imperial society at large. It showed how, from challenging the wealth holders above the peasantry, the army was able to encroach even upon the status symbols of the equestrian class. Significantly, this was not a simple attempt to emulate the Mediterranean elite. Already by the 3rd century soldiers' dress had long since ceased to track the styles of the Mediterranean, as fighting men opted to adopt styles of garments worn by those living on *both* sides of the Empire's frontiers.[102]

Having explored the way in which individual soldiers contributed to the wider creation of Roman military material cultures, it is now only appropriate to see how currents in imperial society helped form the battlefield identities of the soldiers themselves.

---

[101] Ibid.   [102] James (1999: 22).

17

Between Roman and Barbarian

Auxiliary Soldiers on the Battlefield

For Richmond, the masks of the *Hippika Gymnasia* reflected a central cultural assumption that underpinned Rome's armies. The men of the *alae* and *cohortes* were different from legionaries.

> In reality, they were of set policy moulded in the Roman convention: on parade they might wear masks concealing their non-Roman features in a classic frame, and on discharge they became Roman citizens. These facts are all symptoms of the same outlook, which does not prevent them from taking a notable place in the main battle scenes, because as Tacitus emphasises a victory won *citra Romanum sanguinem* was a credit to the commander-in-chief.[1]

There is some truth in this view, but the overall picture is markedly more complex. Notions of cultural difference underpinned the distinctions that existed, and therefore were subject to various changes during the first couple of centuries AD. This chapter explores how the distinction between different troop types was maintained on the battlefield, and assesses the ways in which it changed over time.

The establishment of a professional army was controversial enough, but the formalized institution of non-citizen units dedicated to Rome's defence probably led to the raising of more than one senatorial eyebrow. It is true that allies of assorted types had lent more than a little assistance in the state's wars for centuries, but the citizen soldier always had pride of place. It was upon him that the duty of protecting the Empire fell; he may have had the occasional attitude problem, but he was a great deal more reliable than barbarian levies. Indeed, in every Roman account of combat, he stood at the heart of the battle line; other units—allies and auxiliaries—formed around him. So if non-citizen units were to be formed, they had to be distinguished from the legions. Such considerations may well have predominated amongst the Roman aristocracy in the 1st century. They certainly seem to have influenced the man at the centre of army reform, Augustus. His particular desire to ensure distinctions between citizen and non-citizen blood, and between free birth and slave birth, most probably had an impact on the form and character of Rome's new armies.[2] The literature of the Principate

---

[1] Richmond (1982: 19), quoting Tacitus *Agric.* 35.2: 'without Roman blood'.
[2] For examples of the thinking of Augustus on citizenship, see Suetonius *Aug.* 40. Augustus' view on distinguishing free-born from freedmen appears in a specifically military context in Suetonius *Aug.* 25.

reflects an ambiguity as to the identity of professional auxiliary soldiers. Romans when it suits the writer, their lack of Roman blood may equally be highlighted when it allows a nicely turned phrase. The *cohortales* and *equites* stood in the gap between Roman self and barbarian other. Their battlefield role and dress reflect how they negotiated this shifting ground. As the realities of service life changed, as more citizens joined the ranks of the *auxilia*, as the *cohortes* and *alae* undertook innovative fighting roles, and as new irregular units joined the army, the reservations articulated above must have seemed increasingly anachronistic. When in AD 212 Caracalla extended the Roman citizenship to many of the Empire's free-born subjects, such ideas became redundant.

Richmond's comments on masks, battle scenes, and blood cited above appear in his celebrated paper on Trajan's Column and thus concern the decades at the centre point of this study. In a later commentary on Tacitus' *De Vita Agricolae* he singled out the ancient writer's comments on the sparing of Roman blood as a theme of special interest. Claiming for the passage a particular significance in the development of Roman tactics, he went on to argue that the account prefigures campaigning entirely with auxiliaries—a progression that he believed manifests itself in Arrian's *Acies contra Alanos*, a work contemporary with the *Tactica*.[3] But there are good reasons for believing that Tacitus' comments, part of his description of the battle of Mons Graupius in northern Britain which took place in either AD 83 or 84, are altogether less helpful than Richmond liked to think. The basic outline of the battle seems plausible enough: the brunt of fighting was borne by cohorts of Tungrians and Batavians; the legions were never brought into action.

Does this really indicate some sort of innovative genius on the part of the Roman commander, Agricola, as his biographer and son-in-law Tacitus suggests? This aspect of the account is deeply suspect. To begin with, by the time of the battle it is highly likely that there would have been many citizens, a significant minority, in the ranks of the Tungrians and Batavians. Furthermore, by the time Tacitus was writing his account, fifteen or so years later, the number would have been higher still. Literary conventions notwithstanding, Tacitus would seem to be assuming an anachronistic view of the composition of these units on the part of his readers. Nonetheless, it is interesting that such a perspective could survive amongst the Roman aristocracy over a century after the first regular auxiliary units came into being. More problematic for the account, however, is the fact that Tacitus essentially contradicts it himself elsewhere in his own works. It is evident from his descriptions that auxiliary units had undertaken the bulk of fighting in many other battles prior to Mons Graupius. In quite a number of these, indeed, they were the *only* troops used by Roman commanders. Ostorius Scapula, for example, defeated the Iceni in AD 51 with a force that consisted entirely of auxiliary troops.[4] Other ancient writers similarly make it clear that even before this time auxiliaries were winning battles while the legions looked on. In *De Ira*, written some time between AD 37 and AD 41, Seneca observes that anger caused even the fearsome Germans to fall to auxiliaries before the legions arrive.[5]

---

[3] Ogilvie and Richmond (1967: 66).
[4] Tacitus *Ann.* 12 31; Rainbird (1969: 11); and Gilliver (1996: 55).
[5] Seneca *De Ira* 1.11.4; Saddington (1982: 106, fn. 115).

Such encounters tend to be dismissed summarily in much scholarly literature because of a prevailing view that a 'proper battle' required legionary participation. But it is important to remember that large-scale battles were the exception in Roman warfare. In the vast majority of instances in which Roman troops were called upon to fight, the smaller battles and skirmishes that held the *pax Romana* together were almost certainly undertaken by the *auxilia*. But even in the larger actions, the auxiliaries were no strangers to the roles commonly allocated to legionaries. Gilliver, for example, observes that in Tacitus' descriptions of Germanicus' tactics at Idistaviso (AD 16) and the operations of Lucius Apronius against the Frisii (AD 23), auxiliary infantrymen are to be found taking the roles traditionally allocated to legionaries—but there is no mention of an intention to save Roman blood.[6] A judicious review of the evidence, therefore, suggests that the significance of *citra Romanum sanguinem* is, as Rainbird suggests, more for the historian than the tactician.[7] The rhetorical device simply served Tacitus' desire to exaggerate the achievements in Britain of his father-in-law, Agricola.[8]

The presence of auxiliaries at the heart of the battle line, as well as in their more traditional, Republican-period locations on the flanks, has inspired more discussion as to their precise role in battle. The best-informed discussion follows due reflection on the way ancient commanders understood their battlefields. Onasander, who wrote on generalship in the 1st century AD, notes the central importance of the topography in any battle.[9] And, as Gilliver has astutely remarked, it is evident that in the four major battles of the early Principate where auxiliary forces were the first into action while the legions stood in reserve, the terrain was unfavourable to the Romans.[10] This leads her to suggest that in such circumstances the *auxilia*, able to fight as 'light or more mobile troops', were preferred.[11]

Gilliver's careful qualification of the capacities of auxiliary soldiers as 'light or more mobile troops' is important, as scholars have repeatedly tied themselves in knots over the classification of auxiliary infantry as 'light' in opposition to legionary infantry as 'heavy'. Often, this appears to result from confusion as to the significance of the terms themselves, both of which, while applicable to some ancient armies, are obviously modern. Light infantry fight in open order and are frequently tasked with skirmishing duties; heavy infantry fight in close order, as a body standing in close proximity to one another in the battle line. The term does not necessarily relate to the weight of a soldier's equipment. Indeed, if it did, all regular auxiliary infantry would appear 'heavy' in comparison with their western

---

[6] Tacitus *Ann.* 2.16 and 4.73; Gilliver (1996: 55–6).

[7] Rainbird (1969: 12). Rainbird is by no means the first scholar to question whether the saving of citizen blood was really the intention. Cheesman (1914: 104), e.g. refers to Tacitus' claim as a 'not very creditable excuse'. In this he is followed by Furneaux and Anderson (1922: 134) in their commentary on *De Vita Agricolae* and by Parker (1928: 258), who sees the explanation as an invention by the historian.

[8] For reappraisal of Agricola's governorship, see Hanson (1991) and Birley (2005: 71–95).

[9] Onasander 15 and 31; Vegetius 3.9.

[10] Gilliver (1996: 58–9) cites Idistaviso (*Ann.* 2.16–18), L. Apronius' ford battle against the Frisii (*Ann.* 4.73), the engagement between Cerialis and Civilis near Vetera (*Hist.* 5.14ff.), and Mons Graupius (*Agric.* 29–37).

[11] Gilliver (1996: 59).

adversaries. A further complication lies in the limits of our understanding of *auxilia* over time and place, and the extent to which units specialized in particular fighting methods. I will return to this point in the next section, but first it is necessary to understand why such widely differing explanations of auxiliary fighting techniques are offered in ancient and modern accounts. The view that auxiliary infantry were light infantry[12] is widespread, and stems in part from trends in the Republican period that saw auxiliaries replacing the old citizen skirmishers or *velites*.[13] It is also not without substance in the literature of the Principate, for example, in Tacitus' account of the battle of Placentia (AD 69), in which the close-order formations of the legions are contrasted with the more open lines of the *auxilia: densum legionum agmen, sparsa auxiliorum*.[14] Von Domaszewski, writing over a century ago and taking the long view, argued that auxiliary foot soldiers progressed from light into heavy infantry,[15] but overall, as we have seen, the literary evidence suggests that auxiliaries were capable of both open and close-order fighting throughout the Principate.[16] By the AD 60s, for example, one contemporary observer, Josephus, is just as happy using the term 'hoplites' of auxiliaries as of legionaries.[17] Furthermore, the decisions of commanders indicate that they were well aware of the capabilities of the auxiliaries at their disposal. The study of the *auxilia* in battle has not been helped by the tendency to see each surviving account of the army in action as a separate step in a long tradition of tactical development. Neither the line of battle at Mons Graupius nor the paper dispositions preserved in Arrian's *Acies contra Alanos* discussed below were intended as the ultimate 'one size fits all' formations of their day.

A further feature of the literary evidence under the Principate is that it dwells less on the fighting role of the cavalry than on infantry. This may owe much to the fact that mounted troops stood outside the Roman tradition of combat and were seen as of less interest.[18] Aside from the small cavalry contingent attached to each legion, the vast majority of the Empire's cavalry came from the *auxilia*. It may also be that one of the most crucial moments in battle, the moment when one side or another broke and cavalry could rule the battlefield, was of less interest to ancient writers, as by this stage great vision and dynamic leadership were no longer held to apply. Yet it was precisely at this time that the deft application of cavalry could have the greatest impact, transforming what might ultimately be an indecisive engagement into a bloody rout. An interesting exception to this general trend of disinterest in the ancient sources is Arrian's *Acies contra Alanos*, but here, perhaps, it is the exception that proves the rule. Arrian's text was written from the perspective of a field commander anticipating a real battle; he could not afford to neglect a vital part of his own forces. Everything Arrian has to say about cavalry,

[12] e.g. Keppie (1984: 182) and Wells (1999: 135).   [13] Cheesman (1914: 10).
[14] Tacitus *Hist.* 2.22. See also *Ann.* 1.51; 2.52; 3.39; 4.73; Vegetius 2.2.
[15] von Domaszewski (1967: 59).
[16] Goldsworthy (1996: 20, 135) and Campbell (1997: 481) challenge the simple view of auxiliary as 'light infantry'.
[17] Saddington (1982: 100) for Josephus' use of the term.
[18] For a survey of Roman cavalry combat, see Goldsworthy (1996: 228–44). Aside from Arrian, our main sources for cavalry in combat under the Principate are Josephus (*Bell. Iud.* 3.12–21, 5.312–13) and Tacitus. Interestingly, some of the Tacitean references to Roman cavalry show them refusing to engage in combat (*Hist.* 2.14 and 4.33, though see also *Ann.* 6.35; *Hist.* 1.79, 3.16).

however, appears to apply to the *auxilia*. There is no indication here or elsewhere that legionary cavalry, so small in numbers, played any significant role in mounted operations against the enemy.[19]

If the literary evidence suggests some difference in combat role between the legions and the *alae* and *cohortes*, what does the evidence of equipment studies suggest? Here it is necessary to accept from the outset the limitations of the archaeological record. An artefact recovered without an inscription noting the owner's regiment or sub-unit may not simply be attributed to a particular troop type on the basis of its findspot. Despite years of research, it remains clear that our knowledge of the deployment of Roman soldiers is, and will always remain, hopelessly partial. Under no circumstances can we simply assume that an item of equipment found within a fort, fortress, or other setting should be associated with one particular unit type or another. Nevertheless, a careful comparison of finds with artefacts that do carry ownership graffiti, or with artefacts depicted in reliable depictions of soldiers from named troop types, may allow significant progress. Furthermore, the results may further illuminate ancient views on the fighting methods appropriate to different branches of Rome's armies.

In a thorough survey of evidence from the northwestern provinces, Maxfield concluded that in the campaigning years of the 1st century AD at least, it was impossible to distinguish legionary garrisons from auxiliary ones archaeologic-ally.[20] Her survey, which also took into account the study of fort buildings, laid special emphasis on the distribution of *lorica segmentata* fragments. Up until the time of her study, scholars had been strongly influenced by the apparent association of legionary troops with this type of plate armour, and of auxiliary troops with mail depicted on Trajan's Column (fig 3.3).[21] Maxfield notes that *lorica segmentata* appears in the archaeological record at so many sites that are not associated with legionaries, including at least one site in a province where no legionaries were stationed, that it becomes increasingly hard to sustain the view that they were the only ones to wear it. She may indeed be right, but there are two points to stress here. First, legionary detachments could turn up in many settings without leaving any epigraphic evidence for their presence. Second—and this is a point Maxfield makes herself—it remains the case that there are no known depictions of auxiliaries dressed in plate armour. But it is entirely feasible that the real distinction lay elsewhere. Bishop and Coulston note a clear demarcation in the sculptural record between soldiers with curved shields (*scuta*) and weighted javelins (*pila*) and those with flat, often oval shields, and spears (*hastae*).[22] They further suggest that the flat shield types derived from those introduced into Roman service by Celtic and Germanic auxiliaries.[23] Such distinctions are not

---

[19] Tacitus does, however, describe the deployment of legionary cavalry in Apronius' battle with the Frisii in AD 23 (*Ann.* 4.73). In this instance they were sent in only after German auxiliary cavalry and infantry.

[20] Maxfield (1986a).

[21] The plate/mail armour distinction is nowhere in evidence on the Adamklissi metopes.

[22] The crucial point here is the combination of shield and javelin/spear. As Busch (2009) notes, there is clear evidence that legionaries used curved rectangular shields, but they used other shield types in the 2nd century too; the shape of the shield, she argues, was determined by the type of combat anticipated, not the unit type involved.

[23] Bishop and Coulston (1993: 195).

Fig. 17.1. First-century marks of distinction: an auxiliary-type figure with a *clipeus* and throwing spears (*hastae*) from a column base found in Mainz (Germany). Landesmuseum Mainz.

confined to the stylized monuments of Rome, but are also found in provincial art in German and Danubian settings. Interestingly, it is also preserved in the literary evidence. Tacitus, describing a battle between the British war leader Caratacus and the invading Romans (AD 51), contrasts the *gladii* and *pila* of the legionaries with the *spathae* and *hastae* of the auxiliaries.[24] Before turning to the issue of sword types, and the limitations of the terms *gladius* and *spatha*, we should test the other associations argued here against the surviving archaeological evidence.

Study of inscribed pieces of Roman military equipment is illuminating (see Figs 17.1–17.4). Though a number of pieces clearly had several owners, there is no known instance where an item of equipment can be shown to have been transferred from a legionary owner to an auxiliary owner, or vice versa. This suggests that auxiliaries were not dressed in legionary 'cast-offs', as has been proposed, though it may also just indicate that units tend to recycle their equipment within

---

[24] Tacitus *Ann.* 12.35. In *Hist.* 1.38 Tacitus specifically notes that there were helmets and shields intended for auxiliaries.

Fig. 17.2. First-century column base, almost certainly from the same building as Fig. 17.1, shows infantrymen with curved rectangular shields, a short sword, and a weighted *pilum*. Landesmuseum Mainz.

Fig. 17.3. Second-century marks of distinction: one of two types of armoured Roman infantry depicted on the Adamklissi metopes (Romania). These soldiers carry oval shields and are depicted in similar armour to their cavalry counterparts.

Fig. 17.4. The other type of armoured infantry is depicted on the Adamklissi metopes is distinguished by the use of curved *scuta* and weighted *pila*.

their own ranks. The only piece of a curved shield to carry an inscription, a richly decorated boss recovered from the river Tyne, clearly did belong to a legionary. Indeed, we know the name of the unit in which its owner served, *Legio VIII Augusta*. Furthermore, a fragment of a similar piece, recovered at Vindonissa, carried the same decoration and regimental symbol and most probably belonged to a soldier in the same legion.[25]

Here we must consider two other fragments of evidence that might at first appear to contradict Bishop and Coulston's conclusions. The first is a shield cover discovered near the Roman fort of Roomburgh in Holland.[26] The cover, which belonged to a rectangular, probably curved, shield, clearly carries the title of *cohors XV Voluntariorum* and the image of a capricorn (see Fig. 17.5). The second is the existence of an auxiliary unit that actually bore the rather elaborate title *cohors II Hispanorum Cyrenaica scutata equitata*. The title strongly suggests that this regiment was actually armed with the *scutum*.

[25] Both cited by Bishop and Coulston (1993: 208). For the Tyne find, see Allason-Jones and Miket (1984: 3.724). For the Vindonissa shield, see Simonett (1935).

[26] van Driel-Murray (1999).

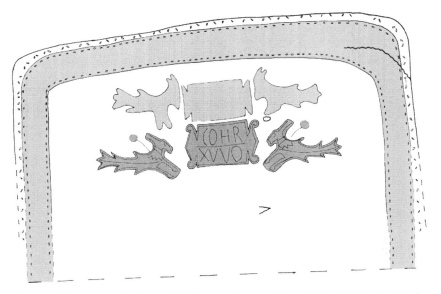

Fig. 17.5. Fragments of a leather shield cover discovered by the Dutch State Service for Archaeology (ROB) near Roomburgh, Holland.

Neither the shield cover nor the Spanish regimental title actually poses a problem for the view that a curved shield and *pilum*/flat shield and *hasta* distinction existed. In the first instance, it may well be significant that the cover belonged to a soldier of one of the *cohortes Voluntariorum*. Though these units subsequently recruited non-citizens into their ranks, their particular origins, drafted from freedmen in the reign of Augustus, entitled them to special entitlements on a par with the legions. It is entirely possible, as van Driel-Murray argues in her study of the cover, that these auxiliaries deliberately carried legionary-style shields to advertise their particular status.[27] Nevertheless, it is worth noting that at their inception they were not treated entirely as other citizen soldiers. Augustus wished to underscore the difference between free-born and freedmen soldiers, and according to Suetonius he did this by keeping freedmen in their own units, not allowing them to mix with soldiers of free birth, and by *arming them differently*—though precisely how this was done remains a mystery and need not necessarily have required a distinction in shield types.[28] In the case of *cohors II Hispanorum scutata*, the very rarity of its title rather implies that it was a distinction for auxiliary units to carry the *scutum*, not the norm. It appears therefore that, at least until the early 2nd century AD, there was a general distinction between the battlefield appearance of citizen and non-citizen units, and that the shield type played an important role in making that distinction apparent.

How is such a view reconcilable with the emphasis on individual choice argued above? That there was a certain amount of control over the shields soldiers used is suggested by two pieces of evidence. First, as we have seen, shields were being

---

[27] Ibid. 52. [28] Suetonius *Aug.* 25.2.

produced at unit level.[29] This allows for a higher level of standardization within
the unit. Secondly there is clear evidence that unit formations were identifiable by
their shields.[30] This literary evidence does, admittedly, focus on decoration, but
the range of decorative schemes that were feasible was determined by the size and
shape of the shield. Soldiers may have enjoyed the freedom to invest in some items
of equipment and to decorate others to their own taste, but there were limits. In
addition to the attractiveness of a collective battlefield identity for the soldiers of
particular units, there is the commander's need for an easy way to identify
members of different contingents.

Did the distinction apparent in shield type manifest itself in the swords that the
soldiers carried, as Tacitus suggests in his lively description of the battle with
Caratacus? Did it mean that legionary and auxiliary soldiers fought in a different
way at close quarters? It is relatively difficult to offer a simple answer to the first
question, but we may note that it is easier to use a long slashing sword with a
lighter flat shield than with a heavier curved one.[31] Scholars normally argue that
up until the 3rd century the legionary was generally armed with a sword called a
gladius, while the cavalry used the *spatha* from the late 1st century BC onwards.
Practice within the auxiliary infantry is seen as more varied.[32] The problem is that
both of these ancient terms were more flexibly applied in Roman times than they
are today; we tend to speak of the *gladius* as a short sword and the *spatha* as a long
sword—a convenient division I shall retain—but the truth is that both terms were
sometimes used for swords of all lengths.[33] Yet there can be no denying that two
different styles of sword fighting were in use, and that these required blades of
different length. The shorter sword and large shield, accompanied by particular
legionary helmet types, suggest a crouched fighting posture designed to allow the
combatant to stab into the belly of his opponent.[34] To drive beneath the flailing
sword of his enemy and execute this intimate blow required the soldier to get even
closer in close-quarter combat than did most warriors of the time. In practice, of
course, other moves might prevail; the *gladius* could be used to chop and slash.[35]
Against the warriors of the Celtic west or the armies of the Greek east, the
discipline of short-sword combat came to appear a distinctively Roman way of
fighting.[36] The *pilum*, 'a short-range, armour-piercing, shock weapon',[37]comple-
mented this style of close-quarter combat. The *spatha*, by contrast, could not be
used in the same way as the *gladius*—it had to be used to parry or slash, while the
hasta could either be thrown in a skirmish or retained for stabbing at the enemy
from behind the shield. The combination of use of slashing sword and spear

[29] See p. 247.
[30] Vegetius 2.18; Dio 64.14.21; MacMullen (1984: 446).
[31] James (2011: 187).
[32] Webster (1986: 151 fn. 4).
[33] For *gladius*, see Bishop and Coulston (1993: 69–71). The term is used for a cavalry sword in *Tab. Luguval.* 16.viii; Tomlin (1999: 132–3). For *spatha*, see James (2011: 29–30).
[34] Connolly (1991).
[35] Even the earliest accounts of the Roman use of the *gladius Hispaniensis* make it clear that the weapon could be used to chop. See Polybius (3.114), writing of the situation in the 2nd century BC.
[36] Coulston (1998: 169). Vegetius 1.12 suggests that the Romans scorned cutters and applauded stabbers.
[37] Bishop and Coulston (1993: 208).

involved a slightly, but crucially, extended distance from the enemy—a form of fighting much more familiar to Rome's enemies. In this respect it may have served to distinguish the fighting techniques of auxiliaries from legionaries during the early Principate. Ultimate acceptance of the *spatha* as the standard weapon of the Roman soldier, legionary and auxiliary, came in the 3rd century AD. Hard to explain as a result of any sudden technological development, this change must surely be understood as a cultural one.[38] With it, all traces of the legionary's distinctive fighting technique disappeared. It was thus in part the fighting style of the auxiliary that defined the new Roman fighting man of the later Roman Empire.

Before concluding, one further source on the distinction between auxiliary and legionary appearance should be noted. In Apuleius' *Metamorphoses* a soldier attempts to confiscate an ass. The description of the soldier, 'whose dress and countenance declare him to be a legionary', suggests that even without his armour a legionary might be distinguishable from other members of the provincial army.[39] It is to be regretted that the author does not elaborate at this point. At the risk of reading too much into what is essentially a tale of fantasy and adventure, it is worth asking what it was about the soldier's dress and demeanour that actually made his legionary identity so clear. At this stage in the tale, only the legionary's sword and staff have been mentioned, neither of which need be diagnostic of legionary troops. Only later, in an entirely new scene where the soldier loads up Aristomenes with equipment not referred to in the first encounter, are the man's helmet, shield, and lance described. Interestingly, these are called *galea*, *scutum*, and *lancea*, all terms paralleled in legionary contexts elsewhere.[40]

Having reviewed the evidence, we may now return to the stock motifs of Tacitean verse and metropolitan propaganda. Taking Trajan's Column, the source of so much confusion about the Roman army, we may note first that there is a determined attempt to distinguish the men with curved shields, the legionaries and praetorians, from those with flat oval shields, the regular *auxilia*. This almost certainly involves considerable artistic licence, but it appears in so many ways (some of them less immediately obvious than others) that it assuredly reflects what was believed to be an important distinction. It is not just that the two troop types are depicted with different armour; other aspects of their dress are also distinguished. The first type always have bare legs, the second always wear *bracae* or breeches. A moral message may be intended here: some of the guardians of Roman norms held the wearing of trousers to be a barbaric habit.[41] In public art, auxiliaries could wear such things, but legionaries could not. The moral message may be conveyed in other scenes too. Auxiliary figures, never legionary ones, are associated with the taking of heads. They appear this way on four scenes on the column, on three scenes from the Great Trajanic Frieze and on one of the

---

[38] Bishop and Coulston (1993: 203) suggest: 'Perhaps the cultural background of western Celtic peoples recruited into the army played an important part in the change over to infantry *spathae*.' See also Elton (1994: 494).

[39] Apuleius *Metamorphoses* 9.39.   [40] Ibid. 10.1.

[41] For *bracae* as barbarian, see Polybius 2.28.7 and Diodorus 5.30.1. Webster (1988: 121 fn. 3) notes that all of the figures with oval shields and none of those wearing *lorica segmentata* appear in *bracae* on the Column.

Adamklissi metopes.[42] This is clearly not coincidental, and most probably reflects a perception that 'barbarian' behaviour even existed within Rome's own armies, though it was confined to the *auxilia*.[43]

Finally, the tasks we see these types of figure perform away from the battlefield give a further clue. The legionary figures build, the auxiliary figures guard—the impression created, with some artistic licence, is that the auxiliary troops were not capable of undertaking the more sophisticated tasks that citizen troops routinely accomplished.[44] In fact we have clear evidence from the reign of Hadrian that auxiliaries did construct temporary and stone-walled camps such as those shown in these scenes, but a real difference probably existed between the ability of different types of unit to undertake more complex engineering tasks.[45] For the Roman viewer, willing to be convinced of Tacitus' claim that wise commanders conserved Roman blood, there was plenty of apparent evidence in the scenes of the Column. These too sought to convey the auxiliary as something of a second-class soldier, less civilized and talented than his legionary counterpart. The prejudice reflects a real division between the troops—one still a feature of military life over a century after the regular *auxilia* came into being.

As the evidence shows, however, the particulars of the auxiliary/legionary division were complex. There was a difference in appearance and there were differences in role. Purists and classical authors might not wish to admit it, but on the battlefield, regular auxiliary units were essentially more adaptable and not necessarily less capable, than their legionary counterparts. Even Tacitus is forced to admit that auxiliary soldiers were able to confront and defeat legionaries.[46] This adaptability appears to have remained the case until the late 2nd/early 3rd century, when cultural change, manifested in the extension of citizenship to free-born subjects within the Empire, made the legal/political underpinnings of the bipartite system redundant. Distinctions in dress, equipment, and use of troops based on this system do not survive in our evidence after this time.

The distinguishing dress of the legionary had largely disappeared by the mid-3rd century. While allowing for the fact that military equipment continued to evolve, we may note that the trajectories that marked later developments owed more to the *auxilia* and the armies Rome faced on her frontiers than to the traditions of the legions. Long swords are now the norm, as (it appears) are the flat oval shields that were once the hallmark of the *auxilia*.[47] The triumph of auxiliary dress is ultimately further reinforced as cavalrymen become the unchallenged new high-status troop type in the Empire, displacing the legionary soldier from his privileged place at the centre of the battle line and tactical thinking.

---

[42] Trajan's Column, scenes 57–8, 60, 183–4, and 302–3, and Adamklissi metope 7. For the Trajanic Frieze, see Leander Touati (1987: nos 67, 70, and 71).

[43] For head-taking and the Roman army, see Goldsworthy (1996: 271–6).

[44] Bishop and Coulston (1993: 209) avoid basing their understanding of the troop type divisions on Trajan's Column, but note that the Column does seek to convey a legionary/auxiliary distinction, and note this important difference.

[45] PP. 76, 149, and 171.   [46] See *Agric.* 36 and *Hist.* 4.20.

[47] Oval shields entirely replace *scuta* in representations of soldiers on public monuments, though we should note the existence of one *scutum* from a 3rd-century context at Dura. For the most recent commentary and literature on this find, see James (2004: 182–3).

Distinctions based on legal status are one aspect of Roman military thinking, but writers both ancient and modern emphasize the significance of other forms of difference within Rome's armies. Ethnic origin, many argue, played an important role in defining the battle tactics and armament of many regular auxiliary units. The final chapter in this section examines this claim, and asks how far this alleged ethnic diversity was actually a genuine reflection of cultural variety in the Empire.

18

Disarming Ethnicity?

'Ethnic' Fighting Traditions in the *Alae* and *Cohortes*

As argued at the beginning of this section, Arrian's colourful account of the *Hippika Gymnasia* celebrates the diversity of traditions that enriched Rome's armies. Elsewhere in the *Ars Tactica* he develops this important theme, making it clear that it was as much a part of the battlefield as the parade ground. Speaking of the range of fighting methods and weapons used by Roman cavalry, he argues that different units of Roman soldiers can be likened variously to the Alani, the Sauromatae, the Armenians, and the Parthians.[1] Continuing in the same vein, Arrian proceeds to link the battlefield practices of diverse auxiliary contingents to their origins. Men should, he argues, use the battle cries native to their 'race'. Thus the Celtic cavalry should use Celtic cries, the Getae, Getic shouts, and the Rhaetians, the war cries of Rhaetia.[2]

Given the emphasis classical ethnography places on the link between martial bearing and ethnic identity, this approach is hardly surprising. Time and again it appears in Roman literature. Tacitus, for example, affords distinctive styles of arms and armour particular significance, regarding it as as much a defining characteristic as language, customs, and religion.[3] Later writers do much the same.[4] Furthermore, the link manifested itself in the most popular of forms. Visitors to gladiatorial games across the Empire knew what a Samnite or a Thracian should look like; they had seen them fight in the arena many a time. Their story demonstrates how stereotypes of ethnic types could survive unchanged in the Roman mind for centuries as 'enduring fictions'.[5] For example, the origins of the Samnite as a stock figure lie in the late 4th century BC, yet Samnites were still making appearances in the arena well into the 3rd

---

[1] Arrian *Tactica* 40.

[2] Ibid. 44.1.

[3] See *Germania* 10 for the role of *patria arma* as an ethnic marker.

[4] The use of weapons and fighting methods as ethnic markers appears in Ammianus Marcellinus (*Res gestae* 31.2.17), Augustine (*De civitate Dei* 14.1), and Isidore of Seville (*Etymologiae* 9.2. 97). For a useful discussion of ethnography in antiquity that includes the role of weapons, see Pohl (1998).

[5] A term used by Woolf (2011) in his compelling dissection of ethnography in the Roman west. Drawing on the image of Gauls in Roman society, Woolf (p. 114) argues, 'The utility of these myths set limits on their revisability'; the same appears true of the groups discussed above.

century AD.[6] Surviving evidence from across the Empire leaves little doubt that there were well-established norms for the appearance of these figures. The audience knew what to expect of them.

Given this tendency to stress the link between ethnicity and armament, it is not surprising that scholars have often sought to identify it amongst the *alae* and *cohortes*. Rome delighted in her mastery of so many peoples—a point confidently emphasized through the very titles of her regiments. Titles such as Briton, Dacian, Parthian, and indeed Thracian carried myriad connotations to the educated Roman. Given the distinctions made between citizen and non-citizen units, might units have preserved distinct arms and fighting tactics recalling their own very distinct origins?

Certainly regiments of the Roman *auxilia* are often described in similar terms in modern scholarship. Webster, for example, argued that 'probably every unit had its own distinctive features, which once established, were jealously guarded. They must have added that gaiety, colour and eccentricity which today seems the prerogative of some of our older regiments.'[7] Wells has recently argued, 'During the first two centuries AD, auxiliary troops frequently used the traditional weapons of their group, and often their traditional combat tactics as well, which could be advantageous to Rome in fighting other indigenous peoples.'[8] Yet while there is clear evidence that this did happen amongst short-lived irregular units, in the *alae* and *cohortes* it occurred in a much more restricted sense and for a limited period.

To appreciate this it is necessary to recognize how significantly individual units could change over time. It is also necessary to factor in the type of regiment and the period of time under discussion. Precisely what types of dress and behaviour are being considered?[9] In terms of military equipment, it is one thing to acknowledge the clear difference between units with specialist weapons, as Arrian is seeking to do with his simple ethnic analogies, and another to claim a situation where each regiment preserved, for example, forms of dress particular to their origins. The use of ethnic battle cries celebrated by Arrian must be seen as just that—the use of a call, not as the perpetuation of more general distinction. And indeed it is firmly linked in the text to something that Hadrian had introduced, an invented tradition, not the survival of ancient practice. The artificiality of the association is only reinforced by the racial terminology Arrian uses. To speak of Celts, Getae, and Raetians is to employ labels imposed by Roman writers upon peoples for whom they had no meaning. It is also likely that some of the formations to which Arrian refers were irregular units, not *alae* or *cohortes*.[10]

---

[6] For the role of Samnium in Rome's view of itself, see Salmon (1967: ix). For Samnite armies of the late 4th and early 3rd centuries BC and Roman perceptions, see Livy 9.40 and 10.38; Dench (1995: 100); Rouveret (1986: 91). Some features, such as the wearing of a single greave, appear to be preserved in the gladiator's appearance (Junkelmann 2000: 103–9).

[7] Webster (1998: 155).   [8] Wells (1999: 135).

[9] These are insufficiently dissected in many discussions of the Roman army. Richmond's (1982: 18–19) classic commentary on *Trajan's Army on Trajan's Column* is a case in point. Comments on the soldiers of the regular *alae* and *cohortes* are mixed in with comments concerning a range of other irregular and allied troops. Of course, it is important to acknowledge here that the Romans themselves were quite capable of blurring barriers between troop types in certain contexts.

[10] Southern (1989: 110).

In fact, the evidence of small finds, funerary reliefs, and monumental art suggests that a far higher level of standardization came to characterize the *alae* and *cohortes* than it did the *numeri* or *nationes*. The latter formations, about which we still know all too little, varied sufficiently to suggest that they may also have exhibited a wide range of dress codes and fighting traditions.[11] Some of these may, perhaps, have perpetuated practices inherited from the communities amongst whom they were formed. The unit of lightermen from the Tigris, *numerus barcariorum Tigrisiensium*, for example, most probably continued to perform their original role while stationed at South Shields. The stylized Moors and bare-chested, club-wielding infantry on Trajan's Column, while reflecting the artistic licence extended to the sculptors, nonetheless probably reflect the preservation of traditional styles of combat amongst irregulars too. Such individuals were, after all, often enrolled for shorter periods of service, but the evidence for the men of the *alae* and *cohortes* suggests a different picture overall. Taken as a whole, the artefact evidence indicates that notions of ethnicity did not play a significant role in determining the equipment soldiers carried. This is also the overall impression that comes from funerary reliefs and from public art. Funerary monuments do, however, offer some important qualifying information. When complete with both representation and inscription, they also enable us to link the origin of a soldier's unit with the way he dresses. One of the most important points that they underscore is that, with a few notable exceptions, while the soldiers generally dress similarly to one another, there is no simple link between the way they dress and the place their regiment was originally raised.[12]

This chapter consists of three case studies, each of which examines claims that *alae* and *cohortes* of particular origins perpetuated distinctive dress. It argues that some such claims are misguided, while many others relate to examples which were either rare or are essentially Roman constructions. While the case of the Batavi indicates the deliberate perpetuation of distinctive fighting traditions, this represents an exceptional case which was bound up with the particular ethnogenesis of a new provincial community.[13] Overwhelmingly, the equipment and dress of the *alae* and *cohortes* should be seen as part of a 'disarming' of ethnic labels. Whatever the literary elite might have fantasized, by the 2nd century AD the arms and armour of *equites* and *cohortales* showed a high degree of similarity. In reappraising established claims to the contrary, I hope this chapter will also go some way to disarming the power of the word 'ethnicity' in discussions of provincial society, where it has for too long been inappropriately used as a blunt instrument.[14]

---

[11] In those cases where forts believed to have been occupied by *numeri* have been excavated, however, the weaponry discovered is virtually indistinguishable from that found at contemporary forts occupied by *alae* and *cohortes*. Oldenstein's (1976) study of military equipment from 2nd- and 3rd-century fort sites on the Upper German and Raetian frontier shows no distinction between the armament of *numeri* and those of auxiliary units.

[12] Simon James (pers. comm.) has made the interesting suggestion that because many middle imperial funerary depictions show soldiers in 'camp dress' rather than in battle order, some of the more exotic and distinctive elements of unit dress may be lost. This is possibly true, but it is worth recalling that in many armies it is precisely in camp dress that unit signifiers are most conspicuously deployed.

[13] Roymans (2004) on Batavian ethnogenesis.   [14] P. 7.

THE PARTHIANS

Clad in baggy riding trousers and deftly firing his bow from horseback, to Roman eyes Maris son of Casitus would have appeared the archetypal Parthian horseman.[15] But this soldier served a long way from the Empire's eastern frontiers. He is commemorated on an early tombstone, possibly Tiberian in date, from Mainz in Germany (see Fig. 18.1).[16] For Maris is an *eques* in *ala Parthorum et Araborum*. In his monument we see clear testimony to the wearing of traditional clothing in Roman service.

Fig. 18.1. Stele of Maris, *eques* in the *ala Parthorum et Araborum* (*AE* 1959, 188). Early 1st century AD. Landesmuseum Mainz.

---

[15] *AE* 1959, 188.   [16] Holder (1980: 287).

Yet less than two centuries later, Rufinus, a soldier in the *ala Parthorum* stationed in North Africa, represented a different picture.[17] His relief is, to be sure, badly weathered. Even fresh, it probably lacked the fine detail and flair of the Mainz monument. Nevertheless, the change is unmistakable. Rufinus has none of the attributes of his predecessor: nothing is to be seen of the distinctive baggy pants; bow and arrow have been replaced by spear and shield. It is possible that the difference may be explained by a different role for the 2nd/3rd-century regiment. But whichever way the monuments are understood, it is evident that traditional forms had no particularly tenacious hold in regimental communities.

How can this dramatic change be explained? Clues to the transformation may be found already within the Maris relief. The relief is not merely of early date, but most probably represents a soldier from the first generation of recruits to the regiment. Not only was this *ala* at the beginning of its history, before the process of standardization began to take effect, it also still contained within its ranks men who actually came from the regiment's places of origin.[18] The unit's title reflected its composition. What the story of Maris and Rufinus suggests is that traditions of dress simply could not survive generations of non-Parthians, decades of standardization, and repeated redeployment around the Roman world.[19]

THE DACIANS

At first sight an altogether more compelling case for the long-term retention of ethnic tradition in Roman service comes to us from Birdoswald in Cumbria.[20] From the second quarter of the 2nd century AD, this was the regimental station of *cohors I Aelia Dacorum*, until the discovery of the Vindolanda tablets the most richly attested auxiliary regiment in Britain. Two 3rd-century dedication stones bearing the long, curved Dacian sword (*falx*) are known from the site (see Fig. 18.2).[21] These swords closely resemble those depicted on the Adamklissi frieze, where they are shown being brandished two-handed with the point facing down. This is different from way the *sica* of the *Thraex* is brandished in depictions of gladiatorial combat and suggests a different, if once related, fighting tradition.[22] Some scholars have argued that the presence of the *falx* on the Dacian cohort's inscriptions indicates that the regiment retained this fearsome weapon, but I believe that the symbol conveys a different message.[23]

---

[17] *AE* 1976, 746.

[18] Petersen (1966) identifies the names on the monument as Persian (Tigranus and Variagnis) and Semitic (Casitus, Maris, and Masicates).

[19] Spaul (1994: 176–7) believes that this unit was stationed in Dalmatia, Germany, and Mauretania Caesariensis in North Africa at various times. See, however, the arguments of Kennedy (1985).

[20] For the argument that the army reinvented Dacian identity in a manner similar to the construction of Batavian identity, see Oltean (2009); I am not wholly in agreement with her thesis, however.

[21] *RIB* 1909 (AD 205–8); *RIB* 1914 (AD 219).

[22] The terms *falx* and *sica* are both used of the weapons of the *Thraex*. For convenience, I will retain the term *falx* for the long two-handed model.

[23] Richmond (1982: 20). Coulston (1981) and Wilmott (2001) evaluate the depiction with care, neither embracing the view that the unit carried this weapon nor wishing to dismiss it. I believe that a more emphatic verdict may be offered.

Fig. 18.2. Dedication slab *c.* AD 219 from Birdoswald recording work by *cohors I Aelia Dacorum* (*RIB* 1914). The inscription is flanked by a *falx* on the right and a palm-branch on the left. Great North Museum, Newcastle upon Tyne.

Advocates of continuity rightly recall the extraordinary psychological impact this curved sword had upon the Roman forces that confronted the Dacians. Certainly it was not soon forgotten. *Legio IIII Flavia Felix* left an extraordinary inscription at Gradishtea Muncelului in Transylvania, a site widely identified with King Decebalus' capital, Sarmizegetusa Regia. Using the images of the weapons of its defeated enemies, the legion carved the F's as if they were *falxes*, the I's as straight swords.[24] The curved sword even featured on what appear to be commemorative decorations in the homes of the provincial aristocracy, if this is the correct interpretation of an impressive mini-*tropaeum* found at the site of a so-called *villa rustica* at Gârla Mare in the territory of Roman Dacia.[25] And of course there are the famous monuments at Adamklissi and Rome, both of which depict warriors with *falx* swords, though the figures at Adamklissi use the sword with both hands while those on Trajan's Column brandish it with one. Yet the fact that the weapon left such an impression on the Romans, both physically and symbolically, does not mean that they automatically sought to adopt it. It is not appropriate to envisage the Dacian *falx* continuing in foreign service in the manner of the Gurkha's kukhri today.

Certainly no *falx* swords, nor indeed anything vaguely resembling them, emerged from excavations at Birdoswald.[26] Furthermore, no curved Dacian swords are attested from any Roman forts outside Romania. The closest parallel is the Oberaden *sica*, but this pre-dates the Birdoswald reliefs by more than 200 years.[27] Absence of Dacian swords from auxiliary forts is not, of itself, proof that they were not used by Roman troops. Absence of evidence does not automatically constitute evidence of absence. It is, however, suggestive.

---

[24] Glodariu and Iaroslavschi (1979: 137). Doru Bogdan, pers. comm.

[25] Pop (2000: 333–5).

[26] Tony Wilmott, pers. comm. For the report on small finds from the site, see Summerfeld (1997).

[27] von Schnurbein (1979: 117–34).

One other find, once advanced as evidence for the swords used by Dacian auxiliaries in regular Roman service must now be reconsidered. This piece which comes from neither Britain nor Germany but from Slovenia has been identified as a sword pommel. It carries an inscription carved by or at the behest of an *optio* in another Dacian *cohort*, cohors II Aurelia Dacorum and was discovered in the second Mithraeum at Poetovio (modern Ptuj).[28] The piece has, however, been reappraised and it is now evident that it is not a pommel, but rather a tessera.[29]

And so we must return to the evidence of Roman public art. As noted above Dacians are depicted fighting with one-handed swords on Trajan's Column. Yet anyone who has had the privilege of examining these weapons will quickly realise that they are just too small for combat against heavily armoured opponents. They exist certainly, and may have become familiar in Rome and the provinces as readily portable momentoes following the ravaging of Dacian properties after the Conquest. They must, however, have been used for other tasks of ritual significance, including perhaps the 'noble suicides' depicted on Trajan's Column, not combat.

The Dacian swords of Trajan's Column are themselves symbols, not technically correct representations, and the Column's artists most probably carved them that way because they had no exposure to artistic compositions showing men fighting with two-handed swords. All the fighting stances on the Column fall into a handful of set stances, all drawn from a classical repertoire, a repertoire entirely alien to the apparently graceless barbarian combat of Adamklissi.[30]

In fact it was the symbolism of the *falx* that had the most lasting impact on Roman perceptions. To the Roman viewer, a Dacian was identifiable by his curved sword. The weapon was an integral element in the Roman elite's understanding of whatever constituted Dacian ethnicity. Reality was not quite so simple. Archaeology demonstrates clearly enough that the Dacians used other weapons, including a range of straight swords.[31] Nevertheless, the extraordinary celebrations that accompanied the conquest of Dacia almost certainly contrived to promote the same associations as those found on Trajan's Column. No doubt part of the vicious gladiatorial spectacle in which Dacian prisoners of war were forced to participate involved the use of this exotic novelty.[32] Word of Trajan's Danubian victories spread far and wide; it even manifested itself in the production of a commemorative Samian pot.[33] In such circumstances, it is hardly surprising that a curved sword often accompanied the personification of Dacia.[34] Indeed, from the

---

[28] The inscription reads IVSTVS OPTIO COHORTIS II AVR(eliae) DACORVM (*CIL* 3.15184, 16). This is the only known reference to the unit. For comment on the inscription and a brief history of the find's interpretation, see MacMullen (1960, 35, no. 34).

[29] I originally found MacMullen's (1960, 35, no. 34) discussion compelling. Further consideration of the piece with Dr Blanka Misic, to whom I am indebted, has led me to abandon this view. I would like to extend my thanks to Dr Misic and to colleagues at the Pokrajinski Muzej Ptuj for their advice and assistance in resolving this point.

[30] Alexandru Diaconescu, pers. comm.

[31] Glodariu and Iaroslavschi (1979) identify three types of straight sword in use by the Dacians.

[32] For what we actually know of the spectacle, see Dio 48.15.

[33] Déchelette (1904: fig. 126).

[34] For the Roman iconography of Dacia, see Petolescu (1986: 310–12).

reign of Trajan onwards, this association is a staple of Roman coinage. It appears on Trajanic *aurei*, *denarii*, and *dupondii*, but it also appears frequently on later issues, continuing to be a popular device right up to the mid-3rd century AD.[35]

So, I would argue that the dedication stones at Birdoswald do not attest an exotic survival or the perpetuation of an ancient tradition, but rather that they represent a Roman notion of what was Dacian. It was a view partly grounded in reality, but it was essentially a coopted Roman device, not a Dacian one. In this way, ethnicity was disarmed. The weapon that once haunted Roman soldiers was reduced to a symbol, albeit a potent one. The Dacian hands which might once have brandished the *falx* now carried swords indistinguishable from those carried by other soldiers of Rome.

THE SYRIAN ARCHERS

To treat all the archers of Syria as if they were part of a single homogeneous group would be to approach the sources in a hopelessly uncritical manner. The Ituraei of the Lebanon and Anti-Lebanon ranges came, for example, from a different society from the subjects of the Emesene dynasty. Yet the frequency with which scholarly commentators have talked nebulously of Syrian, eastern, or 'Oriental' archers means that it is necessary to examine the claims for distinctive dress amongst these units altogether in one place.

That archers continued to dress differently from other units until well into the 2nd century is suggested by representations on tombstones and imperial propaganda monuments. On the basis of surviving evidence, however, it is impossible to claim that distinct forms of dress *endured* on the basis of ethnically based regimental traditions; it is altogether more likely that they simply reflect dress considered appropriate for archery specialists.

Funerary reliefs commemorating troopers of the *ala I Ituraeorum sagittar-iorum*, such as one from Tipasa in Mauretania Caesariensis, do depict the men as unarmoured, shieldless, and either bareheaded or wearing a light cap.[36] The Tipasa relief most probably dates to the mid-2nd century AD, when the regiment came to North Africa as part of the expeditionary force of Porcius Vetustinus.[37] Though this image may reflect a prevailing fashion in tombstone art at this time, that of depicting soldiers without armour, it does parallel another example from the Danube erected to a man of the same regiment.[38] But even if these soldiers did fight unarmoured—and we must remember that not all reliefs that depicted the deceased in martial pose necessarily showed him in full battle dress—it is far from clear that this was understood to be an ethnic trait, rather than a style of dress that naturally suited mounted archers.

---

[35] Cristian Gazdac, pers. comm. The *falx* appears, e.g. on Trajanic issues (*BMC* III no. 145; *BMC* III nos 146–9, 175–84, 887–8 and p. 195) and continue into the 3rd century AD.

[36] For the Tipasa relief, see *AE* 1955, 131); Benseddik (1977: 34–5).

[37] *CIL* 16.99.

[38] Cheesman (1914: 128) notes that the relief suggests that horse archers 'carried no shield, and possibly no body armour, and wore a leather cap in place of a helmet'.

Fig. 18.3. Archers are amongst the most distinctive figure types on Trajan's Column, as this close-up from the spiral frieze shows, but how accurate were these representations?

Much of the debate about the dress of archers has not, in fact, revolved around the examination of funerary reliefs, but focuses rather on the eye-catching bow-carrying figures with flowing gowns and conical helmets on Trajan's Column (see Fig. 18.3). There are two reasons why such a focus is ill advised. First, contrary to what commentators frequently allege, we do not know whom these figures represent—they may not even be regular auxiliary troops.[39] Secondly, a glance at the Column's base is sufficient to show that these figures are dressed in a mixture of exotic weapons captured in the wars, rather than necessarily worn by Roman soldiers. Bishop and Coulston see the archer figures as a *mélange*, conjured out of barbarian *spolia*.[40] These representations must be understood as artistic creations, therefore, in the same way as the Column's Sarmatian cavalry, odd fish-like figures dressed in scale body stockings,[41] or the same monument's native irregulars, carved as if a conglomerate of Hercules clones. Nevertheless, so with the archers as with these figure types the artists were still trying to convey some meaningful distinction to the viewer, however stylized the manner.

Scholars have been quick to spot archaeological parallels for the distinctive helmets worn by the Column's archers. Robinson, for example, saw in a conical

---

[39] Claims for this association may be found in Richmond (1982: 19) and Rossi (1971: 102).
[40] Bishop and Coulston (1993: 22, 119).
[41] Coulston (1985: fn. 85; 1989: 34).

bronze helmet discovered near Dakovo, in Bosnia, a clear analogy, and on this basis suggested that the piece once belonged to an auxiliary foot archer of 'Levantine' origin.[42] He nevertheless draws attention to features of the piece that were not specifically eastern in origin, noting both its construction and the Roman gods that decorated it. Indeed, he saw the helmet as illustrative of a larger process, whereby objects inspired by indigenous forms 'swiftly became Romanized as these (auxiliary) units began to lose their identity'.[43] Similar pieces, dated stylistically to the late 2nd or early 3rd century AD, have subsequently been interpreted in a similar light. Conical helmets from both Intercisa in Hungary and Bumbeți in Romania are linked to the presence of archers.[44] In the Intercisa case, the association appears compelling, for the artefact was dredged up from the bed of the Danube almost adjacent to the fort itself—the famed station of *cohors I milliaria Hemesenorum sagittariorum equitata civium Romanorum*.[45] Consider-able caution is clearly vital when applying regimental affiliations to unstratified finds, but here at least we may confidently associate the piece with an auxiliary unit of some sort; the helmet carries two *T(urma)* inscriptions.[46]

Yet while such pieces, conical in form and lacking a neck-guard, hardly constitute a large group, their distribution does raise some problems for the thesis that they are particularly associated with eastern auxiliaries. All the known examples come from the Balkans—none is actually known from the East. On the basis of our current knowledge of the artefacts themselves, it would be more accurate to attribute a Danubian as opposed to a Syrian pedigree to them.[47] The situation is further complicated by the depiction of an archer discovered at Housesteads on Hadrian's Wall (see Fig. 18.4). This figure is commonly identified as a Hamian archer, not on the basis of any clear epigraphic evidence, but rather on the basis that he is an archer, and *cohors I Hamiorum sagittariorum* was stationed a few forts further down the line of the Wall. Unencumbered by the extraordinary flowing robes seen on the Column, his tunic and coat of mail appear to be of entirely conventional appearance. He does appear to wear a conical cap of sorts, but the relief is badly weathered, making interpretation of its form difficult. There is actually a strong possibility that this figure is not a soldier at all, but a hunting deity.

Altogether clearer is the fact that the Housesteads figure carries an axe and a composite bow, a weapon distinguished by its pronounced recurving profile. These bows, which do indeed originate in a Levantine or Asiatic tradition, are built up of horn and sinew formed around a thin wooden core. The grip and ends (or ears) of the bow are then reinforced with bone or antler laths. Such laths are

---

[42] Robinson (1975: 83, 85). The piece is now in the Archaeological Museum in Zagreb (Inv. No. 9229). The actual findspot is not known. The association with Dakovo is with the donors, local monks, who donated the piece to the Museum.

[43] Robinson (1975: 83, 85).

[44] Bumbeți: Petculescu and Gheorghe (1979). Intercisa: Szabó (1986).

[45] Szabó (1986: 421).

[46] Of interest to students of nomenclature will be the fact that none of these names in this inscription has Semitic properties. This leads A. Mócsy, in a comment incorporated into Szabó's paper, to note that, if the helmet does indeed belong to the Hemeseni, they had most probably begun to recruit locally by the time it was in use (Szabó 1986: 424).

[47] Bishop and Coulston (1993: 119).

Fig. 18.4. Second/third century AD relief depicting an archer and discovered near House-steads on Hadrian's Wall. Great North Museum, Newcastle upon Tyne.

known from Bar Hill on the Antonine Wall regimental station of the Hamii during the 2nd century AD.[48] Furthermore, images of this bow type are repeatedly linked to eastern archers on public monuments, such as the Column, and funerary stelae from around the Roman world.[49] Yet such weapons probably lost any exclusively ethnic connotations very early. Indeed, the sheer range of sites to have produced laths indicates a far wider pattern of use. Such pieces are often discovered in contexts pre-dating the large-scale recruitment of Syrian archers into the *auxilia*, suggesting that this bow form quickly became widely used throughout Rome's armies and was adopted irrespective of the regiment's place of birth or specialization.[50] This impression is reinforced by the absence of evidence for the use of any other bow type during the early Principate, despite the fact that units of all types were trained in archery.[51]

---

[48] Coulston (1985: 224–5).

[49] For another clear example, see the stele of Monimus Ierombali f., of *coh. I Ituraeorum* (*CIL* 13.7041).

[50] Bishop and Coulston (1993: 79 and fn. 24) note examples from Oberaden and Dangstetten (Augustan), Velsen (Claudian), Waddon Hill (Neronian), Risstissen (late Neronian/early Flavian), and Vindolanda (late Flavian).

[51] See Davies (1977: 265–7) for a survey of the ancient sources on bow use in the Roman army.

Both explicitly and implicitly, the many scholarly claims concerning the distinctiveness of Syrian archers are grounded in a belief that these units continued to receive recruits from their place of origin. Such a practice might indeed help foster the retention of certain traditions, not least in dress. Yet, as I hope I have demonstrated, there were no special recruiting practices for the Syrian units.[52] The unquestioned pre-eminence of Trajan's Column as a source for military dress for so long further reinforced the view that these regiments differed in appearance. Reviewed, the image of the Syrian archer appears in a different light. Several of the features attributed to him lose their ethnic significance. The composite bow was simply the best form of bow available at the time, and was therefore widely used. The absence of a shield and, in some cases, of armour may have appeared merely expedient. As for the helmets, the metalwork, form, and decoration of the handful of examples known to date raise fundamental questions as to whether the label 'Syrian' is any more appropriate than the label 'Roman'. The fact that none appear to pre-date the 2nd century suggests that, at the least, they emerged from a fusion of influences within the Empire, not from a sudden infusion from the exotic east.

THE BATAVI

If it had been Roman practice to perpetuate distinctive styles of ethnic dress and combat in the *auxilia*, then it would surely have been the case that the Batavi of all people would surely have preserved theirs. Not only did Batavian regiments continue to draw recruits from their regiments' ancestral homelands, but the Batavi enjoyed the additional distinction of providing a significant proportion of the emperors' horseguards. But the evidence for the Batavi suggests that even here some qualification may be required.

Despite the suggestion that a ceramic mask depicting a frightening warrior with a big top knot, wild moustache, and beard might represent one of the emperor's Batavian guardsmen,[53] there is no evidence to be seen in the reliefs of Batavian soldiers found in Rome or the provinces that they looked markedly different from other auxiliaries. It is true that the mask, which was found in Italy, recalls Martial's poem about the Batavi:

> I am a potter's jest, the mask of a red-haired Batavian
> Though you make fun of it, a boy fears this face.[54]

But the piece could easily indicate any standard Germanic barbarian type.[55] What is clear, however, is that there is a strong association of the Batavian with exceptional horsemanship.

One equestrian skill in particular has gained the admiration of ancient and modern writers alike: Batavian cavalry were famed for their capacity to swim rivers in full armour alongside their mounts. Tacitus notes these talented

---

[52] P. 139.   [53] Speidel (1994b: 24).

[54] Speidel (1994b: 24) for translation. For the mask, see Brit. Mus. Blacas collection, GR 1867-5-8.644. For the poem, Martial *Epigrams* 14.176.

[55] Speidel (1994b: 24 and pl. 11).

horsemen in the preamble to his account of Batavian involvement in the crisis on the Rhine during the Civil War of AD 69.[56] Cassius Dio, writing a century after Tacitus, found these swimming abilities so impressive he accords them special mention, and he makes it clear that he was not the only one to be impressed. When the Batavi swam the Danube, the historian tells us, the barbarians on the other bank were so amazed at their prowess that they abandoned thoughts of war with Rome and instead sought Hadrian's mediation in their internal disputes.[57] The episode appears as a superb piece of Roman theatre, exhibiting native skill in the service of imperial propaganda.

A well-known poetic epitaph celebrates the performance of just such deeds by a soldier named Soranus in the summer of AD 118:

> I am the man, once well known to the river banks in Pannonia,
> brave and foremost among a thousand Batavi,
> who, with Hadrian as judge, could swim the wide waters
> of the deep Danube in full battle kit.
> From my bow I shot an arrow which, while it hung in the air
> and fell back, I hit and broke with another.
> Whom no Roman or foreigner ever outdid,
> no soldier with the spear, no Parthian with the bow,
> here I lie, on this ever-mindful stone have I bequeathed my deeds
> to memory.
> Let anyone see if after me he can match my deeds.
> I set my own standard, being the first to bring off such deeds.[58]

These and other noted episodes in the historical sources have led to confusion about the capacities of Batavian auxiliary units. We might note that even in Tacitus' celebrated description, the swimming horsemen are only a 'select' part of the Batavian forces; but it is the 2nd-century evidence that has misled scholars, myself included, most fundamentally.

The identity of the 'thousand Batavi' has been much disputed. Some have argued that the unit concerned was the *cohors III Batavorum milliaria equitata* and others that it was the *ala I Batavorum milliaria*, both units which had indeed served in Danubian armies.[59] Yet the most convincing interpretation now seems to be that the 'thousand Batavi' are in fact members of the imperial horseguard and that the epitaph of Soranus belongs to the small genre of literary memorials to members of the emperor's bodyguard.[60] It has long been appreciated that while the term 'Batavi' was sometimes used rather loosely by ancient writers, it also became synonymous with a type of guardsman rather than an ethnicity.[61] Indeed, it is notable that the deceased is referred to as 'of the Batavi' rather than as

---

[56] As, e.g. in Tacitus *Hist.* 4.12.   [57] Dio 69.9.

[58] *CIL* 3.3676 = *ILS* 2558. Translation from Davies (1968c) and M. P. Speidel (1994b: 46).

[59] Davies (1968a; 1968c) associates the inscription with *cohors III Batavorum milliaria equitata*. The *ala I Batavorum milliaria* is known to have been in the region. It was in Pannonia Superior by AD 112 and then moved to Dacia Superior, where it is recorded on a series of diplomas, the earliest of which dates to AD 144 (*CIL* 16.90).

[60] M. P. Speidel (1994b: 46 and 174, n. 56; 2005: 73–80) would rather see these soldiers as members of the emperor's guard.

[61] van Driel-Murray (2003: 204).

'Batavian'.[62] There is, however, another point in this debate that is often over-looked. Dio's description of swimming Batavians credits their aquatic prowess to the training they received from the emperor, not to the perpetuation of native traditions. Furthermore, in adding 'as they were called' to the appellation 'Bat-avian', he implies that this 'ethnic' title may have little to do with the origins of the men themselves.

Taken together, the evidence cannot be taken to indicate the perpetuation of traditional fighting skills in regular Batavian auxiliary units. Indeed, far from promoting equestrian skills amongst these Batavian units, the authorities determinedly kept the number of regular cavalry regiments down—only one *ala Batavorum* is recorded—and this despite longstanding pressure from the Batavians themselves for the employment of more cavalrymen.[63]

Taken together, these case studies reveal pragmatism rather than the survival of any romanticized view of ethnic soldiers in Roman circles. Vergil may have repeatedly associated imperial ethnicities with armament, but in practice, Rome's armies took what was useful and disseminated it widely, abandoning the vast majority of weapons and fighting traditions that it deemed less effective. As the tombstone of Maris of the *ala Parthorum et Araborum* demonstrates, some auxiliary soldiers displayed 'ethnically' distinct dress and fighting techniques in the Julio-Claudian period. This should occasion no great surprise. The new units were part of an evolving process, and initially many consisted largely of men from the same area of origin. Regularity was not expected. But as notions of military identity in Roman service evolved, as the origins of units became no more than a distant memory, as those intakes that had once lent meaning to ethnic and national titles themselves died out, such distinctive forms of dress disappeared. Occasionally, perhaps, when new units were formed, the pattern was repeated.

Only in exceptional cases do regiments demonstrably perpetuate associations that point to their place of origin. But such associations reflect Roman perceptions of ethnicity and/or notions of military necessity. Both explanations probably hold good for the special character of the Batavi. Units drawn from this people were distinctive in both recruitment practice and in their association with the imperial guards. Overall, however, a growing standardization, evidenced through wide-spread copying of basic forms of equipment, transformed the *auxilia*. Items that once held deep cultural significance to a particular people were re-labelled and re-presented as more generic markers of Roman military identity. Even regimen-tal symbols, such as the curved sword of *cohors I Aelia Dacorum*, point more to the Roman genius for appropriation than to a genuine ethnic survival. The same thing applies to the different tactics ascribed to Rome's subjects, as Arrian's account of the *Hippika Gymnasia* makes clear. Units were expected to show mastery of tactics believed to have come from diverse peoples, regardless of where they themselves originated. In the world of arms and tactics, therefore, the processes which characterized the 'imagined community' of the soldiers overwhelmingly vanquished the 'ethnic' trappings of the early levies.

---

[62] Ibid. 204 n. 17.   [63] Tacitus *Hist.* 4.19.

Part VI

Pen and Sword

Communication and Cultural Transformation

19

The Spoken Word

The spoken word was, as it has been throughout history, a most sensitive barometer of social change and exchange. In the Roman army, as in the wider Empire, this was not just a matter of Latin and Greek, but of different *forms* of these two great classical languages and use of a multiplicity of other indigenous tongues. A particular challenge lies in the fact that our knowledge of daily speech is wholly dependent on archaeologically recoverable data and literary sources. Even the rich and varied pool of information that survives in inscriptions, papyri, and graffiti inevitably stresses written languages. Although at least twelve languages other than Latin or Greek made use of such forms,[1] our understanding of non-classical languages in the Empire remains poor, and the evidence is only occasionally good enough to allow us to reconstruct basic colloquialisms or patterns for common usage. Furthermore, the fact that what evidence we do have was left by those who made use of writing reminds us that it is not wholly representative—even in highly literate societies, writing was only used by certain people in certain contexts. References to the spoken word in the literary sources, meanwhile, are often brief and highly charged. Aside from the attempts of comic writers to imitate common speech, relatively little evidence survives for Vulgar Latin, a term used for Latin departing from the literary norm.[2] Though ancient authors show an interest in notions of 'correct speech', they seldom offer extended comment open to more detailed analysis. Comments on speech were often designed to convey a particular agenda, such as to emphasize the alleged or real provincialism of a particular individual.

Complicating any attempt to assess the role and character of the spoken word is the fact that multilingualism was widespread in the ancient world. Amongst multilinguals different languages were often, as they are today, used in different contexts. It does not follow that those whose written records survive today in Greek or Latin necessarily preferred to use these languages in other settings. The military communities used various tongues, so too did the civilians of the interior. The papers composing the late 1st/early 2nd-century family 'Archive of Babatha', for example were written in three languages, Nabatean, Aramaic, and Greek.[3] The family of Moab, to which the documents belonged, was clearly wealthy and used to using written documents, but there is no reason to believe that illiterates did not also use different languages for different contexts. Modern studies show that the highest concentrations of multilingualism often coincide with the highest

---

[1] Harris (1989: 175).   [2] Adams (1977: 1).   [3] Yadin (1962: 235, 258).

concentrations of illiteracy.[4] Similar patterns in the ancient world would obviously be hard for the modern scholar to access and analyse, but it would be folly to doubt their existence. In our discussion of how service in the *auxilia* probably increased a soldier's exposure to either Latin or Greek, we need to remember that this would often mean that he was able to add another language to his vocabulary, not necessarily abandon his own.

The Roman soldier, be he citizen or non-citizen, was bound by, and enjoyed the benefits of, Roman law. From the early Principate on he was obliged to swear an oath to the emperor on enlistment and repeatedly thereafter. This oath, which marked his membership of a special group within society, would have been made in Latin or Greek. It had to be made in Latin or Greek because these were the only languages that the Romans considered acceptable for matters of such great import. Occasionally other civilians would take the oath at the same time, underscoring their association with the military community at the same time as they articulated their allegiance to the emperor.[5]

In addition to swearing the oath, the adoption of a Latin or Greek name, a very personal thing, was sometimes demanded by his superiors if they found a man's native name too difficult to pronounce. We have both explicit and implicit evidence for this practice, which is not the same as changing one's name on receipt of citizenship. As an explicit example, we might cite the case of a serving soldier writing to his brother, giving both his Roman name, Valerius Paulinus, and his native name.[6] It is highly likely that the sharp contrast between the indigenous names of fathers and the Roman names of their serving sons—a familiar feature of many epitaphs—reflects this practice. The Thracian trooper Longinus, whose epitaph is discussed in detail in the final chapter, is a classic example. His familiar Roman name is in sharp contrast to the rare name of his father—a name on which scholars still disagree.[7]

From the beginning of his service, then, the soldier was reminded of the particular importance to both the state and the army of one or both these two languages. They were inextricably linked to his identity as a servant of the state, and a soldier of the Empire. This association was not merely symbolic, it was necessary in the linguistic milieu of the provinces, a milieu in which troops often had to communicate with people of widely differing origins. Not only would the ability to speak Latin or Greek have been necessary for the performance of certain regimental duties, it was also necessary for soldiers in a unit to act together. Though this was less vital amongst irregular units and allied troops which received orders in their native tongue, and which were normally collocated with larger formations responsible for their supplies,[8] it clearly became of fundamental importance for much of the *auxilia* at an early date.

As regiments became regular formations, and particularly as they began to operate independently, the situation would have changed rapidly. Units required a *lingua franca* if they were to operate at all; Roman commanders and junior officers

---

[4] Hamers and Blanc (1989: 31–59); Hanson (1991: 159).   [5] Arrian *Periplus* 2.

[6] *P. Cornell* I.64.1.

[7] *RIB* 201. What constituted a 'Roman' name could change overtime. Tomlin (1988: 97) notes that names of very different origins could become part of a regional pool of names.

[8] Pseudo-Hyginus *De Munitionibus Castrorum* 43 refers to commands given in native languages.

would have been introduced, recruits from different areas would have joined, and the regiments, now operating independently, would have had to dispatch troops to a wide variety of places and people to procure supplies. The extraordinary picture of movement and interconnectivity that emerges from the papyrus report of *cohors I Hispanorum Veterana* illustrates this perfectly.[9] On one day in the early 2nd century, soldiers from this regiment headquartered at Stobi in Macedonia were seeking supplies, manning patrols, or being transferred to units in at least four other provinces. One contingent was travelling to the Haemus mountain range of Thrace, which theoretically fell within the orbit of the 'Greek east', but two contingents were in distant Gaul! It is difficult to imagine how the men deployed on these duties could have functioned effectively in so many different linguistic milieux without some Latin or Greek. Interpreters may well have been used, as we will see, but to get from Macedonia to Gaul, for example, involved crossing many language barriers. In that particular case the detachment must have frequently relied upon Latin to make itself understood; it would hardly be expected that the troops would continually use different local languages.

Knowledge of Latin or Greek, depending on where the unit was stationed, also aided communication with other contingents. From an official point of view this was not always a good thing. The Batavian cohorts of the AD 60s offer a good example of the particular risks that arose from the spread of a common language. At this time the Batavians units were not only drawn from the same people, they were famously commanded by their own tribal officers.[10] There is every reason to believe that officers and men were quite capable of communicating with one another in their native tongue. Yet in at least two incidents, claims made by Batavian soldiers sparked clashes with legionary soldiers. Both suggest that there was fairly widespread knowledge of Latin amongst the Batavians. In the first, they are described by Tacitus as going up to legionaries and taunting them with tales of their own martial prowess; in the second an accusation of theft brought to culmination longstanding tensions between them and the men of the Fourteenth Legion.[11] It is possible that some of these claims were made in other languages that the legionaries could understand, but given the number of exchanges involved, it is clear that much of it must have been in Latin. We will return to the wider implications of these episodes and the use of Latin in Batavian tribal society below.

Exposure to languages other than Latin and Greek was also an inevitable part of a soldier's life. Though local recruitment may often have ensured that soldiers did speak the same language as their civilian neighbours, we have seen that this enlistment practice was far from universal. Many served in regions where they encountered different languages. Differing patterns of deployment would have influenced the amount of contact soldiers would have had with native languages. In the east, for example, many men would have served in cities with linguistically heterogeneous populations. Even within these densely populated areas it is possible that language played a part in distinguishing the military community from everybody else, but this can prove difficult to demonstrate even where there is extensive documentary evidence. Pollard has, for example, considered the role of

---

[9] *RMR* 63.　　[10] P. 116.　　[11] Tacitus *Hist.* 2.27 and 2.66.

language use in the 2nd- and 3rd-century setting of Dura-Europos.[12] At one level the linguistic situation here is clearly complex—documents survive in Greek, Latin, Palmyrene, Syriac and Aramaic—but the preference amongst both soldiers and civilians when it came to *writing* was clearly for Greek.[13] The picture that emerges suggests that bilingual exchanges were possible, but it still leaves us in doubt as to how far the different communities spoke differently from one another. Where men or units were moving into a new area, it is probable that a soldier's desire to learn and use the local language must have been influenced by relations with the local population. Intercommunication with local communities in the aftermath of conquest, for example, may have been less attractive to soldiers (and vice versa) than that with a community where an informally agreed *modus vivendi* existed.

Interpreters no doubt played a vital role in communications between military and civilian populations.[14] The words *ut interpreteris* preserved on a fragmentary tablet from Vindolanda do appear to suggest the presence of an interpreter at the fort.[15] It dates to a time in the late 1st century when the newly arrived auxiliary units may have been linguistically isolated among the local population. The importance of such men at a later date, when units were well established, and may even have begun to recruit locally, is difficult to gauge. Whatever the situation locally, interpreters must have been crucial for military operations across the Empire. Before going on to discuss the nature and cultural significance of the languages spoken by soldiers serving in the auxilia, though, we should consider the communication problems that would have arisen as units lost their ethnic homogeneity.

During the formative period of the *auxilia* many units would have had native commanders, men whose leadership position demanded that they serve as inter-mediaries, switching language as circumstances required. Best known to us of these early commanders is Arminius, the man who in AD 9 inflicted the destruction of three legions and thousands of auxiliaries upon Rome. In a striking encounter on the banks of the river Weser, Arminius confronted his brother, a man still loyal to Rome.[16] Speaking in their native language the two men heatedly argued over allegiance to Rome. Interestingly, it was Arminius who peppered his harangue with Latin—Latin, Tacitus tells us, he had learnt in Roman service as commander of native auxiliaries. This ability, so clearly crucial to the operation of the Roman army, is here used to condemn it—further proof that while improved communication may facilitate imperial control, it does not necessary instil allegiance to Rome.[17]

Partly because of the difficulties Roman officials had with native leaders, from the early Principate onwards most auxiliary units received commanders from elsewhere.

These were men who served a few years with the regiment before proceeding to the next level of their careers. It seems most unlikely that more than a handful of these officers would have troubled to learn the native tongues of their charges during their time in command. We can only hypothesize as to the amount of direct contact ordinary soldiers had with them, but we must assume that in units of 500 or 1,000 strong, it was minimal, and that orders and information were

---

[12] Pollard (1996: 217–19).   [13] Ibid. 218; Kilpatrick (1964: 217).   [14] Adams (2003: 760).
[15] *Tab. Vindol.* II.213.ii.1; Bowman and Thomas (1994: 188).   [16] Tacitus *Ann.* 2.10.
[17] Adams (2003: 21) discusses the changing of languages or 'code switching' in this episode.

channelled through junior commanders. This assumption is partly based on our knowledge of the internal command structure of these regiments, and partly on the analogy of modern units of similar size. Commanding officers most probably addressed their regiments in Latin or Greek at special occasions. The Romans set great store by such speeches, as the fanciful battle accounts of the great historians illustrate. At certain periods, and in certain units, subordinate officers may have translated orders from above to their men. Yet quite often sub-unit officers were themselves transferees, and may or may not have been able to speak the native language of the *milites*.[18]

Study of the known career paths of pre-Trajanic centurions, decurions, and *immunes* is illuminating in this regard.[19] The importance of being able to speak the native language of a unit became less important as a factor in posting personnel over time.[20] The presence of a Spanish decurion in the *ala Pannoniorum*, for example, suggests that it had ceased to be an important factor in some units at an early date.[21] Cloutius was appointed to the rank in the Augustan period, when the regiment was stationed in Dalmatia.[22] It seems highly unlikely that Cloutius learnt Pannonian prior to his posting; the assumption appears to have been that this was not necessary because he could communicate with his troops in Latin.[23] This is in itself interesting, for the size of command to which decurions were appointed was not large. It seems unlikely, therefore, that these officers would have routinely depended on under officers to translate and relay their commands, though they may have required some help when discussing issues of greater complexity with their soldiers.

As units began to draw recruits from new areas—a process that could start very soon after their formation—their linguistic homogeneity would have started to dissolve. Yet soldiers still had to communicate with one another; while many must have learnt something of the languages spoken by the natives in the area where they were stationed, the classical languages, in however debased a form, provided a useful medium for interaction. Altars dedicated by soldiers from the Vellavian district and the *pagus Condustris* serving in the British-based *cohors II Tungrorum equitata c. L.* remind us that tribal and cultural groups would have existed alongside one another within many regiments.[24] The troops recorded on these mid-2nd-century inscriptions were most probably recruited by a returning regimental *vexillatio* that is known to have been serving in Raetia at this time. When the detachment rejoined its regiment in Britain, it brought with it groups culturally quite distinct from the rest of the unit.[25] Latin would have been the only mutually intelligible means of communication.[26] We may note in passing that the soldiers chose to emphasize their distinct origins in Latin upon conventional Roman altars.

---

[18] Tacitus refers to the transfer of centurions and soldiers to a unit upon formation in the *Agricola* (28).
[19] Holder (1980: 86–95).   [20] Ibid. 88.   [21] *CIL* 3.2016.   [22] Holder (1980: 283).
[23] Velleius Paterculus claimed that the Pannonian rebels of AD 6, many of whom were auxiliary soldiers, knew Latin (II.1.10.5).
[24] *RIB* 2107 and *RIB* 2108.   [25] A *vexillatio* from the unit was in Raetia in AD 147 (*CIL* 16.94).
[26] Although some Celtic may have been spoken in the Vellavian district of Germania, our evidence suggests that the local languages were Germanic (Neumann 1983).

The ability to communicate with one's fellow soldiers was not simply a matter of professional necessity; it was also essential if a man were to 'fit in' and interact socially with his colleagues. Linguistic case studies of men in modern British army infantry units have observed that pressure on men from their peers to adopt or abandon particular dialects may be considerable; changes in speech patterns are sometimes regarded as essential to an individual if he is to achieve acceptance. The importance of such acceptance in a close military environment means that many were found to conform even when they valued their own way of speaking more highly than that which they adopted.[27] There is no direct evidence that such processes were at work in the Roman army, but this example reminds us that social acceptance is sometimes determined by the way one speaks. It is evident that from an early period it became necessary for auxiliary soldiers to speak and understand some Latin or, if stationed in the east, Greek, if they were to operate within their units at all. But on a day-to-day level ordinary soldiers may also have been under pressure to acquire at least some of the other languages spoken by their *commilitones*.

In Palmyrene *numeri*, for example, where the survival of the men's native language is evident from the enduring use of Palmyrene text in inscriptions from locations as diverse as Transylvania and Algeria, initial reinforcements into the ranks must have found some command of this Semitic tongue essential, if only to speak with their fellow soldiers. Soldiers' Palmyrene necessarily incorporated military loanwords, and we find Latin ranks, formations, and roles transliterated on Palmyrene inscriptions.[28] Yet, less than a couple of generations after each of the Palmyrene units had made its way out to Dacia and Numidia, local Latin became the dominant language even amongst the rank and file.[29] Thus even the irregular units raised from non-citizens ended up succumbing to the process of linguistic incorporation that ultimately transformed provincial society.

Ultimately it remains difficult to assess what the spoken language of the barracks, as opposed to the language of the *principia* and parade ground, really was in any given unit. It is entirely possible to imagine a situation where a different language was spoken amongst senior officers from those in the ranks. Latin or Greek would have been the official language of the camp in regular units, the language of orders and administration, but casual conversation between messmates may have been conducted in any one of a multitude of tongues. Ironically, the best indications of the use of native languages are to be found in a close reading of Latin documents produced in military contexts. In *Bilingualism and the Latin Language* Adams has documented many telling examples.[30] Crucially, what emerges from this is a sense not just of a different military Latin, but of different military Latins flavoured with distinct local and regional elements. Local languages and the mother tongues of the soldiers would have influenced current vocabulary, pronunciation, and even, to some extent, grammar.[31] Such speech

---

[27] McCrum, Cran, and MacNeil (1986: 140–41) for a modern example of this phenomenon.
[28] Millar (1993: 328) discusses the impact of Latin loan words in Palmyrene military contexts, noting particularly their use on *CIL* 3.7999 = *CIS* 2.3.3906 (Dacia) and *CIL* 8.2515 = *CIS* 2.3.3908 (Numidia).
[29] Ibid.   [30] Adams (2003).   [31] Thomas (1980: 104).

could clearly appear upsettingly alien to a Latin speaker from Rome: Tacitus recalls, for example, disgust at the *horridi sermone* of Vitellian soldiers,[32] but it was nevertheless still able to convey important Roman concepts to the soldiers themselves.

To understand how this works, we need to examine more closely soldiers' Latin. *Sermo castrensis* was already an acknowledged form of Latin in the late Republic,[33] but it continued to evolve during the imperial period. As a soldier's language littered with vulgarisms and technical terms, it served to distinguish the soldier from other Latin speakers. Technical terminology played a part, of course. Just as Arrian justifies the extensive use that he makes of foreign words in his *Tactica*, an account of the procedures of Roman cavalry units, by stating that he can find no acceptable synonyms for them in either Latin or Greek, so must many words have entered military parlance.[34]

Some terms evolved out of the poetic or humorous instincts of the soldiery. We know of a few of the words that originated as military slang because they also subsequently enjoyed wider usage. The soldiers' tent was known as the *papilio* or butterfly because its sides resembled wings and it unfurled from a small chrysalis-like package; the word has survived in modern English as *pavilion*. Camp slang for a Persian heavily armoured cavalryman was *clibanarius*, 'oven-man', from the Latin for oven *clibanus*. Unfavourable locations for camps were called 'mothers-in-law'.[35]

As Adams shows, the impact of native languages on *sermo castrensis* took several forms. For soldiers in the *numerus Melenvensium* stationed in Africa, the men's experience of Germanic languages affected their Latin speech in a distinctive way. Rather than the familiar *contubernales* (tent-mates) widely favoured across the armed forces, they referred to their comrades as *concibones*.[36] The term is formed of the collective prefix *cum* (with) and *cibus* (food). It conveys the same sense as *contubernales*, meaning in this instance mess-mates or more literally those with whom one takes food. Adams notes that there was a clear parallel for *concibones* in Old High German, and concluded that the term must have been a calque developed by German solders as they acquired Latin.[37]

Hints of Germanic languages behind the Latin spoken in a *numerus* in Africa can be contrasted with the impact of local languages upon the Latin spoken at another African outpost. Third-century documents from Bu Njem in Tripolitania indicate that Latin was very much a second language for many in the fort. As with many an inexperienced Latin learner, the soldiers often use the nominative form of a noun where ordinarily even 'substandard' users would know that another case was required.[38] Alongside grammatical differences are local words that give the Latin of Bu Njem a distinct flavour. As in all military installations, the receipt and administration of stores was of crucial importance. In this instance though, four different non-Latin words—seemingly representing Punic, Libyan, and other local dialects—are used in the documents to designate the same amount of commodities.[39] These words are incorporated quite routinely into Latin texts

---

[32] Tacitus *Hist.* 2.74.   [33] Wolffin (1902).   [34] Arrian *Tactica* 33.1.
[35] Hyginus *De Munitionibus Castrorum* 57.   [36] See *CIL* 8.9060 = *ILS* 2627.
[37] Adams (2003: 279).   [38] Adams (1994: 96–102).
[39] Marichal (1992: 101) cites the use of *siddipia, asgatui, seleusa,* and *sbitualis*.

as in *O. Bu Njem* 77, where a local camel driver with the Libyan name of
Iassuchthan conveys seven *sbitualis* of *triticum* (wheat). Adams observes:

> The soldiers sent out to deal with local transporters...must have been able to
> communicate in the local language, and the entry of the terms into Latin thus reflects
> a bilingual background. Soldiers recruited locally who were native speakers of the
> African language(s) will have been responsible for the borrowings into their second
> language, Latin, which as the supraregional language of the Roman army, can truly be
> described as a link language.[40]

Much the same dynamic can be observed in the accounts and lists recovered
from Vindolanda. A fragmentary list dating from *c.* AD 92–103, when *cohors VIIII
Batavorum* was in residence, records items received by a man with the Celtic
name Gavo.[41] Though the list is written in rather unexceptional Latin, and here
commodities are measured in the rather more conventional unit of the *modius*,
several distinctive Celtic words appear. In addition to the word *sagum*, for cloak—
a word that had long since received widespread acceptance in Latin usage—we
find the terms *bedocem* and *tosseas*.[42] The first may be of Celtic origin and the
second clearly is, referring as it does to a form of regional dress—as in *tossia
Britannica*—a traditional rug or coverlet. Of particular interest here is the fact that
the military community is contributing to the evolution, dissemination, and
perpetuation of regional Latins.[43] Some of these terms subsequently make an
appearance in non-military documents.[44]

Distinct a form of speech as it may have been, *sermo castrensis* was still Latin,
and as such was capable of communicating those concepts which played a
defining role in the character of the Empire. It is to these concepts that we now
turn. One way to appreciate how this operated is to turn the analysis around.
Rather than looking at loanwords making their way into Latin, we need to look at
Latin loanwords in ancient languages. Such a switch in focus has the advantage of
reaffirming the degree to which ideas in imperial society could and did range
between language groups.

We have already seen how terms for Roman military ranks and formations
were absorbed into languages as diverse as Greek and Palmyrene, but it is clear
that the impact of Latin was far greater. Languages of the Celtic west, for example,
clearly bear its stamp. These loanwords were introduced, of course, at different
times and in different fields, but some interesting generalities may be observed.
Speaking of Welsh, for example, Zimmer notes, 'the majority of the loanwords
were borrowed from the language of the Roman army'.[45] In a more general
analysis of the three Brittonic languages that preserve traces of speech in Britain

---

[40] Adams (2003: 455).   [41] *Tab. Vindol.* II.192.

[42] Adams (2003: 455). In their commentary on the text, Bowman and Thomas (1994: 160) note the
possible Celtic origins only of the second term. For *tossia* as a Celtic term for bedcover, see André
(1966/7).

[43] Adams (2003: 441). A. R. Birley has drawn my attention to another debate over the term
souxtum, which appears in *Tab. Vindol.* II .301.3. Adams (1996) has suggested that this may be a
Celtic (mis)spelling deriving from the Latin term for expense, *su(m)ptum*, but Birley points out the
existence of the Gallic/Celtic term *souxtu*, for cooking pot, discussed by Lambert (2000; 2004).

[44] Notably the *tossia* in the famous 'Marbre de Thorigny' (*CIL* 13.3162).

[45] Zimmer (1990: 280).

in the Roman period, Jackson also identifies an impressive array of military terms that date to that time. These go far beyond the terms *castellum* and *castra*, preserved in place names, to include an array of technical terms such as *arma*, *imperator*, *legio*, *lorica*, *miles*, *militaris*, *papilio*, *pedites*, *sagitta*, *spolium*, *vagina*, and *vigilia*.[46] The introduction of a new vocabulary for warriors is part of the transformation of society—affirming the permanent place in provincial society of the professional soldier. Yet while some of these words could have been readily adopted by civilians, others of a slightly more technical form were probably first absorbed by Celtic soldiers in the service of Rome. Their specificity would have ensured that more widespread adoption would only take place later.

Roman legal terminology also enjoyed more widespread usage in military stations—in auxiliary forts no less than in the camps of the legions—than it did in many civilian settlements. Terms such as *heres* and *ex testamento* became familiar features in auxiliary epigraphs from at least the reign of Tiberius. Those who commissioned the monuments understood that their privileged status allowed them the freedom to choose, as heir, whomever they desired. Ulpian records that a man gained the right to make a will as soon as he joined the army.[47] He had no right to do so before then unless he was a citizen. Juvenal also notes that soldiers alone had the right to make a will while their fathers were still alive.[48] This right under Roman law was unique in the ancient world, and auxiliaries were the only non-citizens in the western provinces to whom it was extended.[49] The terms defined the special relationship of the heir to the deceased, and the obligations it entailed. Use of this term on funerary monuments indicates that such complex, quintessentially Roman ideas, which could only be conveniently conveyed in Latin, came to enjoy widespread usage among the *auxilia*. The right to make a will unfettered by legal stipulations was first granted to soldiers by Julius Caesar on a temporary basis, but it was then extended by Titus, before being confirmed by a succession of emperors.[50] In a rescript to Statilius Severus, for example, the emperor Trajan emphasized the validity of soldiers' wills irrespective of how they were articulated, noting that though witnesses were required, a written document was not.[51] Even without the ability or inclination to produce a written will, the auxiliary was empowered by these distinctive notions of property and inheritance. It is clear that the linked concepts of heirs and wills must have had profound significance in provincial society. They liberated and they bound, legitimizing any soldier's decision to abandon the obligations of his ancestors and binding him afresh to those he chose to name.[52] Just how much of an impact they could have is clear from the surviving will of Antonius Silvanus, a cavalryman in the *ala Mauretana* stationed in Egypt.[53] Dating to AD 142, the will outlines the provision for Silvanus' son, who is to become sole heir to his soldier

---

[46] Jackson (1953: 79).

[47] Ulpian 20.10. This is in respect of property acquired in military service. The ruling dates from the reign of Augustus.

[48] Juvenal *Sat.* 16.51–5.   [49] Thomas (1976: 405–7).

[50] *Digest* (29.1.1–2).   [51] Ibid. 29.1.24.

[52] We may contrast here, e.g. the rules of fixed succession found amongst many German tribes (Tacitus *Germania* 40).

[53] *FIRA* 3.47.

father's property. Silvanus' brother also benefits, as does his slave, who will be given his freedom, and the mother of his heir. Reference to the latter, Antonia Thermutha, is interesting, as it reflects the frustration of family life in the military community. If Silvanus simply described Antonia as his 'wife' in the will, this could well have invalidated it, because serving soldiers had no right to marry.[54] Finally, the regiment's commanding officer receives 50 denarii, a standard procedure to ensure that the will would be honoured. Excepting perhaps Silvanus' brother, whose occupation and place of residence are unknown, all those involved in the will, either as heirs, beneficiaries, stewards, or witnesses, form part of the extended military community of which he was a part. There is little sense here of his considerable fortune benefiting other provincials of his acquaintance. By many such acts, the military community was again distinguished from wider society.

From all this we can see that obligations and opportunities alike ensured that the army provided a uniquely favourable environment for Latin learning. As Adams observes, 'The Roman army was undoubtedly the most potent force during the Roman Empire behind the learning of Latin by speakers of Greek and vernacular languages, and behind the consequent spread of bilingualism.'[55]

The Greek that was the language of the camps across much of the east was also susceptible to the formative processes that generated *sermo castrensis*. This is not just a matter of adopting the vocabulary of time (which was widely adopted in civil settings too), rank structures, or unit titles, but also involved the adoption of more specific terminology. Thus, for example, even in the military parlance of Greek-speaking Egypt, we find Latin terms. The Latin word *aegri*, for example, served for soldiers unable, due to health, to undertake their duties.[56]

Of course the picture of language use was not a neat one. While the overwhelming use of Greek in documents read and written by soldiers in Egypt leaves little doubt as to its importance in their daily speech, men in the armies of other provinces in the Greek east might have behaved differently.[57] In Thrace, for example, Latin makes a poor showing in any documents produced outside the province's two coloniae. Imperial decrees are invariably shown reproduced in Greek.[58] Yet auxiliary troops seem to have used Latin, even in private settings, to a higher degree than their provincial counterparts. Thus, although an *immunis* serving in *cohors I Aelia Athoitarum et Berecorum* who died at Losenec was commemorated in Greek, a *miles* from the same regiment made a dedication to Hercules in Latin.[59] Furthermore, the regiment itself used Latin where other official agents used Greek, notably in commemorating its construction of a temple at Kabyle.[60] For some men in Greek areas, Latin was the tool they chose to use to assert military status.[61] Overall, though, it is clear that Latin and Greek were equally good vehicles of communication for soldiers between soldiers.

---

[54] Campbell (1994: 159). For the legal problem, see *FIRA* 3.19, where the prefect of Egypt cannot rule in favour of the return of dowry held in the estate of a dead soldier because this would appear to recognize the legality of the marriage.

[55] Adams (2003: 761).   [56] *O. Claud.* I.86–94, 96; Adams (2003: 458).

[57] Bagnall (1986: 5); Adams (2003: 527).   [58] Sharankov (2011).

[59] Greek: *AE* 1961, 315. Latin: *AE* 1979, 554.

[60] *SEG* 42.646. What makes dedications by this unit all the more interesting is that it appears the regiment originated as locally raised militia (Roxan, pers. comm., quoted by Spaul 2000: 476). This if anything ought to have reinforced its 'Greekness'.

[61] *CIL* 3.125 from Syria, a soldier's epitaph, recording the man's title in Latin though the text is in Greek.

While the spread of Latin and Greek eased face-to-face communication across the Empire, the wider spread of bilingualism was no less significant. Bilingualism facilitated a deeper interpenetration of concepts across languages, ensuring that concepts central to imperial incorporation entered the speech of men and women who could speak neither Latin nor Greek. Administrative terms, units of time, and military terminology all found their way into indigenous languages. None could have gone unnoticed by the average soldier. Yet for all their impact, these processes were not uniform. Even in the army, where we can see these processes at their most intense, the sheer diversity of units, recruits, and deployments ensured significant variation.

Latin provides the basic 'link language' for the soldiers of the west, and it also permeates the Greek spoken in the military communities of the east, but it emerges as necessarily sensitive to a plethora of local factors. An auxiliary soldier might, therefore, speak Latin, for example, but his form of speech need not simply be a form replete with military jargon—not simply a *sermo castrensis*—but also a notably localized form. In some cases, that localized form may owe much to the native language of the majority of the soldiery, but it would also reflect the language of those locals with whom the soldiers did business. The processes underpinning the spoken word echo those of the material world. Just as the material culture of Rome's provinces reflects broad differences between the west and the east, so it reflects smaller regional patterns. The men of Bu Njem in the 3rd century had similar concerns to those of Vindolanda in the 1st, but where traces of their Latin survive, it is marked by different terminology and sometimes even different grammatical idiosyncrasies. Thus while *sermo castrensis* was a feature of the 'imagined community' of the army and served to distinguish units from their fellow provincials,[62] the local elements in a soldier's speech distinguished his regional affiliations too. This went beyond the Latin of the west and the Greek of the east. Even when Roman armies drawn from the same half of the Empire were brought together, there could be a marked difference in speech. Thus Tacitus, recalling the horrific events of AD 69, found it inconceivable that the armies of Otho and Vitellius 'whose habits and speech were so distinct' could ever reach agreement.[63] Language could divide Roman soldiers as well as unite them.

Auxiliaries certainly played their part in the evolution of provincial language. Drawn from multiple language groups, obliged to acquire some sort of competence in Latin or Greek, creating new words, phrases, and constructions in the process, they contributed to the spread of regional forms of the great 'link languages'. As we will see in our discussion of the written word, this was a matter of crucial import to the incorporation of provincial society. It marked the local absorption of the systems of words and ideas that tied the Empire together.

---

[62] James (1999: 16, 23).   [63] Tacitus *Hist.* 2.37.

20

The Written Word

For sheer drama, there is no document from the Empire to match the report from El-Mweih.[1] Though one of many thousand texts discovered on potsherds (*ostraca*) in Egypt, this one is striking, for the text summarizes the events of a lethal and sustained attack by sixty raiders on the *praesidium* (military station) of Patkoua (see Fig. 20.1). Precisely where Patkoua lay remains unknown, but the text indicates that it must have been somewhere on the important road between Coptos and Myos Hormos. The raid began at 2 in the afternoon and fighting continued till nightfall, resuming the following day. Civilians around the *praesidium* proved particularly vulnerable, and the raiders carried off a woman and two children when they withdrew. A follow-up patrol found the body of one of the young captives later.

Documents such as these must have once been commonplace in the Roman world; references to banditry are certainly legion, but it is rare to possess so graphic an account. The battle report on this amphora sherd tells us something of still wider importance than conflict and loss on an Egyptian road in the early 2nd century. At the bottom of the report is the injunction to distribute the report to 'prefects, centurions, *duplicarii* and *curatores*' along the road. Swift transmission of written intelligence was clearly essential to the security of Rome's presence on the route to the Red Sea, just as it was to multiple other regions across the Empire.[2] The pen was more crucial to the success of the Empire's armies even than the sword. Only through the rapid passage of such information could such relatively small forces reach and respond to threats. Of particular interest is the originator of the report, one Antonius Celer, an *eques* of *cohors II Ituraeorum*, who participated in the fighting and passed a report on it to the centurion Cassius Victor. We might note three points here. The first is the fascinating circumstance by which a trooper, serving in a regiment raised from a people once notorious in Syria for raiding and banditry, is found in Egypt operating against precisely such depredations. This alone is a tremendous testimony to the transformative impact of Rome's institution of the *auxilia*. Second, this ordinary trooper—not a senior officer—is the genesis of a 'paper trail', a source of documentation on matters of literally life-and-death importance. Finally, the matter-of-fact way that the whole tale was communicated not in Latin, but in Greek, is worth noting.

This chapter examines further the role of the written word in provincial society through the experience of the *auxilia*. Most of the examples will be more mundane

---

[1] *O. Krok.* 87; Cuvigny (2005).   [2] Bowman (1994a: 24).

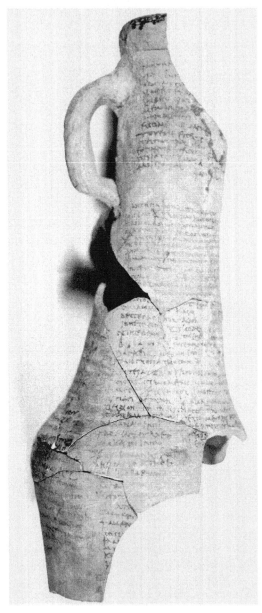

Fig. 20.1. Fragments of an amphora covered in graffiti unearthed at El-Mweih, Egypt. The report by Antonius Celer, an *eques* of *cohors II Ituraeorum*, recording an attack on a Roman station was written on the neck of the vessel (*O. Krok.* 87).

than those found above, but that makes them no less important. While it is clear that Latin enjoyed a particular significance, it was not, as has often been argued, the official language of the Roman army. The chapter shows how the military offered extra incentives to use the written word, and how the soldiers may in turn have promoted use of the written word in wider society. But to understand the importance of all of this it is necessary to understand more generally the role of literacy and writing in ancient society.

LITERACY, THE WRITTEN WORD, AND THE ROMAN EMPIRE

The impact of the written word upon Roman society must be measured not by the proportion of its members who were literate and still less by the number who wrote Latin, but rather by the proportion whose lives it governed. The point is made most strongly by Alan Bowman in his study of the Vindolanda tablets: 'The relatively small size of the literate group needs to be set against the fact that a much larger proportion of the population behaved according to conventions which depended on the presumption that written communication was a normal means of regulating society.'[3] It was entirely possible for an individual to use writing without putting pen to papyrus (or *stilus* to tablet): others might readily perform the service for him or her. Similarly, the life, rights, and entitlements of an illiterate might be fundamentally transformed by information stored in written form. As Hopkins argues, 'The Roman empire was bound together by writing. Literacy was both a social symbol and an integrative by-product of Roman government, economy, and culture. The whole experience of living in the Roman empire, of being ruled by Romans, was overdetermined by the existence of texts . . .'[4] The Roman Empire was by no means the only empire to have depended on writing, but it could only have taken the form that it did through multiple innovative ways of using written documentation that ranged from case law to the taking of the census.

The essential feature of incorporation was its dependence on literate modes of communication, not on mass literacy. Imperial administrators recognized two key languages in official documents, despite the existence of many other forms of writing. Latin and Greek enjoyed clear pre-eminence, leading one eminent scholar to see the spread of their use as a 'single phenomenon . . . sustained by a continuous cultural tradition'.[5] Though there are problems with this approach, most notably in the fact that Greek was used much more extensively to articulate both non-Hellenic and non-Roman ideas,[6] there is a value to considering the two together when studying writing in provincial society. Certainly in the army, Greek was used almost as extensively in military documents in the east as Latin was in those found in the west.

Emphasis on the written form of these languages had many consequences. It made literacy more desirable. It also appears to have encouraged indirectly the

---

[3] Ibid. 82.   [4] Hopkins (1991: 144).
[5] Harris (1989: 22).   [6] Bowman (1991: 124–5).

growth of other forms of written expression in contexts the authorities might never have considered. Our assessment needs to take both of these aspects into account.

It has been estimated that fewer than 10 per cent of the population of the Roman Empire under the Principate were literate in either Greek or Latin.[7] While this estimate—which is to a large degree dependent on the concentrations of stone inscriptions recorded—is widely accepted, it raises further questions. A particular difficulty facing those trying to assess the degree to which this varied by social group and through time is the sheer challenge of defining literacy in provincial contexts.

Current UNESCO definitions of illiteracy and functional literacy encourage us to think of literacy as a package with three interdependent elements—reading, writing, and numeracy.[8] This view, and the governmental interest in pursing its dissemination, is modern. Reading and numeracy skills may be possessed independently;[9] even within modern education systems, the idea of teaching the three elements concurrently is a relatively recent innovation.[10] When studying the ancient world, it is important to remember that even those who only possessed one or two of these skills were often significantly advantaged.

Establishing what proportion of Rome's subjects and soldiers could read, write, and/or calculate numbers is challenging for a number of reasons. Evidence for the first is hard to evaluate, and that for the second and third is often misleading. Attempts at calculation draw from both the contents of documents and the features of Roman social infrastructure conducive to the dissemination of these skills. Clues most often drawn from the latter consist of signatures, illiteracy formulae, handwriting, and age-rounding. Yet the presence of a signature on a text or graffito need not indicate that the signatory was literate, despite scholarly claims to the contrary.[11] Documentary evidence makes it clear that there was no ancient consensus on this point. The 2nd-century scribe Petaus argued for the literacy of a colleague on the basis of his signing ability,[12] but a number of contemporary documents refer to their signatories as *illiterati*.[13] Furthermore, the addition of a signature and closing greeting text written in another hand may indicate that the signatory was not capable of writing more, but they may also indicate that he or she was literate and merely dictating for convenience or even fashion. Horsfall remarks that illiteracy formulae may also deceive.[14] Some of those who employed scribes or claimed illiteracy may have done so because they felt uncomfortable writing *legal* documents. 'Bad' handwriting is also open to various interpretations; it need not, of course, indicate the work of 'semi-literates' or 'slow writers' as is sometimes suggested; if it did, many medical professionals in Britain would be regarded as functionally illiterate. Finally, age-rounding—the practice of rounding up an age to the next unit of five or ten years—demonstrates

---

[7] Harris (1989: 22).

[8] UNESCO defines an illiterate as someone who 'cannot with understanding both read and write a short simple statement about his everyday life' (Harris 1989: 3). Hanson (1991: 162) discusses definitions of functional literacy.

[9] McKitterick (1990: 3); Horsfall (1991: 64).

[10] As Furet and Ozouf (1982: 11 n. 13) observe in their discussion of literacy in modern France.

[11] See here Cressy (1980); Furet and Ozouf (1982: 7 and 17).

[12] *P. Petaus* II.   [13] Harris (1989: 4–6) for a discussion of 'signature literates'.

[14] Horsfall (1991: 71). For example, in *P. Oxy.* xvii.2111.1–12 an advocate claims that a woman previously described on a contract as illiterate could write (Hanson 1991: 24).

ignorance of age, not illiteracy or even innumeracy.[15] We know much, for example, of Aurelius Isidoros of Karanis, who according to his documents aged twelve years in a mere ten, and yet who was able to calculate the taxable value of land precisely.[16] But—and here is the greatest challenge—even if these oft-cited clues did incontrovertibly demonstrate the literacy or illiteracy of those who produced them, it would be difficult to ascertain how representative they were of the wider population. The difficulty is exacerbated by the nature of the archaeological record. The bulk of documentary evidence for routine use of documents in civilian provincial settings, for example, comes from Egypt because the conditions there are good for the preservation of papyri. Egypt's adminis-tration may well have been less atypical than is often alleged,[17] but this does not mean that literacy rates there were representative of other provinces. Indeed, the long-established scribal traditions and village schools probably contributed to a higher level of literacy.[18]

Attempts to estimate the dissemination of literacy skills by examining the presence or absence of conditions conducive to them are also fraught with difficulties. Despite occasional references to schools by historians and the discov-ery of reliefs depicting teaching scenes, it is difficult to assess the availability of elementary education for the mass of provincials. Even if it were possible to establish the numbers of schools, establishing how much teaching went on in the home would be impossible. The cost of writing materials is also sometimes employed to estimate the proportion of literates in a society. Yet this argument takes us nowhere. Leaf-tablets and *ostraca*, mere potsherds, were so cheap that there can be little question of people not being able to afford to write.[19]

Other archaeological attempts that will prove more fruitful have been explored in regions which lacked a major history of writing before their absorption into the Empire. A recent survey of findspots of *stilus* pens from southern Britain, for example, has shown that they are well represented even at seemingly low-status rural settlements.[20] The authors provide an important service by illustrating this fact and emphasizing the degree to which writing skills must have been dissemin-ated geographically; but even this falls far short of qualifying or challenging earlier estimates as to the proportions of literates.

While attempts to quantify the size of the literate group are inevitably frus-trated, given the limited value of our definitions and demographic data, they carry a further risk. They can also obscure our awareness of the degree to which writing permeated the provincial environment and the diverse ways it manifested itself from place to place. Acceptance of writing as a better medium is not, of course, automatic; written communication has attracted suspicion in many societies,[21] not to mention those anthropologists who have documented its impact, most notably Lévi-Strauss.[22] Accordingly, while writing played a primary role in

---

[15] Duncan-Jones (1977: 336).

[16] *P. Cair. Isid.* discussed by Hanson (1991: 186 n. 102).

[17] Bowman and Rathbone (1992).

[18] Legal practices (Hopkins 1991: 153 n. 49) and the existence of well-established cities may have resulted in a wider knowledge of Greek and higher literacy rates (Harris 1989: 13).

[19] Bowman (1991: 128).   [20] Hanson and Conolly (2002).

[21] Clanchy (1979: 150); Pattison (1982: 37).   [22] Lévi-Strauss (1973: 299).

binding together the Empire, it does not follow that all those who used writing used it in the same ways.

WRITING IN THE *AUXILIA*

Military communities experienced more concentrated exposure to imperial conventions of written communication than any other part of provincial society below the urban elite. In what follows we will see this demonstrated by both text and archaeological discovery. Certainly evidence from the *auxilia* furnishes us with an exceptionally rich range of examples that reveal individual responses to the obligations and opportunities writing generated. Though sources as diverse as the tax register of Karanis and the *stili* of southern Britain indicate that writing was widely present even in rural society, it remains true that a large proportion of individuals remained unable to write. In general, it is clear that the rural settlements from whence most auxiliaries came were less likely to generate large numbers of literates than the larger towns.[23] As we will see, however, there is some reason to believe that this changed over the first three centuries AD, a further symptom of the ongoing incorporation of provincial society.

On entering the army many auxiliaries would have found themselves in a more literate world than that to which they were accustomed. The particular importance, mundane and symbolic, of the written word to those serving in the *alae* and *cohortes* can be evaluated by examining writing in military contexts. It must be emphasized that the aim is not to suggest the existence of mass literacy within the army, but rather to demonstrate that the military environment was essentially defined by writing and was accordingly highly conducive to the acquisition of writing skills.

Literate modes of communication played a fundamental role in the Roman army. The Empire, employing only a relatively small number of regular officials, depended upon unpaid local worthies and the army to fulfil a bureaucratic role in the provinces.[24] Soldiers were, for example, charged with the collection of taxes and the investigation of crimes, both tasks that required maintaining written records.[25] The army famously made extensive use of the written word for its non-civic duties. Vast quantities of 'paperwork' characterized the Roman military's management of troops and resources. Documentation recorded such varied phenomena as the state of a regiment's horses and the delivery of equipment, the issue of pay, and the taking of leave. Most of it, though, concerned the men themselves; it was first and foremost about keeping soldiers under command, detailing their duties, overseeing their movements, delivering their pay, and ensuring that their material needs were met. A Roman army without bureaucracy would not have been a Roman army.

---

[23] While it is possible to find many exceptions to Harris's claim that 'very small settlements and truly rural patterns of living are a hindrance to elementary education', his general point remains valid (Harris 1989: 13).

[24] Jones (1964: 1057).   [25] All tasks documented extensively by Davies (1973).

Writing was at once the guardian of a soldier's entitlements and the instrument of his control. Text was a palpable sign not only of his absorption into the imperial system but also, through him, that of his family; but it did not simply classify him and document his life, it physically surrounded him. Writing was a conspicuous feature of every Roman garrison town, fort, and fortress in the Empire. This much is clear when we consider the material culture of these installations. Significantly, many of these centres have yielded markedly more evidence for writing activity than have towns several times their size.

Excavations at military sites make this point clearly. Much attention has been, and will be, paid to the tablets of Vindolanda, but the evidence from the site has much more to tell us about writing than just the texts themselves. Rather over 200 *stilus* pens have been discovered at the site to date.[26] This is an impressive number, but it is all the more significant when we consider it alongside the quantity of such pens found elsewhere in the same province. To put this haul in context, in the prosperous and apparently more sophisticated regions of the south, the area often termed the 'civil zone', there is widespread evidence for *stili*, but they appear in nothing like the same concentration. Though a survey by Hanson and Conolly demonstrates that *stili* were found at 124 rural sites in this region, in the vast majority of cases only one or two such pens were found at each site.[27] While this small number reflects the smaller sizes of these sites, it nonetheless underscores the comparably thin distribution of active writers. More compelling a contrast, perhaps, comes from the numbers of *stili* recovered at Silchester, a town with a long history of contact with the Roman Empire stretching back before the conquest. It had a population at least twice that of Vindolanda, was occupied longer, and has been excavated far more extensively, but it has only produced about 160 pens to date.[28]

To stay with the same province for a moment, if we consider the distribution of graffiti, we see a similar pattern. Detailed analysis of the context of graffiti shows that a disproportionately high proportion of all examples recovered come from military sites—a factor which, while assuredly linked to the density of occupation and the heightened risk of loss, also reflects an environment peculiarly favourable to the written word. The point about loss is important, because while some graffiti can be quite articulate and informative, most are relatively basic, consisting of little more than a mark or name, and many serve simply to mark ownership of objects. In a military situation, where weapons and expensive armour are involved, the need for effective ownership marks is particularly acute. Carefully crafted ownership graffiti on metalwork, pottery, and leatherwork can therefore be added to the more casual scribbling found on walls. But to all this we can add the fact that forts were quite literally littered with letters. At Vindolanda, where some attempt had at least been made to burn and destroy the tablets, many nevertheless appeared in contexts that clearly represented flooring or the dumps that helped build up working surfaces. At Mons Claudianus in Egypt, *ostraca* were also

---

[26] Birley, Birley, and Birley (1993: 16); Hanson and Conolly (2002: 155 n. 35).

[27] Hanson and Conolly (2002: 157–8). Table 1 lists 50 non-villa sites of which only 4 have produced 3 or more *stili*. Table 2 lists 74 villa and probable villa sites of which only 15 have produced 3 or more such pens.

[28] Boon (1974: 62–4); Fulford and Timby (2000: 373).

dumped in and immediately around the fort in their tens of thousands, raising the walking level substantially in several areas.[29]

There was no danger of being left with nothing to read in a Roman fort. From spearheads to luggage labels, writing was everywhere. Everyone in the military community was exposed to the written word on a daily basis, be it stamped on clay, painted on wood, carved on stone, or moulded in metal. Building inscriptions stood above fort gates, and on a wide range of structures throughout the fort interior. They recorded the date that construction took place, who completed it, and sometimes why it was undertaken. Pride of place in these texts always went to the name and titles of the reigning emperor, thus emphasizing the builders' allegiance to the Imperial House. Of course, the emperor's relationship with his soldiers is one of the great themes of Roman history: it could make or break any ruler. And traces of both making and breaking appear in the written word, just as in the art of the camps. Many inscriptions, for example, bear the hallmarks of *damnatio memoriae*; the emperor's name has been deleted. The symbolism here is obvious: the destruction of his name and image was supposed to purge Roman society's collective memory of the man himself. The integral place of auxiliary bases within imperial communications networks ensured that once the decree went out, their walls would soon have resounded to the sounds of chiselling as offending names and faces were swiftly erased.

The discussion of these dedications leads us to question how far they would have had an impact on those who passed them daily. The presence of a text does not automatically mean that people will attempt to read it. Indeed, to those incapable of reading it may remain no more than a series of patterns of limited relevance, more decorative than informative. For those who have acquired some reading ability, however rudimentary, such inscriptions may appear in a quite different light. It has been plausibly suggested 'that public inscriptions in the Roman world provided a large-scale and abundant (if not richly amusing) reader for any child who learned his letters informally'.[30] This is certainly what one of Petronius' freedman characters appears to have done, when in a rant, he boasts that while he may have had little formal education, he 'knew the letters of stone'.[31] The phrase suggests an important distinction between reading abilities that we may be less inclined to make today. Reading monumental inscriptions composed of capital letters, interpuncts, and standard formulae would have been much easier than handwritten correspondence. Even without the problems of different handwriting styles, cursive scripts would have presented greater difficulties to those unaccustomed to reading. Cursive script often looks as though it is written in a different alphabet from that used for inscriptions. Bowman and Thomas note that the Romans themselves could have great difficulties reading the tablets, and cite Plautus' remarks that the letters appeared as *gallina scripsit* or hen tracks.[32] It is possible that many soldiers' reading ability was restricted to capital-letter texts, and it is interesting to note that some Latin military papyri and many graffiti were themselves written in capitals rather than in cursive script.[33] This may have been to make them easier to understand, but it may also suggest that the writer was

---

[29] Bingen (1996).   [30] Horsfall (1991: 62).   [31] Petronius *Satyricon* 58.7.
[32] Bowman and Thomas (1983: 53); Plautus *Pseudolus* 13ff.   [33] e.g. ChLA 7 and 219.

unable to write letters in cursive. Tomlin considers the latter to be a 'tempting' explanation of capital-letter texts among the Bath curse tablets, and suggests that they might indicate this type of literacy.[34]

For those capable of taking in the information presented in formulaic capital-letter texts, there were plenty of other examples of writing to try their skills on. The roofs of buildings bore tiles and antefixes, often stamped with a regimental title. Signs over doors indicated the buildings' functions, and a vast range of regimental property, from handmills to bread stamps, was marked with the name of the unit or sub-unit to which it belonged.[35]

Not all examples of writing in the military community were official, of course. Some of the written documents were commissioned or produced by soldiers and their associated civilians to express something a little more personal. The religious life of the garrison, for example, not only found expression in the ceremonies of the imperial cult, observed in the regimental shrine and on the parade ground, but also in a range of other shrines and temples in the neighbourhood. As we saw in an earlier chapter, such establishments benefited considerably from their military clientele. Soldiers regularly dedicated altars at these places, often inscribing them with the formula *votum solvit libens merito*, declaring that in doing so they were discharging a vow. The expense involved in commissioning altars ensured that the donors were often from the higher ranks, but groups of soldiers sometimes shared the cost, as did the men of the Vellavian district who joined the Tungrian cohort at Birrens in Scotland,[36] or found a cheaper alternative. A possible example of the latter was discovered at Carvoran on Hadrian's Wall.[37] The succinct, roughly carved inscription,

DE(A)E HA/MMI(AE)/SABI(NUS)/F(ECIT)

suggests that it was a home-made effort and not the work of a professional stonecarver. The dedication and the name of the dedicator imply that it was produced by a *miles* of *cohors I Hamiorum sagittariorum,* the unit then stationed at the fort. Whoever dedicated the inscription, it is important to note that the donor was sufficiently convinced of the value of a written dedication to proffer this offering. Such dedications were clearly not the exclusive domain of the officer class. The wording of an altar inscription, as of an epitaph, was of greater interest to the ordinary soldier than the title of the emperor on a building inscription. It conveyed information about a local individual, his beliefs, and his life. We might, therefore, expect that these were the words an individual would take the trouble to read if they were to read anything.

Use of the written word is one thing, of course, but applying it in new ways is quite another. Many of the men who served in the *auxilia* came from peoples who first made extensive use of writing in cult contexts when they were absorbed into the Empire. Even then, the use of the written word in cult was hardly universal—so its familiarity at military bases across the Roman world speaks articulately of a

---

[34] Tomlin (1988: 86).
[35] Signs over doors: Cagnat (1913: 495); handmills: e.g. *CIL* 13.11954a; bread stamps: e.g. *CIL* 13.6935.
[36] *RIB* 2107.   [37] *RIB* 1780.

transformation wrought through writing and the processes of incorporation. The same applies to funerary memorials. The association of writing with monuments to the deities and to the dead was not universal; it would have been alien to soldiers from many backgrounds before they commenced their military service.

Yet tombstones and grave markers came to constitute perhaps the most personal contribution by members of the military community to the literate environment within which they lived and died. Just how important these monuments were to the individuals who erected them and were commemorated by them is demonstrated by the epitaphs themselves. Some are written in verse, others carry a personal message. Mócsy has even argued that spelling mistakes on some epitaphs indicate that soldier-commemorators wrote out initial drafts of the text themselves.[38] It must not be forgotten that those tombstones that survive only represent that element within the *auxilia* that considered the commemoration of their lives in writing a worthwhile investment. Those who could not or would not pay for a stone monument may have sought a cheaper wooden alternative, with or without text. Yet while it is impossible to say what proportion of auxiliaries invested in written monuments, we may observe that even the humblest *milites* are recorded on elaborate stone memorials, and that proportionately far more such monuments survive attesting soldiers than civilians in many parts of the Empire.[39] The tombstone was not a uniquely military phenomenon, but it did enjoy a high profile in areas occupied by the army. It is one of the reasons why we know so much more about soldiers and their families than almost any other group below the elite. Interestingly too, this latter group are well represented as both commemorators and commemorated. Occasionally, they depart from local convention by adding a particular personal touch to the epitaph, as in the case of the siblings of a trooper from the *ala Vocontiorum* interred at Cologne.[40]

In seeing each Roman military base as a place of writing, it is vital to see it in its wider context too. For military stations were of crucial importance to the broader network of written communication. The events at Patkoua are but one, local, military example of this, but it is clear that the implications were much wider. When the sailor Apion wrote to his father in Egypt, from his base in southern Italy, he used the device of sending the letters to an auxiliary cohort, *cohors I Apamenorum*, whence they would be forwarded.[41] The auxiliary camp was therefore a place full of letters and a hub in the larger network of communication; but, as further analysis reveals, it was also well suited to fostering writing in a particular range of ways.

While altars and tombstones are perhaps the most enduring testimony to active use of writing by soldiers, their friends, and their families, they are certainly not alone. The emphasis on the written word that we have charted manifested itself in an impressive range of documents commissioned by or written by these groups. Together, this evidence overwhelmingly indicates that the army valued literacy enormously and soldiers learnt to value it too. Possession of reading and writing skills assured some men better working conditions, and better pay; it was surely a vital qualification for promotion to certain posts. Many a soldier would have

---

[38] *CIL* 6.2552; 2662; Mócsy (1974: 261).   [39] Mann (1985: 205–6).   [40] *CIL* 13.8655.
[41] *BGU* II.423; Maxfield (1995: 22).

echoed Petronius' sentiment that 'there is bread in it'.[42] Certainly, the sailor Apion and the legionary Iulius Apollinarius were aware of the benefits. Apion thanks his father for teaching him handwriting and for his 'good education', hoping, 'if the gods are willing, to advance quickly'.[43] Apollinarius had already seen positive results attributable to his literacy, namely his promotion to *librarius legionis*, when he wrote to his mother and told her how glad he was not to be 'cutting stones' alongside those less privileged.[44] A great deal is known about literate officers and may be assumed about clerks, but our knowledge of the distribution of reading and writing skills among the *milites* is patchy. Few today would subscribe to Horsfall's view that 'the illiterate soldier was seriously disadvantaged and a positive encumbrance, to be taught urgently'.[45] Many documents show that this could not have been the case. A list of receipts for hay-money issued to troopers of the *ala Veterana Gallica* demonstrates that only 22 of the 64 men recorded on legible entries could actually sign for themselves.[46] If Horsfall's understanding were correct, the *ala* would have been scarcely operational, but there is no reason to assume this was the case. What emerges, rather, from this example is that soldiers encountered a lot more documents. If they had to provide receipts for hay-money, for example, they were assuredly doing so for many other commodities that came to them from the state. Certainly they were involved in the production of far more written documents than were the contemporary peasants at Karanis.

Before going any further, it is important to consider the relevance of data from more general Roman military contexts to the discussion of the written word in the *auxilia*. It will be important to distinguish this latter category from that associated with the legions. Harris notes that he uncovered many examples of illiterate auxiliaries in the papyrological evidence, but that he only found only one illiterate legionary, a veteran.[47] In the case of the best-documented of all provinces from the perspective of military paperwork and personal correspondence, Egypt, it certainly appears that there a higher proportion of legionaries than auxiliaries could write.[48] Hopkins suggests that legionary recruitment practices may well account for this postulated phenomenon, arguing that the legions drew their men from the propertied and educated classes.[49] Whatever the reason, the overall impression of lower literacy rates in the *auxilia* than in the legions may also have been reflected in the administrative efficiency within some auxiliary units. Writing in the 1st century AD, for example, Pliny noted that the accountants of the *ala Milliaria* in Syria were the only auxiliary ones in the whole province who were efficient—the rest were unsatisfactory.[50] Mention of *alae* in turn raises a further possibility. Cavalry troopers appear far more likely as the authors of written texts than do infantry soldiers. Though by no means all cavalry troopers were

---

[42] Petronius *Satyricon* 46.7, i.e. there is a chance to earn one's crust.
[43] *BGU* II.423.   [44] *P. Mich.* 466.
[45] Horsfall (1991: 63). Interestingly, Horsfall was led to these conclusions by observing Gurkha units in the modern British army (1991: 63 n. 23). This is not, however, a useful analogy, because Gurkha soldiers today serve within the framework of a highly literate army, and are employed by a country that actively promotes mass literacy.
[46] *RMR* 76.   [47] *P. Mich.* ix.551; Harris (1989: 253–4).
[48] Bowman (1994a: 96).   [49] Hopkins (1991: 137).   [50] Pliny *Ep.* 7.31.

literate, I believe that a higher proportion of *equites* than foot soldiers were using writing.

Such generalities are of some interest when comparing military units; but the military community itself contained many individuals of varied status, and it is important to consider how their participation in written communication varied. The most systematic way to examine this is to go through the ranks and appointments that made up most auxiliary units, considering along the way the likely backgrounds of those under examination. We will therefore do this, starting with officers and working down through the rank structure to the *milites*.

Sitting atop the hierarchy of letter producers within every auxiliary unit was the commanding officer. Though these units were often commanded by senior centurions, their commanders were most often tribunes or prefects, and of equestrian status. We can see through their correspondence that these men and their families were well equipped to participate in the wider imperial network of influence, peddled through writing. Letters and patronage were the instruments that tied them into the Empire's web of power. One letter from the archive of Flavius Cerialis, commanding officer of *cohors VIIII Batavorum* at Vindolanda, for example, shows Cerialis writing to a senior official in the hope that the man will intercede with the governor on his behalf.[51] The text is frustratingly incomplete, but the vital point, that this officer was as much as dependent on patronage as the men below him were on his, is clear.

The vast majority of these men would have enjoyed a traditional Roman education, an education which placed the highest value on oral skills, but in which reading and writing, while receiving comprehensive attention, were regarded as mere technologies. Senior officers, much like high-ranking executives today, were accustomed to dictating letters, and often only wrote the closing greeting themselves. Certainly this was the practice followed by Cerialis. The surviving draft of one of his letters preserves the use of *et hiem* (erased) and then corrected with *etiam*, clear testimony of a phonetic dictation error.[52] That Cerialis used Latin and communicated in this way is all the more interesting when we remember that the man probably owed his position as much to the fact that he was a leading Batavian loyal to Rome as to anything else.[53]

At this level of command, it is clear that officers were expected to be able to master Latin, even if, as in the east, they frequently used Greek. Two centuries after Cerialis, and in the very different setting of Egypt, another regimental commander whose correspondence is well known to us was also clearly expected to do so. Abinnaeus, commander of the *ala* at Dionysias, had to conduct most of his correspondence with the local community in Greek, but his exchanges with senior imperial officials were still in Latin.[54]

The highest levels of literacy and engagement in literary culture were also found amongst others in the *praetorium*. Vindolanda has also furnished us with examples of correspondence between the wives of commanding officers. Best known of these is the birthday party invitation to Cerialis' wife, Sulpicia Lepidina, from Claudia Severa, wife of another equestrian officer.[55] To this must be added

---

[51] *Tab. Vindol.* II.225.   [52] Ibid. II.234.ii.2.   [53] P. 116.
[54] Bell et al. (1962).   [55] *Tab. Vindol.* II.291.

evidence suggesting the teaching of Latin to younger members of the family. Two fragments of a tablet carrying a line from the Aeneid were found in the same context as papers from the Cerialis archive.[56] The impression that they form part of a writing exercise is reinforced both by the word below, which may be read as *segn*(iter) (slack), and by the widespread use of Vergil as a source for such purposes.[57] Though his writings were used in this way across the Empire, it is worth noting that they have made an appearance in military settings as diverse as Britain, Egypt, and Israel.[58] It is not possible, unfortunately, to identify the status of the copyists with any certainty, though the editors of the Israeli example found at Masada associate the find with legionary soldiers.[59] Evidence discussed below may prove that individual auxiliary soldiers benefited from this double dosage of imperial culture, acquiring literacy through exposure to Vergil. We can clearly see that the work of the most articulate exponent of the Augustan ideal found its way into their camps.

Most of the information the governor received from auxiliary units would have had to pass through the hands of the commander; regular reports on the status of the regiments must have been essential. Accordingly, the format taken by excavated reports has attracted a great deal of comment, and several attempts have been made to classify them.[60] As our principal interest here is in writing and the soldiers, an extended discussion of this classification would be inappropriate. It is important to note, however, that the difficulty some commentators have had in reconciling new discoveries to these classifications may reflect real diversity in practice.[61] While no doubt commanders provided, and governors needed, certain types of information, there is absolutely no reason to assume that the style of internal reporting was uniform across Rome's armies.[62] Indeed, the diversity of returns strongly suggests that it was not. Variation between units, which may have followed the favoured practice of particular commanders, or between provincial armies, which followed the traditions established by governors, should be expected. These differences were not ultimately of great importance, but they do remind us of how military units, and particularly provincial armies, could differ from one another. We will certainly see hints of this diversity below, for example in the different styles of leave passes.

Below the level of the commanding officer, centurions and decurions performed similar roles in cavalry and infantry units respectively. Their job required that they could not only read but write as well, something made quite clear in the literary sources. Martial boasts that a centurion serving near the Black Sea could read his poems,[63] a reminder of the way that the army's communication networks could also facilitate the spread of literature. On a more mundane level, Appian notes that centurions had to submit daily reports.[64] The latter need not, of itself,

---

[56] *Aeneid* 9.473 in *Tab. Vindol.* II.118.   [57] Birley, Birley, and Birley (1993: 38).

[58] Bowman and Thomas (1994: 66).

[59] *Doc. Masada* 721 is from *Aeneid* 4.9; Cotton and Geiger, with Thomas (1989: 16).

[60] Fink (1971: 179–81).

[61] See Fink (1971: 179) for diverse practice in monthly reports; Bowman and Thomas (1994: 74–6) on *renuntium* texts, not found within Fink's classification.

[62] As a British army subaltern in the early 1990s I was struck by the difference in procedures for delivering strength reports when I transferred between units.

[63] Martial 11.3.   [64] Appian *BC* 5.86.

indicate that the officer was able to write, as he could have dictated the text to a clerk, but other evidence suggests that he almost always was. Documentary material from all over the Roman world reveals the extensive range of purposes for which centurions and decurions were required to write. Not a single example of an illiteracy formula, a feature of many documents in the first three centuries AD, has been found to be written on their behalf. In addition to the daily returns referred to by Appian, these officers wrote crime reports, witnessed purchases, procured animals, and wrote to their seniors and subordinates. Literacy was clearly a crucial qualification for these posts. But this in turn raises the question as to where the men came from; were sufficient literate soldiers available in the ranks of the *auxilia* to fill these appointments?

The origins of auxiliary centurions and decurions are discussed elsewhere in this volume, but it is worth reiterating that many of these men had not worked their way up through the ranks but rather were direct appointments.[65] Gilliam argued that the state sometimes made direct appointments 'to obtain literate and educated men to help deal with the paper-work and administrative functions of the army'.[66]

A similar picture of transferees, direct appointments, and in-unit promotions emerges when we look at the origins of other junior officers in the *alae* and *cohortes* who needed to read and write. The ranks immediately below *centurio* and *decurio* were *optio* and *duplicarius* respectively. These men were also closely involved in the production of written documents. At Vindolanda in Britain it was the *optiones* who prepared the daily reports. *Optiones* also sometimes appear on tombstones carrying a bag of writing tablets. In Egypt an *optio* witnessed the discharge of a legacy.[67] Our evidence for the origins of *optiones* is poor, and it is difficult to make any useful generalizations from it. In the case of the *duplicarii*, however, eleven pre-Hadrianic inscriptions survive. Although the quantities involved are small, it is interesting to note that four of these were Roman citizens from birth (at least three were legionaries first), three of the remainder came from the same ethnic background as the regiments in which they served (and may therefore have been promoted internally), and at least three were non-citizens of different origin to their regiments.[68] This suggests a similar mix to that found among the centurions and decurions, reminding us that a significant number of those performing literate functions within the *auxilia* may never have served as ordinary *milites* within their units.

A higher proportion of the other posts within the centuries and *turmae* were probably occupied by men who started their careers as private soldiers. Of the twenty-two pre-Hadrianic *signiferi* (standard bearers) identified from inscriptions by Holder, only two appear to have been citizens.[69] This would seem to suggest that the system of transferring legionaries which was attested for senior officers of the century/*turma* was not employed here. The finding is interesting in the light of Vegetius' discussion of recruitment. He advises commanders to take note of

[65] P. 112. This does not seem to have been the case with the legionary centurionate: see E. Birley (1988a: 189–205).
[66] Gilliam (1957: 168). For discussion of the background of centurions, decurions, and *principales*, see Holder (1980: 86–99).
[67] *P. Mich.* 435. i.7–12.   [68] Holder (1980: 92).   [69] Ibid. 931.

literate and numerate new arrivals because they are good potential *signiferi*.[70] It is always dangerous to generalize too much from Vegetius' observations, but this remark may be understood to indicate that men with such skills constituted a small proportion of most recruit intakes, and that commanders were expected to draw from these rather than to organize any instruction for illiterates to prepare them for promotion.

This in turn touches on a wider debate about the ways open to serving soldiers to acquire writing skills. Dietz has suggested that the figure *[p]ollione coh(ortis)* recorded in a papyrus from Dura was in fact that of a unit Latin teacher.[71] Whether or not this is the correct interpretation, it is certainly without parallel within the *auxilia*. Yet, as A. R. Birley has noted, there is evidence that traditional writing exercises were being undertaken in the *barracks* at Vindolanda.[72] Vergil's writings were a popular source for such exercises, and it is interesting to find fragments of them copied out, not in the central range of buildings, where they might perhaps be attributed to the commanding officer's family, but in an altogether more humble setting. The presence of writing exercises would not necessarily indicate the presence of a formally appointed teacher, of course, but it would suggest that, for the reasons discussed here, some soldiers found it beneficial to develop their writing skills.

Whether or not formal or informal teaching was at work, Vegetius' remarks are important because they stress how important it was for the *signiferi* to be able to perform clerical and accounting duties. Proof that they were indeed expected to perform such roles comes from the many pay documents which have been recovered which were processed, written, and signed by standard-bearers. Thus when new recruits arrived to join *cohors I Lusitanorum*, the six *signiferi* of the cohort recorded the money each man deposited in the regimental savings and copied receipts to Longinus Tituleius, the regiment's senior centurion.[73] It is, however, of interest to note that some men may have attained this position without being able to write. We know, for example, of an illiterate *signifer* from the Pselkis *ostraca* discovered at Dakka, Egypt.[74]

Regular production of written documents was also a responsibility of the *tesserarii* and the *sesquiplicarii*, men respectively third-in-command of centuries and of *turmae*.[75] Indeed, the title *tesserarius* derives from *tesserae*, wooden tablets which bore the password which the officer circulated.[76] Accounts of the dissemination of orders in written form have led some authorities to believe that all soldiers must have been able to read if the orders were to be received and understood. Best, for example, infers this from a passage in Polybius, and goes on to generalize about the imperial period from this understanding.[77] Polybius records that *equites* (*hippeis*) drawn from the legions received written instructions as to which guard posts they should check. Yet the particular *equites* referred to in the text were not ordinary soldiers. The legionary cavalry served as messengers, and normally came from better-educated and wealthier backgrounds. Furthermore, even if Best were

---

[70] Vegetius II.20.   [71] Dietz (1985).   [72] A. R. Birley (2009: 277–8).   [73] *RMR* 74.
[74] *RMR* 78. Fink believes that the Pselkis *ostraca* may have been issued to soldiers of *cohors II Ituraeorum equitata* (1971: 311).
[75] Breeze (1974: 245).   [76] Webster (1998: 117).
[77] Best (1967: 122–7) from Polybius (6.35.8–6.36.2).

correct in his assumption that Polybius described an army in which all soldiers could read, his conclusions could not be applied to the *auxilia* of the Imperial period; the organization and social composition even of the legions themselves had changed considerably by this time.

The role Polybius ascribes to the *equites* seems to have devolved onto the *tesserarii* over time, and seems to demand that they were, at least, able to read. Relatively little is known of the auxiliary *tesserarii*. Two surviving references to them on papyrus are, however, entirely consistent with the functions known to have been performed by their legionary opposite numbers. In the first text, a *tesserarius* of *cohors III Augusta Thracum* signs in Latin a deed of sale written in Greek.[78] The episode is indicative of a pattern found on other papyri, where writing in either Greek or Latin is sufficient. In the second, a *tesserarius* of *cohors XX Palmyrenorum* appears on a daily report.[79]

The appearance of *sesquiplicarii* only in regiments with cavalry and of *tesserarii* only in infantry units supports Breeze's theory that the two performed much the same function.[80] It is therefore interesting to note that the much more extensive data recording *sesquiplicarii* suggests that the vast majority of those who held the rank started their careers in the *auxilia*.[81] The overall impression is that soldiers at this level did need to be able to read, and that many of them were promoted from the ordinary *milites* and *equites*.

Before concluding this survey of the use of the written word by officers, it is important to comment on the *curatores*. This term may be an appointment, rather than a rank—and we know that at least in the Egyptian desert the title *curator praesidii* could be held by a centurion or decurion, but often it could be held by more junior officers such as *duplicarii* and *sesquiplicarii*.[82] *Curatores* appear frequently as the recipients of correspondence.[83] In some cases the fact that they receive commands from decurions indicates that they indeed are junior in rank, most probably members of *turmae*.[84] It is striking that the men who held these temporary postings were expected to be able to act on the receipt of written information, and one cannot escape the conclusion again that a fair number of soldiers in the lowest ranks were able to read.

Military bureaucracy was so powerful that all soldiers were made personally aware of the value of written records throughout their service, even when not every man could create them himself. The information that the written word conveyed could result in very definite material benefits to the individual. It also served to define his financial status and safeguard his legal rights. In this way, it will be argued, auxiliary soldiers participated in literate modes in a wider variety of ways and to a far greater extent than their provincial peers.

Just as Cerialis sought influence, favour, and patronage through his correspondence, so too did individual soldiers. Would-be recruits able to bring *litterae commendaticiae* (letters of recommendation) with them on arrival at their regiments could find that such letters made a difference to both their service

---

[78] *P. Dura* 101.   [79] Ibid. 65R.   [80] Breeze (1974: 245).   [81] Holder (1980: 95).
[82] A. R. Birley (2002: 47) suggested that *curatores* served as second in command to decurions on the basis that they are named alongside *optiones*, the second in command to centurions, in Vindolanda *renuntia*.
[83] e.g. *O. Flor.* 7, 11, 13, 16, 15; *O. Claud.* 357, 359.   [84] Bagnall (1976: 22–3).

conditions and promotion prospects.[85] The lesson was one of great relevance to life in wider provincial society too—the Empire was bound together by such networks of patronage, all of which ultimately culminated in the person of the emperor himself.

Sponsors were prepared, and asked, to struggle with a language that they clearly had trouble writing to help the career of a friend or relation.[86] *Litterae commendaticiae* reflect the immense importance of patronage throughout Roman society; auxiliary soldiers who learnt to exploit this system could have benefited considerably. The most celebrated example of this system in action comes from Egypt and concerns one Claudius Terentianus, the son of a veteran, and a man whose military career involved service in the fleet, an attempt to enlist into an auxiliary cohort, and eventual enrolment in the legions. His correspondence with his father, dating from the early 2nd century and written while he was still an unhappy sailor, is intensely illuminating. Initial failure to enter the legions was, he was certain, because one of his referees had let him down. He laments:

> And if god should will it, I hope to live frugally and to be transferred to a cohort. Here, however, nothing can be done without money, nor will letters of recommendation be of any use, unless a man helps himself.[87]

His hopes were therefore fixed on getting into a cohort, but to achieve this he mentions not just letters of recommendation but money and, seemingly, further lobbying in person. Even to enter the navy he had had to rely on letters of recommendation.[88]

Once enrolled, as Terentianus' letter itself suggests, money soon became an issue. Soldiers are rarely indifferent to the matter of pay and the paperwork associated with it. There is nothing to suggest that the Roman soldier was exceptional in this regard. Indeed, pay demands feature largely in Tacitus' accounts of military unrest. Certainly, many of the surviving military papyri and wooden tablets concern soldiers' pay, savings, and deductions for equipment. From the moment he joined his regiment, a man's financial status was the subject of extensive documentation. The *tirones* (recruits) who arrived at *cohors I Lusitanorum* received receipts for the deposit of money credited to them at the very start of their service.[89] The issue of pay statements became a regular feature of their military lives from then on. As we have seen, soldiers were not the only individuals in the provinces to whom Latin or Greek receipts were issued. Civilians were, for example, given receipts to prove that they had completed their compulsory annual public service and had paid customs duties.[90] The regularity with which soldiers received fully itemized pay statements was, however, unique in provincial society. Army regulations also required that all auxiliaries submitted a written statement to the regimental pay office on receipt of their *stipendia* or salary payments. The discovery of such a document at

---

[85] Watson (1974: 496).   [86] The poor Latin of *P. Mich.* 8.468, 35 demonstrates this clearly.
[87] *P. Mich.* 8.468, 35–41. For translation and insightful discussion, see Davies (1989: 11). I take the phrase 'unless a man helps himself' to indicate personal lobbying of staff at the unit concerned.
[88] Davies (1989: 11).   [89] *RMR* 74.
[90] Préaux (1954: 83–7) discusses receipts for public service. For written receipts for customs duties, see, e.g. *P. Grenf.* II.50h.

Vindonissa, Switzerland, has had important consequences, not only for our understanding of soldiers' pay, but also for our knowledge of the uses of writing within the *auxilia*. Speidel reconstructed the Vindonissa text as follows:

> Asino Ce[1]ere, Non[io] co(n)s(ulibus), XI K(alendas)
> Aug(ustas). S(upra) s(criptus) Clua, eq(ues) Raetor(um)
> tur(ma) Albi Pudentis ac(e)epi * (denarios) L
> [e]t stipendi proximi * (denarios) LXXV.[91]

Though the wording of the document is simple—the date by consular year, the name of the recipient and his unit, the *turma* in which he served, and the sum he was paid—it actually tells us a great deal more. First, the wording of the document makes it evident that Clua was a soldier in a regular Raetian auxiliary regiment. It is interesting to find that at this early date (AD 38), an auxiliary soldier of native origin was capable of producing such a text. The possibility that Clua was merely copying out a formula, and that he was incapable of composing anything himself, remains. If, however, that were the case there would have been some strange inconsistencies in the formula itself. These are the omission of the consul Nonius' cognomen, Quintilianus, and the writing of the letter 'e' in two different ways, as E and II. Such irregularities may perhaps be better attributed to one individual's idiosyncratic writing style than to an official template prepared by regimental clerks. A further point of interest is the dating of the receipt. Speidel notes that 'dating by suffect consuls outside Italy was very uncommon and may shed some light on military administration customs of the early empire'.[92] This is perhaps another example of the army, almost uniquely among communities in the provinces, employing an essentially 'Roman' device—in this instance a device for the measuring of time.

Soldiers were accustomed to give written receipts for much more than their pay, however. There are, for example, the receipts submitted by the troopers of *ala veterana Gallica* in Egypt in the late 2nd century for hay-money.[93] Forty-two of the sixty-four legible receipts were written for illiterates. Looked at from another angle, most of the remaining texts, almost a third of the sample, seem to have been written by the individual whose name appears on them. Even amongst the twenty-two there were multiple gradations of writing skill, with sixteen different variations shown in the spelling of the accusative singular of the same word.[94] Interestingly, one of the entries appears to be partially written in the Latin alphabet, rather than the Greek used for the rest of the document.[95] There are two points to make here. First, the unit worked on the assumption that all soldiers, whether or not they were able to write, should be able to furnish the regimental clerks with receipts when such documents were required. As we have seen, civilians were sometimes required to submit written documents too, but the vast majority of provincials would surely not have had cause to do so with the regularity that was demanded of the soldiery. Second, it is interesting to note

---

[91] M. A. Speidel (1992: 90–91). The analysis of the document that follows is based on his own assessment of the text.

[92] Ibid. 91 n. 28.   [93] *P. Hamb.* i.39.   [94] Fink (1971: 284).

[95] Col. xvi.1–9 according to Fink (1971: 284).

that a possible 'literacy' rate within this auxiliary unit is significantly higher than the 10 per cent generally proposed for the civilian population in the provinces.[96]

Surviving documentation also demonstrates how writing at army installations also touched the lives of civilians within the wider military community. Three texts found together within a building at Vindolanda show how these individuals participated within a pattern of exchanges dependent on writing.[97] Each was written by a civilian trader who came to the camp from elsewhere.[98] The first documents the issuing of wheat, both to men who are obviously soldiers but also to one Amabilis at a nearby shrine and to Lucco in charge of the pigs.[99] The second is a cash account which records not simply soldiers, but also an individual listed as the companion/unofficial spouse of the *vexillarius*.[100] Not a soldier, therefore, but someone attached to a soldier and here clearly benefiting through the writing based system used to supply the fort. The third document, written on the back of the first, is interesting—for it suggests that the trader who was dealing with all these individuals was nonetheless regarded by many of them as something of an outsider.[101] He had suffered a beating, quite probably from the soldiers, and his attempts to get justice from the officers on the spot had been frustrated. The whole episode recalls Juvenal's satirical commentary on the benefits of army service, in which he asks what kind of justice a civilian might expect in a military camp.[102] Describing himself as 'a man from overseas', he addresses himself to a higher authority, the governor or perhaps even the emperor, in what appears now to be a draft for a petition. Here we see juxtaposed writing both as an agent that links the military community of Vindolanda together through the supply of their daily bread and as an instrument that can reach beyond the confines of that community, right up to the most powerful individual in the province.

Another form of document that had a profound importance to ordinary soldiers concerned debt. Soldiers borrowed money both from their unit and from one another. Debt certificates written by or on behalf of military personnel have been discovered at a number of sites. They are often witnessed by an officer of some sort. This could indicate that the army sought to encourage soldiers to record personal loans in order to avoid potentially inflammatory disagreement over debts, though I am unaware of any other evidence for such a procedure. Certainly, on one of the Florida *ostraca* a trooper writes to his *curator* to inform

[96] Harris (1989: 254).

[97] *Tab. Vindol.* II.180, 181, 344; Bowman and Thomas (1994: 122). Nos 180 and 344 were on different sides of the same tablet.

[98] Bowman and Thomas (1994: 122 and 330). As the editors note, the 3 texts are written in the same hand.

[99] *Tab. Vindol.* II.180, lines ii.10 and ii.27 respectively.

[100] Ibid. II.181.14–15. Restored by the editors as *contubernalis Tagamatis vexsillari*. This leaves open, of course, the possibility of the individual as the 'tent-mate' or 'comrade' of Tagamatis, but as both the editors of the texts and Birley observe, the term is probably used in its other sense here—that of concubine, partner, or common-law wife (Bowman and Thomas 1994: 130; Birley 1990: 30).

[101] *Tab. Vindol.* II.344; Bowman and Thomas (1994: 329–34). The presence of the term *maiestatem* (i.4–5) strongly suggests the final text was intended for the governor, while the reference to our man's overseas origins is *hominem trasmarinum* (ii.15).

[102] Juvenal *Sat.* 16.5–34.

him of his financial difficulties.[103] This may, of course, just reflect an individual situation rather than a practice demanded by army policy. Officially encouraged to do so or not, it is clear that soldiers were using debt certificates from an early period. In one case, dating to AD 27, we even find a debt certificate issued by an illiterate auxiliary cavalryman to an illiterate auxiliary infantryman.[104] This is a fine example of how, even at an early date, auxiliaries came to value text even when they could not write, or perhaps even read, themselves. In addition to these records, which have been found amongst many of the major collections of military documents, we also have examples of other texts soldiers would have carried amongst their possessions. At least in the Egyptian Desert they also received documentation recording pay advances. These records were clearly issued to all serving soldiers, not just junior officers, as demonstrated by an *ostracon* of 30 January, AD 144 recording an advance to Eupraktos, an infantryman in a *cohors Ituraeorum*.[105]

The right to take leave when they had earned it was no doubt highly valued by the soldiers. Regimental headquarters were, therefore, advised to record soldiers' leave entitlements.[106] This was an important procedure and one that served to give an appearance of fairness, while at the same time ensured proper control. The first indication of desertion might be the late return of soldiers from leave, and reports were quick to note it, as we see from the Dura papyri.[107] If leave was granted, further written documentation was required in the form of a pass. An example of a furlough pass was discovered among the Florida *ostraca*, all of which are believed to have been sent by or to junior ranks of *cohors I Augusta Praetoria Lusitanorum equitata* in Egypt.[108] The document was written in Greek on a potsherd. The leave-taker's name was inserted into an underlined space left for the purpose when the main text was first written. Twelve texts involving applications for leave survive from Vindolanda, six of which are addressed to Cerialis and two to other regimental commanders, one of whom was the prefect of the *cohors I Tungrorum*.[109] Bowman and Thomas note that while these letters follow a certain formula, they differ from the Egyptian examples. This is another example of regional variation in military procedures. For, in this case, the applications were not simply chits in which the soldier's name was filled in; each was written in a different hand.[110] The applicant's rank is not normally given, but Bowman reasonably suggests that a number must have been from 'the lower ranks'.[111] In this case, then, writing was not only the medium which ensured the soldier received what was due to him, it also provided him with certification should his absence from his home base be challenged.

At the end of twenty-five years' service, those auxiliaries who did not already possess it received Roman citizenship. Again, this was marked in writing. The army was careful to ensure that the date of discharge was calculated correctly, and many documents record soldiers' enlistment dates and/or the length of service completed.[112] Soldiers therefore had a very personal interest in this kind of

---

[103] *O. Flor.* 4.   [104] *P. Vindob.* L135.   [105] *O. Claud.* 582.
[106] Vegetius II.19. For leave in the Roman army, see Bagnall (1976: 19–20).
[107] e.g. *P. Dura* 82.2.20.   [108] *O. Flor.* 27.   [109] *Tab. Vindol.* II.166–77.
[110] Bowman and Thomas (1994: 77).   [111] Bowman (1994a: 88).
[112] e.g. *P. Mich.* 164.

documentation. Once again the written word served to ensure that they received what was due to them, when it was due to them. On the acquisition of citizenship many auxiliaries also obtained diplomas, inscribed bronze sheets which could be produced as proof of their new Roman legal status, and that of their family. The diplomas were copies of bronze originals displayed at the heart of the Empire, in Rome itself.[113] It is perhaps thought-provoking to remember that many of those whose names appeared on these bronzes would never have visited Italy or even Europe. We will return to these documents in a later chapter, but for the moment it is sufficient to remember that for some men, diplomas were of the greatest importance. Some were even buried with them.[114] To others, such as Marcus Ulpius Fronto of *cohors I Batavorum*, his wife, Mattua, and their three daughters, Vagatra, Sureia, and Sata, they meant even more.[115] The appearance of named family members in the text reminds us that their rights were also recorded and protected by this document. Perhaps this goes some way to explaining why their early 2nd-century diploma was found in a *late* 2nd-century context in the military *vicus* at Regensburg- Kumpfmühl (Germany)—it had been preserved by the family into later generations.[116] Long after the end of a man's military career had ended, it appears that the written word defined and secured his status and that of his family in a way unparalleled in civil society.

Amongst the vast numbers of documents to survive from Roman Egypt, it is possible to identify many examples of auxiliary soldiers exploiting this medium for essentially private concerns. Thus we learn that in AD 90 M. Anthestius Gemellus of *cohors III Ituraeorum* takes time out from his regimental duties to represent his mother in rescheduling a loan; this was a task that clearly required an ability to work with written documents.[117] Another soldier, Dioscurus, had a rather more mundane use for writing. In the mid-2nd century he wrote to his fellow soldiers and *curator*, sending each a lettuce and bemoaning the fact that he has yet to receive acknowledgement of the cabbages he had sent—a full three days before! Again, the correspondence is delightfully ordinary and marked by an assumption that there was nothing to delay a swift exchange of letters between soldiers if one's correspondents could only be bothered to reply.[118]

Amongst the Greek *ostraca* discovered in Wâdi Fawâkhir, for example, it is also common to find men ending their messages with a request to pass on greetings to their comrades-in-arms.[119] The general content of these *ostraca*, with their references to cavalrymen and carters, indicate again that they are concerned with the most humdrum activities of auxiliary soldiers.

Even when families were separated by substantial distances, it is clear that letter-writing enabled individual members to support one another. The process ensured in many ways that the routine activity of the army actually had a still more profound impact on civilians than it might otherwise have done. Saturnalis wrote to his mother at Karanis from Pselkis (Darra), site of the winter camp of *cohors II Ituraeorum*, 800km away. He advised her that she has a new grandson.

---

[113] Many military diplomas bore the legend *descriptum et recognitum ex tabula aenea quae fixa est Romae in muro post templum divi Aug. ad Minervam.*

[114] Roxan (1985: 93).   [115] *RMD* 86, dated to 16 Dec., AD 113.

[116] Dietz (1978: 44–8; 1979: 63–6); Maxfield (1995: 40 n. 42).   [117] *P. Mich.* IX.568–9.

[118] *O. Claud.* 226.   [119] *O. Wâdi Fawâkhir* 9, 12, 13, 23.

This, it must be noted, is part of a stream of regular correspondence, for Saturnalis had written several times that month, but what is interesting is that he then talks of sending his family to her while he is away on outpost duty. Such a journey is no mean consideration for a family with a young child, but perhaps families were not permitted at outposts, or possibly thoughts of raids, such as the one on the Patkoua *praesidium*, preyed upon his mind.[120]

What is arguably most striking about the contents of these documents is that so many of them request, acknowledge, or accompany necessities. It is clear that this correspondence made a material difference to the lives of the soldiers and of their families. In addition to items of dress, men at the more remote sites were obviously also often concerned with supplements to their rations.[121] Clearly, army provisions were not so extensive that the soldier could not still benefit from regular exchanges with friends and family. Any unable to correspond in this way would have clearly felt the difference.

Similar patterns of exchange emerge from the other end of the Empire. A favourite example must surely be the very first tablet ever to be recovered from Vindolanda; this fragmentary text, which lacks both the name of sender and addressee, nonetheless has a familiar tone to it. Love and concern seem to permeate the message. Practical help, marked by the sending of essentials, is matched by the wish that the recipient lives in the greatest good fortune (harmony?) with his *contubernales* and with others, diligently named, in his circle. How many doughty young warriors have received just such missives from concerned parents over the centuries? The tablet's importance lies in its very banality, delighting Latinists with the first reference to underwear known from Roman military contexts. For the care package included not just underwear, but also sandals and socks. I repeat that we do not know the identity of the addressee, but there is a remarkable amount here that echoes the correspondence of ordinary *milites* from camps across the Roman world. Before turning to those parallels, though, we might note the presence of two women in this document. Sattua, whose name echoes recalls those of Mattua and Sata, the wife and daughter of the Batavian diploma-holder Fronto, is responsible for the socks.[122] Elpis, the other woman, is clearly in the circle of the recipient at Vindolanda—further evidence, not just for the presence of women associated with the lower ranks, but also for their involvement in this network of written communication.

The desire that the recipient pass on wishes to his *contubernales* is of passing interest here; though the term can be used generally to refer to colleagues, and for groups as diverse as slaves and staff officers, it is most generally understood in its sense as tent-mate.[123] It appears in other texts at Vindolanda, however, notably in two cases where the authors berate their correspondents for not writing more frequently—again a valuable testimony to the common expectation that the exchange of letters was routine and uncomplicated. In one of these texts, best wishes are passed on to civilian elders and a 'sister'; in another, the

[120] *P. Mich.* III.203; Maxfield (1995: 26–7).

[121] Maxfield (1995: 27–9) offers excellent examples of gifts sent between soldiers and their families.

[122] *Tab. Vindol.* II 346. Bowman and Thomas (2003: 336) discuss this and consider other options for the origin of the name. The diploma cited above is *RMD* 86.

[123] Bowman and Thomas (2003: 130, 296). Tacitus *Agric.* 5 uses the term to denote a staff officer.

correspondence addressed to Paris of *cohors III Batavorum* may involve a slave.[124] In much of this sort of correspondence, where we see the exchange of greetings, there is also again the exchange of goods.

Recent work by Dutch archaeologists has raised questions concerning the wider cultural implications of such correspondence. Might the writing skills men learnt and exploited during their military service have become more widespread within the civilian communities with which they were most strongly associated? The Batavi appear to be an ideal test case. Not only are there early examples of Batavian soldiers writing in Latin, but there is also evidence for a special and ongoing relationship between the Batavian homelands and units stationed abroad.[125] Might the return of veterans, coupled with the correspondence between soldiers overseas and their families, have helped foster literacy, and even language change, in the tribal lands of the Batavi?

In an impressive analysis, Derks and Roymans sought to argue that the presence of seal-boxes in the archaeological record might be indicative of writing practice, claiming that they were used to seal documents, and noted that there was a striking concentration of these artefacts within the *civitas Batavorum*.[126] While admiring the range and detail of their survey, I believe that it in fact shows something rather different, for I am more convinced by recent work on seal-boxes that shows that they were used to secure, not documents, but bags of coins.[127] What is interesting, though, is to focus on the scenarios that Derks and Roymans consider when looking at the linguistic impact of Roman service on a host society. They believe that the sheer intensity with which the Romans re-cruited in the Batavian tribal area would have led to the growth of a writing culture in the *civitas*. They argue that few families were left untouched by the process, which involved raising at least nine cohorts and one *ala*, in addition to guardsmen, legionaries, and men for the fleet. Theirs is an attractive argument. It links the experience of incorporation into military life to that of the incorporation of a community into imperial networks of communication; but it must be treated carefully. As the authors would be the first to acknowledge, they are arguing that it is the intensity of the community's link to the recruitment process that generates this distinct pattern. Other parts of northern Gaul which also produced many recruits for the *auxilia*—albeit not in quite such numbers—do not show this pattern. The process may have worked between soldiers and families, but the transformation was less marked in society as a whole.

It is, therefore, entirely possible to admire this model without then accepting all of its conclusions. Derks and Roymans believe that 'most Batavian auxiliary soldiers enjoyed informal training in writing and reading Latin while in the army'.[128] Yet, as we have seen, the levels of writing achieved amongst auxiliaries ranged wildly, from contingents in which two-thirds could not sign for hay through to individuals capable of composing, or having composed, sophisticated messages. There are no reasons to think that Batavian cohorts would have produced more literates, and some to suggest that they might on average have

---

[124] *Tab. Vindol.* II.310: elders/parents? (*parentes nostri*) and 'sister'. *Tab. Vindol.* II.311: Paris.
[125] For an early use of Latin by a Batavian soldier, see Bowman, Tomlin, and Worp (2009).
[126] Derks and Roymans (2002: 97).   [127] Charles Andrews, pers. comm.
[128] Derks and Roymans (2004: 102).

produced fewer—for in the relative homogeneity of Batavian cohorts, Latin's value as a *lingua franca* would have been less. So the use of writing is what is important here, not how many could write for themselves; but their argument goes on to see in the presence of written documents 'a radical transformation in the spoken language'.[129] Indeed, they suggest, 'There are good reasons for assuming that here, much in the same way as in Spain or S. Gaul, the original native language gave way to vulgar Latin in the first two centuries AD.'[130] It is an attractive idea—it may even be right—but the tablets themselves do not prove it, and no further evidence is advanced to do so. We live at a time when the growing rapidity of communications is often invoked as the prime suspect in language death. Yet, alongside that sad reality, there is another more uplifting one. As we look at the global triumph of English, for example, we can see that it has frequently been gained through English's acquisition as a second language. Situations emerge where bilingualism becomes prevalent, while the native language remains vibrant: modern Holland is a prime example. Is it absolutely necessary to assume that this could not have been the case there 1,800 years ago? In some parts of the Roman world, Latin and Greek may have had an additional advantage over native languages in that they were also written languages. It may very well be, therefore, that through contact with the *auxilia* the Batavian communities had a higher rate of bilinguals amongst them, rather than a declining number of speakers of their native tongue.

[129] Ibid.   [130] Ibid.

Part VII

Auxiliary Veterans and the Making of Provincial Society

21

Veterani and Other Veterans

At the heart of the Museum of London's fine Roman gallery stands a reconstructed *triclinium* or dining room (see Fig. 21.1). Red panels framed in yellow ochre, green, and black decorate the plastered walls. Beneath the panels runs a dado band painted to give the impression of rich marble veneer. Small glass windows allow light to enter the room and a brazier provides heat. Bronze jugs from Italy, glass from Germany, and Samian pottery from Gaul complement the image of quiet prosperity, while a fashionable floor decorated with black and white tessellated circles completes the picture of good living in Londinium *c.* AD 100.

In evoking this scene, the team at the Museum of London drew on excavated evidence from a house discovered at Watling Court near the city's Roman fort.[1] To stress the relative wealth of the owner, they contrast the Watling Court house with a reconstruction of contemporary craftworkers' quarters discovered only a few hundred metres away. There the floor is of flattened earth, glassless windows are covered with waxed cloth, and the walls lack elaborate decoration. Both the contrast and the captions raise the question: who was the owner of the Watling Court house and how did he acquire his wealth?

The display board answers succinctly: 'The house at Watling Court was owned by a wealthy man who was used to the Roman way of life. He was a retired (veteran) auxiliary soldier. His bronze military diploma, which granted him citizenship and allowed him to marry, was found in the house.' Having reviewed the site archive in detail, I find this explanation of the house's ownership an attractive one, but the opening statement of the display board inevitably invites further reflection.[2] How far did military life really prepare the auxiliary to be a prosperous and accomplished participant in 'the Roman way of life'? What does the presence of a diploma really tell us? Is the story of Watling Court likely to be representative of a wider trend or a reflection of what we want to believe?

---

[1] My thanks to Jenny Hall, formerly Keeper of the Roman Collections of the Museum of London, for discussing the exhibit with me and for making available the documentation that went into the display. While the display was principally based on material from Building D at Watling Court, elements of the wall plaster decoration were based on those found at Roman buildings excavated at Southwark Street. The vessels were added for effect; actual fragments found associated with the building included Black Burnished Ware and parts of Dressel 20 amphorae (Perring, Roskams, with Allen 1991: 42).

[2] See Perrings, Roskams, with Allen (1991) for site report. The fragmentary diploma (*RMD* 83) was recovered in destruction deposits associated with the 'Hadrianic Fire' of London (*c.* AD 120).

Fig. 21.1. Reconstructed *triclinium* based on evidence recovered from Building D, Watling Court, London. The original building was destroyed by fire *c.* AD 120. Museum of London.

Certainly, the view of the honourably discharged auxiliary continuing to do his bit for Rome in retirement remains a popular one.[3] Whether as respected man about town, exemplar of *romanitas*, or bulwark of imperial security, he is often attributed a significance that in reality he probably frequently lacked. When Webster, for example, argues, 'The cumulative effect of this steady extension of the franchise could hardly have been foreseen with up to 5000 men ready for discharge each year from the *auxilia*',[4] we are left to wonder what the cumulative effect really was. More citizens undoubtedly, but what did that mean in social, cultural, and economic terms? I argue below that it clearly had very different implications over time and space. Military service, this book argues, acted as a cultural hall of mirrors, exaggerating some attributes of provincial society while diminishing or eliminating the impact of others. It did not automatically generate turbo-charged agents of 'Roman' culture.[5] Indeed, in some cases the transition from a highly regularized military lifestyle to civil life could have been catastrophic for both ex-soldier and society.[6] An important failing in our understanding of Rome's veterans lies in our tendency to assume that all of them reintegrated naturally. It is a failure exacerbated by lack of recognition that not all veterans necessarily held recognized status as *veterani*. Indeed, there was also the *missicus*, a figure seldom discussed by scholars. He was a soldier discharged without

---

[3] Millar (1981: 5).   [4] Webster (1998: 143).   [5] As Cherry rightly notes (1998: 93).
[6] Though there is no direct parallel between either societies or service conditions, it is thought-provoking to note that today, ex-servicemen represent a disproportionately large group within the homeless population of Britain's major cities. A life in military service does *not* automatically equip a veteran for a successful civilian career.

honourable discharge, before completing his period of service.[7] As 3rd-century entries in the *Digest* demonstrate, Roman law was not only careful to distinguish between honourable, dishonourable, and medical discharge and to grant privileges in accordance with these categories,[8] it also sometimes granted privileges dependent on the number of years served, demonstrating that many men must have left before their twenty-five years of service were fulfilled.[9] Without the fuller privileges that came with honourable discharge, *honesta missio*, a man may have found himself disadvantaged rather than advantaged in civil contexts. Seasoned ex-soldiers included two groups routinely ignored in discussions of the army: the deserters and others dishonourably discharged. Though it is difficult to quantify the size of these groups of ex-soldiers, the presence of such individuals in provincial society should not be forgotten. Accordingly, they will be considered at the end of this chapter.

Even if all soldiers *had* left the army appropriately groomed for life as cultural emissaries, doubts would remain as to their likely impact on society as a whole. Recent analyses have consistently emphasized that veterans represented only a small fraction of the overall population and that in many areas they were hardly present at all. Furthermore, most specialists would now dispute Webster's figure of an annual discharge of 5,000 auxiliary veterans, preferring a lower figure of between 3,000 and 3,600 men.[10] What is perhaps more important is the total number of auxiliary veterans alive at one time. Attempting to estimate the number living in any given year during the 1st and 2nd centuries depends heavily upon a range of poorly documented factors.[11] It is reasonable, however, to assume a figure of between 36,000 and 50,000 auxiliary veterans.[12] There were other veterans of course, from the legions, the fleets, and the imperial guard. When their numbers are also considered, it may be argued that there were between 82,000 and 120,000 honourably discharged veterans in circulation, a total of 0.2–0.3 per cent of the estimated population of the provinces.[13] Given that these individuals were not evenly distributed across provincial society, it is clearly necessary to examine the pattern and experience of discharge at a local level if we are to understand its impact. This involves more than simply asking whether or not veterans were sufficiently numerous and cohesive to be a force for change in a given area. It also raises questions of the degree to which the rights of veterans and their families were interpreted differently locally. Changing patterns of treatment over time have to be considered and so, finally, does the degree to which veterans of different types of unit were treated the same.[14] Studies of returning veterans in other later societies indicates that even where explicit expectations were high that veterans would act as agents of transformation, they often opted to conform to local

---

[7] This term seems to die out in the Flavian period (Holder 1980: 48–9).

[8] *Digest* 49.16.13.3. Categories are *missio honesta*, *missio ignominiosa*, and *missio causaria* respectively.

[9] See *Digest* 27.1.8.3 on exemptions from guardianship.

[10] Cherry (1998: 97) suggests 3,000; Scheidel (2010: 432) argues for 3,000–3,600. I now reject the higher figure advanced in my earlier work (Haynes 2001: 63).

[11] For the difficulties with such estimates, see Scheidel (2010: 425–32), who teasingly asks whether reconstructing the demography of the Roman army should be deemed 'mission impossible'.

[12] Cherry (1998: 98).   [13] Ibid.   [14] Pollard (2000: 161).

conventions rather than trigger change.[15] Each of these questions demands a response.

The need to scrutinize these questions does not, of itself, challenge the basic point that the honourably discharged *veteranus* was a privileged figure in provincial society.[16] Indeed, for the *auxilia*, the fleet, and the guard, the archaeological evidence itself underscores this point. Bronze diplomas, such as the one discovered in Watling Court, provided their holders with written assurance of their rights. Significantly, there is no direct legionary equivalent to these documents, a fact that underscores the existence of genuine ongoing differences between legionary and auxiliary troops.[17]

The diploma is in several respects a privileged artefact. It has been intensively studied, widely debated and historically, promptly, published. About a thousand diplomas of all types have been discovered.[18] Surviving auxiliary diplomas do not quite span the period covered in this study—the earliest known example dates from AD 54 and the latest to AD 206—but they do cover much of it.[19] The date range is longer when we recall that issues to the *equites singulares*, many of whom originated in provincial *alae*, are known from as late as AD 237.[20] Diplomas are known to have been issued by every province that had an auxiliary garrison, and on many of them, a very telling formula is displayed. It assures the owner, who in most cases could surely never have visited Rome, that a record of his rights was displayed in Rome itself, even detailing where it could be found there.[21] All emanated from the emperor. The diploma thus has the appearance of an imperial artefact *par excellence*, a gift of the core to the peripheral. All of this makes diplomas an attractive source of information for those seeking to appreciate varying patterns in both recruitment and discharge across the Empire.

Yet it is important to be clear precisely what these artefacts can tell us.[22] The powerful impression of universality that emerges when one encounters the same bronze form on sites across the Empire should not disguise the diversity they embody. Variations in text are discussed elsewhere, but it is important to stress now that these are not, as is sometimes assumed, discharge certificates. Indeed, diplomas issued under Claudius and Nero made no reference at all to honourable discharge; their text makes it clear that they were issued to serving soldiers.[23] It was only after AD 110 that diplomas were exclusively issued to veterans.

A further important consideration is the fact that even this substantial collection of diplomas represents a minute sample of the original number issued.[24] This

[15] In rural France in the late 19th and early 20th centuries, returning veterans were often regarded as suspect rather than admirable, and often conformed to local practice rather than advancing the cultural ideals of their political masters (Weber 1977: 296–8).

[16] Wesch-Klein (1998: 191); Stoll (2001a: 199–202).

[17] For detailed study of the privileges of veterans in the different branches of service, see Link (1989).

[18] http://www.romancoins.info/MilitaryDiploma.html. Elizabeth Greene, pers. comm.

[19] Earliest AD 54 (*CIL* 16.2) and latest AD 206 (Eck 2011).   [20] *CIL* 16.146.

[21] Some were displayed on the Capitoline at the base of the monument to the Claudii Marcelli in front of the treasury, others behind the temple of Divine Augustus near the statue of Minerva.

[22] Eck (2003) offers a comprehensive introduction to the range of ways diplomas illuminate imperial administration.

[23] Alföldy (1968b); Mann (1972: 233).   [24] Roxan (1989).

has important implications in itself, but when combined with the amount of actual information available on the artefacts' findspots it becomes a major concern. In a growing number of cases these diplomas first come to the attention of scholars after they have reached the international antiquities market. Their place of discovery often, therefore, remains a mystery. Furthermore, even where the provenance of these diplomas is known, the detailed archaeological context so crucial to interpretation is frequently missing.[25] Finally, even where material is recovered by excavation, it regularly emerges in contexts related to its reuse. It is clear that many diplomas were regarded as sources of scrap metal at the time of their deposition. We frequently find them after they have been collected, transported, and hacked to pieces. The findspot of a diploma need not, as is too often assumed, mark the presence of a veteran.

Those patterns that can be observed only complicate attempts to offer Empire-wide analysis. This is partly due to the fact that the diplomas were not actually a gift *per se*; individual auxiliaries had to decide whether or not to buy them.[26] This probably explains why a disproportionate number of diplomas discovered belonged to cavalrymen—yet another archaeological indicator, incidentally, of the difference between the lives and status of cavalry and infantry: cavalrymen were paid more and appear to have had more disposable income.[27] It may also help explain why there are some extraordinary differences in the number of diplomas discovered in different provinces. Thus Britain, with its sizeable army, has produced seventeen diplomas compared to thirty-one known from Mauretania Tingitana, despite the fact that the African province had a much smaller garrison and has been much less extensively excavated.[28]

Generally the archaeological evidence indicates that individual choices, informed no doubt by local conditions, played a fundamental role in the way that ex-soldiers settled into provincial society. There is clear evidence to suggest that veterans varied in the degree to which they chose to stress their military past. When Dasens son of Dasmenus was honourably discharged from *cohors II Hispanorum equitata* around AD 50, he and his wife celebrated by naming their luckless offspring Emeritus and Emerita. Their third child escaped with the tribal name Turuna.[29] Yet where detailed documentary evidence is available, it is clear that *veterani* were in no way systematic in advertising and asserting their status.[30] Not only was this identity clearly less important for some men then others, but there were also times when the status was useful and times when it clearly was not. Here it is also interesting to note that in the birth of modern France, expectations by government agencies that veterans, having been exposed to new ideas, would transform village society often proved illusory. At the local level these men often blended back into local society. This was especially the case where they found

---

[25] Haynes (2001: 74).

[26] Roxan (1986: 266). Against this view, see however Eck (2003: 71–2, 82). I remain convinced that diplomas were not issued to all veterans.

[27] Dušanić (1980) was the first to note the preponderance of cavalry diplomas.

[28] See fn. 4 for figures; the figure comes to 18 if the alleged provenance of *RMD* 146 is accepted.

[29] *CIL* 16. 2; Saddington (1997: 496).   [30] Alston (1998: 218).

themselves a minority in the community.[31] It may well be that many auxiliary veterans, particularly in rural areas, responded similarly.[32]

Settlement evidence from Britain offers some interesting examples of the choices of *veterani*.[33] With the exception of one inscription found in Africa, all monuments recording veterans of auxiliary units serving in Britain were found in Britain.[34] There are ten stone inscriptions which definitely refer to auxiliary veterans, and an eleventh found at Chesters on Hadrian's Wall that may do so.[35] With the exception of a tombstone found at Lincoln, all are found near military camps.[36] Indeed eight, or if we include the Chesters monument, nine, are found associated with auxiliary forts. The impression is therefore of a preference among men to stay close to the military community; but the overall distribution is also likely to reflect the distribution of good building stone. Mann has observed that these men did not necessarily stay close to their former units; for some of them, therefore, it might have been sufficient simply to be around the army.[37] The Lincoln exception may actually hint at another pattern, based on rank. For it records a decurion, a junior officer who may have been better placed for transition back into civil society than members of the rank and file. Reinforcing the sense that extramural settlements attracted or retained veterans is the evidence from Vindolanda, which may contain references to as many as four veterans.[38] While one reference clearly alludes to a veteran at Catterick, the fragmentary texts on which the others appear probably indicate the presence of men much closer to home, men who were part of the immediate Vindolanda community.

The diplomas suggest a greater range of choices. At least twenty-three diplomas belonging to men who served in Britain have been found beyond the province.[39] A strong case can be made that many of these men were returning to their native lands; interestingly, the largest single group of these appear to represent men who were returned to Thracian territory having been recruited there years before, a finding that reinforces Margaret Roxan's belief that 'Thracians go home!'[40] Of the

---

[31] Weber (1977: 297).

[32] Mann (2002: 187) argues: 'In civil society, while legionary veterans seem to have been not unwilling to be known as such, being more defiant and self-confident in their self-styled role as "citizens-in-arms", auxiliary veterans, even though Roman citizens, seem to have lacked this self-confidence, and apparently were less inclined to reveal their status as veterans.' Unfortunately he does not cite the data that supports this view.

[33] The veterans of Britain have been the subject of two classic studies, E. Birley (1982b) and Mann (2002). This analysis supplements their findings with the latest available data.

[34] *CIL* 8.5800.   [35] Mann (2002: 185).   [36] *RIB* 266.

[37] He suggests veterans showed a preference for 'sheltered, low-lying, river valley sites' (2002: 187).

[38] *Tab. Vindol.* II 187.i.11; *Tab. Vindol.* III 581.22; 593.ii.2 and 670 B 2. The latter refers to a veteran at Catterick. Bowman and Thomas (2003: 48) believe that *veteranus* is a personal name, which may seem strange, but see Speidel (1987: 61–2) for a decurion of this name serving in the *ala I Cannanefatium*.

[39] I am grateful to Paul Holder for discussing these with me. Diplomas from the province of Britain found overseas are *CIL* 16.43 and *CIL* 16.69; *RMD* 151, 168, 184, 226, 240, 251, 293, 294, and 450; Eck, McDonald, and Pangerl (2004: 68, 72); Eck, Holder, and Pangerl (2010: 189); Eck and Pangerl (2008a: 227; 2008b: 17, 19, 21); Weiß (2006: 245; 2009: 250). Two further diplomas may possibly be attributed to the provincial army: Weiß (2012: 192) and Paul Holder, pers. comm.

[40] The holders of *RMD* 184, 240, and 293 all appear to be of Dacian/Thracian origin, and if Birley (pers. comm., see above, p. 139) is correct, the recipient of a further diploma believed to have been recovered from Bulgaria (Eck, Holder, and Pangerl 2010: 189) may also be a returning Thracian.

seventeen diplomas found in Britain, it is noteworthy that eight were found at or near military bases, while the remainder are divided between town and country locations.[41] The discovery of diplomas in varied civil settlements both hints at the potential freedom of the settlers and also offers tantalizing support to those who see in the discharge of auxiliaries evidence for linkage between the military and civil worlds. Yet even here there are ambiguities. There is a real possibility that even in the allegedly 'demilitarized' south, veteran settlement was influenced by military networks. Reflecting on the Watling Court diploma, Roxan conjectured that the soldier settler might be doing the same thing as some of his peers—settling close to the fort in which he had served. Even in this growing and cosmopolitan metropolis, it is possible that veteran's cultural orbit, his immediate friends and associates, were overwhelmingly found within the city's military community.

Other provinces, as we shall see, provide different evidence which suggests different dynamics, but for the moment it is worth reiterating the limitations of our sample even in this intensely investigated province. In the early AD 120s, the time of the Hadrianic Fire that destroyed the Watling Court house, there were at least 13 alae and 37 cohorts in Britain discharging veterans.[42] This could have resulted in as many as 420 auxiliary veterans entering provincial society per annum, or 4,200 men in the entire decade of the AD 120s. It is chastening to realize that while this decade produced a notable peak in diploma finds from Britannia, only nine diplomas issued to veterans of auxiliary units are known for certain from this period.[43] Part of the explanation for this may lie in the fact that some auxiliary veterans received locally produced discharge certificates instead—a less expensive choice and one sufficient for most purposes.[44] We know this because one was discovered in the Fayum in Egypt dated to AD 122.[45] Such documents are still less likely to survive on average than the bronze diploma, and accordingly records of the men they documented have been lost. In the British case we may note that in addition to the absence of other diploma documentation, no surviving stone inscriptions can be confidently dated to this time. To assess the nature and impact

A further diploma of uncertain date may also relate to this phenomenon (Holder, pers. comm.). See Roxan (1997: 487) for the observation.

[41] At or near military bases: *RMD* 8 (Middlewich), *RMD* 83 (London), *Britannia* 39 (2008) 381 (Brompton), *RMD* 97 (Chesterholm), *CIL* 16.93 and 115 (both Chesters), *RMD* 420 (Ravenglass). Paul Holder has kindly advised me of an unpublished diploma from Healam Bridge, a site with a Roman fort nearby. At major towns: *RMD* 145 (Caistor St Edmund), *CIL* 16.82 (Wroxeter) and *CIL* 16.130 (Colchester). *RMD* 146 is alleged to come from York, but there are some doubts as to its precise provenance; it is not included in the 17 noted above. Diplomas from rural sites include *Britannia* 35 (2004) 349 (Great Dunham), *CIL* 16.48 (Malpas), *RMD* 360 (Aldwincle), *CIL* 16.70 (near Stannington), *CIL* 16.88 (Walcot).

[42] Based on units averaging 400 for quingenary and 800 for milliary regiments, and on *CIL* 16.69, which records the units discharging troops in AD 122. The discharge rates are calculated following the formula used by Cherry (1998: 96–7).

[43] *RMD* 360; *Britannia* 39 (2008), 381; *AE* 2004, 1900; *CIL* 16.69; *CIL* 16.70; *CIL* 16.88; *RMD* 240; *AE* 2007, 1768.

[44] For the claim that soldiers bought diplomas rather than receiving them automatically, see above, p. 343, fn. 26. For discharge certificates, see Mann and Roxan (1988).

[45] See *CRAI* 1905, 402 = *AE* 1906, 22 = *ILS* 9060 = *CIL* 16, Appendix i. The document was awarded to L. Valerius Noster of the *ala Vocontiorum*. It was produced by the staff of the prefect of Egypt.

of veteran settlement in provincial society, it will clearly be necessary to look beyond these traditional sources of data and to scrutinize a wider range of evidence.

THE RIGHTS OF VETERANS

One can almost hear the frustration in the prefect of Egypt's tone. Confronting a group of petitioners for the second time, he repeats his earlier verdict. 'I told you before that the situation of each of you is neither similar nor identical, for some of you are veterans from the legions, others from *alae*, others from cohorts, others from the fleet, with the result that your legal rights are not the same.'[46] The exchange survives in a papyrus copy of a decision passed by the prefect, preserved with a record of his first impromptu hearing which had taken place outside an army camp. This fascinating document, dating to AD 63, is sometimes cited in discussions of veterans' rights, but in many ways it raises more questions than it answers. Why is it that these men felt that they could make common cause? Had the processes of imperial incorporation already advanced to such an extent that all former servicemen at least saw themselves as part of a single body of veterans? Certainly the unqualified use of the title *veteranus* in daily correspondence might imply that one veteran was much like another.[47] Legal opinion commonly uses the terms *veterani* or *veterani milites* without further qualification.[48] Neither veterans nor their children may be beaten or condemned to the beasts, to the mines, or public works. They were not obliged to take public office and were exempted from certain customs dues, though they must contribute to the cost of roads and pay property taxes.[49]

Yet legal rulings were one thing, the reality of provincial life another. It is far from clear that all veterans received their rights. As Alston has astutely observed, the degree to which the authorities were inclined to favour *veterani* might depend very much on political factors at the time.[50] It is quite likely that on a day-to-day basis some officials were either ignorant of ex-soldiers rights or at least sought to leave them in ignorance. The unfortunate Dionysius Amyntianus, a veteran of the *ala Apriana*, lost forty days discharging a liturgy to which he might not actually have been liable. We know of his frustrations not because of a complaint against the justice of the liturgy, but because having carted blankets to a legionary base in attempting to fulfil the duty, he wrote to say that he had found nobody there to receive them.[51] Another veteran of the same *ala* complained in AD 153 that he had been beaten by a *strategos* who had wilfully ignored his status.[52]

The veterans' appeal of AD 63 demonstrates that other uncertainties existed in the minds of veterans, but it is obvious that for the prefect there was no such ambiguity. He was explicit in emphasizing that different categories of veteran could not enjoy the same status. Precisely what the nature of that difference was is unspecified, though it touches on citizenship. It is possible that the distinction is

---

[46] *FIRA* 3.171. Translated by Campbell (1994: 206).   [47] Alston (1995: 60–61).
[48] The arguments are best summarized by Wolff (1986: 98–100).
[49] *Digest* 49.18.1–3.   [50] Alston (1995: 158).   [51] *P. Oxy.* 36.2760.   [52] *SB* 4.7523.

intended really to distinguish the sailors from the soldiers, but if so his division of the men into four categories seems excessive. It is also possible, as Campbell suggests, that the distinction under discussion was particular to Egypt.[53] In later years, at least, changes in local practice were to have consequences for the standing of *veterani* in Egyptian society. Thus when in AD 130 Hadrian established the new city of Antinoopolis, a lavish memorial to his lover, an entire new status group appeared in the province. The Antinoopolites, the citizens of this new foundation, were a privileged group indeed. They enjoyed many exemptions from liturgies, even beyond the bounds of their own city. Significantly, one of the reasons why we know this is because the relevant judicial rulings are recorded on a papyrus relating to an auxiliary veteran's appeal for exemption from the duty of acting as a guardian.[54] Iulius Niger, formerly of the *ala veterana Gallica*, made this appeal, not on the basis of his privilege as a veteran, which allowed for no such exemptions, but on the basis of his status as an Antinoopolite. With an active council protecting and perhaps even enhancing these rights, Antinoopolite status became more potent even than veteran status. Thus we see some former soldiers specifically citing that they are both *veterani* and Antinoopolite. Being an ex-soldier was clearly not enough, on its own, to ensure top treatment in Roman Egypt.[55]

Yet to return to the prefect's ruling, the most likely explanation for the different treatment of veterans is that it is linked to the *praemia militiae*, or discharge bounty, which was granted either in land or its cash equivalent.[56] From the time of Augustus, legionaries received this award, at first valued at 3,000 *denarii*.[57] While it is clear that ex-soldiers enjoyed the same legal privileges, outlined above, there is no evidence that former auxiliaries received the same discharge bounty as their legionary counterparts.

Most scholars believe that auxiliaries did not receive the *praemium*, but our 1st-century sources allow some ambiguity.[58] Reference to the arrangement in the *Res Gestae* refers simply to 'the soldiers', making no distinction between arms of service.[59] Similarly, Suetonius' account observes that the emperor standardized conditions for all armies, fixing length of service and the size of the *praemium*, according to the rank.[60] This brief statement could obscure distinctions between units of different status. It is even possible that the *auxilia* are ignored here. The epitaphs of auxiliary soldiers clearly demonstrate that they did not enjoy a fixed length of service at this time.[61]

---

[53] Campbell (1994: 207).   [54] *SB* 5.7558.   [55] Alston (1995: 63–6, 129–31).

[56] Wenger (1942: 373); Wolff (1986: 100–101); Link (1989: 112).

[57] For the value of the award, see Dio 55.23.

[58] For the argument that auxiliaries did not receive *praemia*, see Wolff (1986: 48). Hopkins (1980: 124) questions whether it was possible to recruit auxiliaries in equal numbers to legionaries without such an incentive. Furthermore, he suggests that it may have been difficult to maintain this distinction with growing numbers of citizens in the *auxilia*. I see no reason for the distinction to pose problems. Conscription could always ensure that numbers were maintained if necessary. Citizens may have had several reasons for choosing entry to the *auxilia*, amongst them family links to units, proximity of unit, lower entry standards, and greater promotion prospects. Given the proportion of men who survived to discharge, we can hardly assume that the retirement bonus was the principal motive for enlistment.

[59] *Res Gestae* 3.16.   [60] Suetonius *Aug.* 49.

[61] See p. 49. The troubles Augustus' successor inherited nevertheless indicate that many legionaries considered that they were obliged to remain in the army long past retirement age.

It is worth noting the motives cited for paying a *praemium*. Suetonius states that it was designed to discourage veterans from revolting on the grounds that they had insufficient funds to enjoy an honest living.[62] It could be argued that this concern would be equally relevant to ex-auxiliaries, but it remains possible that Augustus was much less concerned about non-citizen soldiers.[63] We know that many of the privileges that benefited auxiliary *veterani*, such as citizenship and the grant of *conubium* (legal recognition of marriage), were either introduced or regularized after his reign.[64] There is, however, absolutely no direct evidence that auxiliaries received a bounty on discharge in the 1st or 2nd centuries, though legionary veterans clearly continued to do so.[65] When 4th-century sources discuss 3rd-century land grants to discharged soldiers, no effort is made to distinguish the arm of service.[66] Coming as they do from the notoriously unreliable *Historia Augusta*, it is dangerous to read too much into these passing references. It is, however, notable that they allude to events in the reigns of Severus Alexander and Probus. In other words, they post-date both the latest known auxiliary diploma (AD 206) and the extension of citizenship to free-born subjects of the Empire under Caracalla in AD 212. By this time the status distinctions between the legions and *auxilia* had become distant memories, as presumably had the rights that characterized their veterans.

Other evidence, too, suggests that legionary and auxiliary veterans could have been treated differently before the 3rd-century reforms. A survey of surviving tombstones indicates that legionary veterans were more likely than their auxiliary counterparts to specify the branch of service from which they came.[67]

One reason why it is important to stress that there could have been significant differences between the legions and the *auxilia* under the Principate is that much, though by no means all, of the discussion of veteran settlement has evolved with particular reference to the legions. Though both Forni and Mann have written illuminatingly on the auxilia, it is their surveys of legionary veteran settlement that have proved particularly influential.[68] In noting the way that the evidence suggests concentrations of veterans in military zones, they have also observed indications that soldiers and ex-soldiers frequently fathered the next generation of legionaries—a pattern that could be taken to suggest the evolution of a military 'caste'.[69] As already noted, however, there is another body of research which draws upon the evidence for which there is no direct legionary equivalent, the diploma. This work, pioneered by Margaret Roxan and now a veritable field in its own right, has tended to stress another dynamic. The title of the single most important collection of synthetic studies in this field, *Heer und Integrationspolitik*, makes its thrust

---

[62] Suetonius *Aug.* 49.   [63] Ibid. 40.

[64] The particular issues surrounding *conubium* are discussed on p. 57, while their intergenerational consequences are considered below.

[65] For legionary veterans, *ILS* 2462, 9085; *AE* 1934, 226.

[66] *Historia Augusta* (*Sev. Alex.* 58.4; *Probus* 16.5). Mann (1983: 65) questions whether these practices were really introduced at this date or emerged earlier.

[67] See Haynes (2001: 76) for data from Britain.

[68] Forni (1953) and Mann (1983). Mann (p. vii) argued that, were a survey of auxiliary veteran settlement conducted in the way he did his survey of legionary veteran settlement, it would show much the same patterns.

[69] Ibid. 65, 67.

explicit.[70] Diplomas, it is argued, help reveal how army veterans integrated into wider society. They also remind us that the *auxilia* could still keep recruiting *peregrini* into its ranks. While recruitment from military families clearly took place too, there was less of a need for it than there was with the legions. We will see accordingly that while there is evidence for military enclaves, there is also evidence both for wider integration and for some significant alienation.

Archaeologically, the most conspicuous monuments to discharged legionaries are the *coloniae*. Their study has also been enormously influential in how veterans are understood within society. Tacitus' famous comment about the dual role of the colony at Colchester, as both a stronghold against rebels and a place where allies might learn their obligations to Rome, has played a formative role in the discussion of both colonies and veterans.[71] Yet recent scholarship has rightly challenged this understanding. The view that colonies were seen as an instrument of pacification must be qualified, not least on the evidence of Colchester's own fate.[72] The view that they served imperial strategy is undermined by the sporadic and disordered pattern of their establishment during the Principate. Even the view of their role in cultural transformation needs to be questioned. In this respect also, the tale of Colchester's role in sparking revolt is a salutary one. Far from being an instrument of *romanitas*, it became a target of the disaffected, alienating rather than inspiring the local population.[73] *Coloniae* could clearly, however, serve as secure bases for imperial enterprise. They were also certainly key centres in the communications network that bound together Roman administration, but they do not automatically transform pacified landscapes. Nor indeed is it even clear that this was the aspiration behind their foundation. Rather, *coloniae* were established essentially to deal with a problem—discharging soldiers. Emperors recognized, as their predecessors had, that failure to satisfy the needs of large numbers of time-expired servicemen could have the most disastrous consequences.

Accordingly, either existing settlements were converted into *coloniae* or, up until the early 2nd century, virgin sites were selected for the role. The last of these extraordinary planned foundations were constructed at Sarmizegetusa in Transylvania and Thamugadi in Algeria. Studying these two cities together is always illuminating, but never more so when we consider the first generation of settlers. It is clear that these were establishments built very firmly with legionary veterans in mind. The same appears to be clear of other *coloniae* founded to settle veterans. Despite the widespread scholarly assumption that legionary and auxiliary veterans settled in similar areas, it is in fact clear that former auxiliaries were rarely found in these cities.[74] The only auxiliaries to be found amongst the earliest generations of inhabitants at Sarmizegetusa and Thamugadi, for example, were neither *milites* or *equites* on discharge, but *decuriones*.[75] As men of importance, there

---

[70] Eck and Wolff (1986).

[71] Tacitus *Ann.* 12.32. For the impact of this remark, see Isaac (1992: 314).

[72] The best critique of the traditional model is ibid. 311–33.

[73] Tacitus *Ann.* 14.32.

[74] Despite his more general argument for a likely convergence of auxiliary and legionary veteran settlement, Mann (1983: vii) acknowledges that markedly few auxiliaries are attested at *coloniae*.

[75] *CIL* 3.1100 was found at Alba Iulia but it records a decurion of *colonia* Dacica Sarmizegetusa who was a former decurion of the *ala II Pannoniorum*, while *CIL* 3.1483 from Sarmizegetusa itself refers to

could have been no suggestion that they had lower status than the legionary veterans amongst whom they moved. The purpose-founded *coloniae*, as opposed to those cities which received the rank of *colonia* as an honour, clearly did not receive all types of soldier. I believe that this must reflect the fact that auxiliaries did not receive *praemia militiae*. It is only later, with Severan investment in the army, that we see auxiliaries living in new *coloniae*, but this is because in this case the new *coloniae* are in fact established settlements promoted by the emperor to reward his supporters and to ensure their continuing sympathy.

Urban *veterani*

One of the most eye-catching inscriptions in the riverside lapidary museum at Saintes in western France commemorates C. Iulius Macer, a local boy made good.[76] The elegantly formed letters of this early 1st-century memorial compare favourably with those on the magnificent contemporary 'Arch of Germanicus' a stone's throw away.[77] Both monuments testify, in their way, to the powerful currents that drew men of the Santones into the cultural orbit of Rome. Both invite the viewer to consider how their authors contributed to the new urban society of *Mediolanum Santonum*.

In honouring the emperor Tiberius, his son Drusus, and nephew Germanicus, C. Iulius Rufus, priest of the imperial cult and builder of the arch, was careful to stress his family's honour too. His inscribed genealogy reveals him as a fourth-generation citizen, a man whose aristocratic Gallic ancestors had successfully navigated the tide of change.[78] We know that he not only built the arch and bridge but was also responsible for the construction of the entire amphitheatre at Lyons.[79]

Macer's memorial, by contrast, makes much less of ancestry but stresses his successful career in the *auxilia*. His thirty-two years' service took him from the *ala Atectorigiana* to the appointment of *evocatus*, commander of 600 Raetian spearmen. At first glance this might appear a splendid rags-to-riches tale—a humble trooper, raised through talent and service to citizenship, and then to (relatively) high command, returning to commemorate his achievements in his home town. Here the tale might stress the army as a source of social mobility and conjecture that the veteran served as a leading light in the new Roman town. Yet impressive though Macer's story undoubtedly is, this reading requires some qualification. Those who have argued that Macer received his citizenship for auxiliary service are almost certainly misreading the evidence.[80] It now seems more likely that he in fact inherited it from his father.[81] A citizen entering the *auxilia* this early is very

---

an ex-decurion within the *colonia*. From Timgad we have a man who had served in the *auxilia*, but he had also been a legionary: *CIL* 8.2354.

[76] *CIL* 13.1041.   [77] Holder (1980: 21, 46) *contra* Kellner (1971: 215).

[78] *CIL* 13.1036.   [79] *AE* 1959, 61.   [80] Holder (1980: 46).

[81] Macer's filiation is given by cognomen, a fact that has confused some readers. While the father's name appears to be given as a non-citizen, therefore, it is in fact being recorded in a manner that was quite commensurate with his having citizen status. Holder (1980: 46) notes another example of a citizen father from the same town whose cognomen is cited in precisely the same way (*CIL* 13.1042–5).

unusual, and we might expect that he received a privileged position in the *ala* from the beginning; indeed he is recorded not as an *eques*, but as a *duplicarius*. Furthermore, excavation demonstrates that the town to which Macer returned was already a thriving settlement long before he was born.[82] It was far from dependent on veterans like him for its growth. Finally, we may note that, while his memorial was clearly designed to impress a local audience, it contains no reference to local office. Did the return of men such as Macer really have the kind of cultural impact so often ascribed to veterans?

Quantifying impact is inevitably difficult; in this case it is dependent on the survival of inscriptions. Perhaps Macer made his own contributions to the evolving fabric of his home town and the evidence has simply disappeared? Yet one thing is clear: overall the evidence does not support the view that former auxiliaries made a big contribution to public life in the major towns.

If the holding of public office is considered as an index of impact, then the contribution of veterans to public life seems to have been limited. Mroszewicz's study of ex-soldiers on the Rhine and Danube shows that only 5.8 per cent of known municipal office holders were veterans of any sort.[83] The overwhelming majority of these had served in the legions and about half the total were officers. Even in this select group, few got beyond membership of the town council. This clearly does not indicate that veterans as a group played a significant role in provincial administration.[84] Elsewhere documented participation rates were even lower; in Britain, with its substantial number of veterans, there are no examples of veterans reaching the *ordo decurionum*.[85] It is probable that low levels of participation reflect deliberate choices by veterans. An Egyptian papyrus dated just before the battle of Actium records Octavian's ruling that veterans could not, against their will, be appointed to magistracies, ambassadorial roles, or the responsibilities of tax farmers.[86] Similar policy clearly remained in force at later periods, a clear indication that there was no wish to see the *veterani* taking on a large role in local government.[87] Even if such a situation were seen as desirable, it was trumped by the imperative to keep soldiers and veterans happy. Most were happier, it seems, to avoid having such honours imposed upon them. They had completed their service to the state and earned their privileges already. Selfless benefaction to the body politic never risked reaching epidemic proportions in the Roman Empire.

If, for whatever reason, veterans generally appear to have been underrepresented in town government, it is worth noting that auxiliaries of the rank and file hardly appear at all. Indeed, there is no known example of an auxiliary *miles* or *eques*, as distinct from a centurion or decurion, becoming a town counsellor anywhere in the northwestern provinces or indeed in Dacia.[88] It is not that they were barred from performing this role; we know that a few men did reach such

---

[82] Maurin (1988).
[83] Mroszewicz (1989: 71). Note also the evaluation of veterans' participation in public life in Wesch-Klein (1998: 196-7).
[84] Ibid. 196.   [85] Ibid. 197.   [86] *BGU* 628 = *FIRA* 1.56.
[87] Much of this later policy emphasizes that soldiers could not be forced to become tax collectors. Indeed, Paul stated that they were only obliged to perform this task if they had let themselves be elected onto the town council: *Digest* 49.18.1-5.
[88] For the northwestern provinces, see Wesch-Klein (1998: 197) and for Dacia, see Ardevan (1989: 85-6).

positions elsewhere. C. Iulius Dexter, for example, began his career as an *eques* in an *ala* and went on to become a magistrate in the colony of Thelepte (Medinet-el-Kedima, Tunisia).[89] But even in this case, Dexter had risen in the ranks before he retired from the army.

Wesch-Klein has argued that discharged auxiliary soldiers probably generally did not have the financial means to acquire a town councillor's post.[90] This is clearly part of the explanation. Whether or not auxiliaries received the *praemium*, it is still quite likely that they were on average less wealthy than their legionary contemporaries. Savings would, of course, vary from soldier to soldier and some auxiliaries were clearly able to build up sizeable sums. One Dionysius of the *ala veterana Gallica*, for example, is known to have accumulated 1,562 *denarii* in his savings.[91] Overall, however, it seems likely that most would have had less. The Severan pay records of one auxiliary unit, which shows soldiers with the consistently small sums of 100 *denarii in deposito* and 75 *denarii in viatico* (reserved for travelling), may reflect official restrictions on savings.[92]

There is only one area of the Empire known to the author where surviving evidence really suggests that veterans could have made a discernible difference to urban development. Surprisingly, perhaps, this area lies in Syria. Despite the fact that veterans were most likely small players indeed within the vast and ancient cities of the Roman Near East, there were some areas in that region that were conspicuously lacking in urban centres. The most notable of these was the Ituraean principality, an area that changed quite dramatically during the Roman period.[93] Here ex-soldiers are found undertaking a range of roles at village level. Veterans appear heading subscription lists, in magistracies (in five instances), as benefactors and founders of settlements, and as tribal patrons.[94] Interestingly, none of these men records his rank or unit, and it is possible that even here former legionaries outnumbered ex-auxiliaries. Only one veteran, a centurion of *Legio III Gallica*, left a record of his military career.[95] He was, however, exceptional—a man capable of erecting a public building at his own expense. The remaining veterans undertake less expensive public service; nevertheless they too appear to enjoy a conspicuous position in local society.[96]

Two things are striking in the evidence for veteran activity in Ituraea. First, the positions these men held are similar in type to those held in major towns. They are, however, held in a humbler environment, where there is less competition from other notables. The second point to note is that however relatively humble these settlements were, they nevertheless clearly reflected the urban pulse. This is all the more significant given the received view of the Principality and its people as difficult and lawless. There is an attractive symmetry to the picture that evolves. An area whose unsettled character makes it ripe for recruiting is brought further

[89] *CIL* 8.2094 = *ILS* 2518.   [90] Wesch-Klein (1998: 197).
[91] *P. Fayum* 105.2.28 and 105.2.44.
[92] As Watson (1965: 153) notes of *P. Berlin* 6.866. This, though, relates to the money held by the unit; soldiers could have had investments beyond the army's reach.
[93] Jones (1931: 271).
[94] Village subscription list (*IGLS* 2399), village magistracies (*IGLS* 1969, 1984b, 1989, 2041, 2546), 'benefactor and founder' (*IGLS* 2413), and tribal patron (*IGLS* 2287).
[95] *IGLS* 2438.   [96] Jones (1931: 270).

into the imperial fold by discharged soldiers.[97] Such a model would appear the
archetype for many analyses of veteran settlement, but even at village level it is
clear that this was far from universal.

Without doubt the richest evidence for the impact of veteran settlement on
provincial communities comes from Egypt. Here, a wealth of papyrological
evidence enables the student to look beyond bronze plaques and stone inscriptions and to see something of the minutiae of daily life. Papyri have a further
advantage too, for they appear in quantity even in those village settlements where
little epigraphic material has been recovered. This allows us to get some grasp on
an otherwise much underrepresented group, veterans in rural society, but the
grasp is only partial. The Egyptian villages from which the biggest relevant
collections come were substantial settlements, some of which may have had
populations of 4,000 or more people. In other provinces, such as Britain, settlements of similar size would be defined as small towns. We shall have to turn to
other evidence to consider the presence and experience of veterans in hamlets and
farmsteads.

Two valuable studies of veteran families in Egyptian village society have
reached similar conclusions. Both Alston and Mitthof emphasize that veterans
appear to have become thoroughly integrated with the general village population,
they did not constitute a separate caste and indeed they do not seem to have had a
distinct impact on the cultural life of their villages.[98] In some cases, rather than
being exotic outsiders, these men were simply returning to the place in which they
grew up before their military careers.

In his analysis Alston offers a detailed case study of Karanis, a substantial village
in the Fayum, an area clearly popular with veterans. In his reading of the
archaeological evidence, he sees little indication of the sort of contrast between
the prosperous and less wealthy townspeople discernible in London. There
is variation in the size of closely packed, dried-brick-built houses, certainly, but
little survives to indicate distinct differences in interior decoration and portable
possessions. Pottery from the village, for example, was overwhelmingly locally
produced, and very little 1st- and 2nd-century fine ware appeared in site assemblages.[99] It is purely through surviving papyri that we can observe that military
families appear to have formed a substantial minority within the community. It is
possible that as many as 14 per cent of the inhabitants were from families with
military associations. This is markedly higher than even the highest estimates for
the Egyptian average. It reminds us again that veterans were not evenly spread
across the provincial landscape; rather, they tended to cluster together even in
areas where there is no fort or fortress nearby.[100] In this case, it is likely that the
presence of a growing number of veterans simply meant that settling in the region
became more attractive to other ex-soldiers. The link was clearly not limited to
one regiment or arm of service; indeed, the population of Karanis contained
veterans from the fleet, the *alae*, the cohorts, and the legions.

---

[97] P. 313.

[98] Alston (1995: 117–42) should be read alongside Alston (1999: 176–96). Mitthof (2000: 377–405).

[99] See Johnson (1981) for the pottery. See also Alston (1995: 229 fn. 22).

[100] Karanis did have a barrack block, strategically located next to the state granary in the village, but
it seems unlikely that this could of itself have been a significant draw to veterans.

Alston's breakdown of the evidence suggests that the impact of veteran settlement here, even in this highly concentrated form, was gradual and spread over several generations, rather than dramatic.[101] Here as elsewhere in Egypt, the sense is not that they constituted a powerful caste, though they clearly gained tangible benefits from their citizenship, enabling them to establish themselves in the landowning class even if not to play a leading role in local politics.[102] Moreover, they do appear to be represented disproportionately strongly amongst the wealthier members of the village.[103] Finally, of course, these families enjoyed some social mobility; succeeding generations could exploit opportunities unavailable to their parents. For the legitimate sons of discharged auxiliaries, for example, service in the legions was now an option their fathers might never have had.

As ever with Egypt, the question is how far this picture is representative of a wider pattern. Unlike in some of the western provinces, key developments in village administration during the Roman period took place here well in advance of the settlement of large numbers of veterans. The agents in this development came not from ex-soldiers, but from a long-established pool of local leaders. At Philadelphia, a village that began to attract a significant number of veterans from the mid-AD 80s, for example, Hanson has demonstrated that imperial administrative procedures had been adopted there at least twenty years earlier.[104] In communities where veteran settlement followed more rapidly upon the absorption of new land and peoples, and where there were fewer Greek or Latin literate members of the local population, the impact of veterans may well have been more acute.

One point that does invite comparison over a wider area, however, is the issue of longer-term impact. Military diplomas across the Roman world attest to the granting of *conubium* to discharged auxiliaries. From at least the reign of Claudius up until *c.* AD 140, this grant ensured that the children of a *veteranus*, whether born during his military service or afterwards, were eligible for citizenship. After AD 140 only those born following his discharge could become citizens. This grant of citizenship along with the privileges discussed above, not just to the father but also to the succeeding generation, assuredly had significant advantages for many families. By the time the third generation—which lacked the exemptions from liturgies, customs duties, and certain taxes enjoyed by parents and grandparents—came of age, most families would have been able to show a marked, if not always dramatic, increase in prosperity and status. While some families may have retained their military connections, induced to do so perhaps by the obligations associated with veteran land grants by the mid-3rd century, others probably took a quite different course. Three generations would have been sufficient to distance others from the army community entirely. And of course there was another possibility. An individual could play off his ancestry to suit his particular circumstances at a given moment.

A notable figure in the Karanis documents is the grandson of C. Iulius Niger, a discharged trooper of *ala veterana Gallica*. Tellingly, the grandson appears under

---

[101] Alston (1995: 117–42).   [102] Mitthof (2000: 401).   [103] Geremek (1969: 56–7).

[104] Hanson (1989: 439) discusses papers from the archive of Nemesion, collector of capitation taxes in the village. She observes that the documents note the beginning of the Roman year, and that the tax office followed a quinquennial cycle when revising lists of villagers' ages. Such practices were established significantly before large numbers of veterans settled there.

many different names in the papyrus archive that records his family's activities; he is described or describes himself variously as Horion, Gemellus, Gemellus Horion, and C. Gemellus Horigenes. Different names clearly suit different purposes. In a property certificate of AD 214 he claims to be a Roman citizen because of his descent from his veteran grandfather.[105] In fact, however, the grounds for the claim on that basis are dubious, as his mother was almost certainly a non-citizen.[106] In many ways, the grandson's life is very different from that of the grandfather. Neither he nor his father appears to have served in the army. The family are prosperous, enjoying extensive holdings in Karanis, and around Karanis.[107] To outward appearances there would be little to associate the two lives. Indeed, there is no reference to the military connection in any of Horion's earlier correspondence. Yet sixty years after his grandfather's discharge, he clearly found the link useful and tried to exploit it.[108]

So far we have considered only the evidence from civilian settlements, but there existed other communities, comparable in size to Karanis, where veterans may have been an altogether more influential group. These were occupants of the extramural settlements attached to forts.

Veterani in extramural settlements

Few sites express this relationship better than the fort and town of Rapidum, near Sour Djouab in Algeria (see Fig. 21.2). Aerial photography, survey, and some twenty seasons of excavation have revealed the history and organization of this settlement, home in the late 2nd century to *cohors II Sardorum*.[109] They have also illuminated the history of an impressive 1,143m-long wall that enclosed a settlement of over 11ha abutting the fort.[110] Two identical inscriptions, one from the settlement's east gate, the other from the west, inform the reader that in AD 167, the *veterani* and *pagani* built the wall from their own resources.[111]

The identification of *veterani* as a distinct group to be specified alongside other parts of the military community is a familiar feature of Roman terminology. Thirty years before the building of the Rapidum wall, Arrian reported to the emperor Hadrian that he had overseen the construction of fortifications by the fort at Phasis in the Caucasus to protect both veterans and traders.[112] Inscriptions recording the communal efforts of *veterani* and others are also attested in the vicinity of auxiliary installations on the Danubian provinces. It is notable that in inscriptions, the *veterani* are invariably the first group named, suggesting

---

[105] *SB* 4.7360.

[106] For a detailed discussion of the archive and the doubtful character of Gemellus Horion's claim, see Alston (1995: 129–32). This is a particularly interesting case, as one might have assumed that he could claim citizenship anyway more directly under the terms of the *Constitutio Antoniniana*. Did he believe that there was in fact a status differential between old and new citizens?

[107] As seen in the census records of AD 189 (*P. Mich.* 6.370). This document lists property belonging to the parents of Gemellus Horion (noted by Alston 1995: 132).

[108] Niger is referred to as a discharged cavalryman in *P. Mich.* 6.428 of AD 154.

[109] Laporte (1989).   [110] Ibid. 101.

[111] *CIL* 8.20834 = *ILS* 6685 (west gate), *CIL* 8.20835 (east gate).

[112] Arrian *Periplus* 9.

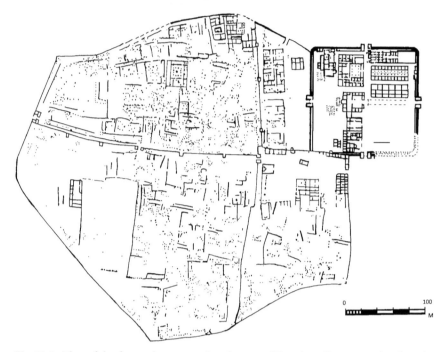

Fig. 21.2. Plan of the fort and extramural settlement of Rapidum (Sour Djouab, Algeria). The fort was founded in AD 122. The walls around the extramural settlement were built 45 years later.

precedence. In some cases, such as the major auxiliary centre at Micia in Dacia, the formula *veterani et cives Romani* is used. It is interesting to see a distinction made between these two groups. The veterans were themselves citizens, but are clearly recognized in this context as a separate group from other citizens, while the *peregrini*, the free-born non-citizens who must have been present in some numbers, do not even get a mention. The *peregrini* were clearly not eligible to participate in all communal decisions and dedications.[113] These patterns of distinction are clearly mirrored in communal activity associated with the legions. Inscriptions commemorating works, decrees, and dedications by *canabae* communities frequently evoke the same formula.[114]

Reviewing the results of excavation at Rapidum gives us some sense of life in this community of *veterani* and *pagani*. The irregularity of the walls of AD 167 indicates that they were built to envelope a settlement that was already well established. It is likely, therefore, that the settlement was already very well established before this time, but that it developed after the foundation of the fort in AD 122. The joining of this new wall to those of the existing fort clearly demonstrates the intimate association of the serving soldiers and the occupants of the extramural settlement.

[113] See Poulter (1987: 395) for the same conclusion.
[114] See, e.g. *CIL* 3.6166 = *ILS* 2474.

Buildings within the interior of the civilian settlement include peristyle houses and at least one classical-style temple—structures familiar in provincial towns but less common in the indigenous settlements of the province. Significantly, perhaps, three of the relatively few dwellings to be substantially investigated at the site were clearly related to olive oil production.[115] Of these, the most substantial lay just 12m from the west wall of the camp. This house, 22.25 × 39.15m, was equipped with an oil press, and a substantial storeroom containing twenty-five oil amphorae. It is tempting, but not essential, to see in this evidence a determination on the part of the oil producers to be as close as possible to their market. The army's appetite for oil, discussed earlier, is well attested. Whether or not the oil producers sought to serve a wider market, the location of Rapidum meant that they were also well placed on local transport networks.

There have been various attempts to calculate the number of occupants at the site. Laporte, who knows the site best of all, has argued for a population of approximately 2,000, of which *c*.500 would have been soldiers.[116] He suggests that about half of those who received *honesta missio* from the resident unit would have settled in the extramural site, the other half moving away, and proposes therefore that there would be about forty veterans living there at any one time.[117] This is, as he notes, 'un calcul très grossier', but it is good to think with. Even assuming a maximum figure, using the formula above and assuming the unlikely scenario that all veterans stayed close by, they would be unlikely to have numbered much more than 100.[118] If, for the sake of argument, we assume an average of three dependants per veteran (an improbably high maximum figure), then the number of individuals from veteran families living within the settlement could potentially have risen to about 400. Even this would see such families as a minority group. Yet for all that, veterans clearly played a leading role in the 'civil' community at Rapidum in the mid-2nd century. Their place on the enclosure building inscriptions demonstrates that they were an impressively assertive group. No amount of statistical conjecture, however, can detract from the fact that veterans were clearly identified as the most privileged and highest-status group amongst the civilians at Rapidum. For many, the draw not only of the familiar, but also of the assured status they could enjoy while living close to a camp, must have been powerful indeed. In the wider civil community, as we have seen, the rights and privileges of the veteran may have been less readily accepted and acted upon.

Sadly little is known of the veterans' families. Only one inscription specifically records a military marriage at Rapidum. This records a soldier of *cohors II Sardorum* and his wife, Sextia Prima.[119] In his survey of marriage epitaphs from the North African frontier zone, Cherry has noted that the recorded wives of soldiers and veterans almost invariably have Roman names, suggesting that intermarriage with the indigenous population was very rare. The sheer weight of the epigraphic evidence for this region supports his argument, suggesting that this was an inward-looking society. Shaw, indeed, used similar arguments from the region to claim that the Lambaesis legion was a 'total institution', and that the practice of soldiers and veterans marrying one another's daughters contributed to the creation

---

[115] Laporte (1989: 110–11, 125–6). [116] Ibid. 16. [117] Ibid. 16 n. 12.
[118] P. 341 fn. 12. [119] *CIL* 8.9198.

of such a culture.[120] Yet it is necessary here to sound a note of caution. First, there may well be evidence for veterans marrying outside the military community at Rapidum. Another inscription found at the site records M. Aemilius Pudens, whose wife has the African cognomen Namgedda. His military status is not recorded, but Laporte thinks it likely that Pudens was a veteran.[121] Second, much of the evidence from other provinces for the presence of local women, and thus the possibility of intermarriage, comes from small finds. Small finds data from these African sites have yet to be examined with this question in mind. Finally, a law from Egypt indicates that veterans' wives might deliberately 'style' themselves as 'Roman' even when they did not have Roman citizenship. An elementary part of this styling might be to use a different name in public settings.[122]

When in the early 3rd century *cohors II Sardorum* left Rapidum, the town remained. Indeed, it went on to have its own town council and to achieve municipal status. It is a pattern that some have imagined as crucial to the urbanization of western provinces, though the dangers of overstating this case have been well noted. Nevertheless, we can reasonably accept that veterans made a contribution to this process. They were in no sense the sole agents of change in the extramural settlements, but they played a role. Frequently their input involved adding their savings and their energies to communities already ordered and established, rather than founding and establishing new centres, but even such a role was far from irrelevant. When the garrison moved on, many may have followed it, but probably some stayed behind helping to sustain another small part of Rome's growing agglomeration of urban centres.

Veterani in the countryside

The 400 'Romans' huddled in a Frisian villa during the brutal tribal revolt of AD 47 must have wished they had the kind of protective walls enjoyed by the *veterani* at Rapidum. Unfortunately for them, they did not. Tacitus passes over their awful fate in a single sentence.[123] Having occupied the home of a former auxiliary, presumably after concluding that it offered some security, this group nevertheless committed mass suicide rather than fall into the hands of the enemy. This moving yet ultimately rather marginal reference is one of very few to refer to an auxiliary veteran in the countryside. Cruptorix, the villa's owner, is described in passing as having been formerly in Rome's service. That is all we know of him, and he ironically, remains our best-known example of an auxiliary villa owner. Yet veterans, both auxiliaries and legionaries alike, are often thought of as rural creatures, taming the countryside by the sweat of their brow.

---

[120] Shaw (1984).

[121] See Laporte (1989: 45–6) for analysis and discussion of veteran families at Rapidum.

[122] *Gnomon of the Idiologus* 53, cited by Scheidel (2010: 424) in his own critique of the use of the 'total' or 'closed institution' model in association with data on soldiers' families from north Africa.

[123] Tacitus *Ann.* 4.73.

The belief that veterans often become farmers is grounded in our classical sources.[124] Farming was, also, the lot of the vast majority of the population. Even in major towns a high proportion of families were directly engaged in agriculture. In the settlements where veterans are known to have established themselves, such as Karanis with its three-storey granary and Rapidum with its olive presses, it is equally clear that farming was an important part of life. The fact that there is relatively little direct evidence for veteran farmers suggests that they are underrepresented in the data.[125]

Absence of evidence has not stopped scholars affected by the perception of veterans as change agents from arguing that such men were important innovators and agricultural pioneers. Veterans appear in the academic literature reclaiming marginal lands, introducing new farming regimes, and pioneering new technology. Such an image has a base in reality—the Theodosian Code famously offered incentives and resources to former soldiers to bring underexploited land under the plough—but the image also requires some qualification.[126]

The Theodosian Code was, after all, a later initiative which reflected imperial intention rather than universal practice. Under the Principate, particularly in the case of the *auxilia*, the situation was probably very different. There is no evidence for similar incentives. As we have seen, there is not even proof that former auxiliaries settled in *coloniae* in newly captured territories or received land grants.[127] If, as our sources aver, they became entitled to conditional land grants in the 3rd century, receiving frontier land in return for an assurance that their sons would follow them into military service, we need to acknowledge the possibility that such land had already been brought under the plough generations before. There is good evidence for extensive exploitation of available land in the frontier zones from at least the mid-2nd century.

It is perhaps in this context that we should interpret the remains of a shattered Jupiter column discovered at Melbach about 3.5km from the fort of Echzell in Hessen, Germany.[128] The column was dedicated by one Lucius Quintionius Servianus, a veteran who had served as a *sesquiplicarius* in the *ala Indiana Antoniniana*. The findspot makes it clear that the column had once stood on a farm close to the road linking Echzell to the fort at Friedberg. The veteran's dedication can be dated AD 211–222. The fact that the farm buildings themselves were only 250m from this road may have encouraged the veteran to set up such an elaborate momument, some 5–6m tall, on what was surely his own land.[129] Veteran farmers whose properties lay further from passing (military) traffic may have been less inclined to mark their identity and beliefs in such a conspicuous manner.

[124] Hyginus Gromaticus, writing in the 1st or 2nd century AD, emphasizes this link, but it is notable that the passage is strongly connected to accounts of early veterans. He refers to the experiences of the men who served under Caesar and Augustus: Thulin (1913: 140–42) ; Campbell (1994: 212).

[125] Alston (1995: 40).

[126] *Codex Theodosianus* 7.20.3.1. The rescript dates from the reign of Constantine.

[127] None of the references to auxiliary veterans found in *coloniae* can be clearly linked to the foundation of the *coloniae*. It is possible that these men moved into the cities, buying property as they did so, significantly after the community had been established and official allotments of land allocated.

[128] Lindenthal, Rupp, and Birley (2001).

[129] Ibid. 200–201. I am indebted to A. R. Birley for this reference.

Overall, though, the degree to which veterans constituted a large, distinct, and innovative group of farmers must be questioned. The problem is not simply one of will. In a world where a man did well if he reached 45, it is unlikely that after 25 physically demanding years of military service, he would have adapted easily to farming. Even after a much shorter period of service, for example, Sulla's veterans had proved notoriously unsuccessful farmers.[130] While acknowledging that their unhappy experience is recorded because Cicero chose to play upon it to advance an argument, and that the actual fate of most veteran farmers is simply unknown, one can remain suspicious of the claims made for the impact of soldier farmers. Statistically, it is evident that even if a high proportion of veterans did in fact take to farming, they would have remained a small minority of the total rural population. Even in areas where circumstances might be thought conducive, such as in the *territorium* of the great fortress of Lambaesis, 600km east of Rapidum, theories of veteran-based transformation no longer appear sustainable. Here, in an area where prosperous legionary veterans were annually discharged into civil society, one might expect some evidence for their impact, but in fact it is impossible to demonstrate that they played any role in local transformation.[131] Rather than acting as change agents, they blended in with the status quo.

Elsewhere, similarly optimistic early assessments of the impact of veteran settlement have also required reappraisal. In his surveys of northern Syria, Tchalenko envisioned veterans spearheading agricultural exploitation of the mountainous terrain of the limestone massif.[132] He saw these individuals as a conspicuous group, dwelling in substantial villas and driving the production of olive oil. Yet reassessment of the evidence undermines this classic image.[133] Though a number of elaborate 2nd- and 3rd-century tombs belonging to Roman settlers have indeed been found in the uplands, as at Quaṭūra on the slopes of Šeih Barakāt, most veterans are attested away from the mountains.[134] Epigraphic evidence shows them in the plains on land long since tamed by generations of farmers. Close study of rural settlement fails to reveal conspicuously different villas for veterans.[135] Even the timing of an upturn in olive oil production fails to fit the model; it can now be dated to the late Roman period.[136]

Auxiliary veterans were on average more likely to behave like Iulius Demetrius: they exploited existing developments rather than pioneered new ones. In AD 227 Demetrius went to the headquarters of his former regiment, *cohors III Augusta Thracum*, to find witnesses for the purchase of a vineyard.[137] The property lay in the Khabur valley in Syria. He was clearly taking over a property owned by a civilian, not launching a new enterprise. As the civilian could not compose the

---

[130] Cicero, *In Catilinam* 2.8. Shaw (1983: 140) draws on this source and others to question the degree to which veterans took to farming.

[131] Shaw (1983: 138–41) critiques Fentress's (1979) argument that veterans played an important role in the transformation of Numidia.

[132] Tchalenko (1953: 382).   [133] Pollard (2000: 247–8).

[134] At Quaṭūra the elaborate late 2nd-century *mausolea* of Aemilius Reginus (*IGLS* 448) and Flavius Julianus (*IGLS* 455) and a *hypogeum* of AD 240 (*IGLS* 447) do indeed convey the impression of an intrusive and prosperous group of Roman settlers. See here Tchalenko (1953: 381), but the problem here lies in assessing the degree to which this site can be deemed representative of more general patterns.

[135] Pollard (2000: 247).   [136] Tate (1992), cited by Pollard (2000: 247).

[137] *P. Dura* 26.

necessary Greek, another veteran wrote his part of the contract for him. All those who signed as witnesses appear to have been auxiliary soldiers below the rank of centurion, and interestingly, all wrote their names and ranks in Latin. Not only does this episode neatly reflect a veteran's ties with his old unit, it also demonstrates a fort's local importance as a centre at which writing skills could be found.

Tchalenko's belief that distinctive villa farms might provide clues as to veteran settlers warrants consideration in other provincial settings. While archaeologists have rightly recognized that there is something inherently blinkered about thinking of rural settlement purely in terms of buildings, it remains the case that attempts to link such buildings to estates are invariably problematic. Can we at least see in the development of villa farms clues as to veteran settlement?

One area where it may be possible to see this is in southwest Germany. Here, archaeologists have identified a quite remarkable pattern of 'colonization'.[138] As army units move up to the limes, new towns and farms are established. What is notable about this is that the new towns are very specifically located on old fort sites,[139] while the new villa farms emerge in areas wholly lacking in recent indigenous farms.[140] Their regular distribution across the landscape suggests that this local transformation was engineered at some level by the authorities. If this is the correct understanding, and I believe it is, it would seem quite possible that some of these lands were allocated, or sold, to veterans to farm. Veterans probably would not have been the only group to benefit from this; civilian settlers may have taken advantage of the initiative too, but it seems likely that they would have been well represented.

What is noteworthy, however, is that even in the northwestern provinces this pattern appears the exception rather than the rule. Certainly there is no parallel for this in the settlement evidence for northern Britain, even if the epigraphic and diploma evidence might tentatively support a strong veteran presence in the so-called military zone. It would appear rather that veterans either made their homes in the extramural settlements or occupied rural residences scarcely distinguishable from those of the indigenous population.

In the south of Britain, however, it is possible to argue from architectural and small finds evidence that veterans did leave their mark on rural society. Black attributes to British auxiliary veterans a range of villas that echo military/imperial architecture in their essentials.[141] For example, there are similarities in plan between some rural houses and the *mansiones*, official travel lodges. He supports his argument with reference to the number of military small finds recovered from a range of villa sites including Gorhambury, Whitton, and Dalton Parlours.[142] Horse trappings and scabbard capes are certainly familiar finds at such sites. Rather than assuming that these finds must have necessarily been dropped by passing soldiers, he raises the possibility that these were the property of veterans.[143] These theories are particularly interesting when the evidence for

---

[138] Sommer (1999a; 1999b).   [139] Sommer (1999a).
[140] Sommer (1999b: 177).   [141] Black (1994).
[142] Though I am less convinced that architectural transformations at these three sites need be associated with the more general argument advanced.
[143] Black (1994: 107–9).

them is compared with data from another part of the northwest, the territory of the Batavi.

The lands of the Batavi on the lower Rhine rank amongst the most intensely studied in the Roman Empire; but their particular importance for this study lies in the fact that they were clearly the home of many veteran soldiers, a large proportion of whom were auxiliaries. A series of groundbreaking studies have examined the likely cultural impact of this intense association with the *auxilia*. Here too, scholars have seen in the introduction of a new architectural form evidence for the impact of military service on veteran settlers. In this case, a different model is advanced, for the traditional byre house remains the dominant form of residence in the first centuries AD, but it is sometimes embellished with a wooden porticus, an architectural form seen as deriving from military rather than civilian sources.[144]

Analysis of the distribution of some 2,700 military small finds from Batavian territory by Johan Nicolay has also yielded interesting results.[145] What emerges from his survey is the fact that a very high proportion of such finds come not simply from military sites and cult centres, but from ordinary villages.[146] Furthermore, he is able to demonstrate that the composition of these assemblages changes over time. During his phase 2 (dated 12 BC–AD 120), for example, militaria found on Batavian territory include not just the range of small finds discovered at British villas, but also fragments of armour and shields, as well as helmets, swords, and daggers. In the next phase, however (AD 120–250/300), a different pattern emerges. Swords are reasonably well represented, but other types of military equipment become scarce. Nicolay argues that the preservation of all this equipment in villages indicates the social as opposed to the military use of such items.[147] He believes that it served as a useful marker of veteran identity. Interestingly, too, he argues a contrast between the way such equipment was displayed in Batavian territory and the way it was displayed in nearby Treveran lands, where it was more likely to be deposited in graves.

The idea that military equipment as a form of veteran identification is intriguing, but it raises a further question as to why so much of it was necessary—I have argued elsewhere that a military belt could have served as a sufficient marker. The comparison with the lands of the Treveri is interesting, though to date there has yet to be an equivalently comprehensive study of military items in civil settlements there or anywhere else. It may be tempting to believe that in the lands of the Batavi old soldiers tended less to die and rather to fade away. The psychological distance between active service and veteran discharge may have been less pronounced in such a military society than it was elsewhere.

Also of interest here are the lands to which the owners of this equipment returned. This area remains a non-villa landscape. There is no hint in the architecture here of a widespread transformation of the built environment following on from the return of veteran soldiers.[148] The addition of porticoes to byre houses represents the most substantial elaboration to be found in this important recruiting area. Other cultural changes resulting from returning

[144] Roymans (2009); Roymans, Derks, and Heeren (2007).   [145] Nicolay (2008).
[146] Ibid. 73–91.   [147] Nicolay (2002).   [148] Roymans (2011: 154).

veterans, notably the growth of literate modes of communication, have been argued; but the settlement pattern shows less of a convergence with ideals of the veteran legacy. What then remained for the men who returned? In her brilliant study of the impact of recruitment on Batavian society, Driel-Murray has posited that farming practices had to adapt to meet the shortage both of menfolk and of land. Examining ethnographic parallels for the situation, she envisions an environment in which women undertook the bulk of agricultural work. Furthermore, she sees the farming regime as ultimately unsustainable. The potential for catastrophe here is clear: a declining subsistence base and underemployed ex-soldiers pontificating on the glory days, surrounded by their arms and armour. This does not sound like an especially wise strategy for managing veteran settlement; rather, it sounds like the unhealthy local consequences of a range of unrelated official policies mediated through a range of private decisions.

Overall, then, it is clear that there was not a concerted policy of veteran settlement. The degree to which legionary veterans had an impact is debatable, but appears small. The impact of auxiliary veterans is even less easy to discern. Where there is evidence, it tends to support the view that soldiers invested in or returned to existing, established farming enterprises. This is an important point in itself. It may be a less glamorous role, academically speaking, but it is not without significance. Where did the soldier's search for investment take him? In some cases, no doubt, it took him to long-established family and communal enterprises. Armed with his savings he could buy into, and no doubt disrupt, long-held farming arrangements. As an outsider, he was also going to need documentation to secure his holdings. Maps or records of holdings were also inevitably important, contributing to the process of documentation which must have represented the single most conspicuous legacy of Rome in many an area. From these stemmed legal implications and an intensification of contact between rural society and the Roman law. Yet before seeing in this some sort of homogenizing effect, it is necessary to remember that even here, the experience of the veteran was primarily dependent on local patterns of life and settlement.

The forgotten veterans

It is striking that most analyses of veteran settlement are unremittingly positive. They may disagree on detail, but they are generally unanimous that veterans found a niche in provincial society one way or the other. Yet it is in fact clear that this was not true of all. A glance at the literature and landscapes of empire reveals another path generally underrepresented by inscriptions, papyri, and artefacts.

The sources are unanimous that *coloniae* and discharge benefits were established partly to ensure the good behaviour of ex-soldiers; but what happened to those men who did not receive these benefits? It is well worth asking whether or not we believe that auxiliaries received them, because it is clear that many who had undertaken military service would not have done so. Roman society would have contained many veterans who had not achieved the full status of *veterani*. A 3rd-century rescript states that men retired on medical grounds after twenty years' service were entitled to honourable discharge with full benefits; but what of those invalided out before that time?[149] Studies of pre-modern armies indicate that between 10 per cent and 20 per cent of soldiers fell victim to debilitating diseases.[150] Then there are injuries sustained in training and also, of course, in combat. Being rendered unfit for military service did not, it should be remembered, mean that a man could not take to a life of armed crime.[151] Even a man discharged honourably and entitled to full benefits may have found himself unfit or unwilling to commit to conventional work that could sustain him. To these individuals we must add two other categories whose existence is unwillingly acknowledged in the literature: men dishonourably discharged and men who deserted. How easy was it for these men to blend back into society? The dishonourably discharged were marked men, quite literally, and would have been quite conspicuous in small communities.[152] Excluded from the privileges of the *veterani*, they may have found the transition to peaceful civilian life especially difficult. Deserters had to endure different problems. The authorities would wish to track them down wherever possible. Again, integration back into provincial society would have been difficult. For some, no doubt, it was manageable, but for others another life might beckon.

Banditry was epidemic in the Roman Empire.[153] For a young man accustomed to weapons and the use of force, it was a genuine option.[154] More optimistic views of the *pax Romana* and its armies tend to ignore the reality of banditry and overlook the behaviour of the troops. Yet there lay behind the façade of imperial power a conundrum of Augustinian proportions.[155] When the forces of Sextus Pompeius were defeated by Octavian, the victor labelled the defeated soldiers 'brigands', hunted them down, and enslaved or crucified them.[156] As soldiers of a vanquished opponent, their military identity was torn from them. Armies defeated in civil wars were intensely vulnerable to such deadly rebranding.

What complicated matters was the fact that soldiers were not infrequently engaged in extortion and armed robbery. What distinguished such behaviour from that of a bandit? In some contexts, even the law-abiding provincial might have found an encounter with roadside robbers preferable. To judge from the Talmud, a chance meeting with bandits might have been better than running into a patrol or even a single soldier out on the take. Confront the soldier and the system is turned on you; outrun the bandit and you have a chance.[157] When soldiers became ex-soldiers, no longer guaranteed food and shelter, would not

[149] Ruling of AD 213 cited in the *Cod. Iust.* 5.65.1. See *Digest* 27.1.8.2–5 for a sliding scale of benefits, depending on time served, at time of medical discharge.

[150] Shaw (1983: 139).

[151] Indeed, it is clear that the authorities recognized that, in practice if not in theory, some men who were medically discharged might recover sufficiently well to apply for reinstatement. A letter of the emperor Gordian indicates that it was thought appropriate to turn such applications down. *Cod. Iust.* 12.35(36).6.

[152] For the marking of dishonourably discharged veterans, see *Cod. Iust.* 12.35(36).3.

[153] Shaw (1984).   [154] Shaw (1993: 314–16).

[155] St Augustine (*City of God* 4.4) famously observes that without justice there is nothing that separates states from gangs of bandits. The same assuredly applies to representatives of states who behave without justice.

[156] Shaw (1993: 315).

[157] This surely is the lesson conveyed in Apuleius *Metamorphoses* 9.39–42. After the ass's owner overcomes a bullying soldier and runs away, he is nonetheless hunted down and dragged away for punishment.

the motive for theft, extortion, and other forms of criminality grow? Adorned in the accoutrements of the soldier, retained from their years of service, they could take rich pickings from luckless civilians.

While it is impossible to quantify the number of men who turned to banditry, it is clear that ancient commentators saw connections between soldiers and bandits. Dio returns to the theme on several occasions, arguing in one instance that the growth of banditry in Italy is directly linked to Severus' decision to open admission to the Praetorian Guard to men from all the legions. Deprived of this source of employment, young Italians allegedly turned to the gladiatorial schools or to banditry to make a living.[158]

It is no coincidence that one of the most notorious bandits of the Roman Empire was himself a deserter. Maternus went from soldier/guardian of the Roman order to an agent of the most terrible anarchy.[159] Deserting his unit, he launched successively larger raids—raids that took on regional significance. His depredations in Gaul and Spain included, we are told, a pattern of throwing open the prisons and allowing their occupants to flee. So grave a threat did he become that three governors received menacing letters from the emperor Commodus, demanding effective action. For the *Historia Augusta*, it seemed no exaggeration to term it a war, the *bellum desertorum*.[160] It is even alleged that Maternus now desired to take over the Empire.[161] There is here an echo of more conventionally mutinous military behaviour. In his commentary on this fascinating 2nd-century episode, Shaw notes how Herodian, its chronicler, plays on the theme of legitimacy.[162] As Shaw stresses, this is key to our understanding of Roman attitudes to banditry.[163] As the enemy within, the bandit, even the suspected bandit, was deprived of all legitimate rights. Whatever his status in Roman society prior to falling under official suspicion, he was liable to torture and gruesome execution. The act of banditry placed him outside the social order, even if the tactics of banditry often meant in practice that he depended especially acutely on local communities to shield and succour him. Maternus' reign of terror ended when he was betrayed by his own people and executed.

Throughout the Principate, it will be remembered, the Empire was marked by internal frontiers. However successful the growth in agriculture was in reclaiming land from the sea and the mountains, there were still areas where there was little real sign of agricultural development. In these areas, where poverty was widespread and the hand of Rome lay light, it is quite probable that former soldiers were among the bandits who waylaid unfortunate travellers. Ironically, as we have seen, even these unpromising realms were sporadically tapped for recruits, so they too could be considered, along with the farmed lands of the frontier, part of the ongoing pattern of incorporation. But banditry remained a factor, armed men beyond the reach of military discipline remained a threat, and accordingly many provincials probably did indeed lead lives of quiet desperation. What contained this situation, as far the imperial authorities were concerned, was the fact that

---

[158] Dio 75.2.5–6.   [159] Herodian 1.10.   [160] *SHA Comm.* 16.2.
[161] Herodian 1.10.3.   [162] Shaw (1993: 335–6).
[163] Shaw's (1993) commentary on banditry reminds us of the practical limitations of rights language in the Roman Empire.

none of their veterans lived for ever. After service in the armies of Rome, most had few years of active life left.

Legacy of the *veterani*

The intensity with which soldiers and their families were bound into the military community clearly left its mark on veterans. Many stayed close to other soldiers, though not always near the units with which they had served. Even villages and towns away from the frontier popular with veterans seem to have had some sort of military draw. Invitations to settle from fellow veterans helped assure the ex-soldier that he need not be totally isolated. Veterans appear to have assisted one another in minor tasks, perhaps allowing each other to enjoy a little additional leverage in local transactions. Even amongst those who did not achieve the coveted status of *honesta missio*, the contacts and lessons made during military service proved important. Ironically, this was probably no less true of the bandit leader Maternus than it was of the prosperous veteran envisaged at Watling Court.

Changing policy towards veterans meant that what it meant to be a veteran changed over time. For many of those auxiliaries discharged under Augustus, the dream of citizenship remained just that, but from the time of Claudius onwards, the *auxilia* became a major source of new citizens in the Empire. From then on until just after the death of Hadrian, auxiliary veterans and their families must have appeared a privileged group. Their elevation marched in step with rapid developments elsewhere in provincial society which saw diverse communities pulled more firmly into the Roman fold. The incorporation of friendly kingdoms, the growth of urban centres, and the consolidation of the frontiers were all developments of this time that were to have lasting implications for the shape and character of imperial society. Within this, the growth of citizenship amongst the families of auxiliary veterans was ultimately sufficiently pronounced to provoke an imperial response. The changes seen on auxiliary diplomas after AD 140 are a reminder that for veterans' families, imperial reforms and initiatives had a real resonance in both positive and negative ways. Not all changes necessarily enhanced social mobility. The change in regulations at this time and the growing tendency, marked from the 3rd century onwards, to link land grants to hereditary service meant that the sons of some auxiliary soldiers had fewer opportunities than their predecessors.

Scholars have frequently argued that it is possible to see the impact of veteran settlers and their families in the archaeology of the provinces. The appearance of fine houses and new farming techniques are marshalled as evidence. A detailed review of the evidence throws this view into question and again reinforces the impression of quite differing material legacies. The tantalizing reference from Egypt to the wives of auxiliary veterans who 'styled themselves Roman' raises questions as to what the material manifestations of such a styling might have been, but it does not offer any neat answers. Indeed, where we do have funerary depictions of veterans' wives they are frequently depicted in local dress, rather than adorned with a view to metropolitan fashion. Even in those areas where we do see a tendency amongst veterans to cluster, as at Karanis, we can see that they merge relatively naturally with the prosperous members of local society. Auxiliary veterans seem to capitalize on what is there, rather than create something afresh. This contributes to the vibrancy of provincial culture and the strength of its networks, but the intrusive 'Roman' elements with which veterans are often associated are outweighed, or at least matched, by other factors. At the auxiliary fort of Intercisa, to take another example, I have argued that the most conspicuous cultural archaeological legacy of veterans was to support the eastern traditions of their homelands over a couple of generations by sustaining the worship of their divine patron Elagabalus. Conversely, in the territory of the Batavi, the most conspicuous aspect of a veteran-heavy society may be seen in the distribution of writing materials.

The degree to which fellow provincials were affected by the return of veterans must have varied to a significant degree according to local tradition. Roxan's astute observation that Thracian veterans are often shown to return to Thrace even after twenty-five or more years of distant service raises questions about more than just enduring links between soldiers and their homes. Despite the justified misgivings of the leaders of the Thracian Revolt, Thrace had had a long tradition of sending mercenaries overseas prior to Roman annexation. Rome formalized this and extended the periods of service, but parts of Thrace may have been culturally better attuned to the disappearance of large bodies of men for sustained periods and the challenge of their reintegration later. Here, perhaps more than in any other part of the Empire save the tribal lands of the Batavi, we may argue that recruitment and discharge contributed distinctively to local provincial culture.

Overall, though, the legacy of the *veterani* was felt most strongly in the lives of the ex-soldier and his offspring. This is clear from the system of rights and privileges, but it is also perhaps suggested by some of the archaeological evidence. Diplomas and military equipment seldom seem to have survived more than a couple of generations before being discarded. During this time many families enjoyed a quiet increase in prosperity.

These observations and our recollection of the fate of the forgotten veterans remind us that the story of auxiliary veteran settlement generally had little to do with dramatic change. The brash green-field *coloniae* that housed a minority of legionary veterans, stamping their mark upon newly conquered landscapes, cannot be seen as representative of veteran settlement and its impact. For the overwhelming majority of discharged auxiliaries the experience was very different.

Yet in all this the theme of incorporation still looms large. Just as the *auxilia* took many of these men, still for the most part in the teens and twenties, and drew them into the bodies of provincial armies, so there was a place for them in civil society when they reached the end of their military life. While some journeyed back to the homes of their youth, none of them made their journeys unchanged. Whatever they made of the lessons and experience of military service in the civil sphere, new networks, and new statuses marked them. Their status meant that they were civilian provincials again, only more so.

Their numbers meant that they were absorbed back into the wider community, but generations later the implications of their military lives were still to be felt. As Horion, the grandson of the veteran C. Iulius Niger, must have felt when he wrote as C. Gemellus Horigenes, there were times when military ancestry could be used to advantage in provincial society.

22

Conclusion

Embodying Rome

Only exceptionally do the words of those who suffered at the hands of Roman soldiers survive. Yet a letter from one such individual, *believed* to have been executed by men of the army of Lower Moesia at about the time the Adamklissi *tropaeum* was erected, is preserved.[1] Writing to the Christian community in Corinth, Clement of Rome likened the Church to an army and drew on technical terminology that would have been familiar to every auxiliary soldier to make his point. Observing that not everyone can be 'a prefect or a tribune or a centurion', he notes that the 'great' cannot exist without the 'small' nor the 'small' without the 'great'. Each individual, he argues, must perform the role they are assigned if the whole *body*, the whole community, is to succeed.[2]

Throughout this volume, an attempt has been made to illuminate the parallelism between the imperial system's incorporation of peoples—classifying them according to scales of rights and obligations while leaving many of their traditions and customs largely intact—and the experience of individual soldiers—pulled into a larger entity, classified, categorized, and yet able to make a range of individual choices which had little to do with Rome itself. Yet a challenge remains. How do we access the lives of the 'small', of individuals, *archaeologically*? Not infrequently, discussions of people within systems have treated individual bodies as the stage on which power is played out.[3] Individuals emerge as passive bystanders, not active agents. Individual bodies are reduced, as Tringham puts it, to 'faceless blobs'.[4] Directing our attention to the way that individuals lived is a way of addressing this problem. But to what extent can we claim to encounter individuals in the archaeological record?[5]

---

[1] Ancient tradition preserved in both east and west holds that Clement of Rome was exiled to that part of the Crimea that fell under jurisdiction of the Lower Moesian army, and was there executed on Trajan's orders.

[2] Clement *First Epistle to the Corinthians* 37.

[3] Meskell (1996: 6–7; 1998). See also Borić and Robb (2009: 4).

[4] Tringham (1991).

[5] There has been much debate over the degree to which searching for agency in archaeology is the same thing as seeking the actions of individuals. See, e.g. Barrett (2001); Dobres (2000); Hodder (2000). I have some sympathy for Gardner's (2004a: 4) observation that this is impossible, but believe that the examples offered below come as close to examining individual lives as we can hope to do in archaeology.

For some, the obvious route is not so much through the approaches adopted so far in this volume but through the study of funerary archaeology. So it is appropriate to consider this approach at the end of the volume. As Reece remarked, cemetery archaeology, digging up the dead themselves, brings the excavator directly into physical contact with the actual people he or she is writing about.[6] Aside from the usual caveats about the fact that the dead do not bury themselves—the essential point being that their internment is by definition outside their full control—there can be no doubt that cemetery archaeology has allowed higher-resolution analysis of individual dress and affiliation.[7] Yet it is important to be clear as to precisely what it can achieve in the case of the *auxilia*.

In pursuit of the agenda set out at the beginning of this volume, emphasizing the need to compare evidence found within fort sites with that found in their immediate vicinity, I worked with Tony Wilmott of English Heritage on the excavation of a cemetery belonging to Birdoswald Roman fort in Cumbria. The intervention was necessitated by substantial erosion at the site. Our discoveries both illuminated and chastened me. The first impression was of the sheer diversity of burial practice within this military community. Commemorative deposits of small quantities of crenulated bone were sometimes left in what was no more than a fold in the ground; elsewhere burnt bone was interred in old jugs, in bags, in cists, and even in one case in a hole that was lined after the ash was placed in it.[8] There were more complex *bustum*-type graves too, where the deceased had been cremated directly over the pit into which his or her mortal remains were laid. What united this disparate group was the fact that all of those within the cemetery had been cremated—a practice that clearly continued strongly amongst military communities long after much of provincial society had turned to inhumation.[9] The cemetery was also conspicuously lacking in grave goods of any kind, save the occasional pots and ancillary vessels discovered. Even here, therefore, the impact of military culture cloaked important elements of individual identity. Cloaked, but not wholly obliterated, however, for while many of the methodologies one might attempt in building individual biographies—isotopic analysis for example—were impossible, other stories did emerge. Of these, the most compelling was associated with 'Urn 33516'. This pot, of Hadrianic/Antonine date, had been placed in a cut dug as close as possible to another vessel of the same date also containing crenellated bone; both lay within a small circular enclosure. Urn 33516, excavated in English Heritage's laboratories at Fort Cumberland, proved to be the only urn containing any artefacts. A small section of mail was discovered, originally provoking speculation that this was a symbolic fragment of military equipment

---

[6] Reece (1988).

[7] For this author, the most exciting example of this is Cool's (2004) study of the cemetery at Brougham. The statistical analyses of correlations between age, sex, and certain artefact types within the Brougham study are appealing. Yet the particular characteristics of the unit and the relative richness of the funerary assemblages mean that the same approach cannot be applied with equal success everywhere. More importantly, it is vital to remember that the correlations revealed reflect associations within funerary ritual; it is impossible to demonstrate that they closely mapped the use of such artefacts in daily life.

[8] Wilmott (2010), who coined the term 'commemorative deposits'.

[9] I exclude from discussion here two inhumation graves that were clearly dug at the site some time after the AD 370s.

indicating a soldier, but afterwards interpreted as part of a chatelaine. Also recovered were a type 3 earring and a possible hairband, suggesting perhaps— but by no means proving—that the urn contained a female burial after all. Along with the ambiguities of the find, and the urn alongside which it lay, is the potent reminder of just how close the military body of each auxiliary soldier often was to other non-soldiers who lived alongside him. Our excavations yielded no grave stelae, though two that probably once came from this cemetery site are known:— one to the children Deciba[lus] and Blae[sus], another to a legionary drawn from Africa[10]—so the team's access to 'individual' stories was limited to that which could be recovered by excavation.

Excavations of military cemeteries remain rare, but the study of funerary monuments in their broader archaeological context still has the potential to illuminate the lives of individual soldiers whose personal experience partly reflected the changing face of Rome. Though their value as sources has been considered from several different perspectives in this volume, a contextualized analysis of four examples will help show how different and how similar a man's life in the *auxilia* could be. Selected from settings that exemplify the evolving character of provincial society, with its sometimes brutal fits and starts, it is possible to see how the mechanisms of incorporation converge.

The life and death of Longinus, a *duplicarius* of the *ala Thracum*, a soldier born near Sofia in Bulgaria who ended his days in Colchester in southern England, illustrates this process admirably (see Fig. 22.1). Colchester/Camulodunum lay at the heart of a classic landscape of conquest and incorporation. Sacred to the war god Camulos and one-time home of the most powerful native ruler, Cunobelinus, Camulodunum underwent a radical transformation in the years following the Claudian invasion. A legionary fortress, converted into a veteran colony, facilitated the shift from tribal centre to Roman stronghold. Yet the initial process of incorporation went horribly wrong, and Camulodunum became the first target for the Boudiccan revolt in AD 60/1.

Amongst the more discrete monuments to this early period of rapid transition is the finely carved tombstone of Longinus.[11] When it was discovered face down a few hundred metres from the Roman city wall in 1928, it appeared to exemplify imperial pride and native anger.[12] Had Boudicca's rebels defaced and overturned the monument as they swarmed through the burning colony? Here was a memorial to a proud Roman soldier, his face hewn off as if in an iconoclastic rejection of all that he embodied. This was after all a man whose life exuded *romanitas*. His very name was a Latin adoption, one that would have come far more easily to a Roman tongue than that of his father, Sdapezematygus.[13] His ability to exploit Roman law, something quite literally life-transforming in provincial society, is attested in the epitaph. Longinus used his special rights as a soldier—powers that most provincials could not have had at this time—to make a will and to choose heirs from outside his immediate kin. His heirs duly honoured this will, erecting the monument in accordance with his instructions. In this respect, we see the

---

[10] *RIB* 1920, 3445.   [11] *RIB* 201.   [12] Richmond (1928).
[13] This reading of his full name, which follows *RIB*, is contested elsewhere but the essential point is not. Longinus is an ordinary Roman name, quite probably adopted when the soldier began his military service. By contrast, the names of his family are decidedly more exotic.

Fig. 22.1. Stele of Longinus, *duplicarius* in *ala I Thracum* (*RIB* 201), England. First century AD.

agency of Longinus, but how far he chose the detail of the tombstone is impossible to tell. All that may be observed is that its decoration notably conformed to a style used by other recent arrivals at Colchester.[14] With its sphinx and harpy decoration, it adopts funerary symbols popular in many parts of the Empire.[15] Even

[14] The Sphinx finial on Longinus' tombstone finds parallel in the oolite sphinx *RIB* 211 found approximately 300yds (275m) to its northeast.

[15] For the Sphinx, see Richmond (1946: 5).

analysis of the source of stone emphasizes Longinus' incorporation into the Roman system; the quarry that provided it was almost certainly under military supervision.[16] The sculpting, too, testifies to a military hand. In a familiar pose that underscored his distance from the native population, Longinus' horse towers over a cowering caricature of a barbarian. The soldier appears as a member of a parallel society that distances him from the native. The two have nothing in common save a shared humanity callously disregarded.[17]

Longinus' tombstone therefore appears to reveal much of his place in the Roman order, but on closer inspection the tale proves more complicated. Recent archaeological excavation at the site where it was initially found recovered the trooper's missing face, suggesting in the process that rampaging barbarians did not defile the memorial.[18] The discovery is a reminder of a key thread within this book: the paramount importance of good contextual evidence for every find. But it is not just in this regard that Longinus' story was more complex.

Within Longinus' lifespan, Thracian society underwent radical changes no less than he himself did. Thracians too had once fallen beneath Roman horses. The story of the Thracian revolt of AD 26, an event that took place when Longinus was but a boy, has been discussed extensively within these pages.[19] The cause of the revolt was another rejection of the demands of imperial incorporation, in this case recruitment for the *auxilia*. As has been noted, such conflicts marked Rome's relations with many provincial societies between the time of Augustus and the revolt of Civilis. The ending of recruitment-related unrest in the late Flavian period marks a new era in imperial time. In achieving ultimate control of local manpower, and with it the right to raise and deploy auxiliary troops in her own, not necessarily local interests, Rome took the final step in consolidating her power across the Empire.

As has been shown, in the case of the Thracians, it is clear that several tribes feared that the demands of the Roman army would utterly transform their society. They believed that communities and families would be broken up, that the young men would be sent far beyond their lands never to return. Longinus' monument reflects the fact that there was substance to these fears, but also that individuals caught up in this process exploited the opportunities afforded by this disruptive imposition.[20] What neither Longinus nor the Thracian rebels of an earlier generation could anticipate, however, was how this process would affect their

[16] Hayward (2009: 98, 100) identified Painswich Hill, close to the fortresses at Gloucester and the Kingsholm site, as the source of the stone. He demonstrated a clear link between the exploitation of the stone there and early military activity.

[17] For a similar observation, advancing the theory that such oppositions were integral to Roman notions of manhood, see Alston (1998: 218): 'One of the most interesting and common of these depictions is of a cavalryman, frequently himself of barbarian stock, riding down a crudely portrayed and often naked, sometimes animalistic, barbarian warrior. Military service was for these men a self-defining role. Service differentiated them from barbarians. It made them men.' Ferris (2000: 158) also discusses the way in which these monuments emphasize the difference between the deceased auxiliaries and barbarians.

[18] The excavations took place under James Fawn and the Colchester Archaeological Group in 1996.

[19] Tacitus *Hist.* 4.46.

[20] Longinus and his family were more probably among the second group than the first; the Thracian revolt concentrated in southeastern Thrace, some distance from his own birthplace.

own society and that of the Empire. As in all such exchanges with Roman administration, local factors played an important role. In the case of the Thracians, it appears that auxiliaries drawn from amongst them generally seem to have responded differently to their time in the army than many of their fellow soldiers. Margaret Roxan's observation that 'Thracians go home' more than any other single group illustrates part of that distinct response.[21] I have suggested that this recalls the region's long tradition of mercenary service, dating back to pre-Roman times. Whatever the reason, the returning soldier was clearly a particular feature of Thracian life. Veterans returned to live in the land of their birth after long years away, contributing to a strong military thread in local provincial society. In a landscape that was relatively under-urbanized in the Roman period this trend was to prove significant, for Rome continued to draw large numbers of recruits from Thracian lands.

A little over two centuries after the death of Longinus, a Thracian said to have begun his rise in provincial society as an auxiliary cavalryman ascended to its very height. The career of the emperor Maximinus Thrax (AD 235–238) exemplifies the network of opportunity that characterized the Empire. Ancient accounts of Maximinus Thrax speak of him as a rough and barbaric figure, a shepherd and sometime bandit from remote lands whose rough Latin preserved more than a mere flavour of his Thracian roots.[22] Senatorial antipathy to Maximinus most probably accounts for much of the negativity and some outright distortion, but there was nothing inherently improbable about a rough frontier soldier becoming emperor, and indeed men of such pedigree were to become increasingly frequent contenders for the purple in the centuries to follow. Such evolutions were entirely possible in the process of incorporation that transformed provincial society at this time.[23] Similarly, the hostility of accounts recalls the ongoing tensions between army and Senate as each sought influence. These tensions drove an evolving conflict which formed both imperial culture and, as we have seen, the culture of the army.

In Maximinus, too, it is possible to see something of the changing face of Rome. In his study of the imperial horseguard, Speidel draws attention to a portrait of the emperor, now in the Capitoline Museum (see Fig. 22.2).[24] As with Longinus its head is broken, but here the culprits are far less likely to have been rebellious barbarians or unfortunate archaeologists than the Romans themselves, commemorating the Senate's courageous decision to strip him of his titles and powers. An inscription records the *saevissima dominatio* that rendered all oaths of loyalty to the soldier-emperor redundant.[25] In an army bound together by oaths, the decision had profound consequences.

---

[21] Roxan (1997: 487). This habit is attested all through our period. For the pattern of veteran settlement within Thrace and Lower Moesia, see Gerov (1988).

[22] Herodian 6.8.1–2, HA Maxim. 2–4. His bandit activities appear in HA Maxim. 2.1, while his Latin is described in HA Maxim. 2.5.

[23] Shaw (1993: 339) sees Maximinus' immediate rise in the context of fragmenting state power.

[24] Speidel (1994b: 69 pl. 6). I found Speidel's discussion of Maximinus, this portrait, and the horseguard particularly useful here.

[25] *AE* 1935, 164.

Fig. 22.2. Bust of Maximinus Thrax. Musei Capitolini, Rome.

Despite the damage inflicted upon it, the portrait preserves something of the identity of the Roman soldier; a brutal military haircut tops a hard face. As demonstrated in the discussion of military routine in earlier chapters, depictions of Maximinus embodied soldierly ideals to an almost absurd degree; even his excessive sweating exemplified the military manifestation of Roman manhood.[26] Yet, as this study has repeatedly emphasized, incorporation generated regional permutations of the very ties that bound the Empire together.

What Maximinus' tale also conveys is the link between imperial incorporation and the rise and fall of regional influences on Rome itself. His rise is linked to the ascendancy of Danubian influence, and though Maximinus himself never got to Rome, it is quite clear that culturally the currents of the Danube mingled with those of the Tiber. Had he visited, he would have found himself most at home in the Lateran area of Rome, for it was there, a few minutes from the forum, that the imperial horseguard dwelt.

There is a tendency to think of the provinces as the exclusive preserve of landscapes of conquest and incorporation, but Rome also carries such traces. Recent estimates suggest that by the time of Septimius Severus between one in 25 and one in 45 of Rome's residents were soldiers of some sort or other, bound as were their *commilitones* on distant frontiers to the emperor's bidding.[27]

---

[26] P. 173.   [27] Coulston (2000: 81).

Furthermore, by Severus' time the delicate balancing act by which imperial security was jointly entrusted to the Italian-born soldiers of the Praetorian Guard and groups drawn from the provinces had shifted in favour of the provincials. In addition to the introduction of new provincial legions, the emperor had increased the number of men in those established guard units that recruited from the *auxilia*. The famous Praetorians had fallen from favour, but the *equites singulares* remained the emperor's trusted companions. Their ranks at this time were filled with the descendants of men such as Longinus and contemporaries of Maximinus—Thracians now found themselves located at the heart of the imperial system. A comparison of the monuments they left at Rome with the one commemorating Longinus at Colchester is instructive.

All these changes reflect the particular features of another of Rome's great cultural revolutions. This time it was the Severan dynasty that drove a transition manifested in the material culture of both military community and civilian society. Though less immediately obvious than much of Rome's past, it is still possible to reconstruct its considerable physical impact on the city. Under St John Lateran, the Pope's own church, for example, visitors may visit the remains of the Castra Nova of the *equites singulares*, and see where Severus demolished extensive palatial houses to accommodate the doubling of his horseguard. The whole complex, along with the garrison that once served within its walls, is a reminder that in important respects the life of the seat of power was tightly linked to that of the provinces.

Thracians were represented in the cemeteries of the *equites singulares* too, but there are illuminating differences between their funerary memorials and that of Longinus. At first glance, the tombstone of M. Aurelius Bithus, a Thracian cavalryman who was based in the Castra Nova and buried in Rome, bears striking similarities to the relief erected two centuries before on the outskirts of Colchester (see Fig. 22.3).[28] Again a horseman dominates the frieze and the inscription is in finely carved Latin letters. But the difference in the detail is crucial. Behind the rider we see a standing figure, almost certainly the trooper's groom. Such servants are an increasingly common feature of rider tombstones, commemorating in part the greater wealth and status of cavalrymen in comparison with their infantry counterparts. A dog, chasing out a boar that appears in a thicket to the right, replaces Longinus' cowering barbarian counterpart. The absence of armour reminds us that the cavalry soldier was able to compete for status in wider civil society too. With the changing rules for citizenship, the auxiliary cavalry of the provinces and of the guard grew further in status. Men even requested transfer from the legions to enter the provincial *alae*.[29] The old equations between high-status legionary infantry and lower-status auxiliary troops were thoroughly forgotten.

Yet to anyone familiar with provincial society along the Danube, there is a further unmistakable message in the memorial of Bithus. The galloping figure with his billowing cloak is an explicit reference to the Thracian Hero, a divine

[28] P. 265. *CIL* 6.3195.
[29] The 3rd-century AD *P. Oxy.* 1666 records a man's desire to transfer from a legion to an *ala* at Coptos, Egypt.

Fig. 22.3. Stele of Marcus Aurelius Bithus, *eques* in the *Equites Singulares* (*CIL* 6.3195). Third century AD. Musei Capitolini, Rome.

being whom Danubian peoples intimately associated with the passage into the underworld. A standard Latin dedication, *D. M.*, 'to the shades of the departed', provides a familiar Empire-wide gloss, but it is the mounted hero who indicates most eloquently Bithus' countrymen's notion of the life beyond the grave. Here again we encounter the monumentalized harmonization of imperial culture and regional culture, the mediation of tension between Roman tradition and indigenous belief. A soldier close to the throne itself saw no contradiction in commemorating his life as a servant of Empire and a son of the provinces. This is a world away from Longinus' 1st-century monument with its diligent adherence to a blander military type, repeated with limited imagination across the Empire.

Away from these landscapes of military dominance, from conquered Britain and from conquering Rome, there is equally strong evidence for the way in which imperial power, through the process of incorporation, could transform ethnic identity. This volume opened with a discussion of Adamklissi and the funerary altar that numbered, amongst others, fallen Batavians. Another part of the Roman world, miles from the Danubian site of the monument and the homeland of the Batavi on the lower Rhine, brings these two elements startlingly close together. In the 3rd century, members of the *equites singulares* were deployed to Anazarbos in Cilicia (near Adana in southern Turkey), a city far behind the frontier. During the reign of Severus, the city was honoured in a manner characteristic of the dynamics of imperial incorporation. It became a centre for the imperial cult, and the venue for massive annual games, a combination that brought greater prestige and wealth, binding it and its citizens ever closer into the network of power that pulled the Empire together.[30] Funerary monuments recording six members of the imperial horseguard have been recovered.

Significantly, two of these memorials reflect sensitivity to local conditions. They also reveal a desire by the soldiers to communicate to the city's population. Here, in this Greek-speaking part of the world far from the martial traditions of the northwest provinces, the soldiers were moved to put up bilingual inscriptions to their dead. Their bilingualism reflects the twin tongues of Empire. The Latin speaks to the community of soldiers, while the Greek speaks to a local audience. Again it is the subtlest variation in the monuments that reveal the most profound shifts in meaning. In one, a Latin text refers to the deceased's regiment as the *equites singulares imperatorum*, while the parallel Greek text renders the unit simply as the Batavi.[31] While in Rome it was never possible to render the unit title in this colloquial manner, here in Cilicia it was different.[32] Yet what is profoundly important about this label is that it owes remarkably little to any real tribal group. In two other Latin altars from the same cemetery, members of *the equites singulares* give their troop name as *numerus equitum Batavonum* text, but in one of these the deceased is described as *natione Pannonius*.[33] To complicate matters further, it is probable that some of the men recorded as serving in this 'Batavian' formation in Cilicia were Thracian, including one whose memorial was composed entirely in Latin, rather than the Greek which dominated the epigraphy of his homeland.[34] Analysis of 210 tombstones of the *equites singulares* makes clear both the transformation of the guard and the transposition of ethnic labelling. From the time of Severus, 70 per cent of the troopers came from the Danube, whereas formerly the largest single group of soldiers came from the northwest provinces.[35] The changing composition is reflected in the varied fashions of the guardsmen's tombstones. The styles of the lower Rhine, for example, steadily give way to the Danubian fashions exemplified by Bithus' monument.[36] By the 3rd century, the guardsmen contained few genuine Batavi in their ranks, but the tribal nomenclature had become synonymous with the guards, and even men who had never seen the lower Rhine were happy to adopt the term as a mark of identity. The Empire's power to integrate, through its capacity to redefine ethnic identity, is admirably illustrated here in stone.[37]

In time, the term 'Batavi' would become still more elastic. It came to be associated with other elite units of the late Roman army, descendants of the auxiliary cavalry, who had metamorphosed from the helping forces of Rome to the cutting edge of her power. One suspects that the proud cavalrymen of the

---

[30] Sayar (1991: 19–40).   [31] Speidel (1994a: no. 688).

[32] The changing status of the city, concern for local readers, and the different rules for writing unit titles that applied in Rome are noted by Speidel (1994b: 62).

[33] Speidel (1994a: nos. 688b and 688d).   [34] Ibid. no 688c records another Aurelius Bithus.

[35] Figures based on 210 documented gravestones of *equites singulares Augusti* (Speidel 1994a: 14–17; 1994b: 83).

[36] For a study of the images see Busch (2003: 679–94).   [37] Roymans (2004).

early Empire, who had so assiduously emphasized their distinct status within the *auxilia*, would have been delighted. But what, one wonders, would Civilis' 'rebels' have made of it all?

If these cavalrymen reveal something of the changes in local and imperial society, and in turn the evolving status of mounted soldiers, what may we learn from the experience of that most fundamental element of any army—the infantry-man? As a general point, it is clear that the auxiliary infantry also enjoyed a growing status over time. As we have seen, from the reign of Caracalla onwards, when the issue of citizenship became less important than whether an individual was considered to be one of the *honestiores* or the *humiliores*, auxiliary troops shared with their legionary counterparts the higher status. Distinctions in equip-ment, pay, and diet are no longer seen. The process of incorporation within the military is largely complete.

A man whose life-story at once epitomizes this pattern and highlights its wider implications for provincial society is P. Aelius Theimes, a Roman citizen of Palmyrene descent. Theimes' tale spans much of the 2nd century, placing him midway in time between the lives of Longinus and Bithus. It emerges from a cluster of finds associated with *colonia* Dacica Sarmizegetusa, a city founded in western Transylvania in the immediate aftermath of Trajan's Second Dacian War *c.* AD 106. In many ways the colony is one of the more spectacular monuments to Roman imperialism. Established on a green-field site some 40km southwest of the major Dacian citadel Sarmizegetusa Regia, from which it took its name, the whole foundation redefined power in the conquered landscape. Lavish marble buildings housed a society with strong cultural links to north Italy. Many of the members of its leading families were indeed drawn from there.[38] Recent study of the city's first forum has illuminated the fierce competition for civic honours, reminiscent of that in Rome itself, amongst its prosperous citizens.[39] It was in this society that Theimes rose to prominence as decurion and duumviralis.

Two separate inscriptions recall Theimes' life: a limestone funerary altar and an epitaph from a funerary precinct or mausoleum. The apparent duplication may seem strange, especially given the slight differences in the textual detail, but this is readily explained, for Theimes clearly opted for a combination of family enclosure and individual memorial of a type popular in Italy at this time.[40] These memorials record that the deceased was a centurion in *cohors I Vindelicorum*, an infantry regiment raised in the Alps but subsequently stationed in Tibiscum, Dacia. Tibiscum was in turn the entry point for many men of Palmyrene descent to Dacia, for it was home of the *numerus Palmyrenorum Tibiscensium*. The most probable explanation is that Theimes' father arrived with the first draft of this unit so that his son was able to move on to senior rank in a unit of quite different origins, a regular cohort of *Vindelici*. In what appears to have been a further example of social mobility, Theimes' own son ended up serving in the Twentieth Legion in Britain. Though rare in its own right as evidence for such mobility over three generations, a pattern that was probably common enough within the

---

[38] Alicu and Paki (1995: 82). [39] Piso and Diaconescu (1999).
[40] Funerary altar *IDR* 3.2 no. 369, *CIL* 3.12587; epitaph plate *IDR* 3.2 no. 370, *CIL* 3.1472.

Empire, what is most striking here is not just the evidence we have for Theimes as soldier and councillor, but also as religious benefactor. His finely carved dedication to Hygeia is an early, in this case mid-2nd-century, example of a statue that resembles many found within Roman Dacia.[41] The goddess he chose to honour attracted devotees across the Roman world, but seems to have enjoyed particular popularity in this province. Coincidentally, the goddess's association with Aesculapius attests to the extent to which Greco-Roman ideas about health and hygiene influenced both the Palmyrene Theimes and his fellow provincials.

Prominent membership of the Roman order did not, of course, conflict with Theimes' Palmyrene identity. While an active member of the town community, he also raised a substantial temple to the *Dii Patrii* of Palmyra at Sarmizegetusa.[42] The temple, excavated in the 1880s, lies some distance to the west of the town but, situated on high ground, was far from inconspicuous. What message did it send to the viewer? A detailed reanalysis based on the original excavator's outstandingly detailed report suggests that the structure's semi-classical exterior housed a sacred place ordered around fundamentally Palmyrene notions of sacred space.[43]

When considered together, all these different monuments to an auxiliary veteran's life illuminate a diversity of human responses to the force of imperial incorporation. For Theimes, who died at 89, links to his homeland remained strong, but he could easily combine being a Palmyrene with being a Roman citizen and magistrate. Other Palmyrenes within the same province negotiated the relationship between Roman status and ethnic identity differently. While Theimes recorded his career and proclaimed his religious affiliations in Latin, contemporaries left bilingual Latin and Palmyrene texts, while one composed a text exclusively in Palmyrene script.[44] This mix recalls the processes of incorporation examined in the discussion of language use above. In other cases the Palmyrene link is still more explicit: soldiers from an auxiliary unit stationed at Porolissum in Dacia Superior set up a statue for their commander in the agora of the great desert city itself.[45] However, the inscription there was in Greek, a further reflection of the impact of empire upon that great cultural centre.

Aspects of Palmyrene culture endured well amongst soldier migrants, but as these examples show, even here there was clearly no obstacle to incorporation with the other diverse peoples of the Empire. Rome's soldiers may have spent their career in parallel societies, distanced from the population at large by routine and by design, but at the end of their service they were nonetheless equipped to contribute to a wider pattern of incorporation. Part of the Empire's success lay in the fact that this contribution in turn worked against the development of larger, ethnically based regions that might more readily split from Rome.

Each of the soldiers discussed above presents a different face of Rome—a synthesis between the experiences of a particular cultural *melange*, a moment in

[41] *IDR* 3.2.152.

[42] *IDR* 3.2.18. For more on the career of P. Aelius Theimes, see *IDR* 3.2.152 and 369–71.

[43] For the excavations, see Téglás (1906: 321–30). Rusu-Pescaru and Alicu (2000: plans 26 and 27) present the building with a classical appearance. Schäfer (2003) offers a convincing reanalysis.

[44] Kaiser (2004a: 565–9).   [45] Seyrig (1941: 231–3, no. 4); Starcky (1949: no. 79).

time, and the needs of the state. Yet each of these episodes, from Longinus trampling a stereotyped barbarian to Theimes venerating his Palmyrene deities, recalls the truth of Tacitus' maxim: 'By the blood of the provinces the provinces are won.'[46] As this study demonstrates, however, the story is about much more than battlefield dominance. The limits of control extended far beyond the edge of the sword. The use of manpower, the development of new military and civilian identities, the currents of religious belief, and the impact of language and law facilitated the ongoing incorporation of individuals and groups into the Empire.

Through this, the Roman auxiliary emerges as a nexus of many of the contradictions and oppositions that the Empire had to reconcile if it was to survive. He is a symbol of much that made provincial society possible. He was (often) a non-citizen who perpetuated the values of the citizen body, a representative of the centre on the peripheries of society, and the embodiment of Rome in a provincial body. Though not always eagerly sought or particularly pleasant, service in the *auxilia* presented hundreds of thousands of men with a network of opportunity outside the confines of local society. In turn it offered them and their families an alternative focus of loyalty and identities that were no longer principally tribal or ethnic, but were rather rooted in the imperial system.

For all the apparent conservatism attributed to 'Roman' society, the Principate is marked by dynamism and constant evolution. Core concepts to which all were obliged to respond provided a crucial framework; they generated the labels that made sense of the social order. Soldier, civilian, freeman, citizen, veteran: all these were words with a power in Roman society quite unlike the one they have in our own. Yet the material evidence reveals that the life to which each label was attached could be lived in very different ways. Conspicuous negotiation of these labels preserved their incorporative power at the heart of provincial society. Study of the *auxilia* reveals that incorporating the Roman world into an enduring Empire was as much about this ongoing negotiation as it was about maintaining the *pax Romana*. Such a conclusion may sit less well with the grand narratives of empire, but the archaeology of the thousands of men who once served in the *alae* and *cohortes* renders it ultimately unavoidable.

---

[46] Tacitus *Hist.* 4.17.

Bibliography

Adams, J. N. (1977) *The Vulgar Latin of the Letters of Claudius Terentianus (P. Mich. VIII)*. Manchester.

Adams, J. N. (1992) 'British Latin: the text, interpretation, and language of the Bath curse tablets', *Britannia* 23: 1–26.

Adams, J. N. (1994) 'Latin and Punic in contact? The case of the Bu Njem ostraca', *JRS* 84: 87–112.

Adams, J. N. (2003) 'The interpretation of *souxtum* at *Tab. Vind.* III 301.3', *ZPE* 110: 238.

Adams, J. N. (1996) *Bilingualism and the Latin Language*, Cambridge.

Agache, R. (1978) *La Somme pré-romaine*, Amiens.

Alföldy, G. (1962) 'Die Auxiliartruppen der Provinz Dalmatien', *Acta Archaeologia Academiae Scientiarum Hungaricae* 14: 259–96.

Alföldy, G. (1968a) *Die Hilfstruppen der römischen Provinz Germania Inferior*, Düsseldorf.

Alföldy, G. (1968b) 'Zur Beurteilung der Militärdiplome der Auxiliarsoldaten', *Historia* 17: 215–27.

Alföldy, G. (2000) 'Das Heer in der Sozialstruktur des Römischen Kaiserreiches', in Alföldy et al.: 33–57.

Alföldy, G. (2005) 'Romanisation: Grundbegriff oder Fehlgriff? Überlegungen zum gegenwärtigen Stand der Erforschung von Integrationsprozessen im Römischen Weltreich', in Z. Visy (ed.), *Limes XIX; Proceedings of the XIXth Congress of Roman Frontier Studies held in Pécs, Hungary, September 2003*, 25–56.

Alföldy, G., Dobson, B., and Eck, W. (eds) (2000) *Kaiser, Heer und Gesellschaft in der Römischen Kaiserzeit: Gedenkschrift für Eric Birley*. Stuttgart.

Alicu, D., and Paki, A. (1995) *Town Planning and Population in Ulpia Traiana Sarmizegetusa*. BAR International Series 605. Oxford.

Allason-Jones, L. (1988) 'Small finds from turrets on Hadrian's Wall', in J. C. Coulston (ed.), *Military Equipment and the Identity of Roman Soldiers: Proceedings of the Fourth Roman Military Equipment Conference*. BAR International Series 394. Oxford, 197–233.

Allason-Jones, L. (1995) '"Sexing" small finds', in P. Rush (ed.), *Theoretical Roman Archaeology: 2nd Conference Proceedings*. Avebury, 22–32.

Allason-Jones, L. (1999) 'Health care in the Roman north', *Britannia* 30: 133–46.

Allason-Jones, L. (2001) 'Material culture and identity', in S. James and M. Millett (eds), *Britons and Romans: Advancing an Archaeological Agenda*. CBA Research Report 125. York, 19–25.

Allason-Jones, L., and Dungworth, D. B. (1997) 'Metalworking on Hadrian's Wall', in W. Groenman-van Waateringe, B. L. van Beek, W. J. H. Willems, and S. L. Wynia (eds), *Roman Frontier Studies 1995: Proceedings of the XVIth International Congress of Roman Frontier Studies*. Oxbow Monograph 91. Oxford, 317–21.

Allason-Jones, L., and McKay, B. (1985) *Coventina's Well*. Chester.

Allason-Jones, L., and Miket, R. (1984) *Catalogue of Small Finds from South Shields Roman Fort*. Newcastle upon Tyne.

Allison, P. M. (2005) 'Mapping artefacts and activities within Roman military forts', in Z. Visy (ed.), *Limes XIX: Proceedings of the XIXth Congress of Roman Frontier Studies held in Pécs, Hungary, September 2003*, 833–46

Allison, P. M. (2006) 'Mapping for gender: interpreting artefact distribution in Roman military forts in Germany', *Archaeological Dialogues* 13.1: 1–48.

Allison, P. M., Fairbairn, A. S., Ellis, S. J. R., and Blackall, C. W. (2004) 'Extracting the social relevance of artefact distribution in Roman military forts', *Internet Archaeology* 17: http://intarch.ac.uk/journal/issue17/allison_index.html

Alston, R. (1994) 'Roman military pay from Caesar to Diocletian', *JRS* 84: 113–23.

Alston, R. (1995) *Soldier and Society in Roman Egypt*. London.

Alston, R. (1998) 'Arms and the man: soldiers, masculinity and power in Republican and Imperial Rome', in L. Foxhall and J. Salmon (eds), *When Men Were Men: Masculinity and Identity in Classical Antiquity*. London, 205–23.

Alston, R. (1999) 'The ties that bind: soldiers and societies', in Goldsworthy and Haynes, 175–96.

Amory, P. (1997) *People and Identity in Ostrogothic Italy 489–554*. Cambridge.

Anderson, A. C. (1980) *A Guide to Roman Fine Wares*. Highworth.

Anderson, A. S. (1985) *Roman Military Tombstones*. Princes Risborough.

Anderson, B. (1991) *Imagined Communities: Reflections on the Origins and the Spread of Nationalism*. London.

Anderson, J. G. C. (1938) *Tacitus: Germania*. Oxford.

André, J. (1966/7) 'Tossia: couverture de lit', *Études celtiques* 11: 409–12.

Ardevan, R. (1989) 'Veteranen und städische Dekurionen im römischen Dakien', *Eos* 77: 81–90.

Arnold, D. E. (1985) *Ceramic Theory and Cultural Process*. Cambridge.

Arnold, P. J. (1991) *Domestic Ceramic Production and Spatial Organization*. Cambridge.

Baatz, D. (1968) 'Romische Wandmalereien aus dem Limeskastell Echzell', *Germania* 46: 40.

Baatz, D. (1973) *Kastell Hesselbach und andere Forschungen am Odenwaldlimes*. Limesforschungen 12. Berlin

Baatz, D. (1993) *Der Romische Limes*, 3rd edn. Berlin.

Bagnall, R. S. (1976) *The Florida Ostraca: Documents from the Roman Army in Upper Egypt*. Greek, Roman and Byzantine Monographs 7. Durham, NC.

Bagnall, R. S. (1986) 'Papyri and ostraka from Quesir-al-Qadim', *BASP* 23: 1–60.

Bagnall, R. S. (1997) 'A kinder, gentler Roman army?', *JRA* 10: 504–12.

Bagnall, R. S., and Frier, B. W. (1994) *The Demography of Roman Egypt*. Cambridge.

Bailey, D. W. (2000) *Balkan Prehistory: Exclusion, Incorporation and Identity*. London.

Bailey, G. B. (1992) 'A Roman shrine near Laurieston?', *Calatria* (May): 1–4.

Baird, J. A. (2007) 'Shopping, eating and drinking at Dura-Europos: reconstructing contexts', in L. Lavan, E. Swift, and T. Putzeys (eds), *Objects in Context, Objects in Use: Material Spatiality in Late Antiquity*. Late Antique Archaeology supplementary volume 4. Leiden, 413–37.

Baird, J. A. (2010) 'Graffiti at Dura-Europos: a contextual approach', in J. A. Baird and C. Taylor (eds), *Ancient Graffiti in Context*. New York, 49–68

Baker, P. A. (2001) 'Medicine, material culture and military identity', in G. Davies, A. Gardner, and K. Lockyear (eds), *TRAC 2000: Proceedings of the Tenth Annual Theoretical Roman Archaeology Conference*. Oxford, 48–68.

Bakker, L. and Galsterer-Kröll, A. (1975) *Graffiti auf Römischer Keramik in Rheinischen Landesmuseum Bonn*. Cologne.

Balfet, H. (1965) 'Ethnographical observations in North Africa and archaeological interpretation', in F. T. Matson (ed.), *Ceramics and Man*. Chicago, 161–77.

Balsdon, J. P. V. D. (1979) *Romans and Aliens*. London.

Banton, M. (1964) *The Policeman in the Community*. London.

Baradez, J. (1949a) 'Gemellae: un camp d'Hadrien et une ville des confins sahariens aujourd'hui ensevelis sous les sables', *Revue africaine* 93: 5–24.

Baradez, J. (1949b) *Fossatum Africae*. Paris.

Bǎrbulescu, M. (1994) 'Africa e Dacia: gli influssi africani nella religione romana della Dacia', in A. Mastino and P. Ruggeri (eds), *L'Africa romana: Kolloquium Oristano 1992*. Sassari, 1319–38.

Barker, P. (1982) *Techniques of Archaeological Excavation*. London.

Bar- Kochva, B. (1976) *The Seleucid Army*. Cambridge.

Barkóczi, L. (1959) 'A new military diploma from Brigetio', *Acta Archaeologica Academiae Scientiarum Hungaricae* 9: 413–21.

Barkóczi, L., Erdelyi, G., Ferenczy, E., Fülep, F., Nemeskeri, J., Alföldi, M. R., and Sagi, K. (1954) 'Intercisa története a római Korban (Histoire d'Intercisa à l'époque romaine)', *Archaeologica Hungarica* 33: 1–285.

Barrett, J. C. (2001) 'Agency, the duality of structure, and the problem of the archaeological record', in I. Hodder (ed.), *Archaeological Theory Today*. Cambridge, 141–64.

Baur, P. V. C., and Rostovtzeff, M. I. (1929) *The Excavations at Dura-Europos: Preliminary Report of the 1st Season of Work (1928)*. New Haven, Conn.

Baur, P. V. C., and Rostovtzeff, M. I. (1931) *The Excavations at Dura-Europos: Preliminary Report of the 2nd Season of Work (1928–29)*. New Haven, Conn.

Baur, P. V. C., Rostovtzeff, M. I., and Bellinger, A. R. (1932) *The Excavations at Dura-Europos: Preliminary Report of the 3rd Season of Work (1929–30)*. New Haven, Conn.

Baur, P. V. C., Rostovtzeff, M. I., and Bellinger, A. R. (1933) *The Excavations at Dura-Europos: Preliminary Report of the 4th Season of Work (1930–31)*. New Haven, Conn.

Bayley, J., and Butcher, S. (2004) *Roman Brooches in Britain: A Technological and Typological Study based on the Richborough Collection*. London.

Beard, M., North, J., and Price, S. (1998) *Religions of Rome*. Cambridge.

Beck, F., and Chew, H. (1991) *Masques de fer: un officier romain du temps de Caligula*. St-Germain-en-Laye.

Becker, A., and Rasbach, G. (2001) 'Waldgirmes: eine augusteische Stadtgrüdung im Lahntal', *Bericht der Römisch-Germanischen Kommission* 82: 591–610.

Bee, R. L. (1974) *Patterns and Processes: An Introduction to Anthropological Strategies for the Study of Socio-cultural Change*. New York.

Bell, H. I., Martin, V., Turner, E. G., and van Berchem, D. (1962) *The Abinnaeus Archive: Papers of a Roman Military Official in the Reign of Constantius II*. Oxford.

Bellen, H. (1981) *Die germanische Leibwache der römischen Kaiser des julisch-claudischen Hauses*. Wiesbaden.

Bellinger, A. R. (1947) 'Seleucid Dura: the evidence of the coins', *Berytus* 9: 51–67

Beneš, J. (1978) *Auxilia romana in Moesia atque in Dacia: Zu den Fragen des römischen Verteidingungssystems im unteren Donauraum und in den angrenzenden Gebieten*. Prague.

Bennett, J. (1980) 'Fort sizes as a guide to garrison type: a preliminary study of selected forts in the European provinces', in W. S. Hanson and L. J. F. Keppie (eds), *Roman Frontier Studies 1979*. BAR International Series 71. Oxford, 707–16.

Benseddik, N. (1977) *Les troupes auxiliaires de l'armée romaine en Maurétanie Césarienne*. Algiers.

Berger, F. (1996) *Kalkriese 1: Die römischen Fundmünzen*. Römisch-Germanische Forschungen 55. Mainz.

Bertolini, D. (1890) 'Novembre: Regione X', *Notizie degli scavi* 339–44.

Best, E. E. (1967) 'The literate Roman soldier', *Classical Journal* 62 : 122–7.

Beutler, F. (2007) 'Claudius und der Beginn der Militärdiplome: einige Gedanken', in M. A. Speidel and H. Lieb (eds), *Militärdiplome: die Forschungsbeiträge der Berner Gespräche von 2004*. Stuttgart, 1–14.

Bhabha, H. (1989) *The Location of Culture*. London.

Bidwell, P. T. (1979) *The Legionary Bath-House, and Basilica, and Forum at Exeter*. Exeter.

Bidwell, P. (1996) 'The exterior decoration of Roman buildings in Britain', in P. Johnson and I. Haynes (eds), *Architecture in Roman Britain*. CBA Research Report 94. York, 9–29.

Bidwell, P. (1997) *Roman Forts in Britain*. London.

Bidwell, P. (2009) 'The earliest occurrences of baths at auxiliary forts', in W. S. Hanson (ed.), *The Army and Frontiers of Rome*. JRA Supplementary Series 74. Portsmouth, RI, 55–62.

Bidwell, P., and Hodgson, N. (2009) *The Roman Army in Northern England*. Kendal.

Bidwell, P., and Speak, S (1994) *Excavations at South Shields Roman Fort I*. Newcastle upon Tyne.

Biggins, J. A., and Taylor, D. J. A. (1999) 'A survey of the Roman fort and settlement at Birdoswald, Cumbria', *Britannia* 30: 91–110.

Biggins, J. A., and Taylor, D. J. A. (2004) 'Geophysical survey of the vicus at Birdoswald Roman fort, Cumbria', *Britannia* 35: 159–78.

Bingen, J. (1996) 'Dumping and the ostraca at Mons Claudianus', in D. M. Bailey (ed.), *Archaeological Research in Roman Egypt. JRA* Supplementary Series 16. Ann Arbor, Mich., 29–38.

Bird, D. G. (1984) 'Pliny and the gold mines of north-west Iberia', in T. Blagg, R. Jones, and S. Keay (eds), *Papers in Iberian Archaeology*. BAR International Series 193. Oxford, 341–63.

Birley, A. (2010) 'The nature and significance of extramural settlement at Vindolanda and other selected sites on the northern frontier of Roman Britain', Ph.D, University of Leicester.

Birley, A., and Birley, A. R. (2010) 'A dolichenum at Vindolanda', *Archaeologia Aeliana*, 5th ser., 39: 25–52.

Birley, A. R. (1971) 'Roman frontier policy under Marcus Aurelius', in S. Applebaum (ed.), *Roman Frontier Studies 1967*. Tel Aviv, 7–13.

Birley, A. R. (1974) 'Roman frontiers and Roman frontier policy: some reflections on Roman imperialism', *Transactions of the Architectural and Archaeological Society of Durham and Northumberland*, n.s., 3: 13–25.

Birley, A. R. (1979) *The People of Roman Britain*. London.

Birley, A. R. (1988) *Septimius Severus: The African Emperor*. London.

Birley, A. R. (2000) 'The life and death of Cornelius Tacitus', *Historia* 49: 230–47.

Birley, A. R. (2002) *Garrison Life at Vindolanda: A Band of Brothers*. Stroud.

Birley, A. R. (2005) *The Roman Government of Britain*. Oxford.

Birley, A. R. (2007) 'Two types of administration attested by the Vindolanda Tablets', in R. Haensch and J. Heinrichs (eds), *Herrschen und Verwalten: Der Alltag der römischen Administration in der Hohen Kaiserzeit. Akten eines Internationalen Kolloquiums an der Universität zu Köln, 28.–30. Januar 2005*.Vienna, 306–24.

Birley, A. R. (2008) 'Cives Galli de(ae). Galliae concordesque Britanni: a dedication at Vindolanda', *L'Antiquité Classique* 77: 171–87.

Birley, A. R. (2009) 'Some writing-tablets excavated at Vindolanda in 2001, 2002 and 2003', *ZPE* 170: 265–93.

Birley, E. (1938) 'Fourth report of excavations at Chesterholm–Vindolanda', *Archaeologia Aeliana*, 4th ser., 15: 222–37.

Birley, E. (1952) 'The epigraphy of the Roman Army', in *Actes du Deuxième Congrès d'Épigraphie Grecque et Latine*. Paris, 226–38.

Birley, E. (1956) 'Hadrianic frontier policy', in E. Swoboda (ed.), *Carnuntina 3*. Graz, 25–33.

Birley, E. (1966) *Alae and cohortes milliariae*', in *Corolla Memoriae Erich Swoboda Dedicata*. Römische Forschungen in Niederösterreich 5. Cologne, 54–67.

Birley, E. (1976) 'Local militias in the Roman Empire', *Beiträge zur Historia-Augusta* 12: 65–73.

Birley, E. (1977) 'An inscription from Crammond and the *Matres Campestres. Glasgow Archaeological Journal* 4: 108–10.

Birley, E. (1978a) 'The religion of the Roman army: 1895–1977', *ANRW* II 16.2: 1506–41.

Birley, E. (1978b) '*Alae* named after their commanders', *Ancient Society* 9: 257–73.

Birley, E. (1982a) 'The dating and character of the tract *de munitionibus castrorum*', in G. Wirth (ed.), *Romanitas-Christianitas: Untersuchungen zu Geschichte und Literatur der römischen Kaiserzeit*. Berlin, 277–81.

Birley, E. (1982b) 'Veterans of the Roman army in Britain and elsewhere', *Ancient Society* 13: 266–77.

Birley, E. (1988a) 'The origins of legionary centurions', in Birley (1988b), 189–205.

Birley, E. (1988b) *The Roman Army: Papers 1929–1986*, ed. M. P. Speidel. Amsterdam.

Birley, E., Birley, R., and Birley, A. R. (1993) *Vindolanda Research Reports*, vol. 2: *The Early Wooden Forts: Reports on the Auxiliaries, the Writing Tablets, Inscriptions, Brands and Graffiti.* Hexham.

Birley, E., and Gillam, J. R. (1948) '*Mortarium* stamps from Corbridge', *Archaeologia Aeliana*, 4th ser., 26: 172–204.

Birley, R. (1990) *The Roman Documents from Vindolanda*. Newcastle upon Tyne.

Birley, R. E. (1977) *The Excavations at Vindolanda: Interim Report*. Bardon Mill.

Bishop, M. C. (1988) 'Cavalry equipment of the Roman army in the first century AD', in J. C. Coulston (ed.), *Military Equipment and the Identity of Roman Soldiers: Proceedings of the Fourth Roman Military Equipment Conference.* BAR International Series 394. Oxford, 67–195.

Bishop, M. C. (1989) 'O Fortuna: a sideways look at the archaeological record and Roman military equipment', in C. van Driel-Murray (ed.), *Roman Military Equipment: The Sources of Evidence.* BAR International Series 476. Oxford, 1–11.

Bishop, M. C. (1991) 'Soldiers and military equipment in the towns of Roman Britain', in V. Maxfield and M. J. Dobson (eds), *Roman Frontier Studies 1989*. Exeter, 21–7.

Bishop, M. C. (1994) 'Roman or native? A new hilt guard from a Roman context', *Arma* 6: 16–18.

Bishop, M. C. (1999) '*Praesidium*: social, military, and logistical aspects of the Roman army's provincial distribution during the early principate', in Goldsworthy and Haynes (1999), 111–18.

Bishop, M. C., and Coulston, J. C. N. (1993) *Roman Military Equipment*. London.

Bishop, M. C., and Coulston, J. C. N. (2006) *Roman Military equipment*, 2nd edn. Oxford.

Black, E. W. (1994) 'Villa-owners: Romano-British gentlemen and officers', *Britannia* 25: 99–110.

Blagg, T. F. C. (1980) 'Roman civil and military architecture in the province of Britain: aspects of patronage, influence and craft organization', *World Archaeology* 12: 27–42.

Blagg, T. F. C. (1984) 'An examination of the connexions between military and civilian architecture', in T. F. C. Blagg and A. C. King (eds), *Military and Civilian in Roman Britain.* BAR British Series 136. Oxford, 249–64.

Bloemers, J. H. F. (1978) *Rijswijk (Z.H.). Die Bult: Eine Siedlung der Cananefaten, I–III.* Nederlandsee Oudheden 8. Amersfoort.

Bloemers, J. H. F. (1980) 'Nijmegen: ROB excavations 1974–1979 in the Roman forts, cemeteries, and *canabae legionis*', in W. S. Hanson and L. J. F. Keppie (eds), *Roman Frontier Studies 1979.* BAR International Series 184. Oxford, 159–209.

Bloemers, J. H. F. (1983) 'Acculturation in the Rhine/Meuse Basin in the Roman period: a preliminary survey', in R. Brandt and J. Slofstra (eds), *Roman and Native in the Low Countries.* BAR International Series 184. Oxford, 159–209.

Bloemers, J. H. F. (1989) 'Acculturation in the Rhine/Meuse Basin in the Roman period: some demographical considerations', in J. C. Barrett, A. P. Fitzpatrick, and L. Macinnes (eds), *Barbarians and Romans in North West Europe.* Oxford: 175–97.

Bloemers, J. H. F. (1990) 'Lower Germany—*plura consilio quam vi*: proto-urban settlement developments and the integration of native society', in T. F. C. Blagg and M. Millet (eds), *The Early Roman Empire in the West.* Oxford, 72–86.

Blok, A. (1977) *Anthropologische perspectieven*. Muiderberg.

Blomart, A. (1997) 'Die *evocatio* und der Transfer 'fremder' Götter von der Peripherie nach Rom', in H. Cancik and J. Rüpke (eds), *Römische Reichsreligion und Provinzialreligion.* Tübingen, 100–111.

Boëthius, A., and Ward-Perkins, J. B. (1970) *Etruscan and Roman Architecture*. Harmondsworth.

Böhme-Schönberger, A. (1993) 'Die reichen Gräber von Goeblingen-Nospelt als Zeichen der Romanisierung zur Germania magna', in V. Beck, W. Ranke, and J. Kuhn (eds), *Reallexikon der germanischen Altertumskunde* 8: 511–23.

Bolindeț, V. (1993) 'Considérations sur l'attribution des vases de Dacie romaine décorés de serpents appliqués', *Ephemeris Napocensis* 3: 123–41.

Boon, G. C. (1967) 'Micaceous sigillata from Lezoux at Silchester, Caerleon, and other sites', *Antiquaries Journal* 47: 27–42.

Boon, G. C. (1972) *Isca*. Cardiff.

Boon, G. C. (1974) *Silchester: The Roman Town of Calleva*. Newton Abbot.

Boon, G. C. (1977) 'Gold-in-glass beads from the ancient world', *Britannia* 8: 193–207.

Boon, G. C. (1984) 'A *trulleus* from Caerleon with a stamp of the First Cavalry Regiment of Thracians', *Antiquaries Journal* 64: 403–7.

Borić, D., and Robb, J. (2009) 'Body theory in archaeology', in D. Borić and J. Robb (eds), *Past Societies: Body-Centred Research in Archaeology*. Cambridge, 1–7.

Boube-Piccot, C. (1994) *Les bronze antiques du Maroc, 4: L'équipment militaire*. Paris.

Bouchier, E. S. (1916) *Syria as a Roman Province*. Oxford.

Bourdieu, P. (1977) *Outline of a Theory of Practice*. Cambridge.

Bourdieu, P. (1990) *The Logic of Practice*. Stanford, Calif.

Bowman, A. K. (1991) 'Literacy in the Roman Empire: mass and mode', in J. H. Humphrey (ed.), *Literacy in the Roman World. JRA* Supplementary Series 3. Ann Arbor, Mich., 119–32.

Bowman, A. K. (1994a) *Life and Letters on the Roman Frontier*. London.

Bowman, A. K. (1994b) 'Letters and literacy on the northern frontier', in A. K. Bowman and G. D. Woolf (eds), *Literacy and Power in the Ancient World*. Cambridge, 109–25.

Bowman, A. K., and Rathbone, D. W. (1992) 'Cities and administration in Roman Egypt', *JRS* 82: 149–69.

Bowman, A. K., and Thomas, J. D. (1983) *Vindolanda: The Latin Writing-Tablets. Britannia* Monograph 4. London.

Bowman, A. K., and Thomas, J. D. (1991) 'A military strength report from Vindolanda', *JRS* 81: 62–73.

Bowman, A. K., and Thomas, J. D. (1994) *The Vindolanda Writing Tablets. Tabulae Vindolandenses II*. London.

Bowman, A. K., and Thomas, J. D. (2003) *The Vindolanda Writing Tablets. Tabulae Vindolandenses III*. London.

Bowman, A. K., and Thomas, J. D., and Adams, J. N. (1990) 'Two letters from Vindolanda', *Britannia* 21: 33–52.

Bowman, A. K., Tomlin, R. S. O., and Worp, K. A. (2009) '*Emptio bovis Frisica*: the "Frisian ox sale" reconsidered', *JRS* 99: 156–70.

Bowsher, J. (1986) 'The frontier post of Medain Saleh', in P. Freeman and D. L. Kennedy (eds), *The Defence of the Roman and Byzantine East*. BAR International Series 297. Oxford.

Bradley, R. (1990) *The Passage of Arms: An Archaeological Analysis of Prehistoric Hoards and Votive Deposits*. Cambridge.

Bradley, R., and Thomas, J. (1984) 'Ritual activity and structured deposition in later Neolithic Wessex', in R. Bradley and J. Gardiner (eds), *Neolithic Studies*. Oxford, 189–218.

Brand, C. E. (1968) *Roman Military Law*. Austin, Tex.

Brashear, V. (1976) 'Soldier's letter', in A. E. Hanson (ed.), *Collectanea Papyrologica: Texts published in honor of H. C. Youtie*. Bonn, 325–9.

Braund, D. C. (1984) *Rome and the Friendly King*. New York.

Breasted, J. H. (1922) 'Peintures d'époque romaine dans le désert de Syrie', *Syria* 3:177–206.

Breeze, D. J. (1973) 'Demand and supply on the northern frontier', in R. Miket and C. Burgess (eds), *Between and Beyond the Walls*. Edinburgh, 264–86.

Breeze, D. J. (1974) 'The organization of the career structure of the *immunes* and *principales* of the Roman army', *BJ* 174: 245–86.

Breeze, D. J. (1977) 'The fort at Bearsden and the supply of pottery to the Roman army', in J. Dore and K. Greene (eds), *Roman Pottery Studies in Britain and Beyond*. BAR Supplementary Series, Oxford, 133–45.

Breeze, D. J. (1982) *The Northern Frontiers of Roman Britain*. Edinburgh.

Breeze, D. J. (1996) *Roman Scotland*. London.

Breeze, D. J. (2011) *The Frontiers of Imperial Rome*. Barnsley.

Breeze, D. J., Close-Brooks, J., and Ritchie, J. N. G. (1976) 'Soldiers' burials at Camelon, Stirlingshire, 1922 and 1975', *Britannia* 7: 73–95.

Breeze, D. J., and Dobson, B. (1969) 'Fort types on Hadrian's Wall'. *Archaeologia Aeliana*, 4th ser., 47: 15–32.

Breeze, D. J., and Dobson, B., (1987) *Hadrian's Wall*. London.

Breeze, D. J., and Dobson, B., (2000) *Hadrian's Wall*, 4th edn. London.

Brilliant, R. (2002) 'The Column of Marcus Aurelius re-viewed', *JRA* 15: 499–506.

Brothwell, D. R., and Brothwell, P. (1969) *Food in Antiquity*. London.

Brunaux, J. L. (1986) *Les gaulois: sanctuaires et rites*. Paris.

Brunt, P. A. (1960) 'Tacitus and the Batavian Revolt', *Latomus* 19: 494–517.

Brunt, P. A. (1974) 'Conscription and volunteering in the Roman imperial army', *Scripta Classica Israelica* 1: 90–115.

Brunt, P. A. (1975) 'Did Imperial Rome disarm her subjects? ', *Phoenix* 29: 260–70.

Brunt, P. A. (1976) 'The Romanisation of the local ruling classes in the Roman Empire', *Travaux de VIe Congrès International d'Études Classiques*. Paris.

Buchenschutz, O., and Ralston, I. B. M. (1986) 'En relisant la Guerre des Gaules', *Rev. Aquitania Supp.* 1: 383–7.

Bujukliev, H. (1986) *La nécropole tumulaire Thrace près de Čatalka, région de Stara Zagora*. Sofia.

Bülow-Jacobsen, A. (1997) 'Lists of *vigiles* (309–356)', in J. Bingen et al. (eds), *Mons Claudianus ostraca graeca et latina II. Claud. 191 à 416*. Institut Français d'Archéologie Orientale, Documents de Fouilles de l'IFAO32, 165–92.

Burn, A. R. (1953) 'Hic breve vivitur', *Past and Present* 4: 2–31.

Busch, A. W. (2003) 'Von der Provinz ins Zentrum: Bilder auf den Grabdenkmälern einer Elite-Einheit. in P. Noelke (ed.), *Romanisation und Resistenz*. Mainz, 679–94.

Busch, A. W. (2009) 'Idee und Wirklichkeit: die Schildbewaffnung römischer Legionäre im 2. Jh. n. Chr', in A. W. Busch and H.-J. Schalles (eds), *Waffen in Aktion: ROMEC Kongress Xanten 2007*. Xantener Berichte 16. Mainz, 323–42.

Cadoux, R. (1978) 'Un sanctuaire gallo-romain isolé: Ribemont-sur-Ancre (Somme)', *Latomus* 37: 325–60.

Cagnat, R. (1889) 'Sur les manuels professionnels des graveurs d'inscriptions romaines', *Revue de philologie* 13: 51–65.

Cagnat, R. (1913) *L'armée romaine d'Afrique*. Paris.

Cain, M. (1971) 'On the beat: interactions and relations in rural and urban police forces', in S. Cohen (ed.), *Images of Deviance*. London, 62–97.

Callies, H. (1964) 'Die fremden Truppen in römischen Heer des Prinzipats und die sogenannten nationalen Numeri', *Beiträge zur Geschichte des römischen Heeres* 45: 130–227.

Camden, W. (1607) *Britannia*. London.

Campbell, B. (1978) 'The marriage of soldiers under the Empire', *JRS* 68: 153–66.

Campbell, B. (1994) *The Roman Army 31BC–AD 337: A Sourcebook*. London.

Campbell, D. B. (1997) 'The Roman art of war', *Britannia* 28: 479–83.

Campbell, J. B. (1984) *The Emperor and the Roman Army 31 B.C.–A.D. 235*. Oxford.

Campbell, J. B. (2002) *War and Society in Imperial Rome 31 BC–AD 284*. London.

Cancik, H., and Rüpke, J. (eds) (1997) *Römische Reichsreligion und Provinzialreligion*. Tübingen.

Cannon, A. (1989) 'The historical dimension in mortuary expressions of status and sentiment', *Current Anthropology* 30.4: 437–47.

Carrié, J.-M. (1993) 'The soldier', in A. Giardina (ed.), *The Romans*. Chicago, 100–137.

Carroll, M. (2001) *Romans, Celts and Germans: The German Provinces of Rome*. Stroud.

Carroll, M. (2006) *Spirits of the Dead: Roman Funerary Commemoration in Western Europe*. Oxford.

Carter, J. C., and G. Mack (2003) *Crimean Chersonesos: City, Chora, Museum and Environs*, Austin.

Casey, P. J. (1982) 'Civilians and soldiers: friends, Romans and countrymen?', in P. Clack and S. Haselgrove (eds), *Rural Settlement in the Roman North*. Durham, 123–32.

Cesano, L. (1922) 'Genius', in E. de Ruggiero (ed.), *Dizionario epigrafico*, vol. 3. Rome, 449–81.

Chantraine, H. (2002) 'Varus oder Germanicus? Zu den Fundmünzen von Kalkriese', *Thetis* 9: 81–93.

Chapman, J. (2000) *Fragmentation in Archaeology*. London.

Charlesworth, M. P. (1934) 'Tiberius', in S. A. Cook, F. E. Adcock, and M. P. Charlesworth (eds), *The Cambridge Ancient History*, vol. 10: *The Augustan Empire 44 BC–AD 70*. Cambridge, 607–52.

Cheesman, G. L. (1914) *The Auxilia of the Roman Imperial Army*. Oxford.

Cherry, D. (1998) *Frontier and Society in Roman North Africa*. Oxford.

Chorus, J. P. (2008) 'Romeinse forten in de Rijndelta: over stammetjes en staanders', in M. Bergmans et al. (eds), *SOJA-Bundel 2007: Symposium voor Onderzoek door Jonge Archeologen*. Groningen, 7–16.

Cichorius, C. (1893) 'Ala', in *Realencyclopädie der classischen Altertumswissenschaft* 1.1: cols 1224–70.

Cichorius, C. (1990) 'Cohors', in *Realencyclopädie der classischen Altertumswissenschaft* 4: 231–356.

Ciugudean, D., and Ciugudean, H. (2000) 'A Roman military grave from Apulum', in H. Ciugudean and V. Moga (eds), *Army and Urban Development in the Danubian Provinces of the Roman Empire*. Alba Iulia, 203–12.

Clanchy, M. T. (1979) *From Memory to Written Record: England 1066–1307*. London.

Claridge, A. (2010) *Rome*. Oxford Archaeological Guide. Oxford.

Clark, J. G. D. (1951) 'Folk culture and the study of European prehistory', in W. F. Grimes (ed.), *Aspects of Archaeology*. London, 49–65.

Clarke, D. L. (1978) *Analytical Archaeology*. London.

Clarke, S. (2001) 'Probably ritual. Assemblage interpretation at the Newstead military complex: towards a more holistic approach', in A. T. Smith and A. Brookes (eds), *Holy Ground: Theoretical Issues Relating to the Landscape and Material Culture of Ritual Space Objects*. BAR International Series 956. Oxford, 73–83.

Clarke, S., and Jones, R. (1996. 'The Newstead pits', *JRMES* 5: 109–24.

Clason, A. T. (1960) 'Some remarks on the faunal remains from the Roman castellum at Valkenburg. *Paleohistoria* 8: 139–47.

Clason, A. T. (1977) *Jacht en Veetelt van prehistorie tot middeleeuwen (Jagd. und Viehzucht von vorgesichtlicher Zeit bis zum Mittelalter)*. Haarlem.

Clermont- Ganneau, C. (1922) 'Empereurs ou dieux?', *Syria* 3: 270–71.

Coarelli, F. (2000) *The Column of Trajan*. Rome.

Coarelli, F. (2008) *La Colonna di Marco Aurelio*. Rome.

Cociş, S. (2004) 'Norico-Pannonian brooches from Roman Dacia', in L. Ruscu, C. Ciongradi, R. Ardevan, C. Roman, and C. Găzdac (eds), *Orbis Antiqvvs: Studia in Honorem Ioannis Pisonis*. Cluj, 406–25.

Cohen, A. P. (1985) *The Symbolic Construction of Community*. London.

Cohen, G. M. (1978) *The Seleucid Colonies: Studies in Founding, Administration and Organization*. Wiesbaden.

Colini, A. M. (1944) 'Storia e topografia del Celio nell'antichità', *APA*, 3rd ser., 7. Vatican.

Collingham, E. M. (2001) *Imperial Bodies: The Physical Experience of the Raj c.1800–1947.* Cambridge.

Collingwood, R. G., and Richmond, I. A. (1969) *The Archaeology of Roman Britain.* London.

Collins, R. (1998) *Spain: An Archaeological Guide.* Oxford.

Collins-Clinton, J. (1977) *A Late Antique Shrine of Liber Pater at Cosa.* Leiden.

Collis, J. (1977) *Pre-Roman Burial Rites in North-Western Europe.* CBA Research Report 22. London.

Collis, J. (1984) *Oppida.* Shefield.

Collis, J. (1984) *The European Iron Age.* London.

Colls, D., et al. (1977) *L'épave Port-Vendres II et le commerce de la Bétique à l'époque de Claude.* Paris.

Condamin, J., et al. (1976) 'The application of gas chromotography to the tracing of oil in ancient amphorae', *Archaeometry* 18: 195–201.

Condamin, J., and Formenti, F. (1976) 'Recherches de traces d'huile d'olive et de vin dans les amphores antiques', *Figlina* 1: 143–58.

Connolly, P. (1981) *Greece and Rome at War.* London.

Connolly, P. (1991) 'The Roman fighting technique deduced from armour and weaponry', in V. A. Maxfield and M. J. Dobson (eds), *Roman Frontier Studies 1989.* Exeter, 358–63.

Connolly, P., and Driel-Murray, C. van (1991) 'The Roman cavalry saddle', *Britannia* 22: 33–50.

Cool, H. E. M. (2004) *The Roman Cemetery at Brougham, Cumbria: Excavations 1966–1967.* Britannia Monograph, Society for the Promotion of Roman Studies. London.

Cooley, A. E. (ed.) (2002a) *Becoming Roman, Writing Latin? Literacy and Epigraphy in the Roman West.* JRA Supplement 48. Portsmouth, RI.

Cooley, A. E. (2002b) 'Introduction', in Cooley (2002a), 9–14.

Cooper, N. J. (1996) 'Search for the blank generation: consumer choice in Roman and post-Roman Britain', in J. Webster and N. Cooper (eds), *Roman Imperialism: Post-Colonial Perspectives.* Leicester Archaeology Monographs 3. Leicester, 85–98.

Cotton, H. M. (1991) 'Fragments of a declaration of landed property from the province of Arabia', *ZPE* 85: 263–7.

Cotton, H. M., and Geiger, J., with Thomas, J. D. (1989) *Masada II: The Yigael Yadin Excavations 1963–1965. Final Reports: The Latin and Greek Documents.* Jerusalem.

Coulston, J. C. N. (1981) 'A sculpted Dacian *falx* from Birdoswald', *Archaeologia Aeliana,* 5th ser., 9: 348–50.

Coulston, J. C. N. (1985) 'Roman archery equipment', in *The Production and Distribution of Roman Military Equipment: Proceedings of the Second Roman Military Equipment Research Seminar.* BAR International Series 275. Oxford, 220–336.

Coulston, J. C. N. (ed.) (1988a) *Military Equipment and the Identity of Roman Soldiers: Proceedings of the Fourth Roman Military Equipment Conference.* BAR International Series 394. Oxford.

Coulston, J. C. N. (1988b) 'Three legionaries at Croy-Hill', in Coulston (1988a), 29.

Coulston, J. C. N. (1989) 'The value of Trajan's Column as a source for military equipment', in C. van Driel-Murray (ed.), *Roman Military Equipment: The Sources of Evidence.* BAR International Series 476. Oxford, 31–44.

Coulston, J. C. N. (1991) 'The *"draco"* standard', *JRMES* 2: 101–14.

Coulston, J. C. N. (1998) 'How to arm a Roman soldier', in M. Austin, J. Harries, and C. Smith (eds), *Modus Operandi: Essays in Honour of Geoffrey Rickman.* London, 167–90.

Coulston, J. C. N. (2000) 'Armed and belted men': the soldiery in imperial Rome', in J C. N. Coulston and H. Dodge, *Ancient Rome: The Archaeology of the Eternal City.* Oxford University School of Archaeology Monograph 54. Oxford, 76–118.

Coulston, J. C. N. (2003) 'Tacitus, *Historiae* 1.79 and the impact of Sarmatian warfare on the Roman Empire', in *Kontakt–Kooperation–Konflikt: Germanen und Sarmaten zwischen dem I. und 4. Jahrh. N. Chr.* Neumünster, 415–33.

Coulston, J. C. N., and Phillips, E. J. (1987) *Corpus Signorum Imperii Romani. Great Britain 1, 6: Hadrian's Wall West of the North Tyne, and Carlisle.* Oxford.

Crawford, M. (1970) 'Money and exchange in the Roman world', *JRS* 60: 40–48.

Creveld, M. van, (1991) *Transformation of War.* New York.

Creighton, J. (2000) *Coins and Power in Late Iron Age Britain.* Cambridge.

Creighton, J. (2001) 'The Iron Age–Roman transition', in S. James and M. Millett (eds), *Britons and Romans: Advancing an Archaeological Agenda.* CBA Research Report 125. York, 4–11.

Cressy, D. (1980) *Literacy and the Social Order: Reading and Writing in Tudor and Stuart England.* Cambridge.

Croom, A. T. (2001) 'Some finds from the 1997–98 excavations at South Shields Roman fort', *Arbeia Journal* 6–7: 68–9.

Croom, A. T. (2002) *Roman Clothing and Fashion.* Stroud.

Croom, A. T. (2011) *Running the Roman Home.* Stroud.

Crow, J. (1995) *Housesteads.* London.

Crummy, N., and Eckardt, H. (2003) 'Regional identities and technologies of the self: nail cleaners in Roman Britain', *Archaeological Journal* 160: 44–69.

Crummy, P. (1997) *City of Victory.* Colchester.

Cuff, D. B. (2011) 'The king of the Batavians: remarks on *Tab. Vindol.* III, 628', *Britannia* 42: 145–56.

Cumont, F. (1923) '"Le sacrifice du tribun romain Terentius" et les Palmyréniens a Doura', *Monuments et mémoires publiés par l'Académie des inscriptions et belles-lettres* 26: 1–46.

Cumont, F. (1926) *Fouilles de Doura-Europos (1922–1923).* Paris.

Cumont, F. (1934) *The Population of Syria.* Society for the Promotion of Roman Studies monograph. London.

Cumont, F. (1956) *Oriental Religions in Roman Paganism.* New York.

Cunliffe, B. (1971) *Excavations at Fishbourne*, vol. 1. London.

Cunliffe, B. (1988) *Greeks, Romans, and Barbarians : Spheres of Interaction.* London.

Cunliffe, B. (1991) *The Iron Age Communities in Britain.* London.

Cüppers, H. (1979) 'Das römische Forum der Colonia Augusta Treverorum', in *Festschrift 100 Jahre Rheinisches Landmuseum Trier.* Mainz, 211–62.

Curle, J. (1911) *A Roman Frontier Post and its People: The Fort at Newstead.* Glasgow.

Cuvigny, H. (2005) *Ostraca de Krokodilô: la correspondance militaire et sa circulation.* Institut français d'archéologie orientale, FIFAO 51. Cairo.

Dabrowa, E. (1981) 'La garnison romaine à Doura-Europos: influence du camp sur la vie de la ville et ses conséquences', *Cahiers scientifiques de l'Université jagellanne* 613: 61–75.

Dabrowa, E. (1986) 'Les cohortes Ituraeorum', *ZPE* 63: 221–30.

Dabrowa, E. (ed.) (1994) *The Roman and Byzantine Army in the East.* Cracow.

Dalton, G. (1981) 'Anthropological models in archaeological perspective', in I. Hodder, G. Isaac, and N. Hammond (eds), *Pattern of the Past: Studies in Honour of David Clarke.* Cambridge, 17–48.

Daniels, C. M. (1959) 'The Roman bath house at Red House, Beaufront, near Corbridge', *Archaeologia Aeliana*, 4th ser., 37: 85–176.

Dannel, G. B., and Wild, J. P. (1987) *Longthorpe II: The Roman Military Works-Depot. An Episode in Landscape History.* Britannia Monograph Series 8. London.

Darling, M. J. (1977) 'Pottery from early military sites in western Britain', in J. Dore and K. Greene (eds), *Roman Pottery Studies in Britain and Beyond.* BAR Supplementary Series 30. Oxford, 57–100.

Davies, H. (1976) *A Walk Along the Wall.* London.

Davies, J. L. (1977) 'Roman arrowheads from Dinorben and the *sagittarii* of the Roman army', *Britannia* 8: 357–70.

Davies, J. L. (1997) 'Native producers and Roman consumers: the mechanisms of military supply in Wales from Claudius to Theodosius', in W. Groenman-van Waateringe, B. L. van

Beek, W. J. H. Willems, and S. L. Wynia (eds), *Roman Frontier Studies 1995: Proceedings of the XVIth Roman Frontier Studies Conference 1995*. Oxbow Monograph 91. Oxford, 267–72.

Davies, J. L. (2002) 'Soldiers, peasants, industry and towns: the Roman army in Britain. A Welsh perspective', in P. Erdkamp (ed.), *The Roman Army and the Economy*. Amsterdam, 169–203.

Davies, R. W. (1968a) 'Fronto, Hadrian and the Roman army', *Latomus* 27: 75–95.

Davies, R. W. (1968b) 'Some notes on military papyri from Dura', *Bulletin of the American Society of Papyrologists* 5: 32–3.

Davies, R. W. (1968c) 'The training grounds of the Roman cavalry', *Archaeological Journal* 125: 73–100.

Davies, R. W. (1969) 'The *medici* of the Roman armed forces', *Epigraphische Studien* 8: 83–99.

Davies, R. W. (1970) 'The Roman military medical service', *Saalburg Jahrbuch* 27: 84–104.

Davies, R. W. (1971) 'The Roman military diet', *Britannia* 2: 122–42.

Davies, R. W. (1973) 'The investigation of some crimes in Roman Egypt', *Ancient Society* 4: 199–212.

Davies, R. W. (1974) 'The daily life of the Roman soldier under the Principate', *ANRW* 2.1: 299–338.

Davies, R. W. (1976) 'Centurions and decurions of Cohors XX Palmyrenorum', *ZPE* 20: 253–76.

Davies, R. W. (1989) *Service in the Roman Army*. Edinburgh.

Davison, D. P. (1989) *The Barracks of the Roman Army from the First to Third Centuries AD*. BAR International Series 472. Oxford.

Dayet, M. (1988) 'Qui était Togirix?', *Revue archéologique de l'Est et du Centre-Est* 13: 82–98.

de Certeau, M. (1984) *The Practice of Everyday Life*, trans. S. Rendall. London.

Déchelette, J. (1904) *Les vases céramiques ornés de la Gaule romaine*. Paris.

de Laet, S. J. (1966) 'Claude et la romanisation de la Gaule-septentrionale', in R. Chevallier (ed.), *Mélanges d'archéologie et d'histoire offerts à André Piganiol*. Paris, 951–61.

Dench, E. (1995) *From Barbarian to New Men: Greek, Roman and Modern Perceptions of Peoples from the Central Apennines*. Oxford.

Derks, T. (1991) 'The perception of the Roman pantheon by a native elite: the example of the votive inscriptions from Lower Germany', in N. Roymans and F. Theuws (eds), *Images of the Past: Studies on Ancient Societies in Northwestern Europe*. Amsterdam, 235–66.

Derks, T. (1995) 'The ritual of the vow in Gallo-Roman religion', in Metzler et al. (1995), 111–27.

Derks, T. (1998) *Gods, Temples and Ritual Practices: The Transformation of Religious Ideas and Values in Roman Gaul*. Amsterdam Archaeological Studies 2. Amsterdam.

Derks, T., and Roymans, N. (2002) 'Seal boxes and the spread of Latin literacy in the Rhine delta', in Cooley (2002a), 87–134.

De Romanis, F. (1997) 'Rome and the *notitia* of India: relations between Rome and southern India from 30 BC to the Flavian period', in F. De Romanis and A. Tchernia (eds), *Crossings: Early Mediterranean Contacts with India*. New Delhi.

Deschler-Erb, E. (1991) *Das frühkaiserzeitliche Militärlager in der Kaiseraugster Unterstadt*. Forschungen in Augst 12. Augst.

Deschler-Erb, E. (1999) *Ad Arma! Römisches Militär des 1. Jahrhunderts n.Chr. in Augusta Raurica*. Forschungen in Augst 28. Augst.

Detschew, D. (1957) *Die thrakischen Sprachreste*. Vienna.

Devijver, H. (1989a) 'Equestrian officers and their monuments', in H. Devijver (ed.), *The Equestrian Officers of the Roman Imperial Army*. Mavors Roman Army Researches 6. Amsterdam, 416–49.

Devijver, H. (1989b) 'Equestrian officers in the East', in D. H. French and C. S. Lightfoot (eds), *The Eastern Frontier of the Roman Empire*. BAR International Series 553. Oxford, 77–111.

Dietz, K. (1978) *Der Bismarckplatz in Regensburg*. Regensburg.

Dietz, K. (1979) *Regensburg zur Römerzeit*. Regensburg.

Dietz, K. (1985) 'Der pollio in der römischen Legion', *Chiron* 15: 235–52.

Dirven, L. (1999) *The Palmyrenes of Dura Europos: A Study of Religious Interaction in Roman Syria*. Leiden.

Dirven, L. (2007) 'The Julius Terentius fresco and the Roman imperial cult', *Mediterraneo antico* 10: 115–28.

Dobesch, G. (1980) *Die Kelten in Osterreich nach den ältesten Berichten der Antike*. Vienna.

Dobres, M.-A. (2000) *Technology and Social Agency*. Oxford.

Dobson, B., and Mann, J. C. (1973) 'The Roman army in Britain and Britons in the Roman army', *Britannia* 4: 191–205.

Domaszewski, A. von, (1895) 'Die Religion des römischen Heeres', *Westdeutsche Zeitschrift für Geschichte und Kunst* 14: 1–124.

Domaszewski, A. von, (1899) 'Die Principia des römischen Lagers', *Neue Heidelberger Jahrbücher* 9: 141–63.

Domaszewski, A. von, (1967[1908]) *Die Rangordnung des römischen Heeres, 2: Durchgesehene Auflage: Einführung, Berichtungen und Nachträge von B. Dobson*. Cologne.

Dommelen, P. van, (2006) 'Material culture and postcolonial theory in colonial situations', in C. Tilley, W. Keane, S. Kuechler, M. Rowlands, and P. Spyer (eds), *Handbook of Material Culture*. London, 104–24.

Doorslaer, A. van, (1967) 'Les nécropoles d'époque romaine en Gaule septentrionale', Dissertationes Archaeologicae Gandenses 10. Bruges.

Dorey, T. A. (1966) 'Caesar: the Gallic War', in T. A. Dorey (ed.), *Latin Historians*. London, 65–84.

Dorey, T. A. (1969) *Agricola* and *Germania*', in T. A. Dorey (ed.), *Tacitus*. London, 1–18.

Douglas, M. (1995) *Purity and Danger: An Analysis of the Concepts of Pollution and Taboo*. London.

Doura-Europos I (1986) *Doura-Europos: études 1986*. *Syria* 63: 1–155.

Doura-Europos II (1988) *Doura-Europos: études 1988*. *Syria* 65: 259–382.

Doura-Europos III (1990) *Doura-Europos: études 1990*. *Syria* 69: 1–151.

Downey, G. (1961) *A History of Antioch in Syria from Seleucus to the Arab Conquest*. Princeton, NJ.

Downey, S. B. (1988) *Mesopotamian Religious Architecture: Alexander through the Parthians*. Princeton, NJ.

Downey, S. B. (2000) 'The transformation of Seleucid Dura-Europos', in E. Fentress (ed.), *Romanization and the City: Creation, Transformations and Failures. JRA* Supplementary Series 38. Portsmouth, RI, 155–72.

Drack, W. (1955) 'Ein Mittellatènschwert mit drei Goldmarken von Böttstein (Aargau)', *Zeitschrift für schweizerische Archäologie und Kunstgeschichte* 15: 193–235.

Driel-Murray, C. van, (1995) 'Gender in question', in P. Rush (ed.), *Theoretical Roman Archaeology: 2nd Conference Proceedings*. Avebury, 3–21.

Driel-Murray, C. van, (ed.) (1996) *Military Equipment in Context* (Proceedings of the 9th International Roman Military Equipment Conference, Leiden, 1994). *Journal of Roman Military Equipment Studies* 5.

Driel-Murray, C. van, (1997) 'Women in forts?', *Gesellschaft Pro Vindonissa, Jahresbericht 1997*. Brugg: Vindonissa Museum, 55–61

Driel-Murray, C. van, (1998) 'A question of gender in a military context', *Helinium* 34: 342–62.

Driel-Murray, C. van, (1999) 'A rectangular shield cover of the *coh. XX Voluntariorum c.R*', *JRMES* 10: 45–54.

Driel-Murray, C. van, (2001) 'Vindolanda and the dating of Roman footwear', *Britannia* 32: 185–97.

Driel-Murray, C. van, (2003) 'Ethnic soldiers: the experience of the lower Rhine tribes. in T. Grünewald and S. Seibel (eds), *Kontinuität und Diskontinuität: Germania inferior am Beginn und am Ende der römischen Heerschaft*. Berlin, 200–217.

Drijvers, H. J. W. (1972) 'Old-Syriac (Edessan)', *Inscriptions* 1.

Drijvers, H. J. W. (1976) *The Religion of Palmyra*. Leiden.

Drijvers, H. J. W. (1980) *Cults and Beliefs at Edessa*. Leiden.

Drijvers, H. J. W. (1981) 'Die Dea Syria und andere syrische Gottheiten im Imperium Romanum', in M. J. Vermaseren (ed.), *Die Orientalischen Religionen im Romerreich*. Leiden, 241–64.

Drinkwater, J. F. (1978) 'The rise and fall of the Gallic Iulii: aspects of the development of the aristocracy of the three Gauls under the early Empire', *Latomus* 37: 817–50.

Drinkwater, J. F. (1983) *Roman Gaul*. London.

Dunbar, L. (2002) 'More AOC archaeology digging at Kintore', *Scottish Archaeological News* 40: 4.

Duncan-Jones, R. P. (1977) 'Age-rounding, illiteracy, and social differentiation in the Roman Empire', *Chiron* 7: 333–54.

Duncan-Jones, R. P. (1990) *Structure and Scale in the Roman Economy*. Cambridge.

Dušanić, S. (1980) 'Review of *RMD* I', *Arheološki Vestnik* 31: 334–5.

Dyson, S. L. (1968) *The Excavations at Dura-Europos, Final Report IV*, pt. 1, fasc. 3: *The Commonware Pottery, The Brittle Ware*. New Haven, Conn.

Dyson, S. L. (1975) 'Native revolt patterns in the Roman Empire', *ANRW* II 3: 138–75.

Eck, W. (2003) 'Der Kaiser als Herr des Heeres: Militärdiplome und die kaiserliche Reichsregierung', in J. Wilkes (ed.), *Documenting the Roman Army*. London, 55–87.

Eck, W. (2007) 'Die Veränderungen in Konstitutionen und Diplomen unter Antoninus Pius', in M.A. Speidel and H. Lieb (eds), *Militärdiplome: Die Forschungsbeiträge der Berner Gespräche von 2004*. Stuttgart 87–104.

Eck, W. (2011) 'Septimius Severus und die Soldaten: das Problem der Soldatenehe und ein neues Auxiliardiplom', in B. Onken and D. Rohde (eds), *in omni historia curiosus. Studien zur Geschichte von der Antike bis zur Neuzeit: Festschrift für Helmuth Schneider zum 65. Geburtstag*. Wiesbaden, 63–77.

Eck, W., Holder, P., and Pangerl, A. (2010) 'A diploma for the army of Britain in 132 and Hadrian's return to Rome from the east', *ZPE* 174: 189–200.

Eck, W., MacDonald, D., and Pangerl, A. (2004) 'Neue Militärdiplome in Britannia, Pannonia Inferior, Pannonia Superior, sowie in Thracia', *Revue des études militaires antiques* 1: 63–101.

Eck, W., and Pangerl, A. (2008a) 'Ein Diplom für die classis Britannica aus dem Jahr 93 n. Chr. unter dem Statthalter Vicirius Proculus',. *ZPE* 165: 227–31.

Eck, W., and Pangerl, A. (2008b) 'Neue Diplome für die Hilfstruppen in Britannia', in H. M. Shellenberg, V. E. Hirschmann, and A. Krieckhaus (eds), *A Roman Miscellany: Essays in Honour of Anthony R. Birley on his Seventieth Birthday*. Gdansk, 17–30.

Eck, W., and Wolff, H. (eds) (1986) *Heer und Integrationspolik: Die römischen Militärdiplome also historische Quelle*. Cologne.

Economist, The (2004) 'Iraq's armed forces: deBaathify, then reBaathify?', 8 May, 42–3.

Edwards, H. J. (trans.) (1986) *Caesar: The Gallic War*. Loeb. Cambridge, Mass.

Elias, N. (1974) 'Towards a theory of communities', in G. V. Bell and H. Newby (eds), *The Sociology of Community: A Selection of Readings*. London, ix–xli.

Elias, N. (1992) *Über den Prozeß der Zivilisation. Soziogenetische und psychogenetische Untersuchungen. Wandlungen der Gesellschaft. Entwurf zu einer Theorie der Zivilisation*. 2 vols, Frankfurt-am-Main.

Elton, H. (1994) 'The study of Roman military equipment', *JRA* 7: 491–5.

Enckevort, H. van, (1999) 'Votivopfer und Paraderüstungen: römische Sattelhörnchen vom Kops Plateau in Nijmegen', *Berichten van de Rijksdienst voor het Oudheidkundig Bodemonderzoek* 43: 141–53.

Enckevort, H. van, and Willems, W. J. H. (1996) 'Roman cavalry helmets in ritual hoards from the Kops Plateau at Nijmegen, The Netherlands', *JRMES* 5: 125–37.

Enloe, C. H. (1980) *Ethnic Soldiers: State Security in Divided Societies*. London.

Erdkamp, P. (2002) 'The corn supply of the Roman armies during the Principate (27 BC–235 AD)', in P. Erdkamp (ed.), *The Roman Army and the Economy*. Amsterdam, 47–69.

Erskine, A. (2001) *Troy between Greece and Rome: Local Tradition and Imperial Power*. Oxford.

Étienne, R. (1970) 'À propos du *garum sociorum*', *Latomus* 29: 297–313.

Ettlinger, E. (1977) 'Cooking pots at Vindonissa', in J. Dore and K. Greene (eds), *Roman Pottery Studies in Britain and Beyond*. BAR Supplementary Series 30. Oxford, 47–56.

Evans, D. E. (1990) 'Insular Celtic and the emergence of the Welsh language', in A. Bammesberger and A. Wollmann (eds), *Britain 400–500: Language and History*. Heidelberg, 149–77.

Evans, J. (1987) 'Graffiti and the evidence of literacy and pottery use in Roman Britain', *Archaeological Journal* 144: 191–205.

Fairon, G., and Moreau-Maréchal, J. (1983) 'Le casque romain de Weyler (Arlon)', *Germania* 61: 551–64.

Farrar, R. A. H. (1965) 'A Romano-British rider relief from Whitcombe', *Proceedings of the Dorset Natural History and Archaeology Society* 86: 104.

Farwell, B. (1984) *The Gurkhas*. London.

Fears, J. R. (1972) 'The cult of virtues and Roman imperial ideology', *ANRW* II 17.2: 827–948.

Fentress, E. W. B. (1979) *Numidia and the Roman Army: Social, Military and Economic Aspects of the Frontier Zone*. BAR International Series 53. Oxford.

Ferris, I. (2000) *Enemies of Rome: Barbarians through Roman Eyes*. Gloucester.

Fiedler, M. (2005) 'Kultgruben eines Liber Pater-Heligtums im römischen Apulum (Dakien) ', *Germania* 83: 95–125.

Fink, R. O. (1971) *Roman Military Records on Papyrus*. Cleveland, Ohio.

Fink, R. O., Hoey, A. S., and Snyder, W. F. (1940) *The Feriale Duranum*. New Haven, Conn.

Finke, J. (1927) 'Neue Inschriften', *Bericht der Römisch-Germanischen Kommission* 17: 1–107.

Fishwick, D. (1969) 'The imperial *Numen* in Britain', *JRS* 59: 76–91.

Fishwick, D. (1978) 'The development of provincial ruler worship in the western Roman Empire', *ANRW* II 16.2: 1201–53.

Fishwick, D. (1987) *The Imperial Cult in the Latin West*, vol. 1. Leiden.

Fishwick, D. (1988) 'Dated inscriptions and the *Feriale Duranum*', *Syria* 65: 349–61.

Fishwick, D. (1990) *The Imperial Cult in the Latin West*, vol. 2.1. Leiden.

Fishwick, D. (1992a) 'Soldier and emperor', *Ancient History Bulletin* 6.1: 63–72.

Fishwick, D. (1992b) *The Imperial Cult in the Latin West*, vol. 2.2. Leiden.

Fitz, J. (1959) 'Der Besuch des Septimius Severus in Pannonien im Jahre 202 u.z', *Acta Archaeologica Academiae Scientiarum Hungariae* 2: 237–63.

Fitz, J. (1972) *Les Syriens à Intercisa*. Brussels.

Florescu, F. (1960) *Monumentul de la Adamklissi, Tropaeum Traiani*. Bucharest.

Flügel, C., and Obmann, J. (1992) 'Waffen in Heiligtümern des Mithras', *JRMES* 3: 67–71.

Fol, A., and Marazov, I. (1977) *Thrace and the Thracians*. New York

Forni, G. (1953) *Il reclutamento delle legioni da Augusto a Diocleziano*. Milan.

Forni, G. (1992) *Esercito e Marina di Roma Antica*. Stuttgart.

Foster, G. M. (1960) *Culture and Conquest: America's Spanish Heritage*. Chicago.

Foster, G. M. (1965) 'The sociology of pottery: questions and hypotheses arising from contemporary Mexican work', in F. R. Matson (ed.), *Ceramics and Man*. Chicago, 43–61.

Fowler, P. J. (1983) *The Farming of Prehistoric Britain*. Cambridge.

Franchet, L. (1911) *Céramique primitive*. Paris.

Francis, E. D. (1975) 'Mithraic graffiti from Dura-Europos', in J. R. Hinnells (ed.), *Mithraic Studies*, vol. 2. Manchester, 424–45.

Frankfurter, D. (1998) *Religion in Roman Egypt: Assimilation and Resistance*. Princeton, NJ.

Franzen, P. (2009) The Augustan legionary fortress at Nijmegen: legionary and auxiliary soldiers', in A. Morillo, N. Hanel, and Martin, E. (eds), *Limes Congress XX Gladius Anejos 2009*, vol. 3. Madrid, 1257–69.

Franzius, G. (1995) 'Die römischen Funde aus Kalkriese 1987–95 und ihre Bedeutung für die Interpretation und Datierung militärischer Fundplätze der augusteischen Zeit im nordwesteuropäischen Raum', *JRMES* 6: 69–88.

Freeman, P. W. M. (1993) ' "Romanisation" and Roman material culture', *Journal of Roman Archaeology* 6: 438–45.

Freeman, P. W. M. (1996) 'British imperialism and the Roman Empire', in J. Webster and N. Cooper (eds), *Roman Imperialism: Post-colonial Perspectives*. Leicester Archaeology Monographs 3. Leicester, 19–34.

Freeman, P. W. M. (1997) 'Mommsen to Haverfield: the origins of studies of Romanization in late 19th-c. Britain', in Mattingly (1997), 27–50.

Freeman, P. W. M. (2007) *'The Best Training Ground for Archaeologists': Francis Haverfield and the Invention of Romano-British Archaeology*. Oxford.

Frere, S. S. (1980) 'Hyginus and the First Cohort', *Britannia* 11: 51–60.

Frere, S. S. (1987) *Britannia*. London.

Frere, S. S., and St Joseph, J. K. (1974) 'The Roman fortress at Longthorpe', *Britannia* 5: 1–129.

Frere, S. S., and Tomlin, R. S. O. (1992) *Roman Inscriptions in Britain*, vol. 2, fasc. 4. Stroud.

Frere, S. S., and Wilkes, J. J. (1989) *Strageath: Excavations within the Roman Fort, 1973–86*. *Britannia* Monograph Series 9. London.

Frézouls, E. (1971) 'Observation sur l'urbanisme dans l'Orient syrien', *Annales archéologiques arabes syriennes* 21: 231–5.

Frézouls, E. (1977) 'Du village à la ville: problèmes de l'urbanisation dans la Syrie hellénistique et romaine', in E. Frézouls (ed.), *Sociétés urbaines, sociétés rurales dans l'Asie Mineure et la Syrie helléniques et romaines*. Strasbourg, 81–93.

Fulford, M. G. (2001) 'Links with the past: persuasive 'ritual' behaviour in Roman Britain', *Britannia* 32: 199–218.

Fulford, M. G., and Timby, J. (2000) *Late Iron Age and Roman Silchester: Excavations on the Site of the Forum-Basilica 1977, 1980–86*. *Britannia* Monograph 15. London.

Funari, P. P. A. (2002) 'The consumption of olive oil in Roman Britain and the role of the army', in P. Erdkamp (ed.), *The Roman Army and the Economy*. Amsterdam, 235–63.

Furet, F., and Ozouf, J. (1982) *Reading and Writing: Literacy in France from Calvin to Jules Ferry*. Cambridge.

Furger-Gunti, A. (1981) 'Frühe Auxilien am Rhein: keltische Münzen in römischen Militärstationen', *Archäoligisches Korrespondenzblatt* 11: 231–46.

Furneaux, H., and Anderson, J. G. C. (1922) *Cornelii Taciti De Vita Agricolae*. Oxford.

Gabelman, H. (1972) 'Die Typen der römischen Grabstelen am Rhein', *BJ* 172: 65–140.

Gabler, D. (1968) 'Arrabona és környékének koplasztikai emlékei',. *Arrobona* 10: 51–78.

Gammon, A. (2004) 'Disciplina: constructing an imperial image from coins and inscriptions', Unpublished paper, University of St Andrews

Garbsch, J. (1978) *Römische Paderüstungen*. Munich.

Garbsch, J. (2000) Römische Paderüstungen', in L. Wamser (ed.), *Die Römer zwischen Alpen und Nordmeer*. Rosenheim, 53–7.

Garcia y Bellido, A. (1963) 'Los auxiliares hispanos en los ejercitos romanos de ocupacion 200–30 a C', *Emerita* 31: 213–26.

Gardiner, J. F. (1993) *Being a Roman Citizen*. London.

Gardner, A. (2004a) 'Introduction: social agency, power and being human', in A. Gardner (ed.), *Agency Uncovered: Archaeological Perspectives on Social Agency, Power and Being Human*. London, 1–15.

Gardner, A. (2004b) 'Agency and community in 4th century Britain: developing the structurationist project', in A. Gardner (ed.), *Agency Uncovered: Archaeological Perspectives on Social Agency, Power and Being Human*. London, 33–50.

Gardner, A. (2007) *An Archaeology of Social Identity: Soldiers and Society in Late Roman Britain*. Walnut Creek, Calif.

Gardner, J. F. (1993) *Being a Roman Citizen*. London.

Garnsey, P. D. A. (1970) 'Septimius Severus and the marriage of soldiers. *California Studies in Classical Antiquity* 3: 45–54.

Garnsey, P. D. A., and Whittaker, C. R. (1978) 'Introduction', in P. D. A. Garnsey and C. R. Whittaker (eds), *Imperialism in the Ancient World* mbridge, 1–6.

Garrow, D. (2005) 'Re-thinking the "structure" in deposition', paper presented at a meeting of the Theoretical Archaeology Group, December.

Gassner, V., Jilek, S., and Sauer, R. (1997) 'Der Töpferofen von Carnuntum', in H. Stigliz (ed.), *Das Auxiliarkastell Carnuntum 1: Forschungen 1977–1988*. Vienna ,179–230.

Gawlikowski, M. (1990) 'Les dieux de Palmyre', *ANRW* II.18.4: 2605–58.

Gazdac, C. (2003) *Monetary Circulation in Dacia and the Provinces from the Middle and Lower Danube from Trajan to Constantine I (AD 106–337)*. Cluj.

Gechter, M. (1990) 'Early Roman military installations and Ubian settlements in the Lower Rhine', in T. Blagg and M. Millett (eds), *The Early Roman Empire in the West*. Oxford, 97–102.

Gechter, M., and Kunow, J. (1983) 'Der frühkaiserzeitliche Grabfund von Mehrum', *BJ* 183: 449–68.

Genevrier, M.-L. (1986) 'Le culte d'Hercule Magusanus en Germanie Infériore', in P. Lévêque and M.-M. Mactoux (eds), *Les grandes figures religieuses: fonctionnement pratique et symbolique dans l'antiquité*. ALB 329. Paris, 371–8.

Gent, H. (1983) 'Centralized storage in later prehistoric Britain', *PPS* 49: 243–67.

Geremek, H. (1969) *Karanis: Communauté rurale de l'Égypte romaine au IIe–IIIe siècles de notre ère*. Warsaw.

Gerov, B. (1988) *Landownership in Roman Thracia and Moesia*. Amsterdam.

Gerstl, J. E. (1961) 'Determinants of occupational community in high status occupations', *Sociology Quarterly* 2: 37–48.

Giddens, A. (1979) *Central Problems in Social Theory: Action, Structure and Contradiction in Social Analysis*. London.

Giddens, A. (1984) *The Constitution of Society: Outline of the Theory of Structuration*. Cambridge.

Gillam, J. P. (1957) 'Types of Roman coarse pottery in northern Britain', *Archaeologia Aeliana*, 4th ser., 35: 180–251.

Gillam, J. P. (1973) 'Sources of pottery found on northern military sites', in A. Detsicas (ed.), *Research in Romano-British Coarse Pottery*. CBA Research Report 10. London, 53–65.

Gilliam, J. F. (1950) 'Some Latin military papyri from Dura', *Yale Classical* Studies 11: 169–252.

Gilliam, J. F. (1954) 'The Roman military *feriale*', *Harvard Theological Review* 47: 183–96.

Gilliam, J. F. (1957) 'The appointment of auxiliary centurions (P. Mich. 164) ', *TAPhA* 88: 155–69.

Gilliam, J. F. (1965a) 'Dura rosters and the *Constitutio Antoniniana*', *Historia* 14: 74–92

Gilliam, J. F. (1965b) 'Romanization in the Greek east: the role of the army', *BASP* 2.2: 65–73.

Gilliam, J. F. (1967) 'The *deposita* of an auxiliary soldier: *P. Columbia* 325. *BJ* 167: 233–43

Gilliam, J. F. (1968) *P. Wisconsin* 14. *BASP* 5: 93–8.

Gilliam, J. F. (1974) 'Jupiter Turmasgades', in D. M. Pippidi (ed.), *Actes du IX Congrès international d'études sur les frontières romaines*. Bucharest, 309–14.

Gilliam, J. F. (1975) 'Notes on Latin texts from Egypt', in *Le monde grec: hommages à Claire Préaux*. Brussels, 766–74.

Gilliam, J. F. (1978) 'Some Roman elements in Roman Egypt', *Illinois Classical Studies* 3: 115–31.

Gilliam, J. F. (1986) 'The ostracon from Mons Claudianus', in *Roman Army Papers*. Amsterdam, 115–17.

Gilliver, C. M. (1993) 'The *de munitionibus castrorum*: text and translation', *JRMES* 4: 33–48.

Gilliver, C. M. (1996) 'Mons Graupius and the role of auxiliaries in battle', *Greece and Rome* 43.1: 54–67.

Glasbergen, W., and Groenman-van Waateringe, W. (1974) *The Pre-Flavian Garrisons of Valkenburg Z.H.* Amsterdam.

Glasbergen, W., and van Lith, M. E. (1977) 'Italische und frühe südgallische *terra sigillata* aus Velsen, Provinz Nord-Holland', *Rei Cretariae Romanae Fautorum Acta*, 17–18.

Glodariu, I., and Iaroslavschi, E. (1979) *Civilizaţia fierului la daci (sec. II î.e.n.–I e.n.).* Cluj.

Goessler, P. (1928) 'Ein gallorömischer Steckkalender aus Rottweil', *Germania* 12: 1–9.

Goessler, P. (1943) 'Neue Steine aus dem Kastell Mainhardt (Württemberg) ', *Germania* 27: 157–68.

Goethert, K. (1989) 'Zur Körper- und Schönheitspflege in frührömischer Zeit: Grab 1026', in A. Haffner (ed.), *Gräber: Spiegel des Lebens*. Mainz, 275–88.

Goffman, E. (1961) *Asylums*. Chicago.

Golden, M. (2000) 'A decade of demography: recent trends in the study of Greek and Roman populations', in P. Flensted-Jensen, T. Heine Nielsen, and L. Rubinstein (eds), *Polis and Politics*. Copenhagen, 23–40.

Goldman, N. (1994) 'Reconstructing Roman clothing', in J. L. Sebesta and L. Bonfante (eds), *The World of Roman Costume*. Madison, Wis., 163–81.

Goldsworthy, A. (1996) *The Roman Army at War, 100 BC–AD 200*. Oxford.

Goldsworthy, A., and Haynes, I. P. (eds) (1999) *The Roman Army as a Community*. JRA Supplementary Series 34. Portsmouth, RI.

Gordon, R. L. (2009) 'The Roman army and the cult of Mithras: a critical view', in C. Wolff (ed.), *L'armée romaine et la religion sous le haut-empire romain*. Lyons, 379–423.

Gosden, C. (2004) *Archaeology and Colonialism*. Cambridge.

Gradel, I. (2002) *Emperor Worship and Roman Religion*. Oxford.

Graf, D. F. (1994) 'The Nabataean army and the *Cohortes Ulpiae Petraeorum*', in Dabrowa (1994), 265–311.

Graf, D. F. (1997) *Rome and the Arabian Frontier: From the Nabateans to the Saracens*. Aldershot.

Grainger, J. (1990) *Cities of Seleukid Syria*. Oxford.

Grant, M. (1990) 'Introduction', in M. Grant and R. Graves, *The Golden Ass*. London.

Green, M. J. (1976) *A Corpus of Religious Material from the Civilian Areas of Roman Britain*. BAR British Series 424. Oxford.

Green, M. J. (1978) *A Corpus of Small Cult-Objects from the Military Areas of Roman Britain*. BAR British Series 52. Oxford.

Greenberg, J. (2003) 'Plagued by doubt: reconsidering the impact of a mortality crisis in the 2nd c. AD', *JRA* 16.2: 413–25.

Greene, K. (2008) 'Learning to consume: consumption and consumerism in the Roman Empire', *JRA* 21: 64–82.

Gregory, S. (1995–1997) *Roman Military Architecture on the Eastern Frontier*. Amsterdam.

Griffith, F. L. (1929) 'Meroitic studies VI', *JEA* 16.

Groenman-van Waateringe, W. (1997) 'Classical authors and the diet of Roman soldiers: true or false?', in W. Groenman-van Waateringe, B. L. van Beek, W. J. H. Willems, and

S. L. Wynia (eds), *Roman Frontier Studies 1995: Proceedings of the XVIth Roman Frontier Studies Conference 1995*. Oxbow Monograph 91. Oxford, 261–72.

Gros, P. (1986) 'Le mausolée des Julii et le statut de Glanum', *Revue archéologique* 1: 65–80.

Grünewald, T. (2004) *Bandits in the Roman Empire: Myth and Reality*. London.

Gudea, N., and Zahariade, M. (1980) 'Spanish units in Roman Dacia'. *Arhiva español de arqueologia* 53: 61–76.

Haalebos, J. K. (1986) 'Ausgrabungen in Woerden (1975–1982)', in *Studien zu den Militärgrenzen Roms III*. Stuttgart, 169–74.

Haalebos, J. K. (1999) 'Nederlanders in Roemenië', *Westerheem* 48.6: 197–210.

Haffner, A. (1984) '145 Grab 33 (1978) Brandgrab', in Rheinisches Landesmuseum Trier, *Trier Augustusstadt der Treverer*. Mainz, 287.

Hainzmann, M., and Visy, Z. (1991) *Instrumenta Inscripta Latina*. Pécs.

Halsall, G. (2000) 'Archaeology and the late Roman frontier in northern Gaul: the so-called 'Föderatengräber' reconsidered', in W. Pohl and H. Reimitz (eds), *Grenze und Differenz in frühen Mittelalter*. Vienna, 167–80.

Hamers, J. F. and Blanc, M. H. A. (1989) *Bilinguality and Bilingualism*. Cambridge.

Hansen, S., and Pingel, V. (eds) (2001) *Archäologie in Hessen: Neue Funde und Befunde. Festschrift für Fritz-Rudolf Herrmann zum 65. Geburtstag*, Rahden.

Hanson, A. E. (1989) 'Village officials in Philadelphia: a model of Romanization in the Julio-Claudian period', in L. Criscuolo and G. Geraci (eds), *Egitto e storia antica dall'ellenismo all'età araba*. Bologna, 429–40

Hanson, W. S., (1991) *Agricola and the Conquest of the North*, 2nd edn. London.

Hanson, W. S., and Conolly, R. (2002) 'Language and literacy in Roman Britain', in Cooley (2002a), 151–64.

Hanson, W. S., Speller, K., Yeoman, P. A., and Terry, J. (eds) (2007) *Elginhaugh: A Flavian Fort and its Annexe*. Britannia Monograph Series 23. London.

Harnack, A. (1981) *Militia Christi: The Christian Religion and the Military in the First Three Centuries* AD. Philadelphia.

Harnecker, J. (2008) *Kalkriese 4. Katalog der römischen Funde vom Oberesch. Die Schnitte 1–22*. Römisch-Germanische Forschungen 66. Mainz.

Harnecker, J., and Tolksdorf-Lienemann, E. (2004) *Kalkriese 2. Sondierungen in der Kalkrieser-Niewedder Senke. Archäologie und Bodenkunde*. Römisch-Germanische Forschungen 62. Mainz.

Harris, W. V. (1989) *Ancient Literacy*. Cambridge, Mass.

Hasebroek, J. (1921) *Untersuchungen zur Geschichte des Kaisers Septimius Severus*. Heidelberg.

Hassall, M. (1983) 'The internal planning of Roman auxiliary forts', in B. Hartley and J. Wacher (eds), *Rome and her Northern Provinces*. London, 96–131.

Haverfield, F. (1911) 'An inaugural address delivered before the first Annual General Meeting of the Society, 11th May, 1911', *JRS* 1: xi–xx.

Haynes, I. P. (1993) 'The Romanization of religion in the auxilia of the Roman imperial army from Augustus to Septimius Severus', *Britannia* 24: 141–58.

Haynes, I. P. (1997) 'Religion in the Roman army: unifying aspects and regional trends. in H. Cancik and J. Rüpke (eds), *Römische Reichsreligion und Provinzialreligion*. Tübingen, 113–26.

Haynes, I. P. (1999a) 'Introduction: the Roman army as a community', in Goldsworthy and and Haynes (1999), 7–14.

Haynes, I. P. (1999b) 'Military service and cultural identity in the *auxilia*', in Goldsworthy and Haynes (1999, 165–74.

Haynes, I. P. (2001) 'The impact of auxiliary recruitment on provincial societies from Augustus to Caracalla', in L. de Blois (ed.), *Administration, Prosopography and Appointment Policies in the Roman Empire*. Amsterdam, 62–83.

Haynes, I. P. (forthcoming) 'Bronze objects from the Liber Pater sanctuary', in I. P. Haynes, A. Diaconescu, and A. Schäfer, *The Sanctuary of Liber Pater, Apulum.*

Haynes, I. P., and Wilmott, T. (2012) 'The Maryport altars. An archaeological myth dispelled', *Studia Universitatis Babeş-Bolyai, Historia* 57.1 25–31.

Hayward, K. M. J. (2009) *Roman Quarrying and Stone Supply on the Periphery: Southern England. A Geological Study of First-Century Funerary Monuments and Monumental Architecture.* BAR British Series 500. Oxford.

Heinen, H. (1985) *Trier und das Trevererland in römischer Zeit.* Trier.

Helgeland, J. (1978) 'Roman army religion', *ANRW* II 16.2: 1470–1505.

Herz, P. (1978) 'Kaiserfeste der Prinzipatszeit', *ANRW* II 16.2: 1135–1200.

Hessing, W. (2001) 'Foreign oppressor versus civiliser: the Batavian myth as the source for contrasting associations of Rome in Dutch historiography and archaeology', in R. Hingley (ed.), *Images of Rome: Perceptions of Ancient Rome in Europe and the United States in the Modern Age. JRA* Supplementary Series 44. Portsmouth, RI, 126–43.

Heyn, M. K. (2011) 'The Terentius frieze in context', in L. Brody and G. Hoffman (eds), *Dura-Europos: Crossroads of Antiquity.* Boston, Mass., 221–33.

Hilgers, W. (1969) *Lateinische Gefässnamen: Bezeichnungen, Funktion und Form römischer Gefässe nach den antiken Schriftquellen. BJ* Beiheft 31. Bonn.

Hill, J. D. (1995) *Ritual and Rubbish in the Iron Age of Wessex: A Study in the Formation of a Specific Archaeological Record.* BAR British Series 242. Oxford.

Hill, J. D. (2001) 'Romanisation, gender and class: recent approaches to identity in Britain and their possible consequences', in S. James and M. Millett (eds), *Britons and Romans: Advancing an Archaeological Agenda.* CBA Research Report 125. York, 12–18.

Hill, P. R. (1997) 'The Maryport altars: some first thoughts', in R. J. A. Wilson (ed.), *Roman Maryport and its Setting.* Cumberland and Westmorland Antiquarian and Archaeological Society Extra Series 28. Nottingham, 92–104.

Hillery, G. A. (1955) 'Definitions of community: areas of agreement', *Rural Sociology* 20: 111–23.

Hingley, R. (2000) *Roman Officers and English Gentlemen: The Imperial Origins of Roman Archaeology.* London.

Hingley, R. (2003) 'Recreating coherence without reinventing Romanization', *Digressus* Supplement 1: 111–19. http://www.digressus.org. Accessed 10.11.06 and 1.07.12.

Hingley, R. (2005) *Globalizing Roman Culture.* London.

Hird, L. (1977) *A Report on the Pottery Found in the pre-Hadrianic Levels at Vindolanda during the Excavations of 1972–1975.* Bardon Mill.

Hobsbawm, E., and Ranger, T. (eds) (1983) *The Invention of Tradition.* Cambridge.

Hock, H. H., and Joseph, B. D. (1996) *Language History, Language Change, and Language Relationship: An Introduction to Historical and Comparative Linguistics.* Berlin.

Hodder, I. (2000) 'Agency and individuals in long-term processes', in M.-A. Dobres and J. R. Robb (eds), *Agency in Archaeology,.* London, 21–33.

Hoddinott, R. F. (1981) *The Thracians.* London.

Hodgson, N. (2003) *The Roman Fort at Wallsend (Segedunum): Excavations in 1997–8.* Newcastle upon Tyne.

Hodgson, N. (2009) *Hadrian's Wall 1999–2009.* Newcastle upon Tyne.

Hodgson, N., and Bidwell, P. T. (2004) 'Auxiliary barracks in a new light: recent discoveries on Hadrian's Wall', *Britannia* 35: 121–58.

Holder, P. A. (1980) *The Auxilia from Augustus to Trajan,* Oxford

Holder, P. A. (1982) *The Roman Army in Britain.* London.

Holder, P. A. (2006) *Roman Military Diplomas V.* London.

Holmes, R. (2001) *Redcoat: The British Soldier in the Age of Horse and Musket.* London.

Hooppell, R. E. (1878) *On the Discovery and Exploration of Roman Remains at South Shields.* London.

Hopkins, K. (1978) *Conquerors and Slaves*. Sociological Studies in Roman History 1. Cambridge.

Hopkins, K. (1980) 'Taxes and trade in the Roman Empire (200 BC–AD 400)', *JRS* 70: 101–12.

Hopkins, K. (1991) 'Conquest by book', in J. H. Humphrey (ed.), *Literacy in the Roman World*. *JRA* Supplementary Series 3. Ann Arbor, Mich., 59–76.

Hopwell, D. (2005) 'Roman fort environs in north-west Wales', *Britannia* 36: 225–69.

Horsfall, N. (1991) 'Statistics or states of mind?', in J. H. Humphrey (ed.), *Literacy in the Roman World*. *JRA* Supplementary Series 3. Ann Arbor, Mich., 59–76.

Husar, A. (1995) 'Celts and Germans in Dacia', in R. Frei-Stolba and H. E. Herzig (eds), *La politique édilitaire dans les provinces de l'Empire romain IIème–IVème siècles après J.-C.*. Bern, 131–43.

Hutton, M. (1970) *Tacitus I: Agricola, Germania and Dialogus*. Cambridge, Mass.

Insoll, T. (2004) *Archaeology, Ritual, Religion*. London.

Irby-Massie, G. L. (1999) *Military Religion in Roman Britain*. Leiden.

Isaac, B. (1990) *The Limits of Empire : The Roman Army in the East*. Oxford.

Isaac, B. (1992) *The Limits of Empire: The Roman Army in the East*, 2nd edn. Oxford.

Isaac, D. and Cociş, S. (1995) 'Fibulele din castrele romane de la Gilău şi Căşeiu. O analiză în context stratigrafic', *Eph. Nap.* 5: 125.

Ivleva, T. (2012) *Britons Abroad: The mobility of Britons and the circulation of British-made objects in the Roman Empire*, PhD thesis, Leiden University.

Jackson, J. (1931) *Tacitus V Annals XIII–XVI*. Cambridge, Mass.

Jackson, J. (1936) *Tacitus IV Annals IV–VI, XI–XII*. Cambridge, Mass.

Jackson K. H. (1953) *Language and History in Early Britain*. Edinburgh.

Jackson, R. P. J. (1988) *Doctors and Diseases in the Roman Empire*. London.

James, S. (1985) 'Dura-Europos and the chronology of Syria in the 250s AD', *Chiron* 15: 111–24.

James, S. (1999) 'The community of soldiers: a major identity and centre of power in the Roman Empire', in P. Baker, C. Forcey, S. Jundi, and R. Witcher (eds), *TRAC 98: Proceedings of the 8th Annual Theoretical Roman Archaeology Conference, Leicester 1998*. Oxford, 14–25.

James, S. (2001a) 'Soldiers and civilians: identity and interaction in Roman Britain', in S. James and M. Millett (eds), *Britons and Romans: Advancing an Archaeological Agenda*. CBA Research Report 125. York, 77–89.

James, S. (2001b) ''Romanization' and the peoples of Britain', in S. Keay and N. Terrenato (eds), *Italy and the West: Comparative Issues in Romanization*. Oxford, 77–89.

James, S. (2002) 'Writing the legions: the development and future of Roman military studies in Britain', *Archaeological Journal* 159: 1–58.

James, S. (2004) *Excavations at Dura-Europos 1928–1937. Final Report VII: The Arms and Armour and Other Military Equipment*. London.

James, S. (2005) 'Large-scale recruitment of auxiliaries from Free Germany?', in Z. Visy (ed.), *Limes XIX: Proceedings of the XIXth International Congress of Roman Frontier Studies*. Pécs, 273–9.

James, S. (2006) 'Engendering change in our understanding of the structure of Roman military communities', *Archaeological Dialogues* 13.1: 31–6.

James, S. (2011) *Rome and the Sword*. London.

James, S., Baird, J. A., and Strutt, K. (2011) 'Magnetometry survey of Dura's Roman military base and vicinity', in P. Leriche, S. de Pontbriand, and G. Coqueugniot (eds), *Europos-Doura Études* 6. Beirut , 1–6.

Jarrett, M. G. (1969) 'Thracian units in the Roman army', *Israel Exploration Journal* 19: 215–24.

Jarrett, M. G. (1994) 'Non-legionary troops in Roman Britain', *Britannia* 25: 7–14.

Jobey, I. (1979) 'Housesteads ware: a Frisian tradition on Hadrian's Wall. *Archaeologia Aeliana*, 5th ser., 7: 127–43.

Johnson, A. (1983) *Roman Forts of the First and Second Centuries* AD *in Britain and the German Provinces*. London.

Johnson, B. (1981) *Pottery from Karanis: Excavations of the University of Michigan*. Ann Arbor, Mich.

Johnson, P., with Haynes, I. (eds) (1996) *Architecture in Roman Britain*. CBA Research Report 94. York.

Jones, A. H. M. (1931) 'The urbanization of the Ituraean principality', *JRS* 21: 265–75.

Jones, A. H. M. (1960) *Studies in Roman Government and Law*. Oxford.

Jones, A. H. M. (1964) *The Later Roman Empire*. Oxford.

Jones, R. H. (2006) 'The temporary encampments of the Roman army in Scotland', Ph.D thesis, University of Glasgow.

Jones, S. (1997) *The Archaeology of Ethnicity*. London.

Junkelmann, M. (1986) *Die Legionen des Augustus*. Mainz.

Junkelmann, M. (1997) *Panis Militaris: Die Ernährung des römischen Soldaten oder der Grundstoff der Macht*. Mainz.

Junkelmann, M. (2000) *Das Spiel mit dem Tod: so kämpften Roms Gladiatoren*. Mainz.

Kaizer, T. (2002) *The Religious Life of Palmyra*. Stuttgart.

Kaizer, T. (2004a) 'Latin–Palmyrene inscriptions in the museum of Banat at Timişoara', in L. Ruscu, C. Ciongradi, R. Ardevan, C. Roman, and C. Găzdac (eds), *Orbis Antiqvvs: Studia in Honorem Ioannis Pisonis*. Cluj, 565–9.

Kaizer, T. (2004b) 'Religious mentality in Palmyrene documents', *Klio* 86:167–86.

Kaizer, T. (2006) 'A note on the Fresco of Iulius Terentius from Dura-Europos', in R. Rollinger and B. Truschnegg (eds), *Altertum und Mittelmeerraum: die Antike Welt diesseits und jenseits der Levante*. Stuttgart, 150–59.

Katona-Apte, J. (1975) 'Dietary aspects of acculturation: meals, feasts and fasts in a minority community in South Asia', in M. L. Arnott (ed.), *Gastronomy. The Anthropology of Food and Food Habits*. The Hague, 315–26.

Keay, S. (1988) *Roman Spain*. London.

Keay, S. (2001) 'Romanization and the Hispaniae', in S. Keay and N. Terrenato (eds), *Italy and the West: Comparative Issues in Romanization*. Oxford, 117–44.

Keegan, J. (1976) *The Face of Battle*. London.

Kellner, H.-J. (1971) 'Exercitus Raeticus', *Bayerische Vorgeschichtsblätter* 36: 207–15.

Kellner, H.-J. (1986) 'Die Möglichkeit von Rückschlüssen aus der Fundstatistik', in W. Eck and H. Wolff (eds), *Heer und Integrationspolitik: die römischen Militärdiplome als historische Quelle*. Cologne, 241–8.

Kennedy, D. L. (1977) 'Parthian regiments in the Roman army', in J. Fitz (ed.), *Limes: Akten des XI Internationalen Limeskongress*. Budapest, 521–31.

Kennedy, D. L. (1980) 'The *auxilia* and *numeri* raised in the Roman province of Syria', DPhil. thesis, University of Oxford.

Kennedy, D. L. (1985) 'The composition of a military work party in Roman Egypt (*ILS* 2483: Coptos)', *JEA* 71: 156–60.

Kennedy, D. L. (1989) 'The military contribution of Syria to the Roman imperial army', in D. H. French and C. S. Lightfoot (eds), *The Eastern Frontier of the Roman Empire*. BAR International Series 553. Oxford, 235–46.

Kennedy, D. L. (1994) The *cohors XX Palmyrenorum* at Dura Europos', in E. Dabrowa (ed.), *The Roman and Byzantine Army in the East*. Cracow, 89–98.

Kennedy, D. L. (1996) *The Roman Army in the East*. JRA Supplement 18.

Kennedy, D. L. (2000) *The Roman Army in Jordan*. London.

Keppie, L. (1984) *The Making of the Roman Army*. Hove.

Killingray, D. (1999) 'Guardians of empire', in D. Killingray and D. Omissi (eds), *Guardians of Empire*. Manchester, 1–24.

Kilpatrick, G. D. (1964) 'Dura-Europos: the parchments and the papyri', *Greek, Roman and Byzantine Studies* 5: 215–25.

King, A. C. (1984) 'Animal bones and the dietary identity of military and civilian groups in Roman Britain, Germany and Gaul', in T. Blagg and A. King (eds), *Military and Civilian in Roman Britain*. BAR British Series 136. Oxford, 187–217.

King, A. C. (1999a) 'Animals and the Roman army: the evidence of animal bones', in Goldsworthy and Haynes (1999), 139–49.

King, A. C. (1999b) 'Diet in the Roman world: a regional inter-site comparison of the mammal bones', *JRA* 12: 168–202.

Kohlert, M. (1980) 'Römische Gesichtsmasken aus Thrakien und Niedermösien', in R. Vulpe (ed.), *Actes du IIème Congrès International de Thracologie*. Bucharest, 223–32.

Kolb. F. (1977) 'Der Aufstand der Provinz Africa Proconsularis im Jahr 238 n.Chr.: die wirtschaftlichen und sozialen Hintergründe', *Historia* 26: 440–78.

Kooistra, L. I. (1996) *Borderland Farming: Possibilities and Limitations of Farming in the Roman Period and the Early Middle Ages between the Rhine and Meuse*. Assen.

Kraft, K. (1951) *Zur Rekrutierung der Alen und Kohorten an Rhein und Donau*. Dissertationes Bernenses 1.3. Berne.

Krasvasilev, L. (2010) 'Royal Thracian tomb', *Archaeology* (March/April): 12.

Kreuz, A. (2007) 'Brei und Brot? Archäobotanische Untersuchungen zur Ernährung der Wachsoldaten des Wp. 5/4 Neuberg am Limes', in A. Thiel (ed.), *Forschungen zur Funktion des Limes: Beiträge zum Welterbe Limes 2*. Stuttgart, 83–9.

Krier, J., and Reinert, F. (1993) *Das Reitergrab von Hellingen*. Luxemburg.

Kropatscheck, G. (1909) 'Ausgrabungen bei Haltern: die Fundstücke der Jahre 1905 bis 1907. *Mitteilungen der Altertums Kommission für Westfalen* 5: 323–75.

Krumeich, R. (1998) 'Darstellungen syrischer Priester an den kaiserzeitlichen Tempeln von Niha und Chehim im Lebanon', *Damaszener Mittelungen* 10: 171–200.

Künzl, E. (1994) 'Dekorierte Gladii und Cingula: eine ikonographische Statistik', *JRMES* 5: 33–58.

Lambert, G. (1990) *Le Luxembourg romain: documents chosis*. Virton.

Lambert, P. (2000) 'Varia III, Gaulish *souxtu*, early Irish *suacht*=cooking pot', *Ériu* 51: 189–92.

Lambert, P. (2004) 'Varia V, Gaulish *souxtu*, addendum', *Ériu* 54: 263–4.

Laporte, J.-P. (1989) *Rapidum: le camp de la cohorte des Sardes en Maurétanie Césarienne*. Sassari.

Lassère, J.-M. (1980) 'Remarques onomastiques sur la liste militaire de Vezereos', in W. S. Hanson and L. J. F. Keppie (eds), *Roman Frontier Studies 1979*. Oxford, 955–75.

Laurence, R., and Berry, J. (1998) *Cultural Identity in the Roman Empire*. London.

Laursen, J. (1982) 'Weapons in water: a European sacrificial rite in Italy', *Analecta Romana Instituti Danici* 11: 7–25.

Lauwerier, R. C. G. M. (1988) *Animals in Roman Times in the Dutch Eastern River Area*. Amersfoort.

Leander Touati, A. (1987) *The Great Trajanic Frieze: The Study of a Monument and of the Mechanisms of Message Transmission in Roman Art*. Rome.

Le Bohec, Y. (1989) *Les unités auxiliaires de l'armée romaine en Afrique Proconsularis et en Numidie sous le Haut-Empire*. Paris.

Le Bohec, Y. (1994) *The Imperial Roman Army*. London.

Le Bohec, Y., Berthet, J., Brizzi, G., and Giuffré, V. (eds) (2003) *Les discours d'Hadrien à l'armée d'Afrique*. Paris.

Le Gall, J. (1976) 'Evocatio', in *Mélanges J. Heurgon: Italie préromaine et la Rome républicaine*. Rome, 519–24.

Le Glay, M. (1972) 'Le commandement des *cohortes voluntariorum* de l'armée romaine', *Ancient Society* 3: 209–21.

Leguilloux, M. (1997) 'Quelques aspects de l'approvisionnement en viande des praesidia du désert oriental égyptien', *Archaeozoologia* 9: 73–81.

Lehner, H. (1908) 'Die Standarte der *Ala Longiniana*', *BJ* 117: 279–86.

Lehoux, D. (2007) *Astronomy, Weather, and Calendars in the Ancient World: Parapegmata and Related Texts in Classical and Near-Eastern Societies*. Cambridge.

Lendon, J. E. (1997) *Empire of Honour*. Oxford.

Lenoir, M. (1979) *Pseudo-Hygin: des fortifications du camp*. Paris.

Lenoir, M., and Licoppe, C. (2004) 'Les *principia* du camp romain de Doura-Europos', in P. Leriche, M. Gelin, and A. Dandrau (eds), *Doura-Europos : Études V 1994–1997*. Paris, 57–64.

Leriche, P. (1986) 'Chronologie du rempart de bricque crue de Doura-Europos', *Syria* 63: 61–82.

Leriche, P. (1987) 'Doura-Europos grecque, parthe et romaine', *Mesopotamia* 22: 57–66.

Leriche, P. (1997a) 'Le *Chreophylakeion* de Doura-Europos et la mise en place du plan hippodamien de la ville', in M. F. Boussac and A. Invernizzi (eds), *Archives et sceaux du monde hellénistique*. BCH Supplement 29. Athens, 157–69.

Leriche, P. (1997b) 'Pourquoi et comment Europos a été fondé à Doura?', in P. Brule and J. Oulhen (eds), *Esclavage, guerre, économie en Grèce ancienne*. Rennes, 191–210.

Leriche, P., de Pontbriand, S., and Coqueugniot, G. (eds) (2011) *Europos-Doura Études* 6. IFPO. Beirut.

Leriche, P., and Gelin, M. (eds) (1997) *Doura-Europos Études IV 1991–1993*. IFAP. Beirut.

Leriche, P., and Mahmoud, M. (1994) 'Doura-Europos : bilan des recherches récentes', *Comptes-rendus de l'Académie des inscriptions et belle-lettres*, 396–420.

Le Roux, P. (1982) *L'armée romaine et l'organisation des provinces ibériques*. Paris.

Lesquier, J. (1918) *L'armée romaine d'Egypte*. Paris.

Levick, B. (2007) *Julia Domna, Syrian Empress*. London.

Lévi-Strauss, C. (1966) *The Savage Mind*. London.

Lévi-Strauss, C. (1973) *Tristes tropiques*. London.

Lévi-Strauss, C. (1983) *The Way of Masks*. London.

Levy, J. E. (1982) *Social and Religious Organization in Bronze Age Denmark: An Analysis of Ritual Hoard Finds*. BAR International Series 124. Oxford.

Lewis, M. (2009) 'Vindolanda's Roman calendar', *Current Archaeology* 224: 12–17.

Lewis, N. (1982) *The Compulsory Public Services of Roman Egypt*. Papyrologica Florentina 1. Florence.

Lewis, N. (1988) 'A Jewish landowner in Provincia Arabia', *SCI* 8/9.

Lindenlauf, A. (2004) 'Dirt, cleanliness, and social structure in ancient Greece', in A. Gardner (ed.), *Agency Uncovered: Archaeological Perspectives on Social Agency, Power, and Being Human*. London, 81–105.

Lindenthal, J., Rupp, V., and Birley, A. R. (2001) 'Eine neue Veteraninschrift aus der Wetterau', in S. Hansen and V. Pingel (eds), *Archäologie in Hessen: neue Funde und Befunde. Festschrift für Fritz-Rudolf Herrmann zum 65. Geburtstag*. Rahden, 199–208.

Link, S. (1989) *Konzepte der Privilegierung römischer Veteranen*. Stuttgart.

Lipper, E. (1982) 'Die Tierknochenfunde aus dem römischen Kastell Abusina-Eining, Stadt Neustadt a d. Donau, Lkr. Kelheim', *Bericht Bayerischen Bodendenkmalpflege* 22–3: 81–160.

Lissi-Caronna, E. (1986) *Il mitreo dei castra peregrinorum*. EPRO 104. Leiden.

Lockyear, K. (2000) Site finds in Roman Britain: a comparison of techniques', *Oxford Journal of Archaeology* 19.4: 397–423.

Lomas, K. (1995) 'Introduction', in T. J. Cornell and K. Lomas (eds), *Urban Society in Roman Italy*. London, 1–8.

Mackie, N. (1983) *Local Administration in Roman Spain AD 14–212*. BAR International Series 172.

Mackintosh, M. (1986) 'The sources of the Horseman and the Fallen Enemy motif on the tombstones of the Western Roman Empire', *JBAA* 139: 1–21.

MacMullen, R. (1960) 'Inscriptions on armour and the supply of arms in the Roman Empire', *AJA* 64: 23–40.

MacMullen, R. (1981) *Paganism in the Roman Empire*. New Haven, Conn.

MacMullen, R. (1984) 'The legion as society', *Historia* 33: 440–56.

Magness, J. (1995) 'Roman military bronzes from Morocco', Review article of C. Boube-Piccot, *Les bronzes antiques du Maroc, IV: L'équipement militaire et l'armement* (1994), *JRA* 8: 489–92.

Mann, J. C. (1954) 'A note on the *numeri*', *Hermes* 82: 501–6.

Mann, J. C. (1963) 'The raising of new legions during the Principate', *Hermes* 91: 483–9.

Mann, J. C. (1972) 'The development of auxiliary and fleet diplomas', *Epigraphische Studien* 9: 233–43.

Mann, J. C. (1974) 'The frontiers of the Principate', *ANRW* 508–33.

Mann, J. C. (1983) *Legionary Recruitment and Veteran Settlement during the Principate*. London.

Mann, J. C. (1984) 'A note on the "Modius Claytonensis"',. *Archaeologia Aeliana*, 5th ser., 12: 242–3.

Mann, J. C. (1985) 'Epigraphic consciousness', *JRS* 75: 204–6.

Mann, J. C. (1986) 'A note on *conubium*', in W. Eck and H. Wolff (eds), *Heer und Integrationspolitik: Die römischen Militärdiplome als historische Quelle*. Passauer Historische Forschungen 2. Cologne, 187–9.

Mann, J. C. (2002) 'The settlement of veterans discharged from auxiliary units stationed in Britain', *Britannia* 33: 183–7.

Mann, J. C., and Roxan, M. M. (1988) 'Discharge certificates of the Roman army', *Britannia* 19: 341–7.

Mann, M. (1986) *The Sources of Social Power*. Cambridge.

Manning, W. H. (1972) 'Ironwork hoards in Iron Age and Roman Britain', *Britannia* 3: 224–50.

Mansel, A. M. (1938) 'Grabhügelforschung in Ostthrakien', *Bulletin de l'Institut d'archéologie bulgare* 12: 154–89.

Mansel, A. M. (1941) 'Grabügelforschung im östlichen Thrakien', *Archäologischer Anzeiger*, 119–87.

Marchand, S. (1996) *Down from Olympus: Archaeology and Philhellenism in Germany, 1750–1970*. Princeton, NJ.

Marchant, D. (1990) 'Roman weapons in Great Britain, a case study: spearheads, problems in dating and typology', *JRMES* 1: 1–6.

Marichal, R. (1992) *Les ostraca de Bu Njem*. Tripoli.

Mason, P. (1974. *A Matter of Honour: An Account of the Indian Army, its Officers and Men*. London.

Mattingly, D. J. (1996) 'First fruit? The olive in the Roman world', in G. Shipley and J. Salmon (eds), *Human Landscapes in Classical Antiquity: Environment and Culture*. London, 213–53.

Mattingly, D. J. (ed.) (1997) *Dialogues in Roman Imperialism: Power, Discourse and Discrepant Experience in the Roman Empire*. JRA Supplementary Series 23. Portsmouth, RI.

Mattingly, D. J. (2002) 'Vulgar and weak 'Romanization', or time for a paradigm shift?', *JRA* 15.2: 536–40.

Mattingly, D. J. (2004) 'Being Roman: expressing identity in a provincial setting', *JRA* 17: 5–25.

Mattingly, D. J. (2006) *An Imperial Possession: Britain in the Roman Empire*. London.

Mattingly, D. J. (2011) *Imperialism, Power and Identity: Experiencing the Roman Empire*. Princeton, NJ.

Maurin, L. (1988) *Les fouilles de 'Ma Maison': études sur Saintes antique. Aquitania* Supplement 3. Paris.

Maxfield, V. A. (1981) *The Military Decorations of the Roman Army.* London.

Maxfield, V. A. (1986a) 'Pre-Flavian forts and their garrisons', *Britannia* 17: 59–72.

Maxfield, V. A. (1986b) 'Systems of reward in relation to military diplomas', in W. Eck and H. Wolff (eds), *Heer und Integrationspolitik: die römischen Militärdiplome als historische Quelle.* Passau, 26–43.

Maxfield, V. A. (1995) 'Soldier and civilian: life beyond the ramparts'. Eighth Annual Caerleon Lecture, National Museum of Wales, Cardiff.

Maxfield, V. A. (2003) 'Ostraca and the Roman army in the Eastern Desert', in J. J. Wilkes (ed.), *Documenting the Roman Army: Essays in Honour of Margaret Roxan.* London, 153–74.

Maxfield, V. A. (2009) 'Aswan and the River Nile: frontier and highway', in A. Morillo, N. Hanel, and Martin, E. (eds), *Limes Congress XX. Gladius* 2009, vol. 1. Madrid, 74–84.

McCrum, R., Cran, W., and MacNeil, R. (1986) *The Story of English.* London.

McIntosh, F. (2012) 'Regional brooch types in Roman Britain: evidence from northern England', *Archaeologia Aeliana*, 5th series, 40: 155–82.

McKitterick, R. (ed.) (1990) *The Uses of Literacy in Early Medieval Europe.* Cambridge.

Meskell, L. M. (1996) 'The somatization of archaeology: institutions, discourses, corporeality', *Norwegian Archaeological Review* 29.1: 1–16.

Meskell, L. M. (1998) 'The irresistible body and the seduction of archaeology', in D. Montserrat (ed.), *Changing Bodies, Changing Meanings: Studies on the Human Body in Antiquity.* London, 139–61.

Meskell, L. M., and Joyce, R. A. (2003) *Embodied Lives: Figuring Ancient Maya and Egyptian Experience.* London.

Messer, W. S. (1920) 'Mutiny in the Roman army in the Republic', *Classical Philology* 15: 158–75.

Metzler, K. (1984) 'Das treverische Oppidum auf dem Titelberg (Lux.)', in Rheinisches Landesmuseum Trier, *Trier, Augustusstadt der Trever.* Mainz, 87–99.

Metzler, J., Millett, M., Roymans, N., and Slofstra, J. (eds) (1995) *Integration in the Early Roman West: The Role of Culture and Ideology.* Luxemburg.

Millar, F. (1981) *The Roman Empire and its Neighbours.* London.

Millar, F. (1993) *The Roman Near East 31 BC–AD 337.* Cambridge, Mass.

Miller, M. C. J., and DeVoto, J. G. (1994) *Polybius and Pseudo-Hyginus: The Fortification of the Roman Camp.* Chicago.

Millett, M. (1990) *The Romanization of Britain.* Cambridge.

Millett, M. (2001) 'Approaches to urban societies', in S. James and M. Millett (eds), *Britons and Romans: Advancing an Archaeological Agenda.* CBA Research Report 125. York, 60–66.

Millett, M. (2002) 'Roman interaction in north west Iberia', *OJA* 20.2: 157–70.

Mitchell, T. (1990) 'Everyday metaphors of power', *Theory and Society* 19: 545–77.

Mitford, T. B. (1950) 'New inscriptions from Roman Cyprus', *Opuscula archaeologica* 6: 1–95.

Mitteis, L., and Wilcken, U. (1912) *Gründzüge und Chrestomathie der Papyrus-Kunde.* Leipzig.

Mitthof, F. (2000) 'Soldaten und Veteranen in der Gesellschaft des romischen Ägypten (1.-2.Jh. n. Chr.)', in G. Alföldy, B. Dobson, and W. Eck (eds), *Kaiser, Heer und Gesellschaft in der Römischen Kaiserzeit.* Heidelberg, 377–405.

Mócsy, A. (1962) 'Hivatali jelvény a sárszentmiklósi kocsisírban', *Fol. arch.* 14: 35–9.

Mócsy, A. (1974) *Pannonia and Upper Moesia.* London.

Moga, V. (1996) 'Inscriptions inédites à Apulum', in M. Porumb (ed.), *Omaggio a Dinu Adamesteanu*. Bibliotheca Ephemeris Napocensis, Clusium. Cluj, 183–5.

Mommsen, T. (1884) 'Die Conscriptionsordnung der römischen Kaiserzeit', *Hermes* 19: 1–79, 210–34.

Mommsen, T. (1905) *Gesammelte Schriften VI*. Berlin.

Mommsen, T. (1954–1956) *Römische Geschichte*, vols 1–3. Leipzig.

Moore, C. H. (1980) *Tacitus II: The Histories I–III*. Cambridge, Mass.

Morales, H. (2007) *Classical Mythology: A Very Short Introduction*. Oxford.

Morillo, A., and Aurrecoecha, J. (2006) *The Roman Army in Hispania: An Archaeological Guide*. León.

Mroszewicz, L. (1989) 'Die Veteranen in den Munizipalräten an Rhein und Donau zur hohen Kaiserzeit (I.–III. Jh.)', *Eos* 77: 65–80.

Mundle, I. (1961) 'Dea Caelestis in der Religionspolitik des Septimius Severus und der Julia Domna', *Historia* 10: 228–37.

Nash, D. (1984) 'The basis of contact between Britain and Gaul in the Late Pre-Roman Iron Age', in S. Macready and F. H. Thompson (eds), *Cross Channel Trade between Gaul and Britain in the Pre-Roman Iron Age*. London, 92–107.

Neer, W. van, (1997) 'Archaeozoological data on the food provisioning of Roman settlements in the Eastern Desert of Egypt', *Archaeozoologia* 9: 137–54.

Neer, W. van, and Ervynck, A. (1998) 'The faunal remains', in S. Sidebotham and W. Wendrich (eds), *Berenike 1996*. Leiden, 349–88.

Neer, W. van, and Lentacker, A. (1996) 'The faunal remains', in S. Sidebotham and W. Wendrich (eds), *Berenike 1995*. Leiden, 337–55.

Neumann, G. (1983) 'Die Sprachverhältnisse in den germanischen Provinzen des römischen Reiches', *ANRW* II 29.2: 1061–88.

Niblett, B. R. K. (1999) *The Excavation of a Ceremonial Site at Folly Lane, Verulamium*. Britannia Monograph Series 14. London.

Nicolay, J. A. W. (2002) 'Interpreting military equipment and horse gear from non-military contexts: the role of veterans', *Gesellschaft pro Vindonissa, Jahresbericht* 2001: 53–66.

Nicolay, J. A. W. (2003) 'The use and significance of military equipment and horse gear from non-military contexts in the Batavian area: continuity from the Late Iron Age into the Early Roman period', in T. Grünewald and S. Seibel (eds), *Kontinuität und Diskontinuität: Germania Inferior am Beginn und am Ende der römischen Herrschaft*. Berlin, 414–35.

Nicolay, J. A. W. (2008) *Armed Batavians: Use and Significance of Weaponry and Horse Gear from Non-military Contexts in the Rhine Delta (50 BC to AD 450)*. Amsterdam.

Nikolov, D. (1976) *The Thraco-Roman Villa Rustica near Chatalka, Stara Zagora, Bulgaria*. BAR Supplementary Series 17. Oxford.

Nock, A. D. (1952) 'The Roman army and the Roman religious year', *Harvard Theological Review* 45.4: 188–252.

Nosch, M. (ed.) (2012) *Wearing the Cloak: Dressing the Soldier in Roman Times*. Oxford.

Noy, D. (2001) '"A sight unfit to see": Jewish reaction to the Roman imperial cult', *Classics Ireland* 8: 68–83.

Obmann, J. (1999) 'Waffen: Statuszeichen oder alltäglicher Gebrauchsgegenstand?', in H. von Hesberg (ed.), *Das Militär als Kulturträger in römischer Zeit*. Cologne, 189–200.

O'Connor, T. (1986) 'The animal bones', in J. D. Zienkiewicz (ed.), *The Legionary Fortress Baths at Caerleon II: The Finds*. Cardiff, 225–48.

Ogilvie, R. M., and Richmond, I. A. (1967) *Cornelii Taciti Agricola*. Oxford.

Oldenstein, J. (1976) *Zur Ausrüstung römischer Auxiliareinheiten: Studien zu Beschlägen und Zierat an der Ausrüstung der römischen Auxiliareinheiten des obergermanisch-raetischen Limesgebietes aus dem zweiten und dritten Jahrhundert n. Chr.* Sonderdruck aus Bericht der Römisch-Germanischen Kommission 57. Mainz.

Oliver, J. H. (1953) *The Ruling Power: A Study of the Roman Empire in the Second Century after Christ through the Roman Oration of Aelius Aristides.* Philadelphia.

Olsen, K. (2010) ‘"Beware the ill-girt boy": tunics, status and masculinity in Roman antiquity’. Paper presented at Roman Archaeology Conference, Oxford.

Oltean, I. A. (2007) *Dacia. Landscape, Colonisation, Romanisation.* London.

Oltean, I. A. (2009) ‘Dacian ethnic identity and the Roman army’, in W. S. Hanson (ed.), *The Army and Frontiers of Rome: Papers offered to David J. Breeze on the occasion of his sixty-fifth birthday and his retirement from Historic Scotland.* JRA Supplementary Series 74. Portsmouth, RI, 90–102.

Oltean, I. A., and Hanson, W. S. (2001) ‘Military *vici* in Roman Dacia: an aerial perspective’, *Acta Musei Napocensis* 5: 505–12.

Oltean, I. A., Radeanu, V. and Hanson, W. S. (2005) ‘New discoveries in the military vicus of the auxiliary fort at Micia’, in Z. Visy (ed.), *Proceedings of the XIXth International Congress of Roman Frontier Studies.* Pécs 351–356.

Omissi, D. (1994) *The Sepoy and the Raj: The Indian Army, 1860–1940.* London.

Opper, T. (2008) *Hadrian: Empire and Conflict.* London.

Otto, W. F. (1910) ‘Genius’, *Realencyclopädie der classischen Altertumswissenschaft* 7: 1155–70.

Owen, O. A. (1992) ‘Eildon Hill North’, in J. S. Rideout, O. A. Owen, and E. L. Halpin (eds), *Hillforts of Southern Scotland.* Edinburgh, 21–72.

Parker, H. M. D. (1928) *The Roman Legion.* Oxford.

Pastor Muqoz, M. (1977) *Los astures durante el imperio romano.* Oviedo.

Pattison, R. (1982) *On Literacy: The Politics of the Word from Homer to the Age of Rock.* Oxford.

Peacock, D. P. S., and Maxfield, V. A. (1997) *Mons Claudianus: Survey and Excavation.* Institut français d’archéologie orientale. Paris.

Peers, D. M. (1999) ‘Imperial vice: sex, drink and the health of British troops in north Indian cantonments 1800–1858’, in D. Killingray and D. Omissi (eds), *Guardians of Empire.* Manchester, 25–52.

Pekáry, T. (1985) *Das römische Kaiserbildnis in Staat, Kult und Gesselschaft. Das römische Herrscherbild III 5.* Berlin.

Pekáry, T. (1986) ‘Das Opfer vor dem Kaiserbild’, *BJ* 186: 91–103.

Perdrizet, P. (1911) ‘Le bronze de Conflans’, *Mémoires de la Société d’archéologie lorraine* 61: 1–8.

Perkins, A. (1959) *The Excavations at Dura-Europos. Final Report V,* pt 1: *Parchments and Papyri.* New Haven, Conn.

Perkins, A. (1973) *The Art of Dura-Europos.* Oxford.

Pernet, L. (2010) *Armement et auxiliaires gaulois (IIe et Ier siècles avant notre ère).* Montagnac.

Perring, D., Roskams, S., with Allen, P. (1991) *The Archaeology of Roman London,* vol. 2: *Early Development of Roman London West of the Walbrook.* CBA Research Report 70. London.

Petculescu, L. (1991) ‘*Utere felix* and *optime con(serva)*: mounts from Dacia’, in V. A. Maxfield and M. J. Dobson (eds), *Roman Frontier Studies 1989.* Exeter, 392–6.

Petculescu, L. (1995) ‘Military equipment graves in Roman Dacia’, *JRMES* 6: 105–45.

Petculescu, L., and Gheorghe, P. (1979) ‘Coiful roman de la Bumbeşti’, *Studii şi cervatari de Istorie Veche şi arheologie* 30: 603–6.

Petersen, H. (1966) ‘New evidence for the relations between Romans and Parthians’, *Berytus* 16: 61–9.

Petolescu, C. M. (1986) ‘Dacia’, *LIMC* 3.1: 310–12.

Petrikovits, H. von, (1952) ‘Troiaritt und Geranostanz’, in G. Marco (ed.), *Beiträge zur älteren europäischen Kulturgeschichte: Festschrift für Rudolf Egger.* Klagenfurt, 126–43.

Petrikovits, H. von, (1975) *Die Innenbauten römischer Legionslager während der Prinzi-patszeit.* Abhandlungen der Rheinisch-Westfählischen Akademie der Wissenschaften 46. Opladen.

Phang, S. E. (2001) *The Marriage of Roman Soldiers (13 BC–AD 235): Law and Family in the Imperial Army.* Leiden.

Picard, G. (1944) *Castellum Dimmidi.* Algiers.

Picard, G. (1963) 'Glanum et les origines de l'art romano-provençal, I: Architecture', *Persée* 21: 111–24.

Picard, G. (1964) 'Glanum et les origines de l'art romano-provençal, II: Sculpture', *Persée* 22: 1–21.

Piso, I., and Diaconescu, A. (1999) 'Testo epigrafico, supporto architettonico e contesto archeologico nei fori di Sarmizegetusa', in *XI Congress Internazionale di Epigrafia Greca e Latina.* Rome, 125–37.

Pitts, M. (2004) 'Military diploma scrapped', *British Archaeology* 77: 8.

Pitts, M. (2006) 'Unique Roman tombstone may leave UK', *British Archaeology* 87: 6.

Pohl, W. (1998) 'Telling the difference: signs of ethnic identity', in W. Pohl and H. Reimitz (eds), *Strategies of Distinction: the Construction of Ethnic Communities, 300-800.* Leiden, 17–69.

Pollard, N. (1996) 'The Roman army as "total institution"' in the Near East? Dura-Europos as a case study', in D. L. Kennedy (ed.), *The Roman Army in the East. JRA* Supplementary Series 18. Portsmouth, RI, 211–27.

Pollard, N. (2000) *Soldiers, Cities and Civilians in Roman Syria.* Ann Arbor, Michigan.

Pop, C. (2000) 'Un petit tropaeum en bronze découvert dans la Dacie romaine', in H. Ciugudean and V. Moga (eds), *Army and Urban Development in the Danubian Provinces of the Roman Empire.* Alba Iulia, 333–5.

Poulter, A. (1987) 'Townships and village',. in J. Wacher (ed.), *The Roman World.* London, 388–411.

Poulter, A. G., and Blagg, T. F. C. (1995) *Nicopolis ad Istrum: A Roman, Late Roman and Early Byzantine City. Excavations 1985-1992.* London.

Préaux, C. (1954) 'Sur l'écriture des ostraca thébains d'époque romaine', *JEA* 40: 83–7.

Precht, G. (1975) *Das Grabmal des Lucius Poblicius: Rekonstruktion und Aufbau.* Cologne.

Price, S. R. F. (1984) *Rituals and Power.* Cambridge.

Raaflaub, K. (1980) 'The political significance of Augustus' military reforms', in W. S. Hanson and L. Keppie (eds), *Roman Frontier Studies XII 1979.* BAR International Series 71. Oxford, 1005–25.

Rainbird, J. S. (1969) 'Tactics at Mons Graupius', *Classical Review* 19: 11–12.

Rankin, D. (1995) *Tertullian and the Church.* Cambridge.

Rea, J. (1977) 'Troops for Mauretania', *ZPE* 26: 223–7.

Reddé, M. (1994) 'Casques de parade et culte impérial', *Latomus* 226: 663–8.

Reece, R. (1987) *Coinage in Roman Britain.* London.

Reece, R. (1988) *My Roman Britain.* Cirencester.

Reece, R. (1997) *The Future of Roman Military Archaeology.* Tenth Annual Caerleon Lecture, National Museums and Galleries of Wales.

Reeves, M. B. (2004) 'The *feriale Duranum,* Roman military religion, and Dura-Europos: a reassessment', Ph.D thesis, State University of New York at Buffalo.

Reinhold, M. (1971) 'Usurpation of status and status symbols in the Roman Empire', *Historia* 20: 275–302.

Remesal Rodriguez, J. (2002) 'Baetica and Germania: notes on the concept of provincial interdependence in the Roman Empire', in P. Erdkamp (ed.), *The Roman Army and the Economy.* Amsterdam, 293–303.

Reuter, M. (1999) 'Studien zu den numeri des römischen Heeres in der mittleren Kaiser-zeit', *Bericht der Römisch-Germanischen Kommission* 80: 357–569.

Ribera i Lacomba, A., with Calvo Galvez, M. (1995) 'La primera arqueológica de la destrucción de Valentia por Pompeyo', *JRA* 8: 19–40.

Richardson, J. (2002) 'The new Augustan edicts from northwest Spain', *JRA* 15.2: 411–15.

Richmond, I. A. (1943) 'Roman legionaries at Corbridge', *Archaeologia Aeliana*, 4th ser., 21: 127–224.

Richmond, I. A. (1945) The *Sarmatae, Bremetennacum Veteranorum* and the *Regio Bremetennacensis*', *JRS* 35: 15–29.

Richmond, I. A. (1946) 'Part of the stem of a Roman monumental *candelabrum* of stone, from York', *Antiquaries Journal* 26: 1–10.

Richmond, I. A. (1955) 'Roman Britain and Roman military antiquities', *Proceedings of the British Academy* 41: 297–315.

Richmond, I. A. (1962a) 'The Roman army and Roman religion', *Bulletin of the John Rylands Library* 45.1: 185–97.

Richmond, I. A. (1962b) 'The Roman siege works of Masada, Israel', *JRS* 52: 142–55.

Richmond, I. A. (1982) *Trajan's Army on Trajan's Column*. London.

Richmond, I. A., and McIntyre, J. (1939) 'The Agricolan fort at Fendoch', *Proceedings of the Society of Antiquaries of Scotland* 73: 110–54

Rilinger, R. (1988) *Humiliores-Honestiores: zu einer sozialen Dichotomie im Strafrecht der römischen Kaiserzeit*. Munich.

Ritterling, E. (1913) *Das frührömische Lager bei Hoffheim im Taunus*. Annalen des Vereins für Nassauische Altertumskunde und Geschichtsforschung 40. Wiesbaden.

Rives, J. B. (1999) 'The Decree of Decius and the religion of empire', *JRS* 89: 135–54.

Robinson, H.R. (1975) *The Armour of Imperial Rome*. London.

Roldán Hervás, J. M. (1974) *Hispania y el ejército romano: contribución a la historia social de la España Antigua*. Salamanca.

Roldán Hervás, J. M. (1983) 'La conquista del Norte de Hispania y la participación de los astures en el ejército imperial romano. ', *Lancia* 1: 119–38.

Rolland, H. (1969) *Le mausolée de Glanum (Saint-Rémy-de-Provence)*. Paris.

Ross, A. (1967) *Pagan Celtic Britain: Studies in Iconography and Tradition*. London.

Ross, A., and Feachem, R. (1976) 'Ritual rubbish? The Newstead pits', in J. V. S. Megar (ed.), *To Illustrate the Monuments*ondon, 230–37.

Rossi, L. (1971) *Trajan's Column and the Dacian Wars*. London.

Rost, A., and Wilbers-Rost, S. (2010) 'Weapons at the battlefield of Kalkriese', *Gladius* 30: 117–36.

Rostovtzeff, M. I. (1934) *The Excavations at Dura-Europos: Preliminary Report of the 5th Season of Work (1931–32)*. New Haven, Conn.

Rostovtzeff, M. I. (1938) *Dura Europos and its Art*. Oxford.

Rostovtzeff, M. I., Bellinger, A. R., Hopkins, C., and Welles, C. B. (1936) *The Excavations at Dura-Europos: Preliminary Report of the 6th Season of Work (1932–33)*. New Haven, Conn.

Rostovtzeff, M. I., Bellinger, A. R., Brown, F. E., and Welles, C. B. (1944) *The Excavations at Dura-Europos: Preliminary Report of the 9th Season of Work (1935–36)*, part 1: *The Agora and Bazaar*. New Haven, Conn.

Rostovtzeff, M. I., Bellinger, A. R., Brown, F. E., and Welles, C. B. (1952) *The Excavations at Dura-Europos: Preliminary Report of the 9th Season of Work (1935–36)*, part 3: *The Palace of the Dux Ripae and the Dolicheneum*. New Haven, Conn.

Rostovtzeff, M. I., Brown, F. E., and Welles, C.B. (1939) *The Excavations at Dura-Europos: Preliminary Report of the 7th-8th Season of Work (1933–34, 1934–35)*. New Haven, Conn.

Roth, J. P. (1999) *The Logistics of the Roman Army at War (264 BC–AD 35)*. Leiden.

Roussin, L. (1994) 'Costume in Roman Palestine: archaeological remains and the evidence from Mishnah', in J. L. Sebesta and L. Bonfante (eds), *The World of Roman Costume.* Madison, Wis., 182–90.

Rouveret, A. (1986) 'Tite-Live Histoire romaine IX, 40: la description des armées samnites ou les pièges de la symétrie', in A. Adam and A. Rouveret (eds), *Guerre et sociétiés en Italie (V–IV avant J-C.).* Paris, 91–120.

Rowell, H. T. (1939) 'The *honesta missio* from the *numeri* of the Roman imperial army', *Yale Classical Studies* 6: 73–108.

Roxan, M. (1973) 'The auxilia of Mauretania Tingitana', *Latomus* 32: 835–55.

Roxan, M. (1978) *Roman Military Diplomas 1954–1977.* Institute of Archaeology Occasional Publication 2. London.

Roxan, M. (1985) *Roman Military Diplomas 1978–84.* Institute of Archaeology Occasional Publication 9. London.

Roxan, M. (1986) 'Observations on the reasons for the changes in formula in diplomas circa AD 140', in W. Eck and H. Wolff (eds), *Heer und Integrationspolitik: die römischen Militärdiplome als historische Quelle.* Passau, 265–6.

Roxan, M. (1989) 'Findspots of military diplomas of the Roman auxiliary army', *University College London Institute of Archaeology Bulletin* 26: 127–81.

Roxan, M. (1991) 'Women on the frontiers', in V. A. Maxfield and M. J. Dobson (eds), *Roman Frontier Studies 1989.* Exeter, 462–7.

Roxan, M. (1994) *Roman Military Diplomas 1985–1993.* Institute of Archaeology Occasional Publication 14. London.

Roxan, M. (1997) 'Settlement of the veterans of the auxilia: a preliminary study', in W. Groenman-van Waateringe, B. van Beek, W. Willems, and S. Wynia (eds), *Roman Frontier Studies 1995: Proceedings of the XVIth Roman Frontier Studies Conference 1995.* Oxbow Monograph 91. Oxford, 483–92.

Roxan, M. (2000) 'Veteran settlement of the auxilia in Germania', in Alföldy et al. (2000), 307–26.

Roxan, M., and Holder, P. (2003) *Roman Military Diplomas IV.* London.

Roymans, N. (1990) *Tribal Societies in Northern Gaul.* Amsterdam.

Roymans, N. (1993) 'Romanisation and the transformation of a martial elite-ideology in a frontier province', in P. Brun, S. van der Leeuw, and C. R. Whittaker (eds), *Frontières d'empire.* Nemours, 33–51.

Roymans, N. (2004) *Ethnic Identity and Imperial Power: The Batavians in the Early Roman Empire.* Amsterdam.

Roymans, N. (2009) 'Die Bataver: zur Entstehung eines Soldatenvolkes', in S. Berke (ed.), *2000 Jahre Varusschlacht Mythos.* Stuttgart, 85–98.

Roymans, N. (2011) 'Ethnic recruitment, returning veterans and the diffusion of Roman cultural among rural populations in the Rhineland frontier zone', in N. Roymans and T. Derks (eds), *Villa Landscapes in the Roman North: Economy, Culture and Lifestyles.* Amsterdam Archaeological Studies 17. Amsterdam, 139–60.

Roymans, N., and Derks, T. (1990) 'Ein keltisch-römischer Kultbezirk bei Empel (Niederlande) ', *Archäologisches Korrespondenzblatt* 20: 443–51.

Roymans, N., and Derks, T. (1994) *Der Tempel van Empel: een Herculesheiligdom in het woongebied van de Bataven.* 's-Hertogenbosch.

Roymans, N., and Derks, T., and Heeren, S. (2007) 'Romeins wordern op het Bataafse platteland: een synthese', in N. Roymans, T. Derks, and S. Heeren (eds), *Een Bataafse gemeenschap in der wereld van het Romanise rijk: Opgravingen te Tiel-Passewaaij.* Utrecht, 11–32.

Rüpke, J. (1990) Domi Militiae: *die religiöse Konstruktion des Krieges in Rom.* Stuttgart.

Rusu-Pescaru, A. and Alicu, D. (2000) *Templele romane din Dacia.* Deva.

Saddington, D. B. (1975) 'Race relations in the early Roman Empire', *ANRW* II 3: 112–37.

Saddington, D. B. (1982) *The Development of the Roman Auxiliary Forces from Caesar to Vespasian.* Harare.

Saddington, D. B. (1991) 'The parameters of Romanization', in V. A. Maxfield and M. J. Dobson (eds), *Roman Frontier Studies 1989.* Exeter, 413–18.

Saddington, D. B. (1997) 'The 'politics' of the auxilia and the forging of auxiliary regimental identity', in W. Groenman-van Waateringe, B. L. van Beek, W. J. H. Willems, and S. L. Wynia (eds), *Roman Frontier Studies 1995: Proceedings of the XVIth Roman Frontier Studies Conference 1995.* Oxbow Monograph 91. Oxford, 493–6.

Saddington, D. B. (2009a) 'How Roman did auxiliaries become?', in A. Morillo, N. Hanel, and Martin, E. (eds), *Limes Congress XX Gladius.* Madrid, 1017–24.

Saddington, D. B. (2009b) 'Recruitment patterns and ethnic identities in Roman auxiliary regiments', in W. S. Hanson (ed.), *The Army and Frontiers of Rome: Papers offered to David J. Breeze on the occasion of his sixty-fifth birthday and his retirement from Historic Scotland. JRA* Supplementary Series 74. Portsmouth, RI, 83–9.

Sági, K. (1954) 'Die Ausgrabungen im römischen Gräberfeld von Intercissa im Jahr 1949', *Archaeologica Hungarica* 23: 61–123.

Salaman, G. (1974) *Community and Occupation.* Cambridge.

Saller, R. P., and Shaw, B. D. (1984) 'Tombstones and Roman family relations in the Principate: civilians, soldiers and slaves', *JRS* 74: 124–56.

Salmon, E. T. (1967) *Samnium and the Samnites.* Cambridge.

Sâmpetru, M. (1984) *Tropaeum Traiani: II Monumentele romane.* Bucharest

Sanie, S. (1981) *Cultele orientale în Dacia romană* 1. Bucharest.

Sauer, E. (1999) 'The Augustan army spa at Bourbonne-les-Bains', in Goldsworthy and Haynes (1999), 52–79.

Sayar, M. (1991) '*Equites singulares Augusti* in neuen Inschriften aus Anazarbos', *Epigraphica Anatolica* 17: 19–40.

Schäfer, A. (2001) 'Götter aus dem Rheingebiet in Dakien und Pannonien', in W. Spickermann (ed.), *Religion in den germanischen Provinzen Roms.* Tübingen, 259–84.

Schäfer, A. (2003) *Tempel und Kult in Sarmizegetusa.* Habilitationsschrift, Humboldt-Universität, Berlin.

Schallmayer, E. (2007) 'Archäologische Ausgraburen an Wp 5/4 "An der Laten Rüdigheimer Hohle" bei Ravolzhausen, Gemeinde Neuberg', in A. Thiel (ed.), *Forschungen zur Funktion des Limes: Beiträge zum Welterbe Limes* 2. Stuttgart, 57–81.

Scheid, J. (1990) *Romulus et ses frères: le collège des frères Arvales, modèle du culte public dans la Rome des empereurs.* BEFAR 275. Rome.

Scheidel, W. (2001) 'Roman age structure: evidence and models', *JRS* 91: 1–6.

Scheidel, W. (2010) 'Marriage, families, and survival: demographic aspects', in P. Erdkamp (ed.), *A Companion to the Roman Army.* London, 417–34.

Schindler, R. (1971) 'Ein Kriegergrab mit Bronzehelm der Spätlatenezeit aus Trier-Olewig: zum Problem des vor-römischen Trier', *Trier Zeitschriften* 34: 43–82.

Schleiermacher, M. (1984) *Romische Reitergrabsteine.* Bonn.

Schlüter, W. (1999) 'The battle of Teutoburg forest: archaeological research at Kalkreise near Osnabrück', in J. D. Creighton and R. J. A. Wilson (eds), *Roman Germany: Studies in Cultural Interaction. JRA* Supplementary Series 32. Portsmouth, RI, 125–59.

Schnurbein, S. von, (1979) 'Eine hölzerne Sica aus dem Römerlager Oberaden', *Germania* 57: 117–34.

Schnurbein, S. von, (1986) 'Dakisch-thrakische Soldaten im Romerlager Oberaden', *Germania* 64: 409–31.

Schönberger, H. (1953) 'Provinzialrömische Gräber mit Waffenbeigaben', *Saalburg Jahrbuch* 12: 53–6.

Schulten, A. (1933) *Masada: die Burg des Herodes und die römischen Lager.* Leipzig.

Schumacher, F. -J. (1989) 'Grab 2215: ein Treverkreiger in römischen Diensten', in A. Haffner (ed.), *Gräber Spiegel des Lebens*. Mainz, 265–74.

Schürer, E. (1973) *The History of the Jewish People in the Age of Jesus Christ*. Edinburgh.

Sealey, P.R. (1985) *Amphoras from the 1970 Excavations at Colchester Sheepen*. BAR Brit Series 142. Oxford.

Seyrig, H. (1941a) '. Postes romains sur la route de Médine', *Syria* 22: 218.

Seyrig, H. (1941b) 'Inscriptiones grecques de l'agora de Palmyre', *Syria* 22: 231–3.

Seyrig, H. (1952) 'Antiquités de la nécropole d'Émèse', *Syria* 29: 204–50.

Sharankov, N. (2011) 'Language and society in Roman Thrace', in I. P. Haynes (ed.), *Early Roman Thrace*. JRA Supplementary Series 82. Portsmouth, RI, 135–56

Shaw, B. D. (1983) 'Soldiers and society: the army in Numidia', *Opus* 2: 133–59.

Shaw, B. D. (1984) 'Bandits in the Roman Empire', *Past and Present* 105: 3–52.

Shaw, B. D. (1993) 'The bandit', in A. Giardina (ed.), *The Romans*. Chicago, 300–341.

Shaw, T. (1982) 'Roman cloaks, pt 1', *Exercitus* 1.4: 45–7.

Sherk, R. (1955) 'The 'inermes provinciae' of Asia Minor', *American Journal of Philology* 76: 400–413.

Sherk, R. (1957) 'Roman imperial troops in Macedonia and Achaea', *American Journal of Philology* 78: 52–62.

Sim, D., and Kaminski, J. (2012) *Roman Imperial Armour: The Production of Early Imperial Military Armour*. Oxford.

Simonett, C. (1935) 'Eine verzierte Schildbuckelplatte aus Vindonissa', *Anzeiger für Schweizeriche Altertumskunde* 37: 176–81.

Slofstra, J. (1983) 'An anthropological approach to the study of Romanization processes', in R. W. Brandt and J. Slofstra (eds), *Roman and Native in the Low Countries*. BAR International Series 184. Oxford, 43–70.

Smith, R. R. R. (1987) 'The imperial reliefs from the Sebasteion at Aphrodisias', *JRS* 77: 88–138.

Smith, W., and Lockwood, J. (1989) *Chambers Murray Latin–English Dictionary*. Edinburgh.

Snape, M. (1993) *Roman Brooches from North Britain: A Classification and Catalogue of Brooches from Sites on the Stanegate*. BAR British Series 235. Oxford.

Sommer, C. S. (1984) *The Military Vici in Roman Britain*. BAR British Series 129. Oxford.

Sommer, C. S. (1988) 'Kastellvicus und Kastell', *Fundberichte aus Baden-Württemberg* 13: 621–2.

Sommer, C. S. (1989) 'The inner and outer relations of the military fort to its *vicus*', in C. van Driel-Murray (ed.), *Roman Military Equipment: The Sources of Evidence*. BAR International Series 476. Oxford, 25–30.

Sommer, C. S. (1991) 'Life beyond the ditches: housing and planning of the military *vici* in upper Germany and Raetia', in V. A. Maxfield and M. J. Dobson (eds), *Roman Frontier Studies 1989*. Exeter, 472–6.

Sommer, C. S. (1995) '"Where did they put the horses?": Überlegungen zu Aufbau und Stärke römischer Auxiliartruppen und deren Unterbringung in den Kastellen', in *Provincialrömische Forschungen: Festschrift für Günter Ulbert zum 65. Geburtstag*. Espelkamp, 149–68.

Sommer, C. S. (1999a) 'The Roman army in SW Germany as an instrument of colonisation', in Goldsworthy and Haynes (1999), 81–93.

Sommer, C. S. (1999b) 'From conquered territory to Roman province: recent discoveries and debate on the Roman occupation of SW Germany', in J. D. Creighton and R. J. A. Wilson (eds), *Roman Germany: Studies in Cultural Interaction*. Portsmouth, RI, 160–98.

Southern, P. (1989) 'The *numeri* of the Roman imperial army', *Britannia* 20: 81–140.

Spaul, J. (1994) *Ala 2*. Andover.

Spaul, J. (2000) *Cohors 2: The Evidence for and a Short History of the Auxiliary Infantry Units of the Imperial Roman Army*. BAR International Series 841. Oxford.

Speidel, M. A. (1992) 'Roman army pay scales', *JRS* 82: 87–106.

Speidel, M. A. (1996) *Die römischen Schreibtafeln von Vindonissa*. Brugg.

Speidel, M. A. (1999) 'Stadt- and Lagerleben', in H. von Hesberg (ed.), *Das Militär als Kulturträger in römischer Zeit*. Cologne, 75–86.

Speidel, M. A. (2000) 'Sold und Wirtschaftslage der römischen Soldaten', in Alföldy et al. (2000), 65–96.

Speidel, M. A. (2007) 'Rekruten für ferne Provinzen: der Papyrus ChLA X 422 und die kaiserliche Rekruiterungszentrale', *ZPE* 163: 281–95.

Speidel, M. A. (2009) *Heer und Heerschaft im römischen Reich der hohen Kaiserzeit*. Stuttgart.

Speidel, M. A., and Lieb, H. (eds) (2007) *Militärdiplome: die Forschungsbeiträge der Berner Gespräche von 2004*. Stuttgart.

Speidel, M. P. (1973) 'The pay of the auxilia', *JRS* 63: 141–7.

Speidel, M. P. (1975) 'The rise of ethnic units in the Roman imperial army', *ANRW* II.3, 202–31.

Speidel, M. P. (1976) 'Citizen cohorts in the Roman imperial army', *TAPhA* 106: 339–48.

Speidel, M. P. (1977a) 'A thousand Thracian recruits for Mauretania Tingitana', *Antiquités africaines* 11: 161–73.

Speidel, M. P. (1977b) 'The Roman army in Arabia',. *ANRW* II. 8: 687–730.

Speidel, M. P. (1977c) 'The shrine of the *dii campestres* at Gemellae', *Antiquités africaines* 27: 111–18.

Speidel, M. P. (1978a) 'The cult of the *genii* in the Roman army and a new military deity', *ANRW* II 16.2: 1542–55.

Speidel, M. P. (1978b) *The Religion of Jupiter Dolichenus in the Roman Army*. Leiden.

Speidel, M. P. (1980) 'Lixa of the Third Thracian Cohort in Syria', *ZPE* 38: 146–8.

Speidel, M. P. (1981a) 'Addendum: Marcus Titius. *ZPE* 42: 272.

Speidel, M. P. (1981b) '*Ala Maurorum*? Colloquial names for Roman army units', *Anagennesis* 1: 89–92.

Speidel, M. P. (1982) 'Auxiliary units named after their commanders: four new cases from Egypt', *Aegyptus* 62: 165–72.

Speidel, M. P. (1982/3) 'The Roman army in Judea under the procurators', *Ancient Society* 13/14: 233–40.

Speidel, M. P. (1983) 'The Roman army in Asia Minor: recent epigraphical discoveries and research. ', in S. Mitchell (ed.), *Armies and Frontiers in Roman and Byzantine Anatolia*. Oxford, 7–34.

Speidel, M. P. (1984) *Roman Army Studies I*. Amsterdam

Speidel, M. P. (1987) 'Horsemen in the Pannonian *alae*', *Saalburg Jahrbuch* 43: 61–5.

Speidel, M. P. (1988) 'Nubia's Roman garrison', *ANRW* II 10.1: 221–4.

Speidel, M. P. (1989) 'Work to be done on the organisation of the Roman army', *Bulletin of the Insitute of Archaeology* 26: 99–106.

Speidel, M. P. (1992) *Roman Army Studies II*. Stuttgart.

Speidel, M. P. (1994a) *Die Denkmäler der Kaiserreiter (Equites singulares Augusti)*. Bonn.

Speidel, M. P. (1994b) *Riding for Caesar: The Roman Emperors' Horse Guards*. London.

Speidel, M. P. (2004) *Ancient Germanic Warriors: Warrior Styles from Trajan's Column to Icelandic Sagas*. London.

Speidel, M. P. (2005) 'Lebensbeschreibungen traianisch-hadrianischer Gardereiter', in K. Vössing (ed.), *Biographie und Prosopographie: Internationales Kolloquium zum 65. Geburtstag von Anthony R. Birley*. Historia Einzelschrift 178. Stuttgart, 73–89.

Speidel, M. P. (2006) *Emperor Hadrian's Speeches to the African Army: A New Text*. Mainz.

Spickermann, W. (2001) *Religion in den germanischen Provinzen Roms*. Tübingen.

Stadter, P. A. (1980) *Arrian of Nicomedia*. Chapel Hill, NC.

Starcky, J. (1949) *Inventaire des inscriptions de Palmyre X*. Damascus.

Stary, P. F. (1994) *Zur eisenzeitlichen Bewaffnung und Kampfweise auf der iberischen Halbinsel*. Berlin.

Stavrianos, L. S. (1957) 'Antecedents to the Balkan revolutions of the 19th century', *Journal of Modern History* 29.4: 335–48.

Stein, E. (1932) *Die kaiserlichen Beamten und Truppenkörper im römischen Deutschland unter dem Prinzipat*. Vienna.

Stîngă, I.(1996) 'L'habitat romain de Gârla Mare: dép. de Mehedinți (II–IIIe siècles apr. J.-C', in *Cahiers des Portes de Fer*. Belgrade, 235–42.

Stoll, O. (1992) *Die Skulpturenausstattung römischer Militäranlagen an Rhein und Donau: der Obergermanisch-Rätische Limes I, II*. St Katherinen.

Stoll, O. (1995) 'Die Fahnenwache in der römischen Armee', *ZPE* 108: 107–18.

Stoll, O. (1998) 'Offizier und gentleman': der römische Offizier als Kultfunktionär', *Klio* 80: 134–62.

Stoll, O. (2001a) *Zwischen Integration und Abgrenzung: die Religion des Römischen Heeres im Nahen Osten*. Mainzer Althistorische Studien Band 3. St Katherinen.

Stoll, O. (2001b) *Römisches Heer und Gesellschaft: Gesammelte Beiträge 1991–1999*. Stuttgart.

Stoll, O. (2010) 'The religion of the armies', in P. Erdkamp (ed.), *A Companion to the Roman Army*. London, 451–76.

Summerfeld, J. (1997) 'The small finds in Birdoswald', in T. Wilmott (ed.), *Excavations of a Roman Fort on Hadrian's Wall and its Successor Settlements: 1987–92*. English Heritage Archaeological Report 14. London, 269–312.

Swan, V. G. (1992) '*Legio* VI and its men: African legionaries in Britain', *Journal of Roman Pottery Studies* 5: 1–33.

Swan, V. G. (1997) 'Vexillations and the garrisons of Britannia in the second and early third centuries: a ceramic view-point', in W. Groenmann-van Waateringe, B. L. van Beek, W. J. H. Willems, and S. L. Wynia (eds), *Roman Frontier Studies 1995: Proceedings of the XVIth Roman Frontier Studies Conference 1995*. Oxbow Monograph 91. Oxford, 289–94.

Swan, V. G. (1999) 'The Twentieth Legion and the history of the Antonine Wall reconsidered', *Proceedings of the Antiquaries of Scotland* 129: 399–480.

Swan, V. G. (2009) *Ethnicity, Conquest and Recruitment: Two Case Studies from the Northern Military Provinces*. JRA Supplementary Series 72. Portsmouth, RI.

Swan, V. G., and McBride, R. M. (2002) 'A Rhineland potter at the legionary fortress of York', in M. Aldhouse-Green and P. Webster (eds), *Artefacts and Archaeology: Aspects of the Celtic and Roman World*. Cardiff, 190–234.

Syme, R. (1958) *Tacitus*. Oxford.

Syme, R. (1971) *Emperors and Biography*. Oxford.

Szabó, K. (1986) 'Le camp romain d'Intercisa : récente trouvaille du Danube', in C. Unz (ed.), *Studien zu den Militärgrenzung Roms III*. Stuttgart, 421–5.

Tate, G. (1992) *Les campagnes de la Syrie du nord au IIe au VIIe siècle*. Paris.

Tchalenko, G. (1953–1958) *Villages antiques de la Syrie du nord*, vols 1–3. Paris.

Téglás, G. (1906) 'A várhelyi syrus templom', *Archaeologiai Értesítő* 26: 321–30.

Țentea, O., and Matei-Popescu, F. (2004) 'Alae et cohortes Daciae et Moesiae. *Acta Musei Napocensis* 39–40.1: 259–96.

Terrenato, N. (1998) 'The Romanization of Italy: global acculturation or cultural bricolage?', in C. Forcey, J. Hawthorne, and R. Witcher (eds), *TRAC 97*. Oxford, 20–27.

Theodossiev, N. (1998) 'The dead with golden faces: Dasaretian, Pelagonian, Mygdonian and Boeotian funeral masks', *OJA* 17.3: 345–67.

Thomas, D. L. (1980) 'The army and the frontier', unpublished DPhil., Oxford.

Thomas, J. (1976) *Textbook of Roman Law*. Amsterdam.

Thompson, L. A. (1989) *Romans and Blacks*. London.

Thorburn, J. E. (2003) '*Lixae* and *calones*: following the Roman army'. *Classical Bulletin* 79.1: 47–61.

Thulin, C. (1913) *Corpus Agrimensorum Romanorum* 1.1. Leipzig.

Tomlin, R. S. O. (1988) *The Curse Tablets in the Temple of Sulis Minerva at Bath*, vol. 2: *The Finds from the Sacred Spring*. Oxford University Committee for Archaeology Monograph 16. Oxford, 59–270.

Tomlin, R. S. O. (1995) 'Addenda and corrigenda', in R. G. Collingwood and R. P. Wright (eds), *The Roman Inscriptions of Britain*, vol. 1: *Inscriptions on Stone*, 2nd edn. Bridgend, 751–800.

Tomlin, R. S. O. (1999) 'The missing lances, or Making the machine work', in Goldsworthy and Haynes (1999), 127–38.

Tomlin, R. S. O., and Hassall, M. W. C. (2003) 'II. Inscriptions', *Britannia* 34: 360–82.

Tomlin, R. S. O., and Hassall, M. W. C. (2004) '. III. Inscriptions', *Britannia* 35: 335–49.

Tonkin, E., McDonald, M., and Chapman, M. (1996) 'History and ethnicity', in J. Hutchinson and A. D. Smith (eds), *Ethnicity*. Oxford, 18–24.

Tönnies, F. (1955) *Community and Association*. London.

Toutain, J. (1967) *Les cultes païens dans l'empire romain*, pt 1: *Les provinces latines*, vol. 1. Paris, 438–64.

Tovar, A. (1968) *El latin de Hispania: aspectos léxicos de la romanización*. Madrid.

Tringham, R. E. (1991) 'Households with faces: the challenge of gender in prehistoric architectural remains', in J. Gero and M. Conkey (eds), *Engendering Archaeology: Women and Prehistory*. Oxford, 93–131.

Trow, S. D. (1990) 'By the northern shores of Ocean: some observations on acculturation process at the edge of the Roman world', in M. Millett and T. Blagg (eds), *The Early Roman Empire in the West*. Oxford, 103–18.

Trudgill, P. (1995) *Sociolinguistics: An Introduction to Language and Society*. Harmondsworth.

Tudor, D. (1963) *Collegium duplariorum. Latomus* 22: 240–41.

Turcan, R. (1996) *The Cults of the Roman Empire*. Oxford.

Ulbert, G. (1985) *Càceres el Viejo: ein spätrepublikanisches Legionslager in Spanisch-Extremadura*. Mainz.

Untermann, J. (1990) *Monumenta Linguarum Hispanicarum, 3: Die iberischen Inschriften aus Spanien*. Wiesbaden.

Urban, R. (1985) *Der 'Bataveraufstand' und die Erhebung des Iulius Classicus*. Trier.

Uslar, R. von, (1934) 'Die germanische Keramik in den Kastellen Zugmantel und Saalburg', *Saalburg Jahrbuch* 8: 61–96.

Uslar, R. von, (1980) 'Germanische Keramik aus Steinkastell und vicus in Heddernheim und aus dem Osthafen in Frankfurt: zur Entstehung der rhein-wesergermanischen Keramik', *Fundberichte aus Hesen* 19/20: 697–724.

Veen, M. van der, and Hamilton-Dyer, S. (1998) 'A life of luxury in the desert? The food and fodder supply to Mons Claudianus', *JRA* 11: 101–16.

Velkov, V., and Gocheva, Z. (1972) 'Die Thrakische Festung Čertigrad im Balkan (ant. Hämus) ', *Thracia* 1: 121–43.

Venedikov, I and Venedikov, A. (1960) *Prehistoric and Antique Relics in Bulgaria*. Sofia.

Verdery, K. (1996) *What Was Socialism and What Comes Next?* Princeton, NJ.

Vertet, H. (1998) 'Lezoux-La Graufesenque et la Romanisation', in J. Bird (ed.), *Form and Fabric: Studies in Rome's Material Past in honour of B. R. Hartley*. Oxford, 127–32.

Visy, Z. (1977) *Intercisa: Dunaújváros in der Römerzeit*. Kecskemét.

Visy, Z. (2003) *The Roman Army in Pannonia*. Pécs.

Vittinghoff, F. (1950) 'Zur angeblichen Barbarisierung des römischen Heeres durch die Verbände der Numeri', *Historia* 3: 389–407.

Völling, T. (1992) 'Dreikreisplattensporen: Anmerkungen zu einem Spornfund aus Hopferstadt, Ldkr. Würzburg', *Archäologisches Korrespondenzblatt* 22: 393–402.

Völling, T. (1993) 'Sporen aus Ringelsdorf, Niederösterreich', *Archaeologia Austriaca* 77: 105–11.

Waateringe, W. G. van, (1989) 'Food for soldiers, food for thought', in J. C. Barrett, A. P. Fitzpatrick, and L. Macinnes (eds), *Barbarians and Romans in North West Europe*. BAR International Series 471. Oxford, 96–107.

Waateringe, W. G. van, (1997) 'Classical authors and the diet of Roman soldiers: true or false?', in W. Groenman-van Waateringe, B. L. van Beek, W. J. H. Willems, and S. L. Wynia (eds), *Roman Frontier Studies 1995: Proceedings of the XVIth Roman Frontier Studies Conference 1995*. Oxbow Monograph 91. Oxford, 161–265.

Wacher, J., and McWhirr, A. (1982) *Cirencester: Excavations 1. The Early Roman Occupation at Cirencester*. Cirencester.

Wagner, W. (1938) *Die Dislokation der römischen Auxiliarformationen in den Provinzen Noricum, Pannonien, Moesien und Dakien*. Berlin.

Wagner, W. (1963) 'Zur ala Pansiana', *Germania* 41: 317–27.

Walker, S., and Bierbrier, M. (1997) *Ancient Faces: Mummy Portraits from Roman Egypt*. London.

Wallace-Hadrill, A. (1989) 'Rome's cultural revolution', *JRS* 79: 157–64.

Watson, G. R. (1959) 'The pay of the Roman army: the auxiliary forces', *Historia* 8: 372–8.

Watson, G. R. (1965) 'Discharge and resettlement in the Roman army: the *praemia militiae*', in E. C. Welskopf (ed.), *Neue Beitrdge zur Geschichte der Alten Welt*. Berlin, 147–62.

Watson, G. R. (1969) *The Roman Soldier*. Bristol.

Watson, G. R. (1974) 'Documentation in the Roman army', *ANRW* II 1: 493–507.

Waurick, G. (1979) 'Die Schutzwaffen im Numidischen Grab von Es Soumâa', in H. G. Horn and C. B. Rüger (eds), *Die Numider*. Theinland, 305–32.

Waurick, G. (1986) 'Helm und Maske', in C. Unz (ed.), *Studien zu den Militargrenzen Roms III: 13. Internationaler Limeskongress*. Aalen, 794–8.

Weber, E. (1977) *Peasants into Frenchmen: The Modernization of Rural France 1870–1914*. London.

Webster, G. (1966) 'Fort and town in Early Roman Britain', in J. S. Wacher (ed.), *The Civitas Capitals of Roman Britain*. Leicester, 31–45.

Webster, G. (1986) 'Standards and standard-bearers in the *alae*', *BJ* 186: 105–16.

Webster, G. (1988) *Fortress into City: The Consolidation of Roman Britain in the First Century* AD. London.

Webster, G. (1998) *The Roman Imperial Army*, 3rd edn. Norman, Okla.

Webster, J. (1995) '*Interpretatio*: Roman word power and the Celtic gods'. *Britannia* 26: 153–62.

Webster, J. (1996) 'Ethnographic barbarity: colonial discourse and "Celtic warrior societies"', in J. Webster and N. Cooper (eds), *Roman Imperialism: Post-colonial Perspectives*. Leicester Archaeology Monographs 3. Leicester, 111–23.

Webster, J. (2001) 'Creolizing the Roman provinces', *AJA* 105.2: 209–25.

Webster, J. (2008a) 'Less beloved: Roman archaeology, slavery and the failure to compare', *Archaeological Dialogues* 15.2: 103–23.

Webster, J. (2008b) 'Slavery, archaeology and the politics of analogy', *Archaeological Dialogues* 15.2: 139–49.

Weeber, K. (1974) '*Troiae Lusus*: Alter und Entstehung eines Reiterspiels', *Ancient Society* 5: 171–96.

Weiss, P. (2006) 'Neue Militärdiplome für den Exercitus von Britannia', *ZPE* 156: 245–54.

Weiss, P. (2009) 'Statthalter und Konsuldaten in neuen Militärdiplomen', *ZPE* 171: 231–52.

Weiss, P. (2012) 'Auxiliardiplome für die Dakischen Provinzen, Pannonia Superior und eine *Provincia Inermis*', *ZPE* 181: 183–201.

Weller, J. (1992) *Wellington in the Peninsula 1808–1814*. London.

Welles, C. B. (1941) 'The epitaph of Julius Terentius', *Harvard Theological Review* 34: 79.

Welles, C. B., Fink, R. O., and Gilliam, J. F. (1959) *The Excavations at Dura-Europos, Final Report V*, pt 1: *The Parchments and Papyri*. New Haven, Conn.

Wells, C. M. (1972) *The German Policy of Augustus*. Oxford.

Wells, C. M. (1997) '"The daughters of the regiment": sisters and wives in the Roman army', in W. Groenman-van Waateringe, B. L. van Beek, W. J. H. Willems, and S. L. Wynia (eds), *Roman Frontier Studies 1995: Proceedings of the XVIth Roman Frontier Studies Conference 1995*. Oxbow Monograph 91. Oxford, 571–4.

Wells, P. S. (1999) *The Barbarians Speak*. Princeton, NJ.

Wenger, L. (1942) 'Noch einmal zum Verfahren de plano und pro tribunali', *ZRG* 62: 366–74.

Wenham, L. P. (1939) 'Notes on the garrisoning of Maryport', *Transactions of the Cumberland and Westmorland Antiquarian and Archaeological Society*, 2nd series, 39: 19–30.

Wesch-Klein, G. (1998) *Soziale Aspekte des römischen Heerwesens in der Kaiserzeit*. Heidelberger Althist. Beitr. und Epigr. Stud. 28. Stuttgart.

Wheatley, P. (1971) *Pivot of the Four Quarters*. Chicago.

Wheeler, E. L. (1978) 'The occasion of Arrian's *Tactica*. *GRBS* 19: 351–65.

Wheeler, E. L. (1996) 'The laxity of Syrian legions', in D. Kennedy (ed.), *The Roman Army in the East*. *JRA* Supplementary Series 18. Portsmouth, RI, 229–76.

Whittaker, C. R. (1995) 'Integration of the early Roman West: the example of Africa', in Metzler et al. (1995), 19–32.

Whittaker, C. R. (2002) 'Supplying the army: evidence from Vindolanda', in P. Erdkamp (ed.), *The Roman Army and the Economy*. Amsterdam, 204–34.

Wiedemann, T. E. J. (1996) 'From Nero to Vespasian', in A. Bowman, E. Champlin, and A. Lintott (eds), *The Cambridge Ancient History*, vol. 10: *The Augustan Empire*, 2nd edn. Cambridge, 256–82.

Wigg, D. G. (1997) 'Coin supply and the Roman army', in W. Groenman-van Waateringe, B. L. van Beek, W. J. H. Willems, and S. L. Wynia (eds), *Roman Frontier Studies 1995: Proceedings of the XVIth Roman Frontier Studies Conference 1995*. Oxbow Monograph 91. Oxford, 281–88.

Wightman, E. M. (1970) *Roman Trier and the Treveri*. London.

Wightman, E. M. (1985) *Gallia Belgica*. London.

Wightman, E. M. (1986) 'Pagan cults in the province of Belgica', *ANRW* II 18.1: 542–89.

Wilbers-Rost, S. (2009) 'The site of the Varus battle at Kalkriese: recent results from archaeological research', in A. Morillo, N. Hanel, and E. Martin (eds), *Limes XX: Roman Frontier Studies*. Anejo de Gladius 13. Madrid, 1347–52.

Wilbers-Rost, S., Uerpmann, H.-P., Uerpmann, M., Grosskopf, B., and Tolkdsdorf-Lienemann, E. (2007) *Kalkriese 3. Interdisziplinäre Untersuchungen auf dem Oberesch in Kalkriese: archäologische Befunde und naturwissenschaftliche Begleituntersuchungen*. Römisch-Germanische Forschungen 65. Mainz.

Wilk, R. (1995) 'Learning to be local in Belize: global systems of common difference', in D. Miller (ed.), *Worlds Apart: Modernity through the Prism of the Local*. London, 110–33.

Willems, W. J. H. (1984) 'Romans and Batavians: regional study in the Dutch eastern river area, II', *Berichten van de Rijksdienst voor Oudheidkundig Bodemonderzoek* 34: 39–331.

Willems, W. J. H. (1992) 'Roman face masks from the Kops Plateau, Nijmegen, The Netherlands', *JRMES* 3: 57–66.

Wilmott, T. (2000) *Birdoswald and Housesteads ware. Project design (CfA project 656)*, English Heritage. London.

Wilmott, T. (2001) *Cohors I Aelia Dacorum*: a Dacian unit on Hadrian's Wall', *Acta Musei Napocensis* 38: 103–22.

Wilmott, T. (2010) 'Birdoswald Roman Cemetery', *Hadrian's Wall Archaeology* 1: 43–6.

Wissemann, M. (1984) 'Das Personal des antiken römischen Bades. *Glotta* 62: 80–89.

Wolff, C. (2003) *Les brigands en Orient sous le Haut-Empire romain*. Rome.

Wolff, C. (ed.), (2009) *L'armée romaine et la religion sous le Haut-Empire romain*. Lyons.

Wolff, H. (1974) 'Zu den Bürgerrechtsverleihungen an Kinder von Auxiliären und Legionären', *Chiron* 4: 479–510.

Wolff, H. (1986) 'Die Entwicklung der Veteranenprivilegien vom Beginn des 1. Jahrhunderts v. Chr bis auf Konstantin d. Gr.', in W. Eck and H. Wolff (eds), *Heer und Integrationspolitik*, Cologne, 44–115.

Wolffin, E. (1902) 'Sprachliches zum Bellum Hispaniense', *Archiv. f. lat. Lex. u. Gram.* 12: 159–71.

Woods, D. (1993) 'The ownership and disposal of military equipment in the Late Roman army', *JRMES* 4: 55–65.

Woolf, G. (1995) 'The formation of Roman provincial cultures', in Metzler et al. (1995), 9–18.

Woolf, G. (1998) *Becoming Roman: The Origins of Provincial Civilization in Gaul*, Cambridge.

Woolf, G. (2000) 'The religious history of the northwest provinces', *JRA* 13: 615–30.

Woolf, G. (2001) 'The Roman cultural revolution in Gaul', in S. Keay and N. Terrenato, (eds), *Italy and the West: Comparative Issues in Romanization*. Oxford, 173–86.

Woolf, G. (2002) 'Afterword: how the Latin West was won', in Cooley (2002a), 181–8.

Woolf, G. (ed.) (2003) *Cambridge Illustrated History of the Roman World*. Cambridge.

Woolf, G. (2004) 'The present state and future scope of Roman archaeology: a comment', *AJA* 108: 417–28

Woolf, G. (2006) 'Pliny's province', in T. Bekker-Nielsen (ed.), *Rome and the Black Sea Region: Domination, Romanisation, Resistance*. Black Sea Studies 5. Aarhus, 93–108.

Woolf, G. (2011) *Tales of the Barbarians: Ethnography and Empire in the Roman West*. Chichester.

Worrell, S., Jackson, R., Mackay, A., Bland, R., and Pitts, M. (2011) 'The Crosby Garrett Helmet', *British Archaeology* 116: 16.

Yadin, Y. (1962) 'Expedition D: the cave of letters', *IEJ* 12: 227–57.

Yegül, F. (1992) *Baths and Bathing in Classical Antiquity*. New York.

Yoshimura, T. (1961) 'Die Auxiliartruppen und die Provinzialklientel in der römischen Republik', *Historia* 10: 473–96.

Zahariade, M. (2009) *The Thracians in the Roman Imperial Army*, I: *Auxilia*. Cluj.

Zampieri, G. (1994) *Il museo archeologico di Padova*. Milan

Zanker, P. (1988) *The Power of Images in the Age of Augustus*, trans. A. Shapiro. Ann Arbor, Mich.

Zimmer, S. (1990) 'Dating the loanwords: Latin suffixes in Welsh (and their Celtic congeners) ', in A. Bammersberger and A. Wollmann (eds), *Britain 400–500 : Language and History*. Heidelberg, 263–81.

Zoll, A. (1995) 'A view through inscriptions: the epigraphic evidence for religion at Hadrian's Wall', in J. Metzler, M. Millett, N. Roymans, and J. Slofstra (eds), *Integration in the Early Roman West: The Role of Culture and Ideology*. Dossiers d'Archeologie du Musee National d'Histoire et d'Art 4. Luxembourg,129–37.

Index

Printed and bound by CPI Group (UK) Ltd, Croydon, CR0 4YY